WOMEN OF PO

Half a century of female presidents
and prime ministers worldwide

TORILD SKARD

Originally published in Norwegian as *Maktens Kvinner* by Universitetsforlaget, Oslo, in 2012.

First published in English in 2015 in Great Britain by

Policy Press
University of Bristol
1-9 Old Park Hill
Bristol BS2 8BB
UK
t: +44 (0)117 954 5940
pp-info@bristol.ac.uk
www.policypress.co.uk

North America office:
Policy Press
c/o The University of Chicago Press
1427 East 60th Street
Chicago, IL 60637, USA
t: +1 773 702 7700
f: +1 773-702-9756
sales@press.uchicago.edu
www.press.uchicago.edu

Cover design by Soapbox Design
Front cover: iStock
Printed and bound in Great Britain by Hobbs, Southampton
Policy Press uses environmentally responsible print partners

Contents

List of figures, tables and photographs

Figures

Tables

Photographs

Acknowledgements

The book did not materialise without support from many quarters. I would like to thank the Norwegian Institute of International Affairs (NUPI) and its director, Sverre Lodgaard, who assisted me in realising the project by offering office space and resources. The Norwegian Organisation of Non-fiction Writers and Translators, NORLA, the Norwegian Ministry of Foreign Affairs and Agency for Development Cooperation (NORAD) and Solvejg Wexelsen Eriksen's legacy provided me with financial support. The libraries at the Nobel Institute and NUPI obtained documentation and materials.

I would also like to thank the women presidents and prime ministers who took of their precious time to give an me interview or check information and thereby heighten the quality of the book. Their contributions are mentioned specifically in the text.

Moreover, I would like to thank a number of professionals and colleagues at NUPI, the Foreign Ministry and other institutions who have supported me and shared their knowledge and insight with me. Special thanks to Lars Alldén, Beatrice Halsaa, Bernt Hagtvet, Bjørg Skotnes, Olav Stokke and the referees and staff at Universitetsforlaget and Policy Press, who have gone through the manuscript as a whole and provided invaluable advice. Further thanks to Yesir Arat, Rolf Berg, Olav Berstad, Arup K. Biswas, Laila Bokhari, Axel Borchgrevink, Ingeborg Breines, Karin Bruzelius, Vegard Bye, Morten Bøås, Mavic Cabrera-Balleza, Jennifer Curtin, Drude Dahlerup, Marianne Damhaug, Visaka Dharmadasa, Øyvind Eggen, Björg Eva Erlandsdóttir, Lisbeth Friberg, Jakub Godzimirski, Bjørn Hansen, Hilde Haraldstad, Cathrine Holst, Anne Holli, Dag Wernø Holter, Eivind Homme, þorbjörg Inga Jónsdóttir, Kari Karamé, Berit von der Lippe, Siri Maria Midré, Elisabeth Nauclér, Aud Lise Norheim, Knut-Are Okstad, Kumar Rupesinghe, Marian Sawer, Erik Selmer, Marie Serra, Kristi Anne Stølen, Esther Suter, Ove Thorsheim, MA. Lourdes Veneracion-Rallonza, Sissel Volan, Julie Wilhelmsen, Merete K. Wilhelmsen, Ivar Windheim, Indra Øverland and Berit Ås who have read longer or shorter sections and given very useful help improving the content.

On a personal level, family and friends have provided support during an unusually extensive and demanding research and writing period, not least my late husband Kåre Øistein Hansen and my late twin sister Målfrid Grude Flekkøy, who assisted in earlier phases and when they were struck by serious illness, Kåre's son Bjørn and his family, Målfrid's family and my brothers and sisters Anne, Halvdan and Åsmund with their families, so the project could be completed nevertheless. Marit Wiklund, Bent Erik Helgeland and the home nursing care in Svelvik also lent a hand. Warm thanks to them all!

A long journey

Generations

In my family, I am a third-generation feminist. I grew up with my parents and maternal grandparents near Oslo in Norway. My grandmother was born in 1871. She was the first farmer's daughter to complete secondary education in her part of the country and became a teacher. She joined the Norwegian Association for Women's Rights (NKF), established in 1884, and fought for the right to vote. It took years of struggle, but universal suffrage was achieved in 1913. My grandmother taught and wrote articles and became a member of a local education committee. However, my grandfather got a PhD, became a university professor and minister of foreign affairs. Surely, he was an impressive man, but my grandmother was also gifted.

My mother got a university degree and fought for women's right to paid work during the recession in the 1930s. She became a senior lecturer at the university and double worked all her life. My father was a university professor, but only men obtained such high positions.

In 1945, a generation after women got the right to vote, Norwegian politics was still a domain for men. There were only seven women in parliament (5 per cent) and one in the cabinet. In addition, feminism was not accepted. At school, I was told by my classmates that I could not be a class representative because I was a girl.

Feminist breakthrough

When I started studying at the university, I joined the NKF and have been an active member ever since. In the 1950s, I met a small group of elderly ladies, impressive pioneers who had fought for equality for decades and would not give up in spite of resistance. There were still some formal rights that were reserved for men, but the pioneers advised me first of all to get involved in politics. Society would not change in practice if women did not take advantage of their formal rights and made change happen.

I attended teachers college and afterwards got university degrees in sociology, psychology and education. At the university, I joined a social-democratic student club. There were not many women and although the atmosphere was friendly, I had a distinct feeling that this was not the place for women's issues. I became chair of the club and even chair of the student parliament, but I did not raise women's issues. When I did, after long hesitation – proposing in the student parliament that a woman physician should be employed in the student health centre to help women students with reproductive health – there was a real uproar. I was accused of 'inviting the students to commit adultery' and had to use my casting vote as chair to get the proposal accepted.

Then, the second feminist wave hit in the 1960s/1970s. All of a sudden, feminist groups popped up here and there. There were protest meetings and demonstrations. 'Women's liberation' was hotly debated, and angry female voices demanded more women in decision-making. In 1971, a 'women's coup' was organised in some municipalities during the local elections. To my great surprise, I was elected onto the City Council of Oslo as the number one from my political party. There was proportional representation, and because I was a woman, feminist voters gave me so many additional votes that I passed all the men who were initially placed at the top of the party list. It was unbelievable. *Because* I was a woman! I got a new go-ahead spirit and decided to fight systematically for women's issues.

I got a job as a lecturer in the social sciences at the University of Tromsø, in the north of Norway. However, it did not last long because, to my astonishment, I was elected to parliament in 1973. The party had to have *some* women! However, while the total number of women members of parliament (MPs) increased, we did not loom large in the parliament hall. There were more than five times as many men. Still, I was elected president of the Upper Chamber as the first woman. The Norwegian Parliament has two chambers that meet separately, which together form the Plenary. My party wanted to show that it was 'pro-women' and the position was prestigious, but not very political.

Chairing the meetings in the Upper Chamber was a simple matter. In the six-member Presidium, consisting of the presidents and vice presidents of the Upper and Lower Chambers and the Plenary, respectively, we were supposed to be jointly responsible for the running of parliament as a whole. But if I had broken a glass ceiling to get in, there was now a glass wall between me and the others and it was quite clear that they would not let me have anything to do with questions of importance. It was frustrating.

However, women MPs from different political parties got together secretly in the women's dressing room in parliament. Here, we discussed women's issues of different kinds and we agreed upon a number that we could promote in our respective parties and get on the political agenda.

Complexity

I was lucky and participated at the World Conference of the International Women's Year in Mexico City in 1975. It was overwhelming, wonderful and exciting, but also confusing. I met sisters and fellow activists, and got new insights and stronger commitment. But when the Finnish Secretary General Helvi Sipilä stated at the opening of the conference that discrimination of women existed all over the world, the Soviet female cosmonaut Valentina Tereshkova protested strongly: she was proof of the fact that the socialist countries were the big exception! The world's first woman prime minister, Sirimavo Bandaranaike from Sri Lanka, was more calm and reflective. We are not here only to demolish discrimination, she noted, but to envision the benefits to the human race of integrating this 'forgotten half of humanity' in development. Shortly after, Imelda Marcos from the Philippines swept into the hall. As there was no woman national leader, the dictator sent his wife, and she explained: 'Woman is not an adversary of man, but his partner. Women are born beautiful, while men are born strong!'

Tough task

Mexico City 1975 was a great inspiration. The vast majority of states in the world committed themselves 'to eliminate all obstacles which stand in the way of enjoyment by women of equal status with men'. But how should it happen? Even in a small egalitarian nation like Norway, there was solid resistance. It was difficult to get women's issues through in parliament, even though the women's movement was broad and active and women MPs from different parties collaborated. Personally, I felt that I was constantly pushed to be *either* a woman *or* a politician, because a *woman politician*, what was that supposed to be?

After four years as an MP, I was exhausted and left parliament before the elections in 1977. I went into women's studies to get a better understanding of opportunities and obstacles. I analysed the 'women's coup' in Norwegian municipalities in 1971 and the role of women in the Norwegian parliament after they got the right to vote in 1913 (Skard, 1979, 1980). I joined a group of Nordic researchers who studied women in politics and we wrote a book together: Unfinished democracy (Haavio-Mannila et al, 1985). We thought that we had insight into the politics of our neighbouring states, but discovered that there was a lot to learn from a comparative women's perspective. At the same time, I became involved in the Norwegian National Commission for the UN Educational, Scientific and Cultural Organization (UNESCO). For the first time, the Commission had a majority of women, and we set about making UNESCO more women-oriented. Several years after the Mexico Conference, the organisation had remained practically dormant.

In 1984, I was appointed UNESCO's first director for the status of women. It was the French Deputy Director General Jean Knapp who asked me. The Nordic countries had a good reputation and I think he said to himself: 'Now, let these insistent Nordic women try themselves and see if they can make UNESCO change!' With headquarters in Paris, I found myself right in the middle of a whirl of studies, discussions, meetings and projects. Prominent women from all over the world came to UNESCO, and I discovered fascinating women leaders whom I had never heard of before.

In 1985, the World Conference on Women was held in Nairobi. But just as uplifting as was Mexico City, Nairobi was equally discouraging and confusing. We knew much more about the situation of women than we did 10 years earlier, but little had happened to improve conditions during the previous decade. On the contrary, neo-liberalism, falling commodity prices, growing debt burdens and structural adjustment had made large groups of women actually worse off than before.

Furthermore, in UNESCO, the efforts to advance the status of women led to few results. Without active support from the director general, Amadou Mahtar M'Bow from Senegal, and no funds, only a secretary and an unqualified assistant, there was not much even the most hard-working director could do. Changing a large institution like UNESCO was also a much tougher job than was generally understood, and I tried later to share my insight and experiences with others (Skard, 2008a, 2008b, 2009).

Political will and resources

Fortunately, I was appointed as the first woman director general in the Ministry for Development Cooperation, later the Ministry of Foreign Affairs, in Norway in 1986. It was amazing. Across party lines, the centre-right coalition government appointed a woman, and even a left-oriented one. I became responsible for Norway's collaboration with multilateral organisations and could continue to exert pressure to strengthen the efforts related to women not just in UNESCO, but in almost all the United Nations (UN) agencies and development banks as well. Norway was a member of many of the executive boards and a driving force internationally in terms of women's issues. We had a strategy for women and gender equality and both ministers and the administration were serious. I was head of a competent department and we had funds. We could support the UN system, women's organisations and specific initiatives and improve the output of the efforts. It was a demanding position, but meaningful. I really felt that we had an impact.

Ministers changed, but the commitment to gender equality remained for a long time. When the issue was given less priority I was happy to go to UN Children's Fund (UNICEF). In 1994, Jim Grant, who was head of UNICEF, wanted to increase the number of women at high levels in the organisation and asked me to become UNICEF's regional director in West and Central Africa. UNICEF was the best UN agency I had seen. I needed field experience to understand more about processes of change, and West Africa was known for the high position women traditionally had in many ethnic groups.

For four-and-a-half years, with headquarters in Abidjan in the Ivory Coast, I covered UNICEF's work in 23 countries, from Cape Verde and Mauritania in the west to Chad in the north-east and Democratic Congo in the south. It was an intense and diverse learning experience about traditions, culture and colonialism, development, solidarity and oppression, idealistic efforts, international arrogance, and local abuse of power. UNICEF was field-oriented and we supported women and children everywhere. I met poor and needy people, young and old, impressive professionals, dedicated local workers, and community leaders. And not least, I got to collaborate with strong market women, queen mothers, women activists and women politicians. More and more, women began to assert themselves both in Africa and other continents, at the grassroots and the top level. These were the richest years of my life, an outcome of which was my book about Africa: *Continent of mothers, continent of hope* (Skard, 2003).

Back to research

A generation after Mexico City in 1975, women made up only 15 per cent in parliaments around the world and even less in governments. How possible would it be to increase women's influence? There were obviously no quick, easy solutions. Conditions were complicated. Still, there had to be ways to move forward.

Seeing how the number of women presidents and prime ministers began to increase in a marked way worldwide during the 1990s and into the 2000s, my curiosity became pressing. The numbers were not large, but the curve clearly went upwards. Was the women's movement scoring a striking success for once – or was something else happening? What made the number of women top leaders suddenly rise so consistently, and what did it entail? There must be something we could learn from what was going on.

I became senior researcher at the Norwegian Institute of International Affairs, received funding and set out on a journey through half a century, taking me to all continents except a few. The result is this book, which I hope will be of use for those who want a more woman-friendly world.

Torild Skard
Svelvik, Norway, May 2014

Introduction

When patterns break

Family photos are often taken when the world leaders get together at top level. Both in the League of Nations and the United Nations (UN), it was the same at every summit: one row after the other had only dark-clad white men. Gradually, they became more multicultural and colourful, some even wore Arab or African dress. However, North or South, East or West, men ruled the sovereign states of the world.

For many years, male dominance was practically total. The number of sovereign states increased and new nations established parliaments, cabinets, presidents and prime ministers, but male dominance continued. All the presidents and prime ministers were men. There were a few ruling queens, but their positions were inherited and their role, to a large extent, was ceremonial.[1]

However, during the last decades of the 20th century, there was a change. Once in a while, a woman suddenly brightened up the family photo with gay colours. Around the turn of the century, there were several women, and by 2010, there were women presidents or prime ministers on practically all continents. They were not many, but, nevertheless, something had happened. Not only men were ruling the world's nation states.

In this book, I ask what happened when the established patterns of male political leadership broke and national top leaders were women instead of men. Why did some women get engaged in political activities that were usually considered a male domain? And how did they manage to climb all the way to the highest political positions, when very few men managed to do so and women had not done it before? Further, when top leaders were women and not men, did it make a difference for policies and decisions?

There were considerable differences economically, socially and culturally from one country to the other and from one period to the other after World War II, but, overall, national political institutions had or acquired sufficient common features to make international analyses and comparisons possible.

Dynamics of change

The book is placed within the field of gender studies. Gender studies can focus on women or men (or both). In this book, women are the main subject. In the political area, women are generally both under-represented and under-researched. There is a need for more knowledge about women's political behaviour and views, about the interactions between women and men in political institutions, and about women's access to, or exclusion from, power. Men have mostly been the subject of studies within political science, and research on male politicians usually lacks a gender analysis. Although I focus on women, I do not see them in isolation from men. In the political area, where men generally dominate, their behaviour and views set the conditions for women's participation and eventual rise to the top.

Increased knowledge about women in politics is not only of academic interest; it is considered important in connection with gender justice. The UN affirms that women and men have equal rights and emphasises that everyone has the right to take part in the government of the country, directly or through freely chosen representatives. The interests of women should be safeguarded in the same way as those of men.[2] There is a loss of talent if women do not have access to power positions, and decisions will be based on a constrained worldview. Furthermore, the legitimacy of government will be reduced and the development of policies promoting democracy and gender equality will be limited.

Decades and decades after women started claiming political rights and the governments of the world committed themselves to recognising and observing these rights, there are still very few women in legislative and executive bodies. In 2010, they constituted 19 per cent of the world's members of parliament (MPs), 16 per cent of ministers and 8 per cent of heads of state and government (IPU and UN DAW, 2010). And even if a new 'record' was set in January 2014, only 22 per cent of the MPs and 17 per cent of the ministers were women and the number of female top leaders actually declined slightly (IPU and UN Women, 2014). This means that women cannot promote their interests and influence the development of society in the same way as men.

However slow, change has taken place. Women's organisations and the UN have systematically promoted change. However, other factors have also influenced events in one or the other direction: hastening change or slowing it down. Taking the women top leaders as examples, I try to get a better understanding of the dynamics of change by studying cases where women succeeded in obtaining the highest political positions at the national level. How did it happen? Was it sheer chance and luck, the result of systematic efforts, or a mixture? And when they got to the top, did they act in the same way as men or did they become 'transformational' leaders?[3]

World history

The descriptions and analyses of the women top leaders that have been made so far present more or less comprehensive biographies, placing them in time and place. But historical and geographic perspectives are limited. To understand how patterns of behaviour develop and change, it is necessary to go back in time. Furthermore, in a world where people, groups and states have become increasingly interlinked, a global scope is needed.

This book takes a broad historic and geographic view to find out why and how women rose to national political office at specific points in time and in different states when they had not done so before. I move from a macro to a micro level and study how the future women presidents and prime ministers were influenced not only by their families, local community and national context, but also by conditions and events at international levels: political, economic, social and cultural.

After World War II, the world became 'one' in a way that was never seen before, at the same time as change processes took place at various levels to an extent that was unknown earlier. New technologies were developed. Production and economies expanded. Living conditions were improved. Nation states were created and more democratic political systems were introduced. Different kinds of regional and international relations were established. Particularly within the framework of the UN, the governments of the world engaged in international, regional and national processes to promote equality between women and men, and a global women's movement gradually grew in strength. This book is a world history seen from the perspective of women's political leadership, focusing on the period after World War II.

Complete overview

As women heads of state and government have been so few, they have not been much studied as a special group. A considerable amount of research has been carried out relating to women and politics more generally, mostly in Western countries, and the focus has first of all been on the recruitment to elected bodies, particularly to parliaments. There is less knowledge about governments and political parties. With regards to the national women leaders, there are various descriptions of individual women, and comparative analyses have been carried out, but they have mainly covered certain aspects of the women's careers and been based on small samples. Comparative analyses of the women heads of state and government worldwide covering more than 50 individuals were first undertaken a few years ago.[4]

As the total number of women presidents and prime ministers remains limited, it is important to include all of them to be able to describe not only variations, but also similarities. However, the selection was not quite simple. Some women were heads of government in countries that were not independent, usually small colonies, dependencies or external territories. As they were controlled by colonial powers, the importance of their positions was limited and these women are therefore not included in my sample.

A number of women were appointed or elected as presidents or prime ministers on a temporary basis. These could serve a good while and exert considerable power. But they could also occupy a position only for a day or two or maybe a few weeks in a purely formal capacity while the holder of the position was absent. In these cases, they were not really attributed the power allocated to the position, and therefore I exclude them from my sample.

Finally, those women heads of state and government are excluded who did not function alone, but served jointly with somebody else or had a position that does not correspond to a presidential or prime ministerial office.

So, this study comprises all the women presidents and prime ministers worldwide in independent states that were members of the UN. The women were appointed or elected to their positions after World War II, which, in practice, means from 1960 until and including 2010, covering about half a century, and they served at least two months or more on a temporary or non-temporary basis. The total number of persons covered by this book is 73 women in 53 states (see the Appendix).[5]

Biographies

The life and work of the women presidents and prime ministers constitute the main material of the book. Within the framework of a brief global history, the women are described chronologically according to different geographic regions. The career of each woman top leader is described within the international, regional and national framework. Background, family, early life and environment are described to clarify why the women engaged in political activities. Which factors made a difference? Although it is not always possible to go in depth, a picture will be drawn that is as complete as possible. Studying the career paths, the focus is on how the women managed to advance and how they were accepted in political positions at the highest level. Regarding the activities of the women executives while they were in power, light is shed on possibilities and limitations and some important aspects of priorities and policies: under which conditions did the women act as top leaders, and to what extent did they represent women?

The analysis is both quantitative and qualitative, but mainly qualitative. The aim is to get an impression of the various factors interacting to permit women to become national leaders. The factors will be quantified globally at the end of the book to get a picture of the whole and to look for patterns or similarities amid the variation. But generalisations will be more tentative than conclusive. The total number of women top leaders still remains small. The aim of this book is not primarily to develop general concepts and theories, but to get a better grasp on historical, institutional and political dimensions and to understand the interplay between global, national and individual levels.

Varied information

Obtaining sufficient and appropriate information about all the women presidents and prime ministers worldwide during half a century has been a complicated task. Some were deceased, and several were very old. In any case, they were spread all over the globe, and those who were still in office were extremely busy. So, I have used many forms of data collection:

- *Direct contact* From 1999, I have personally interviewed or received replies to written questions from 14 women top leaders from five regions.
- *Biographies* Several of the top leaders have written autobiographies and there are a number of shorter and longer, authorised and non-authorised, biographies. These do not cover all the women, but all have been portrayed in various encyclopaedias on paper or the Internet, though the information is sometimes brief.
- *Research* From the beginning of the 1990s, there has been an increasing number of research studies describing and analysing selected groups of women top leaders from various perspectives. The book is based on research in anthropology, history, psychology, sociology and, above all, political science, but efforts are made to avoid undue specialised language.
- *Media articles* As top leaders, the women's activities have been covered by various mass media and they have also written articles themselves.

On this basis, it has been possible to access comprehensive material from different sources, but the quantity and quality vary considerably. Some women top leaders have received very much attention, while others have not. And the reliability of many sources, as well as the understanding of various types of information, must be considered carefully.

Women top leaders were pioneers who were involved in tough power struggles. Often, they aroused strong feelings. At times, they were portrayed with great admiration as heroines or stars because they succeeded in a demanding role usually reserved for men. At other times, they were painted in black because they were not 'real' women or did not meet with expectations. In addition, they held political views that were, by definition, controversial in one camp or the other. The book seeks to draw a picture that is as balanced and realistic as possible about the life and work of the women, providing a fairly specific description going beyond simple stereotypes. In addition to concrete facts and assessments made by social scientists and biographers, statements by the women executives themselves have also been included to clarify their motivations and views.

Generally, facts and assessments have been checked so that there is usually more than one source, and research colleagues and diplomats who have specialised knowledge of the various countries and leaders have provided valuable help and critical comments (see the Acknowledgements).

Plan of the book

The text provides a coherent presentation, but it is also possible to read parts about certain leaders or regions. The presentation is structured geographically and chronologically. It starts with a description of the first women top leaders who came to power in various parts of the world during the period 1960–75.

Chapter Two presents a brief account of insights relating to women in politics in general, and women top leaders specifically, based on previous research. A basis is provided for the biographies that follow: a general background; historical, economic and cultural factors of relevance; and political institutions and concepts that will be used in the book.

Chapters Three to Ten describe different regions of the world, starting with women who rose to the top in Western industrial states around 1980. Afterwards, women presidents and prime ministers in South Asia and East Asia, Latin America and the Caribbean, sub-Saharan Africa, and Eastern industrial countries are portrayed. Finally, Chapter Ten includes women in Western nations who came to power from 1990 to 2010.

Only those states, small or large, are included that have or have had a woman at the top, that is, those where a woman succeeded. It has not been possible to carry out a similar analysis of the nation states where women did *not* succeed. They are the most numerous, by far.

In the two final chapters Chapter Eleven provides a summary of the regional chapters, while Chapter Twelve sums up different factors influencing the women's careers, searching for similarities and patterns on a global scale in the midst of variation. The importance of women's qualifications and women's movements, democratisation and political parties, the electoral system and quotas is discussed and positive changes suggested to increase women's access to political leadership.

The first woman prime minister in the world, Sirimavo Bandaranaike. She was prime minister in Ceylon/ Sri Lanka three times: 1960–1965, 1970–1977 and 1994–2000.
Image: http://scanpix.no

Chapter One

Breakthrough on several continents

Sirimavo Bandaranaike: first woman in Ceylon

Women's place

It created a sensation when a woman suddenly rose up as prime minister of Ceylon in 1960. The news went around the world. A female prime minister – was it possible? And in Ceylon? Not an industrialised country with a developed democracy, but a poor island in Asia that had recently been a British colony! In Britain, people were both enthusiastic and sceptical. Some welcomed a woman in government. The dream of the suffragettes had suddenly come true. A London newspaper noted that we had to invent a new word: 'stateswoman' instead of statesman. But could a woman like Sirimavo Bandaranaike fill the position? She was chosen because of her husband. Never before had anyone come to power in a flood of tears. Who was behind her pulling the strings? In Ceylon, opponents dismissed her as merely a 'kitchen woman'. To this, she replied: 'A woman's place is everywhere and anywhere duty requires her to be and *also* in her kitchen!' (Seneviratne, 1975:204, emphasis in original; see also Malhotra, 2003: 232).

Throughout the ages, mostly men had command of the world. In modern times, with democratic systems, women got the right to vote. However, very few women participated in politics, and those who did, almost never obtained important positions. Politics was a matter for men. A female top politician was unthinkable.[1]

'Weeping Widow'

How could it be that Sirimavo Bandaranaike broke the prevailing pattern of gender roles and became prime minister of Ceylon not only once, but three times, and one of the most important political leaders in the country?[2]

She was called the 'Weeping Widow' when she travelled around in her white mourning garments in what was then Ceylon (later Sri Lanka) in 1959. Western newspapers showed pictures of a pale woman with dark shadows under her eyes, describing her as both 'voluptuous' and 'seductive' (Gooneratne, 1986: 160).

Mrs B, as people called her, was a rarity when she engaged in politics. In ancient times in the country, queens sometimes led men to victory over enemies and rivals. But in modern Ceylon, men dominated, even after women got the right to vote in 1931. Sirimavo's husband, SWRD Bandaranaike, was a politician. He was educated in Oxford, became a lawyer and played a central role in Ceylon's transition from a colony to an independent state.

Ceylon was a poor country, divided into castes and classes with different ethnic groups, mostly Sinhalese, who were generally Buddhists, while the Tamils were Hindus. The British ran plantations and governed the colony with the help of a small group of high-caste men, who were strongly Westernised, many of them Christians. The needs and culture of the population were generally neglected. However, throughout the 1900s, democratic reforms and welfare measures such as food subsidies, education and health services were gradually introduced.

After underhanded negotiations between the British and the Sinhalese elite, Ceylon became independent in 1948 as a Commonwealth realm with a governor-general representing the Queen. There was no nationalist mass mobilisation, like in India. After independence, the political leadership in Ceylon remained in the hands of Westernised men from the local elite. The health and education of the population were relatively good, and social justice was promoted through welfare measures. The political system was developed according to the British model with a House of Representatives mainly elected by universal suffrage through a simple plurality vote and a smaller Senate consisting of designated members. In addition to the two main political parties, a number of smaller parties participated in the elections. A cabinet with a prime minister was formally appointed by the governor-general, but was responsible to parliament.

In the interwar period, SWRD was minister for local administration. After World War II, he entered the coalition government led by the United National Party (UNP) and was responsible for local administration and health. He came from the elite, but broke out and made common cause with the people, becoming a socialist and a nationalist. He converted from Christianity to Buddhism and spoke Sinhalese. In 1951, he left the government and founded a new, more left-wing party, the Sri Lankan Freedom Party (SLFP). Five years later, in 1956, he managed to unite the opposition, won the elections and became prime minister.

Chaotic situation

The time when SWRD started to put his ideas into practice was a creative and productive, but also turbulent and violent period. He was described as both a utopian idealist and an ardent opportunist, a progressive and a parochialist, an egalitarian and an imperious snob (Manor, 1989: 1). He got rid of the British bases and made Ceylon a non-allied country. Bus companies and Colombo harbour were nationalised. Wages were increased, workers got rights and disadvantaged groups were drawn into politics. Welfare policies, including free education and health services, were institutionalised. SLFP went to the polls promising to make

Sinhala the official language and give Buddhism an honourable position. The Tamil minority reacted very negatively to this, and it led to communal riots and bloody confrontations. SWRD was hailed as a hero of the people, but in 1959, three years after he came to power, he was assassinated by a Buddhist monk. It was Ceylon's first political murder.

The murder created a chaotic situation. Party members and opponents fought for power. With SLFP's founder and supreme ruler gone, who would lead the party forward? There was no internal party democracy. Everything revolved around the leader, and no successor was appointed. The men surrounding SWRD did not have what was required for effective leadership and were also marked by bitter conflicts. In the ruling families, a family member usually took over when the head of the family fell away. Since SWRD was dead, the widow was fitting. After a few months, key party members asked her to take over. She was acceptable to the various wings of the party and could provide the leadership the country needed in difficult times (De Silva, 1999: 59; Malhotra, 2003: 235–6).

Under British rule, women organised themselves and demanded political rights. But the organisations were mainly run by elite women. Women generally benefited from the welfare measures, but apart from small leftist parties, nobody in politics focused on the 'woman question'. In 1960, all in all, only seven women had been elected to the House. They belonged to political families and introduced what was called the 'substitute syndrome', which meant that women were elected to replace a father or a husband. Husband-and-wife combinations also occurred. One of the woman MPs became Ceylon's first female minister in 1956; incidentally, the only one in SWRD's government.

Dynasty comes through

Initially, Mrs B. refused to take over from her husband. She had stood by SWRD's side for 20 years, but never imagined a political career for herself. During the period of mourning, she publicly expressed her distaste for politics. She is reported to have said that she 'would not take the prime ministership even if it was handed to her on a platter!' (Weerakoon, 2004: 97). She also had to take care of her fatherless children: her daughters, Sunetra and Chandrika, 16 and 14 years old, and her son, Anura, aged 10 (Opfell, 1993: 6).

However, the situation was critical for the SLFP. Elections were soon to be held. Sirimavo Bandaranaike belonged to the elite, and being the daughter of a noble Kandy family, she was brought up to serve. She sought support in front of the Buddha altar in her small meditation room and then accepted, hesitantly, to participate in the election campaign. 'I am not seeking power for myself', she declared, 'but I have come forward to help the SLFP candidates, so that the Party can continue the policy of my late husband' (Seneviratne, 1975: 174–5). She spoke briefly, but concisely. There was a spark of hope in her words, and she communicated a sense of trust. Ordinary people could rely on her as they had relied on her husband.

SLFP did not obtain enough seats in March 1960 to form a government. The party only won 46 seats in the House of Representatives, while the UNP got 51. But the UNP government did not last long, and new elections were held in July. Then, the widow accepted to run as party leader, though she felt awe and humility for the task. She said:

> I will carry out the policy of my husband. With his victory the common man for the first time enjoyed the real fruits of democracy. They were able to walk with dignity and speak without fear. They could voice their needs to a government that served their interests and not those of a privileged few. I would personally have preferred to keep away from politics and lead a quiet and secluded life. But it is a duty which I owe to my late husband that I should make whatever humble contribution I could towards the welfare of the millions of people in this country whom he loved so very much and who were devoted to him; who looked up to him as their saviour. (Seneviratne, 1975: 176–7)

Sirimavo Bandaranaike was unanimously elected as party leader, and this was no temporary function. She kept the position for several decades and led the party as determinedly as her husband had done before her.

Prophecy fails

The first task was to conduct an election campaign. The hero of the people was gone, but the widow carried on his legacy. She visited every constituency where the SLFP had a candidate, and spoke and played her husband's speeches on tape. She was not a candidate herself.

Within the family, opinions of Sirimavo's political role differed. A young nephew of SWRD, Felix Bandaranaike, worked actively behind the scenes to make sure his aunt would take over, so that the position as party leader would remain in the family (Malhotra, 2003: 236). But the conservative men shook their heads:

> Sirima [her given name, the supplement *vo* signifies respect] can't achieve anything by it. What does she know of politics? In her husband's time Sirima presided over nothing fiercer than the kitchen fire. And think what Ceylon's like – would people ever tolerate a woman at the top? She'll end by spoiling her personal reputation and ruining the family name. (Gooneratne, 1986: 160)

Rarely has a prediction turned out to be so wrong. Under the new leadership, the appeal of SLFP increased. The party won a roaring victory and gained 75 of the 151 seats in the House. The prime minister had to be a member of parliament (MP); 44-year-old Sirimavo Bandaranaike was appointed a member of the senate and elected prime minister. When she first got a job, she stated that she had the courage and strength to take what might come (Seneviratne, 1975: 180). Thus, a national political career began that was to stretch over 40 years, until 2000. Sirimavo Bandaranaike became a dominant force in Sri Lankan politics, was prime minister three times for a total of nearly 18 years, and her daughter Chandrika continued the family tradition.

Only a 'kitchen woman'?

Sirima Ratwatte Dias Bandaranaike worked as a housewife when she became head of government. She lacked higher education, administrative knowledge and political experience, but was not without qualifications in general. As members of the Ratwatte family and the ruling aristocracy in Kandy, her parents were informed, socially oriented people. Her mother was a traditional doctor and her father was a district leader and member of the Senate. Sirima was born in 1916 and grew up in a Buddhist cultural tradition, but was sent to Catholic school in Colombo. She was the oldest of six siblings, and after 11 years of schooling, she came home and took over much of the housework.

Sirima accompanied her father around in the district, and when there was drought and flooding followed by a deadly malaria epidemic, she took care of the sick with her mother. The woman's role was in the home and in humanitarian work. Sirima joined Ceylon's largest Buddhist women's organisation, Mahila Samiti, and worked actively to improve the economic and social conditions in rural areas. In particular, she helped to increase the return on the rice fields, strengthen women's education and spread knowledge of family planning. She held several positions in the organisation, including president. When Sirimavo was asked to take over from her husband, she felt that she was not only known as SWRD's wife; she had long played a role in public service (Seneviratne, 1975: 105).

When SWRD and Sirima married in 1940, it was called the 'Wedding of the Century' (Seneviratne, 1975: 76). It was an alliance between two of the most powerful families in Ceylon, and the highlands were united with the lowlands. The marriage was arranged, but Sirima was consulted along the way. She was 24 years old; her husband was 17 years older. They had different characters and backgrounds, but both had a generally left-wing nationalist stance.

SWRD was already well established as a politician. The home was like a public place. People often dropped in, were welcomed and well taken care of. His biographer, James Manor (1989: 3, 281, 323), thought that he had a strong need to assert his authority and was a bit of a male chauvinist. Although Sirima was her husband's friend and confidante, she had little influence on his policy. Sirima's biographer, Maureen Seneviratne (1975: 99, 176–7, 187), also draws a picture in which the wife primarily listened in relation to her husband. The difference in age and education, as well as personality and gender, might have had an impact. Sirima kept a low profile and fulfilled her traditional role as mother and housewife. At the same time, she received an extraordinary political education from her husband and his acquaintances. Although she did not agree in all things, she came mostly to share SWRD's views. Eventually, she assisted her husband during election campaigns and made interventions.

Succeeding a legend

Sirimavo Bandaranaike was intelligent and quick to learn, and had great inner strength, courage and commitment. She was more resolute than her husband. Once she had decided something, no one could persuade her from it. Some describe her as the most impressive and charismatic leader Ceylon ever had, while others think that she was perhaps too forceful. She claimed no particular political philosophy. SWRD became legendary after his death. He was considered a national hero who democratised the country's government. In SWRD's name, the widow would lead the country forward and implement his promises. More important than the fact that she was a woman was the fact that she represented her husband and the family. But traditional beliefs in the goddess of power in the population may have contributed to her having been accepted. Nevertheless, SWRD's policy was not without problems: his promises were very ambitious and his decisions were partly controversial. In practice, the policy was determined not only by SWRD, but by Sirimavo also, and it is claimed that she pushed through more far-reaching measures than her husband would have done.[3]

The year 1960 was a difficult time. Rapid population growth and falling commodity prices led to a critical economic situation with high unemployment and difficulties in maintaining welfare measures. Sirimavo Bandaranaike nationalised the oil companies and the national bank, promoted industrialisation and local production, carried out a land reform, and strengthened the economy of the rural population. She continued her husband's pro-Buddhist and pro-Sinhalese policies and brought the school system under public control. The policy was not universally popular. Tamils rebelled, and the army was sent into the provinces. If somebody thought that a female top politician would always be kind-hearted and peaceful, they were wrong. There were long periods of martial law. After two years, the military and police tried a coup, but failed.

In addition to being prime minister, Bandaranaike was minister for planning, foreign affairs and defence. She took a strong interest in international affairs and stood forward as a world leader. She attended the Commonwealth conferences, was a founding member and leader of the Movement of Nonaligned States, and mediated in the conflict between India and China in 1962.

'Huge win' for women

When she was elected, Bandaranaike had a very special message for women:

> I will emphasize that what is essential for the women of Ceylon is simple living, decorum and dignity – and an upholding of old-world traditions of

which unfortunately we have only very little now. My victory is really their victory; it is really a tremendous victory to them. (Seneviratne, 1975: 180)

When Western newspapers marvelled that a country like Ceylon could have a female leader, she replied:

> The women of Sri Lanka have never been chattels, never been in enforced servitude to the male sex. Whatever 'servitude' we render, is voluntarily undertaken, because there is a deep rooted respect for the dual and different roles of father and mother in our society. According to Buddhist tradition, the family is a sacred unit and due all honour, and neither man nor woman are considered superior one to the other. (Seneviratne, 1975: 187)

In her speeches, Bandaranaike often referred to the fact that she was a woman. She was proud that as a woman who did not have a higher education, she was the prime minister. She perceived herself as the 'Mother of the People' and could base her opinion on the fact that she was a woman and a mother, for example, as when she called for peace between nations (Weerakoon, 2004: 123) or opposed children being exposed to radioactive radiation (Seneviratne, 1975: 184–5). But she did not express a special interest in women's issues or women as a target group (Seneviratne, 1975: 179; Rupesinghe, 2008). She did not come to power as the result of an active women's movement, and it is unclear how much impact her gender actually had on her policy. Some claim that she tried to strengthen the position of women, while others disagree.

Both maternal health and women's education were strengthened in the 1960s and 1970s, so Ceylon stood out compared to other countries in the region. Universal primary education was introduced for both girls and boys. But it is possible that the welfare measures were mainly viewed in a humanitarian perspective, not as a woman-focused policy, and that it was so well established that the prime minister did not need to support it specifically.

Sirimavo Bandaraike's rise to power did not lead to any important role for women in politics (De Silva, 1999: 60). The SLFP leadership remained a male forum. In 1960, only two women were elected to the House of Representatives. One was from the SLFP, but partly in opposition, and the other belonged to a small Communist/Trotskyist party. So, the Bandaranaike cabinet was made up only of men. Many had worked with SWRD. Her nephew Felix Bandaranaike became minister of finance, but had to resign when he wanted to reduce the rations of rice people were given for free. Later, he became minister without a portfolio.

The proof

The cabinet had to resign due to disagreement about government control of the media, and the SLFP suffered a disastrous defeat at the elections in 1965. Bandaranaike travelled around the country to strengthen the party, select candidates and contribute to their election. But the party only got 41 of the 151 seats in the House of Representatives. Bandaranaike was elected along with three other women and became the first woman leader of the opposition. If it was a consolation, the world got its second female prime minister in neighbouring India shortly after, in January 1966, and Indira Gandhi became a close friend of Sirimavo Bandaranaike.

The conservative cabinet was unable to reduce inflation and unemployment. And in the elections in 1970, Bandaranaike got her revenge. The Socialist Front obtained 91 seats (of 151), the largest majority since independence. Six women were elected, and all belonged to the Front. Sirimavo Bandaranaike became prime minister again. If her entry onto the political arena the first time could be explained by referring to her husband, her re-conquest of power after five years of absence could not be attributable to him. Now, she had 'proved herself', as it was said, having become politically more mature and created her own platform and her own name – and was appreciated and controversial, like her husband also was. She said herself that she had 'learned to judge herself impersonally, in a more detached manner, as a politician first, a woman later' (Seneviratne, 1975: 198).

Dramatic defeat

Sirimavo Bandaranaike reappointed many from her first cabinet and increased the number of ministers to include representatives of various ethnic and religious groups and the small leftist parties. Although SLFP's women's section was strengthened and women's representation in parliament increased, she appointed only a single woman minister, and not until 1976, after the International Women's Year in 1975. Siva Obeyesekere was related to Bandaranaike and was first secretary of state for health, as her husband had been, and then minister of health.

The International Women's Year brought the 'woman question' to the fore, and several measures were implemented. Among others, Bandaranaike took the initiative to establish a government agency for women, which later became the Ministry of Women's Affairs. Both the main parties included women's issues for the first time in their programmes, but the references were brief both in the SLFP and the UNP, and women continued to be poorly represented in political office. In the parties, most women worked at the local level. There were very few at higher levels. The national party leaders preferred men, and women were accepted only when they came from prominent political families.

Bandaranaike continued the policy of her first government in the second, but now somewhat more to the left. Yet, young Marxists in the south of the country organised an armed rebellion when barely a year had passed. Like her predecessors, Bandaranaike kept a small Sri Lankan army, and now India and Pakistan sent troops to Colombo to aid the prime minister in crushing the insurgency. After this, the defence budget was doubled.

In 1972, a new constitution was adopted establishing the country as the Socialist Republic of Sri Lanka, and foreign banks and plantations were nationalised.

Buddhism was given first place as the nation's religion, which increased opposition among the Tamils. Bandaranaike tried to create patron–client relations with Tamil communities and allowed the use of Tamil in the administration and the judiciary. But a separatist movement, headed by armed groups such as the Tamil Tigers (LTTE), demanded an autonomous state in the north and east. Sri Lanka had been perceived as a model for third world democracy, but now developments tended towards civil war. At the same time, the economy of the country worsened, with oil crises, drought, inflation, rising unemployment and food shortages. Dissatisfaction and strikes spread. The prime minister declared a state of emergency. Extending her term of office and nationalising the country's largest newspaper groups did not increase the popularity of the top leader.

In the elections in 1977, the SLFP suffered a dramatic defeat and only won eight of the 168 seats in the House of Representatives. Only five women (3 per cent) were elected: Bandaranaike along with four women from the UNP. However, Bandaranaike was accused of corruption and abuse of power and was expelled from parliament for seven years after a special presidential commission found her guilty of 'undemocratic excesses' (Malhotra, 2003: 239).

Thirty-four from the family

It was the family connection that brought Sirimavo Bandaranaike to power. As a national leader, she was the first political widow. To solve the problems, her family helped her, and she also strengthened the family's power. As prime minister, she did something her husband, SWRD, did not. She appointed relatives in important positions. Felix Bandaranaike was given a ministerial post, and Sirimavo's brothers were, respectively, her private secretary, Supreme Court judge, export director and head of the state-owned plantation company. In 1975, a newspaper noted that 11 of the prime minister's close relatives were placed around in management positions and asked if everything should stay in the family. In 1999, at least 34 from the Bandaranaike–Ratwatte family held high posts. Bandaranaike was not alone in building up a dynasty. The leaders of the UNP (popularly known as the 'Uncle Nephew Party') also belonged to the same family and secured influence for their relatives long before the Bandaranaike family began. In 1999, 75 people with Senanayake–Jayawardene connections had important positions (Malhotra, 2003: 237–43).

Sirimavo Bandaranaike sent all her children abroad to study: Sunetra in Oxford, Chandrika in Paris and Anura in London. After studying political science and economics, Chandrika came back and got involved in her mother's reform efforts. Sunetra was her mother's personal adviser, while Anura was elected to parliament and served as opposition leader while his mother was banned from the House. But who would be Bandaranaike's successor? After much back and forth, Chandrika was selected, possibly because she was the most dynamic and charismatic and most engaged in the conditions of the poor. She was, first, Vice Chair, and, later, leader of the SLFP. Most people in Sri Lanka, including Anura, expected the son to be the next head of the family dynasty, although he was the youngest. When it became clear that his mother preferred Chandrika, Anura went over to the UNP and became a minister in their government. Sunetra got involved in artistic activities (*Current Biography*, 1996; Malhotra, 2003: 240–2).

Civil war

In a new constitution in 1978, the UNP government strengthened the position of the president, creating a dual system with a directly elected president as combined head of state and government who appoints the prime minister and the cabinet. The prime minister is head of the party in parliament. The parliament was reduced to a single chamber, with 225 seats elected by a modified system of proportional representation. In 1980, Sri Lanka signed the United Nations (UN) Convention on the Elimination of All Forms of Discrimination against Women (CEDAW), but no women became members of the UNP cabinet.

The government supported a free market economy, which initially led to economic growth. But the regime became increasingly violent, authoritarian and repressive. In 1983, civil war broke out between government forces and Tamils, with terrorism and military action. Many years of martial law followed.

After a long time, the divided left managed to join forces, and the steadfast Sirimavo Bandaranaike ran for election as president in 1988, at 72 years old. But the UNP male candidate won, with 50.4 per cent of the vote, while Bandaranaike got 44.9 per cent. However, she did not give up, and the year after, she managed to get into parliament again, even though the SLFP did badly in the election and only got 67 seats (of 225).

It was only possible in 1994 to establish a People's Alliance, which won enough seats (105 of 225) to form a government together with some small parties. The UNP government lost the election, among other reasons, because of the Mothers' Front. The Front was formed in 1984 to protest against the disappearance of family members and became one of Sri Lanka's most important women's organisations. In 1992, the Front had 25 000 members, mostly poor women, and they forced political parties to take women seriously during the electoral campaign.

Chandrika Kumaratunga became prime minister, at 48 years old – the third in the family. But she went further and was elected the first woman president later that year, with 64 per cent of the vote.

Mother and daughter

Twelve women were elected to parliament (5 per cent) in 1994, including seven from the People's Alliance. Two women (3 per cent) became ministers. One was responsible for Women and Social Affairs, and President Kumaratunga appointed her mother as prime minister. Formally, the position was far less important than before, but Bandaranaike was still a major influence. It was the first time that a country had both a woman president and woman prime minister and, in addition, mother and daughter. But women's political representation in general was among the lowest in Asia.

In 1999, Kumaratunga was re-elected as president, but the following year, Bandaranaike resigned as prime minister. Her health was poor, and she wanted to give her daughter the opportunity of reorganising the cabinet before the election of a new parliament. On the way home, after having voted in the election, Bandaranaike had a heart attack and died, aged 84 years old. Thus, four decades of pioneering work as a woman in politics was over, with victory and defeat. The world's first female prime minister had been a legend for a long time. She was internationally recognised, and for many in Sri Lanka, she stood out as 'Mathiniya' (the undisputed leader). But Bandaranaike was also criticised for her weak involvement in women's issues and her uncompromising attitude towards the Tamil minority (De Silva, 1999: 60; Kirinde, 2000; Rettie, 2000: 5).

The story of Chandrika Kumaratunga continues in Chapter Four.

India's 'Empress' Indira Gandhi

India's first prime minister

Indira Gandhi was not offered the position on a silver platter like Mrs B. Still, it was a legacy. Indira was the only child of the 'Father of the Nation', Jawaharlal Nehru.[4] After independence in 1947, India became a federal republic with a number of self-governing states. The federal government was structured in accordance with the British model, with a two-chamber assembly, comprising a lower house, the House of the People, and an upper house, the Council of States. The House was directly elected by simple plurality, while Council members were indirectly elected, by state assemblies, and there were also some designated members. The titular, executive head of the federal government was the president, elected by a large electoral college and acting in accordance with advice from the prime minister. *Real* de facto executive power was wielded by the prime minister and a council of ministers drawn from the majority party or coalition within the federal parliament and responsible to the House.

Nehru was India's first prime minister and ruled the country continuously for 18 years. He became known for his struggle for 'neutrality' and was one of the founders of the non-aligned movement. He was an ardent defender of liberal democracy and went against anything that had a smack of nepotism, so he did not prepare for his daughter to succeed him (Malhotra, 2003: 60; Steinberg, 2008: 68). A senior male politician, Lal Bahadur Shastri, took over after Nehru's death. But before long, Indira nevertheless became prime minister.

The Nehru family traced their ancestry to high-caste Brahmins from Kashmir. Indira was born in 1917 and grew up with her paternal grandfather, Motilal Nehru, who was an influential, wealthy lawyer in Allahabad. He was a warm admirer of British culture and sent his son, Jawaharlal, to school in England, where he graduated as a lawyer. But both father and son joined the Congress Party and fought for independence. Mahatma Gandhi played an important role with his Non-Cooperation Policy and had great influence on Jawaharlal Nehru. The family became engaged in political work, boycotted everything British and gave up their luxurious lifestyle for hand-woven cloth and simple Indian food. Over 15 million Indians enrolled in the Congress Party, and it became a leading force in the nationalist movement. People with very different backgrounds and beliefs participated, also many women. The party mobilised against caste differences, poverty and ethnic and religious barriers. The Nehru family was divided, but both Motilal and Jawaharlal became party leaders and, like many others in the family, they were fined and imprisoned by the colonial power.

Kamala Kaul was a teenager when she married the 10-years-older Jawaharlal, and she gave birth to Indira when only 18 years old. The marriage was arranged, and while Kamala belonged to the same caste, her upbringing was in accordance with Hindu tradition, with a minimum of schooling, and so she was looked down upon by her female in-laws. Indira was attached to her mother and perceived that the hostility from the rest of the family was unfair. In her autobiography, she writes that her mother had a very strong character in a quiet way (Gandhi, 1980: 11). Kamal's courageous and persistent support enabled Jawaharlal to join Mahatma Gandhi and change their whole way of life, even though the family was originally against it. Gandhi appealed especially to women, and all strata and groups of the population poured into the streets to demonstrate. Kamala was one of them (Jayakar, 1995: 10–11, 34–6; Frank, 2002: 18; Steinberg, 2008: 17).

In the midst of politics

Indira grew up in a centre of national politics. Being more prophetic than she could have imagined, the famous Indian writer Sarojini Naidu in a letter of congratulations to Jawaharlal Nehru at the birth of his daughter, called Indira 'the new soul of India' (Masani, 1976: 13). And the atmosphere surrounding the child was indeed special: stimulating and engaging, but it was also tense and disturbing. In addition to a large number of family members and servants, the house was constantly full of visitors: British and Indian, intellectuals and peasants. Suddenly, the police would break in and arrest the adults, leaving Indira alone for weeks and months to get along as best she could. Her schooling was frequently interrupted, and she was primarily taught at home. Before she was a teenager, she saw her father sentenced to jail several times. Her mother also spent considerable time in prison. Among the visitors, Indira made friends with Mahatma Gandhi, but could otherwise be quite lonely. Her mother was often sick and isolated. There were few children to play with, and her father was away a lot: if not in jail, he was often travelling. But he was strongly involved in his daughter's well-being, wrote long letters and gave her advice. He was ambitious on his daughter's behalf, but wanted her to choose a career based on her own interests. In prison, he wrote a world history for her in letter form. Indira also travelled with her parents around India and Ceylon and went to Switzerland, where her mother received treatment for tuberculosis. Indira attended the international school and visited European countries with her father.

Indira's mother, who had felt the disadvantages of being a woman, became a feminist and an ardent advocate of girls' education. The family was disappointed when she gave birth to a girl, not a boy, and there were no more children. But Motilal Nehru wanted boys and girls to be treated equally, and Indira's experience was that gender did not matter. She could do what she wanted. She became very independent, but was at the same time insecure and withdrawn. She felt that she could not trust her parents, but had to protect them as best she could. Even as a youngster, her games were primarily political: she let the dolls fight as freedom fighters and police, gave speeches to the servants, and organised the children she knew as couriers and spies to help the leaders of the Congress Party. It hit her hard that her grandfather died in 1931, when she was 13 years old. Then her mother died in 1936, when she was 18. Her father was in jail when Kamala's health deteriorated. Indira took her mother to a sanatorium in Switzerland, but was unable to save her life.[5]

Her father's right hand

After her mother's death, it was decided that Indira should continue her education in England. A family friend and comrade-in-arms, Feroze Gandhi (not related to Mahatma), was a student at the London School of Economics, and Indira attended Somerville College in Oxford, where she read modern history. However, she did not complete her studies. Her health was poor and she failed her Latin exam. In 1941, she returned home to India and married Feroze Gandhi. She chose her spouse herself, in spite of her father's objections because Feroze had a different religious and social background. 'Mixed marriages' raised storms of protest at the time, and their married life was not easy. They were both politically active and fought for India's independence, but they did it in different ways and did not always agree. Feroze accepted that his wife had a career, but when she was successful, he both liked and disliked it. Nothing became easier when both were arrested in 1942, which Indira experienced as highly traumatic. When they were released, they moved in with the Nehru family, and their son Rajiv was born in 1944.

When Nehru assumed leadership of the interim government, he appointed his son-in-law, Feroze, who needed a steady job, to the position of managing director of the *National Herald*, a newspaper founded by Nehru in Lucknow, 500 km from Delhi. The couple moved there, but Indira soon started commuting to Delhi with Rajiv to act as hostess and personal assistant to her father. When he asked her, she felt that she could not say no. Nehru was a widower and faced awesome responsibilities creating a new state at the same time as violent clashes took place between Hindus, Moslems and Sikhs. Millions of people moved between the two newly established states, India and Pakistan, and the assassination of Mahatma Gandhi did not make things easier.

There were marital difficulties, and before long, Indira moved home to her father with her two sons – Rajiv and Sanjay, who was born in 1946 – while Feroze remained in Lucknow. She travelled with her father at home and abroad, was his confidante, and looked after meetings and visitors in addition to the household in Delhi. Feroze sought the company of other women, and relatives and governesses helped take care of the children. In 1952, both Nehru and Feroze were elected to the House. At the same time, Feroze was appointed managing director of the *Indian Express* newspaper and moved to Delhi. However, he did not feel at home in the aristocratic Nehru family with the roles of 'Son-in-law of the Nation' and 'Husband of the First Lady'. In 1960, Feroze died of a heart attack.[6]

In her father's footsteps

While she acted as her father's right hand, Indira Gandhi established contacts and acquired political insight, but, outwardly, she did not distinguish herself very much. She founded a school for destitute children, did relief work in Moslem and Hindu refugee camps, and was active in the women's section of the Congress Party. When India's first general election was held in 1951/52, Congress Party workers asked her to stand for parliament, but she refused. Her sons were too young, she pointed out. Equally important was the fact that both her father and her husband stood for election, and she was campaigning for them. In 1956, she suddenly became member of the Congress Working Committee, the party's highest political body. She had not sought membership, but many of her father's political colleagues regarded her as a conduit to the prime minister and a potentially useful tool. Although she kept a low profile, she ran into problems in 1959, when she was elected president of the Indian National Congress (Masani, 1976: 97-121; Gandhi, 1980: 76, 80; Jayakar, 1995: 153–5; Frank, 2002: 231–41).

It was not the first time a woman was leader of the party, but it was the first time after independence. Since the foundation in 1885, the Congress Party was open to women, and some from the elite became members. In the interwar period, there were three women presidents: the Indian poet Sarojini Naidu and two British women, Annie Besant and Nellie Sengupta. An early women's movement demanded political rights and achieved limited suffrage for women in 1935. Universal suffrage was first adopted after independence in 1950.

In the years that followed, female representation in political positions was very small. A woman leader of the country's dominant party was a rarity. Initially, Indira Gandhi was reluctant. She was sure she could not manage. All the big people would bully her, and she would have to answer back. But she was pressured into doing it, and she went to the task with determination and energy when she was elected. It was an intense and stormy period, and after a year, she refused to continue. She was drawn in all directions, Feroze was furious and she developed health problems.[7]

Nehru was prime minister until his death in 1964. Indira Gandhi had originally planned to travel abroad, but agreed to become member of the Council of States and minister of information in the Shastri government instead. Then something unexpected happened: Shastri died before two years had passed. Nobody had taken this into account, and the party was divided. The ultra-rightist Morarji Desai thought that he was entitled to be prime minister, but central party bosses did not want him because of his authoritarian style. Instead, they suggested Indira Gandhi. She was not identified with any caste, region, religion or faction. She had a clean record, was in fact a national leader and was popular among Hindus, Moslems, other minorities and the poor. She could also attract female voters. The party bosses thought that as a young and inexperienced woman, she would be weak and easy to control. With the appeal of her magic name, she could be a 'vote-catching device' and later be replaced by a more suitable leader. Elections were to be held in a year.

Indira Gandhi herself was reticent and agreed mostly out of duty when she was asked. In her autobiography, she notes: 'I don't think I really debated at all whether I could do it or not. I was really quite numb after my father's death' (Gandhi, 1980: 115). But Desai worried her because his policies were diametrically opposed to hers and those of her father. And she felt that she had it in her to become a leader. She quoted from a poem by Robert Frost to her son Rajiv: 'To be king is within the situation and within me' (Jayakar, 1995: 179; Malhotra, 1989: 88). Before she went to parliament, she visited the memorials of Indian independence, Mahatma Gandhi and Pandit Nehru.

For once, there was a fight in the Congress parliamentary group regarding the prime minister, and Indira Gandhi won, with 355 votes against 169. She would never have made it if she had not been Nehru's daughter. Her parentage was an enormous asset in a country where heredity commanded reverence. When she came out of parliament, a jubilant crowd threw flowers to her and cheered 'Long live Indira' and 'Long live the red rose' (Jawaharlal's symbol).[8]

Tough task

Indira Gandhi became prime minister for the first time in 1966 and influenced Indian politics during nearly two decades. She was prime minister several times, for 15 years in all, before she was assassinated in 1984. Her son then took power.

The beginning was all but easy. At 48 years old, she was younger than her predecessors. She was also inexperienced and, in addition, a woman. Her party colleagues did not take her seriously as a politician. She was treated with downright discourtesy, called among others 'a dumb doll', and the bosses reminded her constantly that she had them to thank for her position. She was elected as her father's daughter at the same time as she wanted to pursue her own policies. While Nehru and Shastri were elected unanimously, Indira Gandhi had a divided party behind her, marked by antagonisms and power struggles. The party bosses decided who should have which posts in the formation of her cabinet, so she assembled a group of personal advisers in what was called the 'kitchen cabinet' (Malhotra, 1989: 90–5; Steinberg, 2008: 26).

The challenges were overwhelming. India is the world's most complex state, with large geographic, economic, social, religious and cultural differences. Each region is unique and contains marked contrasts between bustling urban centres and quiet rural areas, where most people live. Hindus are the majority of the population, but there are also Moslems, Christians and other religious groups. The numerous castes and caste-like groups are ranked, each according to others, with most being traditionally associated with a profession. In addition to Hindi and English, there are 17 recognised regional languages and hundreds of local dialects. When Indira Gandhi came to power, the population of 400 million grew rapidly, but productivity was low and international economic conditions were unfavourable. Approximately half of the population was extremely poor, while wealth and power were in the hands of rich farmers and landowners, capitalists, and the upper-middle class in the cities. The position of women varied more than could be imagined, but, nearly everywhere, they had a lower status than men and less education and employment.

Nehru shaped India with a secular state, a socialist economy and a non-aligned foreign policy. There was a strong focus on the public sector, with government planning and the expansion of education, especially in the cities and at higher levels. Heavy industry was developed and (limited) land reform was introduced. The policies challenged proprietors and the business community, but improved the conditions of religious minorities and low-caste Hindus. In order to finance the development plans, India received assistance from abroad and food was imported.

Indira Gandhi took over at an extremely difficult time. India had recently gone through two wars (with Pakistan and China) and was drained of resources. There was drought, food shortages and inflation, and poor groups were impatient to get better conditions. The dissatisfaction led to unrest and protests. The Congress Party was supreme in Indian politics after independence, but its hegemony had gradually weakened. In order to ensure victory at the elections, the party had established a system of local 'big men', who mobilised voters and afterwards received government support when the party came to power. Thus, the pro-poor Congress Party was in reality dominated by prominent, rich landowners. The party apparatus was heavy, and warring factions hampered the work. Indira followed up the main features of her father's policies and wanted to increase the party's popularity among the large, poor masses, but she depended on central party bosses who had other interests.

The prime minister takes action

The newly elected prime minister set to work in a pragmatic way. She tried to get help from the US, but succeeded only partially and sought assistance from the Soviet Union instead. She visited all the Indian states, travelling more than 50,000 km in order to get support, and won the election in 1967, but the majority was reduced. She became member of the House and was elected prime minister again. Now, she decided herself who would join the cabinet, Desai became deputy prime minister with the finance portfolio.

Her opponents did everything they could to discredit her. There was a long tug of war between Indira Gandhi and the party bosses, leftists and rightists, which ended with the party being split up in 1969. Indira Gandhi lost much of the party apparatus, but got control over the Congress (R) – for Ruling – Party, generally known as the New Congress, and not only the cabinet, but also the central party leadership and state leaders. She continued to govern with the support of other political parties. Politically, the prime minister moved towards the left, nationalised a number of commercial banks and abolished the privileges of the former princes. This was immensely popular in the population. When Indira Gandhi stood for election in 1971, a year early, answering the slogan of her opponents 'Remove Indira' with the slogan 'Remove Poverty', she achieved a two thirds majority in the House (352 of 518 seats).

Soon after, Indira Gandhi won admiration for the way she handled the crisis that arose when the Pakistani army cracked down on East Pakistan in 1971 in order to prevent a free Bangladesh. Atrocities mounted and refugees poured into India, but the prime minister mastered the situation, using political and diplomatic means and waiting as long as possible before she took military action. Then India won the 14-day war with Pakistan and Bangladesh became independent. Indira Gandhi was described as a superb leader, the 'Empress of India', liberating the people of Bangladesh, cutting Pakistan down to size and making India the pre-eminent power in the region (Malhotra, 1989: 134, 141). It was also noted that President Yahya Khan of Pakistan might have been less bellicose and rigid if the Indian government had been headed by a male prime minister, not a woman (Genovese, 2013: 7).[9]

From democracy to dictatorship

Indira Gandhi's position of power was now unique, but India faced one of the worst economic crises since independence. The armaments and refugees from Bangladesh cost dearly, and there was a severe drought. In addition, when the international oil crisis came, the prices went way up. Food shortages and unemployment spread, and inequalities increased.

The New Congress Party had internal problems and struggled with incompetence and corruption. Gandhi's leadership style was increasingly personalised and authoritarian. In 14 years, there were no internal elections in the party. The action against poverty was modest, and the World Bank and International Monetary Fund (IMF) required retrenchment measures in order to provide assistance. Peasants and workers revolted, but were struck down with an iron hand. In 1974, Indira Gandhi declared a nationwide railway strike illegal and 30,000–40,000 railway workers were arrested and their families thrown out of their government-owned houses. At the same time, Indira Gandhi's leadership received two serious blows. The party lost the state elections in Gujarat, in which she had invested heavily, and she was convicted of corruption and violation of the election law in 1971. Mass actions prepared a 'total revolution' to force the prime minister to resign.

Indira Gandhi's position was threatened, but she herself was of the opinion that she was the only one who could handle the situation. To maintain power, she changed the rules of the game from democracy to dictatorship. In June 1975, she declared a state of emergency, arrested opponents, censored the press and banned political organisations. The repression was so tough that it was compared with British colonialism. The prime minister declared that the emergency measures were necessary to fix the economy, and she presented a 20-point action programme.

During the 19 months of emergency rule, measures were carried out to control prices, protect small farmers and increase productivity. But the conditions of the poor were not fundamentally changed, and forced sterilisation, slum destruction and random arrests created strong counter-reactions. When Indira Gandhi called an election in 1977, she suffered a resounding defeat. Her party alliance obtained only 189 seats in parliament against the opposition's 345, and neither she nor her son Sanjay was elected to the House. It was the end of the 30-year hegemony of the Congress Party in Indian politics, and the opposition took over with the aging Desai at the head of a coalition of five parties.[10]

Unexpected revenge

Others would have given up; but not Indira Gandhi. At the age of 59 years, she was without work, income or residence and had also lost her staff. She was arrested and brought to court, but the 'prosecution' turned into 'persecution' of what was referred to as a 'lone and defenceless woman', increasing many people's sympathy for their former icon. The Congress Party was split again, and now the new party was squarely called Congress Party (I) – for Indira. She presented herself at a by-election and became member of the House by a wide margin. Meanwhile, the Desai government, apart from restoring civil liberties and democratic procedures, turned out to be dysfunctional, marked by incompetence and infighting. Soon, the coalition broke down.

'Elect a Government that Works', Indira Gandhi demanded, and the woman who was supposed to be 'thrown into the dustbin of history' obtained two-thirds majority of the votes in the general election in 1980. Her Congress alliance rose to 374 of the 542 seats, even though she practically had no party organisation anymore. Her son Sanjay was also elected to the House. Though he was the youngest, he had come forward as his mother's crown prince, especially during emergency rule, and he became secretary general of the party. In some circles, India was now called the 'Land of the Rising Son' (Malhotra, 2003: 87). But Sanjay died suddenly in a plane crash. Indira Gandhi immediately made her other son, Rajiv, her political heir, although he had so far not shown any interest in politics and Sanjay's widow, Maneka Gandhi, claimed to succeed her husband. Rajiv became an MP and secretary general of the party.

During the following period, Gandhi focused on foreign policy, travelled around the world and became a central figure in the movement of non-aligned states. At home, she increased her power over the party and liberalised the economy, which was improving due to the 'green revolution' in rural areas. But little was done to improve social conditions, and there were still ethnic, religious, linguistic and caste-based conflicts, with assaults and murder, abuse of power by the police, and tribal rebellion. The military were deployed several times to stop outbreaks of violence. When the government sent a thousand Indian troops into the holy Golden Temple in Punjab, Indira Gandhi's fate was in reality sealed. Four months later, she was killed by two of her security guards, who were Sikhs. It was in 1984, and she was 67 years old.[11]

In contrast to the complex deliberations that took place when Indira Gandhi became prime minister for the first time, Rajiv Gandhi was now appointed extremely fast. He took over his brother's seat in the House, rapidly called an election and as leader of the Congress Party (I), obtained the largest majority in the House that the party had ever had.

Head of government and a 'dumb doll'

A number of books have been written about Indira Gandhi and assessments vary. She became one of the great leaders of the 20th century, but was a very complex and controversial political figure. She was appreciated for her foreign policy and strengthening of India's unity, integrity and position as a state. Her resolute leadership in war reassured many Indians. Although Sikhs and Hindus criticised her for the attack on the Sikh temple and brutality in the fight against terrorism, many – who were afraid of a new division of the country – supported her zero tolerance for separatism. She was a secularist, believing that people of all religions should coexist within the state. Opinions of her economic policy differed. On the positive side, the green revolution in agriculture, the nationalisation of banks and the growth of the economy were emphasised; on the negative side were the persistent poverty and inequality between regions and the rich and poor. She received the strongest criticism for her leadership style of centralisation of power and the weakening of political institutions: the judiciary, parliament and the party. But some claim that she actually strengthened democracy because people reacted so negatively to the state of emergency, and after some time, Indira Gandhi herself called an election.

It is easy to underestimate the obstacles Indira Gandhi faced. One of these was undoubtedly the discrimination of women. Gandhi acknowledged that men and unfortunately even women were conditioned by the male-oriented Indian society, women having lower status and fewer possibilities than men. She thought that there must be an end to the discrimination. Women should not imitate men, but get the same opportunities as them to develop their talents and personality. Both women and men should be liberated from obscurantism and superstition and the narrow confines of outdated thoughts and habits. The movement for women's liberation should not deteriorate into some kind of confrontation between men and women. Men and women together could help create a better society and a better world, she stated. When she became prime minister, she declared:

> I'm no feminist. I'm a human being. I don't think of myself as a woman when I do my job. According to the Indian Constitution, all citizens are equal, without distinction regarding sex, language or State. I'm just an Indian citizen and the first servant of the country. (Gandhi, 1980: 113, 186–9; see also Jayakar, 1995: 265–7; Frank, 2002: 293–4)

The political scientist Jana Everett (2013: 153–73) describes how Indira Gandhi's work was shaped by the patriarchal political system, where women who came to power, did it on men's terms and had to forget that they were women. When Indira took energetic action, she was typically enough referred to as 'the only man in a government full of ladies'. Otherwise, she was met with derogatory characteristics such as a 'dumb doll' and a 'mere chit of a girl' by her male fellow party members. To destroy the Congress Party was perhaps not particularly constructive, but the party did not manage to deal with the political challenges then under way, and Indira Gandhi's struggle against hostile-minded elites made her lose confidence in party leaders and bureaucrats. She focused instead on direct contact with the masses and won by using populist appeals, centralisation of power and ad hoc solutions. However, this had negative consequences in the long run.

Indira Gandhi's gender was not solely a negative factor; among others, it contributed to her election as prime minister, and Everett notes that Indira could use the fact that she was a woman in a powerful way. It was no coincidence that she was called 'Mother Indira' and was hailed as a Hindu goddess – energising, but also destructive. She became an image of women's power in a country where people from religion and history were acquainted with vigorous goddesses and powerful queens. As a leader of the Indian Self-Employed Women's Association said: 'If Indira Gandhi could be a prime minister of this country, then we all have opportunities' (Everett, 2013: 170; see also Steinberg, 2008: 9–10).

Family and class

An active women's movement, which became one of the world's largest and most diverse, promoted the interests of Indian women in various areas, but it was not the movement that brought Indira Gandhi to power. That was family and class. As head of government, she appointed some women as junior ministers, but none as cabinet ministers. During different periods, she herself took over several ministerial portfolios: foreign affairs, finance, interior and defence. She did not try to promote women leaders, either. The representation of women in parliament remained at a low level. Ever since independence, India had development plans emphasising education, health and welfare for women, but the funding was frequently reduced, and the 10-point programme Indira presented in 1967 did not include any specific initiatives for women.

A census in 1971 revealed the limits to women's gains in the course of 20 years, despite legislative changes, the expansion of education and the access to public positions. The government appointed a Committee on the Status of Women, which came up with a series of reform proposals and gave inspiration to dynamic women's research. The prime minister herself conducted the activities related to the International Women's Year, but the 20-point programme she presented in 1975 did not encompass any special initiatives for women. Sanjay Gandhi, however, added a few points, including literacy, family planning (which became very controversial) and the abolition of dowry, among others. During the Decade for Women, several new women's organisations were created, some independent and some affiliated with political parties. In 1980, India signed the CEDAW (it was ratified in 1993). An Equal Remuneration Act, guaranteeing women equal pay for equal work, was passed, and a Women's Department in the Ministry of Labour and Employment and a Coordinating Bureau for Women in the Ministry of Welfare were created.

Even though the government was not the only actor, far from it, and it is not clear which role Indira Gandhi herself played, the status of Indian women was to a certain extent improved during the 1970s and 1980s. The changes were not dramatic, but fertility was reduced, life expectancy rose and more girls and women got education. However, the uneven sex ratio did not improve (100:93 in favour of men), employment rates of women went down and women's participation in politics remained low.[12] When Indira Gandhi died in 1984, there were 43 women (8 per cent) in the House and 24 (10 per cent) in the Council of States.

Within Indian women's studies (Swarup et al, 1994: 370–1), Indira Gandhi was perceived as the archetype for women who were trying to obtain not only political representation, but also a place in the power structure of post-independence India. A symbol of both accomplishments and contradictions, she represented the tokenism in women's ascent to power and the underlying limits of the efforts of the women's movement to attain equality and political representation. Gandhi's rise to power was due less to the strength of the women's movement than to a combination of other factors, such as her family background in the nationalist movement and the Congress (I)'s need for a compromise candidate.

Many biographers conclude that Indira Gandhi was an extraordinarily complex person. An admixture of the 'good, the bad, the ugly', the Canadian political scientist Blema S. Steinberg writes (2008: 45). Having flirted with socialism, Gandhi became a pragmatic politician who was prepared to allow capitalism to flourish, with all of its pluses and minuses. Gandhi was strongly goal-oriented, primarily motivated by power and utility. While she had an extremely open approach to the public, her populism was coupled with political impropriety. She was largely competitive and controlling in her relations with the party and other politicians, and not particularly characterised by the cooperative or empathetic leadership styles that have been associated with female leadership (Steinberg, 2008: 10, 45, 67, 110-1; see also Gupte, 2009: 106-25, 445-548).

But the real test of a political leader is how he or she tackles society's problems, the Sri Lankan political scientist Ralph Buultjens notes. Did the leader leave the country in a better shape than when he or she found it? He concludes that: 'In a larger sense, Indira Gandhi meets this test well.' She coped well with many difficulties (war, oil crisis, economic slump and emergency), managed to sustain the unity and integrity of India, was a real secularist and 'the single most exposed and heard political figure in all of history' (Gupte 2009: 107, see also 106-25, 445-548).

No matter how controversial Indira Gandhi was in her time, she became highly appreciated later. A poll conducted by *India Today* magazine in 2001 concerning the best prime minister that India had ever had gave Indira Gandhi 41 per cent of the vote, while Jawaharlal Nehru only received 13 per cent.

Golda Meir takes charge – and Dalia Itzik follows

Unexpected death

No sooner had Indira Gandhi become prime minister in India than she was joined by a woman prime minister in Israel. Golda Meir was not supposed to become prime minister. When it came into question, she was only going to be a caretaker for a short while, until the central male politicians in the government party, Mapai (Labour), figured out who was going to take over. Golda Meir herself hesitated. In her autobiography, she stresses that she never planned to be prime minister. But her party comrades thought that she only pretended – that she, in fact, had been dreaming of becoming prime minister for many years (Meir, 1976: 316; Burkett, 2008: 232–3). Nevertheless, when she got her chance, she was 70 years old, her health was not good and she had recently retired to take it easy and enjoy her life as a grandmother. 'I honestly don't want the responsibility, the stress and strain of being prime minister', she declared (Meir, 1976: 317).[13]

An unexpected death brought Golda Meir into the limelight. Suddenly, the country's top political leader was gone, and the void needed to be filled rapidly. Golda was a widow, but she had no family connections to the prime minister they now wanted her to succeed.

The man, who suddenly suffered a heart attack and died, was Levi Eshkol. He took over as prime minister when Israel's founding father, David Ben-Gurion, stepped down, and governed during a period of high tension in the Middle East. After Israel won the Six-Day War in 1967, defeating Egyptian, Jordanian and Syrian armies and sweeping back into lands they had taken in the Suez–Sinai War and later returned, there were no serious diplomatic negotiations, and hostilities continued along the Suez Canal. In addition to the continual threat of war, Israel faced high inflation, labour strikes, housing shortages, high unemployment and a persistent flood of new immigrants.

When Eshkol died in February 1969, the situation for the Israelis was too serious to risk a paralysing leadership contest. It was also important to avoid an open conflict between the two popular Mapai heroes: the Deputy Prime Minister Yigal Allon and the Minister of Defence Moshe Dayan. A poll indicated that 45 per cent of Israelis wanted Dayan as prime minister, 32 per cent wanted Allon and 3 per cent wanted Golda Meir. As soon as Eshkol was dead, the hullaballoo started, with the two top men quarrelling overtly (Burkett, 2008: 230–3).

The new prime minister had to take over command immediately. Golda was the only person with sufficient authority and confidence in the party to keep it together, and with her experience, she could get going at once. With doubt and fear, Golda agreed to take temporary responsibility for the government until elections could be held and a new prime minister put in place: 'I have never failed to accept party decisions, and I shall not refuse now', she said; 'I have faced difficult problems in the past, but nothing like the one I am faced with now in leading the country' (BBC News, 7 March 2014).

Allon and Dayan agreed to step aside for the time being, and Meir was accepted by the Labour Party as prime minister on 7 March 1969. She was the only nominee put forward before the Central Committee and was selected with a large majority: none opposed, though there with some abstentions. When the result was clear, tears rolled down Golda's cheeks, and she held her head in her hands (Meir, 1976: 315–17; Burkett, 2008: 234).

Stand-in consolidates her position

Israel had a parliamentary political system with a single assembly, the Knesset. It was elected using proportional representation, in which the whole country was a single constituency. This encouraged the formation of a large number of, often changing, political parties, and from the founding, Israel was ruled by successive coalition governments led by Mapai, or the Labour Alignment after 1967. A ceremonial president, chosen by the Knesset, designated the prime minister, who had to be an MP. As prime minister, Golda Meir maintained the national unity cabinet that had been formed in 1967 after the Six-Day War, won an overwhelming vote of confidence in the Knesset and got going.

The cabinet spanned from leftist idealists to militant conservatives, and they had difficulty agreeing on anything. Meir was strong, decisive, overbearing and intolerant; if necessary, scolding ministers as if she had been their mother. Ministers grumbled, but gave in. As prime minister, she kept an unusually high pace and did not think that government managed to do enough. So, she created her own mini-cabinet, the 'kitchen cabinet', which met on Saturday evenings to make important decisions (Burkett, 2008: 236–8; Thompson, 2013: 193–4).

Things did not turn out the way the party elite had imagined. No sooner had Golda Meir been selected as prime minister than Egypt launched the 'War of Attrition'. It was not a full-scale military confrontation, but entailed large-scale attacks, and Israel retaliated. The war required broad mobilisation, and military spending weighed heavily on the Israeli economy. Golda did not hesitate. She actively opposed salary increases and strikes in order to reduce inflation and went to Washington DC to ask President Nixon for financial assistance and military equipment. The initiatives did not pay off immediately, but as elections in October 1969 were approaching, Meir was no longer an interim figure who was supposed to retire as soon as the major contenders for leadership had sorted things out. She was simply 'the prime minister', the undisputed leader of the Labour Party. Furthermore, her grandmotherly appearance and unpretentious style did not diminish her popularity. She won the general election with the largest support an Israeli party ever got (46 per cent). Meir became prime minister again, and this time it was not by default: she gained the position on her own merit (Meir, 1976: 318–31; Thompson, 2013: 189–90).

Golda Meir had an extensive political career, and it was not based on family relations. She climbed up the ranks herself. She starting fighting for a Jewish state at an early age and had 40 years of political experience when she was asked to head the government. She was the first woman to hold this high office in an industrialised country. Indeed, Israel is situated in the Middle East, but the new state was essentially established by immigrants from industrial countries and was marked by this.

Against the conventions

Golda Mabovitch was born in Kiev in 1898 in what was, at the time, the Russian Empire (nowadays, Ukraine). Her family was Jewish, and her early childhood was characterised by poverty, violence and fear. The Czar was implementing a Russification programme, and the Jews were subject to strict control and persecution. Golda's father was a skilled carpenter, but he could hardly provide for the family. Of eight children, only three daughters survived: Sheyna, who was nine years older than Golda, and Zipporah (called Zipke, later Clara), who was three years younger. When Golda was five years old, her father emigrated to the US to get a better livelihood. Her mother moved to Golda's grandparents in Pinsk with the three daughters. The Jewish ghetto was a hotbed of radical activity. Intense and intelligent, the 14-year-old Sheyna was drawn into the socialist Zionist movement and her little sister Golda watched from the sidelines. In 1906, the family left for the US. They went to Milwaukee in Wisconsin, where Golda's father worked off and on in the workshops of the railroad. Despite opposition from her husband, Golda's mother opened a small grocery store to add to the income, and Golda had to assist.

Golda was a bright and active girl and became an excellent student. In addition, at the age of 11, she organised fundraising to buy school books for the children who could not afford them. In her spare time, Sheyna took Golda along to a group of Russian emigrants who debated politics and Zionism. After primary school, Golda wanted to go on to high school, but this caused a conflict with her parents. They thought that more education was unnecessary for a young girl and could even be detrimental to her marriage prospects. But Golda would not give in, so she moved to Denver to live with Sheyna, who had married and established herself there.

Politics, philosophy and history of religion fascinated the young Golda, and Sheyna's house was full of people discussing socialism and Zionism. Ideologically, they were committed to social equality, but they did not concern themselves with women's emancipation. The fundamental and overriding social issue was the problem of Jewish existence. Here, Golda got her basic training and soon became a member of the Labour Zionist organisation. She also met Morris Meyerson, a Jew from Lithuania, who was interested in poetry, art and music. He was some years older than her and worked as a sign painter. Although he was not very interested in politics, Golda admired him 'enormously', not only for his encyclopaedic knowledge, but for his gentleness, his intelligence and his wonderful sense of humour (Meir, 1976: 33). After a while, Golda moved back to Milwaukee to attend teachers' college. But she got more and more involved in the Zionist movement and left school. She spoke on street corners and in public meetings, organised a protest march against pogroms in Pinsk, sold a Zionist newspaper and travelled around to raise funds. This was very unusual for a young woman at the time, but Golda was unusual in her engagement and self-confidence.

Golda became firmly convinced that the Jews had to have their own homeland if they were to survive and determine their own destiny. So, she decided to immigrate to Palestine. For a long time, this vision seemed illusive, but when Great Britain in 1917 supported the idea of Palestine as a Jewish homeland and rapidly put the entire area under British military rule, the situation was all of a sudden totally changed. Morris Meyerson did not particularly want to go to the Promised Land, but accepted Golda's decision, and they married in 1917.[14] In 1921, the couple left friends and family in the US and went to Palestine together with Sheyna and her two children. Sheyna's husband soon followed, as did Golda's parents after a few years.[15]

Hard life in the Promised Land

It was a tough transition. Golda and Morris first lived in a kibbutz (a collective farm). Golda enjoyed it, but Morris had difficulties bearing the hardships of rural labour and the communal way of life, so they moved to Jerusalem. Here, Morris got a job as a bookkeeper. Their son, Menachem, was born in 1924 and their daughter, Sarah, in 1926. Morris was a relatively conventional person, and Golda tried as best as she could to fulfil a traditional role as mother and housewife. But the four years in Jerusalem were the worst Golda Meir ever experienced. Her husband earned very little, and they only managed to rent two rooms without gas, electricity or heating. Even if the housewife taught private pupils and washed clothes to get some extra cash, they were so poor that Golda was afraid the children would go hungry. However, it was not only the poverty, but also the loneliness, that made her so wretched. Instead of actively helping to build the Jewish national home, she sat cooped up in a tiny flat in Jerusalem concentrating all her energy on making do with Morris's wages (Meir, 1976: 78).

In 1928, Golda got a job as secretary of the Women's Labour Council of the General Federation of Jewish Labour, Histadrut. It was the first and last women's organisation for which she ever worked. She was attracted to it not so much because it concerned women, but because she was interested in the work it was doing, particularly agricultural training (Meir, 1976: 88). Histadrut appointed Golda Meir after an internal conflict where male leaders, headed by Ben-Gurion, felt that women's accusations of discrimination undermined the legitimacy of the organisation, and Golda supported the position that women should submit to the organisation, not fight separately (Sharfman, 1994: 384–5).

In practice, Golda became head of the Histadrut women's section, a position that required considerable effort and a lot of travelling, and she had to live in Tel Aviv. Moving became the beginning of her political career and the end of her marriage. Golda took the children with her, while Morris stayed in Jerusalem. They remained friends and never formally divorced, but they did not live together again. Morris died in 1951.

As a single mother, Golda struggled to combine her responsibility for the children with her professional work. This was a dilemma that worried her during most of her life. When she was away from home, she had feelings of guilt and was afraid that the children did not get what they needed. But Golda could not give up her work. The creation of a Jewish state was what gave her life meaning. So, if necessary, she or her family had to make sacrifices to achieve it. She made sure others took care of Menachem and Sarah when she could not do it herself, and pointed out that they grew up as healthy, productive, talented and kind people (Meir, 1976: 90).

In his book about his mother, Menachem describes the home as warm and well-run. The children felt forlorn when their mother took off on a trip, but, apart from that, Golda did not differ significantly from the working mothers of many of their schoolmates. And when their mother was with them, she was really there – 'attentive, kind, considerate, witty and a healer of wounds' (Meir, 1983: 25–9) – and she wore herself out taking care of Sarah when she fell seriously ill.

Golda Meir worked hard and was away from home when necessary. She had charm, and was intelligent and engaged. There were romances with several of the leading men in the movement. The leaders realised that Golda could have a useful function. She spoke excellent English and had good connections in the US, so she was sent on round trips to raise funds for the Jewish settlers and the Histadrut, a task she accomplished beyond all expectations. She joined the Secretariat, the core of Histadrut, and was the only woman member of the close inner circle. She helped create the Labour Party and build a Jewish shipping business. During World War II, she served as a liaison between the Jews in Palestine and the British administration, and, at the same time, she fought against Britain's refusal to open the door to Jewish immigration. When the British cracked down on the Zionist movement in 1946, she took over as head of the political department of the Jewish Agency, which represented the Jewish community in Palestine.[16]

'We have our state'

Great Britain withdrew from Palestine following the UN resolution in 1947 on the partition of Palestine into an Arab and a Jewish state. The resolution (A/RES/181) was adopted by the General Assembly in face of vehement opposition. It was endorsed by a vote of 33 for, 13 against and 10 abstentions, and was supported by both the US and the Soviet Union. But the British abstained, and the Arab League and Arabs in Palestine protested. Violence in the region escalated, and Golda Meir first went to the US to raise money, then secretly to King Abdullah of Transjordan to prevent hostilities. She raised an astonishing $50 million, and David Ben-Gurion later noted that it was a Jewish woman who got the money to make the state possible (Burkett, 2008: 138; Steinberg, 2008: 124).

However, Golda Meir did not become member of the provisional government. Equality between women and men was part of a socialist Zionist ideology, and formally everybody had the same rights. Universal suffrage was introduced at the same time as the state of Israel was established. Women were also supposed to participate in economic production, but traditional gender roles were not much changed, so child care and housework remained 'women's work' and men dominated in politics. Golda became a member of the Jewish People's Council, but they were only two women among 35 men.

Ben-Gurion was head of the Jewish Agency and argued that it was necessary to have at least one woman in the provisional government. However, to make everything fall into place among the coalition partners, only men were included: 13 in addition to Ben-Gurion himself. Golda Meir was deeply insulted, but remained silent. Her loyalty to Ben-Gurion was so strong that she used to say she would jump from the fifth floor if he asked her to (Burkett, 2008: 182; Steinberg, 2008: 128). No sooner was the declaration of independence signed than Golda was sent to the US to raise more funds to cope with the five Arab armies that crossed the borders of the new state. Then, she was sent to Moscow as ambassador; although leaving Israel the moment the state was established was more difficult for Golda than she could say (Meir, 1976: 191).[17]

Modern Deborah

The first election to the Knesset in 1949 resulted in 13 women MPs (11 per cent), among others, Golda Meir. Ben-Gurion became prime minister, and now he included Golda in the cabinet as the only woman. She was minister from 1949 to 1966, being first responsible for labour and social affairs, then foreign policy.

When Golda Meir was nominated as minister, there were counter-reactions from religious quarters because she was a woman. To this, the reply was that Deborah was a judge in ancient Israel – a position that was far more important than a minister (Meir, 1976: 210)! Meir chose to be minister of labour after she refused to become deputy prime minister. She wanted to get something done and see results. Her experience from Histadrut came in handy when she had to provide hundreds of thousands of Jews, many poor, who flocked to the new state with food, shelter and jobs. Meir proceeded pragmatically, travelled to the US to raise money, built houses and roads, and enacted social welfare policy.

Golda Meir became most famous as foreign minister. It was during this period that Ben-Gurion reportedly said that Meir was the only man in the cabinet. This was obviously the greatest possible compliment that could be paid to a woman, Meir noted. But she doubted if any man would have been flattered if she had said about him that he was the only woman in the government (Meir, 1976: 89)!

Ben-Gurion designated Golda Meir as foreign minister to end the conflict he had with her predecessor and gain control over international relations himself. Golda was no fan of diplomacy and did not like a job that mainly consisted of talking, and it did not make things easier that in substantive matters, she was actually Ben-Gurion's marionette. But she did as she was told and enjoyed developing a policy of cooperation with the newly independent states of Africa. She remained as minister for 10 years (Meir, 1976: 263–90; Burkett, 2008: 183–5).

Meir was appointed in June 1956. In July, Egypt decided to nationalise the Suez Canal and block the passage of Israeli ships. Together with France and Britain, Israel went to war in October. In the course of six days, the Israeli forces conquered almost the entire Sinai Peninsula and the Gaza Strip. The Egyptian military bases were destroyed, and thousands were taken prisoner. The UN obtained a ceasefire, but in the world organisation, Meir not only garnered sympathy for herself and her country; she also became known for her uncompromising stance in the conflict with the Arabs, defending Israel's right to exist.[18]

Close to disaster

The constant travel and the strain of international politics wore Golda Meir down. In January 1966, when she was 67, she retired to what she thought would be a quiet home life with children and grandchildren. But the Mapai Party was about to be torn apart by internal power struggles. Friends asked Meir to come back, become secretary general of the party and reconcile the differences. She stood outside of the various factions, held on to the fundamental principles of a socialist Zionism and had shown that she could bring about cooperation and collaboration. Less than a year after she retired, she was again in the centre of the whirl, and she managed to stabilise the party and develop a working labour coalition. When she retired in 1968 after completion of the tasks, she thought that this time it was over. But it did not turn out that way.

Golda Meir became prime minister in 1969 just after one war and resigned in 1974 shortly after another. Although she was not directly involved in the decisions concerning the Six-Day War, she supported military action once it appeared to Israel that war was inevitable and endorsed the decision to retain control of the

West Bank, Gaza and Golan Heights. After the war, Meir believed peace was assured. But, in fact, the level of conflict was heightened. Mediation initiatives failed, and ceasefires did not lead to peace. In 1973, the Egyptians and the Syrians attacked. It was on Yom Kippur, the most holy Jewish festival. The intelligence services did not work well enough, so the Israelis were taken by surprise and suffered heavy losses. Only when Israel received massive reinforcements from the US were the attackers repelled.

A disengagement agreement was negotiated, but Golda Meir was deeply shaken. It had nearly been a disaster for the country. The fact that the Israeli military was invincible had proven to be a myth, and many lives could have been saved if she as prime minister had mobilised faster when the first warning signals came. In her autobiography, she wrote: 'I will never again be the person I was before the Yom Kippur War' (Meir, 1976: 357–8). The government was also criticised. Meir offered to resign, but the party said no. Elections were to be held on 31 December, and despite the criticism, Meir was re-elected. The coalition received fewer seats than before. Yet, Meir formed a coalition government again. A commission of inquiry exonerated both Meir and the defence minister for direct responsibility for the government's unpreparedness for the Arab offensive, but Meir was completely exhausted. She left the prime minister's office in June 1974, at the age of 76. Four years later, she died.[19]

Overriding dream

Golda Meir lived during extraordinary and turbulent times, and, as is true for Indira Gandhi, her legacy is also mixed. Meir was praised for her role in building and defending the state of Israel, but was criticised because she encouraged settlement on the West Bank, denied Palestinians their rights and failed to pursue negotiations with Egypt. While Indira Gandhi was motivated primarily by a concern with power, Golda Meir's most important motivation for assuming high political office was her ideological convictions. Her life centred above all around the realisation of the dream of a homeland for the Jews. Golda Meir did what she could to strengthen the new state with a mixture of ideology and pragmatism, and she could be extremely tough and demanding (Steinberg, 2008: 144, 172–4, 205–8). She was described as a 'Stalwart Lioness' (*Current Biography*, 1979: 47) and the 'Iron Lady' of Israeli politics, long before the epithet was coined for Margaret Thatcher (Butt, G, 1998).

Conflict with the Arabs and war dominated the agenda while Golda Meir was member of the Israeli government. When it came to understanding the Arab–Israeli conflict, defending Israel's interests and the use of force, Meir fit solidly into the mainstream of her peers (Thompson, 2013: 193). But her son points out that she was not the unforgiving, narrow-minded, militaristic woman portrayed by some people. She had a desperate desire for peace, he claims, which she repeated incessantly. But she did *not* want peace at any price and certainly *not* at the price of Israel's annihilation, which she was convinced was the main goal of the Arab states (Meir, 1983: 186).

Golda Meir worked for a society based on justice and equality. When she became prime minister, she hoped that she could do something to help solve Israel's social and economic problems. Between 1949 and 1970, over 400,000 units of public housing were built, and there was not a single place that did not have a school, a kindergarten and, in most cases, also a nursery school. But there was a gap between those who could and those who could not cope economically. Some measures were implemented to reduce poverty, but it was not easy in the midst of armed conflict (Meir, 1976: 331–3).

Not a feminist, but ...

When Golda Meir was young, she refused to be bound by traditional conventions and fought against her parents to get an education. She had to pay a price when she chose to marry and have a family at the same time as she was active outside the home. Nevertheless, she took up a political career and obtained several very important positions, though her career was not the same as a man would have had. No other women in Israel were near to acquiring as important posts as Golda.

Golda Meir acknowledged that women had dilemmas and problems. In particular, it was more difficult for women than for men to live their own lives both inside and outside the home because they had to work double. But she accepted this as a fact without raising objections and wondering if the ideals of equality were being betrayed. In fact, she emphasised:

> I have lived and worked with men all my life, but being a woman has never hindered me in any way at all. It has never caused me unease or given me an inferiority complex or made me think that men are better off than women – or that it is a disaster to give birth to children. Not at all. Nor have men ever given me preferential treatment. (Meir, 1976: 89)

Such an idyllic picture does not mean that Meir actually escaped discrimination. When she ran for mayor in Jerusalem in 1955, for example, two religious representatives refused to support her because she was a woman, which meant that she was not elected. Golda Meir was enraged – as if women did not do what they should and even more to build the Jewish state!

Meir stated that she was not a great admirer of 'the kind of feminism that gives rise to bra-burning, hatred of men or a campaign against motherhood' (Meir, 1976: 89). In her view, the energetic, hard-working women in the labour movement, who taught girls to work in agriculture, represented a completely different, constructive feminism. Kibbutz women were among the world's first and most successful fighters for true equality. However, Golda did not support the kibbutz women when they resisted working in the kitchen to obtain equal burdens with men. 'Why is it so much better to work in the barn?', she asked and began energetically reorganising the kitchen (Meir, 1976: 67–8). Both in Histadrut and as a cabinet minister, Meir promoted measures that improved the conditions of women and particularly working mothers, which she herself had experienced, but it was more a question of improving social conditions than women's position specifically.

Meir did not comment upon her own unique position or the general absence of women in public life. When she became prime minister, she took over a cabinet with only male ministers, and after she resigned, the cabinet still only consisted of men. She was a member of the Knesset until 1974, but during this time, the number of elected women actually went down, to eight (7 per cent). Only in the 1980s did another woman became member of the Israeli cabinet, and it was not until the 1990s that the representation of women in the Knesset reached the level of 1949. In 2014, Israel was among the Western countries with the lowest proportion of women in parliament (23 per cent) and the cabinet (18 per cent).

Dalia Itzik, Acting President of Israel

However, Israel got a female Head of State, Dalia Itzik, in 2007. She acted as Israel's president for six months, when the male president, Moshe Katsav, from the right-wing Likud, took leave because of accusations of rape and other offences.

Dalia Itzik was born in Jerusalem in 1952 in an Iraqi–Jewish family. She was educated as a teacher and obtained a bachelor's degree in literature and history and a degree in law. She married Danny, who was employed in the electric corporation, and they had three children. In the Labour Party, she became a member of the Central Committee, was deputy mayor of Jerusalem in charge of education and was elected to the Knesset in 1992. She was a minister three times, in charge of the environment, industry and commerce, and communication. In 2006, she joined Kadima, a new centre-liberal party, and became speaker of the Knesset during 2006–09. As speaker, she was also deputy head of state. She was the first woman to obtain this position, and in a parliament with only 14 per cent women. But the role as head of state was largely ceremonial.

Dancer Isabel Perón takes over in Argentina

'Spiritual Leader of the Nation'

The first woman to become president of a nation lived on a different continent, in Latin America. In 1974, Isabel Perón came to power in Argentina, a country with a strong presidential executive. But she had very little political experience. She came to power because of her husband, succeeding him after his death, and her leadership did not go very well. Her days of glory were few, turbulent and destructive.[20]

Many compare Isabel, who was the former President Juan Perón's third wife, with his more glamorous second wife, María Eva Duarte, or Evita, as she often was called. But the two had little in common except that both came from humble beginnings. Evita was born out of wedlock. Her father was a large landowner, while her mother was poor, one of the outcasts. Evita grew up with a hatred of the powerful and a demand for justice for the 'shirtless'. She was beautiful, dynamic and worked as an actress after she quit school at the age of 15. She became the mistress of the widower Juan Perón, and they were married in 1945. When he was elected president of Argentina in 1946, she became First Lady. At the same time, she served informally as a minister of health and labour. The Eva Perón Foundation raised large sums of money from public and private sources for schools and social institutions that were neglected by the state. Evita also kept close contact with the labour movement, listened to their complaints and mediated when conflicts arose. She worked tirelessly and efficiently in a non-bureaucratic way and became immensely popular.

Argentina became independent in 1816, and as the country was industrialised and urbanised from the end of the 1800s, women went into paid work and became involved in politics. A series of women's protests were organised against discriminatory laws and practices. Women demanded education and suffrage, worker protection, equal pay, and the right to divorce. Some reforms were implemented, but very limited. Women got the right to vote only in 1947 with the support of Evita Perón. The First Lady also founded a Perónist women's party. At the elections in 1951, the Perónists got many votes from women, and their representation was unusually high, with 24 women (16 per cent) in the Chamber of Deputies. In 1955, the number increased to 34 (22 per cent), but when Perónists were not permitted to stand for election in 1958, the number of women was reduced to only four (2 per cent). Evita tried to become vice president, but the army was opposed, and in 1952, she died. Shortly after, she was given the title of 'Spiritual Leader of the Nation' by the Argentine Congress (Fraser and Navarro, 1996: 158).

Perón's envoy

Juan Perón, born in 1895, was a farm boy, but based his power on the military and the industrial working class. He went to military school, rose through the ranks and became colonel. In 1943, he participated in a military coup against the conservative government and became minister of labour, minister of war and vice president. Then, he won the presidential elections in 1946 and ruled as a de facto dictator for nearly 10 years. He founded the populist Perónist Party, demanding social justice and economic independence. He wanted to follow a nationalist 'third way' between communism and capitalism and focused on industrial development and state intervention in the economy to ensure economic and social benefits for the working class. The party obtained broad support under his authoritarian leadership, but the policies provoked the upper class, the rural population, intellectuals and parts of the military. Inflation, corruption and oppression also led to growing popular discontent. In 1955, Juan Perón had to flee during a military coup.

It was during the flight, when Juan came to Panama, that he met Isabel, actually María Estela Martínez Cartas, often called Isabelita. She was a nightclub dancer, born in 1931. Her father was a bank clerk and died when she was little. Her mother had to support the five children as best she could. Isabel grew up in Buenos Aires and left school after sixth grade to play the piano and go to dancing school before she was engaged in a dance group. The aging politician was attracted to the young beautiful woman – she was 35 years younger than he was – and he hired her as his personal secretary. Before long, they were living together. Isabelita served as a housewife and secretary and was trained to be her husband's political representative (*Current Biography*, 1975: 313).

These were turbulent times in Latin America, and the couple moved from country to country until they settled down in Spain. There, they got married in 1961. Juan Perón wanted to return to Argentina, but the authorities would not allow it and refused the Perónist Party to participate in elections. Nevertheless, Perón maintained control over the party, which was the strongest political force in the country, and Argentinians kept coming to Madrid. The couple had no children, and Isabel Perón went back to their homeland several times on behalf of her husband. She travelled around and talked about her husband, supported his candidates in the provincial elections, tried to unite disputing factions in the party, and discussed the possible return of the party leader with the authorities. As her husband's envoy, she played her most important and successful political role (Opfell, 1993: 56–9; Weir, 2013: 259–60, 267).

Argentina was not particularly poor, but the political situation between 1955 and 1983 was extremely turbulent because of economic stagnation, social conflicts, the suppression of rights and extensive violence. Short-lived civilian governments were followed by a series of military dictatorships, and in response, young Perónists began to engage in guerrilla activity. The situation became more and more untenable, and in 1973, it was decided to hold elections in which the Perónists could participate, and return to civilian rule. After 18 years in exile, Juan Perón came back and was elected president with over 60 per cent of the votes. At the same time, the representation of women in the Chamber of Deputies increased from four to 21 (9 per cent) and in the Senate from none to three (4 per cent).

His wife as vice president

Perón was elected with his wife as vice president, the first woman vice president in Latin America. There was no agreement on another running mate. Before the election, people waited in suspense for the party leader's choice of running mate. During his long political life, Juan Perón had never designated a political heir, and now he was 77 years old with poor health. The choice of his wife was not popular, but Perón insisted. Some of the adverse reaction stemmed from simple Latin American *machismo* (exaggerated masculinity). But, first and foremost, many considered her an incompetent puppet. Some feared that the leader was trying to concentrate more power in his own hands; others that the right wing would be strengthened by the influence of Isabel Perón's ultra-conservative secretary, José López Rega. People also reacted against what they perceived as an attempt to create a new version of Evita. Mrs Perón, herself, generally remained silent about her own views. She stressed her loyalty to Perón and said modestly: 'I cannot offer you great things; I am only a disciple of Perón' (*Current Biography*, 1975: 31–2).

Many hoped Juan Perón would unite the nation, but he did not manage to control either the country or his own movement. In exile, he supported the left wing of the party and the most aggressive trade unions, but when he came back, he became attached to the military and other right-wing groups. This led to a worsening of the conflicts between the various Perónist factions. At the same time, the economy deteriorated, with inflation, shortage of goods and strikes. Isabel Perón copied Evita's looks, promoted the interests of Argentinian women and supported measures such as the freezing of prices and wages. But she lacked her predecessor's popular roots, energy, charisma and political skills. In addition, the president fell ill three months after the election, and during half a year, Isabelita had to chair the cabinet meetings and travel abroad on her husband's behalf. Just before he died on 1 July 1974, Juan Perón transferred all his authority to her. She was 43 years old and not only the world's first woman president, but Latin America's youngest head of state (*Current Biography*, 1975: 32–3).

Incompetent head of state

Isabel Perón could have held new elections, but instead she took on the positions as head of the Perónist movement and head of state and government, and she promised to follow Juan Peron's policy 'without an iota of change' (*Current Biography*, 1975: 33). This was accepted due to her husband's death. She was perceived as his heir. But she also encountered resistance, and in fact it was Minister of Welfare José López Rega who took control. The Perónist movement was now not just divided, but extreme factions were at war with each other, and bomb attacks, political assassinations and kidnappings became more widespread. In particular, Rega's guard 'La Triple A' (The Argentine Anti-communist Alliance) developed into right-wing 'death squads'. Labour demonstrations were brutally struck down. Left-wing groups were attacked and counterattacked.

As president, Isabel Perón was not supported by any power group and changed ministers constantly. In the course of 21 months, ministers were changed 28 times, and as far as one knows, all of them were men. Salaries and subsidies were kept at a high level, but increasing consumption combined with falling exports and capital flight worsened the trade balance and economic problems. Inflation soared. Retrenchment measures were opposed by the trade unions. The country was moving towards chaos and anarchy. There were extensive strikes and violence increased, while the government did little to stop developments. Eighteen months after her husband's death, in March 1976, Isabelita was removed by the military in a bloodless coup, placed under house arrest and charged with fraud and corruption (Weir, 2013: 261–2).

It is a generally accepted view that Isabel Perón's performance as top executive was poor. When she was deposed, the country was on the brink of disaster. Some believe that she could not have prevented it. She inherited a country in deep economic crisis, which reinforced the political and military crises so that it became impossible to govern. Others believe she at least was partially responsible for the country slipping into the 'dirty war', a long period of repression and violence where women, men and children were persecuted and tortured, and thousands of Argentinians 'disappeared'.

The widow wanted to continue her husband's policies, but they only consisted of a vague and authoritarian nationalist populism, and Isabel Perón lacked political knowledge, experience and leadership training, particularly in a crisis situation. Contrary to her husband's advice, she primarily relied on a narrow, extremely right-wing circle, where José López Rega was a key figure, and this provoked the military. The action she took did not improve the security situation and the economy. On the contrary, and in 1975, a Perónist government was for the first time met with a general strike. The woman president reacted in an anti-democratic and repressive manner and gave the military more authority. It is recorded that 600 people disappeared and 500 were murdered during the Perónist regime during 1973–76. 'La Triple A' alone is supposed to have killed several hundred people (Selmer, 2007b; Weir, 2013: 261–4).

Hopeless situation

The political scientist Sara Weir wonders to what degree gender mattered for Isabel Perón's political work. She became head of state in a country marked by strong anti-feminism and opposition to women's political power. Perónism was anti-feminist, though it opened the door for women politically. Evita Perón was not a feminist. She supported and strengthened her husband's position in doing charity work. Isabel was not a feminist, either, and she was not successful in mobilising women through appeals to traditional family (women's) values. The other possibility, using political power in more traditional (male) ways, was closed to women in Argentine society. Under such circumstances, no woman could have succeeded as president, in Weir's view. And she adds: 'It is unlikely that Isabel Perón would have been successful in the presidency even if the political system had been more open to women. She lacked the political skills and popular support necessary to govern effectively' (Weir, 2013: 265-7). Feminists also criticised her lack of qualifications.

In 1981, Isabel Perón was convicted of two charges of corruption and went into exile in Spain. In 2007, she was arrested on charges of human rights violations during her presidency, but the Spanish authorities did not comply with the Argentinian demand for extradition, and Isabel remained in exile in Spain.

Friend of the Central African Republic's dictator: Elisabeth Domitien

Imperious and bitter lady

Also, in Africa south of the Sahara, a woman rose to the top at a relatively early stage, but nearly nobody knew about it in the Western world. The Central African Republic (CAR) was ruled by the supreme dictator Jean-Bédel Bokassa, and people did not know much more about conditions in the country. Moreover, if there was a prime minister, it would only be one of Bokassa's henchmen, it was said.

In 1999, I came to the CAR. When I asked for Elisabeth Domitien, I was told that she had really been prime minister and I could go and see her. It turned out to be a long interview. Elisabeth Domitien did not speak French, only the national language of Sangho, and her niece Marie Serra translated.[21]

The former top politician was marked by her high age, but there was an extraordinary strength in her eyes and authority in her voice. To me, it seemed extremely unlikely that she would only have been one of Bokassa's 'henchmen'. She had also worked in politics for 25 years before she became prime minister, and had acquired power and influence on her own, independent basis.

The photographs on the wall told of an eventful life, with journeys around the world. The French President Valéry Giscard d'Estaing presented her with the Legion of Honour in Paris and next to a cross with Jesus Christ there were decorations from Gabon, Congo and Chad. But Elisabeth Domitien herself felt unappreciated and forgotten. No one cared about those who had served their country, she sighed, neither men nor women: "Had Bokassa been here, I would not have been neglected the way I am now. Without my coffee plantations, I don't know how I would have managed" (interview in Bangui, 8 December 1999).

Plundered colony

Ubangi-Shari in French Equatorial Africa, later the Central African Republic, is richly endowed with fertile soil, minerals, wildlife and forests. But the people were exploited and plundered, first by the slave traders, then by the French colonialists. Forced labour was used to extract timber, rubber, coffee, cotton and diamonds, and uprisings were crushed with a heavy hand. When the country became independent in 1960, it was among the poorest in the world, with a population of only 1.3 million. People made a living as best they could, cultivating the soil, but the average life expectancy was not more than 37 years and very few could read and write.

An organised liberation struggle began after World War II. The Catholic priest Barthélémy Boganda founded an independence movement, The Movement for Social Development of Black Africa (MESAN), and he was supposed to be the father of the new nation. But he was killed in a mysterious plane crash in 1959. A close relative, the former teacher David Dacko, took over in 1960 and became the first president of the CAR. It was neo-colonial independence. Dacko governed in an authoritarian way, with French administrative and military support. The country soon became a one-party state with MESAN as the sole legal party. Some of the economy was nationalised, but forced labour continued, and French companies retained control of most of the diamond exports, plantations, timber concessions and foreign trade.

Women's leader

Elisabeth Domitien was born in 1925 in Bangui, the first urbanised area in the country. The family's plantations were also there. Her father was employed in the postal service and her mother was a farmer. Elisabeth was the oldest child and the only daughter, and she worked in the field and helped to sell products. She also earned money sewing. The Catholic Church had established schools in the area, and Elisabeth was allowed to get an education. But the nuns in colonial Africa had a narrow view of women's role (narrower than the Central Africans themselves) and gave only rudimentary reading and writing instruction to girls. Besides religious instruction, they were first and foremost supposed to learn sewing and cooking. Elisabeth therefore never came to master either the art of reading or the French language. But she learned to deal with numbers and worked as a farmer and businesswoman. She grew peanuts, corn and bananas for the local market and coffee for export. In addition, she traded in textiles as a wholesale dealer.

Elisabeth Domitien's niece, Marie Serra, explained that women in traditional African farming communities were respected as important economic actors and could have significant influence and independence. Her aunt had a strong personality, was enterprising and went forward undaunted, solving all sorts of problems. The women gathered around her, and she became an informal leader in the community. In the village, the custom was that women had the last word in all sorts of questions. They kept the family secrets, and for the men, a woman's word was holy. Polygamy was common, and women could also give advice to the husband with regards to a new wife. But the women did not come forward. They told the men what their opinion should be before decisions were taken. Elisabeth Domitien was special, because she came forward. It was unusual, but was tacitly accepted because people appreciated what she did.

At the age of 20, Elisabeth Domitien got involved in the liberation struggle. She mobilised the population with her speeches in Sangho, helped unite different groups and created a sense of national identity. The MESAN had a women's group with a president, a men's group with a president and a president for the whole party. Domitien became head of the women's group and of the whole party. She worked closely with Boganda and became president of the party in 1953. Later, she collaborated with Dacko and Bokassa. Among other things, she travelled abroad with them. Elisabeth Domitien came from a different ethnic group than the three male leaders – she was Ngbaka, while they were Bobangui – but all belonged to the same region, where the Europeans arrived relatively early and were engaged in missionary work.[22] Domitien served as political adviser both to the party leaders and to ordinary people, trying to reconcile different interests and improve the living standards of the population.

Elisabeth Domitien married twice, but lived all the time in the capital Bangui. Her first husband was Jean Baka, who worked as an accountant in a river company and commuted back and forth between Bangui and Brazzaville. Today, Brazzaville is the capital of Congo, but at that time, the whole region was a French colony. They had a daughter, Beatrice, in 1941 (or thereabouts), but were divorced. Later, Mrs Domitien married Mr Ngouka-Langadji, who was mayor and ran a coffee plantation in the Mobaye region, some distance east of the capital. The man had several wives and did not move when he married Elizabeth. She lived alone in Bangui, and her husband came to visit.

Thug becomes megalomaniac

Jean-Bédel Bokassa was the son of a village chief who was murdered when he protested against abuse by the colonial power. A week later, his mother took her own life in despair. Jean-Bedel was six years old. His grandfather sent him to a missionary school, and at 18 years old, he entered the French army. It was in 1939, and in World War II, he fought in Indochina and Algeria and received several medals for bravery. Bokassa was a lieutenant when he was called home by his cousin, David Dacko, to take care of the military in the new state. As the only Central African officer, he became commander in chief.

It is unclear if Bokassa responded to economic problems, corruption, failed development projects or rivalries within the security services. But he seized power in a coup on 31 December 1965, abolished the constitution, dissolved parliament and appointed himself as the head of the party, state and government with legislative and executive power. It was a 'sultanistic' regime, based on a mixture of fear and rewards,[23] where Bokassa exercised unlimited power at his own discretion, without being hindered by laws or rules, ideology or value systems. He recruited his assistants personally from different areas and their positions derived from their purely personal relationship with the ruler, submitting to him.

Bokassa ruled the CAR for 14 years. With French assistance, industry, transport, health and education were developed, and initially the dictator enjoyed a certain popularity. But the policies were volatile and arbitrary, with widespread corruption, waste and abuse of power. The population was brutally oppressed by purges, imprisonment and murder. Eventually, megalomania took over. In 1972, Bokassa declared himself president for life; in 1974, as marshal; and in 1976, as emperor, with a coronation ceremony that cost a third of the state's revenue.

The dictator had a cabinet in which the ministers changed constantly. In the first 10 years, the cabinet was rearranged 44 times. Information about the period when Elisabeth Domitien served as prime minister also varies. She said herself in 1999 that she held the position a bit more than two years, from 6 June 1974 (decree no 74/271) to August 1976. But other sources believe that the term of office was shorter, from January 1975 to April 1976.

In any case, it was very unusual for a woman to obtain such a position. But Bokassa knew Elisabeth Domitien well from MESAN. He appointed her as vice president, and in 1973, she led the first national congress of Central African farmers. She was clever and industrious, appealed to the population, and served as a unifying force, which Bokassa needed. In addition to being vice president of the party, she was now given a newly created, even more central and visible, position as prime minister. The International Women's Year Conference was to be held in Mexico in the summer of 1975, and Bokassa wanted to draw positive notice to himself internationally by appointing a woman in a leading position. As prime minister, Domitien herself wanted to "empower women and develop the agriculture as well as women's and men's trade in agricultural products and get the president to meet people's expectations" (interview in Bangui, 8 December 1999).

The dictator also promoted other women. While Elisabeth Domitien was prime minister, there were in addition four woman ministers. They were responsible for finance and planning, commerce, industry, and women's issues. Although the cabinet was large, with a total of 35 members, such a representation of women (11 per cent) was quite unusual. Bokassa was known for his many wives and mistresses, but he also sought to promote talented women in society. One might ask, however, how much it meant under a dictator like Bokassa.

"I told the truth"

Some believe that Elisabeth Domitien was not prime minister 'for real' because she was not elected, but appointed by a dictator. However, the degree of democracy is highly variable around the world and there are many countries where the prime minister is not elected, but appointed by the president. Bokassa gave no room for independent actors, but this did not necessarily mean that a 'prime minister' could do nothing. She could, among other things, influence the dictator and his decisions. Elisabeth Domitien was no novice and had her own political platform.

As prime minister Elisabeth Domitien was not the head of government. Bokassa had this role, and he appointed the ministers. Domitien was 'primus inter pares' (first among equals) with a responsibility for the whole and in addition deputy head of state. When Bokassa was absent, she served as president. A secretary helped her read and deal with the documents. In principle, the cabinet would discuss the president's decrees, but it is doubtful how much this actually happened, and if the ministers had some influence, it was first and foremost on a personal basis.

When I asked Domitien what she achieved as prime minister, she replied that she helped strengthen the income and position of women. Women as well as men came to her with problems, and she gave advice, tried to find solutions and, if necessary, requested assistance from the president. She advised the president regarding the recruitment of women to government, and she gave women possibilities to go abroad and widen their horizon. "In matters concerning women,

Bokassa always consulted with me", she assured me. But did he do as she said, I wondered. "Bokassa respected me, because I told the truth", said the former prime minister. Marie Serra added:

> "When it came to women, Bokassa would always agree with my aunt. But he did not always listen to her otherwise. Sometimes, she and the president quarrelled. They were two strong personalities. But Bokassa could apologise after they had an argument, and even after she no longer was prime minister, he sought advice from her. She also visited him at the palace, when she thought he was doing wrong." (Interview in Bangui, 8 December 1999)

Elisabeth Domitien was criticised by some people in the CAR for the support she gave to Bokassa. During the interview in 1999 Marie Serra explained that they referred in particular to the ceremony in which he appointed himself marshal, and Domitien stated: 'You are the needle, we are the thread. We follow where you go.' In her view, the population should follow the leader. At the same time, she demanded that the president should respect the people and safeguard their interests. All sorts of people came to her to ask for help, and she was not afraid to voice her opinion, even to the president. Domitien got many people out of jail after they were arrested without trial. People called her 'La Dame de Fer' (Iron Lady), Marie Serra told me, because of her courage, integrity, honesty and righteousness. She also served as a model for women and gave them new visions.

Abrupt end

When Bokassa wanted to proclaim himself emperor and the prime minister opposed, it was over. Elisabeth Domitien had to resign. She continued, however, as vice president of the MESAN.

Attempts were made to overthrow Bokassa many times. In 1979, they succeeded. A massacre of demonstrating schoolchildren was too much even for the French. Having paid for Bokassa's coronation, they now intervened with military means, supporting a coup and reinstating David Dacko as president. He arrested Elisabeth Domitien and confiscated her possessions (plantation, vehicles, etc), accusing her of supporting Bokassa. Her husband was very proud when his wife became prime minister, but when she was imprisoned, he disappeared. After two years, she was released, but, later, her house was pillaged during unrest. People said that it was a present from Bokassa. While she was prime minister, Domitien got a salary, servants and a car with a driver, but she continued to cultivate the land and do business. There were no pensions or privileges when her political career was over.

In 1981, the military gained control again and ruled for 12 years. In 1993, it was replaced by a civilian government, and Ange-Félix Patassé was elected president. Then, Domitien received compensation for the unjust treatment she had been exposed to. She was also asked to get involved in politics again. But she refused: 'There is so much gossip and slander. It is best to stay away', was her bitter comment to me.

When I visited her, the former prime minister lived in simple conditions in a popular part of the capital, Bangui. There was no conspicuous luxury, just a few low brick buildings around a small courtyard. Elisabeth Domitien received her guests wearing a plain African cotton dress in a living room with simple furniture: two deep sofas and a coffee table. Her daughter, Beatrice, was dead, as were her brothers. At 74 years old, Mrs Domitien lived with only three nephews.

After my visit to Bangui, Elisabeth Domitien was included on the list of women prime ministers of the United Nations, and when she died in 2005, she was buried with official honours.

Though she was a women's leader, Elisabeth Domitien did not think it was her task as prime minister to organise women, and few participated in politics during the military regime in the 1980s. After Patassé took over as president, a few women became ministers and this also happened when the military took power again in 2003 and Patassé was replaced by François Bozizé. But in March 2013 the unrest escalated, president Bozizé was removed by rebel groups and the CAR got its first Moslem president. The economic situation was catastrophic. There was widespread violence and massacres, Christians against Moslems, and the French troops and African peace forces were unable to protect the population. At least one million people were put to flight. In this chaos a woman was suddenly made interim president by the National Transition Council in January 2014.

Fifty-nine-year-old Catherine Samba-Panza, lawyer, wife of a former minister and the mother of three children, defeated all the male candidates. She was Christian, but moderate without any clear political profile. She had a solid French education in law and a successful career in private business, fought for human and women's rights in NGOs and was vice president of the national mediation dialogue in 2003. Recently she was the mayor of the capital, Bangui. In the situation it was further positive that she had a regional affiliation: born in N'Djamena (in the neighbouring Chad) with a father from Cameroon and a mother from CAR. Accepted both by the Moslem rebels and their opponents and supported by France and the EU, the US, African Union and the UN she became 'Queen Catherine'. But she lacked political and administrative experience, had few resources at her disposal and was not permitted to present herself at the planned forthcoming elections later in the year. She appointed a cabinet with a male prime minister and a third women ministers and her daughter helped her as principal private secretary (Soudan, 2013, 2014).

Game of chance

Different backgrounds

Modern nation states were male-dominated everywhere. Then, in the course of a few years, five women on different continents served in top political positions that had previously been reserved for men. What made women suddenly obtain roles that were out of the ordinary for their gender?

Looking at the women's backgrounds and careers, there are few similarities. They were spread all over the world (see Figure 1) and came from countries with different histories, economic development, social conditions, culture and religion. In Argentina, the majority of the population was of European descent and Roman Catholic faith. In Israel, most were Jews; in India, Hindus; and in Ceylon, Buddhist Sinhalese. The CAR comprised 80 different ethnic groups, some with traditional religions and some Catholic or Protestant. With the exception of Elisabeth Domitien, the women top leaders came from the majority population. Argentina had been an independent state for more than 150 years when a woman came to power, while Ceylon and India had only recently become independent of British, and the CAR of French, colonial rule. Israel was being established by immigrants.

Figure 1: Countries with women heads of state and government, 1945–75

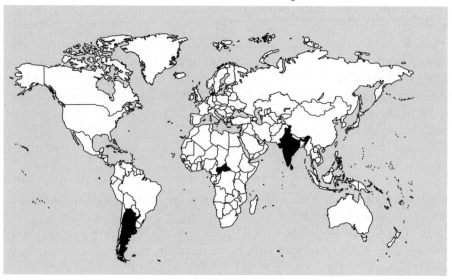

Source: Compiled by the author.

The five women came to power at different times, but all the countries had significant economic problems, and in four, there was political and social unrest. Four of the women made war or struck down opposition by force, and in the fifth case, the superior president did.

Although economic activities and the structure of society differed, all the five countries were generally clearly male-dominated. Men had control over the economy as well as politics. But in rural Africa, women had considerable influence behind the scenes, and a women's union was created in the CAR in connection with the liberation struggle. In Ceylon and India, goddesses were important in traditional beliefs, and, historically, the countries had strong queens. In both countries, women joined forces to fight for their rights. Argentinian women also did so when the country became industrialised, and Evita Perón formed a special women's party. In Israel, equality was central to the socialist Zionist ideology and Histadrut had a special woman's unit. How feminist these various organisations were is not clear, but they raised demands on behalf of women, and this might have played a role in creating opportunities for women politicians. The International Women's Year led to the promotion of Elisabeth Domitien, but the other women became top leaders before 1975.

Three of the women came to power in parliamentary democracies (Ceylon, India and Israel). In Ceylon, women received voting rights before World War II, while they were achieved in Israel in 1948 and in India in 1950. In all three countries, women obtained the most important political executive position, and Sirimavo Bandaranaike was prime minister for more than 17 years, Indira Gandhi for 15 and Golda Meir for a little more than five. The two other women received top positions partly in a dictatorship, partly in a difficult transitional situation. In Argentina, women received voting rights in 1947, but the regime was often authoritarian, without elections, and in the CAR nobody had the right to vote. Isabel Perón acquired a powerful position, while Elisabeth Domitien's influence was severely limited. None of them were in office for more than one or two years.

None of the five women had expected to rise to the top of society. All rose to power by chance. In four cases, unexpected deaths were decisive factors, while in the fifth case, it was an unpredictable dictator. None of the women were considered the most qualified for the position as top leader, but in three cases, there was disagreement about the male candidates. In the two other cases, the leader was determined by the president.

Family and competence

Gender was an important factor in the careers of all the women, but in partly different ways. For Bandaranaike, Gandhi and Perón, family relations were essential. Both Mrs B. and Mrs Perón became widows. They had no political careers of their own. All three were housewives and were partly ill-prepared for an executive position, though they had functioned as political assistants: Indira for her father, Sirimavo and Isabel for their husbands. In any case, family proved to be more important than gender and competence when the successors to the deceased leaders were chosen. Sirimavo Bandaranaike was requested to take over after her husband because she was a member of the family and the party could not agree upon a male leader. Isabel Perón was accepted because her husband had empowered her. Mrs B. had earlier done voluntary humanitarian work and soon developed political skills, which enabled her to stand on her own feet, but Mrs Perón failed in this.

In India, there was a conflict regarding the choice of prime minister, and Indira Gandhi was proposed as the daughter of a former, deceased prime minister. She had acquired competence through collaboration with her father in his position for many years and also had organisational and political positions herself. But those who supported her primarily wanted to avoid the male opponent and thought that a young, relatively inexperienced woman would be easy to control.

For both Golda Meir and Elisabeth Domitien, the competence they had acquired was crucial. Golda Meir had a professional career in trade union work, while Elisabeth Domitien was a self-employed farmer and businesswoman. Both had long political experience and obtained high positions before they became prime ministers. The fact that they acquired the last position was due to chance, but it was not illogical. In the party and government, Meir's proficiency was recognised and her skills were needed. For Domitien, it was important that she had a high position in her capacity as woman.

Both Domitien and Meir broke with traditional roles at a young age and thereby developed political qualifications that were unusual for women. Domitien came forward as a leader of women and could thereby provide the president with important support from this part of the population. When Bokassa wanted to show the world that he was a pioneer with regards to equality, he appointed her as prime minister. Meir engaged early in political agitation, something that was unusual for a woman. Histadrut gave her tasks and she was promoted. When she was included in the cabinet, it was because the political leader thought that there should be at least one woman. Then, she proved that she was just as capable as her male colleagues.

New women's role

Three of the top women grew up under poor conditions, while Bandaranaike and Gandhi belonged to well-to-do and powerful families. Nevertheless, none of the women got formal higher education. Gandhi studied at university, but did not pass the exam, and Meir had incomplete teacher training. Bandaranaike and Perón only had a high school education, and Domitien was illiterate, even though she was a skilful speaker and could do arithmetic.

All the women married before they rose to power in politics, Domitien twice, and both Domitien and Meir were actually, if not formally, divorced. With the exception of Isabel Perón, they all had children (Elisabeth Domitien had one; Indira Gandhi and Golda Meir had two each; and Sirimavo Bandaranaike had three) and during periods of time, were solely responsible for them. Meir, in particular, worked hard to combine child care with a job and politics while the children were small. Family and servants helped Gandhi. For Bandaranaike, it was simpler because her children were older when she obtained political positions. In any case, all the women gave priority to political activities.

The women top leaders had different political affiliations. Bandaranaike and Meir were socialists, while Isabel Perón was a Perónist. Gandhi wavered pragmatically between different approaches and it is also difficult to place Domitien. All five were contested, but two ruled for many years and only Isabel Perón was evaluated in a mainly negative way. Indira Gandhi was assassinated, but was, as Bandaranaike, Domitien and Meir, both criticised and recognised.

Only Elisabeth Domitien was perceived as a representative of women when she became top leader. The others were expected to promote the interests of their husband/father, party and the nation. All five women national leaders probably served women's interests by just doing that: being women national leaders. Thereby, they proved that it was possible for women to obtain such a position, even if it was extremely unusual, and all of them were more or less solitary swallows. Several underlined their femininity by coming forward as mother figures, but none declared that they were feminists. Nevertheless, with the exception of Isabel Perón, all of them supported measures that benefited women: Bandaranaike was inspired by the International Women's Year, and Meir did it before she became prime minister. Both Bandaranaike, Gandhi and Meir were criticised because they did not do more. As women, the top leaders were also reproached for their use of force and violent means – all except Domitien, but, here, the superior president did it. Several were also described as 'men' or 'iron women'. For feminists, the question became pressing: what kind of leaders should women actually be? Was the most important thing that they came to power and governed in the same way as men, or should they promote another, more 'feminine', policy, whatever that might be? If this was the case, the first were not particularly inspiring, even if they were ever so courageous and strong.

Out of the ordinary

It was out of the ordinary that women became national leaders and the women's backgrounds and careers were very different. Still, the question arises as to whether it was only a coincidence that five women emerged as top leaders around the world within a relatively short period of time. Had the situation of women and traditional roles changed so that women were more willing than before to participate in political activities? All the women experienced that they were treated differently than men because of gender, but, all the same, maybe the resistance to women in politics was less than before. In any case, the political situation was difficult and the political system was under pressure. Maybe this gave more openings for women.

More women top leaders were to come in the years that followed, however.

Women demonstrating on 19 June 1975 at the NGO Tribune during the International Women's Year
Conference in Mexico City.
122986: UN Photo/B Lane

Chapter Two

Women in politics: background, approaches, research

This chapter presents a brief account of insights and approaches relating to women in politics in general, and women top leaders specifically, based on previous research. It is difficult to generalise historical and societal developments in the way I do in this chapter without becoming superficial. But the aim is to provide some overall aspects as a background for the biographies that follow, where there will be more details. The chapter describes historical, socio-economic and cultural factors of relevance, political structures, and concepts that will be used in the book.

Overview

By the end of 2010, a total of 73 women had been presidents or prime ministers in 53 countries spread across the globe. They lived and worked in North and South, West and East, in Asia, Africa, Latin America and the Caribbean. Only in the Arab states and the small Pacific island states there had been none. In total, nearly 30 per cent of the countries in the world had a woman head of state or government at one time or another after World War II. Although the women were few in number, the fact that they rose to the top in national governments constituted a worldwide phenomenon.

It is also a recent phenomenon. The women came to power in the course of half a century, from 1960 to 2010. Most of them rose to the top after 1990. Whereas 20 women became presidents or prime ministers during the 30 years from 1960 to 1990, this figure was more than doubled in the 20 years that followed. From 1991 to 2010, a total of 53 women rose to the level of national leaders (see Table 1, Figure 2 and Appendix). In 2010, there was a total of 281 presidents and prime ministers in United Nations member states worldwide, and of these, 18 were women. Women comprised only 6 per cent, but that was more than before.

Table 1: Women presidents and prime ministers in different countries and regions, 1960–2010

Region	Number of women	Number of countries
Industrial countries	**36**	**25 out of a total of 59 = 42%**
Western	23	15 out of a total of 31 = 48% Israel 1969, UK, Portugal 1979, Iceland 1980, Norway 1981, Malta 1982, Ireland 1990, France 1991, Canada, Turkey 1993, Ireland, New Zealand 1997, Switzerland, New Zealand 1999, Finland 2000, 2003, Germany 2005, Switzerland, Israel 2007, Iceland 2009, Switzerland, Australia, Finland 2010
Eastern	13	12 out of a total of 30 = 41% Yugoslavia 1982, Lithuania, GDR 1990, Poland 1992, Bulgaria 1994, Lithuania, Latvia 1999, Georgia 2003, Ukraine, 2005, Moldova 2008, Croatia 2009, Kyrgyzstan, Slovakia 2010
Developing countries	**37**	**28 out of a total of 133 = 21%**
Asia	**11**	**7 out of a total of 22 = 32%**
South Asia	7	4 out of a total of 9 = 44% Sri Lanka 1960, India 1966, Pakistan 1988, Bangladesh 1991, Sri Lanka 1994, Bangladesh 1996, India 2007
East Asia	4	3 out of a total of 14 = 21% Philippines 1986, 2001, Indonesia 2001, South Korea 2006
Sub-Saharan Africa	**10**	8 out of a total of 45 = 18% Central African Republic 1975, Burundi, Rwanda 1993, Liberia 1996, Senegal 2001, São Tomé 2002, Mosambique 2004, São Tomé 2005, Liberia 2006, Gabon 2009
Latin America and the Caribbean	**16**	**13 out of a total of 33 = 39%**
Latin America	10	9 out of a total of 20 = 45% Argentina 1974, Bolivia 1979, Nicaragua 1990, Guyana 1997, Panama 1999, Peru 2003, Chile 2006, Argentina 2007, Costa Rica 2010, Brazil 2010/11
Caribbean	6	4 out of totally 13 = 31% Dominica 1980, Haiti 1990, 1995, Jamaica 2006, Haiti 2008, Trinidad and Tobago 2010
Arab states	**0**	**0 out of a total of 19 = 0%**
Pacific	**0**	**0 out of a total of 13 = 0%**
World	**73**	**53 out of a total of 192 = 28%**

Note: Regions are delimited according to the United Nations Development Programme (UNDP, 2011a: 174), with a few modifications. Country groups are defined not only geographically, but also politically/socio-economically. Western countries include Western Europe and other countries with similar societal features: North America, Cyprus, Malta, Turkey, Israel, Australia, New Zealand and Japan. Eastern countries include Eastern Europe, transitional states in South East Europe and the Commonwealth of Independent States. In total, the number of industrial countries in the table amount to 27 instead of 25 because Germany is included among both Western and Eastern countries (GDR) and both the former Yugoslavia and Croatia are included, although Croatia was earlier a part of Yugoslavia. The years indicate the first time a woman became president or prime minister.

Figure 2: Women heads of state and government, 1945–2010

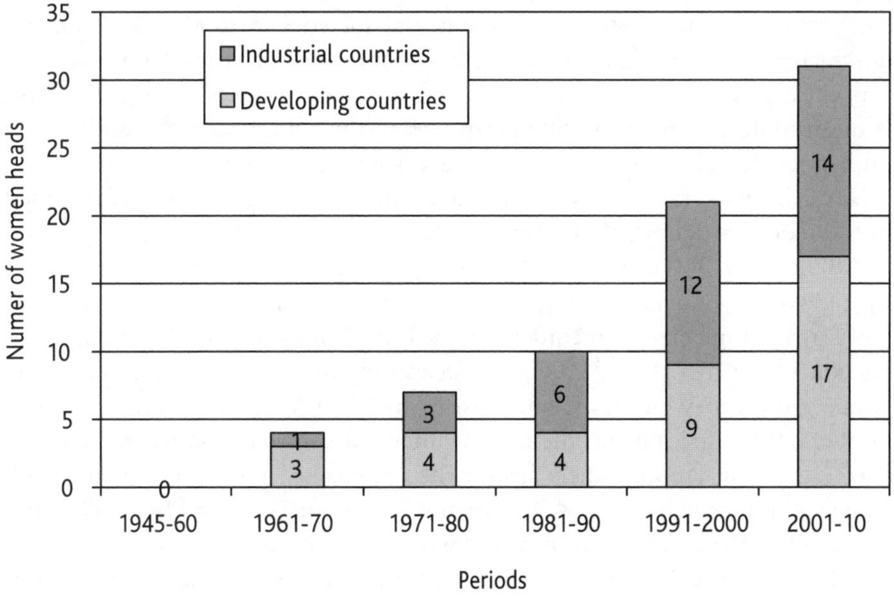

Source: Compiled by the author.

Glimpses back in time

Male dominance

Looking back in time and around the world, there is much that is not known about the origins and extensiveness of male dominance. In all known human societies, gender provides the basis for a fundamental division of social functions. But the anthropologist Alice Schlegel (1977: 353–6) underlines that division of functions does not necessarily lead to stratification; rather, it can lead to balanced complementarity. Sexual stratification is not pan-human, but rather poses a problem that must be explained, for each society, in terms of the forces to which it is responsive, and cross-culturally, in terms of the variables that exist across societies. The emergence of sexual stratification in any society is multidimensional. The forms it acquires are the unfolding consequences of many different kinds of forces intermingling over time. In this respect, stratification or equality are responses to economic, political, social and ideological conditions internal to the society or impinging on it from its relations with other societies.

The anthropologists Michelle Z. Rosaldo and Louise Lamphere (1974: 3–13) sum up that some anthropologists argue that there are or have been truly egalitarian societies, and all agree that there are societies in which women have achieved considerably social recognition and power. None have observed a society in which women have a publicly recognised power and authority surpassing that of men. Everywhere, we find that women are excluded from certain crucial economic and political activities, that their roles as wives and mothers are associated with fewer powers and prerogatives than are the roles of men. It seems fair to say, Rosaldo and Lamphere conclude, that all contemporary societies are to some extent male-dominated, and although the degree and expression of female subordination vary greatly, asexual asymmetry is presently a universal fact of human social life. It means different things in different places and is not a necessary condition of human societies, but a cultural product accessible to change.

Nevertheless, evidence of women rulers extends to the beginning of recorded history and throughout all geographic regions of the world. Guida M. Jackson (1998) included 360 woman rulers in her biographical encyclopaedia. In ancient Egypt, women enjoyed very high status for several thousand years. The names of 150 Egyptian queens are recorded before Indo-European and Semitic nomads penetrated the area around 2,000 BC, weakening the position of women. Many ethnic groups in West and Central Africa had female chiefs, queens or queen mothers. West Africa boasts the most women African rulers on record. Women also waged war, among others against the colonialists. Nowadays, women still enjoy exceptionally high status in tribes along the Guinea Coast. Much of Central and Eastern Africa was matrilineal and women could inherit leadership.

In India and the Arab states, conditions for Islamic women varied throughout time, but there were a number of queens. When there was no male heir, the mother or wife would take over. This also happened in other parts of the world. In Burma and Thailand, women enjoyed rare equality throughout history, and in ethnic groups living on islands in Indonesia and the Philippines, women also had a high status. Some of the strongest women rulers reigned in China and equally strong were some of the concubines. By far the majority of women rulers of whom we have record ruled in Europe. Lapp women enjoyed a high position and legends of Celtic queens abound. In the rest of Europe, few women ruled in their own right, but as regents or duchesses. When men marched off on crusades, women ruled.[1]

Colonial rule led to the Europeanization of the globe and the spread of Islam and Christianity worldwide contributed to the strengthening of male dominance in many societies. Despite the differences between them, both Islam and Christianity emphasise the subordination of women to men. Colonialism arose out of strongly male-dominated Western societies, and the European masters governed the colonies according to their patriarchal customs. In addition to oppression and exploitation of the original population in the colonies, millions of slaves and indentured labour were moved involuntarily to other continents. In both cases the colonial powers changed the status of women. Sometimes, conditions were improved for women with extremely weak positions (eg local slaves), but in many cases, and particularly where women traditionally played a major role, their position was weakened. They lost traditional rights, and it was neither understood nor accepted by the colonial powers that women could exert political influence. They were supposed to be subordinate to men.[2]

Female resistance

Female resistance to subordination and oppression has manifested itself worldwide in various forms throughout history. Often, it was expressed by individual women or small groups. Growing opposition from women was noted in the 1600s, and during the Age of Enlightenment, the American War of Independence and the French Revolution, questions were raised and requests for women's rights were presented by writers and activists. The ideas spread throughout Europe, North America and Oceania. The first wave of an international feminist movement arose during the 1800s in what were to become industrial countries, starting with women's organisations in the US and the UK, then France, Germany and the Nordic countries. In addition to ideas of liberation and rights, the movement was a reaction to structural changes in society.

The development of modern technology led to the restructuring of production. The introduction of machines and factories changed the lives of many women dramatically. The family was no longer the main production unit. Women lost their work and went to the cities to earn a living. There, they became part of an emerging working class. Demands were made for better conditions and rights related to marriage, education, employment and income. Women from different social strata had different interests, but the struggle for suffrage was widespread.

During the 1800s, men obtained the right to vote in many countries. But women's demands for the right met with considerable opposition. A number of international women's organisations were created, mainly based in Europe and the US, to promote suffrage, democratic rights and peace. They collaborated with the League of Nations in Geneva. The League was an unprecedented form of intergovernmental collaboration aimed at ending wars. Women saw the League as a powerful arena for promoting peace, human rights and women's equality. For the League, women were a valuable lobbying support group. In Latin America, an emerging women's movement demanded recognition of equal rights by the International Conference of American States and the first intergovernmental body to address issues related to the status of women was created there in 1928.[3]

The United Nations

Confirmation of equal rights

When World War II ended in 1945, the representatives of 50 allied states got together in San Francisco to create a new intergovernmental organisation to maintain peace and security. At the time, women had the right to vote in 30 countries. In the parliaments that existed, there were 3 per cent women, and in the cabinets, there were virtually only men (IPU, 1997: 83). As a consequence, nearly all of the 3,500 participants at the founding conference of the United Nations (UN) were men. But there were a few women delegates, among others, from Latin America, and of the 42 non-governmental organisations (NGOs) that had access to the conference, some were women's organisations. They managed to get 'the equal rights of men and women' into the UN Charter and the Commission on Human Rights and the Commission on the Status of Women (CSW) were created (UN, 1945; Skard, 2008a).

The Universal Declaration of Human Rights was adopted in 1948. On the basis of a proposal from the CSW, the UN recommended that all women should have the right to vote, and in 1952, a UN Convention on women's political rights was adopted. Here, it was established that women had the right to run for election and to hold all government positions. But it took more than 30 years from the UN was created until gender equality in political life was put high on the international agenda.

During the 1960s and 1970s, a second wave of feminism arose, especially in the global North, with new forms of mobilisation and activism. Women created different kinds of feminist groups. Vocal women's organisations popped up in great numbers, demonstrating and demanding their rights. Studies and research were started up to analyse the situation of women. A special focus was on women, power and politics (see among others Currell, Jacquette and Kirkpatrick, all published in 1974). Many women's activists stressed that personality characteristics and the behaviour of women and men were little, if at all, constrained by biology. 'Gender', as distinct from biological sex, was defined as the set of social meanings attached to the categories of male and female. A system of social structures and practices in which men dominate and oppress women was characterised as 'patriarchal' and gender was seen as a socially constructed relationship of inequality. This system and also differences between women and men in political powers, social roles, images and expectations could and should be changed.[4]

Governments responded to the new feminist activism and the UN proclaimed 1975 as International Women's Year. The first major International Women's Conference was held in Mexico in the same year and 1976–85 was declared the United Nations Decade for Women: Equality, Development and Peace. The Mexico Conference was a milestone. It was the largest conference ever held on the status of women: 133 states were represented and women dominated among the government delegates. In a special NGO forum, 6,000 members of women's organisations participated and 1,500 journalists assured more extensive media coverage than any previous UN conference.

The Mexico Conference emphasised the importance of promoting the equal status of women and men. A World Plan of Action was adopted and a special fund for women created to support positive action (later named UNIFEM, Snyder, 1995) as well as an institute for research and training (INSTRAW). Major international women's conferences followed in Copenhagen in 1980, Nairobi in 1985 and Beijing in 1995. They assessed developments and adopted new action plans. Each time, the conferences were larger and the recommendations on measures to strengthen the position of women were more extensive. Stronger and more diverse women's organisations emerged, getting together at the NGO forums, and an international feminism developed (see Figure 3).[5]

Figure 3: Growth in women's international non-governmental organisations (WINGOs)

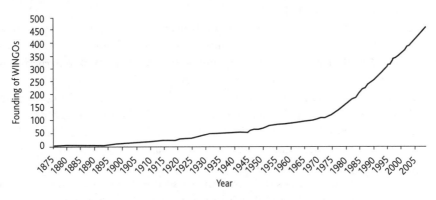

Source: Paxton and Hughes (2007: 178, Figure 6.1; 2014: 185, Figure 7.1).

Action to be taken

Although the term 'feminism' was not included in the UN vocabulary, the world's governments endorsed extensive declarations and action plans, acknowledging that discrimination against women was a persistent problem worldwide and calling for equality between women and men. This implied changing men's and women's traditional roles, strengthening the position of women, and expanding their activity to include all aspects of society. Governments committed themselves to adopt action plans, establish mechanisms, revise legislation and implement concrete measures to promote gender equality.

The UN Convention on the Elimination of All Forms of Discrimination against Women (CEDAW) was adopted in 1979, and it became a basic instrument. It comprises women's legal position, civil and political rights, education, economic and social activities, gender roles, family, and cultural factors. It is not sufficient that the CEDAW was adopted in New York. Governments are supposed to take further action: accept and ratify the CEDAW and follow up in their countries. Women's organisations can request compliance, and on the basis of regular country reports the UN assesses actions and developments and advises on further progress.

The CEDAW became one of the conventions with the most widespread support. In 2010, 186 countries, more than 95 per cent of the world's states, were party to it. A number of governments had reservations regarding various paragraphs, and in some cases ratification only entailed a formal, political decision without any intention of follow-up. In any case, implementing and fulfilling the provisions of the convention is a much more demanding task than accepting words on paper. Nevertheless, many governments took action. Things moved forward, albeit slowly, varying from country to country. A study of 123 countries from 1981 to 2003 shows that over time countries that ratified CEDAW minimized political inequality between men and women more so than countries that did not. Although CEDAW might not be the cause of women's improving situation, it at least generally indicates a shared commitment to women's political equality (Paxon and Hughes, 2014: 193–7).

In most countries, but not all, women eventually got the right to vote. It took many years before women obtained political positions of some importance. In the first decades after World War II, very few women were elected to parliaments and female ministers were a rarity. Even during the Decade for Women, the representation of women in parliaments increased by only one percentage point, from 11 to 12 per cent. The Nairobi Conference in 1985 emphasised equality in political participation, and in 1990, the Economic and Social Council of the UN (ECOSOC) adopted quantitative goals for the number of women in positions at decision-making levels (ECOSOC res. 1990/15).

Five years later, progress was still very limited, so the Beijing Conference 1995 changed the focus, emphasizing that it was not the women, but the institutions that had to change. 'Gender mainstreaming' was launched as a major strategy to empower women and transform structures of inequality and a series of measures were recommended to achieve this in an extensive Platform for Action. Governments should among others establish the goal of gender balance in governmental bodies and public administrative entities and take positive action to build a critical mass of women leaders, executives and managers in strategic decision-making positions. The UN system, in particular the Committee on the Status of Women (CSW) and the General Assembly, reviewed the follow up of the Beijing Platform on a regular basis and urged states to accelerate their efforts to fully implement the Platform. The women's movement also used the platform actively.

But in practice, it proved difficult to mobilise sufficient political will and resources to integrate gender everywhere and particularly strengthen the share of women in positions of power. In 2000, the UN adopted eight Millennium Development Goals and one of them was to promote gender equality and empower women by 2015. In 2010, the UN was reformed and UN Women was established to increase progress towards the goals. But a survey in 2012 showed that while 135 countries had closed more than 90 per cent of the gender gaps in health and education, they still remained wide with only 60 per cent closed of the gap in economic participation and 20 per cent of the gap in political empowerment (Hausman et al, 2012).[6]

Changing world

The advocates for women's rights faced a dramatic world in 1945, one devastated by war. Countries were marked by widespread suffering, economic and social inequalities, oppression and exploitation, and political and military tension, related, among other things, to the Cold War. But there were also liberation, reconstruction and development efforts, international collaboration, and technological advances. During the decades that followed, a revolution in living conditions and political systems took place that had far-reaching consequences for the status of women and their participation in politics.

Nation states

During the colonial period, the majority of the world's population was conquered by European powers. The first wave of independent states came between 1800 and 1850, when a number of new states were established in Central and South America. The second wave of nation-state formation occurred from the 1940s to the 1980s, with the decolonisation of Africa, Asia, the Arab states, the Caribbean. The third wave, and the most dramatic, came in the 1990s after the dissolution of the Soviet Union, mainly in Central and Eastern Europe and Central Asia. Before the end of the 20th century, nearly the entire world consisted of independent nation-states. By 2010, the number of states that were members of the UN had increased to 192.

For most women, the formation of nation-states was accompanied by formal legal equality and secularism in government, which disentangled the power of the state from the power of religious denominations. This expanded women's political opportunities and the increasing number of states, in principle, provided more openings for national leadership. In recent decades, however, the rise of ethnic, communal and regional forces have increasingly challenged national control of politics.

At the end of the colonial period, political systems were established in the colonies according to Western male-dominated patterns. The important positions in the new political parties, parliaments and cabinets were taken over by indigenous (often Western-educated) men, and women were excluded, even where they traditionally had participated in decision-making processes or actively resisted the colonial power. The colonial set-up largely continued in the new, independent states.[7]

Economic crises

During colonialism, the developing countries were integrated into the capitalist economy of the European powers. When the colonies became independent, an extractive capitalism continued, in most cases, practised by indigenous elites and multinational corporations. Developments were uneven, both between countries and within each country. Where productivity and standards of living improved, women and men did not benefit equally. Often, men's share of resources and their control over women's lives increased.

In the industrial countries, rapid technological, economic and social development took place after World War II, though the economy was organised differently in communist countries in the East and capitalist countries in the West. Production, consumption and trade increased, and people got better health, more education and higher incomes.

In the 1970s and 1980s, higher oil prices and a deep recession in the West hit the world economy and led to economic crisis in many developing countries. They were stricken by debt burdens, inflation and declining levels of income. Attempts to introduce a new, more just, world order failed, and an expanding neo-liberalism characterised the structural adjustment programmes that countries had to implement to get balance in the economy. These usually entailed changes in the economic policies to reduce the power of the public sector and organised labour and increase the power of the commercial agriculture, private industry and export sectors. Increasing unemployment, decreasing earnings and reductions in public social expenditures generally hit women harder than men (UN, 1991, 1995; Nelson and Chowdhury, 1994: 4–6; UNDP, 1995a).

Neo-liberalism was tested in Latin America and was a key element in the transition to capitalism in Eastern and Central Europe. After the debt crisis in Latin America in the 1980s, Asia was hit by a financial crisis in the late 1990s, Turkey and Argentina in 2000/01, and in 2007 and the years that followed, the whole world economy was more or less affected by crisis.

Human development

Despite economic difficulties and a growing population, there was significant long-term progress in human development, not only in industrialised, but also in developing countries. Most men and women eventually got better health, more education and greater access to goods and services, though gender gaps persisted. [8]

Thinking that more women would engage in political activities when living standards improved, because women got better health, more education, more vocational work and higher income, two worldwide surveys were made in 1998 by Lane Kenworthy and Melissa Malami (1999) and Andrew Reynolds (1999). [9] The surveys showed that women's political representation was in fact related to countries' socio-economic development level (see Figure 4). Reynolds stated that the proportion of women in parliament (but not in the cabinet) was determined by how much education women generally got, how long their life expectancy was and how good the economy was that they had. [10] But Kenworthy and Malami found that education or vocational work were not essential in general. Instead, *what kind of occupations* women had was crucial. In particular, professions such as a teacher, lawyer, journalist and so on could provide useful qualifications and motivation for political activities. [11]

But other factors may also have an impact. At the end of the 1990s Ronald Inglehart and Pippa Norris (2003) analysed surveys of people's views on gender equality and women's role in politics in 62 countries on different continents. Significant differences appeared. Both with regards to general ethical values and the view of women in politics, the culture was most egalitarian in countries with high socio-economic levels. The attitudes influenced politics so that countries with an egalitarian culture generally had a relatively high representation of women in parliaments.

Figure 4: Percentage of women in parliaments in 173 countries by level of development, 1970–2005

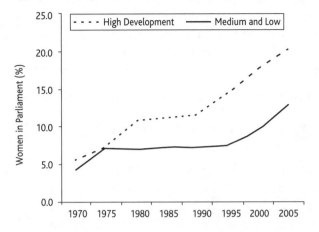

Source: IPU (1995, 2005a) and United Nations Population Fund (2005),
reproduced in Paxton and Hughes (2007: 131, Figure 4.3; 2014: 135: Figure 5.1)

Cultural changes

Over the past few decades, there has been a communication revolution that has increasingly made the world into one. Not only goods, technology and money, but also people, knowledge and ideas, move across borders with increasing speed. The reporting of news, mass media and the Internet are dominated by the West, and the impact of Western culture, entertainment and advertising has become strong around the world, particularly in urban areas. This can reinforce gender stereotypes and the discrimination of women. But women's activism and top leaders can also attract attention on national and international media and women's activists use the Internet to promote an international women's movement with networks and websites.

People also travel much more than before, among other reasons, to get education, jobs and income. The migrants comprise both men and women. In many, particularly industrial, countries, cultural diversity has increased, but ethnic-religious tensions have also been intensified. In different religions, there has been a noticeable rise in fundamentalism. The growth of various forms of Islamic fundamentalism in particular has influenced the view of men and women in many countries, sometimes even internationally.

Prevailing attitudes affect both women's motivation for involvement in politics and the support or resistance they experience. Religious opinion leaders frequently stress traditional women's roles, but the situation can be complex. In South Asia, for example, Buddhism, Hinduism and Islam present images of powerful women, and older women in particular can play important roles in the family (Hodson, 1997: 36–7). On a global level, Kenworthy and Malami (1999) and Reynolds (1999) noted that the religious orientation of the population was important for women's share in the parliaments (and cabinets). The proportion was generally lower in countries with a predominantly Moslem population than in countries marked by other religions, though Islam did not prevent all women from being active in politics at a high level. The update in 2010 shows that differences have been markedly reduced, the impact of religion being mitigated by other factors (see Table 2).

Table 2: Average percentage of women in parliament, by country's dominant religion

Region	1970	1980	1990	2000	2010
Protestant	5	9	12	17	20
Catholic	4	9	9	13	20
Orthodox	11	18	5	8	17
Moslem	4	6	5	5	13
Mixed	3	6	10	16	19

Note: A country is coded as mixed if no one religion is dominant – that is, if at least 50% of its population does not adhere to a single religion. The table does not include countries classified as having indigenous or other religions such as Judaism, Hinduism, or Buddhism.

Source: Paxton and Hughes (2014: 109, Table 4.1).

In the biographies in this book, both socio-economic and cultural factors will be studied for women in general in the country and for the women top leaders.

Democratisation

When the UN General Assembly proclaimed the principle of democratic government, the great majority of member states endorsed it, though many had different forms of authoritarian government. In the following years, emphasis was placed on strengthening the political role of states and democratic forms of government.

There were not only waves of independent states, but also 'waves of democratisation', periods when democratic institutions emerged in many countries. Decolonisation led to many countries becoming independent, with formally democratic political institutions. But most of the new states in Africa were soon ruled by dictators. Some European countries also got authoritarian rulers. By contrast, the small states in the Caribbean and the Pacific were democratised.

In the 1980s, a 'wave of democratisation' swept across Latin America. This was partly related to a policy change of the US, from supporting dictatorial regimes to promoting 'democracy' and neo-liberal economic policies. After the dissolution of the Soviet Union, a 'wave of democratisation' arose in several parts of the world in the 1990s. Countries in the former Eastern bloc adopted democratic forms of government and market liberalism when they became independent. When dictatorial regimes were no longer supported as part of the Cold War, developing countries also began to democratise, not least in Africa (see Figure 5).

Figure 5: Global trends in governance, 1946–2012

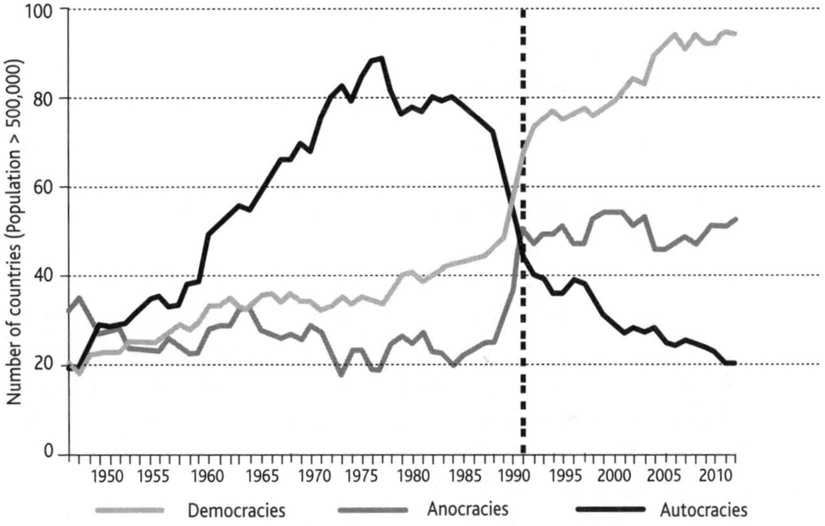

Note: Anocratic governance is a system placed somewhere between democracy and autocracy. The power is spread between elite groups competing for power.

Source: Center for Systemic Peace, Polity IV Project (see: www.systemicpeace.org)
© Center for Systemic Peace 2014

Around the year 2000, the political scientists J. Denis Derbyshire and Ian Derbyshire (2000: 27–45) registered that about one quarter (47) of the world's 192 states had authoritarian regimes. They ranged from military dictatorships and absolutism, to communism and authoritarian nationalism.

The remaining three quarters of the world's states were formally democratic. Half (74) were described as 'liberal democracies', with both representative government and individual freedoms. There was majority rule through free elections, a choice of political parties and limitations on the power of government. The liberal democracies were mostly found in Northern and Western Europe, Central America and the Caribbean and the Pacific.

The other states (71) were designated as 'emergent democracies'. In the past few years, they had a system with many of the characteristics of liberal democracies, but they lacked stability. Most had at least one undemocratic coup or change of government since 1987. These states were particularly found in sub-Saharan Africa, Eastern and Southern Europe, and Asia.[12]

Democratisation implies a strengthening of political rights and civil liberties. But neither Kenworthy and Malami (1999) nor Reynolds (1999) found any clear connection between the degree of democracy[13] and the number of women in the parliament (and cabinet). But the view on women in politics was important. Both surveys showed that women's chances to obtain political positions increased the longer women had political rights. In this book, questions related to women's political rights and the degree of democracy in the country will be followed up in connection with the women who managed to become top leaders.

Political structures and actors

In a broad sense, 'politics' can encompass all social relations that involve power, governance and authority, while a narrower definition limits it to public decision-making. The focus of this book is mainly on what takes place in and around formal political institutions at the national level: elections, government formation and state management. Women have, to a great extent, been involved in informal political activities of various kinds, from local action and groups to voluntary organisations and social movements, around the world. They have tried to influence the development of society. But the formal political institutions have been a domain for men, and it is in these institutions that the struggle for power over national policies, administration and resources primarily takes place, though the division of power may vary.[14]

Many factors have an impact on women's participation in formal political institutions. Most of the research in recent decades has been done in rich industrial countries. Gradually, studies have also been carried out elsewhere, and international comparisons have been made, but they are not numerous.[15]

Women's movements

The second feminist wave took a variety of forms, spanning from consciousness-raising groups and demonstrations, to professional organisations and women's caucuses. The movement played an important political role, though most of the groups and organisations were autonomous. They stressed identity with women as a group, used explicitly gendered language about women and demanded representation of women as women in public life. The movement benefited from the democratisation processes and, at the same time, helped to strengthen them. Studies note that the increases in women's participation in parliaments and cabinets in the 1980s and onward would not have been possible without women's movements that steadily pushed for women's political representation. They changed political expectations, redefined political interests and remade political networks. This allowed individual women to rise to and exercise power, and in this book, the contacts of the women top leaders with different parts of the women's movement will be examined.[16]

At the same time, the women's movements challenged the conventional notion of 'politics' as first and foremost the management of the state and the economy. Many of the most pressing issues for women in the North involved women's personal and intimate experiences. Therefore, politics should include power aspects of all human relationships where one group dominates another. Such a broad view on politics was met with resistance. But the struggle of the women's movement for reproductive rights and the work of the UN related to population issues pressed governments to deal with questions related to women and private circumstances. Eventually the agenda came to include legislation related to sexual orientation and measures to prevent violence against women.

Women's activism spread globally, but when women from all over the world came together at the international NGO forums, Western women were criticised by women from other regions. They claimed that white, middle-class, heterosexual women from the North could not necessarily represent other women because they had not experienced racial, class, colonial and heterosexual domination. The focus was therefore placed on intersectionality: the relationship between gender, on one hand, and ethnicity, nationality, class and sexual orientation, on the other. Women experienced oppression and possessed power in varying configurations and degrees of intensity according to the intersection of gender and the other characteristics. Injustice had more than one dimension and instead of one feminism, there could be many 'feminisms'. But even with the differences that existed, women in specific historical times and places could establish political goals in common and act together (McCann and Kim, 2003: 12–23).

At the beginning of the 21st century, women's movements were strongest in the global South, often supported by UN agencies, international women's NGOs, regional commissions and Western aid agencies. On each continent, the women's movement took on a special character, raising issues and organising according to local conditions and needs (Ferree and Tripp, 2006: 3–75).

'Feminism'

The term 'feminism' can be defined in different ways, but a common central element is a commitment to ending women's subordination in relation to men. It is also formulated as eliminating the discrimination of women due to sex or reducing gender inequalities. As the word 'feminist' has been stigmatised in many contexts, women often declare that they are not 'feminist', but nevertheless express clearly feminist views. This makes it difficult, at times, to distinguish between different kinds of women's activism. In this book, however the women label themselves they will be considered 'feminist' if they hold the view that something is wrong with the treatment of women and it is therefore necessary to advance their status and, explicitly or implicitly, challenge gender hierarchies and forms of women's subordination.

The large international women's conferences of the UN were intergovernmental conferences, and governments had the responsibility to follow up on the outcomes. This implied a 'state feminism' of a completely new kind, imposing new demands on leading politicians, not least ministers, and state administrations. In many countries, women's policy agencies were established at different levels of government to promote gender equality: a separate ministry or department, a special office, a coordinator, or advisory bodies. Their task could be to introduce women's status and gender equality in a specific policy area, bring in gender perspectives more broadly, or through formally feminist policies, promote women's rights and strike down gender hierarchies. In many countries, active 'woman-friendly' policies were pursued, improving the status of women in general or various groups of women in particular.

The concept of 'state feminism' was put to use in Scandinavia, where women made significant advances in terms of political power and were beginning to make their presence felt in most areas of welfare state policy. 'State feminism' was seen as the interplay between women's agitation from below and integration policy from above (Hernes, 1987: 11). The term was used in various gender studies, but created some confusion about what 'feminism' was actually supposed to be. In 'state feminism', the distinction between state and civil society could become blurred and it was unclear if women's policy agencies were accountable primarily to governments or to a women's movement.

In many countries, a 'state feminism' was also practically unrealistic. The political establishment remained strongly male-dominated and the essential components for good governance were lacking: state capability, responsiveness to the needs of the citizens and accountability. In many cases, the states were not only weak and unstable, but even 'failing'. In many developing countries, the 1980s were a 'lost decade', with extensive economic problems, and neo-liberal policies entailed the weakening of the state, privatisation, reduction of public services and increasing unemployment. Women got more access to paid work and financial services, but the majority of women got precarious, low-paid jobs and poverty became 'feminised'. At the same time, women's activists were seeking state support for gender justice and the strengthening of the position of women.

In the 1990s, one of the biggest achievements of the international women's movement was the introduction of a women's rights paradigm into various global governance regimes. But this progress coincided with the spread of the neo-liberal global order and the economic crises from 2007 hit worldwide, including rich industrial countries, leading them to introduce extensive austerity measures. These usually led to a weakening of the state and public policies. Income equalities increased while social services were reduced, leading to more marked differences between the well-off and poor, men and women, urban and rural areas, and different ethnic groups. Although there was some progress with the women's rights paradigm, women's activists in 2013 expressed great concern that the neo-liberal transformation was undermining gender equality and the protection of women's rights, and there were difficult discussions about effective feminist strategies in different contexts.[17]

Resistance to change

Over the years, social science research, primarily in Western societies, has probed into the social systems that create and maintain gender inequality, and underline that they make themselves felt at all levels, from the upbringing of children to productive activities and the exercise of societal power.

Inequalities based on ethnicity, social class and gender manifest themselves differently, but all are an integral part of the structures and practices in families, schools, workplaces and governing bodies. They are deeply rooted, resistant to change and long-lasting, and because gender inequalities mark so many institutions they are difficult to change or remove. Inequalities in one institution (such as the school) can enhance and be enhanced by inequalities in another (such as the workplace). Inequalities are made legitimate by prevailing ideology and gender stereotypes. These not only indicate how women and men 'are' and how they should behave, but systematically support the allocation of unequal status, resources and power to the two genders.

Gender stereotypes are quite similar across cultures. Women are generally associated with compassion, care and friendliness, while men are associated with assertiveness, aggression and control. The stereotypes facilitate men's access to power, while they complicate the access of women. The unequal position of women and men strengthens the expectation that men should rule and women support. Politics and leadership go together with men and masculinity.

Dominant groups have an interest in maintaining the unequal distribution of power, and the more power in question, the greater the interest. Women who try to change the system or acquire roles that are usually reserved for men, for example, in politics, often meet resistance and negative reactions of various kinds (Connell, 1987; Eagly et al, 2004; Wharton, 2005).

Both a vertical and a horizontal division of labour between women and men are frequent in political life. The *vertical* division reflects the gender power relationship. Almost without exception, the higher up one moves in the power hierarchy, the fewer women there are to be found. The proportion of democratically elected women representatives in parliaments and local councils is far smaller than their proportion of the electorate. Women's share of senior parliamentary posts and often also of cabinet members is less than their proportion of parliamentary members. There are usually fewer women at party leadership level than their share of the party membership. This division of labour has been called a kind of 'iron law', but it is not absolute and invariable, as has been seen during recent decades, particularly in connection with the use of gender quotas.

There is also a widespread *horizontal* division of labour, entailing that women are concentrated in the education and social sectors, while men are clustered in the productive sector. This 'sectorisation' operates in parliaments, committees and cabinets and has been criticised because women should also participate in planning, finance and so on. The division of labour might be the result of exclusion by more influential men; however, the areas where women are concentrated are also those where women usually have the most experience (Haavio-Mannila et al, 1985; UN, 1991, 1995, 2000, 2010).

Political parties

Political parties play a key role in the political life and development of a country. After 1989, the number of one-party states declined sharply, and there was greater scope for political pluralism. At the close of the 20th century, there were only a few states without political parties.

Around the world, parties were created with different policies, sizes and working methods. While some had internal democratic processes to decide on policies and measures, others were ruled with an iron hand by a powerful front man (or, exceptionally, woman). Some parties acted primarily as fund-raising and election machinery, while others contributed actively to the development of national and international policies. In any case, political parties were placed between the citizens and the governing bodies and usually played a crucial role as gatekeepers for recruiting candidates for parliaments and executive positions (see Figure 6; also Lovenduski and Norris, 1993: Goetz, 2009; Krook and Childs, 2010, Lovenduski, 2010).

As with politics in general, political parties have been and still are strongly male-dominated. On the basis of reports of women in politics from 43 countries worldwide, Barbara J. Nelson and Najma Chowdhury (1994: 15–18) concluded that formal political institutions, primarily political parties, constituted major obstacles to women's participation in politics on an equal footing with men. Formal politics were often characterised by a male culture and ethics, as well as an aggression and competition that were perceived as masculine. The maleness of politics had two aspects. Partly, politics were rooted in fraternalism, a brotherhood of men that excluded women. Partly, they functioned in a patriarchal way with patron–client relations that reiterated patriarchal father–son family structures and excluded women from many of the material rewards in politics.

Social networks and alliances are common in political activity, but they acquire a special character when they are based on patron–client relations or patronage. Then, political leaders establish personal ties to their followers for mutual benefit. The ties can be based on family, class, ethnic or cultural affiliation, party membership, and so on. The (male) leaders provide resources (privileges, benefits, services), while the followers provide support (votes in elections). Patron–client networks can involve corruption and other abuses of public positions (Brinkerhoff and Goldsmith, 2002; Utas, 2012). A survey by Transparency International in 64 countries worldwide showed that the general public considered the political parties as the institution most affected by corruption, followed by parliaments, the police and the judiciary (2004).

The approaches of women's organisations towards political parties have varied: at times, collaborating; at times, keeping a distance because of lack of faith in the party culture and working methods. Since the 1980s, there has been increased pressure from women on the outside, but also from the inside, to obtain institutional change. More women have joined political parties, engaged in mainstream politics and worked for increased women's representation at decision-making levels. They

Figure 6: Parliamentary recruitment system

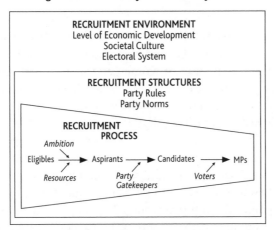

Source: Matland and Montgomery (2003). By permission of Oxford University Press.

have proposed changes in the political agenda, party reforms, the introduction of gender quotas, new means of policymaking and new government structures.

Women's sections and networks have become widespread means of organising women in political parties. They can help women get to the top. But, at times, the sections isolate women instead of integrating them into the party as such. Generally, change has been limited and slow. By 2012, 40 to 50 per cent of party members globally were women, but women held only about 10 per cent of the leadership positions in political parties (Figure 7). Fifteen years earlier, the percentage of women leaders was roughly the same.[18]

Figure 7: Women and men in leadership positions in political parties worldwide in 2012

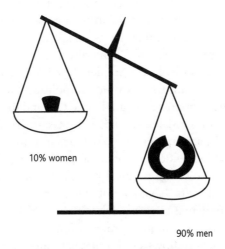

10% women

90% men

Source: Compiled by the author.

Numbers count

In the 1970s, the sociologist Rosabeth Moss Kanter (1977) studied men and women in corporations in the US and observed that their behaviour varied with the proportional representation of women and men in each group. In 'skewed' groups with few women, they became 'tokens'. They got special attention. Differences between them and the men were exaggerated and gender stereotypes were used to describe them. They became symbols: 'mother', 'seductress', 'pet' or 'iron maiden'. They were exposed to special performance pressures and were surrounded by organisational, social and personal ambivalence entailing stress and personal costs. A mere shift in absolute numbers could change the social interaction. A 'skewed' group had 15 per cent women or less. If a group became 'tilted', with women amounting to around 35 per cent, the minority could begin to influence the culture of the group and alliances between minority group members could become a possibility, according to Kanter.

Analysing behaviour, Kanter did not focus on women and men as such, but on the proportion of social categories such as women/men, that is, the organisation of the institution. Her thinking was followed up by the women's movement and researchers in several countries focusing on women in politics. What would change with more women? If there was a 'critical mass' of, for example, 30 per cent, a fundamental change might happen, making it possible for women to change their performance, the social climate, the political discourse and the policies and obtain more power. The significance of numbers changed. It was not only a question of descriptive representation: a share of women in political bodies according to their share in the population. It was also a question of substantive representation: women representatives being able to promote women's policy interests (Dahlerup, 1988, 2006; Dahlerup and Friedenvall, 2010).

In 1990, the Economic and Social Council of the UN (ECOSOC) recommended goals of 30 and 50 per cent women at decision-making levels. But progress was slow and it was realised at Beijing that it was not sufficient to eliminate barriers to ensure 'equal opportunities' for women and men. 'Equal opportunities' were in practice not really equal due to the direct and hidden discrimination of women. Inclusive measures had to be implemented to obtain 'equality of result' and actually increase the number of women in political positions. *Gender quotas* became the most widely supported action by the UN and the Inter-Parliamentary Union. Quotas could be legislated candidate quotas, reserved seats in parliament or voluntary political party quotas. In 2010, around 50 states had introduced gender quotas by law in elections to national parliaments. In approximately 40 other states, at least some of the political parties had introduced gender quotas for their own candidate lists. It was a 'fast-track' policy measure in contrast to the well-known incremental track model, where gender equality would come, slowly, in due course (see www.quotaproject.org).

The use of positive action shows a political will to move from rhetoric to reality. But many countries only accepted voluntary or limited quotas, so the effect was not as great as could be expected (see Table 3). As the quotas mainly were related to parliamentary elections, the impact on cabinets and the top political leadership was not certain and the question of the promotion of women-friendly policies remained open. A 'critical minority' of women was important to prevent them from being only token participants, but it was insufficient to ensure that women's interests were taken properly into account. Systematic changes had to take place in the political institutions, particularly the political parties and parliaments, so that they effectively combatted de facto discrimination against women.[19]

Table 3: Women members of parliaments and cabinet ministers worldwide in 2010

Region[a]	Average percentage of women			
	Parliament		Cabinet	
Industrial countries[b]		21%		20 %
Western		25 %		29 %
Nordic	42%		50%	
Others	22 %		25%	
Eastern		17 %		11 %
Developing countries		18%		15%
Asia		19%		9%
South Asia	18%		7%	
East Asia	19%		9%	
Pacific		6%		9%
Sub-Saharan Africa		20%		20%
Latin America and Caribbean		22%		20%
Latin America	24%		23%	
Caribbean	15%		16%	
Arab states		10%		7%
World		19%		16 %

Source: Based on IPU and UNDAW (2010).

Notes: [a] The regions are the same as in Table 1. The information is based on 187/188 of 192 countries. Parliaments include unicameral parliaments or the lower houses of parliament. Vice prime ministers are considered as cabinet ministers, but prime ministers only when they are also responsible for a sector ministry. The percentages are calculated for regions, continents and the world as a whole, so individual countries may weigh more or less according to the size of the parliament and cabinet.

[b] Western countries include Western Europe, Malta, Turkey, Israel, Canada, USA, Australia, New Zealand and Japan. Eastern countries include Eastern Europe, transitional states in South-East Europe and Commonwealth of Independent States.

Parliaments and cabinets

After 1995, women's political activity and representation in formal bodies increased around the world, although the variation was considerable. Some states introduced positive measures such as quotas, but few changed the electoral laws to get more women into decision-making positions. Overall, the representation of women in parliaments grew from ten per cent in 1994 to 22 per cent in 2014. It was a noticeable increase, but represented only a 0.6 percentage-point increase a year. There was a long way to go to reach the goal of 30, not to mention 50, per cent of women members of parliament (MPs) in the world. But 39 countries had 30 per cent or more in 2014, of which one country (Rwanda) had more than 50 per cent (actually 64 per cent). These countries had usually introduced positive measures of one kind or the other. In contrast to them, there were four countries that did not have a single woman parliamentarian and ten had only one (IPU, 2014a, 2014b).

With regards to cabinets, there were a total of 6 per cent female ministers in 1994, and the proportion rose to 17 per cent in 2014 – more than double. 36 countries had 30 per cent women ministers or more, of which three had 50 per cent or more (Nicaragua, Sweden, Finland). There were eight countries that did not have a single woman minister, while 32 had one (UNDP, 1995a, IPU and UN Women, 2014).

In a democracy, elections are held to choose members of the national parliaments. The most widespread voting system is a form of proportional representation, with party lists in multimember constituencies. In 2000, this was used in approximately half of the world's states. Simple plurality or 'first-past-the-post' electoral systems, where the candidate who gets the most votes is elected, was used in around one third of the states. Alternatively, an absolute majority could be required using single-member constituencies. This system was applied in 15 per cent of the states (Derbyshire and Derbyshire, 2000: 93).

There are a number of variations in the systems and conditions, but it has generally been registered that it is crucial for the representation of women in parliament for the country to have a woman-friendly electoral system. A system of plurality or majority vote in single-member districts often makes it difficult for women to be elected. They have better chances when party lists with proportional representation are used in multimember districts. Proportional representation is also the best system for enforcing quotas. But the size of the electoral district and the number of seats in the parliament can make a difference. In the elections in 2012, proportional representation globally delivered 25 per cent women in parliaments; first-past-the-post, 14 per cent; and mixed systems, 17.5 per cent (see Figure 8).[20]

Figure 8: Percentage of women in parliaments: majoritarian versus proportional electoral systems

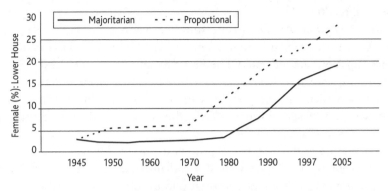

Note: Based on 24 established democracies.
Source: Matland (2005).
Reproduced by permission of International IDEA from *Women in parliament: Beyond numbers*
© International Institute for Democracy and Electoral Assistance 2005

Ideological directions

A wide spectrum of parties has come into existence, varying from country to country. It is often difficult to know for sure what they represent. Policies and party designations are unclear or have varying meaning. There may also be differences in the parties' practices in relation to the ideology or platform they invoke. Roughly, the political parties can be categorised as follows:

- Leftist parties, including: parties to the far left, such as communist parties; to the left, such as socialist, social-democratic and labour parties; and to the centre-left, such as radical and social-liberal parties.
- Rightist parties, including: parties to the extreme right, such as fascist, Nazi, authoritarian and extreme nationalist parties; to the right, such as conservative and Christian-democratic parties; and to the centre-right, such as agrarian parties.
- Centre parties, including, among others, liberal parties advocating freedom, democracy and justice.

Studies have registered that left-wing parties have more women in parliaments and cabinets than more conservative parties (Reynolds, 1999: 567–70; Tremblay and Bauer, 2011: 184). But there are women national leaders from different parties and this will be looked into further later in the book.

Executive systems

Authoritarian and democratic regimes have different forms of executive systems. The authoritarian executives include military rulers, dictators, monarchs or communist leaders, and they are spread across the globe. In 2000, democracies had three forms of executives: half of them had a limited presidential system; around

40 per cent, a parliamentary system; and 10 per cent, a dual system (Derbyshire and Derbyshire, 2000: 47).

The roles of 'president' and 'prime minister' are not the same in the three systems. With a presidential system, often inspired by the US, the executive and legislative functions are separated. The president plays the central executive role as head of both state and government. He/she is usually elected directly, but can be elected by parliament, and governs with an advisory cabinet of non-elected members who are chosen and appointed by the president and who are responsible to him/her. The cabinet may include an advisory prime minister. With a 'limited presidential executive' the presidential powers are limited by the legislative powers of parliament and the need for approval by parliament of certain executive actions. Limited presidential regimes are mostly found in sub-Saharan Africa and South America.

With a parliamentary system, sometimes referred to as the Westminster model because it originated and is found in its clearest form in the UK, the roles of head of state and head of government are separated. Generally, the head of state (an elected president or a monarch) has a mainly ceremonial role, while the head of government has the executive political power and appoints the cabinet. The prime minister is not elected directly. Both the prime minister and the cabinet are drawn from the parliament and are directly responsible to it. Usually, the prime minister is the leader of the party that has the majority or the most seats in the parliament, but this can vary. There may be a vote of no confidence. Parliamentary regimes are most frequent in Northern and Western Europe, Central America, and the Caribbean.

Some countries, mostly in Eastern Europe after the dissolution of the Soviet Union, introduced dual executives, where the power is more or less evenly divided between the president and the prime minister. Here, there are always two elected top leaders, while there may be only one in the other systems: one president or one prime minister (Lijphart, 1992, 1999; Siaroff, 2003).

Regarding the different forms of executives, the political scientist Farida Jalalzai (2013b: 44-56) finds that female national leaders around the world occupied weaker posts with less concentrated authority than male leaders. Generally, more women were prime ministers than presidents, and the majority shared power with another chief executive (president or prime minister). The women fell into five groups. Most were dominant or weak prime ministers, while some were dominant presidents. A few were powerful or weak presidents. The analysis will be followed up later in the book.

Different paths

There is usually a long way to go to acquire a top position in national politics. The structures of political institutions are hierarchical and the competition to rise to power is fierce. The different executives also have different recruitment patterns. In parliamentary systems, it is necessary to first be elected to the parliament before it is possible to get to the top. In presidential systems, the president is most often elected directly and the background of the candidates can vary considerably. In both cases, it is important to have support from a political party.

Previous studies of women top leaders show that they followed different paths to get to the top. Some women were outsiders and did not participate in political activities before they rose to executive power. Some gained office through chance circumstances or 'inherited' power from family, father or husband. It was also notable that many women rose to the top in situations of social and political turmoil, where established institutions were weakened, possibilities for unusual solutions were opened up or there was suddenly a political vacuum (Tripp, 2008; Genovese, 2013: 336-7; Jalalzai, 2013b: 14-21).

Studying how national women chief executives managed to advance to the top in politics, Francine D'Amico (1995: 15-30), Research Fellow in International Studies, drew up several paths. In this book, we will apply the paths with slightly revised definitions. We will refer to: a) 'substitutes', who take over a family member's position of power; b) 'insiders' or climbers in the political parties, who obtain a position of power through the party; and c) 'outsiders', who obtain a position of power on the basis of occupational activities or participation in NGOs or at grassroots level outside the political parties.

Woman in a man's world

The expectations and demands related to women entering the male-dominated political area depend on the reasons for participation. If the representation of women is primarily seen as a democratic right, policies will not necessarily be expected to change. But if women are perceived to represent special interests because they are women, the question arises as to whether their participation makes a difference. To do so, women must be able to assert themselves on their own basis in the political institutions.

Women who get involved in formal politics often encounter a complex social and psychological reality.[21] Different institutions have their distinctive features, and what happens depends upon who a woman is, where she enters and on what basis. If a woman becomes a member of a political party or is elected to the parliament, it is usually expected that she, like other newcomers, learns the accepted practices of the institution. She can be appreciated as a new member, but she can also be challenging because she differs from the majority.

If women politicians want to succeed in male-dominated political institutions and have a career, they are usually obliged to accept the dominant male culture and become 'one of the boys'. In particular, the first women to enter such institutions have to adjust their behaviour to that of the majority. When they are co-opted or assimilated into the established culture, they use men's language about issues men consider important. But this makes them more or less invisible as women. They melt into the landscape without changing the terrain they operate in. The dilemma is whether women change the institutions before the institutions change them, as noted in feminist quarters (Peterson and Runyan, 1999).

Co-optation occurs when women are exposed to active pressure to think and act like the (male) majority. This can take many forms, from friendly discussions to sanctions, or threats of sanctions, if they do not adapt. Co-optation can also take place when words and ideas that the majority finds objectionable are suppressed or may appear to be accepted, but are emptied of content. More women may be accepted in politics, but not feminist demands. In order to keep women in 'their place', men can use dominance or 'master suppression' techniques, according to feminist research. These aim at maintaining the status quo, with male dominance in spite of the participation of women. The techniques entail that men, among other things, make women invisible and ridicule them, withhold information from them, condemn them whatever they do, or inflict guilt and shame (Ås, 2008).

Women politicians and leaders often experience double binds because they encounter conflicting expectations. On the one hand, they are supposed to comply with the female role by promoting women's demands and being cooperative, warm and altruistic. On the other hand, they are supposed to comply with the role of politician by promoting the policies of the (male-dominated) party and being self-assertive, competent and competitive. If women are confident and efficient, they are easily criticised for not being 'feminine'. If they are kind and caring, their political ability is questioned. How should they behave? As politicians or women? Whatever, it may be 'wrong'.

Double binds have as a consequence that female politicians are met with scepticism: are they capable enough? A double standard is created, and women are subjected to closer scrutiny and stricter demands than men. While men are described as 'strong' and 'reliable', women are described as 'controversial' and 'weak'. This contributes to greater difficulties for women being recognised, and, in practice, they are discriminated against. It does not improve the situation that issues of particular interest for women generally have low status in male-dominated politics (Murray, 2010: 7–13).

Feminist leadership?

Studies have been made of the efforts of male and female politicians to promote gender equality. The Inter-Parliamentary Union (IPU, 2008: 43-59) interviewed parliamentarians worldwide and found that women MPs were the most ardent supporters of women and redefined legislative priorities to include women's concerns and perspectives. In particular, the efforts to combat gender-based violence led to results, and child care, pensions, gender-equality laws and electoral reform appeared on the agenda. Although women were key actors, men slowly began to address such questions as well. Not all female parliamentarians raised women's issues or felt a responsibility for them. Some were primarily interested in 'male areas', such as finance and foreign policy. Some who wanted to promote women's interests encountered obstacles: they did not get the support of colleagues or they came into conflict with the party (IPU, 2010; Palmieri, 2011).

The social anthropologist Anne Krogstad (1999b: 47-62) studied the media presentation of women chief executives in different countries and noted that the images differed. Three categories inspire the analysis in this book. Some women chief executives conformed to the norms and values of male-dominated politics, acted in the same way as their male political colleagues, fought on their terms and became the first among equals. But they were not engaged in women's issues – whatever they might be – and could be criticised because of this. Other women top leaders tried to be as matter-of-fact as possible, making a compromise between men's and women's interests. They could emphasise that they were not 'women', but 'politicians', and try to be 'both tough and caring'. But there could be difficult balances to be struck. The third group challenged male domination and promoted feminist policies. They took 'critical action' such as recruiting other women, introducing gender quotas, passing laws or establishing institutions supporting women. To avoid political battles, some referred to their roles as mothers, but this could weaken their status as politicians.

The different categories are not mutually exclusive. The behaviour may change at different times and in different situations, though it mainly falls into one category. What the categories actually involve can also change over time in different parts of the world. In any case, the questions arise: what does it mean to promote women's interests? What interests and how? Some women's issues are also highly controversial, particularly those relating to sexuality and procreation: divorce, contraception and abortion, homosexuality, prostitution, and sterilisation. In this book, public statements, policy decisions, legislation, expenditures and measures to improve the status of women will be considered 'women-friendly policies' if they are in accordance with the CEDAW and the Beijing Platform for Action. But it is mostly impossible with the available information to know the effects of the policies in practice.

The political scientist Michael A. Genovese (1993: 217; 2013: 343) noted that none of the women national leaders he studied challenged in any fundamental way the patriarchal power structure of their societies. To do so would have been political suicide, he states.

Most of the women executives have risen to the top later than the women Genovese studied and the political climate and conditions have changed. With an increasing number of women in decision-making bodies or positions, it can be easier to promote women's interests and gain support for them, though women may disagree among themselves about what this should be.

Women national leaders under scrutiny

Since 1990, several books have been published with international biographical overviews of national women leaders. Relevant information from these sources is used in this book.

In 1993, the journalist and teacher Olga S. Opfell described the careers of 21 women leaders who came to power between 1960 and 1992. The author Laura A. Liswood travelled around the world in 1993/94 and interviewed 15 women presidents and prime ministers. In 2007, she interviewed four more and published an updated version of her book. The political scientist Michael A. Genovese chose a different approach. Together with university colleagues, he carried out individual studies of seven important national women leaders from different countries and published in 1993. Twenty years later, he presented a revised version together with Janie S. Steckenrider, with three additional biographies. In 1995, Francine D'Amico analysed 28 national women leaders since World War II and, together with Peter R. Beckman, edited a book with biographies of four of them.

In 2005, the political scientist Robert P. Watson, together with Alicia Jencik and Judith A. Selzer, presented brief biographical data concerning 52 women top leaders. In 2006, the political scientist Gunhild Hoogensen and the historian Bruce O. Solheim published brief biographical overviews of 22 women chief executives from different regions, mostly prior to 1995. The women were placed in a regional context, but little information was provided about individual countries. The same was true of the collection of biographical data published by the political scientist Jane S. Jensen in 2008, comprising 64 women top leaders.

The political scientist Farida Jalalzai has studied women chief executives worldwide for a number of years and published several articles in addition to a book. She first described the political and educational background of 44 top leaders (2004) and then looked into institutional and structural factors that made a difference when 49 women leaders came to power (2008). She analysed the president of Liberia, Ellen Johnson Sirleaf, in particular (2013a). In her book (2013b) she outlined important patterns related to women's executive paths and the power of women who became presidents or prime ministers during the years 1960–2010. She compared them to their male predecessors and women who failed to win top positions.[22]

Jalalzai combines qualitative and statistical methods, providing both international overviews and geographic comparisons. The book provides essential insight that I have benefited from in my book. In relation to hers, my book presents a broader historical perspective, bringing in the geographic contexts and international developments influencing women's access to power to a greater extent, and the biographies are more developed, bringing in more of the women's background and environment and the experiences of women themselves.

Recent studies with more limited focus include the work of the political scientist Aili Mari Tripp (2008), who collaborated with four colleagues to examine the political background of four women national leaders who came to power in 2005/06, and Rainbow Murray (2010), who edited articles on women's campaigns for executive office: five who succeeded and four who did not.

Following chapters

The research that has been done on the women top leaders provides essential information at a time when important insight is lacking. The factors and forces that can have an influence on the rise of a woman to the national leadership of her nation state are numerous and diverse. In the biographies, efforts will be made to draw a complex and realistic picture in order to get a grasp of the forces in play and thereby understand how the exceptional could happen: that a woman became president or prime minister.

Summing up, the key questions are: which societal conditions on various levels contributed to the women's rise to the top? How were the women motivated to do something as unusual as engaging in politics and becoming national leaders? How could it be that male-dominated political institutions not only allowed women to participate, but also let them acquire some of the key power positions? And what importance did the fact that women obtained these positions then have? Did it make a difference?

The biographies are presented by region and chronology and divided up according to the number of women leaders in each region. The text starts with the early women leaders in the Western industrialised countries. The later leaders in these countries are described in a later chapter. Asia is so vast that it is given two chapters and Latin America and the Caribbean have a chapter each. Due to the relatively few women top leaders, the whole of Sub-Saharan Africa is presented in a single chapter as is the whole of the Eastern bloc. The regional information is summarised in Chapters Eleven and Twelve.

The British Prime Minister Margaret Thatcher (left) and the Norwegian Prime Minister Gro Harlem Brundtland in front of 10 Downing Street, London, on 1 April 1987.
Image: Getty Images

Chapter Three

Western industrial countries (I): women are able – in various ways

The world's first democracies

Common features in culture and politics

The revolutions in England, France and the US in the 1600s and 1700s had a profound influence on the societies in Europe and North America.[1] Thinkers such as Voltaire and Rousseau spread ideas about liberty, equality and brotherhood. They did not talk about sisterhood, but women like Olympe de Gouges and Mary Wollstonecraft advocated for women's rights. In the course of the 1800s increasingly democratic constitutions were adopted, and elected parliaments were established in many parts of Europe.

Although their histories vary, Western industrial countries are grouped here because they have common societal features. In addition to Western Europe and North America, Turkey, Malta Cyprus, Israel, Australia, New Zealand and Japan are included.[2] In the past there were divisions, conflicts and wars between countries, but after World War II they have been characterised by rapid modernisation, high socio-economic growth and increasing collaboration. The creation of the North Atlantic Treaty Organisation (NATO) and the European Community were of particular importance.

Most of the Western industrial countries have ethnically been relatively homogeneous nation states marked by a Christian heritage, but some have indigenous people within their borders, or there are noticeable tensions arising from regional differences in language, culture and religion. At times, these have led to armed conflict. Nevertheless, the political systems are relatively similar. Almost all countries are stable democracies, the majority with parliamentary and multi-party systems. A few have presidential or dual systems.

Politics in these countries has been a male domain, with the exception of a few countries with royal women rulers. In the last century, the most important have been the queens of Denmark, the Netherlands and the UK. After Queen

Elizabeth 1 and Queen Victoria, the UK got Queen Elizabeth II. Her duties are mainly ceremonial, and she is Britain's longest lived and second-longest reigning monarch, and is formally the head of state not only in Britain, but also in a number of Commonwealth countries, including Australia and Canada. The Netherlands had three ruling queens in a row, and Denmark had a reigning queen for nearly 40 years.[3] Queens have a certain symbolic power, but they are not elected. The positions are inherited, and there is no evidence that female monarchs have stimulated the recruitment of women to leading positions in politics in general, though the British queen has appointed some women as governors-general.

Early industrial development

Western countries were industrialised relatively early, but the basis for economic activity and income differed, and developments were uneven. Eventually, almost all countries had a form of mixed economy, with a market economy and relatively well-developed school systems and social services. But the specific arrangements were the subject of political controversy and varied from country to country and from time to time. In the Nordic countries, the organisation of a welfare state by labour movements had special significance. Western industrial countries became among the richest in the world, with widespread urbanisation and education, high average income, and long life expectancy.

The industrial development drew women into paid employment, but the work was generally hard and poorly paid. Good education, better jobs and positions of power were reserved for men. In some countries, especially in England and the US, an activist women's movement was created as early as the 1800s. This inspired women in other places to organise, but the Catholic Church was a conservative force that delayed the development of women's rights in Southern Europe especially. In some Western countries, women received the right to vote before World War I, while others had to wait until the end of World War II or even later.

Regardless of when women got the right to vote, there were few women in important elected positions until the 1970s. A liberal-democratic system and formal rights theoretically gave women the possibility to participate in government, but, in practice, it did not happen. After World War II, however, economic development gained momentum, which, among other things, led to women getting better health and more education. This also made it possible for more women to get into various kinds of paid employment. Many people thought that economic prosperity, higher education and more women in the labour force would remove the barriers preventing women from political involvement. But politics generally remained a male-dominated part of society, with women often conspicuously absent in important decision-making bodies.

The second feminist wave

The first wave of feminism during the last part of 19th and first part of the 20th century largely focused on the struggle for voting rights in industrial countries. The second wave of feminism emerged in the 1960s in the US. Until 1960, there had only been two women ministers and a maximum of 3 per cent women in the House of Representatives. A majority of the women had paid employment in addition to the responsibility for house and home. But the notion of 'the happy housewife heroine' (Friedan, 1963) was far from reality for many, and the image of the successful career woman was also distorted. The women worked for lower wages than men in factories and as maids, secretaries, teachers and nurses, while, with few exceptions, only men had highly paid and prestigious jobs.

The new wave of feminism arose almost simultaneously with the civil rights movement among black people in the US and was, to some extent, inspired by it. The new women's movement attracted great attention. Full of anger and enthusiasm, women created awareness-raising groups and organisations, acquired knowledge, and took action. They sabotaged the crowning of pretty girls, stormed publishing houses, demonstrated against advertising, demanded the right to paid work, day care and self-determined abortion, opposed the traditional family, threw away their bras, and protested against all forms of oppression of women. The movement in the US created ripple effects in other countries. In Western countries, in particular, where conditions were reminiscent of those in the US, the new feminist wave had great importance. The International Women's Year in 1975 led to increased mobilisation, focusing on the position of women in politics and government. In 1979, the UN Convention on the Elimination of All Forms of Discrimination against Women (CEDAW) was adopted, and during the 1980s, it was ratified by most Western countries, except the US.[4]

The representation of women in parliaments and cabinets increased, especially in some countries. A few got women top politicians. After Golda Meir in Israel, a first group went to the top around 1980, with women executives in four corners of Europe: the UK, Malta, the Nordic countries and Portugal.

Margaret Thatcher: Conservative Iron Lady

Admired and reviled

One of the national female leaders looming highest in the 20th century was Britain's Margaret Thatcher.[5] She was the object of an extraordinary personal fascination all over the world. She was deeply divisive and controversial and, besides the nickname 'The Iron Lady', she was called 'Her Malignancy' and 'TBW' ('That Bloody Woman') (Campbell, 2009: 380; Genovese, 2013: 294). Decades after she left office, at her funeral in April 2013, strong emotions of both admiration and anger were expressed in the British population.

Her record was unequalled. She was the first elected woman to lead a major world power, Britain's first woman prime minister and the first woman to lead the Conservative Party – accolades yet to be repeated. She was prime minister for more than 11 years, longer than anyone in the 20th century, won three consecutive general elections, reshaped much of the British political landscape and is considered to be one of the most important prime ministers in British history. Further, she is one of only a few British prime ministers to have an approach recognised as an 'ism' – not even an achievement by Churchill. Hand in hand with Reaganism in the US, Thatcherism set the template for the development of the world economy at the time. For better and worse, Thatcher became one of the transformative figures who shaped the 20th century.[6]

The 19th-century women's suffrage movement was large and militant. In 1918, women over 30 got the right to vote, and in 1928, women obtained suffrage equal to men. But though the country had fostered a number of woman rulers, intellectuals and artists throughout history, very few women were elected to political office. At the end of the 1960s, women mobilised again for political equality, but representation remained low. The British population of about 60 million was characterised by marked class divisions. The electoral system was not favourable to women and party elites had a strong grip on the political recruitment processes. Parliament has two chambers. Elections for the House of the Commons are by plurality vote in single-member constituencies, while members of the House of Lords are appointed in different ways. The prime minister and cabinet members are predominantly members of parliament (MPs) (a few members of the House of Lords are included) and are accountable to parliament.

How could a woman, first, get to the top in a male-dominated political party such as the Conservative Party and then change its policy from the consensus that the Conservative Party's Churchill and the Labour Party's Attlee established as prime ministers after World War II to a completely different direction? Was it due to special circumstances, unusual personal talents or just chance?

Her father's daughter

Margaret Roberts was born into a lower-middle-class family in Grantham, England, in 1925, the younger of the two daughters of Beatrice and Albert Roberts. Albert was a successful modest grocer with two shops. The family lived above one of them and all gave a helping hand. Before she married, Beatrice was a professional tailor, but afterwards she worked as a housewife. Albert served as a Methodist preacher, and Margaret's childhood was marked by her parents' faith and austere lifestyle. Her father was also a local politician and served as school governor, borough councillor, alderman and finally mayor of Grantham. His politics was a natural extension of his business and he supported the Conservatives.

As an adult, Margaret would speak of her mother in a condescending manner: 'I loved my mother dearly, but after I was fifteen we had nothing more to say to each other' (Ogden, 1990: 38). In her autobiography, she added that her mother managed the household, did a great deal of voluntary social work and made possible all that her husband and daughters did. 'From my mother I inherited the ability to organize and combine so many different duties of an active life', Margaret (1995a: 106–7) noted. Her father became the biggest influence on her life, however. He was her teacher, mentor, guru and guide and prepared her for a masculine political world. Father and daughter had long political discussions. Margaret was taught the right upper class accent and her father took her to the council meetings to learn how to debate issues. Ultimately, life was about character and he instilled in her the habit of hard work, tireless community activity and an exceptionally powerful moral sense to do what was right without being afraid of being different. Margaret came to believe in private enterprise. Winston Churchill was her hero and she soon engaged in Conservative Party activities. She had politics in her blood, she said (1995a: 85), and at only 10 years old, during the election campaign in 1935, she began as an errand girl for the local Conservative parliamentary candidate.[7]

Margaret's father regretted that he had little formal schooling and wanted his daughters to get the best possible education. The oldest was not particularly interested in reading and was more closely attached to her mother, so Albert tried to get the five years younger Margaret to manage what he himself had not achieved. Margaret went to a girls' grammar school and did well. In 1947, she earned a bachelor's degree in chemistry at Somerville, one of the oldest women's colleges in Oxford. She was less than enthused with chemistry, but a degree in science offered good job opportunities. Her passion, however, was politics. She joined the Oxford Union Conservative Association and became, first, secretary, then treasurer and finally president.

After graduation, Margaret began working as a research chemist but was also still active in politics. In 1948, the local party chief was looking for a candidate to run in Dartford, a strong Labour seat. Margaret was only 23 years old, but accepted and defeated the four men on the shortlist. She was the youngest woman parliamentary candidate. In a Labour constituency, the Tories had little to lose, but could get some publicity by presenting a person out of the ordinary. There were only 4 per cent women in the House of Commons at the time. Some older women in the party gave Margaret advice. She ran an energetic campaign and received international as well as national publicity. She lost the general election in 1950, but the Labour majority was reduced. She ran again in 1951 and lost again.[8]

Mother of twins

At one of the political meetings, Margaret met Denis Thatcher, a wealthy, conservative businessman. He was 10 years her senior and had been divorced for a time. They married in 1951 and for Mrs Thatcher, marriage did not entail that she had to choose between career and marriage. On the contrary, the marriage relieved her of financial worries and the traditional demands of housework. Denis was sufficiently rich to provide for her and enthusiastically supported her career while he was doing business and playing rugby football. In fact, he became an important advisor for his wife. Margaret joined the Church of England and began to study law. She specialised in patent and tax law and started practising as a barrister.

In 1953, she and Denis had twins, Carol and Mark. But she did not let the children interfere with her ambitious goals. In fact, she applied for her bar finals while she was still in the maternity ward and passed them a few months later. She hired a combined nanny and maid, sent the children to kindergarten and later to private boarding schools, and continued with her professional and political activities. She was a concerned and conscientious mother and assured everyone that she was never more than 20 minutes away if the children needed her. But as an adult, Carol reported that she felt that she came second of the two children and drew a devastating picture of Margaret's remoteness as a mother.[9]

When the twins were a year old, Margaret tried again to be a candidate for parliament, but was refused by several constituency associations. The selection committees wondered how she could have time enough for the constituency with her family commitments. Margaret assured them that she could fulfil her obligations, but felt that beneath the criticism there was the view that the House of Commons was not really the right place for a woman anyhow (1995a: 94).

It was a struggle to be accepted by the party as a candidate for a safe Tory seat in the House. But Thatcher did not give up. She felt that she had something to contribute as a Conservative politician. She found out all there was to know about local and national politics, got professional help with speaking skills, weighed every word in her speeches, which she memorised by heart, and mobilised male politicians as supporters. In 1958, when the twins were five years old, she managed to be nominated as the Conservative candidate for a safe seat in the Finchley constituency of North London, in competition with more than 150 potential candidates. At the final, there were four: three men and a woman. In the first round of voting, Thatcher obtained 35 votes against 34 for her nearest rival. On the second round, when two candidates had dropped out, she got 46 against his 43. It was a close race, and it is not clear what made the difference. The fact that Thatcher was a good-looking young person, committed and an excellent debater must have weighed more heavily than prejudices against women. Some of the opponents were so angry, however, that they refused to follow standard practice and make the final decision unanimous.

In 1959, Margaret Thatcher ran an intense election campaign against the two male candidates from Labour and the Liberal Party. She canvassed Finchley more thoroughly than anyone ever before, and with the help of a conservative wave of public sentiment, she was elected to the House of Commons with more votes than her predecessor. Nationally, the Conservatives won a landslide and increased their margin in the House of Commons to 100 seats. Margaret Thatcher had special reason to be thrilled: 'I'm dead lucky: my husband's work is in London, we live in the London area, my constituency is in the London area, Parliament is in London, everything just happens to gel' (Liswood, 2007 [1995]: 253). She was elected as the youngest MP along with 24 other women (still not more than 4 per cent) and kept her seat for 33 years, until 1992.[10]

'Thatcher the milk snatcher'

Once Margaret Thatcher was elected, her career got moving. Guided by her father and experienced male colleagues, she began as one of the very few women to rise in the ranks. She did not have access to the network of old upper-class men in the House, but she was intelligent and worked tirelessly. She made the issues of money and economics, of which women were traditionally held to be ignorant, into her strong suits. And it made a deep impression when she gave a weighty speech in parliament for 27 minutes without a script. The Conservatives were in power, and after two years, she was offered a junior post in the ministry of pensions and national insurance.

The predominantly male parties were under pressure from a growing women's movement demanding room for women. In the Labour Party, Barbara Castle became minister and the only woman in the cabinet when the party took over the government in 1964. The Conservative Party leader, Edward Heath, then made Thatcher chief opposition spokeswoman on pensions, and later on housing and land. After the Conservative defeat in 1966, she joined the shadow treasury team, where she won attention with her spirit and fearlessness in attacking the Labour Party budget. She was moved to cover fuel and power, then transport and finally education. Later, she said that she did not contribute much nor was she asked to do so during these years, but she gained knowledge and experience (1995a: 144).

Things changed in 1970, when the Conservatives took over the government. Thatcher was appointed minister of education in Edward Heath's cabinet. It was not a very happy experience and she particularly got into trouble when she cut the school milk programme in an effort to protect the main education budget from general cuts in public expenditure. This led to an outcry. The minister was called 'Thatcher the Milk Snatcher', 'The Lady Nobody Loves' and 'The Most Unpopular Woman in Britain'. Denis told his wife that she did not have to put up with such abuse and asked why she would go on. With tears running down her cheeks, Margaret replied: 'I'll see them in hell first. I will never be driven anywhere against my will' (Ogden, 1990: 112). And the prime minister supported her. She was not close to Heath, but she was the only woman in the cabinet and did her best for the party and the government.[11]

For want of somebody better

The 1970s were a turbulent time in Britain, with economic recession, strikes and riots. The Conservative government lost power, and Labour took over in 1974. Having suffered defeat in three of the four elections during a 10-year period, many in the Conservative Party were ready for a change of leadership. Margaret Thatcher was among those who thought Edward 'Ted' Heath should go, because she disagreed with many of his policies. But none of the party members in central positions was willing to challenge the party leader. Before Heath, party leaders were selected by party seniors behind closed doors, but Heath was chosen by election among MPs. This democratised the process, also giving 'outsiders' a chance. When the last with important posts said 'no', Thatcher wrote in her autobiography:

> I was on the edge of despair. We just could not abandon the party and the country to Ted's brand of politics. I heard myself saying: 'Look, if you are not going to stand, I will, because someone who represents our viewpoint *has* to stand'. (1995a: 266, emphasis in original)

Thatcher was not one of the aristocrats who dominated the party, but came from the lower-middle class and was perceived by many as rather provincial. In addition, she was a woman. But she got recognition from colleagues, because it was hard work, courage and skill, not wealth and privilege, that brought her forward. She, herself, declared that 'any woman who understands the problems of running a home will be near to understanding the problems of running a nation' (Dale, 2010: 108). She did well in political debates, was more persistent than Heath and many agreed with her that the party should return to fundamental conservative principles and defend middle-class values. In February 1975, she initially got 130 votes against 119 for Edward Heath. The majority was not large enough to be elected, but Heath withdrew, and in the next round, Thatcher got 146 votes and clearly defeated the next candidate, who got 79. Thus, she beat four male candidates. She was nobody's first choice, but was elected as the leader, as it was said, for want of somebody better, or as a result of a series of accidents.[12]

Unlikely candidate goes to the top

As a newly elected party leader, Margaret Thatcher was met with awe, anxiety and, at times, contempt from her colleagues. She was compared to her predecessor and could compete with Heath in commitment and effort, but she was blank in foreign policy. She engaged in hectic travel, where she met the Indian Prime Minister Indira Gandhi, among others. The Indian leader made a strong impression on Thatcher. She sat at Mrs Gandhi's feet and wanted to know: how had she made it to the top, and how had she stayed there? The newly elected British leader seemed to gain confidence witnessing another woman successfully wielding power (Young, 1989: 120; Steinberg, 2008: 216).

The Labour government was unable to solve the economic problems, and Thatcher started to develop an economic model in sharp contrast to the consensus that had prevailed since World War II. Churchill and Attlee had emphasised a mixed economy, with full employment, public ownership of industry, space for trade unions, active state management and the development of a welfare state. This meant an active government, significant public spending and high taxes. The foreign policy entailed support for NATO, independence for the colonies and Britain as a nuclear power. It was Attlee, in particular, who followed up the agreement. But in the 1970s, problems arose due to the global recession, oil embargo, low economic growth, rising unemployment and inflation, and the government handled them poorly. Thus, it became politically possible to challenge the earlier consensus.

The year 1979 became the 'Winter of Discontent', with record cold and strikes in the public sector. Hospitals, schools, garbage disposal and funerals were affected, and Labour lost the election. The Tories came to power promising to regenerate the economy and Margaret Thatcher became prime minister at 54 years old. The victory was not overwhelming. The election was more about getting Labour out of office than getting the Conservatives in. People wanted change, but it was not clear what kind of change. Polls showed that Thatcher was less popular than both the Labour Party leader and the Conservative Party in general. But if gender played a role, other factors were evidently more important. In a desperate financial situation, an unlikely candidate rose to the top.[13]

Conviction politician

Margaret Thatcher wanted to give Britain new strength on the basis of a free market philosophy. Her aim was to break with the policies of the post-war era and bury collectivism, 'socialism' and welfarism. Specifically, she wanted to reduce regulations and liberate private enterprise, cut income taxes and public expenditures, privatise publicly owned industries, and restrict the power of the trade unions. She based her foreign policy on national self-interest, strengthening defence, fighting against the Soviet Union and communism, and supporting the US and NATO. Her extraordinarily close relationship with President Ronald Reagan became an important political alliance, as they shared similar views of the world. However, she had a reserved approach to the European Union (EU).

The Conservative Party got a majority in 1979 (of 43 seats). Thatcher kept most of the Heath ministers and began to implement her policy. As production fell and inflation and unemployment rose, violent riots broke out in the inner cities and disagreement within the Conservative Party grew. But the prime minister was unmovable. She was a conviction, not a consensus, politician, she explained (1995a: 448), and the market had to rule, no matter how great the social cost. In fact, the problems redoubled her faith. It was that difference, a matter of character not of wisdom, which both sustained the policy's wavering friends and routed its paralysed enemies, according to her biographer, Hugo Young (1989: 206–7).

Amid recession and high unemployment during the first years, Thatcher's ability to retain power was helped by the unpopularity of the Labour Party, the growth of the Social Democratic Party and the Liberals, and the Falklands War. When the Argentinians invaded the British overseas territory in 1982, Thatcher struck back, defending the interests of the Empire. Despite gross errors of judgement, Britain emerged victorious from the conflict and the position of the prime minister was dramatically changed. She was portrayed as a warrior, even a warrior queen, a national hero who gave Britain back her grandeur: 'Britannia Ruled the Waves'. In the general elections in 1983, the Tories won a convincing majority (of 144 seats).[14]

Thatcher continued her policies and the sale of state utilities accelerated. The miners' strike in 1984 became a decisive victory for her individualistic and anti-socialistic views. Radical miners were forced back to work after a year-long bitter strike with considerable violence, without their demands being met. But she did not manage to solve the Northern Ireland problem in spite of an Anglo-Irish Accord, and her dealings with the European Community were less successful. She was also criticised because she allowed US planes to take off from the UK to bomb Libya. Dissension within the government became more evident. But the economy was improving and the Conservatives won a new, overwhelming victory in the general elections in 1987.[15]

With a parliamentary majority of 101 seats, there were few restraints imposed upon the prime minister. She now felt that she could introduce domestic reforms at top speed to implement her 'New Right', and her stance became more overbearing and imperious. Controversial reforms included the education and national health services, and water and electricity industries. In addition, a local government community charge (the 'poll tax') was enacted in 1990 amid widespread demonstrations and rioting. The economy was affected by recession, and Thatcher's scepticism towards the European Community led to increasing discord in the Conservative Party. In 1989, the Chancellor of the Exchequer resigned in protest. The electoral prospects for the party seemed to be dimming, and in 1990, Thatcher's leadership was openly challenged.

In the first round, Thatcher got most votes as party leader, 204 against 152 for the male opponent, with 16 abstentions, but it was not enough to be re-elected (falling two votes short). She was determined to continue the fight, but minister after minister asked her to leave the position as party leader and prime minister, and on 22 November 1990, she resigned. Her protégé, John Major, took over. An era in British politics was over – or that was what many people thought. But Thatcher was not ready to be silenced and during the Conservatives' remaining seven years in office, she acted as a back-seat driver, voicing her criticism more and more publicly and undermining the efforts to reunite the party around a new agenda.[16]

Powerful prime minister

Margaret Thatcher's record was mixed, making her both intensely admired and deeply abhorred. When she visited Oslo in 1986, the official dinner had to be postponed because of the most ferocious demonstrations for 15 years. The protests were against Thatcherism: from the unemployment and environmental pollution to the compliant attitude towards the apartheid regime in South Africa (Young, 1989: 487). In 2002, she was ranked number 16 on a television poll's list of the '100 Greatest Britons', which was the highest placement for a then living person.

In 2003, she was placed as number three on the list of 'The 100 Worst Britons', while the business magazine *Forbes* the year after ranked her as number 21 of the world's 100 most powerful women (*Forbes*, 2004).

Biographers describe Margaret Thatcher as one of the most powerful prime ministers of the 20th century. She was a woman and had limited experience when she was elected, lacked support from a majority of the party leaders and called for a new and radical policy. Yet, she accomplished most of what she wanted and changed British society.

As a leader, Margaret Thatcher was strong, resolute and courageous, a moral crusader. For most issues, she saw things in right and wrong and getting her way meant everything. She did not tolerate challenges to her power and developed a highly personal style of leadership, trying to dominate allies and adversaries into submission. She worked longer hours than anybody else and her conscientiousness enabled her to repeatedly beat down colleagues and opponents by sheer mastery of detail. In addition, she used fear, threat, intimidation and other means of persuasion. If necessary, she could abandon commitments and revert to dissimulation. In this way, she managed to force her will upon her cabinet, but on many occasions, she also lost the vote. The government course became somewhat chaotic. Compared with her predecessors, Thatcher was generally more ideological, more ambitious, more confrontational and more autocratic (Genovese, 2013: 292). Her assertive style was essential to her success, but her bullying also contributed to her fall.

Thatcher managed to neuter the trade unions, privatise most of the public sector and introduce market forces into practically every area of national life. In this way, she rewrote the whole agenda of politics, gradually forcing the Labour Party to also change its policies. She made Britain more prosperous, and her policy was copied by numerous countries. But she was largely insensitive to the needs of the poor. Wealth was unevenly distributed, inequalities increased and social cohesion reduced. The lower classes constituted a growing portion of the population. Further, local governments became less powerful, while the state was centralised. The prime minister kept close control of the party and the cabinet, at the same time as she concentrated power in a prime minister's role that was stronger and more intervening than before. She thereby crippled the Conservative Party. The party retained a slim majority in the general elections in 1992 despite losing 41 seats, but it was the last outright Conservative victory for decades. The elections in 1997 resulted in a landslide victory for Labour.

It is too soon for long-term assessments of Thatcher and her policies, but in 2009, her biographer, John Campbell (2009: 500–1), noted that the widespread optimistic view that Thatcherism would infinitely assure ever-growing prosperity on a tide of financial ingenuity and deregulated credit was shattered the year before, when the 2008 'credit crunch' directly caused by the irresponsible lending of deregulated banks and other financial institutions in Britain and the US plunged the world into the worst recession since the 1930s.[17]

Advantage of being a woman

According to the political scientist Michael Genovese (2013: 297–301), the fact that Thatcher was a woman proved to be one of the greatest advantages in her career – from an early stage, when the Tories needed a 'woman' before she had shown what she was capable of, to her work as prime minister. Well brought-up Englishmen in the upper and middle class did not know how to deal with Thatcher. They had no experience with strong, self-confident women in politics and did not know what an appropriate response would be. This uncertainty was exploited by Thatcher. She took advantage of her gender when it could serve her interests. She was careful about her looks and how she expressed herself. She was a master of gender-style flexing, varying her behaviour according to the situation, sometimes using feminine wiles, acting as a nanny, or as a bully, coaxing, cajoling, flattering, yelling or even weeping. She could appear as a docile wife, an androgynous leader, the mother of the nation or a warrior queen. The impression was both contradictory and confusing, and many men found it hard to stand up to her.

Margaret Thatcher's behaviour was perceived as traditionally 'female' and, at the same time, clearly 'male'. She was described as 'the best man in the country'. 'There was not a man to match her.' Governing in a 'man's world' of politics, it might have been necessary to act like one. At the same time, people criticised Thatcher because 'she was not a real woman' and was, at times, unduly rough. Thatcher, herself, underlined that there was no difference between men and women in style of governance (Liswood, 2007: 251).

As head of government, Margaret Thatcher used the gender differences as a political tool. She was always a lone woman surrounded by senior male politicians. There were only a few women in junior positions. The men were often relatively weak and willing to take orders, and she often changed ministers.

In the European Community, Thatcher, as other European leaders, asserted her country's interests. But she was the first woman to have a place at the highest level of diplomacy and created surprise, admiration and resentment. The French President François Mitterand expressed it this way: 'She has the eyes of Caligula and the mouth of Marilyn Monroe' (Harris, 1995: 65).[18]

Anti-feminist

The women's movement made it possible for Margaret Thatcher to pursue a political career, and she became famous because she was a woman. In her turn, she changed and challenged the prevailing ideas about women's role, was more powerful than the men who surrounded her and proved that a woman could lead the nation with the same strength and competence as a man. In this way, she became a role model beyond the borders of her country. But feminists criticised her for being an honorary male for all practical purposes.

Thatcher used her femininity for what it was worth and could speak up for her sex. But women were not part of her revolution. When she was one of a few Conservatives to support legalisation of abortion and decriminalisation of male homosexuality, it was due to personal experiences as a barrister, not involvement in women's situation. She failed to recognise the marginal position of women, in politics and in society more generally. In fact, she saw mainly men. Women – except herself – were invisible to her. In spite of the recommendations of the international women's conferences and Britain becoming party to the CEDAW, in 1986, issues related to women had little or no place in Thatcher's programme. In her view, the battle for women's rights had largely been won, and she disapproved of quotas and sex equality legislation. Not only did Margaret Thatcher refrain from advancing the cause of women, but her dismantling of the welfare state had, in fact, negative consequences for them (Webster, 1990: 168–73; Genovese, 2013: 298–9).

Compared to other Western European countries, women were included relatively late in British politics. Thatcher had difficulty with women and deliberately excluded all but one, who filled a minor portfolio, from her cabinet. While she was in power, female representation in parliament went from 3 to 6 per cent, and the number of conservative women rose from seven to 17, but this did not influence their number in cabinet. The prime minister did not contribute to strengthening the position of women in public life in general, either. In fact, though she always worked outside of the home herself, Thatcher often enjoined women to stay at home, raise families and assume traditional roles (Webster, 1990: 168; Steinberg, 2008: 9). When she retired in 1990, there were hardly any women in high positions in the state administration, in the judiciary and in government in general.

Feminists criticised Thatcher, but she dismissed feminists as women who wanted something given to them that they were not willing to work for. As Golda Meir and Indira Gandhi had 'made it' in a man's world without the need for special treatment, so had Thatcher, and in her view, so could every other woman. When she became prime minister, it was because she worked hard and was the best. It was not a victory for women, but for someone in politics (Webster, 1990: 68).

After Thatcher resigned, the picture changed gradually. Much attention was paid to political parties and the recruitment of women candidates, and due to actions predominantly by the Labour Party, the representation of women increased. In 2014, 23 per cent of the members in the House of Commons were women and 16 per cent of the cabinet ministers. This was lower than most Western countries, and there was no new woman prime minister.[19]

Solitary swallows in Malta and Portugal: Agatha Barbara and Maria de Lourdes Pintasilgo

True socialist in Malta

Although Margaret Thatcher became most famous internationally, she was not the only woman national leader in Western European around 1980. Women rose to the top under very different circumstances: in Malta, Portugal, Iceland and Norway.

Agatha Barbara was born in Malta in 1923.[20] The location of the islands south of Sicilia gave them great strategic importance. They were conquered by a succession of powers, Great Britain being the last, and Malta became a vital naval base. Highly urbanised, with 200,000–300,000 inhabitants, the country was one of the smallest and most densely populated in the world, and the population suffered from poverty, disease, illiteracy and unemployment. Agatha's father worked for the British Navy as a tug master, a skilled pilot of tugboats, but was very poorly paid. Her mother struggled to feed the nine children on her husband's wages. Agatha was the second child and the eldest daughter in the family. She saw that her father did not get the pay increase to which he was entitled when he was promoted to captain because he could not read and write. She became very interested in education and pleaded with her parents to find money to send her to secondary school, but World War II prevented her from continuing to college. Nazi planes bombarded the island, and Agatha had to work as an air raid warden and supervise one of the kitchens set up by the British military to feed the population.

Afterwards, Agatha became a school teacher. There was high unemployment and growing social unrest. She felt that those governing the island did not bother about how people were living, and there was no social justice. So she chose politics over a family, realising that she could not have everything, and joined the burgeoning independence movement (Dunn, 2001). She became a member of the Malta Labour Party (MLP) and was very active in party affairs, became member of the MLP Executive Committee, headed the party women's branch and founded the Women's Political Movement in Malta.

From 1947, Malta had limited self-government with a parliamentary system. There was a single-chamber assembly elected using a modified form of proportional representation. Demands for voting rights for women were raised by the Women of Malta Association and the MLP against loud protests from the Church, and the proposal was adopted by a narrow majority by the constitutional assembly: 145 against 137. The clashes with the Church spurred Barbara to show what women could do, so when people encouraged her to stand for election the same year, she accepted. She became the first and only woman among the 40 MPs, and she was the only woman candidate to successfully contest every election since, until 1982, when she resigned to become president.

The number of women in parliament increased to four in 1951. But then the representation was one, two or a maximum of three until the 1990s, even though the number of seats in parliament was increased to more than 60. However, in the 1950s, one of the principal political leaders was a woman, Mabel Strickland, daughter of a former prime minister, a journalist and a newspaper editor who led the conservative Progressive Constitutional Party.

Woman-friendly minister

Agatha Barbara became known as a warm defender of economic and social reforms. She was Malta's first and, until the end of the 1990s, only woman cabinet minister. When the MLP came to power for the first time in 1955, Prime Minister Dom Mintoff appointed Barbara as minister of education. He wished to follow up MLP's policy to strengthen the role of women in politics. Barbara made a name for herself by undertaking comprehensive reforms: introducing full-time compulsory basic education for all, establishing a teacher training college and special schools for the disabled, making secondary school free, and providing science classes for both girls and boys.

However, relations between the British and the Maltese deteriorated, and Mintoff resigned in 1958. Protests erupted on the streets, a national strike was called and a state of emergency was declared. Barbara participated in the demonstrations and was sentenced to 43 days of hard labour, serving 32 of them. Afterwards, she was responsible for the day-to-day management of party publications and the Freedom Press, the party's printing house.

In 1962, the British relinquished their direct-rule hold over Malta and the islands were granted full independence in 1964. The conservative Nationalist Party won the elections. When Mintoff came to power again in 1971, Agatha Barbara was appointed minister of education again. She also now carried out extensive educational reforms. Compulsory basic education was extended from the age of 14 to 16, trade and technical schools were established, and university fees were abolished. In 1974, she became minister for labour, culture and welfare. She worked hard to reduce unemployment and improve workers' pay and conditions and industrial relations. She also introduced a law on equal pay for women and men, paid maternity leave, a 40-hour working week and retirement and unemployment benefits. In addition, she brought about a democratisation of culture and set up a number of national museums.

In 1974, Malta became a republic, with a president elected by parliament. The president appointed the prime minister and, on the latter's recommendation, other ministers. Executive power was exercised by the cabinet, which was drawn from and collectively responsible to parliament. Malta remained a member of the British Commonwealth and initially had a defence agreement with Britain. But in 1979, when the agreement expired, Malta declared itself neutral.

Avoiding civil war

In 1976, Agatha Barbara became deputy chair of the MLP parliamentary group, but not of the party, and deputy prime minister. For shorter periods, she served as deputy for Mintoff. In 1981, elections led to a constitutional crisis because the National Party (PN) won a majority of the votes but only got a minority in parliament: 31 seats against 34 for MLP. PN boycotted parliament and organised protests. Nevertheless, Mintoff took power, but instead of becoming minister, Barbara was now elected as the first woman president at 59 years old. Usually, the position of president was mainly ceremonial. But in a crisis situation, it became important. Why Barbara was chosen is unclear, but she had a long political career, a high position in the MLP and international contacts. At the same time, Mintoff was preparing his resignation as party leader and prime minister in 1984 and had not singled out Barbara, but the deputy chair of the party (a man), to take over. Barbara, herself, thought that it was hard to be president. She had little taste for formality and felt barred from active politics. But she was loyal and accepted the responsibility. Mintoff then took the unusual step of allowing her to participate in the cabinet's deliberations as the only woman.

As president, it was Barbara's main task to resolve the country's constitutional crisis, and she managed to do this. The conflict escalated, with strikes, confrontations and violence, but Barbara prevented the situation from evolving into civil war. She organised dialogue between the two sides, and the PN representatives agreed to meet in parliament. The election system was then changed before the next elections so that the distribution of seats better matched the votes. In addition, the role of the president consisted of representing the country abroad, and Barbara visited many countries to strengthen Malta's position as an independent nation and promote the country's policies. She was also involved in humanitarian efforts to help children, families and disabled people in need. In 1987, her term expired, and she withdrew from politics.

Persistent traditions

In her work, Agatha Barbara designated herself as a socialist, but hardly a feminist, although she made an invaluable contribution to women. She was actively involved in the political organisation of women and helped strengthen their position. Primarily not as president, but as minister, she implemented reforms that gave women in Malta better health and education and improved their economic and social conditions.

Malta only became party to the CEDAW in 1991, with several reservations. Malta was one of the Western states with the fewest female MPs, despite the fact that the country had elections with proportional representation, which was usually an advantage for women. Barbara would have liked to see more women in parliament. She believed that women could be as good as men in politics, and sometimes better. The absence of women from politics was, in her view, particularly due to their difficulties reconciling a demanding job with family obligations, especially with young children. She, herself, remained single and childless all her life (Dunn, 2001). Researchers have pointed out that the problem was not a lack of candidates, the electoral system or voter behaviour, but the failure of party elites to recruit women candidates. Catholicism was the official religion in Malta and the influence of the Church was strong. The Maltese held some of the most conservative views about the role of women in all of Europe. In the party organisations, women were more or less restricted to auxiliary and support roles (Lane, 1995).

In 2014, Malta had only ten female MPs (14 per cent) and in the small cabinet there were only two women ministers (also 14 per cent). But Agatha Barbara got a female successor, when the Labour politician Marie Louise Coleiro Preca was elected President of Malta in April 2014.

Three Marias in Portugal

We will make our way back to the root
Of our own anguish, all by ourselves, until we can say
'Our sons are sons, they are people and not
Phalluses of our males.' We will call children
Children; women women and men
Men. We will call upon a poet to govern
The City.[21]

The large audience at the UN Educational, Scientific and Cultural Organization (UNESCO) in Paris gasped. It was the representative of Portugal speaking – a backward, closed country striving to get out of prolonged military dictatorship and colonial war – and on the platform was a woman reading from *The three Marias* – a book that was seized by the Portuguese government in 1972 and the women who wrote it arrested and brought to trial.[22]

Maria de Lourdes Pintasilgo continued her intervention unabated:

> The revolt against the political regime in Portugal took the form of an outcry from women regarding liberation. They demanded that all divisions should be abolished, physical as well as psychological, between male and female, masters and servants, dominant parents and helpless children and between lovers who were separated by forces beyond their control. This should not only happen by altering women's consciousness, but by changing the exploitative social order that made women remain 'the last colonial territory'.[23]

Such a salty feminist intervention was not commonplace in the world organisation. People were confused and shocked, and even more so because Maria de Lourdes Pintasilgo was known for her strong ties to the Catholic Church. She was international vice president of the Graal, a Catholic order of worldly women, and served as female liaison between the Catholic Church and the World Council of Churches.

Women's revolution

It was the autumn of 1978, and there were not many women in the hall, but they cheered. Portugal's representative was not just anybody. She was an educated engineer and had a high position in a large industrial company before she became minister in the first provisional government after the 'Carnation revolution'.

After more than 40 years of dictatorship, with discrimination and oppression, democracy was restored after the Portuguese Colonial War and the bloodless 'Carnation revolution' carried out by the military in 1974. It was a revolution also for women. Their position was very difficult. The dictator, Salazar, improved social conditions and women received education. In 1980, women accounted for more than 40 per cent of the students in higher education, and Portugal had more women in technical professions than any other Western country. But the living standards of the 10 million inhabitants was relatively low, personal freedom was restricted and the war in the colonies took human lives and resources. Women were affected and lost rights that they had acquired earlier through strong queens, female artists, intellectuals and an active women's movement.

In the early 1970s, women journalists started to attack the injustice in Portuguese society, and the three women authors – Maria Isabel Barreno, Maria Teresa Horta and Maria Velho Da Costa – described the Portuguese women's plight in their provocative anti-fascist and feminist book *The three Marias*. The book came to play a central role in the revolutionary movement. It was banned for 'offense against public morals'. But the authors were released after a national and international feminist protest campaign in which Maria de Lourdes Pintasilgo actively participated. In 1976, Portugal's new constitution introduced not only a democratic political system, but also gender equality and full voting rights for women (they got a partial right to vote in 1931). In the years that followed, the status of women was drastically changed, with new rights and opportunities.

Unmarried, religious feminist

In connection with the 'Carnation revolution' in 1974, Maria de Lourdes Pintasilgo, first, became secretary of state and, the year after, Portugal's first woman minister, with responsibility for social affairs. She was born in 1930 in a middle-class family. Her father worked in the wool business, but abandoned the family soon after Maria's birth. At seven years old, she was sent to school in Lisbon, where she was drawn into Salazar's youth organisation. But she moved towards the Left, made contact with Graal and helped establish it in Portugal despite opposition from high-level Catholics. As a believer with progressive views, she was so progressive that many older priests thought that she was dangerous. But people supported her, and she was one of Graal's leading international figures in the 1960s.

In a country where intellectual freedom was limited, and there were few opportunities for women, Maria de Lourdes Pintasilgo (like a good deal of other women) chose to study an 'apolitical' technical 'man's' subject like chemistry. She loved philosophy, but the sciences were not so politically exposed and she could easier demonstrate the abilities of a woman. In 1953, she graduated in industrial chemistry and began working as an engineer in a large Portuguese company producing cement. Here, she eventually became project director. In 1960, she became the first female member of one of the advisory organs of the dictatorship and worked with a government programme for development and social change. From 1970, she was head of the National Women's Commission, and in 1971, she went into battle for feminism, defending the three Marias, women's power and a just society.

In 1976, she was sent to Paris as Portugal's first UNESCO ambassador and member of the Executive Board. She was an outspoken and courageous figure in the international milieu: politically independent, very religious and, at the same time, an ardent feminist, she was an unmarried, single woman known for broadmindedness and joyful exuberance. She was an active partner when the Nordic countries tried to make UNESCO more woman-friendly.[24]

Short fresh breeze

The political situation in Portugal was turbulent, with conflicts between the military and tensions between different power groups. The economy was also in great trouble. In 1976, the first democratic elections in 50 years were held. A president and a parliament were elected in a system where the president and prime minister were supposed to share power. The parliament was elected using proportional representation. An independent former general, António Ramalho Eanes, was elected president with the support of all major parties. The Socialist Party obtained just over a third of the seats in parliament and formed a minority government. But the political constellations varied, with frequent changes in the cabinet, and in July 1979, the president decided to organise new elections.

At 49 years old, Maria de Lourdes Pintasilgo was called home to head an interim government. She refused membership of any political party and stood outside of the controversies of immediate importance. However, she was politically not far from the Socialist Party, with broad experience, so she was a prime minister that the president could trust. She, herself, stated that the election of a woman was 'a totally logical result of the participation of women on equal footing with men in the revolution' (1984: 572; see also Brill, 1995: 128). But she was the fourth prime minister after the new constitution was adopted and affirmed the principle of equality, and was to function for just five months in anticipation of new elections, with a technocratic transitional government. Furthermore, the cabinet consisted only of men. There were 5 per cent women in parliament, but the new prime minister was unable to get other women to join the cabinet, even if she tried. She met with different reactions. While some spoke of new hope and 'a fresh breeze', others were furious. Conservative MPs went so far that some of the house desks cracked under the fury of their fists. Maria Pintasilgo remarked to a friend: 'You know, they never forgive me for having dared to enter their world' (O'Shaughnessy, 2004: 2).

Despite her short term, Maria de Lourdes Pintasilgo pushed to modernise the outdated social welfare system. She made social security universal and improved health care, education and labour legislation. But a centre-right alliance won the election in 1980, and Prime Minister Pintasilgo had to resign. Women also continued to be extremely poorly represented in parliament and the cabinet. Maria de Lourdes Pintasilgo became member of the President's Council, and in 1986, she ran as the first woman candidate for president. She ran as an independent with the support of the non-communist Left, but was unsuccessful. The following year, she became an independent member of the European Parliament with the support of the Socialist Party and served until 1989.

In 2014, Portugal had 31 per cent women in parliament and 21 per cent in the cabinet.

Vigdís Finnbogadóttir and Icelandic red stockings

High time for a woman

The Icelandic women's movement has a long history, with both highlights and quieter periods.[25] During the International Women's Year in 1975, Icelandic women attracted great attention when they organised a general strike to show how important women's undervalued work was. Many women worked outside the home, but they were often poorly paid, and there was a great shortage of kindergartens. Women over the age of 40 got the right to vote in 1915, and the age limit was lifted in 1920. But 55 years later, there were only 5 per cent of women in parliament, and in the cabinet there had only been one single woman.

But the women's movement was active, and 90 per cent of the Icelandic women went on strike. The 'Women's day off' paralysed a large part of society and feminists around the world were full of admiration: how could they achieve something like that! Iceland, a small island far out in the North Sea dependent on agriculture and fishing, the most sparsely populated country in Europe, with only a little more than 200,000 inhabitants – the women must be good organisers! This was surely true, but being small could also have its merits. In Iceland, around two thirds of the population lived in the capital region, and in a situation of rapid economic development, Reykjavik became a centre for women's activism.

Iceland's Parliament has a single chamber elected with proportional representation and and a directly elected president. The president appoints the prime minister and the cabinet on the basis of their parliamentary support, and they are collectively responsible to parliament. There were always coalition governments because of the number of political parties.

At the presidential election in 1980, the women's movement focused on getting a woman. Although the role of the president was essentially apolitical and ceremonial, it was not without significance. The president represented the nation as a whole and was the country's figurehead. Besides, the election was direct, so to present a candidate, it was not necessary to go through political parties. After much persuasion, a woman accepted to run for election against three male candidates, all independent, and the woman was elected with 33.6 per cent of the vote, while her nearest rival got 32.1 per cent. At 50 years old, Vigdís Finnbogadóttir became the world's first democratically elected woman president.

President Vigdís

Vigdís Finnbogadóttir, herself, had not thought of a political career. She was born in 1930 in Reykjavik, where her father was an engineer and professor. Her mother was an active feminist and headed the nurses' trade union for 35 years. They had two children: Vigdís and then a son a year later. Her father was very ambitious on behalf of his children. Vigdís was able to study language and literature in France, theatre history in Denmark, and French philology in Sweden before she graduated in English, French and pedagogy at the University of Reykjavík. She married a physician in 1954, but divorced in 1963, and at the age of 41, she adopted a daughter, becoming the first single woman who was allowed to adopt a child.

After graduation, Vigdís Finnbogadóttir taught French in schools and on TV, instructed French drama at the university, and worked with experimental theatre. In 1972, she became director of the Reykjavik theatre. She was a well-known personality from TV and cultural activities when she agreed to run for president. She had never been a member of a woman's organisation, but was a feminist in private, and friends convinced her that it was high time that a woman ran for election to become president of the country (Dahlerup, 1985: 340–1; Jensen, 2008: 74).

Although she was politically independent, the Left supported her because she was against the US naval base at Keflavik. As the only member of NATO, Iceland did not maintain a standing army, air force or navy, but had a US base near the airport. Fans of Vigdís (as the Icelandic people called her) were afraid that her status as a divorced single mother would be used against her during the election campaign, but this did not happen. She travelled all around the country, made contact with people and acquired a thorough knowledge of thinking and living conditions. She did not talk about politics, but about Icelandic culture and identity.

In her position as president, Vigdís believed that she was not discriminated against, but she was often asked how she could manage the job without a husband. She replied: 'If I were married, I wouldn't be standing here,' adding that she thought she was the only president in the world who did the dishes and went shopping (Dahlerup, 1985: 342; Jensen, 2008: 156).

Sixteen years on top

Vigdís Finnbogadóttir became very popular. She was re-elected as president in 1984 without opposition, got 92 per cent of the votes against another woman in 1988 and was then re-elected without opposition in 1992. In 1996, she did not run for election. All in all, she was Iceland's president for 16 years.

Politics in Iceland was very male-dominated, and a woman president was not always shown proper respect. It was the president's job to sign new legislation, and we are told that Finnbogadóttir refused to do so once. But this is not correct. It was in October 1985, the 10th anniversary of the 'Women's day off'. The women planned to celebrate the day by staying at home again. In the morning, however, the minister of transport decided to issue a provisional law to stop the ongoing wage strike among the flight attendants that incidentally took place on the same day. But he did not contact the president. She heard about the matter on the radio. So, when a government employee came with the text for the president's signature, she replied that she wanted to talk with the prime minister. She was willing to sign the law (otherwise there would have to be a referendum), but she wanted to delay implementation until the day's demonstration was over. Obtaining contact with the prime minister took so long that the president managed to do this; a gesture the women's movement knew how to appreciate.[26]

It was primarily through the media that Vigdís Finnbogadóttir could exert influence. The executive power was with the prime minister and the cabinet. Vigdís attracted considerable attention internationally as well as nationally – much more than a male president would have done – and spoke publicly on many occasions. She emphasised the role of small nations and filled the front pages of the newspapers around the world when she hosted a crucial summit between the US President Ronald Reagan and the Soviet leader Mikhail Gorbachev in 1986. The two most powerful men in the world met under the auspices of the female president of one of the world's smallest nations. The negotiations broke down at the last minute, but contributed nevertheless to end the Cold War.

Vigdís Finnbogadóttir had as her motto: 'Never let the women down'. Women have been treated so badly that you must support them, she said (Haugstad, 2006). As president, Vigdís worked specifically to promote girls' education and emphasised her role as a model for young women not only in Iceland, but also elsewhere. She stressed, however, that she was elected president not as a woman, but as a human being, and that she was as much the president of men as of women. 'A woman experiences life in a different way than a man. The best result is achieved by letting both women's and men's experiences of an issue affect the outcome', she underlined. She saw it as her task particularly to fight for Icelandic language and culture, and she also found a role as an environmental activist (Dahlerup, 1985: 336; Paton et al, 1995b: 142).

Women's Party

AlthoughVigdís Finnbogadóttir mainly had symbolic power, there were significant changes in the position of Icelandic women during the time she was president, and she was part of the change process. She was brought to the top by a feminist wave when she was elected, and women activists did not give up afterwards. Many women were dissatisfied with social conditions, and the representation of women in parliament did not increase, although women put on pressure. In practice, the electoral system was an obstacle. Even with proportional representation only one or two candidates were usually elected from each constituency, so the competition was fierce. Moreover, the leaders of the four male-dominated established parties did not consider the low representation of women to be a problem, although there were no women in the cabinet in 1980 and only three (5 per cent) in parliament.

Vigdís was independent and could interact with a dynamic women's movement. The first general elections after she became president were in 1983. To strengthen women's influence, a special Women's Party was created before the elections. It obtained 5.5 per cent of the votes and got three representatives out of 60 in parliament. In the elections that followed, the Women's Party obtained from three to six representatives. The party also helped increase the representation of women in general. In 1983/84, three of the four established parties adopted internal gender quotas. In 1995, there were a total of 16 women MPs (25 per cent). In addition, from 1983, a woman was a member of the cabinet. The representation of women also increased in the municipal councils, and in 1995, women made up half of the city council of Reykjavik, with a mayor from the Women's Party (Styrkársdóttir, 1999: 83–90).

Representatives from the Women's Party raised issues such as incest, sexual abuse, violence against women, low wages and kindergartens, and proposals and new laws were adopted. As the other parties got more women among their representatives, the support for the Women's Party went down. In 1999, the Women's Party became part of the new social-democratic alliance Samfylkingin (the Group Together), which came to power 10 years later under the leadership of Jóhanna Sigurðardóttir. She was also the country's first female prime minister (see Chapter Ten).

Norway's 'Mother', Gro Harlem Brundtland

Child of the Labour Party

Just afterVigdís Finnbogadóttir was elected president in Iceland, Norway got its first woman national leader in 1981, when Gro Harlem Brundtland became prime minister. Unlike her Icelandic sister, she got the central political executive role in her country. Norway has a parliamentary system similar to the Icelandic one, except that the head of state is a hereditary monarch and therefore not elected. As in Iceland, the prime minister is head of government, and the government is based on parliamentary majority. Parliament is elected with proportional representation.[27]

Gro Harlem Brundtland had an extraordinary political career. It was the Labour Party and the women's movement that brought her to power. She grew up in the central milieu of the Labour Party, even though the family had an academic background and lived in a very posh part of the capital, Oslo.

Gro Harlem's mother, Inga, was originally Swedish, and she met her husband, Gudmund, through the Nordic socialist student collaboration. She was a student of law, while he studied medicine. They got married in 1938 and joined a commune in Oslo. The commune consisted of two families and several others, including Gudmund's mother and sister and sometimes a maid. There were several people who could take care of the children. Gro was born in 1939 and her brother, Erik, in 1940. Soon, Norway was attacked by the Nazis. Both parents became engaged in the resistance, and the children led an unsettled life, including as refugees in Sweden. Here, Gro got to know her Swedish grandmother, who was an extraordinary woman. Divorced with two children, she was the first woman lawyer in Stockholm's administration.

Both Gudmund and Inga resumed their university studies when the war was over. Inga finished the first part of law school, even though she got a 'peace child', Lars, in 1946. The last child, Hanne, was born much later. Gudmund passed his medical degree and worked as a physician. When he received a scholarship and the family travelled to the US for a year, it was the end of law studies for Inga. Back home, she took a job as a secretary and worked for the parliamentary group of the Labour Party. In 1955, Gudmund became minister of social affairs, then minister of defence, in the Labour government. The Labour Party was in power from 1945 to 1963, with a majority in parliament until 1961. The party reconstructed the country after the war, developed industry and built up a welfare state with expanded education and social security.

Gro went to primary school in Oslo and joined the Labour Party's children's organisation, Framfylkingen (the Onwards Group). In her autobiography, she writes that the Fram leaders Werna Gerhardsen, the prime minister's wife, and Rolf Hansen, the Labour Party secretary, were the most important adults for her in her childhood in addition to her parents (Brundtland, 1997: 18–49; 2002: 3–20).

Physician and mother of four

In secondary school, Gro participated in the creation of a socialist pupil organisation, and at the university, she joined the Labour student group. But she devoted herself primarily to her studies. She took a master's degree in medicine in Oslo and a master's at Harvard School of Public Health in the US, specialising in mother–child care and breastfeeding. Back in Norway, she started working in the Directorate of Health, and in 1970, she became assistant chief physician at the Oslo health board. She combined the roles of mother and student, physician and researcher.

It created quite a stir in political circles when Gro married a conservative young man in 1960. But Arne Olav Brundtland was no dogmatic right-wing extremist. He was, above all, an intellectual. He came from a family of teachers, studied political science and was editor of the conservative student paper *Minerva*. His goal was to be a researcher. He was an open, tolerant and sociable fellow and made friends with several of his male colleagues who were active in the Labour Party. During the 1960s Gro and Arne Olav had four children in quick succession, three boys and a girl.[28]

Politician by chance

The second wave of feminism mobilised Norwegian women for equality on a broad basis. The economy was expanding, and women, who acquired more education than before, entered the labour market in increasing numbers. But they encountered obstacles and discrimination. In political bodies, there were only a handful of women, even though Norway was one of the first countries to give women the right to vote (in 1913). Independent feminists and female members in the political parties collaborated, taking action to get more women into politics.

Traditionally, Norway was a poor agricultural country; for centuries, a colony under Denmark and then in union with Sweden before it became independent in 1905. Class differences were small, egalitarian norms strong and popular movements widespread, though the country was extremely outstretched and sparsely populated. So, when women demanded democratic rights with sufficient force, it had an effect. In the general elections in 1973, the proportion of women in parliament went up from 9 to 16 per cent. In 1974/75, the Liberal and Socialist Left Parties introduced women's quotas of 40 per cent, and both parties elected women party leaders.

It is said that Gro Harlem Brundtland (known as Gro) entered politics in 1974 by chance. The Labour Party came to power after the general elections in 1973, but a woman minister suddenly fell ill and died. One of the male ministers happened to see Gro on TV and suggested that she should become a member of the cabinet instead. In the Norwegian system, it was not necessary to be an MP to become a cabinet minister, though most of them were. Admittedly, Gro was politically inexperienced, had participated little in the party and had not been a member of either the municipal council or parliament. But the cabinet needed a woman, and she would be relatively young in an assembly that had begun to turn grey. The party's top leadership was familiar with Gro through her family, and the way she fought for the government's proposal to introduce self-determined abortion, with both commitment and expert knowledge, was impressive. That was what she was doing on TV.

The request came as a surprise to the young woman physician, who was fully occupied with work and children, and she had to respond quickly. Her entire childhood and youth were marked by the labour movement and the struggle to promote social democracy with solidarity, equality and justice. So, the answer had to be 'yes'.

But for a husband to serve in the 'wife' position in a political relationship was not only rare, but unheard of at the time. However, Arne Olav said: 'I'll take the home front – but on one condition: that I am the boss and in charge. I don't want interference and criticism if there is no milk one day' (Brundtland, 1996: 65). They were, indeed, a modern couple in the spirit of equality. Arne Olav had working parents who shared the housework and he learnt quite a bit himself after he married Gro. But now he took over in a completely different way and made a great effort – unusually great for a husband at the time – to support Gro in the demanding political positions she acquired. He did the ordinary housework, organised the household and took care of the kids, was a 'decoration' on ceremonial occasions, assisted her on journeys, and gave advice on policy issues. In this way, he played a pioneer role, disregarding provocative remarks about his manhood and subordination to a woman. Later, he wrote two books about his married life with Gro (Brundtland, 1996, 2003).

Gro Harlem Brundtland did not become minister of social affairs, though that is what she would have preferred. This demanding field was left to a more experienced man, but she was appointed minister of the environment. Many thought that this was an 'easy' ministry, but it was no simple matter to balance 'growth and protection'. Gro was the youngest in the cabinet and, in addition, a woman. She had high ambitions on behalf of the environment and came into conflict with other ministers. But environmental policy became increasingly central to the work of the government, and Gro won important victories, the protection of Hardangervidda, Europe's largest continuous mountain plateau, being one of them. And when there was an uncontrolled blowout on the Bravo oil platform in the North Sea, she was suddenly on the TV screens worldwide and was admired for her effective coordination of the recovery efforts.[29]

There must be a woman

Only six months after Gro became minister of the environment, she also became deputy leader of the Labour Party. It was the International Women's Year, and only having men in the top leadership was a drawback for the party. The Labour Party had been the largest in Norway since World War II, but no women had been a member of the leadership. Around the country, many people suggested that Gro should have an important position in the party. She made a positive impression in the abortion debate, and her family affiliation was reassuring, although some had objections because she did not belong to the working class. A preparatory committee registered the proposals and supported Gro as deputy leader, and the party Congress applauded the choice. Gro, herself, was not sure how she would manage still another position. But the women's branch of the party put on pressure, as she writes in her autobiography: 'I couldn't say no. How could we hope to achieve equality, if the women said no?' (1997: 150–4; see also 2002: 80).

In 1977, the Labour Party did well in the elections, and the government continued, even though it did not have the majority (76 of 155 seats). The proportion of women in parliament increased to 24 per cent, and Gro Harlem Brundtland was elected. But she did not attend as long as she was a minister, according to the rules. However, in 1979, she was dismissed from the cabinet against her will. The municipal elections that year were the worst for Labour since World War II, and the party was in crisis. Prime Minister Nordli preferred having the party leader in the cabinet rather than Gro. So she became head of the Standing Committee on Foreign Affairs in parliament and joined the International Commission on Disarmament and Security Issues under the leadership of the former Swedish Prime Minister Olof Palme. Gro supported Norway's membership of NATO, but thought that something had to be done to halt the arms race and wanted, among other things, the Nordic countries to constitute a nuclear-free zone (Brundtland, 1997: 326–62; 2002: 111–29, 160–75).

Then, in 1981, Gro Harlem Brundtland suddenly became prime minister. It was not planned. But the government was getting worn out. The polls were poor, and general elections were approaching. In the midst of it all, the prime minister had health problems. On 29 January, he resigned, assuming that the party veteran Rolf Hansen would succeed him. But Rolf Hansen was not willing and referred to the deputy leader of the party. The leader, Reiulf Steen, was out of the question. Thus, Gro Harlem Brundtland was selected. She was only 41 years old, but took on the task for some months until the party Congress was held. Then, the party leadership could be clarified in a proper way (1997: 266–7; 2002: 130–35; Henderson, 2013: 59–62).

Prime minister and party president

Gro was the youngest prime minister in Norwegian history, and, in addition, she was a woman. The appointment aroused general enthusiasm. She was soon everybody's 'Gro'. People talked about 'Gro-time' and 'Gro-wave'. The opinion polls leapt upwards. The 'Green Goddess' was going to save the Labour Party from defeat. As a young, fresh breath, she could also attract new, younger voters. Being a woman was a key issue – Norway's and Scandinavia's first female prime minister. 'She will call the boys to order,' it was gleefully noted. 'A feminist in the cabinet!' Gro had not been a member of the women's branch in the Labour Party, but she fought actively for women's reproductive rights and emphasised that there should be more consideration for the needs of the family and children in the different phases of life. So she became an active advocate for gender equality.

Two months after her appointment, Gro Harlem Brundtland left the Labour Party Congress not only as prime minister, but also as the Labour Party's first woman leader. She declared openly that the positions of party leader and prime minister should be united into one role. Support for her personally, not least in the remote districts, was visible to all. Reiulf Steen resigned as leader when the

Congress opened, and Gro took over without opposition. Steen's supporters and older workers were sceptical. But Norway was about to become party to the CEDAW. The party's women's branch was on the offensive and got support for the principle of gender quotas. Two years later, this was confirmed so that both men and women should be represented by at least 40 per cent at all elections and nominations. The fact that the largest party in the country accepted this was a turning point for the representation of women in Norwegian politics (Brundtland, 1997: 301–10; 2002: 135–59).

'Get rid of her'

All the threads were gathered in Gro's hands. She became the undisputed front figure for 15 years and was prime minister during three terms, 10 years in all.

But the rise to the top was sudden and unprepared. Gro took over most of her predecessor's cabinet ministers and got going. The economic situation was difficult and required austerity measures. In many European countries, the Conservatives were moving forward. The Labour Party was divided, and in a few months, elections were to be held. The electoral campaign was a hard test for a fresh politician. She was confronted with one of the most knowledgeable and experienced male politicians, the Conservative leader Kåre Willoch, and the campaign was particularly hard because she was a woman. It was 'damned if you do, damned if you don't'. If she behaved like a typical 'female', getting touched or crying, she was criticised for being too emotional. If she was assertive or tough, she was criticised for being too 'masculine', not 'human' enough. Her appearance, dress and family life came under scrutiny by the media, and the political Right harassed 'The quarrelsome woman from Bygdøy' (a posh part of Oslo) in an unusually malicious way in the campaign: 'Get rid of her' (Henderson, 2013: 75–6).

The general elections were held seven-and-a-half months after Gro took over. Although the polls indicated increasing support, the Labour Party did extremely badly and only obtained 66 out of 155 seats in parliament. Kåre Willoch became prime minister, leading, first, a Conservative, then a non-socialist coalition, government. During his government, market forces in society were strengthened. People with employment and income became more prosperous, while the numbers of unemployed and underprivileged increased. Gro was head of the opposition and of the Foreign Affairs Committee.

In 1983, Gro also got an important international position as head of the UN World Commission on Environment and Development (Brundtland, 1997: 311–25; 1998: 50–98; 2002: 191–231).

Historic 'women's cabinet'

Before the general elections in 1985, the Labour Party launched an ambitious social programme and managed to increase its number of seats in parliament to 71 out of 157. At the same time, the representation of women increased from

26 to 34 per cent. Labour did not get enough seats to form a government, so there was a new non-socialist coalition government. In the period that followed, Norway experienced the worst economic crisis since World War II. The country had become an oil-producing nation, but the price of oil plummeted, with negative consequences for the state budget and balance of payments. Banks got into trouble, and employers locked out the employees. The austerity policies of the Willoch government failed, and he had to resign. In 1986, a minority Labour government was formed with Gro as prime minister (Brundtland, 1997: 408–24).

The cabinet was historic. When Gro became head of government for the first time, she tried to increase the number of female ministers, but only managed to add one more, so there were four all in all (25 per cent, including Gro). But, in the meantime, the party had adopted gender quotas. Gro followed up, and eight of the 18 members of her second cabinet were women (44 per cent). It was a worldwide sensation, and the cabinet was immediately named the 'women's cabinet', even though men actually were the majority and Gro's inner circle consisted mainly of men. The woman ministers got their names inscribed on a monument at the girls' school in Sakai, Osaka, Japan, showing that a dream of women's awakening had become a reality (Brundtland, 1998: 7–23; 2002: 232–40).

Mother of the Nation

Gro's women's cabinet lasted three-and-a-half years, until the 1989 elections. Although it was a minority government, Gro Harlem Brundtland's position as a national leader was strengthened. To implement her policies, the prime minister had to be a skilled negotiator to get support from other parties in parliament to obtain the necessary votes. Gro was criticised for being arrogant, direct and aggressive. At the same time, her determination, skill and leadership abilities were appreciated. Internationally, she was a rising star. When Margaret Thatcher came to visit, the newspapers wrote about 'the Iron Woman against the Super Woman'. Gro was the 'Iron Woman' – 'tougher than any man'.

Gro opposed Reagan's plans for rearmament and weapons in space and carried out a drastic turnaround to solve the major economic problems. It entailed increased taxes and, at the same time, cutbacks in public expenditures and a law on wages. The policies were controversial. The government was particularly criticised because of rising unemployment. At the 1989 general elections, the Labour Party experienced its worst setback since World War II, obtaining only 63 out of 165 seats.

A new non-socialist coalition government was formed, this time with the Conservative Jan Syse as prime minister. But it only stayed in office for a year due to internal disagreement concerning relations with Europe. So, the Labour Party took over, again with a minority government, the cabinet consisting of nine women (including Gro) and 10 men. Becoming prime minister for the third time and now without an effective opposition was a great triumph for Gro Harlem Brundtland. She truly became the 'Mother of the Nation' and a 'Queen'.

The government operated from 1990 to 1996, though there was still a non-socialist majority in parliament after the 1993 elections: the Labour Party did not get more than 67 seats out of 165. The economy was going better, but in the referendum in 1994, Gro lost the big battle about Norwegian membership of the EU. She supported closer European cooperation and went for membership, but the no's got the majority of the votes. Many people, particularly in the north, felt that Brussels was much too far away, and that the EU was undemocratic. Gro, however, made Norway, together with other countries in the European Free Trade Association (EFTA), part of the EU internal market. This decision was made without resorting to another referendum (Brundtland, 2002: 240–381).

In 1992, Gro withdrew from the position as party leader for personal reasons: her youngest son suddenly died, and she wanted more time with her family. In 1996, she also withdrew as prime minister. It was her personal choice. She was at the peak of her power and popularity and felt that her policies had created results that truly mattered for most people (Brundtland, 2002: 427). But four years with a shared political leadership – party leader and prime minister – was long enough, and she wanted to do other things. Her retirement was timed so that it was possible for her successor to prepare for the 1997 elections. But the Labour Party only got 65 of the 165 seats and a non-socialist government was formed (Brundtland, 1998: 24–442; 2002: 382–428; Henderson, 2013: 64–72).

Gro did not stay long out of the circus ring. With a clear majority, she was elected director-general of the World Health Organization in 1998, a post she retained until 2003. Afterwards, she became a founding member of the Elders, a group of elderly statespeople who helped resolve contentious issues (Brundtland, 2002: 429–71).

Consensual leadership

Gro Harlem Brundtland was not only the first woman prime minister in Norway, but, with the exception of the first prime minister after World War II, she was also the post-war prime minister who stayed in power the longest, all in all, about 10 years. Under her leadership, Norway was reshaped and its international position was enhanced.

She did not become prime minister as the direct result of elections where the Labour Party obtained a majority in parliament. Usually, a total of seven parties were represented, and when the non-socialist parties failed to form viable governments, Gro Harlem Brundtland took over, representing the largest party. But without a majority, she had to ensure support for her policies partly from the Left, partly from the Right. This was an extremely challenging situation, as the Norwegian Parliament could not be dissolved, but Gro managed it with a combination of determination and pragmatism.

Scandinavian politics have been described as a politics of compromise, based on consensual, open, rationalistic and deliberative policymaking. Gro was a resolute and enthusiastic leader, goal-oriented and, at the same time, flexible; outspoken and, at the same time, cooperative. On her first day as prime minister, she told her staff: 'This will be all fun!' (1997: 274; 2002: 138). As head of government, she tried to create a team with optimism, go-ahead spirit and solidarity. Her leadership style was in sharp contrast to that of Margaret Thatcher – not only did they belong to different political parties, but Gro was a consensus- and coalition-builder while Thatcher was a hierarchical top-down leader. In taking decisions, Gro was willing to study all aspects of a problem before she made up her mind, and collaborate closely with colleagues and other partners. On the international level, Gro strived to use Norway's soft power as a small, peaceful nation to attract and co-opt, rather than coerce and force, as a means of promoting non-violent conflict resolution and reconciliation, to a great extent, through the UN (Henderson, 2013: 62–4, 72–4).

Gro was a social democrat with a vision of society that combined a market economy with a strong role for the state in ensuring social security and progressive change. But from 1986, Gro governed in times of recession, and her economic policies were disputed. She moved from planning to market: privatised state enterprises; liberalised the market; 'modernised' industry and commerce; and brought Norway closer to the EU. She was criticised for turning her policies towards the Right, relying on collaboration with capital-owners rather than the working class. But a number of social reforms were introduced, and unemployment was on the way down when she withdrew.

At Gro's 70th birthday in 2009, she was particularly praised for her efforts for the environment and gender equality. Regarding the environment, she put political will behind the demand for protection and important decisions were reached, though environmentalists lost their case over the development of the Alta River in Northern Norway. As an environmentalist, Gro had greater significance internationally. The UN Commission was a pioneering organisation, placing the challenges of sustainable development, energy consumption, population problems and global poverty on the world agenda. Producing the report *Our common future* (World Commission on Environment and Development, 1987) took five years of extensive travelling and hard work, but was a milestone for which Gro received many awards.

Norway's 'matriarchy'

Gro Harlem Brundtland experienced discrimination against women in her political career, but she also had the ability to turn the situation into an advantage for herself and other women politicians. The women's movement helped her rise to power, and it was a part of her political platform all the time. After 1986, there was, all in all, more than one third women in parliament, and in the Labour group, there was more than 40 per cent. Women strengthened their position in several parties, and issues close to their heart such as care and equality emerged on the political agenda. Some people talked about 'the political matriarchy of modern history in Norway'. After the Labour Party, non-socialist parties also got female leaders, and in 2011, five of the seven parliamentary parties had a woman at the top.

Unlike Margaret Thatcher, who was gender-averse, Gro was described as gender-aware (Henderson, 2013: 76). She was a role model not only in the sense of demonstrating that a woman was able to be a national leader; she showed that women could make a difference by using her position to actively strengthen the status of women. When the American feminist magazine *Ms.* in New York chose Gro as the Woman of the Year in 1988, the editor, Gloria Steinem, justified it by stressing that Gro was the first top leader ever elected on the basis of a feminist wave who then carried the wave on. All in all, Gro appointed 20 women in her cabinets and was known for her efforts to ensure that women could participate on equal terms with men in working life and society.

In course of the decade from 1986, there were more female than male students, and the proportion of female employees approached that of men. Maternity leave was considerably prolonged, and paternity leave was introduced. The capacity of kindergartens was more than doubled, and caring work eventually entailed pension rights. The reforms were all the more remarkable in light of the bad economic times. After Gro withdrew, women continued to have at least 40 per cent of the members of the cabinet, regardless of the political colour, and in 2009, the red–green government went up to 53 per cent. In parliament, the percentage rose to 40 per cent in the general elections in 2013, and Norway got a blue two-party minority government consisting of the Conservative and Progress Party. There were 47 per cent women ministers and the cabinet was headed by Norway's second woman prime minister, Erna Solberg, from the Conservative Party. 52 years old, with a University degree in the social sciences, married to a business man and the mother of two children, Solberg has a long political career. She started in local politics joining the Young Conservatives in the 1980s, was elected to parliament in 1989 and re-elected five times, became leader of the Conservative Women's Association, served as minister for regional affairs from 2001 to 2005 and was elected leader of the Conservative party in 2004.

Gro Harlem Brundtland not only worked for equality nationally; she brought the population issue and the status of women into the international debate on the environment and caused a stir when she boldly advocated the right of women to control their own bodies and called for the decriminalisation of abortion at the UN Population Conference in Cairo in 1994. At the International Women's Conference in Beijing in 1995, she attacked 'genderised apartheid' and asked participants to go home and change values and attitudes in the boardrooms, local communities, governments and the United Nations headquarters. "Women power is a formidable force", Gro said (Brundtland, 1995).

Gro Harlem Brundtland did not get as much publicity as prime minister as Margaret Thatcher, coming from a small country in the periphery of Europe with only 4 million inhabitants. But Gro sent a strong message for change: women should become national leaders and use their authority to make a difference in a woman-friendly way.

Rising wave of feminism

Various differences

Although the five women rose to the top in the same region and at about the same time, the variation is striking. They came from both Northern and Southern Europe. Two became national leaders in extremely small states, two in somewhat larger and one in a major power. Two of the countries had middle incomes (Malta and Portugal), while the other three were better off, with high income levels.

When the women became national leaders, Malta was establishing itself as an independent nation and experienced a constitutional crisis, which Agatha Barbara as president was requested to solve. Portugal was in a difficult transition between dictatorship and democracy, and Maria Pintasilgo was brought in as an interim prime minister pending elections. The three other countries had well-established liberal democracies. But there were difficulties of other kinds. The UK had pressing economic problems, which brought the Conservative Party headed by Margaret Thatcher to power. She became leader of the party because none of the men would challenge the leader in office, though many criticised him. In Norway, the Labour government was in a vulnerable situation and Gro Harlem Brundtland was appointed prime minister because no suitable male candidate was willing to take over. Vigdís Finnbogadóttir was a candidate in a regular presidential election, but ran as a protest against the male-dominated political parties.

The five women had different political affiliations. Most of them were oriented to the Left: Barbara and Brundtland represented Labour parties, while Pintasilgo and Finnbogadóttir were independent, but they leaned towards the Left. Only Thatcher belonged to a conservative party.

The political systems in the five countries were not the same. Three of the countries had both a president and a prime minister, while Norway and the UK, with hereditary monarchs, only elected prime ministers. Vigdís Finnbogadóttir and Agatha Barbara became presidents with limited power in largely ceremonial roles. In Portugal, Pintasilgo was prime minister, but the power was shared with the president. Only Gro Harlem Brundtland and Margaret Thatcher obtained powerful positions as executive prime ministers.

Maria Pintasilgo acted only in a temporary capacity for a few months, while Agatha Barbara retired after one term. The three others were in office for a long period of time. Vigdís Finnbogadóttir remained the longest, at 16 years. Although her role was mainly ceremonial, she attracted considerable attention as the first democratically elected woman president in the world and made the most of her position. Margaret Thatcher functioned continually for 11 years, while Gro Harlem Brundtland served 10 years all in all, with two interruptions. Both played an important role and had considerable political impact.

Active women's movement

Although circumstances varied, all the women rose to the top in connection with a growing women's movement expressing strong and audible demands for increased representation of women in political positions. This pressure gave women more courage to participate and created opportunities they would otherwise have been denied. In democratic elections, it could suddenly be advantageous for a party to have a woman in a visible position to attract votes, especially if competing parties had such women.

During the 1970s and 1980s, the willingness of women to stand as candidates for president or parliament increased. During this period, a total of 37 women ran as presidential candidates in nine Western countries. Nearly all lost, but not all, and the number of women in parliaments and cabinets rose, although there were large differences from country to country. This was also the case with countries that got a woman top leader. In Iceland and Norway, the representation of women in parliaments and the cabinets rose clearly above the average for Western countries, while Portugal, the UK and particularly Malta remained at relatively low levels. In Malta, very few women were elected.

Usually, the candidates for high political positions represented political parties. But Vigdís Finnbogadóttir was elected directly as president outside of the parties. She had never belonged to any party and was presented by the women's movement as a special woman candidate. Maria Pintasilgo did not belong to any political party either. Under the Portuguese dictatorship, it was no easy matter to get involved in politics. When she was assigned national tasks, it was on the basis of her scientific and cultural competence and, after the revolution, also as a representative of the women's movement. Agatha Barbara was active in the Labour Party all her life and she was elected to parliament with the support of women. As there were no other women MPs when her party came to power, she became minister and later president. Both Gro Harlem Brundtland and Margaret Thatcher grew up with their respective political parties. Thatcher also struggled hard to become an MP. Both were recruited to the party cabinet because the party needed a visible woman at the top.

None of the women inherited their top positions from their family, though the parents were politically involved and helped their daughters acquire an interest and understanding of politics in many cases. Both Thatcher and Brundtland had close relationships with their fathers, who were active in politics, and the treatment her father was exposed to by the British authorities made a strong impression on Barbara. Apart from Thatcher, all had gainfully employed mothers, and the mothers of Gro and Vigdís were also engaged in political and trade union activities.

In Western industrialised countries, many women got an education and an occupation. All of the top women also acquired extraordinary qualifications. Although none of them came from the upper classes, they had more education and higher status than most women in their countries. Four belonged to the middle class and obtained one or more university degrees. Only Barbara came from the working class and did not get higher education. All were economically active in good to very good positions. Brundtland worked as assistant chief physician and Thatcher as a research chemist and barrister. Finnbogadóttir became director for a theatre and Pintasilgo was project director in a large industrial company. Barbara was a school teacher and then managed the party printing house.

Women's double burden of family and work has often been an obstacle to political involvement. Both Barbara and Pintasilgo remained single, and Finnbogadóttir was divorced with an adopted daughter before she was elected president. However, Thatcher and Brundtland married at an early age and had children: Thatcher two and Brundtland four. They got help at home, and their husbands supported their wives in a way that was very unusual at the time and was crucial for the women's careers.

For and against feminism

The five Western women top leaders worked in countries with different religions: Catholicism (2), Protestantism (2) and the Anglican Church (1). It was possible for women to become national leaders in countries with different Christian denominations. But the time in office was shorter in the Catholic than in the other countries.

The five women had different attitudes towards feminism. Pintasilgo and Finnbogadóttir considered themselves to be feminists, though it was only Pintasilgo who actually joined the women's movement. And there were clear limits, in different ways, to what the two could accomplish for women during their time as top leaders. Barbara did not call herself a 'feminist', but she founded a women's organisation and made significant efforts to improve the situation of women, especially before she became president. The one who, without doubt, did most for women was Brundtland. She did not join the women's movement, but fought for women's rights before she became prime minister. In office, she endeavoured to empower women and strengthen their position in different ways. Although Thatcher benefited from the women's movement, she was a pronounced anti-feminist and saw no reason to support women.

As models, Gro Harlem Brundtland and Margaret Thatcher came forward as opposites. Margaret Thatcher was the 'Iron Lady' above all. She shed light on the central dilemmas facing women in politics. In a powerful Western country and a strong Conservative Party, Thatcher demonstrated for all that women *were able* in a male-dominated world: they were able to serve as prime minister and lead a great nation, like a man, in war and in peace. All over the world, women looked at Thatcher and thought: if Thatcher can do it, another woman must also be able!

But *what* was Thatcher able to do? Just that: lead like a man or even a bit more in a 'masculine' way. She did *not* demonstrate how a woman could lead in *another* ('softer') way than men. She was a striking example of how women's participation in politics did *not* necessarily mean that they made a difference, that the policies became more beneficial for women. She also made it clear that a woman who broke with the traditional female role and became involved in politics was not necessarily politically to the left. And as a Conservative with the New Right policy, Thatcher actually weakened the position of women in British society.

Gro Harlem Brundtland also showed that women were able. She did not come from a great power, but Norway had stronger egalitarian values and a more democratic tradition than the UK. This was useful, but not sufficient, when Gro decided to create a 'women's cabinet' and sent a striking message to the world that it was possible for a woman top leader to do something not only to improve women's living conditions, but also to empower them. A female prime minister could create a positive circle, where women supported female politicians, who in turn helped to empower women. While Thatcher remained a solitary swallow as a woman national leader, Brundtland was surrounded by both women and men and received broad support from women in different walks of life.

The Prime Minister of Pakistan Benazir Bhutto speaking at the UN General Assembly in New York on 3 October 1996. She was prime minister from 1988–1990 and 1993–1996.
190830: UN Photo/Milton Grant

Chapter Four

'Roaring She-Tigers' in South Asia

Poor and populous South Asia

Feudal patriarchy

In the second half of the 20th century, South Asia was the world's poorest region, the most illiterate and the most malnourished and sick, and women were the hardest hit. Still, South Asia became the region with the highest frequency of women national leaders: four of the nine countries have or have had a total of seven women heads of state and government.[1]

The four countries are all post-colonial states. They were subject to the British Empire and won their independence after World War II – India and Pakistan in 1947, Sri Lanka in 1948, and Bangladesh, first, as part of Pakistan in 1947, then as an autonomous state in 1971. Gradually, they became members of the movement of non-aligned states. They were all agricultural countries, but natural conditions and economic development varied. In the years following independence, they generally had very low incomes, Bangladesh among the lowest in the world, though, by the end of the 1990s, Sri Lanka became a middle-income country. There were great social and economic inequalities related to geography, class, gender and caste. Elites got a Western university education, while poverty was widespread, particularly in Bangladesh and India, and partly in Pakistan.

The region was characterised by historical and cultural wealth, and the countries were marked by considerable diversity. In India, most people were Hindus; in Bangladesh and Pakistan, Moslems; and in Sri Lanka, Buddhists. However, minority groups presented nationalist claims on the basis of ethnicity, language and religion. The situation of women varied. In some places, they had greater freedom and higher status than in others. But, practically everywhere, feudal patriarchal social structures made women more or less subordinate to men. Strict gender roles, including *purdah* (seclusion of women) in Pakistan, Bangladesh and India, were often deeply rooted. Even though women worked hard in the household and the informal sector, their efforts were usually invisible and neglected. They lacked education and health services, and were economically dependent and marginalised. In paid employment and public life, female participation was generally small.

Few women in politics

The struggle for universal suffrage took time in South Asia, and, afterwards, women had to fight to be able to make use of their political rights. In the early decades of the 20th century, women became involved in social and educational work and a few even in politics. In India, this was promoted by Mahatma Gandhi and organisations like the All-India Women's Conference. In Sri Lanka, women got the right to vote in 1931, but independence was negotiated by male-dominated elites without broad popular involvement. On the Indian subcontinent, extensive liberation struggles contributed to the mobilisation of women. Both in India and Pakistan, women got universal suffrage in connection with independence: Pakistan in 1947 and India in 1950. In Pakistan, a strong All-Pakistani Women's Organisation was created in 1949. In Bangladesh, the women's movement arose out of the nationalist movement and the new state confirmed universal suffrage in 1972.

India and, later, Pakistan became federal states, while the others had centralised national governments. India and Sri Lanka established democracies after independence, but the conflict between the Sinhalese majority and the Tamil minority in Sri Lanka gradually increased in strength and violence. Bangladesh and Pakistan fluctuated between democracy, autocracy and military rule. Pakistan, in particular, was highly militarised. All the countries established political institutions more or less according to the British model, but there was chronic discord related to national issues, and the politics were unstable.

Women participated in national social movements and struggled for peace, democracy and better living conditions. After the 1970s, when there was a wave of democratisation with emphasis on human development, the breadth of women's organisations increased, and the movements became relatively strong. Laws were revised, and special measures were adopted to strengthen women's participation in politics. However, traditional beliefs about the role of women (emphasising their responsibility for the private sphere), opposition against female politicians, voters' lack of trust, fear of mental and physical violence, and lack of self-confidence, in addition to poverty and illiteracy, prevented many women from engaging in political activities. The highly visible female top leaders stood in sharp contrast to the extremely modest representation of women in the political system in general.

Benazir Bhutto: daughter of the East

Pakistan's difficult start

Her father was decisive for Benazir Bhutto, who suffered a fate even more dramatic and tragic than Indira Gandhi.[2] Pakistan was established as an Islamic state and Islam was the one unifying force in a country which was very populous, but geographically, ethnically and linguistically extremely diverse. The majority of the population was Sunni, with a substantial Shi'a minority. The political framework was weak, and the country was ruled by a powerful military bureaucracy, tribal leaders and a landowner aristocracy. Constitutional crises, prolonged military rule, economic instability, frequent political unrest and regional and cultural differences influenced the development. Nevertheless, a women's movement was active. Fatima Jinnah, sister of the 'Father of the Nation', played an important role. She even ran for president in opposition to the incumbent dictator in 1965, but lost by a narrow margin, which many believe was due to fraud.[3] Being involved in politics was difficult in general, and women were particularly inhibited. Political parties were inefficient, at times forbidden and often extremely corrupt. The participation of women in public life was hindered not only by feudal structures, but also by fundamentalist movements, military rule and Islamisation programmes supported by the state. The few women who got political positions belonged to prominent elite families.

Unlike India, the transition from a colony to independence in Pakistan did not take place under firm political leadership with well-developed state machinery. The head of the Moslem League and the founder of the nation, Mohammed Ali Jinnah, died in 1948, and his right hand man was murdered in 1951. The country thereby lost the architects of the new state, which had to be built from scratch. Pakistan did not get a constitution until 1956. Before two years had passed and elections could be held, there was a coup and martial law was introduced. Field Marshal Ayub Khan was the first of several military dictators. He appointed a cabinet of both civilian and military personnel, and Zulfikar Ali Bhutto became minister, first, for energy and trade, then foreign affairs. The Bhutto family was among the largest landowners in the Sindh province, with enormous wealth, and dominated local politics for many years. The family was Sunni Moslem, and Zulfikar Bhutto was sent to Berkeley and Oxford to study. The young man chose political science and law and was influenced by Western culture and socialist ideas. After graduation, he taught at the Sindh Moslem College before establishing a law office in Karachi. Zulfikar Bhutto was eloquent, clever and politically ambitious and was soon Ayub Khan's closest associate.

Pakistan's first elected civilian leader

As minister, Zulfikar Ali Bhutto became internationally known. He collaborated with other Moslem states, the US and China. In the Kashmir conflict, he took an uncompromising attitude towards India and fell out with Ayub Khan, and so he withdrew from the cabinet. The dissatisfaction with Khan was considerable, and in 1967, Bhutto created his own party, the Pakistan People's Party (PPP), with the motto: 'Islam is our faith, democracy our polity, socialism our economy – all power to the people!' PPP attracted large crowds, and Bhutto was arrested. But protests led to his release, and Ayub Khan resigned.

A new general, Yahya Khan, took over and finally organised general elections in 1970. Bhutto was supported by a broad movement of workers, farmers, activists and students, and the PPP won a sweeping victory with 81 of the 138 seats from West Pakistan. Sheikh Mujibur Rahman got all but two of the 162 seats from East Pakistan. The leadership in the West would not accept that the East should play a dominating role in the new state, and a bloody war broke out, with the result that Bangladesh was established as an independent nation after Indian intervention. Yahya Khan resigned and handed power over to Bhutto. In a situation of martial law, he became the country's first democratically elected civilian leader.

Zulfikar Ali Bhutto stayed in power for five-and-a-half years, first as president, then as prime minister. The constitution was restored in 1973, making the country a federal Islamic republic with a parliamentary system and basic human rights. The country got a titular president and a federal parliament with a national assembly and a senate. The National Assembly was elected directly by simple plurality, while the Senate was elected by provincial assemblies and tribal areas. The prime minister had executive political power, and the cabinet was accountable to the National Assembly. Discrimination on the basis of race, sex and religion was forbidden. At the same time, Islam was compulsory in schools, and a ministry was established for religious issues. Measures were also implemented to improve the status of women: education, 13 reserved seats for women in the National Assembly, access to government posts (some women were also appointed) and a women's rights committee.

Bhutto nationalised industries, fixed minimum wages, encouraged workers to organise and took land from the feudal lords and gave it to the landless. Further, he turned Pakistan into a nuclear power and made peace with India. The policies were criticised by industrialists, landowners and religious fundamentalists. In particular, Bhutto was accused of a concentration of power and an authoritarian leadership style, with repression of dissidents, personal persecution, imprisonment and murder.

At the general elections in 1977, PPP won an overwhelming victory and got 155 seats out of 200 in parliament. Ten women (5 per cent) were elected. But Bhutto was accused of fraud, and unrest followed, with violent confrontations. After four months, General Zia ul-Haq intervened and took control in a bloodless coup. A state of emergency was declared. Zulfikar Ali Bhutto was arrested, accused of murder and executed in 1979.[4]

Chosen child

Benazir was Zulfikar Ali Bhutto's firstborn. Her mother, Begum Nusrat Ispahani, was Bhutto's second wife and a Shi'a Moslem of Iranian origin. She was the daughter of a rich businessman who operated, first, in Bombay, then in Karachi and sent his daughters to college. While the Bhutto women lived in *purdah*, Nusrat drove unveiled around in a car. But she was very pious, and after marriage, she lived according to tradition and wished that her daughters should also do so. But

Zulfikar Ali Bhutto wanted a secular, Westernised home, released his daughters from traditional duties and encouraged them to get an education. He also requested his wife to engage in politics, and she was elected to parliament and became head of Pakistan's delegation to the International Women's Conference in Mexico in 1975. Together, Nusrat and Zulfikar had four children, two boys and two girls. Benazir was born in 1953 and was her father's favourite. As the oldest child in the family, she got special attention, even though she was a girl and a boy was born soon after. Girls and boys should have the same opportunities, her father said. He wanted to lead both the country and his children into the 20th century.

From an early age, Benazir was brought up to be her father's political heir. The region was full of powerful women, and Benazir learned about famous statesmen and female Islamic rulers, about Sirimavo Bandaranaike, Indira Gandhi, Joan of Arc and Fatima Jinnah. Her father had a huge library, and he wrote long letters to his daughter when he was away. He took her with him to political meetings, and she had a deep love and admiration for him. Both parents travelled a lot, and from when Benazir was little, she had to take responsibility for the house together with the servants. They had an English governess, and Benazir attended Catholic convent school in Karachi and received private instruction in Islam at home (Mernissi, 1993; Academy of Achievement, 2000).

At 16 years old, Benazir went to the US to study, first, at Radcliffe, then a women's college in Cambridge, Massachusetts, that integrated with Harvard University (1969–73). Afterwards, she went to Oxford (1972–77). She wanted to be a diplomat and graduated with degrees in comparative government and politics, philosophy and economics. She participated in the women's movement and got involved in anti-war activities. She was elected head of the reputable Oxford student union as the first foreign woman, and she got to know Margaret Thatcher. In between, her father took her to meetings in the UN Security Council, the 1972 Simla negotiations with India (Indira Gandhi), which officially ended the 1971 war between the two countries, an Islamic summit and political talks in China and France.[5]

Prosecuted and fearless

In prison, Zulfikar appointed his wife as head of the PPP, and the party bosses accepted it as a compromise. Nusrat's health was poor, but she could not refuse. When General Zia ul-Haq seized power, Benazir had just returned home after completing her studies, while her brothers and sister remained abroad. Her father asked Benazir to carry on his work and, at 24 years old, she took over his tasks, including responsibility for the family farm, and became spokeswoman for her mother and the party. The seven years that followed were an ordeal. Mother and daughter campaigned to get Zulfikar released, and when he was executed, they mobilised PPP supporters to protest. By killing Zulfikar Ali Bhutto, General Zia got a dangerous opponent out of the way. But if Bhutto was controversial in person, he soon became an idol after his death, a hero of the people and a martyr.

Zia ruled with an iron fist, and mother and daughter were taken into custody, detained and placed under house arrest, released and detained again and again, together and separately. For more than two years, Benazir was in solitary confinement. It was inhuman. But if she had been protected and pampered before, the persecution made her fearless and unyielding. She was the only one who could take up the mantle of her father, and she had faith in herself. She said that she had always felt that she could become prime minister if she wanted to, but she did not want to because she had seen the assassination attempts on her father. She did not want the fear, the worries. But her father's execution changed that. They could not let the dictator win and let her father's blood and the blood of all those others who had died go to waste (Academy of Achievement, 2000: 5–6).[6]

Both women got sick, but did not give up. Because of international pressure, Nusrat was permitted to travel abroad for medical treatment in 1982 and Benazir in 1984.

'A little punk girl'

Formally, mother and daughter chaired the PPP together, but it was Benazir who did the job. Nusrat wanted her daughter to lead a normal life, but Benazir thought of everybody in Pakistan who looked to her with hope. Her flat in London became the centre of the party's battle against dictatorship. PPP was a gathering of different groups: Marxists, feudal landowners, business people, minorities, women and poor. Zulfikar Bhutto united them, but when he was gone, the various factions fought among themselves. Benazir Bhutto tried to mobilise them to work together, but lacked her father's authority. As a descendant of the party's founder, she was entitled to leadership. She was well-educated with personal charisma, but she was a woman. Not only that: she was young – she could have been the daughter of one of the old party 'uncles' – and inexperienced, both politically and organisationally. She had spent the most of her adult life incarcerated or abroad. The 'uncles' perceived her as 'a little punk girl' and thought that she would mostly serve as a symbol.

There was internal strife, divisions and splintering. Many party bosses sought more fertile pastures in the camps of opponents. Gradually, Benazir Bhutto became the supreme leader of the PPP in exile and at home. She did not build up a strong party organisation, but in spite of her upper-class background, many ordinary people saw her as a representative of democracy and social justice. During the Zia regime, PPP was the only credible national political force of importance.

In Haiti, the dictator Duvalier was overthrown, and in the Philippines, the dictator Marcos suffered the same fate. In Pakistan, General Zia was pressurised into repealing the state of emergency, and Benazir Bhutto returned in 1986. It was an act of great courage in the uncertain situation. She came home as the flag-bearer of the Bhutto name, the daughter of a martyr, a victim of the general's persecution herself, a hope for democracy, freedom and progress, and a world-famous superstar. She referred to herself as the sister of the people, always brought with her a large picture of her father and was greeted by large, enthusiastic crowds, but was arrested and released (Anderson, 2013: 93). Elections were to be held in 1988, and shortly before, General Zia suddenly died in a plane crash, the cause of which was never determined. PPP won 92 of the 203 contested seats in the National Assembly and was the largest party, even if it did not have the majority. By the use of quotas, 10 per cent were women, and Benazir Bhutto became prime minister.[7]

'Kill the heretic!'

Benazir Bhutto was Pakistan's second democratically elected civilian leader. She was the first woman national leader in a Moslem country in modern times. She was also one of the world's youngest heads of government, at 35 years old, and the first to be elected and then give birth while she was in office.

Youth and beauty, combined with the fact that she was elected by the people in a militarised Moslem country, where she had previously been imprisoned and persecuted, instantly made Benazir Bhutto a media event worldwide. She appeared as a female idol and, at the same time, modern, traditional and timeless, with her elegant white scarf. She became a symbol of women's capability, despite opposition. Perhaps what most people thought was impossible was possible after all. It was seen as a victory for women internationally and nationally. In Pakistan, women were inspired to surmount traditional barriers. It was generally not considered decent for Moslem women to have an occupation, but now women said: 'The prime minister is a woman, why can't we go out to work?' (Academy of Achievement, 2000). Above a certain social class, a person was perceived as being almost without gender and it was generally not considered inappropriate for a woman to take the political role of an imprisoned or dead family member. Benazir Bhutto stood forth as Zulfikar's descendant and heir, and there were no male members of her family left in Pakistan. So, she felt that, in a way, she transcended gender. Everybody knew the circumstances that had forced her out of *purdah*, the pattern of landowning families (Bhutto, 1988: 140).

In addition to ubiquitous male resistance to female leadership, Benazir Bhutto was faced with the special challenge of seeking power in a Moslem country whose traditions decree the subordination and seclusion of women. She was attacked for being anti-Pakistani, Western and immoral. Although the Constitution of 1973, which was approved by the country's religious parties, had declared women eligible to become head of government, Moslem leaders claimed that female leadership broke with Islamic principles, and fundamentalists questioned whether a woman could serve as a prime minister, according to Moslem law. There were riots in Sindh, and fundamentalists across the country protested. 'She has usurped a man's place!' was the hateful call. 'She is a heretic who must be killed!' But the Shariah Supreme Court ruled after the election that she could remain in office (Bhutto, 1988: 317–22; Academy of Achievement, 2000; Bennett, 2010: 70).

Young mother as prime minister

As a woman, Benazir Bhutto had difficulty dealing socially with her male colleagues. The fact that she was unmarried became a political liability. It was considered a worrisome deviation, and she had to get permission from the family to do the simplest things. Also, it would immediately be a scandal if her name was linked to a man. General Zia kept her under surveillance to catch her with a man. On the prompting of her family, Benazir therefore decided to get married in 1987 and to do it the traditional way. The family chose Asif Ali Zardari, who was of the same age, came from a politically active landowning Sindh family and was educated as an economist in London. Benazir accepted the choice, but as a feminist and to honour her father, she kept the Bhutto name.

The couple had three children, two daughters and a son. The first was born just before the elections in 1988. Although Benazir Bhutto was healthy and strong, it was no easy matter to combine the role as mother with demanding political duties. Stress made her give birth four weeks early, and she was told to take complete rest. There is little information about the arrangements she made. Benazir herself boasted about how she started campaigning just a month after the baby was born. She took the child with her to official occasions, which attracted attention, and the prime minister's jet got a combined office and nursery full of toys and papers, nannies and small children. Nevertheless, the mother was absent a great deal, which gave her serious concern. During periods, the children stayed in Karachi, where family and servants took care of them, while Benazir Bhutto commuted back and forth to Islamabad and Rawalpindi. The situation was not helped by the fact that her husband Asif Zardari was also often absent. For safety reasons, the children sometimes were sent to Benazir's sister in London or placed in a boarding school in Dubai.

Benazir Bhutto thought that the public focus on her gender was at times too much. But it was brought out not only by her defence of women's rights, but by the fact that she was the mother of young children. When she was absent because of child care her mother, Nusrat, served as prime minister. It made a good impression in the Western media when the Pakistani prime minister on an official visit stepped out of the helicopter carrying her infant son as a symbol of beauty, power and motherhood. But in Pakistan, she was criticised, and it became a popular joke that the only thing Benazir Bhutto managed to deliver as prime minister was a baby.[8]

Power without possibilities

The military dictatorship undermined law and order, national institutions, the political system, a free press, religious freedom, and civil rights. Corruption and crime became widespread national industries. Zia ul-Haq gave strong support to fundamentalist groups and brought state laws in accordance with Islamic religious law, the Shariah. He also revised the constitution in 1985, giving the president, who was indirectly elected, a dominating position. The president could appoint and dismiss the prime minister and the cabinet and dissolve the parliament. He also increased the number of reserved seats for women in the National Assembly (from 10 to 20), but the policy of reserved seats formally lapsed after the elections in 1988.

After the elections, Benazir Bhutto did not automatically become prime minister. She had to negotiate the conditions with the interim president and when she was appointed, her influence was very limited. With a plurality, but not a majority, in the National Assembly and a Senate that was dominated by anti-PPP parties, she could not get any reform legislation passed. To achieve a majority in parliament, she had to enter into a coalition. The collaboration with Muhajir Qaumi Movement, MQM, was fragile because the movement differed from the PPP in many ways. MQM represented the interests of the Moslem Indians who fled to Pakistan in 1947. Bhutto appointed a cabinet of more than 50 ministers in a parliament of 237 members to increase her support, but it made the work inefficient, and she had to accept that both the president and the minister of foreign affairs came from the general's regime. She, herself, took responsibility for defence, atomic energy, finance, economy, information and establishment.

Benazir Bhutto faced a strong army and a hostile president, and she encountered resistance not only from an aggressive opposition, but from the whole Zia establishment of military-friendly, extremely right-wing and religious narrow-minded followers. She tried to make use of her own people, among others, her mother and father-in-law, but they were not always equal to the tasks, and she was criticised for using her family and relying on feudal landowners instead of young intellectuals and technocrats.[9]

Ideals and realities

At the inauguration as prime minister, Bhutto declared that she wanted to:

> [build] a progressive and democratic Pakistan, free from all kinds of exploitation … promote the lofty Islamic principles of amity, brotherhood, equality and tolerance … and work for national unity based on justice and equality. Ours is the message of peace and hope. (Shaikh, 2000: 123–4)

After 11 years of dictatorship, Bhutto represented a change of regime. There were high hopes for what she could accomplish, and her electoral promises contributed to this. She immediately created a sense of freedom by strengthening human rights. She gave amnesty to all political prisoners and exiles, lifted restrictions on the media, non-governmental organisations (NGOs) and student and labour unions, and protected minorities' rights (Bhutto, 2008: 198).

The women's movement was enthusiastic. Benazir Bhutto was evidently elected as a woman. In her campaign, she depicted herself as a strong Moslem woman. 'Moslem women have a heritage to be proud of,' she emphasised (Bennett,

2010: 70). She attacked Zia's Islamisation programmes and opposed all laws discriminating against women. But, at the same time, she noted: 'I never thought of myself as a woman. I am, of course, but I'm more a person who was caught up in dictatorship' (Weaver, 2002: 190). She projected herself in different ways, both as an emancipated modern woman and a traditional devout Moslem (Akhund, 2000: 314–26; Weaver, 2002: 190–4).

As prime minister, Benazir Bhutto promoted women's organisations and made efforts to empower women. She included four women deputy ministers in her cabinet and a quota for women was reserved in government service. She established a Ministry of Women's Development and a Women's Development Bank, created a woman police force and opened all-women police stations. She extended educational opportunities, set up institutions to help train women in family planning, nutritional counselling, child care and birth control, and created university women's studies programmes. Women's participation in international sports was legalised and supported (Bhutto, 2008: 198–203). A proposal reintroducing reserved seats for women in the National Assembly was presented, but Bhutto's government was dismissed before a vote could take place. Bhutto did not (and most probably could not) change the civil laws based on Shariah and was criticised bitterly by women's rights activists for her failure to do so.

In addition to structural obstacles, the Bhutto government lacked funds to improve the lives of the numerous poor and illiterate in a population of more than 100 million. Since independence, money had been diverted away from economic and social development to the army and intelligence service. And after years of martial law, Benazir inherited a dismal economy marked by an enormous national debt, unemployment and inflation, and loans from the international financial institutions required economic austerity measures. Bhutto privatised public-owned utilities, but the budget was weighed down by heavy military spending. The country depended on foreign loans just to keep the government afloat. But the prime minister managed to increase foreign aid from the US, among others, to strengthen the social sector.

The security situation was deteriorating, with a growing communal threat and a confrontation between democracy and the army. Benazir Bhutto strengthened the process of democratisation and agreed to a military alliance with the US. Due to national interests, she kept Pakistan's nuclear programme. But attempts to bring about peace and cooperation with the indigenous population, the *Muhajir*, in Sindh and India were short-lived, and in 1989, MQM withdrew from the government.[10]

Only 20 months

Benazir Bhutto gave exciting speeches, appealing to the people as a struggling daughter and sister. But completely different skills were required to control a troubled, chaotic and violent country. She was criticised for the lack of clear policy. The party she inherited from her father stood for an unclear populism. Trying to place it as a pragmatic leftist centre party, Bhutto had difficulties elaborating a concrete programme. She was not always sure of her own views, and there were different opinions in the party. In addition, she was afraid of provoking the army and Islamists. When asked if the government would try to cut the defence budget, she replied: 'Not unless we want the army to take over again' (Akhund, 2000: 129). In the West, Bhutto was seen as a liberal democrat fighting oppression, and her image in the Pakistani population was strong. But those with whom she worked perceived her as authoritarian and intolerant, with a poor grasp of government and administration (Anderson, 2013: 97–8).

After 20 months, the prime minister was removed by the president. She was accused of incompetence, abuse of power and corruption. Corruption was extremely common in South Asian politics, but the allegations struck Bhutto with particular force because she came forward as a guardian of morals, and her husband and father-in-law were subject to scrutiny.

New general elections were held, and the PPP only got 45 of the 207 seats in the National Assembly, while the opposition, the Islamic Democratic Alliance (the IJI alliance), got 105, despite the fact that the difference in the percentages of the votes between the two groups was less than 1 per cent. Nawaz Sharif became prime minister.

Stained halo

Three years of wandering in the wilderness of opposition followed. Nawaz Sharif reinstated press censorship and banned student unions, reversed social programmes and reforms for women and girls, and strengthened the military. But he also had problems and was removed in 1993, accused of corruption. When new general elections were held, PPP obtained 86 of the 207 seats in the National Assembly, while Sharif got 72. Only four women were elected, among others, Benazir Bhutto and her mother. Benazir became prime minister again. It was quite an accomplishment. For the first time, a Moslem woman was re-elected as prime minister. And nobody could now say that she was only elected because of her father.

This time, Bhutto was in power for three years. The constitution was not changed, but she no longer faced a hostile army and president. She still had to work with a coalition government; this time, with smaller parties and independents. The economy was precarious, but with assistance, especially from the US, living conditions improved: schools were built, children were immunised, villagers got electricity and family planning was strengthened. Bhutto received a medal from the World Health Organization for her efforts in the area of public health. Pakistan became party to the UN Convention on the Elimination of All Forms of Discrimination against Women (CEDAW) in 1996, though with reservations, and senior women judges were appointed.

Some believe that Benazir Bhutto's second period was worse than the first because mismanagement and corruption, particularly in the prime minister's closest circle, became more extensive. It can be argued that her record did not differ significantly from others in Pakistan at the time – but the expectations were different. Bhutto herself held the view that the accusations were politically motivated. But even if they were used politically, they were not necessarily groundless. In such a thoroughly corrupt society as Pakistan, it took a lot to keep one's way pure, and it is claimed that conditions got worse during Bhutto's government. She was also charged with corruption in Europe. In Switzerland, a sentence was passed that Bhutto and her husband said that they would appeal. When Benazir was killed, investigations were ongoing concerning assets worth millions connected with the family name placed at different locations abroad.

Even her marriage, which was supposed to be a positive factor in Benazir Bhutto's life, became a burden. The family emphasised that her husband did not have political ambitions of his own, but he became a political disaster for his wife. Asif Ali Zardari was elected as a member of parliament (MP) in 1990. He was highly corrupt and got nicknames such as 'Mr 5 per cent' and 'Mr 10 per cent' because of the commissions he took for services. After Benazir Bhutto was removed as prime minister in 1990, Asif Zardari was arrested for corruption and jailed until 1993. Then, he became MP again, and his wife appointed him as minister. Now, he was called 'Pakistan's real ruler', and there was an outcry when he became minister of investment in 1996. Not long after Benazir Bhutto was dismissed. Her husband was arrested and imprisoned without trial until 2004 on a range of charges, including blackmail and murder. Then, he was released and left the country. None of the cases resulted in conviction despite almost 11 years behind bars. And in 2010, he became Pakistan's president.

A particularly tense situation arose when Benazir Bhutto's brother, Murtaza, returned home after 16 years in exile and demanded to be accepted as his father's rightful heir. Nusrat gave him a hearty welcome, but not Benazir. In exile, her brothers engaged in a militant group to avenge their father's death, and Murtaza was charged with terrorism. A serious dispute followed. When Benazir's mother preferred her son as her husband's heir, Benazir felt betrayed and accused her mother of male prejudice (Anderson, 2013: 104). Mother and son publicly came out against Benazir, and Murtaza ran for election in 1993 with his own party against the PPP. As a consequence, Nusrat was set aside as 'co-leader' of the PPP and Benazir became supreme leader for life. The feud ended in 1996, when Murtaza was shot and killed by the police. The prime minister's husband was accused of contributing to it, while Bhutto blamed 'high officials' (Bhutto, 2008: 209). The second brother was poisoned in mysterious circumstances while living in exile in France.[11]

Exile and death

For the second time, Benazir Bhutto was accused of corruption and mismanagement by the president and removed in 1996. This time, it was a president representing the PPP who overthrew her. With the all-time lowest voter turnout – 17–20 per cent – the PPP lost the elections and obtained only 18 of the 207 seats in the National Assembly, while Nawaz Sharif got 137. Sharif became prime minister again, but economic crisis, corruption scandals and a failed military adventure in Kashmir put the civilian government into disrepute. In 1999, General Musharraf took power in a coup. This time, Nawaz Sharif was exposed to legal action and went into exile.

Benazir Bhutto was also exposed to legal action. In 1999, a high court in Lahore sentenced her to five years in prison for corruption. With her husband in prison, Bhutto fled arrest and sought refuge, first, in London, then in Dubai. She lived with her family and travelled around the world, gave speeches and wrote articles. She promoted a view of Islam as a religion of peace and equality that was being politicised and exploited by extremists and fanatics, and under dictatorship, extremism festered and grew, threatening not only Pakistan, but the whole world. When she returned to Pakistan, she brought with her the unfinished manuscript of a book, *Reconciliation – Islam, democracy and the West*, which was published in 2008, after her death.

It was only possible to go back to Pakistan in connection with the elections in January 2008. Benazir Bhutto went after Musharraf granted her amnesty. She came home in October 2007, poised to win the subsequent election, the third restoration of democracy in Pakistan's history. The welcoming procession was overwhelming, but it was attacked by bombs and more than 130 people were killed. And on 27 December, Benazir herself was murdered at a public meeting in Rawalpindi, the same town where her father was hanged in his time. The culprit was apparently a militant affiliated to the terrorist network Al-Qaeda, but the case was never solved.

Benazir's husband, Asif Ali Zardari, and eldest son, Bilawal Bhutto Zardari, took over the leadership of the party. They collaborated with Nawaz Sharif and got a large majority of the parliamentary seats. Zardari was relieved of the corruption charges (with no proof that they were untrue), and in September 2008, he was elected president of Pakistan. Now, it was the husband who became head of state by virtue of his deceased wife – not vice versa. And he usually appeared with a large photograph of Benazir Bhutto by his side.[12]

Disputed role

The whole world followed Benazir Bhutto's political struggle, moved by her courage and determination: how she dared to come forward as a Moslem woman under very difficult circumstances, demanded to be taken seriously as a political leader and did not give up in spite of resistance. For many, she became a strong symbol of women's potential empowerment. She was not only elected prime minister twice, but was the undisputed leader of one of Pakistan's two largest parties, in fact, the only national leader the country had. Although action was limited, she supported democracy, economic and social justice, and women's causes. Bhutto was very conscious of her role as a woman and 'found it difficult to tolerate gender inequality in any form' (Bhutto, 2008: 288). If neither culture nor Islam were a positive help, she showed that they were not *insurmountable* obstacles to women's political representation. But her tragic death demonstrated the challenges in a society marked by feudal patriarchy, the military, inequalities, repression and violence.

After her death, Benazir Bhutto was hailed a hero and martyr. But how should her performance actually be evaluated? Views differ. It is underlined that Bhutto contributed to democratic restoration in Pakistan, but democracy remained extremely fragile. Neither of Bhutto's two administrations completed their term and she could not even start her third before she was killed. She is strongly criticised for her poor governance, corruption and lack of action. Even her supporters, it is claimed, generally consider Bhutto's tenures as prime minister as failures (Anderson, 2013: 80). But as a woman, Benazir Bhutto was a pioneer, and she achieved *something* in an extremely difficult situation. Some actually see her gender as her best accessory, signalling a departure from the generals and the mullahs and promising modernity to a nation with a complex of inferiority (Stan, 2007). But her power was extremely curtailed and she encountered fierce resistance from different quarters. Although she might have done more, the election of Bhutto was a milestone for gender equality and she should be remembered for what she did for women, especially Moslems (Bennett, 2010: 80, 204).

Bhutto made women's access to political power in Pakistan more legitimate, and representation increased, albeit slowly. In the 1970s, educated middle-class women created a number of organisations demanding women's rights. Campaigns were organised, but they were directed more towards the mighty state apparatus than the weak, unreliable political parties. PPP was progressive, modern and secular, but like the other parties, there were few women in decision-making positions. Less than 5 per cent of all party members were women. Women's branches were established to mobilise voters, not to strengthen women's influence in the party. The PPP party board had only three women out of 21 members in 1999, and the Moslem League – Nawaz Sharif's group – had only five of 47. All the ministers in Benazir Bhutto's first cabinet were men, except her mother, who was deputy prime minister without portfolio. In the second cabinet, Benazir was the only woman. And the male dominance was equally massive in Nawaz Sharif's cabinets.

Before 2002, never more than six women were elected to general seats in the National Assembly. In addition, some women obtained reserved seats before 1990. General Musharraf repealed many anti-women laws and under international pressure, he reintroduced and increased the women's quota to 60 (20 per cent) in the elections in 2002. Then, the number of directly elected women also increased. But, all in all, in 2014, there were only 67 women (21 per cent) in the National Assembly. In the Senate, there were 16 per cent. In the cabinet there were no women.[13]

Khaleda Zia and Sheikh Hasina in Bangladesh

Bengali sovereignty

Out of the bloody birth of Bangladesh as a state emerged two female heirs who both claimed the right to lead the nation. Sheikh Hasina and Khaleda Zia were just as unknown internationally as Benazir Bhutto was known. Bangladesh did not have the same strategic and military importance as Pakistan, and the women did not appear in Western media with the same romantic image as Benazir Bhutto. But from 1991, they alternated being in power in Bangladesh, practically completing three full terms in succession, which is unique, and then – after an interruption – a fourth term, after which Sheikh Hasina was re-elected in 2014.[14]

Sheikh Hasina is the daughter of Mujibur Rahman. Mujib came from a middle-class family in a remote Bengali village. He was a clerk and as a young law student at Islamic College, he fought for Pakistan as a separate Moslem state. But the new state comprised two very different parts, one part east and the other west of India. East Pakistan was the most populous and it had a linguistically and culturally homogeneous population in contrast to the multi-ethnic character of the West. But political and economic power was concentrated in the West, and the eastern part was treated more like a colony. Injustice, exploitation and political disempowerment made the East want to secede from the West.

When Urdu was declared Pakistan's only official language, Sheikh Mujib broke with the Moslem League and founded the Awami League (AL) in 1949 to defend the rights of the Bengali. The military dictatorship suppressed national claims and Mujib was imprisoned several times. He was called *Bangabandu*, friend of Bengal, and when Bangladesh became independent after the war in 1971, he was the leader, first, as president, later as prime minister, with the title 'Father of the Nation'.

'Father of the Nation' slaughtered

Many doubted that the new state was sustainable, with overcrowding and poor access to resources, weak institutions, and extensive war damage. Most people ran primitive farms where they cultivated rice and jute on the low Bengal delta, but storms and floods often ruined the land. Poverty and illiteracy were widespread. In addition, industries and infrastructure were underdeveloped, and communications and villages were destroyed by the armed conflict. In 1972, a constitution was adopted based on nationalism, secularism, socialism and democracy. A parliamentary system was introduced with a ceremonial president and single-chamber parliament elected by simple plurality. In foreign policy, the country was non-aligned. In the elections in 1973, the AL obtained 293 of the 300 seats in parliament.

Of the around 150 million Bangladeshis, more than 80 per cent are Moslems. The university teacher of religious studies Clinton Bennett underlines that the culture in Bengal predisposed people towards a tolerant, open, pluralistic, gender-equal and human–rights–affirming worldview. There has been a long tradition of strong Bengali women allowing nobody to dominate them. In the 19th century, women entered the political domain, and they played major roles in the language and independence struggles. In the constitution, women and men were given the same political rights (Bennett, 2010: 80–108, 137–63).

With substantial international assistance, a massive reconstruction of Bangladesh took place, and more than 10 million refugees were repatriated. Bangabandu embraced a broad socialist commitment to a centrally controlled economy, wealth distribution and welfare provision. He nationalised industries, initiated land reform and developed water, electricity, schools and health services. Two women were appointed in the cabinet, and reconstruction, agriculture and education programmes were oriented towards women. Quotas for women were also established: 15 seats in parliament and 10 per cent in the state administration. The women were appointed by the ruling party.

But economic conditions were difficult. Production and wages fell, while prices rose. In 1974, the country was hit by devastating floods and famine, and dissatisfaction grew. The AL was accused of corruption, and the security situation deteriorated. People were divided between freedom fighters and 'collaborators', revolutionary socialists and supporters of market economics. In response to the criticism, Bangabandu chose an authoritarian solution. He declared a state of emergency, changed the country into a one-party state with a presidential form of government and appointed himself as president with extraordinary powers. This created strong reactions, and in 1975, the president with his family and two key employees were slaughtered in Bangabandu's home by a group led by military officers. Shortly after, the entire leadership of the AL was killed.

Military and murder

This was the beginning of 15 years of military rule, with only a brief intermission in 1981/82. The situation following the assassination of Bangabandu was chaotic and confused, with coups and counter-coups. In 1977, army chief Zia ur-Rahman, a war hero, took power. Zia was the son of a chemist, took military training and made a valiant effort in the liberation war. He was one of the first officers in the Pakistani army who joined the rebels. When Yahya Khan struck, he presented a historic declaration of independence for Bangladesh over the radio on behalf of Sheikh Mujib.

After General Zia took over as head of state, he gradually relaxed martial law, ended press censorship and allowed political parties He changed the constitution, replacing 'socialism' with 'economic and social justice' and 'secular' with 'faith in Almighty Allah'. In 1978, he organised presidential elections, which he won. Zia tried to stimulate the economy with a free-market policy and worked hard to combat poverty. He obtained considerable international assistance, stimulated agriculture and industry, and built infrastructure and schools. In addition to the Islamists, he tried to appeal to women. His rule coincided with the UN Decade for Women and Bangladesh became one of the first countries in the world to have a unit for women in the office of the president, and it was soon made a separate ministry headed by a woman. Zia appointed women police and increased the number of reserved seats to 30. He also established a Ministry of Religious Affairs and introduced compulsory Islam studies in school. Zia's Bangladesh National Party (BNP) won the general elections in 1979, with 270 seats out of 300.

But in 1981, General Zia was assassinated by a group of officers. The civilian Vice-President Abdus Sattar became acting president and organised elections, which he won. But then General Hussain Mohammed Ershad took over, abolished the constitution, dissolved parliament and imposed martial law again. The regime was characterised by repression and coercion. Political activities were prohibited, and when elections were eventually held, it was in strictly controlled forms. Ershad mostly pursued the same policies as Zia. He appointed a woman in the cabinet and ratified the CEDAW (with reservations). However, the regime entailed a setback for women, because Islamisation was emphasised and Islam was declared the state religion (Hakim, 1992: 16–153).

Daughter and widow

The AL was at a loss after Bangabandu's death. The leader of the largest fraction approached Sheikh Hasina and asked her to take over. Hasina and her younger sister, Rehana, escaped the massacre because they happened to be abroad. Hasina was elected as leader of the AL in 1981, while she was still in exile.

The BNP was also marked by internal dissension when the leader disappeared. The situation became acute when General Ershad began arresting members of the party. Khaleda Zia, the widow of the founder of the party, was included in the BNP leadership as a symbol and a unifier. She became vice-chair in 1983 and chair in 1984.

The two women had in common that they assumed the mantle of one of the nation's murdered founders. Although Moslems pointed out that female leadership was contrary to Islam, they were elected because they were relatives of the martyrs and could mobilise sympathisers and supporters. None of the women belonged to rich, aristocratic families such as Sirimavo Bandaranaike, Indira Gandhi and Benazir Bhutto. They were more middle class and had not been educated in the West, either. When they were given high political positions, both were housewives. But there the similarity also ends.

Politics in the blood

In Dhaka in 2003, I interviewed Sheikh Hasina, who was leader of the opposition at the time, in her office. She was wrapped in a cream-coloured sari from head to toe and a large portrait of her father loomed over her on the wall:

"I had politics in my blood from early childhood. There was never any question if I would participate in politics or not. I learned from my mother and father that we had to do something for the people. But it is very demanding. If you make somebody rich, it's easy. But it is very difficult to work for the common people. Some circles will try to take the power from you. But I am fighting for democracy just as my father fought for the country."

Both her grandparents and her mother, Sheikh Fazilatunessa, supported Bangabandu's political activities, Sheikh Hasina told me. The house was open, and the mother took care not only of the five children, two daughters and three sons, but also the AL, when her husband was in prison. She organised the activists, gave guidance and kept the finances in order. Hasina was born in 1947, and her father was locked up during most of her childhood. As the oldest of the children, her task was to go to Mujib with messages and come home with instructions. When he was not in prison, her father was busy with the party organisation. Hasina learnt politics from both her parents and admired her mother's courage and perseverance.

Although it was a conservative Moslem family, boys and girls were not treated differently, and it never occurred to Hasina that as a girl, she should have no role in politics. Sometimes, her mother tried to hold her back, but then Hasina got support from her grandfather. She wanted to be a teacher and got higher education. First, she went to high school and college for girls, and then graduated from the University of Dhaka with a bachelor's degree in humanities. She demonstrated against the military dictatorship, was elected vice president of the student union and secretary of the AL student unit.

In 1968, Hasina married a fellow student from the University, the nuclear physicist MA Wazed Miah, but chose a designation referring to her father, not her husband: 'Sheikh Hasina'. She soon gave birth to a son and a daughter. She was pregnant with their first child when she was put under house arrest with her mother and siblings during the liberation war. Afterwards, she did not engage much in politics. Her brother, Kamal, was chosen to be her father's heir, and she had her own family to take care of. When Bangabandu was murdered with his wife and sons, Hasina was in West Germany, where her husband was studying. It was impossible to go home. They could be killed, too. So, Hasina settled in London and New Delhi with her family.

It was not until the fifth anniversary of her father's death that Sheikh Hasina went public and spoke at a meeting in London. This was noticed and helped establish Hasina as a political leader. She wanted to complete her father's work, but it was not easy to move home in the insecure situation. It required considerable courage. But she went and told the crowd that welcomed her: 'I have lost my parents and my beloved ones. I have nothing more to lose. I dedicate myself to the cause of the people and promise to restore democratic rights' (interview 2003). The eight- and nine-year-old children were left with her sister. After a couple of years, they also moved to Bangladesh, but their mother could not take care of them, so they were sent to boarding school in India and sometimes stayed with their father in his small apartment in the nuclear energy quarter in Dhaka.

Wazed Miah was a student leader, but never engaged in politics after he married Sheikh Hasina. He pursued his own professional career, became an internationally renowned scientist and the head of Bangladesh's Atomic Energy Commission. It was not easy to be husband of the prime minister, and Hasina felt strongly that she let the children down, but the people and the country had to come first (interview 2003). In spite of difficulties and marital discord, the couple did not break up. In 2009 Wazed Miah died.[15]

Mother and housewife

Unlike Sheikh Hasina, Khaleda Zia had never imagined that she would engage in politics. She was raised to be a good wife and homemaker. She was born in 1945 in a traditional Moslem home in Jolpaiguri in India as the third of five siblings. Her father, Iskandar Mazumder, was originally from Feni, which later became part of Bangladesh. He was a businessman, and her mother, Tayeb, was a social worker. When India was divided, the family moved to Dinajpur in East Pakistan, and Khaleda went to the local school for girls. At 15 years old, she married the nine-years-older Zia ur-Rahman, who was a captain in the Pakistan army. However, she completed high school before she joined her husband on his transfers. They had two sons, whom she took care of. When the liberation war broke out, she was put in prison, but released after some months. In the independent Bangladesh, her husband rose in the military ranks, but Khaleda was not very interested in politics and public life. Even when she was First Lady, she was shy and withdrawn, stayed mostly with the children, and participated little in her husband's social life.

After General Zia's death, groups in the BNP wished to involve Khaleda to defend her husband's policies. The idea was strengthened by the AL electing a female leader. But Abdus Sattar was preferred as the BNP leader. He soon retired, however. Khaleda Zia hesitated, partly on account of her children. It was only when the party was in serious danger that she accepted the position as leader. She said:

> Shahid Zia ur-Rahman's ideal was to create a just society without oppression on the basis of Bangladeshi nationalism. As the wife of the great leader, I will fulfil his ideals and urge all patriotic and progressive political parties and groups to contribute together on the basis of national unity in the people's struggle for democracy. (Hakim, 1992: 10–11)

Some in the BNP doubted whether she would manage the task, but she was unanimously elected as party leader. It soon turned out that she was extremely quick to learn and proved to be a strong and popular politician. A public opinion poll in 1984 showed that she had considerable support as a possible presidential candidate.[16]

Women's duel

Although the AL and the BNP had different policies, they both fought for democracy. The AL formed a 15-party alliance and the BNP a seven–party unit to fight against Ershad's military dictatorship. It took time, but eventually the two competitors managed to present demands together for the abolition of martial law, release of political prisoners and democratic elections. It was a long and arduous battle, with demonstrations, rallies and strikes. Disagreement, conflicts and splintering arose within the movement. Both Sheikh Hasina and Khaleda Zia made changes in the leadership of the parties. Both were arrested and detained a number of times, but showed impressive persistence and did not give up.

The largest women's organisation in Bangladesh, the independent and left-oriented Mahila Parishad, was founded in 1970 and fought for women's rights. With regional and international support, the breadth of women's organisations grew in the 1980s. They protested against Ershad's Islamisation and stood in front of the democracy movement. At the end of the decade, a coalition of 20 organisations presented a 17-point platform of women's demands.

Like General Zia, Ershad created his own party, the Jatiya Party (JP), and organised elections. The AL participated in the general elections in 1986, while the BNP boycotted them. Sheikh Hasina said that the protests should continue in parliament, but Khaleda Zia maintained that the elections were rigged. In any case, the opposition continued, and in 1990, Ershad resigned because massive popular resistance, with strikes and disruptions, virtually paralysed the country. He was immediately arrested for corruption and sent to jail.

Both Sheikh Hasina and Khaleda Zia came forth as winners. And both were undisputed authoritarian leaders of their parties with a personalised management style. In total, 75 parties and alliances contested the general elections in 1991, but the two parties were the main opponents: the AL in the centre-left calling for a mixed economy and a secular orientation, and the BNP in the centre-right with a more Islamic outlook and a free-market economy. Both parties had measures benefiting women on their programmes. The two leaders engaged in intense electoral campaigning and spoke at hundreds of meetings. The difference in voter support was small. Both Khaleda Zia and Sheikh Hasina were elected to parliament, but the BNP got most seats: 169 of a total of 300, while the AL got 92. Most of the 34 elected women also supported the BNP.

The constitution was amended, reintroducing a parliamentary system with a ceremonial president elected by parliament and a prime minister with executive power, who was an MP and accountable to parliament. The prime minister selected the ministers, and the cabinet was appointed by the president.

Of the two main contenders, the one with the clearest Islamic ethos obtained the most votes, even though she was a woman. Analysts attribute it to Begum Khaleda's uncompromising battle against military rule (IPU, 1991). She became the first woman prime minister of Bangladesh at 46 years old, and the second woman prime minister of a Moslem country.

Fifteen years followed with women at the top. Khaleda Zia and Sheikh Hasina alternated in power, the AL with the support of JP and the BNP with the Islamic Jama'at-i-Islami (JI). The reintroduction of democracy in 1991 led to an increase in the religious Right, and JI, being a mixture of a political party and religious movement, played a key role in the elections in 1996 and 2001.

Khaleda Zia was prime minister first during 1991–96, and then the 48-year-old Sheikh Hasina took over during 1996–2001. It was an extremely even election, with the AL getting 146 seats and the BNP 116 (out of 300). In addition, most of the 30 seats reserved for women were held by the AL. In 2001, the BNP took revenge, with 193 seats against the AL's 62 (out of 300). The women's quota expired in 2000 and only six women (2 per cent) were elected. Khaleda Zia was prime minister for the second time during 2001–06 (Malhotra, 2003: 303–14).

Crisis and imprisonment

Fifteen years with women national leaders ended in political crisis. The 2006 elections could not be held due to manipulations, unrest and violence. A state of emergency was declared. Sheikh Hasina and Khaleda Zia were accused of corruption and taken into custody, along with thousands of others in politics and government, while a transitional government had the task of organising elections. What had happened?

Some factors can by highlighted. Bangladesh had nearly always experienced authoritarian rule, first under colonialism, then as part of Pakistan and finally during the years following independence. The AL started with a parliamentary democracy, but the culture and institutions were not developed for this kind of government, and the regime slid into authoritarian rule. This was reinforced by the military regime. Then, suddenly, democracy was to be introduced in 1991, with fundamental freedoms and a parliamentary system. Elections were held and power alternated between the two largest parties. The media and civil society worked without government control, and the military stayed in the background.

But the democratic institutions functioned poorly. During the military regime, patron–client relationships and corruption were institutionalised, and this continued, even increased, under the democratically elected governments. The leaders had mostly experienced authoritarian leadership. The parties lacked internal democracy, and regardless of which party was in power, the negotiations in parliament were boycotted by the main opposition party. A two-party system established itself, but there was little dialogue. The two leading ladies rarely met and there was little control of executive power. Democratically elected leaders began to exploit state power for their own gain, supporters were rewarded and opponents punished. Bangladesh acquired a leading global position with regards to corruption.

The little power-sharing made the difference between losing and winning state power vital. Political life became increasingly polarised and characterised by confrontation, despite the decreasing political differences between the two main parties. Street agitation, strikes and violence were used to undermine the government, as was done during the military regime, instead of following the democratic rules of the parliamentary system.

During the period 2001–06, the state became even more politicised than before. Violence and Islamist terrorist acts became more extensive, and the perpetrators were often protected by the government. It is claimed that thousands of opponents were killed. Sheikh Hasina survived a grenade attack on an AL opposition rally in 2004. Khaleda Zia's two sons, among others, were accused of corruption and extortion. Khaleda Zia tried to establish her son, Tareq, as her successor and appointed him 'senior co-secretary' in the BNP. Together with supporters, he established a parallel cabinet located in the party leader's office. He was soon considered the country's most powerful person. When the BNP started to manipulate rules and appointments in 2005 to influence the 2006 elections, the opposition reacted so strongly that the country was on the border of civil war, and the military intervened after consultation with Western donor countries (Jahan, 2007).

Women's failure?

When I was in Bangladesh in 2003, many expressed the view that the administration of the country was poor because of the personal animosity between the two women top leaders. People sighed and exclaimed: 'Indeed, these women!' Without disregarding the bitterness of the rivalry, it seemed clearly unjustified to simply relate it to gender. Aggression is usually not a particularly feminine characteristic, and many factors were evidently at play.

The two women got their leadership positions as part of a dynastic succession. Because of kinship, they were set to restore the legacy of the father and the husband, respectively, and thus entered into a rivalry between families. At the same time, politics caused both women great pain. People very close to them were murdered. And it did not improve the relationship between them that General Zia, first, and then Khaleda Zia gave immunity not only to the army for what it had done during the state of emergency, but also to those who murdered Mujib, Sheikh Hasina's father. Trials for the murders in 1975 only began in 1996.

The two women continued to suffer in the struggle against a brutal military dictatorship, where they had to adopt strong measures and take the consequences of them. Extraordinary courage, determination and perseverance were required. This was particularly the case because they were women and worked in a role that many thought women were not capable of. They were met with considerable scepticism, especially in the countryside.

At the elections in 1991 and 1996, women's issues were more focused than before, but neither the AL nor the BNP really emphasised them or actively worked to promote women's participation in politics. Neither Sheikh Hasina nor Khaleda Zia considered themselves as 'feminists', and they stated that they did not represent the women's movement. On their side, women's organisations gave women a voice, but perceived politics as 'dirty' and were reluctant to participate in political parties.

Although the party leaders were women, both the AL and the BNP were strongly male-dominated parties, with few women in leading positions. At the turn of the millennium, there were 5 per cent women in the executive boards. Women were mobilised for campaigns and protest marches, but not for governing bodies and public offices. Both Hasina's and Zia's inner circles of advisors consisted of men (Majumdar, 2012).

After some years, Khaleda Zia appointed a woman as minister of women's affairs in her first cabinet. One also became minister of state for culture. In the second cabinet, there was one woman out of 27 ministers. Zia's eldest sister was responsible for women and children. Another woman was again minister of state for culture. But the cabinet was reorganised several times. In the AL, some outstanding women participated, including two party secretaries who were the only two women in Hasina's first cabinet. They were responsible for 'heavy' ministries: the Ministry of Agriculture and the Ministry of Environment. Other prominent women were pushed aside after Hasina took over the leadership. Both prime ministers were personally responsible for a number of ministries, such as defence, planning, education, health, information and energy (Ahmed, 2005).

New start

The military-led state of emergency lasted for nearly two years. Anti-corruption campaigns, mass arrests and suppression of political parties, media and intellectuals were implemented to transform the political landscape. But it was easier said than done to reform institutions and systems, and attempts to create a third political force as an alternative to Hasina and Zia failed. The pressure increased to organise general elections, and they were held in December 2008. 'From failure to success', satisfied international observers noted. The election laws and the election commission were strengthened. A total of 11 million false names were removed from the voter lists, and photographic voter lists of an international format were introduced.

Hasina and Zia were released to run election campaigns. Both promised to reduce food prices, prevent corruption and terrorism, and bring an end to the violent street confrontations. With a record voter turnout, Sheikh Hasina was swept into parliament with a two-thirds majority. A total of 32 parties stood for election. But, as before, the fight was mainly between Hasina and Zia. Hasina led an alliance of 15 parties, including a restored Ershad JP. After time in jail, Ershad publicly admitted guilt and got involved in politics again. Zia had an alliance with four parties, including the Islamist party JI. Hasina's alliance got 263 of the 300 seats, while the BNP alliance only got 33, not including the 45 seats reserved for women.

That Hasina should win by such a large majority was surprising. But Khaleda Zia was accused of abuse of power and violence, in addition to corruption, while she was prime minister during 2001–06, and many were opposed to her close association with the Islamists and the military. Sheikh Hasina promised to reduce poverty and unemployment, provide health care for all, and rid the country of illiteracy. In particular, women and young people voted for her to get a change (Jahan, 2007; Kumar, 2007; Alamgir, 2009; Eicher et al, 2010).

The new parliament got a record number of directly elected women (19), so the total was 64 or 19 per cent. Prime Minister Hasina announced that she would raise the number of seats reserved for women from 45 to 100 and make them directly elected. In the cabinet, however, only three women ministers (13 per cent) were appointed: for foreign affairs, agriculture and post and telecommunications. In the BNP national council meeting in 2009, Khaleda Zia was re-elected as party president with her son, Tareq, as senior vice president.

Progress after all

The conditions in Bangladesh and the polarised political situation did not make it easy for any government regardless of party to solve social problems, improve the economy and strengthen democracy. In addition, both Zia and Hasina had to deal with devastating natural catastrophes. And it is debatable how different the BNP and AL actually were when it came to practical politics. Both placed themselves in the centre, but the BNP government was clearly the most pro-Islamic.

The AL government distinguished itself by prosecuting Mujib's killers, resolving the conflict with India over water by signing a 30-year Ganges water-sharing treaty and making peace with the indigenous minorities in the Chittagong Hill Tracts, thereby ending the 23-year-old insurgency and bringing an area inhabited by nearly 5 million people out of violence. During her time as prime minister, Sheikh Hasina received a number of prizes and awards, particularly for her efforts for peace, democracy, development and human rights. During Khaleda Zia's term, Bangladesh began to participate in UN international peacekeeping efforts.

When it came to economic policy, the differences were small. Both parties sought and received extensive international aid to build infrastructure, schools and health services and restructure the economy. They complied with the International Monetary Fund (IMF), encouraged investment and micro-credit, and gave assistance to the poor. In addition, Bangladesh had strong NGOs that partly functioned as a kind of parallel to the state. With considerable support from international donors, organisations such as the Grameen Bank and BRAC (Bangladesh Rural Advancement Committee) played a very important role in the strengthening of the poor, especially women, and the extension of education. Women's organisations were also engaged in a wide spectrum of social activities

Despite governance problems the period from 1990 was characterised by marked progress. There was steady economic growth. Per capita income increased and poverty was reduced, though Bangladesh continued to be a low-income country with widespread poverty, illiteracy and health problems.

And the progress benefited women. Khaleda Zia introduced free, compulsory primary education with scholarships for girls and promoted micro-credit for village women. In 2004, she reintroduced reserved seats for women and increased the number to 45, divided between the parties according to their mandates. But the alliance with Islamic fundamentalists hindered her, and violence against women became more and more of a problem in her second term. In 2004, *Forbes* rated Zia as number 14 of the 100 most powerful women in the world; in 2005, as number 29; and in 2006, as number 33.[17]

Sheikh Hasina launched a national policy for the advancement of women. Two reservations to the CEDAW were removed and several gender-related laws were passed, including the Violence against Women and Children Act. She appointed women to important positions and promoted measures to increase women's participation in the labour force and improve their health and social security. She also introduced a quota for women of one third in local politics, and 14 000 women were elected to local government (UNB, 2012).

In 2010 the United Nations Development Programme (UNDP) stated that Bangladesh was making notable progress with regards to gender equity, education, health, food production and reduction of population growth (UNDP, 2010b). Later, per capita income continued to increase, but advances in human development were limited (UNDP, 2013).

The increase in girls' education was especially remarkable. Basic education for all became a reality, and the number of girls in secondary school was more than tripled so that a gender balance was nearly achieved among the pupils. Significant progress was also made in the fight against maternal mortality and in 2010 Bangladesh received a UN Award for its remarkable achievements in reducing child mortality. In 2013, the country further received UN recognition for halving the incidence of hunger (Reuters, 2010; Ahmad; 2013).

Old patterns persist

It was no easy task to govern Bangladesh, ensuring institutional stability, justice and security, strengthening democratic structures and processes, and promoting economic and social development. A month after Sheikh Hasina took office as prime minister for the second time in 2009, a mutiny was staged by the military force in Dhaka because members were unhappy with pay and conditions. Around 70 people were killed before the government could end the uprising. Governance was not made easier by the serious economic crisis that the world was facing at the time. Hasina implemented economic reforms and expanded the social budget. Per capita income continued to increase and there was progress, although limited, in human development (UNDP, 2013).

The US business magazine *Forbes* ranked Sheikh Hasina as number 79 of the world's most powerful women in 2009, but did not have her on the list later. To begin with, Sheikh Hasina was praised for stopping the rise in religious extremism, but delayed prosecutions and convictions for war crimes committed during the

Bangladesh War of Independence, among others, of leading members of the main Islamist party JI led to protests and demonstrations. In 2013, the party was banned by the high court in Dhaka from taking part in the forthcoming general elections because its charter put God above democratic process. The BNP and its alliance called for general strikes and blockades and strong concerns were voiced regarding the undemocratic political culture and the government's lack of a conciliatory approach towards political opposition and the military (Islam, 2013). To ensure free and fair elections, the BNP required that a neutral caretaker system should be put in place to prevent election-rigging by the party in power. When this was refused by the AL, there were demonstrations and protests and the major opposition parties boycotted the election. International election observers were withdrawn, but elections were held on 5 January 2014, nevertheless, though marred by violence and unrest. People were killed and polling centres set on fire. A large number of seats remained uncontested. In spite of the problems the tenth parliament was constituted with 231 seats for the AL of the 300 directly elected, and Sheikh Hasina was sworn in as prime minister. She stressed the importance of 'equal participation of women alongside men in political decision making as this only could help achieve the real development and progress of a nation' (UNB, 2013). Nevertheless, only a single woman minister was appointed in her 30-member cabinet. Hasina herself was responsible for defence, home affairs and foreign affairs.

Critical women

Both the two women prime ministers improved the situation of Bangladeshi women, though they declared that they were not 'feminists'. Part of the women's movement was also highly critical of them, because they failed to address women's rights and men's dominance due to pressure groups and the balance between different interests. When they emphasised education for girls, for example, it was to enhance the overall development, not to promote social justice or women as a group, was the claim.

Quotas for women were also controversial. Some women's organisations supported them because women got access to decision-making bodies without the usual political, social and financial costs. In addition to the patriarchal and religious resistance to women in politics, male patron–client networks and lobbies and the use of black money, muscle men and violence during the national elections in Bangladesh were so widespread that it was not easy for women to stand for election. Also, the electoral system of plurality vote was unfavourable to them. With quotas, the representation of women in parliament rose close to 69 (20 per cent) in 2011 and 2014.

Others believed that quotas prevented women from being nominated and elected to ordinary seats. And since the quota was filled by indirect election, it was under the control of political parties, and the women were not accountable to any constituency (Kabir, 2003; Basu, 2005: 16–20). Against protests from women's rights organisations demanding direct elections, the system with indirect elections was maintained when the number of reserved seats was increased to 50 (not 100) in 2011.

Epilogue in India: Pratibha Patil

Shaky dynasty

After Indira Gandhi's death, her son Rajiv was prime minister of India for five years.[18] But he suffered defeat in the elections in 1989 and a coalition government was formed without the Congress Party (I). Then, in 1991, Rajiv Gandhi was assassinated while he was campaigning in the south, probably by a representative of the Tamil Tigers. During the 1990s, the Congress Party (I) went through a prolonged crisis. After Rajiv Gandhi's death, the party asked his widow, Sonia Gandhi, to take over. She was the person most people could agree upon. Sanjay Gandhi's widow, Maneka Gandhi, was politically active and a minister in the coalition government, but she represented the opposition. After Sanjay's death, Maneka fell out with her mother-in-law regarding political succession, and Indira 'threw her out of the house', as it was said. Maneka then formed her own political party and later went over to the Indian People's Party (BJP), a pro-Hindu party in opposition to the Congress Party (I).

To the surprise of many people, Sonia Gandhi refused to become president of the party. She was politically inexperienced and had lost three of her closest relatives in politics. She was also the object of threats from Hindu fundamentalists because of her foreign origin and dynastic connection. Sonia Maino was born in Italy in 1946 to Italian parents. Her father was a building contractor, and she grew up under modest circumstances in a traditional Catholic family. At 17 years old, she travelled to Cambridge to work and learn English. Here, she met Rajiv Gandhi, who studied engineering. They married in 1968 and moved in with Indira Gandhi in New Delhi. Rajiv was a pilot, and Sonia took care of the two children. She had a close relationship with her mother-in-law and helped her as a personal assistant, but Rajiv and Sonia kept out of politics. When Sanjay died, and Rajiv felt that it was his family duty to replace his brother when his mother wanted it, Sonia felt uncomfortable. But she supported her husband as prime minister, travelled with him and ran an active campaign against Maneka Gandhi when she stood for election to the House of the People against Rajiv.

Others took over the leadership of the Congress Party (I), but it did not work out. In 1996, the party lost the election and was in full disintegration. Sonia was unable to see the party that her family had lived and died for fall apart in this way. She put duty before her personal considerations and agreed to go into service. As 'Mother India's daughter', she went out to help the poorest and promote a secular government, and in 1998, she was elected president of the Congress Party (I). Many believed that she saved the party from extinction, and the dynasty was restored. Sonia Gandhi was attacked for being foreign, although she had been an Indian citizen for many years and people swarmed to hear her when she travelled around the country in an Indian sari and gave speeches in Hindi with a foreign accent. From being a 'sphinx', she soon became a passionate speaker. In 1999, she was elected to the House of the People and became leader of the opposition.

After two defeats, the Congress Party (I) won enough seats in 2004 to form the government. It came as a 'political bombshell' when Sonia Gandhi refused to take over as prime minister. She referred to an 'inner voice', but threats and boycotts related to her foreign origin in addition to the grim fate of her husband, brother-in-law and mother-in-law may have played a role. She continued, however, as president of the party and the parliamentary group, while a senior male party colleague and former minister of finance, Manmohan Singh, became prime minister. Sonia's son became a member of the House of the People. Under the leadership of Sonia Gandhi and Manmohan Singh, the Congress Party (I) did well in the elections in 2009. The party's electoral alliance almost got the majority. In 2004 the magazine *Forbes* considered Sonia Gandhi as one of the 100 most powerful women in the world, and this was maintained practically every year afterwards. From 2010 to 2013 she was ranked among the ten most powerful (Kidwai, 2010; www.forbes.com 2013; PS, 2013).

Unforeseen promotion

In July 2007, something happened. India got a new woman top leader. But this time, she was not the prime minister. For the first time, a woman was elected as president of India. At 72 years old, Pratibha Patil became head of state for five years with the support of the centre-left. The rival candidate was the former vice president, an 84-year-old man from the BJP.

The Congress Party (I) launched Pratibha Patil. She was not a member of the Gandhi family, but was close to it. She was born in 1934 in a prosperous and progressive Hindu Maratha family. Her father was a local politician, and after primary school, Pratibha took a master's degree in political science and economy and a law degree, which allowed her to practise as an advocate. She married a teacher and professor, and together they started up a series of measures for the underprivileged, women and children. These included hostels for working women, a cooperative sugar factory and a cooperative bank, as well as schools for disabled and poor children. Pratibha engaged in social work and the couple had two children, a boy and a girl.

Pratibha Patil became involved in politics at 27 years old at the request of senior male executives in the Congress Party. She had a long career in the state politics of Maharashtra, including as minister. When the Congress Party split in 1977, Patil did not break off with Indira Gandhi, as most leaders of the state party did. Patil protested against the arrest of Indira Gandhi and the jailing of her for 10 days. Then, she led the Congress Party (I) in opposition in the state. When Sanjay Gandhi was killed, it is said that Pratibha Patil took care of Indira Gandhi's kitchen. She became a minister again in the state government when the Congress Party (I) came to power, and Rajiv Gandhi appointed her as head of the party in Maharashtra. She was elected to the Council of State in 1985, where she was vice president, and to the House of the People in 1991. She was the director of a national federation of cooperative banks, and in 2004, she was named the first woman Governor of India's largest state, Rajasthan (Gayathi and PS, 2013).

Compromise candidate

A woman candidate was not really what the Congress Party (I) had planned. The first choice for the position as president was the former minister of the interior. But the left-oriented allies of the party would rather have the minister of foreign affairs. Instead of the two men, the end result was a compromise woman. She was proposed by Sonia Gandhi. Pratibha Patil had held important positions on behalf of the Congress Party (I) and Mrs Gandhi hailed her candidate because in the 60th year of India's independence, they had a woman president for the first time (BBC, 2007a). Maybe most importantly, Patil was known for her support of secularism and loyalty to the Gandhi family. Patil underlined that she particularly wanted to work for socially inclusive economic growth, education and the empowerment of women (Embassy of India, 2007). She achieved two thirds of the votes in the election, which took place in an electoral assembly consisting of members of the national and state parliaments. Around 4,500 MPs and state legislators were eligible to vote.

However, there was a heated debate. Patil was accused of poor qualifications, corruption and unethical behaviour, which was rejected by the Congress Party (I). Also among feminists, opinions were divided. Some claimed that should it be a woman, the government ought to have honoured a person who had distinguished herself more in the struggle for women and the disadvantaged. Others thought that it did not have great importance. Although the president of India was the head of state and military commander, the role was mostly ceremonial (Guha, 2007). When Patil's term ended after five years and she retired in 2012, opinions also differed. In various Indian media, she was criticised, among other things, for expensive foreign visits, tokenism and loyalty to the Congress Party, while she was appreciated for commuting a number of death sentences to life.

Regardless of the high positions some Indian women acquired, women remained largely absent from political life at the national level. At the local level, it was different. Here, quotas for women of one third of the municipal councils were introduced in 1993, and in 2009, were extended to 50 per cent. A proposal to reserve a third of the seats for women in the national and state assemblies has not obtained sufficient support. In 2014, there were only 11 per cent of women in both the House of the People and the Council of State. The situation at the state level was about the same. In the cabinet there were four women ministers (9 per cent). As far as there are data, women were missing in decision-making bodies in all the political parties, and the Congress Party (I) was no exception. The women who came to the fore were mostly Hindu from the upper castes and classes, and many were recruited on the basis of family ties. At the same time, statistics showed that many women's lives needed to be improved: nearly half of the women were illiterate compared to a quarter of the men; half as many women as men participated in the labour force; and maternal deaths were among the highest in the world.

Chandrika Kumaratunga of Sri Lanka

Her mother's favourite

As the president of Sri Lanka, Chandrika Kumaratunga had an important role. She was both head of state and head of government. Admittedly, she was elected with the promise to delegate authority from the president to the prime minister, establishing a dual system, but in practice, not much became of it. She felt that she needed all the authority she had to deal with the problems she was facing.[19]

Chandrika Kumaratunga was born in 1945, and as the daughter of two prime ministers, she got more politics in her childhood than most children. Family friends felt that she was close to her father and was interested in politics from when she was quite small. She, herself, said that she was curious about what was happening in the world, and she wanted to serve the people like her parents did. Most of all, she wanted to be a doctor. She did not wish to go into politics because she saw how much it required, and how much her parents had suffered. Her father was murdered when she was 14 years old (Gluckman, 1996).

After secondary education in Colombo, Chandrika travelled to Paris to study and remained there for five years. She graduated in political science, was active in the student uprising in 1968, wrote for the newspaper *Le Monde* and prepared a PhD in development economics. But her mother asked her to come home at the beginning of the 1970s, and she was given a central role in the efforts of the Land Reform Commission and, later, the commission establishing collective farms. She was the editor of a daily newspaper, joined the Sri Lanka Freedom Party (SLFP) and became executive committee member of its Women's League. When the SLFP lost the majority in 1977, she became a consultant for the UN Food and Agriculture Organization (FAO).

In 1978, Chandrika married a movie star and politician Vijaya Kumaratunga, and they had a son and a daughter. Chandrika was a member of the SLFP board, but she differed politically from her mother. In particular, she reacted against Sinhala nationalism and adopted a more conciliatory approach to the Tamil separatists. Together with her husband, she founded a separate party in 1984, which advocated power-sharing with the Tamils. Here, she first became vice president, then president. But in 1988, her husband was murdered right before her eyes by Sinhalese extremists who opposed any agreement with the Tamils. For safety reasons, Chandrika took the children with her and travelled to Britain, where she took up research work.

In 1991, Chandrika came back at the request of her mother. She joined the SLFP again, and in 1993, was elected as the chief minister of the politically important Western province (where the capital Colombo lies). She was known for her courage and energy, idealism and intellect, but so far she had mainly supported family members in politics and had not expected to go to the top herself (Gluckman, 1996).

For 17 years, the United National Party (UNP) ruled the country. But now, Kumaratunga entered a meteor-like career. She became president of the SLFP, and in 1994, she ran for parliament for the People's Alliance, an alliance with the SLFP and some small leftist parties. At least 50,000 people had been killed since the civil war began, and she stood for election on a platform requiring peace and negotiations with the Tamils. In addition, she wanted to help the 40 per cent of the population still living in poverty. She travelled around and held meetings, and with the support of two smaller parties, the People's Alliance obtained enough seats to form a government. Both Bandaranaike and Kumaratunga were elected, and the daughter became prime minister, while the mother was minister without portfolio (*Current Biography*, 1996).

Vain peace attempt

Since her father's and mother's time, the political system had been altered and the position of president had become the most important. A few months after the general elections, the 49-year-old Kumaratunga ran for president, and she was elected by a massive popular vote (64 per cent), while the UNP candidate (also a woman) only got 34 per cent. Now, the mother became the prime minister with responsibility for defence and foreign affairs.

Chandrika Kumaratunga had to rule a country with ethnic conflict, security problems, terrorism, power outages, water shortages and economic downturn. She took over the ministry of finance, tried to liberalise the economy and privatised public enterprises that her father had built up. At the same time, she tried to fight against poverty through welfare measures to obtain a 'free-market economy with a human face'. The economic situation improved. More people got electricity and water, and education and health were developed. A special body was established for the protection of children's rights (PresidentCBK, 2008).

But this was overshadowed by the conflict with the Tamils, which made Kumaratunga's presidency very turbulent. It was commonly said in Colombo that her father planted the seeds of the ethnic conflict, her mother nurtured them and now their daughter was left to reap the bitter harvest. It was a stop-and-go process. As president, Kumaratunga was chief of the army and the police. In addition, she took on the job of minister of defence and minister of the newly created Ministry of Ethnic Policies and National Integration. She tried to quell the Tamil insurgency through negotiations. She wanted to design a constitution for a diverse society, where Tamil wishes could be fulfilled without dividing the country. But she encountered insurmountable obstacles in trying to get the parties to the table. And when the violence just continued, she fell back on a military strategy. But this was also very problematic.

In 1999, Kumaratunga was re-elected as president despite the fact that she was nearly killed by a suicide bomber just before the election, and one eye was destroyed. It was the first time since independence that a head of government was re-elected, but she only got 51 per cent of the vote against 43 per cent for the rival male candidate from the UNP. At the general elections in 2000, the People's Alliance held their position, but there was disagreement within the Alliance, and several supporters withdrew. Kumaratunga called new elections in 2001, but then the People's Alliance did not get enough seats to form a government, so Kumaratunga had to govern with a prime minister from the UNP, Ranil Wickremesinghe.

Sri Lanka had never before had a president and prime minister from different parties, and the constellation was difficult. First, Kumaratunga accepted that the prime minister could appoint the cabinet, but in 2003, she dissolved the parliament, took over the Ministries of Defence, Interior and the Media, and called new elections. The peace process was resumed, and Wickremesinghe made progress in getting the Tamil Tigers to the table and arranging a ceasefire. But Kumaratunga said that the UNP made too many concessions to the Tamils. In 2004, a new United People's Freedom Alliance took over the government with a number of parties, including the SLFP and JVP (*Janatha Vimukthi Peramuna*, People's Liberation Front), a Sinhala nationalist left-wing party.[20] Kumaratunga's brother, Anura Bandaranaike, joined the cabinet after he reconciled with his sister and joined the SLFP again. But it was a difficult coalition, and rising prices and unemployment, as well as the Asian tsunami, made nothing easier.

In 2004, *Forbes* placed Kumaratunga as number 44 among the world's most powerful women, and in 2005, as number 25. But in 2005, she had to resign because she had served two terms as president. Her successor from the SLFP, Mahinda Rajapaksa, won with a meagre margin, 50 per cent of the votes against 48 per cent for the UNP candidate. In 2006, Rajapaksa also became president of the SLFP. The JVP pushed for a decisive war against the Tamil Tigers. It went back and forth, but then the war escalated. In 2009, the Tamil Tigers were defeated by government forces and 300,000 people were forcibly displaced.

Alone at the top

Chandrika Kumaratunga has stated that she never felt discriminated against as a woman in politics, nor did she experience that men disputed her authority (BBC, 2007b). But she was not only a woman; she belonged to the ruling elite, had a good education and inherited political capital from her parents. Neither Chandrika nor her mother represented the broad masses, and as women, they remained relatively solitary swallows in the political landscape. Most women's organisations in Sri Lanka were social welfare organisations. Eventually, some began to organise themselves, especially in the cities, to influence the government in a woman-friendly direction. In 1993, they developed a women's charter in collaboration with the women's ministry, and before the elections in 1994, they requested the parties to take up women's issues. The government of the People's Alliance followed up. A national plan of action was elaborated and measures were implemented to combat violence against women.

In connection with the civil war, women were involved partly in human rights and peace organisations and partly in militarised rebel groups, in addition to the Mothers' Front, which protested against the disappearance of family members. During elections, women participated in campaigns and voted, but few were engaged in political parties. There was only 2–10 per cent women in the decision-making bodies of the parties, even when the president was a woman. The women who got positions in Sri Lankan politics belonged mostly to the elite and carried on the legacy from male relatives – husbands, fathers or brothers. In 1994, the presidential election was actually a 'widow's duel' between Chandrika Kumaratunga and Srima Dissanayake, the wife of the UNP's presidential candidate who was assassinated shortly after he was nominated (Kiribamune, 1999a).

Women in Sri Lanka became top politicians while the representation of women in parliament was among the lowest in Asia. In 1993, Sirimavo Bandaranaike argued that more women should become MPs because women's issues were not taken into account. They had, in particular, family problems that men did not have, such as physical violence (Liswood, 2007: 75). But in the 1990's, the proportion of women in parliament was less than 5 per cent. At the elections in 2000, 22 parties and 91 independent groups proposed only 117 women of a total of 5,048 candidates. A number of women's organisations joined forces, demanding a quota for women of 30 per cent of the MPs. But this was not accepted. In 2014, the proportion of women in parliament had increased, but only up to 6 per cent. Kumaratunga said that the situation was so insecure that people were afraid to participate in politics. At the same time, she acknowledged that she could have done more for women and equality while she was in power. In her cabinets, there was at no point more than a maximum of two women. In total, they were four, all from political families. In 2014, there were still only two women ministers (3 per cent).

Regarding the low representation of women, researchers have pointed to: the importance of the elite character of political life, where leaders strengthen the family's power more than women's; the women's movement being unable to change the political institutions, including the electoral system; and the lack of a democratic culture that can, among other things, be open to affirmative action for women (Attanayake, 2008).

Dynasties and violence

Crisis of governance

Women's place in politics is related to South Asia's specific forms of society. Analysts describe a widespread crisis of governance in the region. Regardless of the political system, power is concentrated in a few powerful individuals distant from most people. They rule in a personal and informal way, bend the rules, and bypass the institutions if it is convenient. This makes democracy into a more or less empty ritual, although elections are held. Moreover, the governance is inefficient and unjust. The rich became richer, while millions of poor people live in poverty and despair (Haq, 1999). The crisis of governance was not caused by the women leaders, but they fell into the pattern. The crisis affected the way they were recruited and how they could govern the country.

The central political institutions in South Asia – the legislature, executive and judiciary – were not developed locally, but taken over from the colonial power and only partially changed after independence. And, in practice, they did not function according to the original intentions. The leading politicians ruled at their own discretion, and the institutions were undermined. The administration implemented extensive measures, but only served the interests of the people to a small extent. And the division between executive and judicial power was not clear, except in India.

After independence, India and Sri Lanka introduced liberal democracy, while Pakistan and Bangladesh were characterised by authoritarian regimes. Sri Lanka was also marked by growing unrest and militarisation. Conflicts left their mark on the region through three interstate wars, two partitions,[21] periodic confrontations, disagreements and partly armed conflict between classes, castes, ethnic groups and nationalities. Murder of political leaders was one manifestation of the violence.

The modern Western institutions were placed in societies with a different structure, working largely informally on the basis of kinship, alliances and patron–client relationships. Instead of following rules, personal connections determined views and decisions. The state was highly centralised, and a few privileged elites controlled access to power and resources. These were, above all, landowners, industrialists, bureaucrats and officers. The landowners were strongly represented in political parties, parliament and the government, and the impact of industrialists increased over the years. In Bangladesh and Pakistan, a military bureaucratic oligarchy constituted a significant part of the ruling elite. All the countries were strongly stratified, with marked social and economic inequalities and a big gap between the rulers and the ruled. Within the power elites, above all, a few family dynasties dominated. And most people considered kinship as more important than achievements for political leadership.

Representatives of the family

There were no women top leaders in Afghanistan, Bhutan, Iran, Maldives and Nepal. And the four countries where women became leaders had different economies, cultures, religions and politics. Historically unique and extraordinary circumstances resulted in women becoming heads of state or government – circumstances that are unlikely to recur in the same way either in their own or other countries. Most of the women came to power in dramatic situations, with murder, coups and sudden death of a leader or opposition to authoritarian forces.

With one exception, South Asian women became top political leaders due to family relations. Five of the leaders were substitutes for deceased male relatives, of whom, all but one were murdered. Two were widows, while three took up the mantle of their dead fathers. In one case, the top leader succeeded her mother (who was not deceased). It was not, first of all, political parties that brought them to power, though practically all the women became party leaders. They were recruited more or less directly into the party leadership and the parties became an important basis for the execution of power. The period varied from the death or the resignation of a prominent political relative until one of the women took up the mantle. Bandaranaike took over the positions as party leader and prime minister very soon after her husband's death, and her daughter did so when her mother was old, even if her mother was still politically active. Indira Gandhi was party leader for a year, but withdrew and then became prime minister later, a couple of years after her father died. Bhutto, Hasina and Zia had to fight for a long time as party leaders before they got to the top. In the meantime, they acquired political insight and experience.

Even if they were substitutes, they did not acquire short temporary positions. All of them came to power 'for real', and as prime ministers, they most often had central executive positions in parliamentary systems with ceremonial presidents. Benazir Bhutto was an exception, having to share power with a strong president, and Sirimavo Bandaranaike also had to do this while her daughter was president. Kumaratunga, on her side, had the most powerful position as president. And several retained their top positions for a substantial period of time.

Without suitable family connections, women had small chances of becoming top leaders. Pratibha Patil was, in this sense, special. Her rise to power was primarily as an insider, climbing up through a political party. But it was the dominant party, and she was close to the important Gandhi family. Political parties usually served as tools for the elite, not as forums for democratic participation or channels for ordinary people to participate in political decision-making bodies. And she did not get a central power position, but became a ceremonial president.

Preference for women

In politically important families, sudden death, often political murder, allowed women to get a chance as top leaders. The deceased left an important gap that needed to be filled. It was generally a person who was regarded as a hero or martyr, and it was natural to look to the martyr's family. But why *women*, wondered the social scientist Rounaq Jahan (1987). In some cases (as with Indira Gandhi and Sheikh Hasina), there was no alternative. But in other cases (Sirimavo Bandaranaike, Benazir Bhutto and Khaleda Zia), there were male family members. The women's lack of experience, however, meant that they were more acceptable to the male party leaders who made the selection, Jahan noted. The women had no political past to defend, and the leaders believed that they would be easier to control. As political newcomers, they could present themselves to the voters as pure and moral, as opposed to the established leaders. In addition, they could appeal to people's sympathy as wives and daughters and come forward as honest and trustworthy in their loyalty to their dead leaders. Here, differences in culture and religion were without significance. By leading a non-violent opposition, women could also contribute to the fight against dictatorship. Perhaps they also were more willing than men to take the risk in a hazardous political world, such as Pakistan and Bangladesh.

For Chandrika Kumaratunga, the situation was different in the sense that the dominant party leader was her mother. Sirimavo Bandaranaike judged differently than male party leaders and appreciated Chandrika's strength and political profile. She preferred Chandrika as her successor instead of Chandrika's older sister or younger brother, a choice that created tension in the family and Chandrika's brother, Anura, went over to the opposition party UNP.[22] Pratibha Patil was also promoted by a female party leader, but it is unclear what counted most: Patil's competence or the fact that she was close to the family and loyal, or maybe it was a combination.

Benazir Bhutto was challenged by a younger brother with the support of her mother. But this was relatively late in Benazir Bhutto's career, and the battle ended when her brother suddenly died after a relatively short time.

Tough power struggles

To participate in politics, women were generally disadvantaged since they lacked the necessary financial resources, time, skills, experience, support, contacts and information. It is significant that no women in South Asia went to the top just because of their own ability. Generally, more was required, and members of resourceful families could get help overcoming obstacles to succeed in a political career. Apart from Khaleda Zia, all the female top leaders came from privileged families, and Khaleda Zia's husband established himself through the liberation struggle. All the top leaders, except Khaleda Zia, grew up in families who were engaged in society and learned politics from childhood. Khaleda Zia had only a conventional upbringing, and she was introduced to politics through her married life, but to a lesser extent than the other widow, Sirimavo Bandaranaike. Both widows had little formal schooling, while the women who followed in their father's or mother's footsteps, got higher education, partly abroad, and much higher than most women. Pratibha Patil also had a well-to-do family and got higher education. Nevertheless, most of the women had to be persuaded by party leaders before they took on the top positions. Such positions entailed not only power and privilege, but a breach of traditional roles, struggle and suffering.

The role as the substitute for a recognised leader was used for what it was worth. In all the countries, women's organisations were fighting for democracy and trying to strengthen the status of women. But if the gender of the women leaders could be an advantage, it could also be a handicap, particularly in the Islamist Pakistan, where men could not accept that they should be led by one of the 'weaker sex'. To obtain the positions of power, the women also had to show that they were able to lead, and be both tough and unyielding. After they had become party leaders, they also outmanoeuvred former leaders and recruited their own supporters.

The fact that the women top leaders were substitutes did not mean that the road to power was simple and straightforward. They inherited a special resource, but they often had to struggle not only to rise to power, but also to remain in office. Especially in Pakistan and Bangladesh, there was also political unrest. The climate was ripe for change, and the regimes were under pressure. This increased the women's chances. But, at the same time, they had to fight against authoritarian regimes for a long time, with incarceration and the risk of death, before they could get a chance. All the substitutes stood for election and thus became legitimate leaders. But then they were deposed or lost elections and had to work hard to come back. It took both courage and steadfastness. The president dismissed Bhutto, first, after one-and-three-quarter years, then after three years. The others usually continued until the end of their term, but the military deposed Zia at the end of her second period and arrested both her and Hasina. Both Gandhi and Bhutto were assassinated. In addition, Bhutto experienced that her two brothers were killed, and Bandaranaike and Kumaratunga that Kumaratunga was seriously injured and her husband killed.

Despite the difficult circumstances the South-Asian women top leaders exercised power for relatively long periods of time. The three women who died before 2010 had all in all been in power for close to 40 years: Bhutto for 5 years, Gandhi for 15 and Bandaranaike for 18. The other women were still active. Khaleda Zia had been in power for 10 and Kumaratunga for 11 years. Prathiba Patil ended her term as president in 2012 after 5 years and Sheikh Hasina was re-elected as prime minister in 2014 after having been in office for 10 years.

Roaring tigers and tame kittens

The main motivation of the substitutes was to carry on the policies of the deceased husband or father. Thus, their work was based on a man's vision and perspectives. The situation was different for Kumaratunga, who collaborated politically with her mother, and she followed up her mother's policies, but only partially. In any case, the woman top leaders functioned in surroundings strongly marked by men, and even if there was an active women's movement, the contact was limited, and the political agenda was, in fact, determined by others.

The top women could be criticised because they did not stand out from their male rivals and follow a 'different' line of politics, or because they served the interests of the family more than the nation or women. After they were elected, the women rapidly developed into leaders in their own right and exercised power the way men did. All of the women proposed measures benefiting women, but they did not call themselves 'feminists', and women's issues were rarely a chief concern. The boldest person defending women's rights was probably Benazir

Bhutto. On the way to power positions, the women often got the support of women's organisations and lobby groups, but at the top, they lacked a support system and structures to promote an alternative leadership style and political agenda. The parties did not focus on issues related to gender equality unless the women's movement pressured them into doing so, and parliament as well as the cabinet and administration were strongly male-dominated. The top women did not recruit women into politics beyond their own family, and it is an open question as to what extent these elite women could represent the wider population. After having evaluated the activities of the top women leaders, the political scientist Andrea Fleschenberg (2008) concluded that they were roaring tigers when it came to being elected and ruling the country, but tame kittens when it came to setting an agenda for women.

Worst in the world

While the region was characterised by a number of women top leaders, women's participation in politics in general was most often very low. In 2014, in South Asia as a whole, there was an average of 18 per cent women in parliaments and 7 per cent in cabinets. Culture and political institutions inhibited the entry of women in many ways. Religion, with discrimination of women and segregation in private as well as public spheres, made politics into an area for men. Authoritarian, militarised regimes gave no room for women, and women and women's organisations kept away from 'the dirty game', in which patron–client relationships, mafia, money, manipulation, muscles and violence played an important role. Quotas for women were established at national level in Bangladesh and Pakistan,[23] but apart from the quotas, it could be difficult for women to be nominated and elected to parliament. The few women who participated in the parties had little leverage, and the parties wanted 'winning candidates', that is, men. Moreover, most of the countries (except Sri Lanka) used a system of majority vote, which was unfavourable for women. Without being an MP, it was impossible to become prime minister or a member of the cabinet in most cases.

At least as important was the weak position of women in general. At the beginning of the 21st century, the region was characterised by unusually large gender inequalities, for example, in health and education. The differences were particularly great in North India, Pakistan and Bangladesh, while Sri Lanka differed from the rest of the region. Considerable progress improved the situation of women generally, but they nevertheless were among the worst off in the world. And patriarchal systems were deeply rooted, with arranged marriages, families following the paternal line, the favouring of sons and the training of girls to be subservient. There was little impetus for women to engage in society and politics, and they often lacked the necessary resources. Where they had more resources, as in Sri Lanka, the violent political climate was a major obstacle.

The President of the Philippines Cory Aquino at a press conference on 11 December 1989.
Aquino was president from 1986–1992.
Image: Getty Images.

Chapter Five

Equilibrists in East Asia

Manifold island realms

Twenty-five thousand islands

As geographically close and interlaced are the South Asian countries, as scattered and dissimilar are the East and South-east Asian – from Mongolia in the north to Indonesia in the south.[1] Here is one of the world's biggest countries, China, but also mini-states such as Brunei and Singapore. Most of the states are on the mainland (Indochina, China and Korea), but there are also extensive island realms (Indonesia and the Philippines). Economic activities, politics, social relations and culture vary across the region, and it is in the two island states that women have become top leaders during the last decades.

Both Indonesia and the Philippines consist of a multitude of islands. Indonesia is the world's largest archipelago, comprising over 17,500 islands, of which about half are inhabited. The Philippines include more than 7,000, but the majority of the people live on 11, of which Luzon and Mindanao are the most important. Historically, geographically and culturally, the islands are very diverse. Traders, missionaries and conquerors visited them and left traces. Philosophical and religious traditions such as Taoism, Confucianism, Buddhism and Hinduism became widespread, in addition to Islam and Christianity. Both archipelagos were exposed to prolonged colonisation, Indonesia by the Dutch and the Philippines by the Spaniards, and they had to fight for their independence. In 1898, Spain had to hand over its Asian colony, the Philippines, to the US. During World War II, the islands were occupied by the Japanese.

With more than 235 million inhabitants, Indonesia is the fourth most populous country in the world, with the largest Moslem population. The vast majority of Indonesians are Moslems. The islands include close to 340 ethnic groups. Javanese make up the largest group, with about 40 per cent of the inhabitants, and they have had a strong influence on the national government. The Philippines has just over 50 ethnic groups and more than 90 million inhabitants, most with Indo-

Polynesian backgrounds. They are essentially Catholic and the Church is strong, but there are also Moslems, particularly in the south.

From egalitarian to hierarchical societies

The ethnic groups on the islands vary from relatively egalitarian hunter-gatherers to complex hierarchical societies based on the cultivation of rice. Most live by traditional farming and fishing. In the Philippines, the Spaniards established rubber, coffee, sugar and tobacco plantations, and the Dutch, in addition to the trade in spices, started sugar plantations on Java. Industrialisation occurred during the last decades and education became relatively common, also among women, who are economically active to a great extent. But economic development has been uneven, with crises, among others, in 1997/98, where Indonesia was among the countries that were hardest hit. Indonesia was a low-income country for a long time, but in 2005, Indonesia and the Philippines were classified as middle-income countries.

Both in Indonesia and the Philippines, there are ethnic groups that have had strong patriarchal social systems with clear subordination of women. But there are also groups that have traditionally practised extensive social equality between women and men. Hierarchy was based on age, with the older being superior to the younger, while the two genders complemented each other as brothers and sisters. Spouses were equal partners in family, economic and social decisions. In Indonesia, there were female rulers in pre-colonial times, but the Dutch colonisers destroyed local forms of leadership and only allowed men to hold authority. In the Philippines, women lost their high formal and informal positions when the Spaniards and Americans came and imposed their Western patriarchal culture on the population.[2]

After independence, both countries established a centralised government, and tensions arose between the leadership of the state and some minority groups. The national government was strongly male-dominated in both countries. First, democratic systems were established with strong presidents, but before long, the military took over. The military regime lasted until the mid-1980s in the Philippines and the end of the 1990s in Indonesia. When the dictatorships fell, women top leaders suddenly appeared on the scene.

Cory Aquino, the Philippines' number one

Elite rule

Under the Spaniards, a strictly stratified society was created, with a landowner aristocracy exerting extensive control.[3] In spite of the poor, landless farmers revolting, the system was carried on by the Americans and marked the society also after independence in 1946. The Philippines acquired autonomy gradually, and democratic institutions according to the US model were introduced, with a strong elected president and an influential Congress with two chambers: the

House of Representatives and the Senate. Both were elected by simple plurality, the House of Representatives in single-member constituencies and the Senate from the country as a whole. The president was head of both state and government and appointed the cabinet. Unlike the British system, in which ministers were usually members of parliament (MPs), the two roles could not be combined according to the US model. Ministers were chosen from various quarters and were confirmed by a Commission of Congress.

The middle class was small and the government apparatus was weak. An elite of the privileged ruled political parties on the basis of patron–client relationships. In the 1970s, about 400 families dominated in industry, agriculture, banking and politics. The economy developed unevenly. At times, things went exceptionally well, but little was done to improve conditions for ordinary people. The US continued to have strong interests in the country, including military bases until the early 1990s.

The country's first woman president, Corazon 'Cory' Conjuangco Aquino, came from the upper class. Her father, Jose Conjuangco, was a wealthy plantation owner and banker and served as elected congressman. Her mother, Demetria Sumulong, also belonged to a wealthy, politically famous family and was an educated pharmacist. She supported the family's political activities.

Religious housewife

Cory was born in 1933 and grew up with two brothers and three sisters. She was number four. Had Cory been a boy, she would certainly have been brought up to work in public service, as the men in the family usually were. Her younger brother went into politics. But she was a girl and was sent to convent schools in Manila and the US. Family values and the Catholic faith were central, and she became a strong believer, with prayer as a daily support. At college, she took exams in French and mathematics. After seven years, she came back to the Philippines in 1953 and started to study law. Here, she met a fellow student and journalist politician, Benigno 'Ninoy' Aquino Jr, from another powerful, politically involved family. They broke off their studies and married in 1955. Thus, three mighty political families were united. Ninoy bought a farm and soon took over the operation of a sugar plantation belonging to Cory's family.

Ninoy Aquino had high ambitions. In 1955, he was elected as the country's youngest mayor, at 22 years old. In 1961, he became the youngest provincial governor, and in 1967, the youngest senator. Cory's role was to be the supportive wife of a politician making his way upwards. But unlike other wives of politicians, she stayed at home and took care of the five children. Ninoy's mother helped him organise the election campaigns.

The political parties were loose groupings based more on personality than policy. Often, they were split up, and politicians changed affiliation and entered into shifting alliances. The Nationalist and the Liberal Parties alternated being in power, but the policies were not basically different. Ninoy went from the nationalists to the liberals at the same time as Marcos went the opposite way. Marcos was elected president in 1965. When Aquino was elected to the Senate two years later as the only opposition politician, he soon acquired a reputation as a critic of the regime.

Martyr of the dictatorship

Ferdinand Marcos was popular to begin with: he built roads and schools and improved agriculture. But he developed a sultanistic regime[4] – a highly personal dictatorship where he ruled by means of fear and rewards for the benefit of himself and his contacts. The extensive and overt repression made communist-inspired insurgency activities expand, and the turmoil increased between Moslems and Christians in the south. Part of the upper and middle classes also disapproved of the regime. To stay in power, Marcos repealed the constitution and set aside the political institutions before the elections in 1972, and declared a state of emergency. Thousands of oppositionists, including Ninoy Aquino, were arrested.

The result was eight hard years in prison, first, with a lengthy trial, then with a death sentence. Unexpectedly, Cory Aquino was thrust into a political role as messenger between her husband and the surrounding world. Ninoy founded the Laban Party ('The People's Struggle') and stood for election from his prison cell. His wife had to hold press conferences and speak on his behalf. He was not elected, but became internationally famous as an opponent of dictatorship. When he had a heart attack in 1980, he was allowed to travel to the US for treatment and settled there with his family. But in 1983, he returned, despite warnings, to resume the political struggle. The moment he set his foot on Philippine soil, he was shot and killed.

Ninoy Aquino's death triggered huge sympathy demonstrations. Ninoy was iconised and the funeral procession in Manila lasted 11 hours, with about two million people. As the coffin was closed, a sobbing Cory bent over and kissed her husband farewell. 'I told him: "Ninoy, I promise, I will continue your struggle"' (Reid and Guerrero, 1995: 21). Until 1986, mass campaigns and demonstrations by organisations and opposition parties continued. Later, the events were characterised as a 'people power revolution'. But there were also other actors: businessmen, the Catholic Church, the old guard of politicians and the military. In addition, the US government, which had hitherto supported the dictator, worried that Marcos would lose control so that the communist insurgency would spread, and the already-weakened economy become even worse.[5]

Widow in yellow

A group of conservative reformists met to consult in the house of Cory Aquino's mother, and Cory chaired the meetings in her role as the widow of a political martyr. Many men wanted to face Marcos, but were not considered suitable or competent enough, or they represented just a small part of the broad people's movement. A person was required that was as unlike Marcos as possible, a person with integrity that could be accepted by all, and also by Washington. Salvador Laurel was the one in the opposition who had the most 'guns, henchmen and gold', which was what usually counted in Philippine elections. But being crafty and powerful, he was too reminiscent of Marcos and what ordinary people were against. Ninoy's brother, 'Butz', was suggested as a candidate, but many thought that he was too left-wing. In Ninoy's party, now called the PDP-Laban after a merger with the PDP, Philippine Democratic Party, Cory's brother was secretary general and he supported Cory. Although a man was best, a woman could also be accepted. There was a cult of feminine spiritual superiority among Catholics, and women had a traditional role as moral guardians. As Mrs Ninoy Aquino, Cory had a special force as an innocent and injured party who did not owe anybody anything and did not seek power for herself, but on the basis of higher values. She could get the support of the Catholic Church, unite the anti-Marcos opposition and transform the race into a battle of political morality.

Marcos suddenly called a 'snap' presidential election to be held on 7 February 1986. Cory Aquino hesitated. She did not want to be in the centre of the political limelight. She was a housewife with little knowledge of politics, paid employment or public life. But her children were for the most part grown up, and she wanted to complete the task Ninoy had started, helping people enjoy the fruits of justice, peace and liberty. When sympathisers collected more than a million signatures to convince her to run, she thought: 'I'd never be able to forgive myself if I have to live with the knowledge that I could have done something and didn't do anything' (Reid and Guerrero, 1995: 23). Dressed in her trademark yellow, she engaged herself in an active campaign, criss-crossing about the country. She drew large crowds to her meetings, often in religious settings, and became the spiritual centre for the anti-Marcos protest. She called for a peaceful, non-violent revolution and promised to lead the country 'in our quest for a better nation for ourselves and our children' (Crisostomo, 1987: 181; see also Reid and Guerrero, 1995: 24).

Revolution without a shot

In a country with a sense of personality cult, Cory Aquino became the newest superstar. It was not due to her feminine beauty. To Filipinos, Cory was presented almost as a saint, Mater Dolorosa, Joan of Arc or the Virgin Mary – in striking contrast to President Marcos. She was called 'Filipina Mary' – making Marcos appear, according to himself, as a mixture of 'Darth Vader, Nero, Machiavelli, Stalin, Pol Pot and maybe Satan himself' (Weiner, 1986). The dictator stressed that Cory was only a woman and could not do a man's job. A woman's place was in the home and she should confine her preaching to the bedroom. Cory Aquino admitted that she 'had no experience in cheating, stealing, lying or assassinating political opponents', but she was honest, sincere and devout. She led a moral crusade against an immoral dictatorship and challenged Marcos to 'stand up like a woman and answer truthfully to charges of cowardice, if he dared' (Komisar, 1988: 83, 90–1; see also Jensen, 2008: 162–6).

Marcos poured hundreds of millions of dollars into his electoral campaign. There was state terror and more than 200 people were reported killed. With a small margin, Marcos was declared the winner. But there were allegations of fraud, and Cory claimed that Marcos had stolen the election. Together with a group of younger officers, the Minister of Defence Juan Enrile and Vice Chief of Staff Fidel Ramos mutinied against Marcos, taking control over two military camps in Manila. When they understood that Marcos controlled most of the army, they asked the influential Catholic Archbishop Jaime Sin to gather people in the streets. Sin and Cory Aquino appealed over the Catholic radio for support of the rebels, and the military uprising was taken over by civilians. During four days, from 22 to 25 February, millions of people demanded that Marcos should withdraw. He sent tanks against the crowd, but the soldiers were greeted with flowers and women in prayer. It turned out to be 'a revolution with a smile', without a shot being fired. And the miracle happened.[6] On the fourth day, Marcos fled with all his company. Cory Aquino was president, at 53 years old.

'Cory's Crusaders'

'Cory's Crusaders' they called themselves, the women who demonstrated to bring Cory Aquino into power. They were numerous and stood in the forefront. Before the Spaniards came, Filipino women had a strong position in local society, but the Spanish and US rulers relegated them to the home and family. Nuns founded the first girls' school in the late 1800s. The Americans focused on education and development of the country, and after the turn of the century, several girls' schools and women's institutes were established, and in 1910, a women's university. Women also obtained important academic and administrative posts. The next step was the right to vote. Universal male suffrage was ensured in 1935. Women organised themselves, presented their claim and won in 1937, after nearly half a million people answered 'yes' in a referendum. While women in the middle and upper classes fought for political rights, women in industry fought for better wages and working conditions. Women also participated in the protests against US colonial rule. After independence, some women were elected to public office, especially at the local level, but also nationally. Yet, politics remained a male domain. From 1946 to 1971, not more than 11 women were elected to the House of the Representatives and seven to the Senate, while four were members of the cabinet for shorter or longer periods of time.

During the Marcos dictatorship, women enrolled in the armed underground movement. Militant nuns and radical activists defended human rights and protested against the US bases and extensive 'sex tourism' that went with them. When Ninoy Aquino was assassinated, a multitude of large and small women's organisations from different social strata entered into broad coalitions against the dictatorship and played an important role, both symbolically and practically. The fact that a woman was the only viable contender and suddenly could become president illustrates the extent of mobilisation and the crisis that the country was in.[7]

'Soft' reign

After the election, the political working days started. Cory Aquino was poorly prepared. Nobody had time to prepare a change of regime. They stood on the barricades one day and found themselves in the halls of power the next. For Cory Aquino, this was her first (and only) job. And when she moved from protests and campaigns to political governance, the forces in action changed. The power she had outside of the formal structures, based on popular support, was replaced by relative powerlessness within the political institutions. She was hailed as a hero of the people, but the fact that she was a woman and represented 'the people' was not appreciated. It could even be a disadvantage when she was supposed to be in charge of the established political system. To begin with, she appointed three women ministers, responsible for planning, social affairs and education, but they only amounted to 10 per cent of the cabinet.

Aquino was elected under a broad opposition banner, personalising the popular uprising as a unifying mother figure. But 'understand that I came to power on the crest of a loose coalition of forces. Two of them were at mortal odds with each other: the left and the military right' (Roces, 1998b: 80), Aquino explained at the end of her reign. As president, Aquino felt that her mission was to be above the political parties, yielding to neither side. So, she did not join any party and did not found a separate 'Cory party' as relatives wanted her to do. Thus, she lost the support and influence that a party could have given her, for example, in Congress. And it did not take long before the broad coalition that brought her to power began to disintegrate.

When she appointed her cabinet, Aquino tried to place it in the political centre to take care of the breadth of the popular movement. But she chose the traditional approach and went after friends and supporters. Thereby, two highly hostile male rivals became members of cabinet. Former Senator Salvador Laurel, who led a group of opposition parties and was Aquino's stablemate during the election campaign, became not only vice president, but also prime minister (which was unusual) and minister of foreign affairs. He claimed to be the actual head of state, which he said Cory Aquino had promised him if he withdrew as a presidential candidate before the election. Opposing him was Defence Minister Juan Enrile, who had hoped to lead a junta after a military coup against Marcos, but instead now found himself as a minister, in addition, under the leadership of a woman whom he perceived as being weak in relation to the communists. Both men called for a new presidential election immediately, and when Aquino refused, they supported coup attempts in the months that followed to give Cory Aquino her 'right' symbolic role.

As a whole, the cabinet represented the established elite, most very wealthy. Catholic businessmen, who gave money to the campaign, became ministers of finance, trade and industry. Folk close to Ninoy Aquino and human rights groups got important positions, while Fidel Ramos continued as army chief. The political views spanned from Left to Right. Intense tugs of war arose within the cabinet, and the president often changed ministers. The various groups supporting Cory Aquino outside of government also disagreed among themselves.

To lead the country, a political programme was required. But apart from continuing Ninoy's battle, getting rid of Marcos and restoring democracy, Cory Aquino provided little political direction. She referred to social reform, land reform and peace with the guerrillas, but only vaguely. She shied away from being a strong leader. To develop a new political culture based on popular participation in contrast to the oppression of the Marcos regime and to survive as a woman in politics, she chose a 'soft' democratic approach, trying to serve the people with altruistic love. She could take a strong stand, but often she kept a low profile and left decisions to the ministers, with the result that the government lacked focus and priorities. The president's moral integrity was not questioned, but she was perceived as weak and indecisive, partly uninterested. As various ministers were replaced, in practice, technocrats down the ranks took over the administration of policies, and the governance developed a clearly conservative character.

Problems everywhere

The new president faced an unruly, impoverished nation devastated by political turmoil and years of misrule and corruption. Although the Philippines was a middle-income country, there were extensive class disparities, large-scale unemployment, an underpaid labour force and massive poverty. Telephones did not work, roads needed repair and schools lacked teachers. At the same time, Marcos had contracted a crushing foreign debt. There was an active communist insurgency, three Moslem secessionist movements and a factionalised military.

President Aquino began restoring democracy. She cancelled the Marcos constitution, dissolved his puppet Congress, reintroduced press freedom, released political prisoners, (including communists, which provoked the army strongly), removed people from positions they had received from Marcos and appointed a constitutional commission. Following a national referendum, the constitution became effective in 1987, maintaining a US-style presidential system, and competitive elections were organised.

The restoration of democracy strengthened the reputation of the Philippines abroad. In 1987, Cory Aquino was designated woman of the year by *Time* magazine. It was only the third time a woman had been given this honour and the first time it concerned a female politician. As president, Aquino sought international help to strengthen the government and improve the run-down economy. She negotiated with the US government, the World Bank and the International Monetary Fund (IMF) and obtained capital assistance and development aid. But, at the same time, it became difficult to fly the flag of the opposition's reluctance to accept foreign debt and US military installations in the Philippines.

Cory Aquino liquidated some trade monopolies, but she left further economic policy and land reform to the new Congress. Here, there was little willingness to reform. When Congress was to be elected, Cory supported candidates from the establishment, often with family ties. Her candidates dominated the elections, and, as a result, the assembly was marked by the elite. To achieve reforms, the president was dependent upon Congress, but the golden opportunity for far-reaching changes had passed. It was impossible to make Congress adopt a real agenda for redistribution of resources to the weakest in society, and poverty reduction and economic reconstruction were slow. At the same time, the old local clans benefited from the situation and re-established the private armies that Marcos had stopped.

The president started peace talks with the communists, but did not get an agreement, so the fighting continued. However, an agreement was reached with the breakaway Cordillera People's Liberation Army (CPLA), known as the Mount Data Peace Accord. Peace was not obtained with the Moslems, either, and supporters of Marcos demonstrated in the streets. Facing nine coup attempts during her term, some supported by Enrile and Laurel in her own government, Aquino was almost toppled in the bloody August 1987 and December 1989 putsch efforts. She punished those responsible, but conformed quietly to demands and sought support where she could to remain in power. The army was strengthened, and Fidel Ramos became minister of defence. Aquino joined forces with strong capital interests and became increasingly dependent on the US. In 1989, she had to get help from US fighter planes to stop the rebels. A series of natural disasters – earthquakes, volcanic eruptions and typhoons – did not improve the situation.

'Mother of Democracy'

Cory Aquino managed to finish her term. 'Success' to her was handing her power over to others. Under the new constitution, the president's office was also limited to a single term. Afterwards, Aquino continued her work in voluntary organisations.

In 1992, the Philippines was a quieter place. The Communist Party was weakened, and the army no longer represented a threat. But the country was constantly turbulent, with poor governance, poverty and corruption. The democratic institutions that were re-established after the Marcos dictatorship were as dominated by the elite as before, so Cory Aquino was characterised as an 'elite restorationist' (Hutchcroft, 2008: 144). And although President Aquino was not accused herself, her family was charged with corruption. The economy grew, but less than in the rest of South-east Asia, while the population increased rapidly. Health and education were generally improved, but not much.

Cory Aquino's greatest achievement was her role in the popular revolution. Without her, it is doubtful whether the uprising against Marcos would have succeeded. She managed to create democratic institutions and stay in power for six years, despite the rebellion, coup attempts and chaotic political conditions. Her emphasis on non-violence, the separation of powers and the rule of the law was an important contribution to the democratisation of the country, and she was given the name 'Mother of Democracy' (Whaley, 2002). When she retired, there was a peaceful transition to a new president. Some said her presidency was 'a miracle', while others thought she 'barely scraped through in a way'.

Cory Aquino demonstrated that a woman could have as much integrity and determination as a male president. But Cory Aquino fell short with regards to social and economic change. Expectations were exaggerated. Strong counter-forces defended the established order, while the opposition was poorly organised. Aquino lacked leadership qualities and was more concerned with process than issue. The US-inspired system also limited the president's possibilities of governing. The president could issue executive orders and sign bills approved by Congress, but only Congress could initiate and pass bills, the approval of both chambers being required for the passage. Special interests – landowners, industrialists and regional politicians – could easily stop reform efforts. Instead of mobilising the population for reform or building a coalition in Congress and the cabinet to push issues forward, the president was content with advice from family. Arguably, she was inexperienced and had a poor administrative grasp, but it is also possible that she was not particularly interested in reform. Her roots were in the landowning elite, and it was difficult to fall out with the US government. When the military bases were terminated in 1991, it was against Cory Aquino's wishes.[8]

Power-loving First Lady

The historian Mina Roces (1998b: 39-50, 75-89) compared Cory Aquino with Imelda Marcos, the wife of the dictator, who was First Lady from 1965 to 1986. She got some formal positions, but as First Lady, she only had informal power. On the other hand, she used it in an unrestrained manner. She interfered with a whole range of policy issues, raised money, conducted large-scale projects and was involved in foreign policy and international diplomacy. She was called Marcos's 'alter ego', and according to some, she was the first female national political leader in the Philippines, if not in name, then at least in reality.

During the state of emergency, the Philippines had what is described as a 'conjugal dictatorship'. It was not uncommon in the islands that women exerted political influence behind the scenes. From the perspective of Roces (1998b: 7), Philippines politics/power is *not* male-dominated, but *gendered:* men generally exercise official power, while women exercise unofficial power via their kinship and marriage ties to male politicians. Imelda took the role as a politician's wife, protector and benefactor to new heights. She became the woman in the post-war period that exploited her unofficial power position the most. Whatever one may think about the policies she pursued (and they were heavily criticised), Imelda Marcos stood in sharp contrast to Cory Aquino, who had the highest official position, but hesitated to use power in a decisive manner. With regards to influence, Roces thought that the character of the person was even more important than the kind of power that they were given.

After Marcos died in exile in Hawaii, the widow turned back to the Philippines in 1991, ran for president twice and lost, but was elected to the House of Representatives in 1995 and 2010, although there were unresolved corruption allegations against her.

Reserved advocate

Cory Aquino thought that politics should not remain a bastion of male dominance:

> There is much that women can bring into politics that would make our world a kinder, gentler place for humanity to thrive in. It seems that it is only when women take matters into their own hands that they are able to secure their rights and privileges as full human beings, equal partners of the menfolk. It is up to the women who are in positions of power and responsibility to push for the equality that women aspire for and deserve. (Aquino, 2002: 143–5)

The Philippines was party to the UN Convention on the Elimination of All Forms of Discrimination against Women (CEDAW) (since 1981) and Aquino appointed women in high positions. Six became members of the constitutional commission, and gender equality was included in the constitution. Aquino did not have many women ministers. Gradually, the number reached seven. In addition, she appointed more than a dozen women to lower positions in the administration – among others, Gloria Macapagal-Arroyo, who became her successor. But Aquino did not address important women's issues such as the right to divorce and reproductive rights. Marcos supported birth control, but Cory did not want to challenge the Catholic Church. She established a commission for the development of Filipino women in general, and women benefited from her emphasis on democratisation and measures for the poor. But a woman in power did not truly empower the most vulnerable women in society.

During Aquino's term, a very small number of the bills passed in Congress were related to women, only 18 in total. And the initiatives were taken by male, not female, legislators. Women's organisations, however, were working tirelessly to promote ideas, frameworks and strategies for social reform (Veneracion-Rallonza, 2008: 234–40).

More women participated in politics, but not many. Whereas two women were elected to the Senate and 19 to the House of Representative, a total of 9 per cent, in 1987, four women were elected to the Senate and 23 to the House of Representatives, a total of 11 per cent, in 1992.

At the presidential election in 1992, two of the seven candidates were women. Besides Imelda Marcos, there was Aquino's former minister of agriculture, Miriam Santiago, who finished as number two with just a few votes less than Fidel Ramos. Even though she lost, it was a victory for women because Santiago ran for office not as a substitute for a man, but on the basis of her own qualifications. Aquino, however, supported Fidel Ramos, though he was a liberal Protestant. As minister of defence and chief of staff, he supported her all the time she was president. But he had been deputy chief of staff under Marcos and was elected president with record-low voter participation, only 5 million or 24 per cent of the votes. But nobody had more votes, and there was no requirement that the winning candidate should have more than half of the votes. Santiago got 4 million or 20 per cent of the votes.

Gloria Macapagal-Arroyo, the Philippines' number two

President's daughter

Nine years after Cory Aquino concluded her presidential term, a new woman rose to the top in the Philippines.[9] Gloria Macapagal-Arroyo (popularly known as 'Gloria' or 'GMA') was not elected as the head of state, but acquired the position by means of a new 'people power' revolution. Unlike her female predecessor, GMA was well prepared. She descends from Lakandula, the last reigning Rajah of Saludong. Her father, Diosdado Macapagal, was president of the Philippines from 1961 to 1965, and she herself worked in the Aquino administration, was a senator for six years and vice president for two.

Macapagal, 'the poor boy from Lubao', was the son of a farmer and a cleaning lady. He received help to go to school and became a successful lawyer. Then, he undertook a PhD in economics. He was a skilled orator and was elected, first, to Congress and then as vice president with support of the Liberal Party. He was the first of peasant stock who became president of the Philippines and was known for his work for the poor, including a land reform (which was rather watered down, however, before it was adopted). He was called 'the incorruptible', but was also, like his predecessors, accused of corruption and lost when he ran for re-election against Ferdinand Marcos. Evangelina Macaraeg was Macapagal's second wife (his first died during the war). As the daughter of a US-trained engineer, she came from better conditions than her husband. She was talented and studied medicine, but gave up her work as a physician when she got married. As the First Lady, she participated actively in her husband's work and took care of his well-being and entertaining.

Gloria was born in 1947 and grew up with two older siblings, a half-brother and a half-sister, and a younger brother. She was raised in two places: in San Juan in the Rival province in the north and in her mother's hometown in the south in Mindanao, where she lived with her maternal grandmother. However, when I interviewed her in Manila in 2003, she told me that she felt that she was the one of the children who was closest to her father. She attended Catholic school in Manila, was a gifted student and became a professing Christian. When her father became president, Gloria was 14 years old. They moved into the presidential palace, and she accompanied her parents on official visits to Italy, Spain, Pakistan and the US.

Having finished secondary school, Gloria went to the US to study at Georgetown University, where she was a classmate of former president Bill Clinton. Her education was cut short after two years, however, when she came home to marry, at 21 years old. Jose Miguel 'Mike' Tuason Arroyo was a law student of the same age from a wealthy, politically active family. They had three children, two boys and a girl. Gloria completed her undergraduate education with a degree in commerce and planned to stay at home to raise her children as her husband wished. But she soon returned to academia. Her husband explained: 'I saw how bored she was, how I was wasting away that intelligence. So I told her she should go back to school, do what she wanted and I'd support her. I've supported her since' (Crisostomo, 2002: 19). Gloria earned a master's degree in economics in 1978 and a PhD in 1985. At the same time, she worked as an assistant professor. Her husband became a lawyer and a businessman.

Diligent senator

Gloria Arroyo did not intend to go into politics, but in 1987, Cory Aquino offered her a position in the Department of Trade and Industry. She became assistant secretary, then under-secretary and, in addition, executive director of the Garments and Textile Board and governor of the Board of Investments. In 1992, she agreed to be candidate for the Senate. The children were fairly grown up and the centre-right LDP, *Laban ng Demokratikong Pilipino* (Democratic Philippine Struggle Party) asked her to run. Macapagal was a good name. GMA had a useful education and did well in the department. Moreover, a woman was needed to balance the great number of men. Gloria was engaged in issues related to society and decided to take her father's well-travelled road. Mike Arroyo found delight and fulfilment in campaigning with and for his wife. He became her manager, fund-raiser, writer, photographer and chief image-maker and helped her to get elected (Crisostomo, 2002: 19–22).

It was an advantage to be a woman in the elections to the Senate, GMA explained to me when I spoke with her. Women usually voted for women, while men did not mind women being elected. It was different in the presidential elections. Then, many people felt that a woman was not tough enough. Men did not like, either, that a woman should make decisions about them. In order to be treated equally as the president, a woman had to be more proficient than a man, GMA emphasised.

Gloria stood for election after her father had given her the green light. Her mother hated politics and warned her against it, Gloria explained, but when Gloria first got involved, she helped her nonetheless. The LDP won a majority, and GMA was a very diligent senator. She filed more than 300 resolutions and bills, ranging from indigenous rights to export development. A number were passed into law. Several concerned women: credit for small entrepreneurs, an increased minimum wage for house helpers and measures against sexual harassment and trafficking. GMA was particularly preoccupied with economics. She advocated a free market with a social conscience, as she called it, and authored laws strengthening the private sector and liberalising foreign investment. When she ran for re-election in 1995, she got nearly 16 million votes, which was a record in the Senate elections. The others who were elected got between 9 and 13 million votes. As a woman, GMA stood out, and she had shown that she was capable.

Movie hero and paragon of virtue

Under the administration of President Fidel Ramos, the country was relatively stable and experienced significant, if uneven, economic growth. Ramos fought actively against corruption and organised crime, tried to bring an end to the military coups and managed to get a peace agreement with Moslem rebels. Limiting armed opposition was beneficial to women, and Ramos issued a number of gender-responsive executive orders and proclamations, inspired by the Beijing Platform. Also, during his presidential term, the number of women-related bills passed in Congress increased to a total of 26. The Party List System Act, Anti-Sexual Harassment Act and Anti-Rape Law were adopted, the last after seven years of active lobbying by women's organisations.

The Asian financial crisis began in 1997. Despite opposition, Ramos implemented economic reform policies that led to economic growth. But in 1998, his term ended.

Then, Gloria Macapagal-Arroyo became the first woman vice president, with record support. Actually, she wanted to run as president, but Ramos said she was 'too young, too ambitious and too inexperienced' (Crisostomo, 2002: 25). So, Gloria agreed instead to be the vice presidential running mate of the House speaker, who was a candidate for president with the support of the conservative Christian Democratic alliance of Ramos. In the election, however, the House speaker was defeated by the more right-wing movie star Joseph Estrada. The voters could vote for a president from one party and a vice president from another. All in all, there were 11 candidates for president and nine for vice president. Despite the fact that Arroyo did not belong to Estrada's party, she was elected as vice president, with 13 million votes, three times as many as Estrada's running mate, a male senator. Estrada himself got 11 million votes. Thus, GMA became vice president and also cabinet secretary of welfare and development. She initiated an early childhood development programme and sought foreign money for welfare projects.

Estrada came from the middle class, but dropped out of school, and in a number of movies, he was the defender of the poor. When he became involved in politics, he was supported by broad segments of poor Filipinos and was elected as senator, then vice president and finally president. But as president, he showed little interest in politics. The media described him as a populist self-glorifier and criticised his dissolute lifestyle with alcohol and mistresses. After a number of financial scandals, Estrada's intervention in gambling led to his downfall.

As a consequence of a 'popular revolution' number two ('People Power 2'), GMA became president. It was declared that democracy was saved, but actually the democratic rules were broken. As in the first 'popular' revolution, the protesters wanted to force a corrupt president to resign. The support ranged from the political Left to Right. Some perceived it as a popular protest from various groups, while others believed that there was a conspiracy of people from the elite, and even the military. At the head stood two former presidents, Cory Aquino and Fidel Ramos, together with Archbishop Jaime Sin. It was claimed that Estrada should be brought to an Impeachment Court. A court was established, but the process was obstructed by allies of the president. Mass demonstrations were then organised to get Estrada to resign. When he did not, a unanimous Supreme Court declared that the position of president was vacant on 20 January 2001. Now there was, unlike the last time, a constitutional successor, and 53-year-old Gloria Macapagal-Arroyo was sworn in as president a few hours before Estrada left the presidential palace.

Philippine tangles

GMA was an 'unintended president', and the change was dramatic. A woman took over from a womaniser, a doctor of economics from a movie star, a workhorse from a man about town. Apparently, Arroyo had broad support as president and she became the president in the history of the Philippines who sat the longest, nearly a decade. But her presidential period was unusually stormy and beleaguered.

In 2003, Arroyo told me: "I will follow in my father's footsteps and do what is right. God will take care of the rest. My father is my role model. My living role model is Cory Aquino." She wanted to win the fight against poverty, strengthen democracy, combat terrorism and improve the morality of the administration and society as a whole, particularly by counteracting corruption and clientelism.

But her leadership was met with protests from the beginning. The popular demand for a change of regime was not as clear and compelling in 2001 as in 1986. As soon as GMA was inaugurated, her legitimacy was disputed. Estrada claimed that he was the legally elected president, and when he was arrested and accused of plunder, the presidential palace was stormed by hundreds of thousands of followers who wanted to force Arroyo to withdraw. It was called a 'popular revolution number three', and this time, it was spontaneously driven forward by poor people. The president declared a 'state of rebellion' and managed to restore peace and order, but for a while, the situation seemed critical.

Arroyo appointed a large cabinet, with people who supported her against Estrada, technocrats and Aquino and Ramos people, including seven women, and in the legislative elections in 2001, her coalition got a majority in both the House of Representatives and the Senate. She initiated measures and worked hard, 16 hours a day, six days a week. But there were problems.

In my interview with her, GMA explained that she went for the presidential position with the intention of improving living conditions, but discovered that she had to start by strengthening institutions: introducing computers during the elections, raising the salaries of soldiers and police, reforming the judiciary, strengthening the market system, making civil society function, and so on.

The economy was unstable. Islamic militants took hostages, and when the president refused to pay the ransom and sent in the military, the families paid anyway, reportedly also to Filipino officers. Groups from the army rebelled. GMA's husband was criticised for interfering too much with his wife's work and, in addition, was accused of corruption. For a period of time, he lived in exile.

Controversies

Since Arroyo was not elected president in 2001, but only took over the 'unfinished' term of President Estrada, she was not constitutionally barred from running for president in 2004. During the period 2001–04 Arroyo projected the persona of an 'Iron Lady'. Now, she reorganised and became head of the presidential coalition. It was a tough battle against four competitors, of which one was a popular male actor who was close to Estrada. She won with a scant lead, obtaining 40 per cent of the vote against 37 per cent for the actor. The GMA coalition also got a majority in Congress, including the election of Arroyo's eldest son. But there were reports of incidents of violence, bribery and fraud. The president was accused of having intervened herself to influence the election result. The matter provoked strong reactions, though there was no solid evidence that she actually committed election fraud. GMA publicly apologised for talking to an election official, but denied any wrongdoing. Yet, the atmosphere became so inflamed that 10 ministers quit and Cory Aquino, who originally backed Arroyo, asked her to resign. Fidel Ramos, however, supported GMA. And she continued.

In the years that followed, Arroyo was exposed to harsh criticism, coup attempts, riots, street protests and bombings. She strengthened her position by establishing ties to key players such as Roman Catholic bishops, top military officers and business leaders. The cabinet was reshuffled several times, and a great number of retired generals participated or headed various government agencies. On photos, GMA stood as a tiny doll in front of a high wall of tough uniformed officers. There could be no doubt about who was in control and 'rescued the damsel in distress', as people said.

Business and government were accused of corruption and cronyism in an atmosphere of impunity. There were scandals and human rights violations. Internationally, there was growing concern particularly regarding disappearances, arbitrary detention and killings of leftists, activists and community and religious leaders around the country by death squads and the army. In 2006, the Philippines was downgraded from the status 'free' to 'partly free' by the US Freedom House, and the country was declared as the most dangerous country for journalists to work in, after Iraq. In 2007, Arroyo declared an 'all-out war' against the communists. In 2008, a number of impeachment demands were presented on the grounds of corruption, extrajudicial killings, torture and illegal arrests. But they did not receive sufficient support in the House of Representatives (at least one third of the members) to be dealt with. And the elections for Congress in 2007 were as hampered by problems as the 2004 elections. GMA won a majority in the House of Representatives, but not in the Senate. Both of her sons became members of Congress.[10]

Weak democracy

The restoration of democratic structures after the fall of the Marcos dictatorship revealed many underlying issues: the role of the military in politics, major economic and social disparities, and the power of the elites and the local clans. There were special problems related to the political institutions. The new constitution was drawn up in a hurry with the aim of representing all interests. It was perhaps the world's longest and was not always appropriate. Congress, the election administration and political parties were weak and ineffective and became characterised by abuse of power and corruption. The entire political process was rotten, declared the speaker of the House of Representatives in 2007 (Hutchcroft, 2008: 151).

President Arroyo tried to reform the democratic structures. She wanted to revise the constitution, but met strong resistance. And as the Philippines suffered one political crisis after another, the country's already weak political institutions were, in fact, further weakened. As before, Arroyo was the 'Iron Lady', and after 11 September 2001, she was a faithful supporter of the US in the war on terror. But her policies alternated and she was also described as the 'Great Compromiser' because of her willingness to accommodate anyone able to help her retain the presidency (Hutchcroft, 2008: 142–4). Estrada was sentenced to life imprisonment for plunder, but, afterwards, he was pardoned by the president. Arroyo abolished capital punishment, but implemented a law against terrorism that worried human rights groups and the Church. When she stepped down in 2010, Moslem and communist insurgencies were festering. For the first time in 30 years, Arroyo declared martial law in December 2009, following an election-related massacre. But unlike President Marcos, who declared martial law in the whole of the Philippines, she only did it for Maguindanao.

Growth without equality

As an economist, it was particularly important for Arroyo to ensure economic growth and reduce poverty. In her inaugural address in 2004, she vowed to create more than six, even ten million jobs in the next six years, develop one, if possible two million hectares of agribusiness land, build economic opportunity for the poor and establish justice for all (Macapagal-Arroyo, 2004).

The economic situation was difficult. She continued the economic policy reforms that President Ramos started, and improved infrastructure and communications, with new roads and airports. Houses were built, jobs were created for the poor and health and education services were strengthened. Assistance, not least from the US, in addition to increasing cash flows from Filipinos abroad, helped boost the economy. The growth was also relatively high compared with other Asian countries, expanding each year of Arroyo's administration. The Philippines was one of the few economies that avoided contraction during the 2008 financial crisis. But when Arroyo stepped down, there was a large budget deficit and poverty increased.

The economic expansion benefited the elites, big business and politicians above all. The Philippines was considered one of the most corrupt countries in the world, at the top of the list in Asia. And Arroyo failed to reduce income inequality. The Philippines lagged behind other East Asian countries, with hunger among the impoverished on the increase, and the impoverished included more than half of a rapidly growing population. The growth was the fastest in South-east Asia (Thompson, 2010).

In 2004, *Forbes* placed GMA as number nine among the world's 100 most powerful women, and in 2005, she was moved up to number four. But in the years that followed, she went down: to number 45 in 2006; 51 in 2007; 41 in 2008; and 44 in 2009.

Dubious profile

Neither Cory Aquino nor Gloria Macapagal-Arroyo was a 'feminist'. Arroyo became known for her statement that 'leadership has no gender'. But to my question as to whether she was interested in women's issues, she replied: "I have had an agenda for women since I started in public service. It consists of two parts: the promotion of economic rights and protection of human rights".

During Arroyo's terms as president, women made social and economic gains. Filipino women in general ranked better than their male compatriots with regards to life expectancy, literacy rates and education. But there were 'layered levels' of discrimination, and the majority of women remained particularly vulnerable (Tarczynski, 2009). The Arroyo government was criticised for a limited implementation of laws and follow-up of women's rights. Non-governmental organisations (NGOs) had to step in instead. A number of women-related bills were enacted into law during Arroyo's presidency, but this was not because Arroyo pushed for their passage. They were the result of the efforts from government and women's organisations. The laws related, among other things, to solo parents' welfare, anti-trafficking in persons and anti-violence against women and children. In 2009, after seven years of lobbying, a Magna Carta of Women was adopted to promote women's rights more generally. It was signed by President Arroyo, although the document had a strong emphasis on reproductive health.

Arroyo's policies relating to population and reproductive rights were the most controversial. Abortion was illegal in the Philippines and Arroyo did not take action to reduce fertility. As Cory Aquino, she went against birth control. The Catholic Church did not favour most family-planning programmes, except natural methods, because they were deemed abortion techniques. So, Arroyo would push for responsible parenthood, she declared, but not use government funds to promote the use of contraceptives (see: www.isiswomen.org). Thus, contraceptive use remained limited, particularly among the numerous poor, and unsafe abortions represented a pressing health problem.

Arroyo appointed a number of women in the government administration, and to begin with, the number of women ministers increased. In 2003, she said that she had nearly 40 per cent women in the cabinet, and they constituted a block that managed to implement women-oriented initiatives, such as microfinance. But there were frequent replacements, and in 2010, the cabinet only had three women ministers (14 per cent). In the House of Representatives, the number of women rose to 56 (21 per cent) in 2010, but in the Senate, there were only four women (17 per cent).

As president, Arroyo could exhibit courage and strength, speaking her mind and taking unpopular decisions. And she managed to stay in office until the end of her second term. But it was noted among Filipinos that while Cory Aquino demonstrated that a woman could have as much integrity and determination as a man, Gloria Arroyo showed that a woman could also be as tough and corrupt as a man.[11]

New Aquino takes over

In 2010, Arroyo could not be re-elected as president, but she ran and became member of the House of Representatives. The elections were the most free and fair since 1965, and the election campaign was marked by the fact that Cory Aquino died on 1 August 2009. Her son, Benigno 'Noynoy' III Aquino, shot up as a leading presidential candidate and took a strong stand against Arroyo. On television, he declared "I do not steal from you", with a picture of his parents in the background, and he was elected as president against eight other candidates, with 42 per cent of the vote. One of the first things that he did was to appoint a truth commission to investigate allegations of fraud and corruption against Arroyo and her administration. Arroyo was arrested and charged, but in 2012, released on bail.

In the meantime President Benigno Aquino supported a bill on reproductive health aimed at giving couples the possibility to use contraceptives if they chose to, though the Bishop said that he might face excommunication. In December 2012, Congress passed a law protecting women's rights to reproductive health after a decade of lobbying from women's organisations and medical professionals, and in 2014 the Supreme Court upheld the law (Amnesty International, 2012; WUNRN, 2014). After the elections in 2013, there were 78 women (27 per cent) in the House of Representatives and six (25 per cent) in the Senate. In Aquino's cabinet there were only four women (16 per cent).

Megawati and Moslem men in Indonesia

Despot and liberator

When Gloria Macapagal-Arroyo was elected president of the Philippines in 2004, she had a sister in Indonesia with less luck.[12] Megawati was also the daughter of a former president, the 'Father of the Nation', and, like GMA, became vice president. The two were of the same age, and their fathers had left politics at the same time. When the Indonesian president had to resign in 2001, as the president of the Philippines also had to, Megawati moved up. She served as president for three years and then ran for re-election. But unlike Arroyo, she lost.

Megawati's father, Sukarno (many Javanese have only one name), led the liberation movement under Dutch colonial rule. He was the son of a schoolteacher from Java and a woman from Bali, went to Dutch secondary school, and studied architecture and engineering in Bandung. In 1927, he was co-founder of the Indonesian Nationalist Party and became its first leader. A women's rights movement was formed and women contributed to the independence struggle. Universal suffrage was introduced in 1941. From 1942 to 1945, the Japanese occupied Indonesia. A constitution was prepared, and when the war was over in 1945, Sukarno immediately declared the country independent. The result was a bitter armed and diplomatic conflict before sovereignty was accepted by the Dutch in 1949, and Sukarno became the country's first president.

The new state had a difficult start. The population was poor, with little education, and the economy was destroyed by war. At the same time, development was hampered by low commodity prices, political unrest and poor economic management. Indonesia was established as a unitary republic based on pluralism and representative democracy. It was described as 'presidential with parliamentary characteristics'. Elections were held in 1955. The government was weak and unstable, however, and there were ethnic/religious antagonisms. The other islands were sceptical of Java's dominance, and there were tensions between the army, Islamic groups and the communists.

Sukarno was a nationalist, Marxist and anti-imperialist. He became a charismatic leader of Afro-Asian nationalism and the movement of non-aligned states. On the home front, a revolt in Sumatra made him declare a state of emergency in 1957, and he introduced a 'guided democracy', legitimised as the antithesis of so-called 'Western' democracy. Parliament was replaced by a designated body, and Sukarno ruled in an authoritarian way as president, with support of the army and the communists. Dutch enterprises were nationalised and major construction projects were initiated in the middle of a declining economy.

For some, Sukarno stands as a revolutionary demagogue and despot who mismanaged the country. For others, he was the nation's father who freed and united the people and made them proud to be Indonesians.

Thirty-two years of dictatorship enough

Under the Cold War realities, Sukarno moved the country to the 'Left'. Indonesia's Communist Party was reportedly the largest outside the Soviet Union and China. The country became increasingly dependent on aid, above all, from China, and there was a growing conflict between the party and the army.

In 1965, there was a coup, and Soeharto-led troops took power. The blame for the coup was put on the communists. The party was banned, and in the riots that followed, thousands of communists were killed. General Soeharto became president, while Sukarno was placed under house arrest, where he died in 1970.

The military rule lasted for 32 years. Military personnel were established at every political level, from ministers to governors and village leaders. They were awarded 155 seats in the People's Consultative Assembly and operated within the commercial sector. In the 1970s, more than 20,000 military served in non-military functions. The Golkar Party became the political arm of the regime, with a wide-ranging national organisation. Only two other parties were allowed – an Islamic party: the PPP, *Partai Persatuan Pembangunan* (United Development Party), and a non-Islamic party: the PDI, *Partai Demokrasi Indonesia* (Indonesian Democratic Party) – with severely limited activities, and the media were censored. The New Order regime, as it was called, denationalised industries and introduced a market economy, opened up for foreign investment, and received aid from the US. Using oil revenues, agriculture and industry were developed. Living standards were improved and the number of poor decreased. Health and education were strengthened. Almost everyone got access to basic education, and family planning was introduced.

People reacted against the rampant corruption that, not least, the Soeharto family and its closest associates benefited from, and the use of authoritarian methods. There were outbreaks of violence and religious and ethnic conflicts. The relocation of landless farmers from Java to other parts of the country increased the antagonisms. When the East Asian financial crisis hit in earnest in 1997, and living conditions were greatly worsened at a stroke, protests occurred in many places. A broad democracy movement emerged and Soeharto was forced to resign in 1998.

A disorderly and sometimes violent transition to democracy followed. Repressive laws were repealed and prisoners were released. The constitution was amended and authority was strongly decentralised to the regions. The president was head of state and government, while a 700-member People's Consultative Assembly was the supreme political assembly, electing the president and vice president every five years. It consisted of 500 members of the House of Representatives and 200 selected representatives from provincial assemblies and functional and political groups. The special representation of the military continued. The House of Representatives was mostly directly elected with proportional representation, but adopted legislation had to be ratified by the president, who appointed cabinet ministers, often technocrats, who were responsible to him. In 1999, democratic general elections were held for the first time in 44 years, and Megawati came out as the winner.

Overtaken by the past

Women's organisations criticised Sukarno for being a sultan with a harem. In all, he had nine wives. After he divorced his second wife, he married Fatmawati, a young woman from Java. With her, he had his first child, a son named Guntur in 1944, then Megawati in 1947 and, afterwards, the daughters Sukmawati and Rachmawati, and finally his son Guruh. Both the boys and girls aroused great enthusiasm, but their childhood was not easy. Their father was preoccupied with his duties, at times, becoming the object of assassination attempts. Fatmawati left Sukarno with Guntur when he took a new wife in 1953. This was much to the dismay of the other children, who were left in the presidential palace, entrusted to the servants and not only one, but eventually several, new wives. Megawati was a devout Moslem at the same time as she followed Javanese tradition. She tried to take care of her younger siblings and was described as a 'soft and motherly' young woman (McIntyre, 2000: 4; 2005: 143).

Despite Sukarno's male chauvinistic attitude to his wives, he valued women's roles in traditional societies and designated the feminist pioneer Kartini (1879–1904) as a 'National Hero'. He proudly supported Megawati's desire to become an agricultural scientist and help improve Indonesia's food supplies. She started studying in Bandung, but dropped out when her father was overthrown by General Soeharto. In 1970, she began studying psychology, but left before completing the course. She married a pilot and had two boys before her husband was killed in a plane crash not long after her father died. An impromptu marriage with an Egyptian diplomat was quickly annulled. In 1973, she married an activist in the Sukarno Party student group. Taufik Kiemas was a man of modest means, but became a successful businessman, managing a chain of petrol stations. Their marriage produced a daughter and Megawati stayed at home as a housewife and took care of the children.

For many years, Megawati remained outside of politics. But the government-sanctioned successor of Sukarno's party, the Indonesian Democratic Party (PDI), was weak and divided. When Sukarno was rehabilitated in 1986, the party leader asked Sukarno's children to support the party in the semi-democratic elections in 1987. They were particularly interested in Guntur, who was very reminiscent much of his father. But only Megawati (and her husband) accepted. Later, she said: 'I had no thoughts of becoming a leader. At the time I felt that since my children were already independent, I might as well become active in politics' (McIntyre, 2000: 8; see also 2005: 152). Megawati participated in political discussions in the family in her childhood, and there was a widespread impression that she wanted to continue her father's work. Her sisters refused because they did not want to associate themselves with any particular party, and the PDI was not radical enough anyway, in their view. Guntur gave priority to his company and was, in general, closer to his mother. Guruh joined in 1992 (and the sisters later).

Silent symbol

Megawati lacked political experience, but she was appreciated as her father's daughter and was considered to be incorrupt. She had charisma and attracted people from different backgrounds. She was perceived as a person who supported the weak and poor, while the elite thought she would influence the business climate in a favourable way. Large crowds showed up, and the PDI increased its support. Both Megawati and her husband were elected to parliament.

Central party members asked Megawati to become the leader of the PDI, which she accepted. She was elected with great enthusiasm in 1993. But the authorities did not accept the election. Both she and the PDI were threatened, followers were arrested, offices were attacked, and several people were killed. Megawati preached non-violence and prevented retaliatory actions. But in 1996, the regime staged a party coup. When Megawati maintained that she was the rightful leader of the PDI, the party split into two factions.

Going against Soeharto was courageous, and Megawati became famous and popular in the opposition. She remained extremely calm all the time and turned into a silent symbol of resistance against injustice and brutality in contrast to the regime's abuse of power. Megawati did not participate actively in the demonstrations in 1998, but ran for election with her own PDI-P (P for *Perjuangan*, 'struggle') Party in 1999. The party was based on her fraction of the PDI and stood up for secular nationalism, pluralism and adjustment. Megawati was the leader and was re-elected in 2000 and 2005. Her brother, Guruh, was responsible for the party's education and culture department. There was internal tension and rivalry within the party and disillusioned members left, including Megawati's two younger sisters, who formed new parties.

In the elections for the People's Consultative Assembly in 1999, a total of 48 parties participated. PDI-P obtained the most votes, with 34 per cent. Then, the Golkar Party got 22 per cent and an Islamic party led by an old family friend, Abdurrahman Wahid, called 'Gus Dur', got 12 per cent. The old PDI only obtained 0.5 per cent.

Swindled out of the presidency

At independence, there was only a small elite of men and almost no women with formal education. Two women ministers were appointed in 1946 and 1947, but none in the 1950s, and in the elections in 1955, women only got 6.5 per cent of the seats in parliament. Later, representation varied, but remained low.

In Soeharto's authoritarian state, there was little room for organisational and political activity, and few women were given positions in the sanctioned parties. During the United Nations Decade for Women (1976-85), a Ministry for

Women was created, with a junior minister outside the cabinet. Indonesia became party to the CEDAW in 1984. Women's living conditions were improved and gender differences in education and income decreased. But only three women participated in the Soeharto cabinets, and women's subordinate position was generally emphasised instead of the diversity of gender roles around the country. Only after 1998 could women's rights organisations freely do their work, and the number of organisations increased. At the elections in 1999, 16 women from the Golkar Party became members of the Consultative Assembly and 15 from the PDI-P. Overall, 40 women (8 per cent) were elected.

The president was to be elected by the Consultative Assembly, and many took for granted that Megawati would get the position, with her high number of votes. She had a strong sense of entitlement, but she lacked experience with lobbying and the new, competitive form of politics. There were few women in the Assembly and other leaders gathered against her, partly to avoid a female president. She was criticised for her three marriages, because she did not cover her head in a pious manner and because she lacked higher education. Megawati was reticent with regards to declarations about what she would do as president. It seemed clear that she, like her father, would emphasise secular nationalism and a strong centralised government, but beyond that? The media saw her as a question mark.

Abdurrahman Wahid was elected with 373 against 313 votes, despite the fact that he came from a minor party and clearly had weak health. Disappointed PDI-P supporters protested furiously in the streets, and the day after, Megawati was elected as vice president, with 396 against 284 votes. Wahid noted dryly: 'We make a perfect team, I can't see, and she can't talk' (McIntyre, 2000: 15). In another public context, he called her 'stupid' and unable to take over his role. Generally, Megawati ignored such sexist remarks, but she replied once that being a housewife did not mean that one did not understand politics (Bennett, 2010: 182).

Moslems change views

Abdurrahman Wahid was respected for his thoughtful and moderate Islam, but as a president, he was no success. He was soon criticised for his erratic leadership style, mismanagement and corruption and was forced to resign in 2001. This time, preparations were done beforehand, and 54-year-old Megawati was unanimously elected as president. After extensive discussions, the majority of Moslem leaders who opposed a female president eventually changed their view and accepted that a woman could acquire the position (Doorn-Harder, 2002). It was not as in Pakistan, where Benazir Bhutto encountered a wall of hatred because she wanted a man's job. However, PDI-P did not have a majority alone, and as vice president, Megawati got the leader of the largest (moderate) Islamic party. He had previously gone against a woman president, but now said that it was better to have a woman than an incompetent and corrupt man. In the interest of national unity, Megawati accepted him.

Her cabinet was a 'rainbow cabinet', with representatives from the main parties, a number of military personnel and professionals from the Soeharto administration. It was no easy task to head such a coalition, and Megawati functioned more as a head of state representing the whole than a prime minister driving through a specific programme. She rarely held political speeches and left most of the business to others. The policies lacked clear goals and were, to a large extent, based on the pillars that were established in society, the Golkar Party and the army.

As the newly elected president, Megawati summarised the tasks she faced: maintaining the nation's unity; continuing reforms and democratisation; restoring the economy; consistent upholding of the law and eradication of corruption; conducting a free and active foreign policy; and preparing for safe, orderly and clean general elections in 2004 (Fic, 2003: 219). It was an overwhelming challenge. The economy was run-down, with a huge national debt. There were separatist movements in several provinces, and the transition to democracy was incomplete.

Megawati was criticised for her lack of action, but she pursued allegations of human rights abuses and established anti-corruption and judicial commissions, auditing bodies, and a constitutional court. The democratisation process continued, albeit slowly and unevenly. She abolished the military-dominated Supreme Advisory Council, but the army regained much of its influence. After initially negotiating a peace in Aceh, she declared military rule, and subsequently a state of emergency, when problems arose. The political situation calmed down, and, in particular, the violence between Christians and Moslems diminished. The economy improved, and the government was praised both domestically and abroad for its handling of economic policy (Bennett, 2010: 191–4). In 2004, there was still widespread corruption, unemployment and lawlessness, but *Forbes* placed Megawati as number eight among the world's 100 most powerful women (the only time she was placed on the list).

'Mother Earth' fails women

Megawati presented herself as a mother figure, who would replace the arrogance and aggression of her predecessors with care and respect. Her supporters called her 'Mother Earth'. But the women's movement blamed her for not helping women: she did not support family planning and neglected important questions such as trafficking, violence against women, guest workers and women in politics. The two male presidents before Megawati set up a commission on violence against women, changed the name of the Ministry for Women to the Ministry for the Empowerment of Women and appointed an active minister. But Megawati replaced her with the head of the governmental women's organisation of the Soeharto regime, who had not distinguished herself as a feminist, which was criticised.

In her cabinet, Megawati only had one woman among 33 ministers, but there were some women at the lower levels. When she was asked why she did not have more female advisors, she said: 'It is still a tradition (in Eastern culture) that the woman has the duty to stay in the background. It's very hard and tough work. I am doing it, yes, but that is why I think I am rather unique' (Jensen, 2008: 186).

Due to pressure from women's organisations, the electoral law was changed before the elections in 2004, and a passage was included stating that the parties would 'carry in their hearts' the desirability of having 30 per cent women among the candidates. It was called a 'maybe quota'. Although the wording was weak, it was perceived as a victory for the women's rights movement. But the results were disappointing. Megawati, for example, went against the use of quotas. She believed that everybody should be treated equally in a democracy (Parawansa, 2005). In the elections the representation of women in the House of Representatives increased, but not by much. A total of 62 women were elected (11 per cent), 19 from the Golkar Party and not more than 12 from the PDI-P. The PDI-P did badly in the elections and only got a total of 19 per cent of the votes.

For the first time, the president was to be directly elected. There were five candidates, including Megawati as the only woman. In the first round, she received 26 per cent of the vote, while the main opposition candidate, the former army general Susilo Bambang Yudhoyono, known as SBY, with his new 'Democratic Party', got 34 per cent. In the second ballot, Megawati lost against SBY, with 39 against 61 per cent.

Woman against the military

Why was Megawati defeated? A significant factor was that she was a woman. While religious leaders had accepted her, many ordinary Moslems were against a female president. Women traditionally had a strong position in some Indonesian ethnic groups, but among the largest groups, the majority were patriarchal with male leadership. In Java, where Megawati came from, men were seen as spiritually and physically stronger than women. The supporters presented Sukarno as an ideal and a martyr, but views were mixed, and Megawati could not run as a new moral alternative in 2004, as she could in 1999, because she had been in power. It was also noted that some people wanted a strong man in an unsafe security situation, and Megawati appeared withdrawn and passive in relation to the more dynamic and aggressive style of the rival candidate. Other factors were also mentioned in the comments, but there was little emphasis on the candidates' policies. Regarding the programmes, both were vague, though SBY was more specific than Megawati. The difference in support was explained mostly by the image of the candidates.

It was striking that a former military officer could succeed in a country that was trying to free itself from military dictatorship. The whole of SBY's education and career were military, but he was one of the few senior officers who had not been directly implicated in the atrocities the army was accused of, and there were no corruption charges against him. SBY was minister for security in the cabinets of both Gus Dur and Megawati, but left both of them because of disagreements with the president. He looked good on TV and presented himself in the campaign as 'new', a man of principles, with a good grasp on democracy and human rights, while able to solve the country's problems. From before, he was best known for his leading role in Indonesia's fight against terrorism, after bombs were detonated in Bali in 2002 and many innocent people were killed.

Ambiguous silence

Megawati did not get the benefit of the doubt. She was the only candidate who had been responsible for the policy during the years before the elections and was blamed for rising prices and unemployment. Many considered her a mediocre leader, who had disappointed her fans. When she was elected, it was hoped that she would have a calming and soothing effect through her ability to listen and be a team player, and her emphasis on community and reconciliation. This also happened, but, at the same time, Megawati came across as careful and uninvolved, distant from most people. She symbolised her father, the first president of the Republic, and was, in a sense, born to rule. According to Javanese tradition, this implied that she should sit as a good queen with charismatic power that manifested itself by reticence, not action (Anderson, 2007: 13–19). It is further possible that the men around her were opposed to her acting as a leader and interfering with their activities. In 2001, part of the central government's authority was also decentralised.

Inconsistencies in Megawati's politics and political beliefs abounded. Her father's legacy was ambiguous, and, at times, she was divided between aspects of her father's views and her own values. She had limited education and political experience, and apart from secular nationalism and a strong, united, democratic Indonesia, it was unclear what she stood for. In some cases, she took a definite stand, while, at other times, she changed her mind. She was particularly criticised for inaction and vacillation in connection with the terrorist attacks. The cabinet was very heterogeneous, and she often got conflicting advice. It was no easy task to implement reforms with collaborators who were not very reformist, and to protect the interests of the weak with politicians from the elite. Because she said little, it is hard to know what she really thought. Some perceived her silence as evidence of political cunning, while others was saw it as a sign of intellectual weakness. She simply did not have anything important to say (McIntyre, 2005: 201–50).

Despite her one-term presidency, the teacher of religious studies Clinton Bennett notes that the first Moslem woman head of a modern state has a place in history. And she was not overthrown, forced out or impeached like a number of male presidents. Instead, she played a significant role in Indonesia's democratic transition (Bennett, 2010: 194).

Poor repetition

Nevertheless, Megawati did not give up. She continued as party leader and ran again as presidential candidate in July 2009, as the only woman against two men. And she lost again. She got fewer votes this time, 27 per cent, while SBY was re-elected in the first ballot with 61 per cent. He formed a new cabinet with 14 per cent women.

Megawati ran with a candidate for vice president who was formerly a lieutenant general, married to a daughter of President Soeharto and convicted of having a role in the kidnapping of anti-Soeharto demonstrators in 1998. SBY chose a former vice president of the Golkar Party. As for SBY, it was particularly noted that his presidency had not been hampered by the continual political and financial scandals that had plagued the work of earlier presidents and that the country had good economic growth and progress in poverty reduction and had managed to come relatively unscathed through the global financial crisis of 2008/09. He was criticised for not being sufficiently action-oriented and not succeeding in the fight against corruption, particularly in the police and the judiciary. However, in the first directly televised programmes showing a debate between presidential candidates, SBY came out with the best marks.

The PDI-P also lost votes in the legislative elections and became the third-largest party, with 14 per cent. The Golkar Party got 14 per cent and SBY's party got 21 per cent. In total, 38 parties participated in the elections. The representation of women increased to a total of 102 (18 per cent). Megawati's husband, Taufik Kiemas, was elected speaker and her daughter was a prominent member of the House of Representatives. In addition, she became deputy leader of the party. In the cabinet, there were only four women (11 per cent) in 2012.

When a dictator falls

Innocent woman against despots

As so for South Asia, it can also be said that there was a governance crisis that weakened democracy in the Philippines and Indonesia. Following independence, the political institutions were largely established according to Western models. State control was centralised in scattered archipelagos with great economic, social and ethnic/cultural differences, and with politics marked by elite power, personal networks and patron–client relationships. The army played a central role, and countries soon got military dictatorships (see Figure 9).

The three East Asian women came to power in a democratisation process, and the political scientist Mark R. Thompson (2002/03, 2004) was struck by how often since the mid-1980s women led popular uprisings against dictatorships in Asia. Four of six successful democratic revolutions (Bangladesh, Pakistan, the Philippines and Indonesia) and two of three unsuccessful revolutions (Burma and Malaysia) were headed by women.[13] Women participated actively in social movements in many countries, but patriarchal barriers prevented them from gaining leadership positions in democracy movements and opposition parties, and they were accordingly – with the possible exception of Indira Gandhi –

Figure 9: Asia and Pacific: regimes by type, 1946–2012

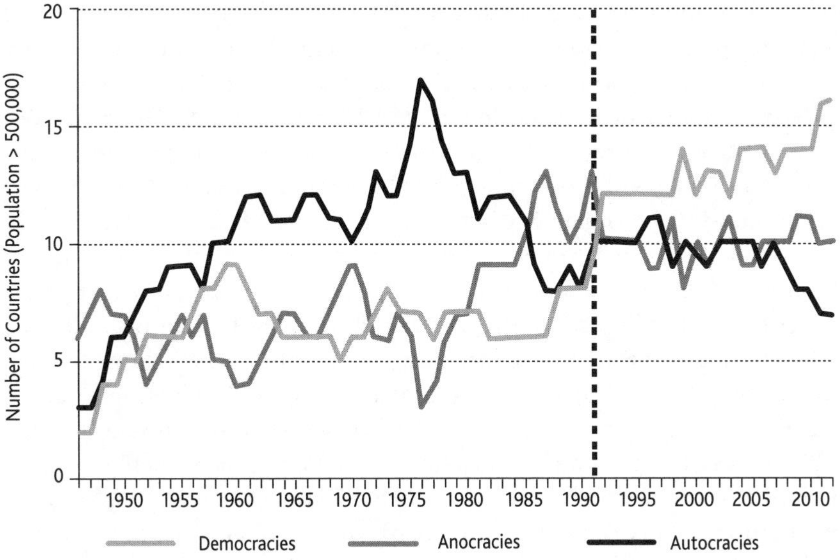

Note: Anocratic governance is a system placed somewhere between democracy and autocracy. The power is spread between elite groups competing for power.
Source: Center for Systemic Peace, Polity IV Project (CSP, 2013) (see: www.systemicpeace.org).

excluded from negotiations between the opposition and the rulers regarding the transition to democracy. In general, very few women became top leaders. How could women be 'over-represented' among the leaders of democratic revolutions in Asia, Thompson wondered.

All the Asian countries have strong patriarchal traditions, with an emphasis on male dominance and women's non-political role in the family. In East as well as South Asia, these traditions, paradoxically, helped the female leaders of democratic revolutions, according to Thompson. Since women were perceived as weak, they were less threatening as political rivals, at the same time as the selfless, decent 'mothers' and 'sisters' emphasised the moral character of the struggle against dictatorship. This was true for Islamic countries as well as for others.[14] Culture only provided part of the explanation for the women top leaders. The prevalence of patron–client systems also plays a role. Although these were not confined to Asia, they seem to be particularly widespread there, and dynastic succession was a common outcome of family-based political networks. Further, political assassinations brought such succession into question more often than they would have been with normal lifetimes.

Family and gender

Women's political representation is low in most of Asia. Even in the most affluent societies, such as Taiwan, South Korea, Singapore and Malaysia, where women have obtained higher education and positions in economic life, there has only been a slow increase of women in politics. The fact that women became leaders in East as well as South Asia was not, first and foremost, due to their expertise, but to their family ties. They belonged to important political families, came to power as substitutes for a deceased relative and brought the political work and vision of the departed father or husband forward. In East Asia, this was most obvious in the case of Cory Aquino. Her husband was a political martyr, and only a few years passed from when he was shot until she became president. Their fathers were important for the other two, but least for Gloria Macapagal-Arroyo. Her father was only president for one period and had a good reputation, but quit in the normal way because he lost the election. Megawati's father, however, had a special position as the founder of the nation and was president for over 20 years before he was deposed and died under house arrest. In both cases, about 20 years passed from their fathers leaving the political arena to the daughters entering.

For all the women, their gender made a difference when they rose to the top. Women generally had the strongest position in the Philippines, where it was not uncommon that they exerted political influence behind the scenes. And as the widow of a martyr, Cory Aquino came forward with moral integrity in contrast to the dictator Marcos, while objections against a women leader were not too strong. GMA could also appeal to female voters. For Megawati, it was more difficult. As an alternative to a military leader, she had the advantage of appearing as a woman with a conciliatory and motherly attitude, but broad Moslem communities went against a woman as president, and in her leadership role, she lacked political dynamism and focus. For all of them, it was a positive part of their femininity that they were considered 'clean', not corrupt and with an unblemished past.

If their gender could be an advantage, none of the women was the first choice in the recruitment for the political leadership positions. In the Philippines, there were a number of men who wanted to stand up against Marcos, but they were either deemed unsuitable, were controversial or were unwilling to get involved. So, Cory Aquino was the solution. In the case of Megawati, the party would rather have her brother when they were seeking one of the Sukarno children. But he refused, and Megawati got the chance instead. Then, she won the 1999 election, but a man was preferred as president. It was only when he turned out to be unfit that Megawati moved up. GMA was first rejected as a presidential candidate because the coalition would rather have a man. But then she got the most votes as vice president, and became president by chance because the man who was elected created too much dissatisfaction.

Both the Philippines and Indonesia had presidential systems without prime ministers and the three women acquired the country's highest political position. But they had to take advantage of the opportunities. Aquino ran for and was elected president, while the other two were elected vice presidents and then promoted. None of them got short-term temporary positions. Aquino was in power for one term – six years – and was happy to hand the position over to somebody else. Megawati and GMA ran for re-election. Megawati lost, while

GMA won a second term after a disputed election. All in all, Megawati was in power for three and GMA for nine years.

Mixed competence

The top women were partly poorly qualified for a political top job. All came from well-off elite milieus, though GMA's father was originally poor, and they grew up in politically engaged families. Cory Aquino was the least prepared for political leadership. She studied French, mathematics and some law, but stayed at home as a housewife after she married and had children. Only when her husband was in prison did she become a messenger and a speaker on his behalf. She was 50 years old when her husband was murdered. From his death until she became president, not more than three years passed of campaigning and opposition activities.

Megawati grew up in the presidential palace, but her mother left her when she was little, and her father was very busy with his political activities. GMA was a teenager when her father became president, and before that, she had partly lived with her maternal grandmother. None of them participated in politics before they were called upon at a mature age. Both married, Megawati three times, and had children. But their children were adults when their mothers got engaged in politics. GMA was 45 years old when she was elected to the Senate and Megawati was 40 years old when she entered parliament. GMA had by far the best education, with a PhD in economics, and the most relevant political experience, with important positions in the state administration and service as a senator. She had Cory Aquino as a role model when she ran for the highest office, and was not the first, but the second, woman president of the Philippines. Megawati did not complete a degree in either agriculture or psychology and worked as a housewife. She was an MP and party leader, but it was quite a different matter to engage in opposition politics under a dictatorship than to function as a top leader in a more competitive democratic system. When she took over as president, she had only been vice president for one-and-three-quarter years.

Strength becomes weakness

All the three woman leaders got exceptionally demanding and difficult leadership roles, with untidy political conditions and uncertainty about the rules, weak political institutions and tensions between authoritarian and democratic courses of action, and contradictions and conflicts, in addition to urgent financial problems. It took a bit of a balancing act. Male leaders would also have had governance problems in such a situation, but the women's problems were probably greater because of the poor correspondence between female and leadership roles.

The same personal qualities that contributed to a successful democratic revolution were unfit for executive authority and the consolidation of democracy. If it could be an advantage in the fight against a dictator that a woman had an unblemished past and differed from traditional male politicians, this became a hindrance to political leadership when the woman acquired the top position. She experienced difficulties exerting power and did not easily master the political game. Male rivals opposed her and even tried to overthrow her because a woman was supposed to rule in name but not in reality. This was particularly noticeable in relation to the police and the military. Military dictatorship strengthened patriarchal forms of governance, and the military continued to have considerable influence even after a change of regime. Cory Aquino and Megawati were especially perceived as weak leaders, but it was not just a question of 'strength' and 'weakness'. Different cultures and leadership styles also played a role.

The women top leaders wished to continue their father's or spouse's visions, as they understood them. In this way, they acted as the men's substitutes. They were radical in the sense that they wanted to replace authoritarian rule with democracy. But what 'democracy' actually should imply, apart from formally elected political bodies, was unclear. Furthermore, there were not only high, but in reality exaggerated, expectations of what the women could achieve. People were often disappointed when the women leaders did not manage to implement measures or significant changes in the system and practices. In both countries, elite control and patron–client relationships continued, and the women presidents were hit all the harder by allegations of corruption and nepotism because they had promised principled governance. GMA was especially criticised. But the women prevented new military coups, and neither Cory Aquino, GMA nor Megawati were removed from their positions by force. Aquino and GMA completed their terms. Megawati failed when she stood for re-election, but the change of leadership took place in a democratic manner.

An active women's movement supported Cory Aquino and GMA in their rise to the top. In Indonesia, women were surprised when Megawati was suddenly an option for vice president, but soon got mobilised. None of the three leaders were feminists and were criticised by women's organisations because they acted in the same way as their male rivals and failed to follow up on important women's issues, particularly related to reproductive rights. But Aquino and GMA implemented less controversial measures that benefited women. All of them appointed women in positions in the administration and politics, and in both countries, women's participation in politics increased. But the two countries did not differ significantly from East Asia in general.

Han Myung-sook: on her own merits in South Korea

Development and democracy

In contrast to the predominant pattern elsewhere in East Asia, there was one woman head of government in recent years who did *not* lead a democratic revolution, and who did not come forward as either a widow or daughter of a prominent male politician.[15]

During a democratisation process, women gain a new power position as voters. The parties become dependent on female votes to win elections and are consequently motivated to appeal specifically to them. One way of doing this is to recruit women and give them high posts. This happened in South Korea.

After the Korean War in 1950–53, South Korea registered record growth in the 1960s and 1970s, with an urban industrial economy and rising income and education, also for women. But the regime was authoritarian, the military budget was among the world's largest and women were subordinate to men. Gradually, the opposition grew, and a democratisation process started. In 1992, for the first time in 30 years, a president with no military affiliation was elected, and in 1997, a representative of the opposition, the veteran pro-democracy campaigner and centrist Kim Dae-jung, was elected president for the first time.

The president was directly elected for a five-year non-renewable term and functioned as head of both state and government. He was assisted by a prime minister and a cabinet that was approved by the single-chamber parliament elected with proportional representation. There were no restrictions on who could be prime minister. But extremely few women were engaged in politics (only 4 per cent of the MPs were women) and the arrangement was complicated when the president did not have a majority in parliament. The parties were very unstable, with splits, splintering, new formations and mergers. This frequently resulted in changes of prime minister and, even more often, of ministers. President Kim Dae-jung appointed eight prime ministers in five years.

In 2003, Roh Moo-hyun was elected president. He was also a centre liberal, but replaced most of Kim Dae-jung's team. He doubled the number of women in the cabinet (from two to four), and at the general elections in 2004, the representation of women in parliament more than doubled, to 13 per cent.

Election tactics

During his term, Roh Moo-hyun appointed seven prime ministers. When the fourth prime minister resigned because of a scandal, he appointed a woman as the fifth in 2006. It was the 62-year-old Han Myung-sook, a former dissident who had been imprisoned because of her opinions. She was born in 1944 in Pyongyang, now the capital of North Korea, but fled south when the Korean War started. She completed master's degrees in Christian theology and women's studies and a bachelor's degree in French. Han Myung-sook was a devout Christian, and in 1968, she married a professor whom she met in the Christian student club. They had a son, but her husband was imprisoned for more than 12 years because of his involvement in the democracy movement. Han Myung-sook was also a social activist and took part in the democracy movement. She was brutally arrested, tortured and imprisoned for two years.

Han Myung-sook worked to improve the status of women and became leader of a women's organisation. When democracy was well-established, she joined a centre liberal party and was elected to parliament in 2000 and 2004. Here, she fought for women's rights, such as extended maternal leave, and became minster of gender equality during 2001–03 and of the environment during 2003/04. For her efforts for women, she was called 'Godmother' of the feminist movement.

When Han Myung-sook was appointed prime minister, it was said that a woman prime minister was supposed to strengthen the party's support because of the president's weak position. It was stressed that Han Myung-sook was 'clean', with no connection to any scandals. And the woman prime minister was approved with 182 of the 264 votes in parliament. This was remarkable, all the more so because Kim Dae Jung had tried to get a female prime minister in 2002, but failed. When he appointed the president of the female university in Seoul, Chang Sang, waves of shock went through the political establishment. For the first time, a prime minister was subject to approval examination by parliament and was rejected by 142 against 100 votes.

Women's groups welcomed the appointment of Han Myung-sook with joy. 'A historic day we will remember', they said. There were two women ministers when Han Myung-sook took over, and she did not change this. But the job as prime minister lasted less than barely 10 months. She visited the United Arab Emirates, Kazakhstan and Uzbekistan to promote economic cooperation, urged Western companies to invest in an economic zone shared by North and South Korea, accepted the expansion of the US military base near the capital Seoul, and was praised for her 'stable state administration'.

Massive wall of men cracks

In 2007, *Forbes* placed Han Myung-sook as number 40 of the world's 100 most powerful women. But in March, she withdrew to run for president at the elections that year. However, she did not succeed in the nominations. The presidential candidates were all men. In 2008, Han Myung-sook ran for re-election to parliament, but was not elected. In 2012, however, she led the largest opposition party, the Democratic United Party, for three months and was elected to parliament.

After democratisation, women in South Korea could rise to the top on their own merits. But even if they had high levels of education and administrative experience, it was not easy. Women leaders represented a break with the established male-dominated society and with Confucian philosophy, which prescribed an unequal relationship between men and women.

When a woman became Korea's first female president, in 2012, she had a very special, high status family background. She was the daughter of one of the founders of modern Korea, the country's longest ruling dictator, Park Chung-hee, who was president from 1963 to 1979. Park Guen-hye was his first child, born in 1952, went to school in Seoul and received a bachelor's degree in engineering. Her mother was assassinated in 1974 and the daughter served as de facto First Lady until 1979, when her father also was assassinated. Ms Park remained single and childless. She joined the conservative Grand National Party and became member of the National Assembly from 1998 to 2012. As leader of the party she was so successful that her supporters gave her the nickname 'Queen of Elections'.

Running for president in 2012, Ms Park travelled all over the country, apologised for human rights abuses committed by her father and promised a new dawn in relation to North Korea. Contrary to the hardline policy of her predecessor, she wanted to establish a 'trustpolitik' and an era of harmonious unification. 61 years old, Park Guen-hye obtained 52 per cent of the votes, while her main opponent, the Democratic United Party's male candidate, Moon Jae-in, only got 48 per cent. Many older people, in particular, perceived Ms Park as a symbol of stability. She was also elected to parliament, where there still were few women, totally 47 (16 per cent). And in her cabinet only 2 women were appointed ministers (12 per cent) (Rauhala, 2012; Alexander, 2013, CNN staff, 2013).

Official portrait of President Dilma Rousseff at the Alvadora palace, the official residence of the president in Brasilia, at the inauguration on 9 January 2011.
Image: http://en.wikipedia.org

Chapter Six

Machismo, marianismo and modernism in Latin America

Violeta Chamorro: Peace Dove in Nicaragua

In Asian style

Suddenly, it was no longer the militant Daniel Ortega who led the war-torn Nicaragua. It was a mild, white-haired grandmother. How could that happen? And how could it work out?

When Violeta Chamorro was elected president, the Ortega Sandinista regime was replaced by a 'democratic' regime, and a successful transition to peace took place. Chamorro has been compared with the women who brought about democratic revolutions in Asia (Thompson, 2002/03). She was a widow. The election meant the end of a bloody conflict. It was the first time that power was transferred from one party to another in a peaceful manner, and the system of government was changed. But was it actually the same kind of revolution?[1]

Dictator's downfall

Nicaragua's history has been marked by invasions and civil war, tyrants and oligarchs, use of force and murder.[2] The country is strategically located between two oceans and was occupied by the Spaniards in the 1500s. Battles, slavery, disease, abuse and escape reduced the Indian population and the inhabitants became a mix of people with Indian, Spanish and African origin. The Spaniards built cities, but the economy was primarily based on agriculture. A patriarchal political system was established, which was influenced by the Catholic Church, business organisations, patron–client networks and the military. Economic and social disparities were large and a small, mighty elite ruled over the masses of poor farmers and workers.

When Nicaragua seceded from the colonial power in 1821 and became an independent republic in 1838, politics were characterised by rivalry and armed conflict between liberals and conservatives. The Conservative Party was based on large cattle farmers, while the Liberal Party represented coffee cultivators and businessmen. They took turns being in power, but all ruled in an authoritarian way. The winners persecuted the losers, tearing down what they had built up, and exploited resources. In 1912, the US sent in the marines to stabilise conditions, and the occupying forces stayed for nearly 20 years. In 1927, nationalistic rebels revolted under the leadership of Augusto Sandino. They had broad support in the population, and to strike them down, a modern national guard was created under the command of Anastasio Somoza García. Sandino was murdered and Somoza García took power.

From 1936 to 1979, Nicaraguans lived under the Somoza family's violent authoritarian rule. Somoza García controlled political power directly as president or indirectly through puppet presidents. He owned or controlled large portions of the economy, had the military support of the National Guard and collaborated closely with the US. There was corruption and nepotism, lawlessness and oppression. Elections were manipulated. In the 1960s and 1970s, industry was developed and the economy grew, but the regime exploited the resources for its own benefit. Conditions were dramatically aggravated when the capital, Managua, was hit by a devastating earthquake in 1972. Opposition spread, but had it not been for the Sandinistas, the Somoza clan would hardly have been divested of power.

The Sandinista National Liberation Front (FSLN) was founded in 1961 as a political–military guerrilla organisation with Marxist roots. The poverty, subjugation and violence made both women and men side with them. In 1955, the country was one of the last in the region to give women the formal right to vote. FSLN adopted the principle of equality in 1969 and women participated in demonstrations, strikes, sabotage and armed battle. They constituted 30 per cent of the revolutionary army and had leading positions. The army defeated the National Guard and overthrew the last dictator in a bloody clash in 1978/79. It is estimated that more than 40,000 of a population of about 2.5 million died in the war.[3]

Married to a martyr

Violeta Barrios Torres belonged to the traditional elite. The family consisted of landowners and generals who were at the head of the liberation struggle against the Spaniards. Violeta's grandparents were engaged in trade and cattle and supported the Conservative Party. Her mother had an old-fashioned Catholic upbringing, while her father grew up in the US. Here, he studied at a technical college, but he did not complete his studies because he had to take over the family properties and moved back to Nicaragua as a ranch-owner. Here, he was an influential member of the local community, but was not involved in politics. Violeta was born in 1929 in Rivas, where her mother took care of her and her four brothers, while her father saw to the properties. Violeta was sent to Catholic school in Nicaragua, then to the US, where she went to college and took a secretarial course. She was not particularly interested in studying and not especially competent either. When her father died in 1948, she quit and came home.

In Nicaragua, Violeta met the five-year-older Pedro Joaquin Chamorro Cardinal, also from a family of conservative landowners. Nicaragua's first president was a Chamorro and later three others in the family were presidents. Pedro's father edited the conservative anti-Somoza newspaper *La Prensa*. Pedro studied law, participated in riots against the dictator, was arrested and was expelled from the university. The family then sent him to Mexico to complete his studies. The year after, the family had to leave the country and moved to New York. In 1948, they returned to Nicaragua. Pedro became co-editor of *La Prensa* and took over as editor when his father died in 1952. His younger brothers Jaime and Xavier and other relatives also worked at the newspaper.

Pedro and Violeta married in 1950, and he came to shape her whole life. They had four children who survived to adulthood – two sons and two daughters – and lived together for 27 years. Violeta was an exemplary wife and mother by Latin American standards: faithful to her husband, children and the Catholic Church. Often, she had problems with her health and life was turbulent, but she stood by her husband's side, ran the household and took care of the children. Pedro not only wrote against Somoza in *La Prensa*, but became involved in attempts at armed resistance and was arrested and imprisoned several times. Violeta was not engaged in politics, but brought food to her husband in prison and went with him when he fled to Costa Rica. The family lived there for several years. But Pedro went back to Managua, resumed his opposition and was murdered in broad daylight in 1978.

The murder of Pedro Chamorro was a provoking factor in the uprising that led to the fall of the Somoza clan 18 months later. After her husband's death, Violeta Chamorro was committed to *La Prensa* and supported the FSLN, but she did not join them. When the front took over in 1979, an executive council with five members was established. Violeta Chamorro was the only woman. They needed a person of character and courage, as well as the name of a national martyr and the newspaper *La Prensa*. Violeta came along because she believed they had a chance to build 'a free and democratic government dedicated to carrying out social reforms while maintaining a place for private enterprise' (Chamorro, 1996: 152). She lacked political experience and kept a low profile. Her role was mainly symbolic. Before a year had passed, she withdrew, officially for health reasons. But the reality was that the council was dominated by the FSLN and Chamorro disagreed with the Sandinista policies.[4]

'New Nicaragua'

The FSLN called for a 'new Nicaragua': socially just and democratic. The FSLN was influenced by liberal as well as radical ideas and wanted to introduce socialism of a special kind, with political diversity and a private sector in coexistence with as state-centred economy. Foreign policy should be independent, particularly of the US. Initially, the FSLN governed with a small executive council and a larger council of state with people from different sectors, where the FSLN had a majority. The police and the military were reorganised and mass organisations were established for workers, women and farmers. The Sandinista women's organisation had 80,000 members.

According to FSLN, a country could only be democratic if rich and poor, urban and rural, men and women were equal. The power of the privileged had to be limited, and resources had to be redistributed to the underprivileged. In practice, this meant agrarian reform, with expropriation, the strengthening of the trade unions and the creation of state farms and cooperatives. The health and education of the poor had to be improved and extensive literacy, immunisation and anti-malaria projects were put into action.

When the FSLN took over, living conditions got better. Nicaragua became party to the United Nations (UN) Convention on the Elimination of all forms of Discrimination Against Women (CEDAW) in 1981, and prostitution was banned. The principles of equal pay and equal parental responsibility were established, and paid maternity leave was introduced. But the liberation of women was to take place primarily through increased involvement in the labour market, in addition to revolutionary struggle, and their economic activity increased in a number of areas. After some years, 30 per cent of the leading positions in the state administration were occupied by women, but there was only one woman minister.[5]

Backyard of the US

Some of the traditional elites backed the Sandinista policies, but most saw them as a threat, and many left the country. But Nicaragua had a more open, tolerant and pluralistic system than before, and opposition was expressed particularly by the Catholic Church, big business and *La Prensa*, even if there were limits. The Sandinistas received aid from President Jimmy Carter and Western Europe. But the US changed its attitude when President Ronald Reagan came to power. He did everything he could to undermine the regime. He implemented a trade embargo and financed an armed contra revolution. The prolonged civil war cost lives and money, and development was set back. The revolutionary transformation of society was replaced with the defence of a revolutionary government under constant attack.

In 1984, elections for president and parliament were held to improve the situation. Seven parties, partly leftist, partly rightist, presented candidates and independent observers described the elections as free and fair. But the largest anti-Sandinista coalition refused to participate, a fact President Reagan used as a pretext for calling the election a 'Soviet-style sham' and escalating the war. Daniel Ortega obtained a two-thirds majority in both elections. A total of 13 women (14 per cent) were elected to parliament, all from the FSLN. There were 21 per cent of women in the Sandinista party group, more than any other party in Central America. A woman was vice president of the parliament, and two became cabinet members.

A new constitution was adopted after discussions at large popular meetings. The law contained broad revolutionary goals, but established a liberal-democratic presidential system to implement them. A directly elected president was to be head of both state and government, with a directly elected vice president and an appointed cabinet. In addition the parliament would be elected with proportional representation. With regards to the rights of women, the constitution was one of the most progressive in Latin America.

But the war continued and cost more and more. It is estimated that over 30,000 were killed and twice as many wounded. Thousands were driven away or disappeared. Austerity measures were introduced and inflation reached record levels. The economy broke down, and Nicaragua became one of the poorest countries in the region. Only towards the end of the 1980s did the Central American presidents succeed in achieving a ceasefire, for which Costa Rica's President Oscar Arias received the Nobel Peace Prize. New elections were held in 1990, and when the Sandinistas lost, the US lifted the embargo and stopped supporting the contras (Close, 1999: 11–36).

'A White Peace Dove'

Violeta Chamorro was more than 50 years old, and her children were grown up, when she left the executive council. Relieved of her duties as wife and mother, she could take an active role in the leadership of La Prensa. The family disagreed about the approach towards the Sandinistas. Violeta's children Claudia and Carlos supported them, and her brother-in-law Xavier wanted to be a positive critic. But Violeta herself and her brother-in-law Jaime wished to express a clear opposition and were supported by her children Pedro and Cristiana. Xavier broke out and edited his own newspaper, while Violeta Chamorro became the strongest critic of the Sandinistas in both La Prensa and the international media. She was a warm advocate of family and motherhood, religion and fatherland, and attacked the regime for being totalitarian and ungodly and violating human rights. As a consequence, the newspaper was censured and periodically closed down. When it supported the US and the contras, it was stopped for a year.

In the presidential election in 1990, Violeta Chamorro ran for a coalition of 14 anti-Sandinista parties: the Nicaraguan Opposition Union (UNO), which received extensive support from the US. The UNO spanned the entire political register from the Right to the communists. Chamorro did not belong to any political party herself and said:

> I will work for peace and freedom. To achieve peace, I will end mandatory
> military conscription and aim at reconciling the family – Nicaragua – which
> has been polarized for too long. I will give back to the people their right
> to choose their leaders through open and fair electoral competitions. And

above all, I will give them honesty, honesty and more honesty, not just in appearance but in full practice. (Chamorro, 1996: 260)

Nobody believed Chamorro had any chance of being elected. But she travelled all over the country and asserted: 'I am not a politician, but I believe this is my destiny. I am doing this for Pedro and for my country' (Saint-Germain, 2013: 125). Like a grandmother, at 60 years old, white-haired and dressed in white, with a gold crucifix, she stood forth and was presented as a 'White Peace Dove'. She made the Catholic Nicaraguans think of Jesus's mother, Mary. And to everyone's amazement, she got 55 per cent of the votes against 41 per cent for Ortega in the most strictly monitored elections in Latin American history. She became Latin America's first elected women president. She also got a majority in parliament, and this time, 15 women were elected (16 per cent): nine from the FSLN and six from UNO (Opfell, 1993: 176–7; Chamorro, 1996: 203–96).

'Useless old bag of bones'

The political scientist Michelle A. Saint-German (2013: 121–8) is of the view that several factors contributed to the victory of Violeta Chamorro. The Sandinistas allowed opposition, and although there were a multitude of different parties, the battle was essentially between two groups: the FSLN and UNO. For many people, the main tasks in the elections were getting rid of the Sandinistas and ending the war and economic problems. It was of less importance who took over.

Ortega emphasised traditional masculine values in the campaign and presented himself as the nation's father with a fighting rooster as his symbol. The cabinet was dominated by men, but women constituted more than 30 per cent of the leadership of the FSLN's management and reacted negatively to Ortega's use of symbols. In the UNO, it took several days of heated debate before Violeta Chamorro was accepted as a presidential candidate. Several men wanted to run, but the enmity between them was so great that the choice of one chased away the others. Only a political outsider could unite the strongly divergent factions. Violeta Chamorro was politically inexperienced and a woman. The male candidate for vice president described her as 'a useless old bag of bones'. But the US was in favour of Doña Violeta, as she was called. She stood in stark contrast to Ortega: as a devout, pure Mother figure, who was going to save the country. Parallels were also drawn with the successful presidential campaign of Cory Aquino in the Philippines.

Violeta Chamorro came to power in a democratisation process, but in the struggle that brought the dictator down, she was a supportive person, not a leader. She became leader of another struggle, afterwards, against the Sandinista regime. The Republicans in the White House branded the Sandinistas 'communists' and 'heartless dictators'. But the political scientist David Close (1999: 11–36), who has analysed the development in Nicaragua, underlines that Nicaragua never was a Cuba or Czechoslovakia. The Sandinista regime could not be called a 'dictatorship', possibly a 'half-democracy' because of authoritarian features such as, among other things, a politicised judiciary. But there were no death squads and few arbitrary imprisonments. Political life functioned remarkably normally, and the regime created a far more inclusive political culture with greater social equality than that before 1979. They did this with a more pluralistic political system than any of the Central American neighbours, save Costa Rica. The FSLN organised the first honest elections in Nicaragua, and the Sandinista government was the first to surrender power voluntarily when it did not get a majority. The elections in 1990 were not about introducing democracy where there had not been any before, but moving from one form of democracy to another, Close points out.

Besieged mother figure

Violeta Chamorro faced an extremely demanding task as head of state and government: create peace, improve the economy and make a democracy work – in a country devastated by war and with enormous inflation, debt and unemployment. In addition, there was long-lasting drought, volcanic eruptions and a fall in coffee and cotton prices. As if this was not enough, it soon became clear that the 'Peace Dove' was presented as candidate for president primarily as a symbol, to be elected, not to govern the country. The same groups that expected the FSLN to hand control over to them after the Somoza clan was overthrown believed that Violeta Chamorro would now give them control after the Sandinistas were defeated. Conservative and liberal politicians were of the view that they morally and pragmatically were entitled to govern the country. Chamorro had neither the experience nor the competence and could best serve as a 'Queen Mother', they thought. Then, they would bring the nation in order, eliminate the FSLN as a political force and ensure that they, themselves, got their legitimate place, economically and socially. The Vice President Virgilio Godoy attacked Violeta Chamorro from the first day and demanded that she withdraw. But she had no intention of doing so, and a quarrel developed between them that resulted in Violeta Chamorro denying him an office in the government building. And she insulted the UNO bosses even more by appointing people to the cabinet who were more loyal to her than to the UNO.

Although the UNO won a majority in parliament, it was not sufficient to change the constitution. And the alliance soon broke down in internal conflict. Violeta Chamorro had to govern without clear support in parliament. She had no popular basis, no party apparatus and no security forces. She also lacked legitimacy as a leader, and attempts at cooperation, peace and reconciliation were perceived as signs of weakness and inability to rule in Nicaraguan culture. Many regarded her as only an interim president. She appointed a cabinet of skilled professionals from the private sector and left the details to them and her son-in-law Antonio Lacayo, who was educated as an economist in the US. He married Cristiana, who now published *La Prensa*, ran Violeta's electoral campaign and became her de facto prime minister. In addition, a small group of family members and close advisers helped her, and relatives and friends got key positions. It was a government of novices from the elite with unwavering faith in free-market blessings.[6]

Violeta Chamorro began by declaring that the war against the contras was over, demobilised, gave amnesty to political prisoners and reduced the military by three quarters. She went against the tradition that the winner takes all and opened government up for participation by everybody. She took the post of minister of defence herself, but kept Ortega's brother as commander-in-chief. This entailed strong reactions and two ministers left the cabinet. She implemented austerity measures and with foreign assistance managed to get inflation under control, but not unemployment, and economic growth was slow. Health and educational services were further weakened and were no longer freely available to all.

If Violeta Chamorro was loved by ordinary Nicaraguans, she was besieged by political opponents. Society was deeply divided. There were outbreaks of violence and strikes, and politics got the character of short-term emergency measures. The president was unable to make citizens agree upon the principles for the governance of the country. But in spite of the controversy, she managed to maintain a constitutional regime, which was a bit of an achievement. She remained alive and in power until her period ended in January 1997. She concluded the civil war and rescued the country from economic ruin. She could not stand for re-election, and the elections in 1996 were highly disputed, with accusations of fraud and administrative failures, but no one was killed. A liberal conservative male president took over with 51 per cent of the votes against 38 per cent for Daniel Ortega from the FSLN.[7]

Challenging and traditional

As a woman, mother and a widow, Violeta Chamorro challenged the stereotypical notion of what a president should be like. At the same time, she fulfilled the traditional expectation that women should participate in politics as an extension of their role in the home, as mothers. She often said that she acted and talked like a woman, but specified: 'I'm not a feminist, nor do I want to be one. I am a woman dedicated to my home as Pedro taught me' (Saint-Germain, 2013: 138). She managed the country like her own family, and the government worked actively to strengthen family values. With her Catholic faith, Violeta Chamorro was against abortion and sceptical about contraception, divorce and cohabitation. There was not much in the UNO's platform that benefited women, either. Although peace was good for them, they were hit by cutbacks in public services, and many had to go over to the informal sector, with low and insecure incomes. The support for feminist organisations, the programme for rehabilitation of street children and prostitutes, and most of the centres for child care were stopped. Violeta Chamorro herself noted that one positive action she had taken was to encourage women to become property-owners, so that they were protected in case of divorce or the husband's death (Tan-Wong, 1998).

It is said that Chamorro inspired the former First Lady in Costa Rica, Margarita Pénon de Arias, to run for president, but Chamorro did not try to increase women's participation in politics. She appointed few women in the administration and only one as minister of health. In 1995, she had a female vice president, but this was decided by parliament against Chamorro's wishes.

Generally, it did not go well for women under Latin America's first elected female president. For the largest, most diverse and feminist women's movement in Central America at the time, the battle became defensive. The organisational experience many women developed under the Sandinistas in the 1980s activated them during the following decade. And in 1994, the FSLN introduced quotas of 30 per cent female candidates on the electoral lists. But in the elections in 1996 only 10 women were elected to parliament (11 per cent) and nearly all from FSLN.

While the liberal conservatives were in power, few women participated in political decision-making. But in the elections in 2006 FSLN's Daniel Ortega surprisingly became president again and was re-elected in 2011. Ortega's policies had become much more moderate during the time in opposition, but the number of women in governing bodies increased dramatically when the FSLN gained influence. In the elections in 2011 FSLN went from 38 to 61 per cent of the MPs and Nicaragua made the greatest progress in the world from one election to the other, practically doubling the number of women in parliament: from 21 to 40 per cent. In 2014 Nicaragua achieved the world record in female cabinet ministers with 57 per cent (8 of 14). At the same time, Nicaragua was one of the very few countries in the world where abortion was illegal without exception.

Third wave of democratisation

Democracy and strong men

Nicaragua was not the only country in Latin America that carried out democratisation processes in the late 1900s. The year 1978 began what is called the third wave of democratisation in Latin America.[8] The dictator in the Dominican Republic was overthrown, and this was followed by a revival or strengthening of democracy in most of the continent. Very often, the military juntas fell because of popular mobilisation.

Of the independent states on the mainland of South and Central America, the great majority were Spanish colonies (16), while Brazil was Portuguese. In addition, three states were colonised by the Dutch and British. The Latin countries gained independence during the 1800s, often as the result of a liberation war. Modern ideas from the French and American Revolutions were felt, at the same time as colonialism left deep traces. In addition, the US was strongly involved in the region, militarily as well as economically, ideologically and politically. The societies were modernised, urbanised and stratified with great economic and social inequalities between the well-to-do and working class, cities and rural areas, and, occasionally, groups with different ethnic backgrounds. The political institutions were weak. Nearly everywhere, power was centralised in a small, mighty upper class that ruled by means of patron–client relationships and violence, often also the military. Sometimes, the Catholic Church and the military had a dominant position.

Over time, stability and unrest, and democracy, dictatorship and mixed regimes, alternated. Before 1978, authoritarian regimes were pervasive. Only three countries could be called 'democracies' (Colombia, Costa Rica and Venezuela). But in the course of some years, virtually all the states introduced more or less democratic systems. Democracy became more widespread and long-lasting than previously on the continent despite variations, declines and setbacks (see Figure 10). The democratisation processes took different forms, but democratic institutions were set up, civil rights were protected and free and fair elections were held with universal suffrage. In 2000, Derbyshire and Derbyshire classified all the countries in South and Central America except five as 'liberal democracies'. Chile, Nicaragua, Panama, Paraguay and Surinam were considered to be 'emerging democracies'.

The majority of countries established centralised presidential systems more or less following the US model. In addition to a parliament, most often elected using proportional representation, a president was directly elected. The president appointed the cabinet and often had one or more vice presidents, but no prime minister. Instead, there could be a 'chief minister', 'head of cabinet' or something like it. In practice, the institutions functioned more or less democratically. In many parts of the continent, a 'strongman culture' prevailed, which resulted in important

Figure 10: South America: regimes by type, 1946–2012

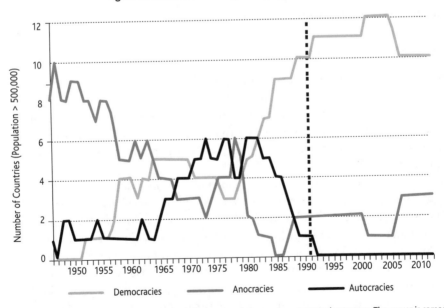

Note: Anocratic governance is a system placed somewhere between democracy and autocracy. The power is spread between elite groups competing for power.
Source: Center for Systemic Peace, Polity IV Project (CSP, 2013) (see: www.systemicpeace.org).

decisions often being taken by the leader alone or in consultation with a few, personally selected advisers, and patron–client relationships were widespread.[9]

Economic crisis

In the 1980s and 1990s – at the same time as the democratisation – Latin America was hit by the worst social and economic crisis since the 1930s. Besides traditional agriculture, commodities were produced for export (meat, wheat, coffee, sugar, bananas, rubber, oil and metals), which resulted in significant revenue, especially in the 1960s. The economies grew, and social conditions were improved. But then the price of oil increased on the world market. The industrial countries were stricken by recession. The demand for commodities and prices dropped, while prices of industrial products and the interest on foreign loans rose. Many countries had difficulties paying interest and amortisation, and the debt crisis was a fact. During the 1980s and 1990s, most countries in Latin America had almost no economic growth per capita. To solve the problems, neo-liberal structural adjustment programmes with austerity measures, privatisation and the weakening of the state were introduced and social spending was reduced. The income distribution became more skewed and poverty increased. The crisis was, in particular, detrimental to women.

In the early 2000s, all the states were classified as middle-income countries, but economic and social disparities were larger than in most regions. And it was remarkable that elected regimes survived despite widespread poverty, huge inequalities and, in most cases, weak economic development. Presidents were defeated or resigned, but the regimes almost invariably continued. Only Peru broke down in 1992. Political factors, such as popular support for democracy, reduced political polarisation and international support for democratisation, especially from the US and the Organization of American States (OAS), seemed to be more important than economic growth and the level of development. But poor administration on the part of governments played a part in undermining democracy (Mainwaring and Scully, 2010a).

Women's struggle

Indian cultures varied, but the Spanish conquistadores dominated in the modern nation states. The Spanish (and Portuguese) were Catholics and brought with them a gender order of machismo, an excessive, aggressive masculinity, and marianismo, a humble, self-denying femininity. The woman was respected if she was passive and subordinate to the man. The distinction between private and public was emphasised, and the public (political) sphere was marked by the values of the Spanish conquistadores: physical strength, manliness and military prowess. Politics was a male arena, tainted by corruption, while the woman was clean and referred to the private sphere. Here, she could exert influence, in the upper class as a powerful matron, in the lower class as a single provider. Eventually, the roles became more varied. But a 'proper' woman had to be careful not to deviate too much from the norm.

After the formation of nation–states, feminist movements emerged across the continent, but the processes of including women in political and social life were uneven and took a long time. Women organised in the 1800s in Argentina, Chile, Mexico, Peru and Uruguay, while other countries followed in the first half of the 1900s. The demand for voting rights was central. International women's conferences dealing with this question were held from 1910 onwards. Women's associations, suffragette groups and women's parties were created. In 1928, an Inter-American Women's Commission at government level was established, and the first feminist wave gave women the right to vote from 1929 onwards. But the right remained a formality under authoritarian regimes.

The second feminist wave emerged in the 1960s and 1970s, and it is ironic that while women's political activism began to flourish globally, Latin American regimes closed down the public spaces that were traditionally used for political activity. Military regimes prevented everybody from exercising civil rights, and broad opposition movements arose. Different women's groups collaborated to fight against oppression. Together with men, women engaged in human rights organisations, grassroots groups doing relief work, radical church-based communities and guerrilla activities. Women were key figures in the struggle against authoritarian rule. But the efforts did not entail real possibilities of gaining political power. When the dictators disappeared, women were usually forgotten. It was not a given that 'democratisation' should mean rights for women. Generally, they were excluded from the whole gamut of formal leadership positions. But they became leaders in civil society, thereby laying the foundations for political influence and, in some cases, formal positions (Htun, 1997, 1998a, 1998b, 2000; Craske, 1999).

Plus and minus

The largest international women's conference of all time was held in Latin America (Mexico) in 1975, the International Women's Year. The conference received extensive media coverage and helped give women's demand for influence strength and legitimacy. In the decade that followed, regular regional conferences on the status of women were held, and women participated with increasing force in democracy movements and protests against the economic reforms of the 1980s. Democratisation led to the mobilisation of groups that were otherwise excluded, and women were given new opportunities for influence. Voluntary women's groups and organisations flourished, along with other grassroots and citizen movements. At the same time, traditional political parties lost credibility and power. Women did not automatically obtain their rightful place in government, but democracy was necessary for women to get a chance to be represented.

The combination of long-lasting struggle for women's rights and the modernisation of Latin American societies contributed to the improvement of women's health and education. This, together with modern contraception, where it was allowed, helped women become more independent and greater numbers went into paid work. Thereby, women acquired useful skills for social and political activities. The possibilities for involvement were, however, hampered by traditional views of the role of women and opposition from the Catholic Church against women's reproductive rights. Moreover, women usually had low wages, poor working conditions and double work. The economic problems in the 1980s and 1990s made it even more difficult for many women to find the time and energy for activities beyond the most necessary. Not only was it harder to raise money, but social services were reduced and weakened. At the beginning of the 2000s, more women than men obtained higher education in many countries. Labour force participation varied, but only about half of the Latin American women had their own income, usually from unstable, poorly paid jobs.

Most countries became party to the CEDAW, and national machinery to promote equality was eventually established, even though many countries had reservations against the convention. Laws were revised, and actions taken. Views on gender roles changed, and women's participation in politics and society became more accepted. But the political institutions were heavily male-dominated and opposed changes that threatened the established position of the power elites. These were also discredited by the authoritarian regimes, and women were reluctant to engage in politics. The representation in party leaderships, parliaments and governments usually remained small and sporadic. In 1994, there were in South and Central American countries on average 9 per cent women in parliaments (or the lower chambers) and 7 per cent in senates and cabinets.[10]

Bolivian revolutionary: Lidia Güeiler Tejada

From accountant to revolutionary

The first woman president in Latin America was overthrown by the military. It was Isabel Perón in Argentina in 1974–76, when a semi-democracy drifted into dictatorship. The second woman president, Lidia Güeiler Tejada in Bolivia, was also overthrown by the military, but, here, the country was moving from dictatorship to a more democratic regime. That was in 1979.[11]

Bolivia was one of the poorest countries in Latin America, with a very heterogeneous population of diverse Indian groups and Europeans, the vast majority Catholics. Women fought alongside men against the Spanish colonial power, but they did not participate in politics after independence in 1825. They did not get a limited right to vote until 1938 and universal suffrage was adopted only in 1952. The country was characterised by political turmoil and military coups. It is said that Bolivia has a regional record of coups, but there were also periods of civilian rule. The longest military dictatorship in the 1900s began in 1964 and ended in 1978. Towards the end of the 1970s, there were significant economic problems and increasing demands for democratic elections from the opposition as well as the US President Jimmy Carter. The dictator Hugo Banzer agreed to hold elections in 1978. This started a chaotic period of two provisional civil governments and three military, two unsatisfactory presidential elections and four coups, until a civilian government came to power in a constitutional way in 1982 (Mayorga, 2005: 151).

In the middle of all this, Lidia Güeiler Tejada became president. She did not belong to any powerful ruling elite and did not inherit the position from a deceased father or husband. She fought a lifelong struggle for human rights, especially for women, was for nearly 35 years a driving force in a leftist revolutionary movement and spent years in prison and exile. She was born in Cochabamba in 1921 and trained as an accountant. At 18 years old, she married Mareirian Pérez Ramírez, a former officer from Paraguay, and had a daughter before they parted. She became a single mother and admitted later that politics – 'my love for my country' – was more important than the needs of her daughter (Davison, 2011). She reacted against the exploitation of the poor in general and women in particular. In the early 1940s, she got a job in the central bank, but was fired when she participated in a strike. Later, she learned that she was actually fired after four-and-a-half years at the bank because of her 'political inclinations' (Bonner, 1980). In 1946, Güeiler joined the underground movement. She married Edwin Moller, a Bolivian trade union leader, and co-founded a left-wing party, but they later divorced.

Güeiler became known among Bolivian women in 1951 when she led a hunger strike with 26 mothers and wives of imprisoned leftist men, and they were released after eight days. When workers and the reformist middle class joined together in what was then a leftist national revolutionary movement (Movimiento Nacionalista Revolucionario, MNR) to fight against the oligarchy of landowners and powerful mining interests and carried out a national revolution in 1952, Güeiler was in the streets. Bolivian women were traditionally socially active and participated in both rebellions and the struggle for independence. In the 1900s, women's organisations claimed political and economic rights, and the MNR became the first party to accept women as members (Salinas, 1994: 115–16).

First woman in parliament

Lidia Güeiler Tejada became a party worker who toiled her way up and forward. As the only woman, she organised youth brigades solely with men. She became a commander in the revolutionary force and the only female leader of a battalion. When the MNR's founder, Victor Paz Estenssoro, became Bolivia's president in 1952, she worked for a while as his private secretary. The MNR emphasised universal suffrage, education and social security, which benefited women as well as men. But the party leaders did not want to share political power with women, and women largely disappeared from the political arena after the revolution was over. Güeiler joined feminist organisations, founded a political women's organisation and continued as about the only woman as an active MNR member. She became the leader of a national women's command and was the first woman elected to parliament in 1956.

The MNR gradually came forward as more centre-right and sought to develop Bolivia into a modern capitalist state with broad social participation. Land was redistributed and mines were nationalised. In 1964, Güeiler ran as vice presidential candidate with the country's most powerful labour leader as candidate for the presidency, but the military took power. Güeiler was imprisoned, tortured and forced into exile. In Chile, she participated in PRIN, the Revolutionary Party of the Nationalist Left (Salinas, 1994: 119-21).

Coup after coup

Presidential and legislative elections were to be held in 1978. The president was directly elected and both chambers of Congress, the Chamber of Deputies and the Senate, were elected by simple plurality. But there were allegations of irregularities and the military seized power twice. Elections were then held in 1979. There was a multitude of political parties. Güeiler founded PRIN-Güeiler, a small leftist party that she directed herself in alliance with the MNR, and was elected to Congress. She also became president of the Chamber of Deputies. In the presidential elections, there was no clear winner. Of the four candidates, two received the same support, 36 per cent, while 51 per cent was required to be elected. In Congress, none of them obtained a majority, either. The president of the Senate then formed a temporary government until new elections could be held in 1980. But it did not take long before he was overthrown by a military coup. This led to protests and strikes. The solution was that 58-year-old Lidia Güeiler Tejada became the country's first woman head of state. She had good relations with both Right and Left parties and was to function until a new president was elected.

It was an unusually turbulent and violent time. As president, Güeiler was head of both state and government. She appointed a cabinet with one military and 18 civilian ministers, including two women, one responsible for social welfare and one for public health and welfare. She would have liked to have more women, but this was not accepted by the powerful factions in Congress. She also changed ministers several times. Güeiler said: 'I am not a feminist. I am a fighter for the involvement of women in the process of the development of the country, but it is not a struggle to be waged exclusively by women' (Bonner, 1980: 86). Together with the female ministers, Güeiler established a public welfare centre for women, children and the elderly, and a women's hospital. But she was criticised because she did not attack the negative attitudes to birth control that existed in the Catholic country (Jensen, 2008: 64–5).

Conservative officers protested against appointments Güeiler made, and workers, peasants and women protested when the peso was devalued and prices rose for gasoline and food. But Güeiler was undaunted. After a violent election campaign, where Güeiler was not a candidate, the military intervened again and took power under the leadership of Güeiler's cousin. By then, Lidia Güeiler Tejada had only been sitting for eight months. She went to France and stayed there until the military regime fell, and her cousin was sentenced to 30 years in prison. Later, she worked as an ambassador and senator and supported the former coca farmer Evo Morales in the presidential election campaign in 2005 (Bonner, 1980; Davison, 2011).

It can be seen as doubly distressing that such a woman-friendly woman president was allowed to rule for such a short time. But in 2010, after active pressure from a couple of hundred women's organisations, Bolivia's leftist President Evo Morales appointed a cabinet with 50/50 women and men after he had managed to include gender equality in the new constitution. The representation of women made a leap upwards to 25 per cent in the Chamber of Deputies and 47 per cent in the Senate. But in 2014, the number of women in the cabinet had gone down to 33 per cent (7 of 21).

Janet Jagan: from Chicago to Guyana

Janet and Cheddi

Violeta Chamorro was Latin America's third woman president, and then, in 1997, the fourth was elected. She was also a widow, but Janet Jagan did not belong to any family dynasty, and her husband was not a political martyr. In fact, she was an immigrant, and her life is an extraordinary story of gender, ethnicity, politics and ideology.[12]

Janet Rosenberg was born in the US in 1920. She grew up in Chicago in a Jewish immigrant family from Czechoslovakia. They belonged to the middle class, but as a student, Janet developed an interest and affinity for socialism. She was trained as a nurse, and in 1942, she met Cheddi Jagan, who studied to be a dentist. He was also interested in socialism. He came from Guyana, where his parents were poor Indian plantation workers. Yet, he went to college and travelled to the US, where he got various jobs to earn money, undertook a bachelor's degree in science and became a doctor in dental surgery.

Unlike most of the continent, Guyana was originally a Dutch colony that the British took over in 1814. The country therefore had more in common politically, culturally and historically with the Commonwealth Caribbean than the rest of Latin America. The abolition of slavery led to a shortage of labour on the sugarcane plantations and the colonial authorities imported Indian workers. In the 1900s, the largest population groups comprised Indo-Guyanese, who were mostly Hindus, lived in the rural areas and traded and cultivated rice, and Afro-Guyanese, who were mainly Christian and lived and worked in urban areas. There were strong antagonisms between the two groups, and economic problems and poor living conditions led to riots and demonstrations. From the 1940s, the British introduced measures to improve conditions and political reforms. The colony gradually became independent, but it was not without frictions. The constitution was changed several times (Merrill, 1992).

In spite of their mixed ethnicity, Janet and Cheddi soon married. In 1943, the couple settled in Guyana, where Janet worked as a nurse in Cheddi's dental clinic in the capital, Georgetown. They had a son and a daughter and the clinic became a centre for contact and activities. Janet made a special impression, particularly in the East Indian community. A white woman as a champion of non-white liberation was remarkable. She even married the son of sugar plantation workers. In addition, Cheddi was a rising political star who would become a champion of his people. To Janet, Cheddi was both a husband and a political partner. She soon became 'indianised', both politically and culturally, and her support of his causes made them a team – the Jagans. Janet became identified as an uncompromising defender and advocate of East Indian interests, and she shared Cheddi's influence, charisma and power. For two generations, the couple were leading figures in the country in the struggle for freedom, equality and democracy (Hinds, 2011: 195–6).

Her own person

When the Jagans came to British Guyana, the colony was undergoing significant changes. There was a rapid increase in the Indian population, in ethnic consciousness and anti-colonial militancy. Both the Jagans got actively involved in the labour movement. Janet joined a campaign to organise domestic workers, and the insight she got into women's problems led her to co-found with other women the Women's Political and Economic Organization (WPEO). It worked in areas such as health, housing and education, which had especially negative effects on women and children. She became WPEO's first general secretary. With her husband, she was also co-founder of the Political Affairs Committee (PAC) to end colonial rule and establish a socialist movement. She became editor of the *PAC Bulletin*. In a colony characterised by male dominance, Janet Jagan's political role was exceptional. Janet underlined: 'From the start, Cheddi and I went in together and started everything together. I have always been my own person' (Jensen, 2008: 19). The 1940s and 1950s were marked by struggle for political rights. In 1945, women got the right to stand for election, and universal suffrage was introduced in 1953.

Both Cheddi and Janet ran for election to the Legislative Council in 1947 as independent labour candidates, but only Cheddi was elected. Janet lost and due to her political involvement, she was deprived of her US citizenship and became a Guyanese citizen only in 1966, after independence. In 1950, when sugar workers were gunned down during a strike, the couple established Guyana's first modern political party, the People's Progressive Party (PPP), to fight for independence. Cheddi was leader, while Afro-Guyanese Forbes Burnham was chairman and de facto deputy leader. Janet became secretary general, a position she held for 20 years. She also edited the party publication, so she wielded considerable influence in the party. After the founding of PPP, Janet Jagan and other women created the Women's Progressive Organization (WPO) in 1953 to involve women in political and organisational activities. Janet held the post of president. She was also elected as the first woman to the city council of Georgetown (Hinds, 2011: 196–8).

Heavy-handed colonial power

The PPP tried to become a mass party and mobilised and trained workers and peasants through public meetings. How many women participated is not clear. Women had little access to public decision-making, but were active at the community level and had a tradition of joining in riots and strikes, running soup kitchens, and collecting money. Janet Jagan reports that they showed up in large numbers at PPP meetings and showered their leaders with flowers when opponents threw stones and eggs (Jagan, 1962).

With a new constitution elections were set for 1953. The PPP triumphed, obtaining 18 of the 24 seats in the legislature. Both Janet and Cheddi Jagan were elected, Janet as one of three women. A government was formed, but power was maintained in the hands of the British-appointed Governor. Cheddi became chief minister and minister for agriculture. Janet was not included in the cabinet, but became the first woman deputy speaker in the legislature. The government expanded the education system and introduced progressive measures to ease the plight of working people. The changes were modest, but opponents alleged that the policy was 'communist', and it was not long before the colonial power intervened, with US blessings. After 133 days, troops were sent in and the constitution was suspended. The PPP headquarters was attacked and both Cheddi and Janet were jailed for several months.

During the British occupation, the divide between ethnic groups deepened, and Afro-Guyanese broke out of the multi-ethnic PPP and formed their own party, the People's National Congress (PNC). Indo-Guyanese remained in the PPP, which became an ethnically homogeneous Indian party, firmly organised around Cheddi Jagan as leader and Janet Jagan as co-leader. Both parties declared that they promoted 'socialism', but the enmity between the two dominant characters, Cheddi Jagan and Forbes Burnham, marked Guyanese politics for many decades.

In new elections in 1957, the PPP regained a majority with nine of the 14 seats. The PNC obtained three. Cheddi Jagan became minister of trade and industry, and Janet, as the first and only woman minister, was responsible for labour, health and housing (there was no chief minister). With the help of foreign aid, improvements were made in health, education, housing, roads and agriculture, but the British governor prevented more radical measures.

In 1961, the election campaign was tough, but the PPP won a majority again. Cheddi became prime minister and minister for development and Janet was appointed senator and minister of home affairs for a period, again as the only woman. The economy grew, people got education and living standards were improved, but the government was met with protest demonstrations and strikes and the worst ethnic violence the country had seen to date. The disturbances were so extensive that the British stationed troops in the country. In 1964, they changed the electoral system from majority vote to proportional representation and the PPP lost influence. The party got 46 per cent of the votes in the elections, but the PNC joined forces with the Conservative Party and formed a coalition government (Merrill, 1992; Hinds, 2011: 198–201).

Authoritarian independence

The PNC government retained power for nearly 30 years, with the support of the US. In 1966, Guyana became independent, and in 1970, it became a republic, non-aligned and member of the Caribbean Community (CARICOM). The political system was first set up according to the British model, but in 1980, it was replaced by a presidential system. The president was elected by the party with the most seats in parliament, was head of state and government, and appointed several vice presidents, a prime minister and other ministers. The president and vice presidents had to be members of parliament (MPs), but not the ministers, although many of them were. Most of the MPs were elected through proportional representation, while others were indirectly elected.

In theory, the PNC supported a socialist one-party state, but, in practice, the policies fluctuated several times from socialism to middle-position capitalism, and governance was poor. In spite of the formal democratic institutions, governance became more and more dictatorial, with party control, the persecution of political opponents and the manipulation of elections. During the 1970s and 1980s, the economy and social conditions deteriorated, which particularly affected women. In 1992, Guyana was among the poorest countries on the continent. The population of about 700,000–800,000 – women as well as men – was relatively well-educated, but there was extensive migration and many of the best qualified left the country (Merrill, 1992).

During PNC rule, Cheddi and Janet Jagan held the PPP together as best they could and fought for democracy, economic development and harmony between the races. Cheddi was leader of the opposition in parliament and took over as PPP secretary general. Janet became an MP and was one of the longest serving. In the PPP, she was member of the General Council, Central Committee and Executive Committee and also served as international secretary and executive secretary. In the 1990s, the Executive Committee of the PPP was gender-balanced. In addition, she reorganised the Union of Guyanese Journalists and was the first president. She was also editor of the *Mirror* newspaper.

The PNC established a women's section, but prevented gender issues from coming onto its agenda. And no national women's organisation was founded uniting the various ethnic groups. A women's office was established in the state administration, and CEDAW was ratified in 1980. Some projects were initiated to promote gender equality, but patriarchal norms and customs were strong and women were discriminated against in politics and economic life. In parliament, the share of women increased, but there were very few women in the cabinet (Valdés and Palacios, 1999; Hinds, 2011: 201–2).

Jagan couple takes over

In 1990, former US President Jimmy Carter went to Guyana to obtain free elections, and in 1992, the veteran Cheddi Jagan was declared 'the first freely elected President of Guyana'. The PPP alliance together with the Civic group (a social and political group of professionals and business people), got 54 per cent of the votes in the freest elections since 1964. But it was a narrow victory, with 32 seats to the PPP/Civic and 31 to the PNC. In parliament, there were 12 women (19 per cent), six from the PPP and six from the PNC. Janet became First Lady and was not appointed to the cabinet. She continued as a newspaper editor and also wrote children's books. The president chose the independent industrialist Samuel Hinds as prime minister, and had three women as cabinet ministers (12 per cent).

Cheddi was a national hero and one of the most charismatic and famous leaders of Latin America and the Caribbean. He had the image of being an ethnic moderate and modified his socialist views so that he promoted a mixed economy with a private sector and economic growth, as long as it contributed to social justice and ecological sustainability. While he was president, the economy grew rapidly. The education system was developed further. A national policy for women was adopted and the first woman chief justice was appointed. However, he died suddenly in 1997, at 79 years old.

After Cheddi Jagan's death, Samuel Hinds moved up and served as president, while Janet Jagan was the first woman vice president, first woman prime minister and minister of mines. In the elections that followed, with some hesitation, she agreed to run as the PPP presidential candidate. She was reluctant to take on the responsibilities associated with the country's highest office, but was aware of the appeal of the Jagan name and wanted to carry forward her late husband's agenda (see: www.rulers.org). In the PPP, she had support as a compromise candidate to maintain party unity in spite of contending factions (Jagan, 1999; Das, 2000).

The PPP/Civic obtained 55 per cent of the votes and 34 seats against 26 for the PNC. Janet Jagan became Latin America's second elected woman president, the first white president of Guyana and the first North American woman to head a nation. In parliament, 12 women were elected (19 per cent), as before, about evenly divided between the PPP/Civic and the PNC.

North American woman top leader

Janet Jagan's candidacy united the PPP, but widened the ethnic gulf in the country. After the elections, people demonstrated in the streets of the capital. They accused the PPP of fraud and claimed that Janet Jagan was unfit to lead the country because she was a white American woman and, at 77 years, was too old. The PNC went so far as to sabotage the work in parliament. To solve the crisis, CARICOM had to intervene and mediate and it was agreed to have an independent review of the elections (which found no evidence of cheating), revise the constitution and hold new elections in three years instead of five. The PNC MPs (except the leader) then took up parliamentary work, but there was continued unrest and strikes as the PNC tried to make the country ungovernable.

President Janet Jagan asked Samuel Hinds to continue as prime minister, with a cabinet with two woman ministers (15 per cent). She strengthened her husband's efforts in the areas of health, education and housing, rural electrification, and the provision of potable water. Further, she was an outspoken advocate for the full emancipation of Latin American women, including equal education, equal housing opportunities, equal pay for equal work and free maternity leave. In addition, she tried to promote regional cooperation. The UN Educational, Scientific and Cultural Organization (UNESCO) gave her the Gandhi Gold Medal for Peace, Democracy and Women's Rights. But the situation was very difficult (Jensen, 2008: 19–20).

In 1999, after 20 months, Janet Jagan resigned as president, officially for health reasons. But the PNC opposition had taken its toll. The (male) minister of finance took over as president, with a male colleague as prime minister, and he was re-elected with a PPP/civic majority in parliament in 2001, 2006 and 2011.

After Janet Jagan resigned as president, she continued as executive member of the PPP and wrote in the party newspaper. In 2009, she died and was hailed as a liberation hero because of her contribution to an independent Guyana and as one of the most important leaders produced by the country.

Women's liberation?

The political scientist and biographer David Hinds (2011: 207–8) notes that much of what Janet Jagan did was overshadowed by the stardom of her husband and the negative perception of her by the Afro-Guyanese. But whether as organiser, parliamentarian, journalist, advocate, minister or leader, she was steadfast and deliberate and an uncompromising partisan. She made a momentous contribution to the shaping of Guyana's politics, he states.

To the question as to whether Janet Jagan was a feminist, Hinds answers 'no'. She organised women and was concerned about women's issues, but this was part of her primary work, which was to strengthen the party as a means to change society, he emphasises. She did not champion 'autonomous women's organizations' (Hinds, 2011: 207).

Hinds does not go into depth and uses a narrow definition of the term 'feminist'. It is clear that Janet Jagan did not describe herself as 'feminist', and she might not fit the mould of many later 'feminists'. But she made important contributions to the emancipation of women in Guyana. She was conscious of her gender and identified with disadvantaged women. She wanted to change society, and women were an integral part of both the goals and means. It was necessary to have a strong political party, but also women's organisations. She stood up for women's rights not only by acquiring positions herself that had previously been reserved for men, but also by organising women to improve the status of women in general.

She started in the 1940s and her efforts spanned a broad range of issues during a long time span: six decades, all in all. In 1975, she declared:

> The women must join the struggle to bring about political and socio-economic changes so that there will be equal opportunities for all, so that we can end unemployment, poverty and hunger, so that genuine democratic institutions can flourish, so that our women can be free and equal citizens. (Jagan, 1975)

In 2012, there were 31 per cent women in Guyana's Parliament and 30 per cent in the cabinet – more than most countries in the region.

Panama's 'new dawn': Mireya Moscoso

Eccentric teacher

In 1999, Latin America got a new woman president, the fifth overall and the third who was elected. It was Mireya Elisa Moscoso Rodríguez de Arias of Panama. As Violeta Chamorro and Janet Jagan, she was the widow of a prominent politician, but her husband was not murdered. He was president several times and died a natural death of old age, as did Cheddi Jagan.[13]

Arnulfo Arias was elected president three times and as many times overthrown by the military. He came from a middle-class family in the province of Panama and was educated as a physician in the US. Yet, he reacted against the strong US influence in his country. Panama was separated from Colombia and established as an independent state in 1903 following a decision in the US Congress. The sole purpose was to build the Panama Canal under US domination. The population of the country was mostly Mestizos and Catholics. Formally, the country became a democracy, but, in reality, it was ruled by a commercial oligarchy and the military, with repeated coups and regime changes.

Together with his older brother, who was a prominent newspaper publisher, Arnulfo Arias founded a nationalist party, the Panamenista Party. In 1931, he helped engineer a coup that led his brother to power as president. He became minister of public works and agriculture. In 1940, he ran himself and was elected president. He created a social security system, strengthened labour laws, took over foreign companies and gave women limited voting rights in 1941, which were made universal in 1946. At the same time, he imprisoned dissidents, deprived non-Hispanics of their civil rights and gave voice to fascist sympathies. After a year, he was overthrown in a military coup, backed by the US. He was elected president again in 1949. Then he suspended the constitution, established a secret police force and was overthrown in 1951. In 1968, he was elected president for the third time, but the military ousted him after only 10 days (Skidmore and Smith, 2005: 367-70).

Secretary and boss

Mireya Moscoso was born in the countryside in 1946 as one of six siblings. Her father was a teacher and farmer, but died early, and Mireya grew up in straitened circumstances. But she got secondary education, worked as a secretary in a government office and became a sales manager in a coffee company owned by Arias. She contributed to his election campaign when he was elected president in 1968 and joined him in exile in Florida after the coup. Here, she studied interior design, and at 22 years old, she married the 67-year-old widower. He was a strong personality who, according to his wife, even decided her hairdo. He gave her education and political training. 'My biggest university was that of Dr Arias', Mireya Moscoso said (Navarro, 1999). In 1978, Arias travelled back to Panama and ran for president again in 1984. He was then 83 years old and lost. Afterwards, he returned to Florida, where he died in 1988.

From 1968, Panama was, in reality, a military dictatorship, although the presidents were civilians. The strongman was at all times a general. But infrastructure was built and social welfare programmes were initiated. Both women and men got education, and some women acquired high positions. When the economy deteriorated, and there was unrest, General Manuel Noriega intervened, cancelled the elections in 1989 and was declared president. Shortly after, the US invaded the country to protect the canal and restore democracy. Several thousand people were killed, Noriega was arrested for drug-dealing, and a new president was inaugurated. During 1990–94, it was decided to disband the army and replace it with only a police force, border guards and the like.

Widow takes up the mantle

After her husband's death, Mireya Moscoso went back to Panama and had various jobs. She married Ricardo Gruber and adopted a boy, but divorced after a few years. Arnulfo Arias was criticised for fascism, racism and mysticism while he was still alive. After his death, he became legendary as a nationalist, and Mireya Moscoso was asked to continue his policies, although few women participated in politics. At first, she refused, but in 1990, she helped create a centre-left Arnulfisto Party to replace the Panamenista Party and became leader of the party in 1991. At the end of the 1990s, it was estimated that the party had more than 100,000 members in a country with over 2.5 million inhabitants and was the second-largest party in Panama. How many women participated is not known, but in the leadership, they amounted to no more than one sixth.

According to the constitution, a president and two vice presidents were elected by direct elections and a parliament by plurality vote. The cabinet was appointed by the president. In 1994, the former First Lady ran for president in what became known as the first fully free elections in the country's history. She travelled around and began all her speeches with a Latin proverb that Arias was in the habit of using, *vox populi, vox Dei* (the people's voice, the voice of God), and lost by a meagre margin (Jensen, 2008: 162). Mireya Moscoso was the only woman of the seven candidates and received 29 per cent of the votes, while the rival candidate got 33 per cent. Moscoso became the main opposition leader, and in 1999, she ran again for president, at 52 years old. Now, there were only three candidates, and Moscoso won with 45 per cent of the votes. The opponent, Martin Torrijos, got 38 per cent. He was the son of the military dictator Omar Torrijos, a reasonably progressive nationalist who deposed Arias in 1968. With high unemployment and a poverty rate of more than a third, both candidates promised to curb the effects of free-market policies. Moscoso was regarded as the one placing the greatest emphasis on social justice, while Torrijos was perceived as more business-oriented (Jensen, 2008: 21–2).

Hopes of thousands of women

During the election campaign, Mireya Moscoso encountered male chauvinistic opposition and was told that she could not be president because she was a woman. She replied: 'I can wear pants just like the men in this country! And I know when to put on skirts, and when to put on pants, too!' (Navarro, 1999). When she became president, she declared that the country was beginning to make real the hopes of 'thousands of Panamanian women over the centuries' to share in the country's leadership (Gonzalez, 1999). But her policies were formulated in a general way. 'I won't forget my roots or my commitment to fight unemployment, poverty and its consequences', she said, 'I want for this country what I want for my son Ricardo, that he have the right to grow up in a democratic country, with guaranteed freedoms, with judicial stability and social justice' (Navarro, 1999).

Women were politically active in Panama before they got the right to vote in 1941. They founded, among others, a women's party in 1923. In 1950, Panama became the second country in Latin America to get a woman minister. But in the years that followed, the organisation of women was difficult and participation in political bodies was very small. Panama became party to the CEDAW in 1981, but it was only in the 1990s that a women's directorate was established and a plan for women elaborated. There was little activism among women, and in the elections in 1994, the representation of women in parliament was 9 per cent. In the cabinet, there were two women (13 per cent).

In 1997, a quota was introduced of 30 per cent women in party and general elections. But there were no sanctions for non-compliance. The parties were requested to use state funds to train women, but only Moscoso's party did this. In parliament, the representation of women was only 10 per cent in 1999, but Mireya Moscoso increased the number of female ministers from two to four, sometimes five (about 30 per cent) and had four female deputy prime ministers. When she retired in 2004, the proportion of women in parliament was 17 per cent, but in the cabinet of her male successor, the number of female ministers was reduced to three. In 2014, there were only 9 per cent women in parliament, while there were six female ministers in the cabinet (32 per cent).

Señora Presidenta from top to bottom

When Mireya Moscoso took office, she was immensely popular. People saw in her a possibility for change. But the Arnulfista Party had only one quarter of the seats in parliament and the Torrijos Party had almost half. Moscoso had to manoeuvre to get sufficient support. As the combined head of state and government, she appointed a 'national unity cabinet' with young professionals from different political camps. But they had little government experience.

During Moscoso's presidency, the country took over the Panama Canal. In 1977, General Omar Torrijos had agreed with President Jimmy Carter that Panama would gain control of the canal by 1999, and American troops pulled out for the first time since 1903. The president elaborated a national security plan, saw to an efficient administration of the canal and set about modernising. But there were problems when she signed a contract regarding US patrols in Panamanian waters to stop illegal drug trafficking and gave the Americans extended authority to conduct inspections of the economy in order to prevent tax evasion and money laundering.

The economy was sluggish to begin with. The profit from the Panama Canal was larger than before, but export earnings fell. Gradually, production, women's education and women's economic activity increased, but income disparities grew, and poverty continued. Despite tax reforms, there was a budget deficit.

Mireya Moscoso attracted most attention with her scandals. The president donated expensive Cartier watches to MPs and was accused of bribery. Thousands of dollars were allegedly stolen from the freezer of Moscoso's secretary, but no one knew where the money came from. Since Moscoso was divorced, her sister acted as 'First Lady', with the privileges it entailed, and the president herself was accused of misuse of public funds for campaigning.

When the president went so far as to remove the chief of social security, there was a general strike. People thought that she had not fulfilled her campaign promises to improve the economy and reduce corruption. At the end of Moscoso's term in 2004, her approval rating was the lowest for any Panamanian president (Hoogensen and Solheim, 2006: 117). She could not run for re-election, and the male presidential candidate of the Arnulfista Party only got 16 per cent of the votes. In parliament, the party won 22 per cent of the seats. There were four presidential candidates, and this time, Martin Torrijos emerged victorious, with 47 per cent of the votes. His party got more than half of the seats in parliament. After Moscoso, he represented a clear leftist alternative, and investigations of corruption allegations were initiated against her. But she moved back to Florida.

Beatriz Merino: independent woman in Peru

Fuji shock

Latin American women leaders after Moscoso had different backgrounds and paths to the top. But none of them were widows. They climbed to the top by using their own skill and perseverance. Families could help the women develop their competence, but only in one case up to 2010 did family ties lead directly to the political top leadership.

One of the world's oldest civilisations exists in Peru. It was the largest state in pre-Colombian America. After 300 years of Spanish colonial rule, the country was multicultural and multi-ethnic 'with all sorts of blood', but the vast majority of the population were Catholics. Peru became independent in 1824 after a hard struggle, and a Creole elite class took power. But the new state was marked by economic problems and political turmoil, with alternating civil and military regimes, democracy and authoritarianism.[14]

In 1980, Peru was one of the first countries to transition from prolonged military rule to democracy. But in 1990, the country found itself in the midst of a social, economic and political crisis that threatened both the political system and civil society. Parallel with the democratisation process, the country was stricken by the worst economic crisis in Peru's history. The standard of living went dramatically down and poverty increased. Guerrilla operations were launched in several places in the country.

The Japanese-born mathematician Albert Fujimori, who was an outspoken opponent of both the establishment and politics, was elected president in 1990, to general surprise. He implemented drastic measures to stop hyperinflation, and when there were protests, he staged a 'self-coup'. He suspended the constitution, arrested opposition leaders and ruled in an authoritarian way for two years. Afterwards, he adopted a new constitution with a strong president who was head of both state and government, and appointed two vice presidents, a prime minister and a cabinet. Parliament was reduced from two to one chamber elected by proportional representation. Fujimori forced through market-oriented reforms, swooped down upon terrorism and was re-elected as president in 1995. Afterwards, he continued to rule in a half-authoritarian manner. In a questionable election, his term of office was renewed in 2000, but then a serious corruption scandal broke out. Fujimori withdrew and fled to Japan. Later, he was charged and sentenced to several years in prison for corruption and human rights violations (Tanaka, 2005: 261–88).

Unexpected support

Female activism began early in Peru, but suffrage was first granted in 1955 by a general who wanted to secure the support of women. Unlike other military regimes, the Peruvian attempted to modernise the country, giving women and men education and possibilities for paid work and expanding social services. But poverty was widespread. From the end of the 1970s, an extensive and diverse women's movement emerged, but the relationship with political parties was tense. A women's commission was established in connection with the International Women's Year and CEDAW was ratified in 1982, but by the end of the 1980s, there were only 6 per cent women in the Chamber of Deputies, 3 per cent in the Senate and none in the cabinet (Vargas and Villanueva, 1994: 576–80; Barrig, 1998: 104–7).

President Fujimori created a women's ministry, got women-friendly laws adopted and introduced quotas for parliament. First, 25 per cent, then 30 per cent, of the candidates on the electoral lists should be women. Furthermore, Fujimori appointed a number of female ministers, state secretaries and leaders in the government administration. The policy was partly controversial, also among women, who believed it aimed more at strengthening the influence of the president than promoting the interests of women. But more women participated in politics. In 2011, there were 22 per cent women in parliament and three women (17 per cent) in the cabinet (Blondet, 2000).

Alejandro Toledo was elected president in 2001. He came from humble beginnings and was an economist in the World Bank. He went against Fujimori and founded his own centre party, Possible Peru. With a small margin, he became the first president of Indian descent, but he inherited weak political institutions and a party system in ruins. He promised to provide people with work and income. The economy was strengthened, and rural women received support. But austerity measures led to protests, strikes and blockades. In the course of a couple of years, Toledo had to declare a state of emergency twice and turn to the army to keep discontent at bay. In June 2003, support for the president was at a record low. Eight out of 10 Peruvians were against him, and when Toledo's second prime minister and the whole cabinet resigned, the president was in a mess. Toledo asked a lot of male politicians to become prime minister, but no one accepted. They did not want to risk their reputation in such a dubious undertaking. Finally, a woman said yes (Fournier, 2003).

Headstrong saviour

Beatriz Merino was no widow. She was born in 1947, was single and lived with an aunt and a girlfriend. Her mother had taught her to be tough, and she graduated in economics in London and undertook a master's of law at Harvard (Jensen, 2008: 91). She worked in the private sector, became senator in 1990 and was elected to Congress in 1995 as a conservative candidate in collaboration with, among others, the renowned author Mario Vargas Llosa. Llosa ran for president against Fujimori in 1990 and lost. Merino joined Peru Possible and ran for vice president in 2000, but was defeated. She was given the responsibility for the tax agency and received recognition for her management of a generally corrupt and inefficient administration. She became director of a programme for women leaders in the Inter-American Development Bank, was the first woman in the Andean

Commission of Jurists and was designated Peruvian woman of the year by the local chapter of the Organization of Women in International Trade.

Mario Vargas Llosa was asked to become prime minister, but declined. He would rather concentrate on his career as a writer. Instead, he is said to have persuaded Beatriz Merino to accept. She had political experience, was highly skilled and supported economic restructuring. Furthermore, she was known and respected by Peruvians for her honesty and for increasing tax revenue. 'In a difficult moment for the country, we will all have to work together', Merino said, 'and I want this cabinet to build a democracy based on consensus, on harmony' (Reuters, 2003). And she added that, with all due respect, she had never submitted herself to the empire of any man and would as prime minister 'co-govern' with Toledo (Jensen, 2008: 52).

Merino was the first woman prime minister in Peru and in Latin America, but not the first woman in a high position in Peru. She scored high in the polls when she was appointed, and the president's support also increased. But soon there were political attacks. She was accused of being a lesbian and finding government jobs for friends, which she denied. However, disagreement arose between her and the president regarding, among other things, the appointment of ministers, where Merino emphasised competence rather than patron–client relationships. Before half a year had passed, she resigned at the request of the president, and the male president of the Congress became prime minister instead of her. He sat for one-and-a-half years before a fifth (male) prime minister took over until President Toledo himself had to go in 2006. In 2009, the Congress elected Beatriz Merino as the first female Ombudsman in Latin America.

Unlikely pioneer in Chile: Michelle Bachelet

Latin America's oldest democracy

Most of the women top leaders in Latin America received little publicity internationally. But there were big newspaper headlines when Michelle Bachelet was elected President of Chile in 2006.[15] It was not just that she was a woman and the first woman elected president of a Latin American country without being a widow or a relative of a prominent male politician. It was about one of the region's most powerful positions as president, and Bachelet was agnostic, socialist and a divorced mother of three children by two different fathers in a country strongly marked by the Catholic Church. 'As the old joke goes, I have all the sins together', Michelle Bachelet commented (Contreras, 2005: 45).

Chile is an old democracy. Throughout history, the country only briefly had military rule. Most of the time, the upper class, the oligarchs and the Right were in the power. In the 20th century, the Right and the Left fought, and when the leftist Salvador Allende was elected president in 1970, not more than three years passed before he was deposed in a military coup supported by the US. The military dictatorship led by General Augusto Pinochet ruled with a hard hand and fought against all opposition by means of disappearances, torture and murder. Market liberalism was introduced, with privatisation and the reduction of government expenditures, with the result that unemployment and poverty rose dramatically. Chile became one of the countries with the largest gap between the rich and poor. It got so bad that the regime gradually changed attitude and intervened to improve the economy (Morgan, 1984: 134–7).

In a tightly controlled referendum in 1980, Pinochet got a new constitution approved. It entailed that a referendum on re-election of the dictator would be held in 1988. Pinochet was the only candidate and he expected to obtain a majority. But a centre-left alliance for democracy, Concertación, was formed with liberals, socialists and Christian democrats, and they managed to get 55 per cent of the votes for 'no', while 44 per cent voted 'yes'. Then, in 1989, a referendum was organised on democracy, a Christian democrat from Concertación was elected president, and Pinochet stepped down in 1990 (Skidmore and Smith, 2005: 109–38).

The constitution of 1989 introduced a presidential system, with an elected president who was head of state and government and appointed a prime minister and a cabinet. The Senate was elected by a mixed system, while the Chamber of Deputies was elected by a simple plurality. Concertación won all the presidential elections until 2010. A president could not be re-elected, and there were, first, two Christian democrats, then two socialists. But rightist forces made themselves felt. The electoral system – which was almost impossible to change – was criticised for being undemocratic because the numbers did not necessarily determine who was elected. It was very difficult for minority groups and women to enter parliament, and right-wing parties were systematically over-represented. Political reforms were carried out, but only gradually because the rightists could block constitutional amendments. Investments were made in infrastructure, and unlike other countries on the continent, Chile achieved exceptional economic growth and stability. Health and education were developed, incomes increased, and the number of poor was more than halved. More women obtained paid work (Angell, 2010).

Victim of the dictator

Verónica Michelle Bachelet Jeri, as is her full name, was the victim of Pinochet's regime and had special appeal in a country that had recently lived through dictatorship. She was born in 1951 in Santiago. Her mother, Angela Jeri Gómez, was an anthropologist and active socialist. Her father, Alberto Bachelet Martinez, was a general in the air force and was stationed on various military bases in Chile and in the Chilean Embassy in Washington DC. The family went with him, and Michelle and her older brother went to different schools. In the US, the young girl was shocked by the racial discrimination and the assassination of President Kennedy. Back again in Chile, she got involved as a socialist in the protest movements in the late 1960s. She did well in school and began to study medicine in the same year that Salvador Allende was elected president.

Her father worked in Allende's administration and was immediately jailed when Pinochet came to power. After months of torture, he died in prison of a heart attack. Michelle Bachelet and her mother were also imprisoned and tortured before they were released and exiled to Australia, where Michelle's brother lived. But they travelled on to East Germany, where Chilean socialists in exile gathered and organised protests against Pinochet. Michelle continued her medical studies and worked at a health clinic. She met a Chilean architect, Jorge Davalos Leopolo Cartes, whom she married and they had a boy and a girl before they parted.

Meanwhile, the family was able to go back to Chile, where Michelle Bachelet completed medical training and specialised in children's diseases and public health. At the same time, she took care of her children and home as a single mother. Afterwards, she said:

> As a young mother and a paediatrician, I experienced the struggles of balancing family and career and saw how the absence of childcare prevented women from paid employment. The opportunity to help remove these barriers was one of the reasons I went into politics. (Bachelet, quoted in *UNESCO Courier*, 2011: 11)

Michelle Bachelet also worked to restore democracy and help the victims of the dictatorship. After Pinochet's fall, she went into the public health service and assisted poor patients. She was an advisor to the Ministry of Health and the World Health Organization and had her third child, a girl, with a fellow physician, Arúbal Hernán Henríquez Marich, but their life together only lasted a few years.

Michelle Bachelet was interested in the relationship between the military and the popularly elected politicians in Chile. She began studying military policy and strategy, first, in Chile, then in the US. She became an advisor to the minister of defence and undertook a master's degree in military research at the army's war academy. She was also active in the Socialist Party, where she became a member of the Central Committee and the political commission. In 1996, she ran for mayor in Las Condes, but lost (Hoogensen and Solheim, 2006: 118–19; Worth, 2008).

Popular minister of defence

Chilean women began to demand education, access to occupations and voting rights at the end of the 1800s. Women's parties were founded in 1922 and 1946, and the right to vote was granted in 1949, but women were not integrated into politics. During the Pinochet dictatorship, when political parties were banned, the women's movement fought against general oppression and economic decline. At the same time, feminists claimed women's rights in civil life, the labour market and with regards to reproduction and the family. But Pinochet strengthened women's role as mothers, opposed their occupational participation and went against divorce, contraception and abortion.

After democracy was reinstated, women's activities flourished, particularly in relation to the state and political parties, but the movement also became less united and independent. Unlike many other Latin American countries, Chile had a strong party system, and it is estimated that women accounted for about 45 per cent of party members at the beginning of the 1990s. But few acquired leadership positions. Some centre-left parties introduced quotas, but there was, all in all, not more than one woman in six in the governing bodies of political parties in 1998. But women organised their own coalition for democracy and women's demands were included in the Concertación programme.

Chile became party to the CEDAW in 1989 (shortly before the elections) and a comprehensive gender equality plan was presented. A women's ministry with considerable resources was created and a number of women-friendly legislative amendments were passed. But Chile was lowest in Latin America with regards to women in the labour market, and Chilean women had greater difficulties than women in neighbouring countries getting into elected bodies. Because of opposition from the Right, it was not possible to introduce quotas at elections, and in the 1990s, women only accounted for 6 per cent in the Chamber of Deputies and the Senate. During the years until 2005, representation increased to 15 per cent in the Chamber of Deputies, but it was lower than the average in the region, and in the Senate, it was only 4 per cent. In 1990, there was only one woman minister. This increased to three, then five, but in 2005, went down again to only three (18 per cent). And it was hard to gain acceptance for a satisfactory feminist agenda. Chile was the only country in the Western Hemisphere with a ban on divorce when it was finally legalised in 2004 (Htun, 1998b; Valenzuela, 1998: 47–74; Craske, 1999).

When the socialist Ricardo Lagos became president in 2000, he increased the number of woman ministers, and Michelle Bachelet became minister of health. Then, in 2002, she became the first woman minister of defence in Latin America. People were uncertain how she would handle the system that had killed her father, but she took a cautious stance, trying to avoid confrontation, and won respect with her toughness without hate. She said:

> I'm not an angel. I haven't forgotten. It left pain. But I have tried to channel the pain into a constructive realm. I insist on the idea that what happened here in Chile was so painful, so terrible, that I wouldn't wish for anyone to live through our situation again. (Bachelet, quoted in Worth, 2008: 14)

Michelle Bachelet cooperated with the army leadership while Pinochet's henchmen were brought to justice. In 2003, the army leadership declared that the army would never undermine Chile's democratically elected government again.

Bachelet became so popular in the polls that she was asked to run for president by the socialists. At first, she did not want to. She had never before held elected office, but nevertheless ended up running because she would not let her supporters down. In addition, her youngest child had reached the age of 12. She became the second Chilean woman to run for president. The first, the Communist Party leader Gladys Martin, did so in 1999 and got less than 4 per cent of the votes (Hoogensen and Solheim, 2006: 199–20).

Gender equality in the centre

The presidential elections in 2005/06 took place under stable economic conditions. The centre-left coalition enjoyed considerable popularity, and after 15 years of uninterrupted rule with little room for women, a certain resentment was felt among people against the traditional male politicians. As a woman, Michelle Bachelet could stand forth as an outsider, someone who was 'new' and closer to the people, with a wind of change. The traditional gender roles helped her. She was perceived as incorruptible, more interested in the nation than trivial party matters and willing to engage in politics in a new way. Some observers believe she had special appeal as a mother figure, being 54 years old, tolerant and pluralistic, who could heal the wounds caused by armed conflict and dictatorship. The mixture of continuity and change helped attract both traditional and new voters, and positive opinion polls were a determining factor in the nomination, making Bachelet the only official candidate of the coalition. The rival candidate, a former woman minister from the Christian democrats, withdrew due to lack of support (Franceschet and Gwynn, 2010: 177–95).

At the elections, Michelle Bachelet ran against three men. The Right did not manage to agree on one single candidate, and two of the men who ran had a history with Pinochet's regime, which was under investigation for human rights violations. Bachelet went out with the slogan 'I'm With You', and added:

> I can do politics differently because I am a woman. People expect women to be more ethical and caring than men. Because I was the victim of hate, I have consecrated my life to turning hate into understanding, tolerance and, why not say it – love. (Bachelet, quoted in Worth, 2008: 12–20)

She focused on equality and social cohesion in the election campaign and worked to reduce the gap between the poor and rich, give the original population more influence, and strengthen the position of women in politics and the economy. She did not call herself a 'feminist', but she came forward with a strong pro-women profile. She demanded women's quotas in elections, gender balance in political positions, kindergartens and equality in the workplace. For once, the debate during the election campaign focused on gender equality and women's status in society.

In the first round, Bachelet got 46 per cent of the votes. It was not enough to get elected under Chilean law. In the run-off against Sebastian Piñera, a centre-right millionaire who was allegedly the country's richest man, she won with more than 53 per cent of the votes. It was a bigger margin than Lagos had in the earlier election, and it was considered a milestone. It benefited Bachelet that Chile was the only country in Latin America with a well-educated middle class, and that democracy worked better than in most countries in the region. But it was decisive that women who had voted for the conservatives before now supported Bachelet (Reel, 2006; Tobar, 2008).

Dauntless lady

Chilean socialism was 'pragmatic' and united liberal economic policies with progressive social policies. It was an important goal to reduce disparities between the rich and poor, which were among the largest in the world. As president, Michelle Bachelet started out with an absolute majority in both chambers and a generous budget. She immediately began to implement 36 measures that she had promised in the campaign to carry out during the first 100 days. They spanned from free treatment for elderly patients to reform of the social security system and the construction of kindergartens and shelters. Health centres were established to distribute contraceptives, in spite of significant protests, but legalisation of abortion was out of the question. Christian democrats were a vital part of the centre-left coalition.

The newly elected president provoked rousing cheers when she saluted the audience with 'Chilean women and men' instead of the usual 'Chilean men and women', and the new cabinet was presented, one by one, in the strong light of the TV projectors – woman, man, another woman, man, still another woman – until the election promise of 50/50 was fulfilled: 10 women and 10 men. The world's feminists rejoiced. And Bachelet maintained a consistent pro-women approach throughout her presidency in spite of considerable resistance and problems.

The debate concerning the appointment of the cabinet started at once. Most of the ministers were highly educated technocrats and only two had previous government experience. And the way ahead was not straightforward: miners went on strike; contraception for teenagers led to an outcry; massive student demonstrations demanded a better quality of education; and serious problems arose in the transport system in the capital. Bachelet replaced ministers. Several experienced party members were brought in, and the share of women went down. Gradually, the government lost the majority in both chambers of Congress because people withdrew from the coalition and became independent. The president had to negotiate with various groups to get proposals through. The miners got higher wages, Bachelet was able to implement an education reform and the minister of transport was replaced. But the Constitutional Court (all men) prevented the morning-after pill from becoming freely available, and in 2007, support for the president was down to 40 per cent.

Chile was a 'macho' country. On the streets, people called Bachelet 'La Gordis' (the fat lady), and Bachelet's warm and inclusive attitude, with the ability to listen and create agreement, was perceived as uncertainty, dawdling and indecision. At the same time, she was criticised for having a bad temper when she was angry, while a man in the same situation would hear that he was a strong leader. But when the global financial crisis hit in 2008/09, the president handled it with an efficiency that silenced many critics. And when her period neared its end, she got 80 per cent support in the polls. *Forbes* magazine ranked her as number 17 on the list of the world's most powerful women in 2006; number 27 in 2007; number 25 in 2008; and number 22 in 2009 (Barnes and Jones, 2011: 109–18).

Progress for women

In spite of economic growth and poverty reduction, Chile remained one of the countries in the region where inequalities were greatest. There was considerable progress for women during Bachelet's presidency, but Chile was still a solid male-dominated society. The cabinet did not always include 50/50 women and men, but Chile was among the world's front-runners, with mostly between 40 and 50 per cent women ministers, and a significant number of women were employed in the state administration. The proposed quota system in the elections was stopped by Congress, and in 2008, there were only 15 per cent women in the Chamber of Deputies and 5 per cent in the Senate. But equality rules were made applicable to all public services and the private sector was encouraged to follow suit. The Ministry for Women was strengthened. Support for mothers was increased, breastfeeding and child nutrition were strengthened, and the number of free nursery schools was multiplied. Women got more education, and thousands of female-headed households received vocational training. Still, Chile was at the bottom in the region, with only two out of five women in paid labour, and executive boards and trade unions with only men. A large number of shelters were established, but one of the world's strictest abortion laws was not changed. Chile was also criticised for a lack of human rights for indigenous people in the country (Angell, 2010: 269–306; Pribble and Huber, 2011; Roberts, 2011).

The constitution limited the president's term to four years and prohibited immediate re-election. So, Bachelet could not run in the 2009 elections. And for the first time in 50 years, since Pinochet, a president from the Right, not the centre-left, was elected. It was a small margin: the millionaire Sebastian Piñera got 52 per cent of the votes against 48 per cent for the male candidate from Concertación. In Congress, the race was extremely close. Neither of the two coalitions obtained a majority. The representation of women went down slightly to 14 per cent in the Chamber of Deputies, while it rose to 13 per cent in the Senate. In the new cabinet, it was reduced to 27 per cent.

With international recognition, Michelle Bachelet was elected the first executive director of the new entity for gender equality in the United Nations, UN Women, in September 2010. Her service during the first term was 'outstanding' according to the UN Secretary General Ban Ki-moon (see: www.un.org). But then Bachelet wanted to go back to Chile. So, she resigned to run for president again in the autumn of 2013. The conservative President, Piñera, was confronted with widespread demonstrations for change. Left-wing Bachelet promised to finance education with higher corporate taxes, reduce the wealth gap, protect the environment and reform the constitution. There were nine candidates, and in the second round, two women were running against each other for the first time. Right-wing Evelyn Mathei's father was a member of Pinochet's junta, and in the final election in December 2013, Bachelet won a landslide victory, with 62 per cent of the votes. But in parliament, Bachelet's New Majority coalition did not get more than 55 per cent of the seats in the Chamber of Deputies and 56 per cent in the Senate, which is insufficient for some of the reforms Bachelet promoted. The representation of women in parliament remained low: 16 per cent in the Chamber of Deputies and 18 per cent in the Senate. In the cabinet Bachelet appointed 39 per cent women (9 of 23).

Cristina Fernández follows up in Argentina

Depressed democracy

In 2007, Latin America got its seventh woman president. This time, it was in Argentina – a country with twice as many inhabitants as Chile – and Cristina Fernández de Kirchner was the second woman who went to the top. But she was the first who was elected. She was not the widow of a deceased president, as Isabel Perón was 30 years earlier, but the wife of one who was very much alive at the time. She and her husband were Argentina's 'power couple', while she pursued her own career at the same time. Her husband helped her to become president, but died in 2010 before her first term was over.[16]

The coup that deposed Isabel Perón in 1976 was the beginning of a civil–military dictatorship that lasted until 1983. Political activity was prohibited and opposition was banned. Around 30,000 people disappeared, were tortured and killed in what was named 'the dirty war'. Human rights violations, economic decline, allegations of corruption and, finally, defeat after the occupation of the Islas Malvinas (Falkland Islands) brought the military regime into discredit. Under strong public pressure, the ban on political activities was lifted, and in 1983, democratic elections were held to choose a civilian president, vice president and parliament.

The democratisation process was turbulent. There were military revolts and economic problems. Under pressure from the military, two amnesty laws were adopted protecting members of the former military regime from prosecution. The Perónist politician Carlos Menem became president in 1989 and launched a neo-liberal policy without precedent in Latin America. The state was supposed to leave everything to the market. Trade and finance were liberalised and agribusiness giants were brought in to cultivate genetically modified soybeans on a large scale for export. State enterprises and public services, including health and pensions, were privatised. The consequence was that small and medium enterprises went bankrupt and farmers were driven from their lands. Debt, unemployment and poverty increased, while a heavy burden of care was placed on women.

In 2001, the most serious economic, social and political crisis in the country's turbulent history occurred. Massive protests resulted in 30 people being killed, and five interim presidents were elected, one after the other, in the course of a week. The democratic institutions were about to collapse, but they did not, even though they were weak and unstable. There was broad resistance among people against military rule, in fact, against the entire political class. The slogan was 'Away with them all'. But the political parties, particularly the Perónists, were strong and civil society was robust (Levitsky, 2005: 63–89).

New radical generation

According to the constitution, the president was directly elected and served as head of both state and government, presiding over an appointed cabinet. Legislative power was shared with parliament. The Chamber of Deputies was directly elected using proportional representation, while the Senate was elected by provincial assemblies and minority groups. In 2003, the Perónists were split, and three of the five presidential candidates in the election were Perónists. Carlos Menem, who had been president twice before, won the first round, but he only got 24 per cent of the votes, while the relatively unknown Néstor Kirchner, who had been governor of Santa Cruz during three periods, got 22 per cent on a record-low voter turnout. Polls forecast a victory for Kirchner and Menem decided to stand down. Suddenly, Kirchner emerged victorious, with the lowest percentage gained by any winner of a presidential election.

Néstor Kirchner represented a new generation of politicians. He was a centre-left Perónist in opposition to Carlos Menem and promised to 'return to a republic of equals'. But he only appointed one woman in his cabinet: his sister, who had a PhD in social work and became minister of social policy.

Kirchner came into office on the tail of a deep economic crisis. The country was deeply impoverished, with a record debt burden. He stressed the need for accountability in government, changed the judges and made dozens of officers in the armed forces step down. The party, the police and the military were reorganised and the amnesty laws repealed so that human rights violations became punishable again. Measures were taken against corruption, and economic policy was changed. Kirchner was not opposed to markets and the private sector, but he was critical of neo-liberalism and the International Monetary Fund's (IMF's) structural adjustment and emphasised instead the need for state intervention, external debt reduction and social inclusion. He introduced regulations and taxes, increased employment in the public sector, subsidised energy and transport, mobilised manpower and industries, and refused to repay debt to the IMF.

IMF experts predicted that the economy would decline again, but Kirchner put the doomsday predictions to shame. The economy grew, infrastructure, housing and education were developed, and wages and social security increased. Poverty was reduced, but not the disparities in income, and there were some high-profile financial scandals. But when Néstor Kirchner resigned in 2007, aged 57, he was the most popular outgoing president in Argentina's modern history.

Kirchner could have run for re-election, but did not. Instead, his wife Cristina ran and was elected.

Thirty years of politics

Cristina Fernández was born in La Plata in Buenos Aires in 1953. Her father was head of a medium-size bus company and supported the Radical Party, while her mother was a trade union leader for government employees and a Perónist. Cristina Fernández was compared with Evita Perón, but Cristina came from the middle class and did not experience poverty first-hand like Evita did. Furthermore, Cristina was given a solid education and met Néstor Kirchner while she was studying law at university. Both completed law school, but Néstor went on and also undertook a PhD. They married in 1975 and had two children, a boy in 1977 and a girl in 1990. Néstor's mother and the extended family helped take care of the children. Both Cristina and Néstor got involved in the Perónist Party in the 1970s, but during the military dictatorship and the 'dirty war', they went to his hometown in the Santa Cruz province in the south of the country and started a law firm.

After civilians took over the reins, Néstor got a job in the provincial administration and was elected, first, as mayor of his hometown in 1987 and then as governor of Santa Cruz in 1991. Cristina was elected to the provincial parliament in 1989 and again in 1993. In 1995, she was the first of the couple to move up to the national level, being elected to the Senate from Santa Cruz. In 1997, she was elected to the Chamber of Deputies, and in 2001, to the Senate again, while Néstor continued as governor.

When Cristina Fernández became president, she had been active in the Perónist Party for more than 30 years and had important posts for 18 of them. She became nationally known as a senator during 1995–97 when she criticised President Menem for illegal arms sales and corruption and was excluded from the party group of the Perónists. At this point, there were only 10 per cent women in the party leadership, and Néstor Kirchner was a relatively unnoticed provincial politician. It was a long time before he decided to run for president (Barnes and Jones, 2011: 105–21).

Quota pioneer

Different women's organisations fought against the military dictatorship. The Mothers and Grandmothers on Plaza de Mayo demanded that the killings and disappearances should be cleared up and became world-famous. During democratisation and the economic crisis, women were engaged on several fronts. They had to seek gainful employment in large numbers at the same time as unemployment was high. To mitigate the distress, women organised relief measures. They participated in political parties and raised women's issues, and organised feminist groups and national women's meetings. Women politicians collaborated with the women's movement, and when democracy was threatened or human rights were violated, protests were mobilised.

In 1985, Argentina became party to the CEDAW. A women's office was established in the state administration, and family law was revised. In 1989, the first woman minister of external relations, Susanna Myrta Ruiz Certi, was appointed by the first civil president after the dictatorship, Raúl Alfonsin from the Radical Party, but she did not stay in office very long. At the time, there were only 6 per cent women in the Chamber of Deputies and 9 per cent in the Senate. The Perónist Party used quotas in the 1950s, and in 1991, with the support of President Menem, quotas were reintroduced during elections to the Chamber of Deputies: 30 per cent of the candidates at the top of the lists should be women. The proposal was put forward by a bipartisan group of women politicians and adopted by a large majority.

Argentina was the first country in Latin America to introduce such quotas, and it led to a dramatic increase in female representation. Argentina's electoral system, with proportional representation for the Chamber of Deputies, was an advantage, and sanctions were introduced so that electoral lists were not approved if they did not follow the quota rule. The women's movement monitored the action of the parties. Along with Costa Rica, Argentina led the continent with regards to women parliamentarians.

In 1998/99, there were 27 per cent women in the Argentine Chamber of Deputies. But other arenas did not automatically follow. There were only 11 per cent women in the cabinet and 3 per cent in the Senate. The party leadership of the Perónist Party had only 6 per cent women; the Radical Party, 8 per cent; and the moderate leftist Front for a Country in Solidarity (*Frente por un Pais Solidario, FREPASO*), 13 per cent. In 2000, the quota law was strengthened, and quotas were also applied to the Senate.

The increased representation of women had consequences, though it did not alter existing political frameworks. A ban on the use and sale of contraceptives was dismantled and access to information and services vital to reproductive health and responsible procreation was mandated. Furthermore, legal exceptions were adopted to the ban on abortion (Carrio, 2005: 164–72; Araújo and Garcia, 2006).

Fernández and Kirchner

Cristina Fernández de Kirchner played a central role in her husband's political activities. But when her husband was inaugurated as president, she made a point of remaining in her seat in the Senate instead of joining him on the podium, to signify that she had her own political position. And she was not content with being 'First Lady'; she preferred 'First Citizen' and ran for re-election to the Senate in 2005 against the wife of a former Perónist president. She won the 'wife duel' by a margin of 25 percentage points. In the Senate, Fernández worked actively to get her husband's bills adopted, lobbied the courts to prosecute atrocities of the 1976–83 dictatorship and defended women's rights.

There were 14 candidates in the presidential election in 2007, among them, three women, several with ties to the Perónist Party. Fernández won, with 45 per cent of the votes in the first round, while the runner-up, also a woman, got 23 per cent. The success of her husband helped 54-year-old Cristina Fernández be elected as president, and many felt that it was time for a woman. Fernández emphasised that she would continue and expand the economic and social reforms her husband had started (Bacon, 2012). The Perónist Party had a powerful electoral machine. It was the only mass party in the country and mobilised through a mixture of patron–client relationships and other appeals. But there were internal divisions, and Fernández received support particularly from the suburban working class and the rural poor. The opposition was extremely weak and fragmented.

The Perónist Party won a majority in both chambers. And women obtained 40 per cent of the seats in the Chamber of Deputies and 39 per cent in the Senate. Argentina was number five on the world-ranking list of women in parliament.

Néstor Kirchner became member of the Chamber of Deputies and also leader of the Perónist Party. In practice, he was his wife's co-president. They governed together and the press referred to the 'presidential marriage'. Cristina also took over most of her husband's ministers (seven of 12) when she appointed her cabinet. Her team only included three women (25 per cent) (Levitsky and Murillo, 2008).

Economic and social reform

As Néstor Kirchner restructured Argentina's foreign debt and achieved macroeconomic growth while he was in office, Fernández could as president build on this with things like improved education and a system of national public health. She hoped to make Argentina a human rights role model in the world (Padgett, 2007).

Fernández had more political experience than her husband when he was elected, but the economy was vulnerable and got into trouble when the global financial crisis struck in 2007/08. Fernández reacted swiftly and launched a massive programme to increase employment and profits. But her nationalisation of private pension funds created turmoil, and when she wanted to raise the export tax on agricultural products to increase income, the landowners and peasants went on strike. There was disagreement about inflation and the correctness of the national statistics was questioned. Fernández was further accused by media-owners of undermining press freedom with new media legislation. The press talked about the president's 'fall', and in the midterm elections in 2009, the Perónists lost their majority in both chambers.

Fernández renewed contact with the international financial institutions (including the IMF) to obtain loans and debt relief and introduced new stimulation measures. Commodity prices were high, exports of soybeans increased rapidly and the economy grew. It became possible to pursue a policy of social transformation, create jobs, raise wages and expand welfare programmes. Energy was subsidised, millions of people got pensions and poor children received benefits. The Universal Child Allocation programme was called the 'most transcendent social policy decision in a long time', by the Plata University (Kyle, 2010).

From 2003 on, Argentina had one of the highest economic growth rates in Latin America, but it stagnated after 2009 and inflation was high. Poverty and unemployment was reduced, but the country remained severely stratified, with large income inequalities. Misery and marginalisation were widespread and environmental problems increased. Welfare policies were also criticised for creating social clients instead of generating economic activity.

With regards to human rights, people responsible for torture, disappearances and mass murder during the dictatorship were put on trial, among others, leading members of the former military junta, and sentences were passed. The largest centre for torture in Buenos Aires was transformed into a human rights centre.

Queen and wife

The Argentine macho culture made a top political career extremely complicated for a woman, and Fernández played different, sometimes inconsistent, roles. Instead of downplaying her gender in a male-dominated environment, she emphasised her feminine appearance, using make-up, wearing expensive clothes and proudly stating that she never lost her place in the house.

When she ran for president in 2007, the media criticised her femininity rather than her policy, her marriage rather than her career. She was not a competent politician, but a spotlight-hungry starlet. *The Times* of the UK mocked her: 'Lipstick goes a long way in dazzling the masses'. The Argentinian press called her a 'courageous doll', but also 'Queen Cristina' and compared her with Evita Péron and Hillary Clinton. *The Economist* stated that Cristina owed her job to a prominent husband: 'For Argentine women, the best route to the political summit is still to be a Perónist wife'.

Fernández underlined that she did not want to inherit anything from Evita or her husband. Everything she had was a result of her own achievements, and her own defects, too. And she boasted that she was elected Senator long before her husband became president. At the same time, there were pictures of Evita at Fernández's meetings during the election campaign, and she said that she would build on and continue her husband's policies. The close political collaboration between the two was also maintained.[17]

While she was still a senator, she was asked if she was a 'feminist', she replied:

> I consider myself feminine. But if you recognize feminism as a political category, you're validating the notion that machismo is a political category. I believe in defending the rights of women and of minorities, but not under the label of being a 'feminist'. (Fernández, quoted in Contreras, 2005: 47)

During the election campaign in 2007, Fernández appealed to her 'sisters in gender' and stated: 'Women today bring a different face to politics. We are culturally formed to be citizens of two worlds, public and private' (Padgett, 2007: 2). She admired her predecessor Evita Perón, but it was primarily due to her passion and combativeness. And Fernández did not address women's issues during the election campaign. Gender equality was not mentioned as a political goal, either. On election night, however, she exclaimed that she felt 'an enormous responsibility to her gender' (Hyland, 2011: 2) (see also Barrionuevo, 2007; Petterson, 2007; Reel, 2007).

Women's groups felt that Fernández did not do enough to improve the status of women when she became president. She was criticised for not being more outspoken about the stark inequalities facing women and not being more active in advancing issues like equal pay. But in 2009, a comprehensive new law on violence against women was approved. In 2010, Argentina was the first Latin American country to allow same-sex marriages and an 'Argentine Bicentenary Hall of Women' was created, exhibiting notable women in Argentine history.

Reproductive rights were a thorny issue. Fernández was against abortion, and laws and policies benefiting women by guaranteeing access to contraceptives and legal abortion went unimplemented. Physicians also refused to perform legal abortions. Thus, unsafe abortions continued to be a leading cause of maternal death. In addition, contraceptives were difficult to obtain (Human Rights Watch, 2010).

Brilliant re-election

Forbes magazine ranked 'la Presidenta' as number 13 of the world's 100 most powerful women in 2008; number 11 in 2009; then as only number 68 in 2010; but as 17, 16 and 26 in 2011, 2012 and 2013, respectively.

A year before the presidential elections in 2011, Néstor Kirchner suddenly died. In the campaign that followed, Fernández did everything to emphasise her role as widow. She dressed only in black, praised her husband's policies and asserted that she would follow them closely. Certain media questioned her capabilities for office and called her 'fake', 'hysterical' and 'mentally unstable' (Dzodan, 2011).

Nevertheless, Fernández ran for re-election as president with the male minister of the economy as candidate for vice president. The opposition was fragmented and Cristina Fernández was elected against six other candidates with the largest margin since democracy was introduced in 1983. As the first woman head of state in Latin America, she was re-elected with 54 per cent of the votes, while the runner-up only got 17 per cent.

The Front for Victory (FPV) headed by Fernández won a majority in both chambers of Congress. The share of women was 37 per cent in the Chamber of Deputies and 39 per cent in the Senate. But the president only appointed three women (18 per cent) in the cabinet.

Cristina Fernández consolidated herself as the single-most powerful woman in Argentina. Her policies were controversial, but after five years of her presidency, research associate Kathleen Bacon (2012) wrote that Fernández had established herself as a 'formidable and independent politician' with enough political courage to break taboos and become a recognisable leader in Latin America. But the general elections in 2013 did not go very well. Discontent related to economic problems, high inflation and high crime strengthened the opposition. The FPV remained the largest party with 29 per cent in the Chamber of Deputies and 32 per cent in the Senate, and the FPV alliance obtained a majority in both chambers. But it is not sufficient to change the constitution so that Fernández can be re-elected again at the presidential elections in 2015. The representation of women remained unchanged from 2011 and Fernández continued with three women ministers.

Pink Wave in Costa Rica and Brazil: Laura Chinchilla and Dilma Rousseff

Small and unarmed

A leftist wave swept over the Latin American continent in the 2000s. It reached a majority of the countries, and women's rights were a part. The 'Pink Wave', as it was called, contributed to women rising to the top not only in Argentina, but also in Costa Rica and Brazil. In 2010/11, three women on the continent were presidents at the same time (Levitsky and Roberts, 2011, Shifter, 2011).

Costa Rica was sparsely populated, with few resources. The colonial power cared little about the country, which became one of Spain's poorest colonies and had few armed forces. The inhabitants were farmers and came to consist of a mixture of different kinds of 'whites'. Catholicism became the state religion. After the country became independent during 1821–38, it was one of the most stable democracies in Latin America, with the exception of a period of military dictatorship in the 1800s and a brief civil war in 1948. A presidential system was established, with a directly elected president and two vice presidents on the same ticket and a parliament elected with proportional representation. Presidential power was limited by parliament having control over the budget. On the other hand, the president appointed the cabinet without approval by the parliament. Over the years, the parties in power alternated, after 1949, between the social-democratic National Liberation Party (PLN) and a loose grouping of opposition parties who eventually called themselves the Christian Socialist Unity Party (PUSC). The economy grew, and education and social services were developed. Despite the severe economic crisis in the 1980s, Costa Rica became one of the most prosperous countries in Central America, and the country distinguished itself by the fact that it had no standing army. But the police force was well equipped and the defence budget greater than that of neighbouring Nicaragua.

In the interwar period, women organised to obtain rights and change the dominant macho culture. Both women and men got an education, and in 1949, women also got the right to vote. The same year, a woman was appointed minister of education, but no women were elected to parliament. A large number of women's organisations and groups were created, and many fought for equality. Costa Rica became a model for progressive social policies that protected women, but long-lasting differences between men and women persisted, especially in terms of employment and politics. Women got fewer jobs and less income than men and were more affected by unemployment. The representation of women in political parties and parliament increased very slowly.

In 1986, there were 12 per cent women in parliament. A woman was elected second vice president, and one was minister. In 1990, a law was passed to strengthen the implementation of gender equality in practice. The parties were, among other things, required to give women training to strengthen their political role. In 1996, quotas were introduced, and Costa Rica went to the top on the continent with nearly gender-balanced leaderships of the political parties. The share of women in parliament rose to 35 per cent in 2010.

Woman number eight

In 2006, the Costa Rican President during 1986–90, Oscar Arias, who got the Nobel Peace Prize for his Central American peace plan, and was president of the PLN, was again elected president of Costa Rica. It happened with a surprisingly narrow margin because Arias backed a free trade agreement that was very controversial. He was also criticised for supporting neo-liberalism. But he received universal recognition for the way he handled the financial crisis in 2008/09.

Laura Chinchilla, also from the PLN, was elected as Arias' first vice president and simultaneously became minister of justice. There were 30 per cent women in the cabinet. Arias wanted Chinchilla to succeed him, and she ran as the presidential candidate for the PLN. At 51 years old, she won the elections in May 2010, with 47 per cent of the vote in competition with five men and a woman, and became the eighth female president in Latin America.[18]

Laura Chinchilla was born into a political family in San José in 1959. Her father was a high government official and Laura got a university education in Costa Rica and Washington DC. She took a master's degree in public policy, specialised in institutional reform, particularly reform of the state, the judiciary and the police, and worked as a consultant for various international organisations. In 1982, Laura Chinchilla married Mario Alberto Madrigal Diaz, but they divorced. In 1996, she had a son with a lawyer, José María Rico Cueto, and they married in 2000. During 1994–98, she was, first, vice-minister and then minister for public security in the PLN government, and during 2002–06 she was a member of parliament (MP) before she became vice president.

During her campaign, Chinchilla was attacked for being Arias's protégée and puppet, and for supporting neo-liberalism and free trade as he did. She was also criticised by women activists because she was opposed to gay marriage and abortion in most cases and answered evasively on women's issues. At her inauguration as president, Chinchilla promised a more inclusive, transparent and green government. Her government would be for all women and men. She would take up the banner of ethics and transparency, work for a more prosperous and competitive Costa Rica, and make the country safer amid growing concern over drug-related violence (News Wires, 2010).

As newly elected president, Chinchilla appointed 39 per cent women in her cabinet, and on her first day at work, she banned opencast mining for environmental reasons and created an anti-drug commission, a network for the care of the elderly and one for the care and education of preschool children. But the PLN did not have a majority in parliament. The two-party system was replaced by three, and the PLN only got 40 per cent of the seats. So, the adoption of measures required alliances with other parties, Left or Right. The situation was not made easier for Chinchilla by difficult challenges: a periodical dispute with Nicaragua about their common border, a growing budget deficit and the threat of increased drug trafficking.

Chinchilla brought the border issue to the International Court of Justice, and it ruled in favour of Costa Rica, but the president decided to build a road in the area that created controversy. Public debt continued to grow and unemployment was high. There was a decline in violence against women and the government attacked drug dealers and seized drugs, but the cartel activity nevertheless increased (AFP, 21 November 2013; Woodbury, 17 January 2014).

In 2010, *Forbes* placed Chinchilla as number 83 among the world's 100 most important women and in 2011 as number 86. Later she was not included on the list. Her approval ratings went down, and in 2014 her term ended and she could not run for a second consecutive term. A male president from the opposition, the centre-left Citizen's Action Party (PAC), was elected, and the PLN only got a fourth of the seats in the Legislative Assembly.

Great power in motion

Laura Chinchilla did not get much international attention, and she wound up completely in the background when, five months later, Dilma Rousseff was elected president of Brazil – South America's largest country, occupying nearly half the continent, and the world's eighth-largest economy. The election was all the more striking because Rousseff was a former Marxist guerrilla and twice-divorced grandmother. Moreover, Brazil had an all-time low participation of women in politics, despite the fact that quotas were introduced in 1997.[19]

Brazil, with its indigenous Indians, was colonised by the Portuguese in the 1500s, and the resources were exploited using slaves. In 1822, Brazil became an independent monarchy and a republic in 1889. After independence, the country shifted from democracy to authoritarian state and military rule. Economic development was also uneven. There were periods of decline and social unrest. Inequalities were large and poverty was widespread. The population ranged from wealthy landowners to poor Indians, from well-off capitalists to destitute slum-dwellers. The inhabitants were both multi-ethnic and multicultural and most were Catholic. The population grew rapidly. In the 1980s, it reached almost 150 million. Agricultural and industrial production rose. Urbanisation spread, and social services were developed. Despite setbacks, Brazil became classified as a middle-income country.

The military took power in 1964, and a strict authoritarian regime lasted until 1985, when a civilian government took over. Brazil is a federal state, and in addition to the state legislatures and governors, a president was directly elected at the national level. The president appointed the cabinet, while the Chamber of Deputies was elected with proportional representation and the Senate by simple plurality. Nearly 30 political parties were formed, but most only aimed at providing a candidate with the opportunity of running for election. Economic problems, neo-liberal reforms, inflation and unemployment led to an unstable political situation. Gradually, the economy improved, but social and economic disparities persisted.

Having run for president and lost three times, Luiz Inácio Lula da Silva, called Lula, was elected in 2002 for the Workers' Party, a party he founded himself. A red coalition took over. With high commodity prices and large oil deposits, the economy grew rapidly. At the same time, Lula introduced more government regulation of the economy, redistribution, jobs and social programmes and brought millions of Brazilians out of poverty. He became immensely popular and was re-elected in 2006. He was then called one of the most successful politicians in his time and had a support rate of 80 per cent when he left office in 2010.

Persistent patriarchy

Among many of the original inhabitants, inheritance followed the maternal line, but the Portuguese weakened the position of women. They suppressed local culture and introduced Catholic European norms. Brazilian society became strongly patriarchal. At the end of the 19th century, a women's movement arose, demanding liberation and rights, and women got access to education and employment. Over the years, women actually got more education than men, but they were exposed to widespread discrimination in the labour market.

In 1921, the Brazilian Women's League was created, and women got the right to vote in 1932. Women fought for democracy, but until 1986, practically no women were elected either to the Chamber of Deputies or the Senate. Women's issues were raised during the International Women's Year in 1975, and a new feminist wave arose. With the onset of political openness, four women (1 per cent) entered the Chamber of Deputies in 1978, eight (2 per cent) in 1982 and 26 (5 per cent) in 1986. The female representatives joined forces and got gender equality into the new constitution. In 2001, women obtained equal rights in marriage. Some women became members of the cabinet, but in 2010, there was only one female minister (7 per cent). In the Chamber of Deputies, there were only 9 per cent, and there were only 12 per cent in the Senate. This was almost the lowest on the continent.

Quotas were introduced in 1997, but did not help. The voters were supposed to choose a party or a person from the electoral list. The candidates on the list were not ranked. According to the quota, 30 per cent of the names on the list were reserved for women. But the parties did not need to fill the list completely with names if they did not want to, and as there could be 50 per cent more names on the list than the number of seats they were competing for, they could have a sufficient number of candidates without including a single woman. And there were no sanctions if women were not nominated. In 1998, only 10 per cent of the candidates on the lists were women, and in 2002, 12 per cent.

Lula's protégée

Dilma Rousseff was born in 1947 and grew up in an upper-middle-class family as the middle of three siblings. Her father was a Bulgarian immigrant and lawyer and her mother was a teacher. Dilma received basic education at a convent school for girls and became a Catholic. Then she went to mixed secondary school, became a socialist and student leader, was married for a short period time, and participated in guerrilla activities against the military dictatorship after the coup in 1964. In 1969, she met the lawyer Carlos Franklin Paixão de Araújo and both suffered persecution and arrest under the military regime. Afterwards, Rousseff studied in Porto Alegre and earned a degree in economics. She stayed together with Carlos Araújo and they had a daughter.

Rousseff and Araújo became founders of the Democratic Labour Party (PTD). The husband was elected to the state assembly, while Rousseff became municipal secretary of the treasury of Porto Alegre. In the early 1990s, Rousseff served as president of the Foundation of Economics and Statistics and was appointed state secretary of mines, energy and communications. After they divorced in 2001, Rousseff joined the Workers' Party, where she supported Lula as president. After he was elected, she became minister of mines and energy during 2003–05 and chief of staff during 2005–10. Lula could then not be re-elected and launched the 62-year-old Rousseff as his successor in the fight for social inclusion.

Rousseff was called the 'Iron Woman', but during the electoral campaign, when she was accused of being a 'Lesbian Child Killer' because she said she would look into the strict abortion law, she promised not to make abortion easier. But she announced that she would build day care centres, strengthen education, develop infrastructure, govern on behalf of all Brazilians, reduce inequality and eradicate extreme poverty. To achieve the latter, a gender focus was needed, as the poorest families were women on their own with children under 10 (Osava, 2011).

Two of the three presidential candidates were women, and Dilma Rousseff was elected with 56 per cent of the votes in the second ballot against the male candidate. The Workers' Party and its allies got 80 per cent of the seats in the Chamber of Deputies and 74 per cent in the Senate. But only 44 women (9 per cent) were elected to the Chamber of Deputies and 13 (16 per cent) to the Senate.

Dilma Rousseff took office on 1 January 2011, presenting herself as 'Presidenta' rather than the gender-neutral 'Presidente' and surrounding herself by female pioneers and artists. Among the 37 ministers, she appointed nine women, which was considered an important step forward, though the target of 11 was not met. She also appointed women as chief of staff and political coordinator of the power base in Congress, which attracted attention. In 2010, *Forbes* placed her as number 95 on the list of the 100 most powerful women in the world and advanced her to number three in 2011 and 2012, and number two in 2013.

Behind a successful woman is a strong man

Democracy and women's rights

Democratisation did not take the same form in Latin America as in Asia. Instead of scattered democracy revolutions, practically the whole of Latin America was marked by an extensive democratisation wave.[20] Although reorganisations took place at somewhat different times and varied from place to place, male dominance in government was generally retained. In 11 of the countries, only men became top leaders during the approximately 30 years that followed: Belize, El Salvador, Guatemala, Honduras and Mexico in Central America; and Colombia, Ecuador, Paraguay, Suriname, Uruguay and Venezuela in South America.[21] But, exceptionally, in nine countries, a woman came to power for a shorter or longer period, but only one in each country (in Argentina, in addition to Isabel Perón, who came to power before the democratisation). And in two cases (Güeiler and Merino), they stayed in office for only a few months.

Despite a long history as independent states with active women's organisations, for many decades, no women rose to the top in Latin America before the International Women's Year in 1975 and the democratisation wave in 1978, with the exception of Isabel Perón, who inherited her position. Democratisation was a necessary condition for women to get access to political power. But democracy was not sufficient. In the three states that had democracy long before 1978 – Colombia, Costa Rica and Venezuela – there were no women top leaders before Costa Rica got a female president in 2010.

In addition to democratisation, there had to be a pressing demand for political participation of women. The demand was strengthened by international support in 1975 and afterwards. But even then, very few women became top leaders and most of them only after 1990. Without the women's movement, none of them would probably have succeeded, not even the widows who relied on the status of their husbands. The women's movement helped women dare take on demanding political office. Closed doors were opened. Women became more acceptable and gradually even useful as politicians, and women's claims were included on the political agenda.

Although they fought for democracy, women in Latin America did not lead democracy revolutions the way they did in Asia. The situation of Violeta Chamorro's struggle in Nicaragua was the most similar. But when she came forward, the dictatorial Somoza clan was already defeated. She appeared in a later phase. There was still a struggle for peace and democracy, but also a battle over various forms of democracy.

It happened that a woman rose to the top while the military were still heavily involved in politics, as was the case with Isabel Perón and Lidia Güeiler. Both were ousted by the military. But most of the women got their positions under civilian rule, although conditions could be confused and marked by conflict. Beatriz Merino was appointed to resolve a crisis in the male top leadership, while Violeta Chamorro, Janet Jagan, Mireya Moscoso, Michelle Bachelet, Cristina Fernández, Laura Chinchilla and Dilma Rousseff all ran as candidates for president in democratic elections and won.

Narrow needle's eye

At the end of the 20th century, all the countries in South and Central America, with one exception (Belize), had presidential systems. Most often, the presidents were directly elected and acted as heads of both state and government with executive power, as well as a ceremonial role. Only three countries (Belize, Guyana and Peru) had a prime minister in addition to the president.

Generally, the more power attributed to high positions, the more difficult it was for women to obtain them. Should women become top leaders in Latin America, in the great majority of cases, they had to become presidents. And the fact that there was only a single top leader with great power limited the possibilities for women to reach the top. There was only one top position to compete for. It was an advantage that the presidents were directly elected. Women voters could be mobilised and the candidates did not have to be endorsed by political parties or be elected to parliament first. But competition was fierce. From 1974, when the first woman ran as a presidential candidate after World War II (in Colombia), until 2010, a total of 62 women presidential candidates tried to go to the top in 47 elections in 16 Latin American countries, and several ran more than once, but they did not succeed. It cannot be said that women did not try, but it was not, in fact, easy to reach the top. It was not easy for men, either, but women were, in addition, constrained by traditional gender roles. They had difficulties being accepted by political parties, fell outside male networks and lacked money to finance election campaigns. Sixteen women became vice presidents in eight of the countries (particularly in Costa Rica and Honduras), but these positions did not usually entail much influence.

Few women managed to go to the top, but those who did, with only one exception (Merino), achieved the highest political position (president) and acquired considerable power, at least formally.

Successor to a strong man

But how did the successful few manage? The pattern of widows taking over political top positions from their deceased husbands, which is found in Asia, also exists in Latin America. Perón, Chamorro, Moscoso and Jagan became presidents in their capacity as widows. But in the Latin American context there was also

244

another form of 'substitute'. In a macho marked culture with a male-dominated political world like the one in Latin America, women had to have the support of prominent male politicians to go to the top. And in three cases they were actually launched and supported by active male presidents as their successors. Fernández succeeded her husband while he was still alive, while Chinchilla and Rousseff were promoted by political male colleagues who could not be re-elected as presidents. The three men were decisive for the women's acquisition of top positions. Their support was visibly brought out in the political contest. They were present all the time, either personally or through photos and references.

Only Güeiler, Merino and Bachelet went to the top mainly on their own merits. Güeiler was president of the Chamber of Deputies when she, by coincidence, was given the task of acting as interim president. Merino had special qualifications as head of the tax agency with a view to becoming prime minister. Bachelet was a cabinet minister. It was emphasised that she was the first woman in Latin America who was elected president on the basis of her own qualifications, without family ties to any leading male politician.

Men's interests

Why would men prefer women as the successors of politically important men? In three cases, they were a political couple, 'diarchy' as it has been called. Juan Perón was 77 years old when he became president in 1973 and made his wife vice president. Before he died, he gave her full authority to continue his work. The Jagan and Kirchner couples worked together politically all their life, and the wives acquired extensive political experience and high offices. When Cheddi Jagan died in office, the party saw it as in their interest that his wife should take her husband's policy further. Néstor Kirchner wanted his wife to take over when he did not wish to continue as president himself, and she intended to follow up his political vision.

Chamorro and Moscoso both ran for election several years after their husbands died, and they were requested to do so by supporters who wanted to gain ground by using their husbands' name and heroic nimbus. Chamorro ran even though many thought that she would not be elected, but they could not agree upon any other (male) candidate. Moscoso hesitated at first, but then ran twice before she succeeded. Merino was requested to become prime minister, because no men wanted the job. She did not stay in office long, either. Chinchilla and Rousseff were also designated by men that they were not related to. Oscar Arias was 66 years old when he became president for the second time, and he took his party colleague, Chinchilla, with him as vice president before he backed her as his successor when his term was over and he could not be re-elected. Lula was president for two terms, while Rousseff was member of the cabinet. During the second term, she was his closest collaborator. Then, she was launched as the new president, when Lula could not run again.

All the top women were politically aligned with prominent men. Although gender may not have been the primary reason for their rise to the top, it made a difference. A woman leader was something new and out of the ordinary, even historic. She could attract attention, signal progress and hold out promises of a better policy. She could particularly attract women voters, and in some places, people thought women leaders had distinctive spiritual power. Especially with regards to the most recent women top leaders, their gender could in itself have been a positive element because women had become more politically attractive than before. But a woman candidate still broke with traditional gender roles, and this could arouse adverse reactions, particularly in religious circles, and be used negatively in the political competition. But if the political legacy of a man carried enough weight, it could offset the handicap of the successor being a woman. The three male presidents may also have thought that it would be easier to train and influence a woman than a man as their political successor.

Variable qualifications

What qualifications did the women have for the position as national top leader? They came from different circumstances – poor, middle-class and rich – and had different educational, working and political backgrounds. The widows largely had the least education. Isabel Perón left school after sixth grade and mainly worked as personal secretary for her husband. She was evidently poorly qualified for a high-level executive political position, but accepted it, nevertheless. Chamorro, Moscoso and Jagan had secondary education and obtained various occupations. Chamorro was a housewife for a while and then worked as editor of the family newspaper for more than 20 years before she ran for president. Moscoso assisted her husband in a supporting role and became president more than 10 years after he died. In the meantime, she had different jobs and was head of a political party to pursue her husband's policies. Jagan worked as a nurse for many years and had an extensive political career from party secretary and editor to MP, minister and First Lady before she became president.

Except Güeiler, the other top women distinguished themselves by higher education. Güeiler's only training was as an accountant, but she had more than 30 years of diverse professional, organisational and political posts before she became president. The others had higher education followed by demanding occupations and high-level positions. Merino was educated as an economist and a lawyer and was elected as a member of Congress before she became head of the tax agency. Bachelet was a medical doctor and became involved in politics at an early age, got important party assignments and was minister twice before she ran for president. Fernández was educated as a lawyer and became member of the provincial parliament, the Chamber of Deputies and the Senate, in addition to being First Lady, before she took over herself. Chinchilla pursued university studies in public policy and Rousseff in economics. Chinchilla worked as a consultant and became an MP, vice minister, minister and vice president. Rousseff participated in political struggle, worked with economics and statistics, was state secretary, and helped found a political party before she joined another and was appointed as Lula's collaborator.

Except Chamorro, all the women top leaders participated in political parties, obtained party positions and were members either of parliament or the cabinet before they acquired top positions. Only Jagan and Chinchilla were members both of parliament and the cabinet, while Moscoso was the only party leader.

When they came to power, all the women were active in politics or working life. Only Fernández and Chinchilla were married. The others were single, widowed or divorced. All except one had children, but the mothers were more than 50 years old and had finished with the most intensive child care by the time they acquired the top positions. The youngest child was 12 years old (Bachelet). In Catholic countries like those of Latin America, it is striking how often the women were divorced, and some more than once.

Male environment

Although there was an active women's rights movement in Latin America, the women top leaders were rather solitary as women in the political leadership. There is only information regarding Güeiler and Jagan that they participated in women's organisations. In addition, Merino was engaged in leadership training for women.

Until the 1990s, women's participation in formal politics was random, scattered and limited. Political parties were very reluctant to include women and give them positions. Eventually, many parties got more than 50 per cent women among their members, but in the governing bodies, there was generally only a small minority, and among presidents and secretaries, there was general extremely few. The countries with women top leaders were no exception in this respect.

With such a male-dominated structure, the parties functioned effectively as barriers to women's advancement in politics and to the active promotion of women-friendly policies. Even though Fernández, Chinchilla and Rousseff were supported by men in the highest position, it is an open question as to how much support they got as women or for women-friendly policies.

In order to accelerate the recruitment of women, many countries introduced quotas, partly statutory for legislative elections, partly voluntary internally in the parties. Before the end of 2010, 11 countries had quotas during elections and four in the parties. This meant that the great majority of countries had quotas of one kind or the other and the number of women in various forums increased significantly. But the arrangements differed and were not always effective. On average, in 2010, there were 20 per cent women in parliament/the lower house, 19 per cent in the senate and 23 per cent in the cabinet of the Latin American countries. The countries with women top leaders generally had higher levels than the others, but the variation was large in both groups.

Fernández was the first woman top leader to lead a country with a significant representation of women in parliament (40 per cent) and Chinchilla followed (with 35 per cent). The others had to be content with less than 20 per cent, and not all were members of their own party. The top leaders could compensate by appointing women ministers, vice ministers and so on. But they could encounter resistance to their choices from party colleagues, and practices varied. Most of the top women appointed one, two or maximum three women in the cabinet. This was also the case with Fernández, despite the broad representation of women in parliament in the time. Moscoso had four women ministers (30 per cent); Chinchilla, seven (35 per cent); and Bachelet struck a record with 10 (50 per cent).

Admired and bullied

As presidents, the women faced serious challenges. The situation was often unstable, with difficult economic and social conditions, and political institutions were sometimes weak. The women had limited leadership experience and the strength and competence of their collaborators varied. A good number of the collaborators were newcomers and of little use, at times, even a nuisance, and many were replaced. Several of the women leaders had to govern with complex political alliances, and Chamorro and Moscoso, partly also Bachelet, Chinchilla and Fernández, lacked a sufficient majority in parliament to implement desired reforms.

It is not possible to draw a complete picture of the work of the women top leaders. Four left office after a relatively short time: Perón, Güeiler and Merino were forced to leave, while Jagan resigned officially for health reasons, but the political situation was very difficult. Three were still in power in 2010/11. The final three completed their terms, and according to the law, they could not run for re-election.

Regardless of criticism and shortcomings, the three top leaders who completed their terms managed to achieve something during their presidencies. Chamorro had the greatest difficulties, with a country ravaged by conflict, but she contributed to ending the war, maintaining a constitutional regime and saving the economy from ruin.

When Moscoso came to power, Panama had financial problems, and the results during her period were mixed. But the country managed to take over the Panama Canal and American troops pulled out.

Bachelet had absolutely the best situation financially and politically when she rose to the top in Chile. She took a strong stand, with an ambitious social and gender-focused policy, and was criticised on that basis. But she was the female president who received the greatest recognition when she retired. In Bachelet's period, the economy grew, poverty was reduced and significant progress was made for women.

The female top leaders represented different political trends. Even if the platforms were not always precise and consistent, it is reasonable to place seven to the left or centre-left and three to the right. In any case, as politicians, the women broke with traditional female roles and undertook a task that was usually assigned to men with behaviour that could be considered inappropriate for women. Some were perceived positively as 'Queen Mothers' or 'Peace Doves'. However, this did not prevent them also being bullied and abused because of their gender, for example, called 'hysterical', 'lesbian', 'the fat lady' or 'a useless old bag of bones'.

Representing who?

It is always a question as to what extent a woman top leader, in practice, represents men and/or women. Apart from Chamorro, who was independent, all represented male-dominated political parties, which meant that they could encounter resistance if they wanted to give priority to women-friendly policies. In the Latin American atmosphere, it was often difficult to signal a strong involvement in women's issues. None of the women top leaders described themselves as 'feminist', either, though some appreciated being called 'feminine'. Several stressed that they were leaders for *both* men and women and did not talk about gender equality. Not all the leaders were particularly concerned about the status of women, and those who were could be hampered by prevailing macho or Catholic attitudes particularly if they mentioned women's reproductive rights.

But the countries varied with regards to gender norms and culture, some being notably more equality-oriented than others. Becoming party to CEDAW, adopting measures benefiting women and introducing gender quotas in politics all signalled a will to promote gender equality and contributed to increasing equality in practice. The personal ties to strong male politicians were a precondition for many of the women top leaders being elected. Seven of the women top leaders saw it as their main task to carry out the political programme of a prominent man. This could set boundaries for their involvement in questions related to women, but not necessarily. Juan Perón and Arnulfo Arias gave women voting rights and Cheddi Jagan introduced a national policy for women. Néstor Kirchner appointed women justices, Oscar Arias emphasised the role of women in peace and Lula improved women's economic and civil rights – in addition to the fact that all three supported a woman as president. In addition, the political climate gradually became more women-friendly than before, but it remains to be seen what this entailed in practice.

Chamorro often stated that she acted and talked like a woman, but the question was: what kind of woman? For her, it was a traditional, economically well-off mother, and in her policies, she was, in practice, practically anti-feminist. Not only was she against abortion and sceptical about contraception, divorce and cohabitation, but she did not support women-oriented measures, either. It did not go well for women as a group under her rule. Many experienced their position as weakened.

The other women leaders (except the two who took office in 2010/11), in practice, did something that was beneficial for women. Moscoso helped draw women into politics and Fernández proposed laws on violence against women and same-sex marriages.

When Güeiler, Jagan and Bachelet spoke about their political work, they referred to women's issues to a great extent. Güeiler fought to bring women into the development process and established a public welfare centre for women. Jagan expressed clear political support for women's rights and developed health and education. But it was, above all, Bachelet who came forward as a politician actively promoting women's interests, and although there were imitations, she made an impact, improving the status of women in many areas. Her policies represented a milestone for women's issues. She expanded the limits of what a woman top leader could do in male-dominated politics.

The Prime Minister of Dominica Mary Eugenia Charles at the Caribbean Conference on
1 December 1983. She was prime minister from 1980–1995.
Image: Getty Images.

Chapter Seven

Lopsided democracies in the Caribbean

Her picture was in the newspapers worldwide, standing beside the US President Ronald Reagan on the president's own platform. They were an odd couple. She was as brown as he was white, and he led the world's most powerful nation, while she came from a tiny, mountainous island in the Caribbean that many people had scarcely heard of. Eugenia Charles was prime minister of Dominica (not to be confused with the Dominican Republic), and, in addition, the chair of the Organization of Eastern Caribbean States (OECS) – not exactly commonplace for a black woman in October 1983. But then she got Reagan to intervene militarily on the Caribbean island of Grenada to remove the leftist regime. Officially, it was declared that the US was trying to protect US citizens and restore order. After the press conference, Charles turned to Reagan and said: 'Mr President, you have big balls!' (*Economist*, 2005).

British heritage and male networks

Islets, struggle and culture

Caribbean history differs from that of Latin America.[1] During colonial times, the islands were an area of rivalry between different European interests: British, French, Dutch and Spanish. Most of the islands became British colonies and, later, members of the British Commonwealth, but some were conquered by other Western powers. Many of the states are very small, with less than a quarter-of-a-million inhabitants. But language and culture are extremely varied, marked not only by West Indian and European, but also African, East Indian, Mayan, Chinese, Cuban, Indonesian, Arabic and other, influences. The religions range from Hinduism and Islam to Christianity and traditional religions.

During the colonial period, conflict arose between white colonisers and black slaves on the plantations and the slaves rebelled. The islands have a common history of struggle against colonialism, slavery and racism, and, more recently, in problems related to economic neo-colonialism and tourism. Beyond sugar and tourism, the islands had little to offer commercially and became stations for trade between Latin America and Europe, but the structures of the colonial plantation society changed little.

Gradually, the influence of the US became stronger. The Cuban Revolution in 1959 not only changed the conditions in Cuba, but was highly significant for the whole region. Politically, militarily and economically, the US tried to prevent other countries from following the example of Cuba. Military bases were located all over the Caribbean and investments were made to stem political unrest. Although the countries remained largely agricultural, the region developed considerable exports of bauxite and oil. Almost all became classified as high- or middle-income countries, with an emphasis on education, health and social welfare. The exception was Haiti, which remained a low-income country. At the same time, the development of the Caribbean as a whole was characterised by economic dependence, large disparities, poverty, unemployment, illiteracy, corruption and violence linked to the international drug trade.

Haiti gained independence in 1804 and the Dominican Republic in 1844, but most territories became sovereign only after World War II and some as late as 1981.[2] Before independence, social and political democratisation took place in the British colonies. Economic activities became more varied, and schools were built. Active trade unions and religious communities sprang up. Areas acquired different degrees of self-government, often as a result of struggle, and when they became independent states, they carried on with liberal democracies, most often, with parliamentary rule according to the British model. Women often got the right to vote in the 1940–1950s, but the leaderships of the new states consisted of educated, black men from the middle class. Policies changed. Coups and authoritarian tendencies were not unusual, but, on the whole, democratic institutions were maintained, so that the Caribbean was described as the largest cluster of liberal democracies among developing countries. In 2000, only Haiti was classified as an 'emerging democracy', in addition to Cuba as 'communist', and both have a special history. There was no 'wave of democratisation' in the region, as in Latin America, either (Meditz and Hanratty, 1987; Duncan and Woods, 2007).

Strong women

Women in the Caribbean included Indians, European wives and servants, African slaves, and Asian forced labour. Traditionally, women had a strong position in some Indian ethnic groups, but male dominance was prevalent and was reinforced by the colonial powers. Men were given leading positions in politics and the economy, while most women belonged to the 'invisible majority' at the bottom of the social ladder. Women had the main responsibility for the home and family, and particularly in the lower economic strata, very many were unmarried and single parents. It became a widespread custom that women helped each other, and the Caribbean got a reputation for having 'strong women'. Female slaves participated in the riots of the 1700s and 1800s, and around 1900, women of European origin created associations to obtain social reforms and education for women. After

World War II, women fought for rights and better pay and working conditions, and in the 1960s and 1970s, national women's organisations and political groups of women were established. The number of organisations increased dramatically, but women's representation in political bodies remained at a low level.

After the International Women's Year in 1975, the UN Women's Conference in Mexico and the follow-up conference in Copenhagen in 1980 (which was headed by a Caribbean woman, Lucille Mair from Trinidad and Tobago), almost all the states got public offices for women, ministries or commissions. The United Nations (UN) Convention on the Elimination of all forms of Discrimination Against Women (CEDAW) was ratified in course of the 1980s and early 1990s. Women received education on the same level as men and, on average, performed better than them at all levels. The West Indian University established a special unit for women and development, and the number of female writers and artists increased. But economic problems had as a consequence that nearly half of the households had a single female parent, while fewer women than men obtained paid employment. Unemployment among women was twice as high as among men, although many women had to support not only the family, but also their unemployed husbands (Barrow-Giles, 2011).

Eugenia Charles: a Caribbean matriarch

Star of the Caribbean

International reaction to the intervention in Grenada was hostile. A superpower had intervened with military forces in the internal affairs of a small state. With a great majority, the UN General Assembly condemned the action as illegal. But Eugenia Charles just scoffed. For her, it was a family matter. In the region, they were kith and kin. 'The Grenadians wanted it, and that's all that counts', she stated, 'I don't care what the rest of the world thinks' (AP, 2005; Cobley, 2006: 123-8)

It should be noted that Eugenia Charles did not take action when leftists seized power in Grenada in 1979. She reacted when the government was deposed by a coup and the prime minister and his colleagues were murdered. That could not go unchallenged. And she was afraid that the Soviet Union and Cuba were behind it and that Dominica could be the next country to fall to communism. In the West Indies, the intervention was immensely popular. Sovereignty, security and development were pressing issues in the small island states, and Charles was the first leader of the regional OECS. Standing beside the US president on the podium of the White House, she was perceived as a star. Now, the region had its own 'Iron Lady'.

It was not her only 'first'. Eugenia Charles was the first Caribbean woman to lead a Caribbean political party successfully and the first woman elected head of government in Dominica and in the Caribbean and she made an impact for almost three decades, half of this period as the Dominican prime minister. She remained in power longer than any other top woman leader in Latin America and the Caribbean.[3]

In the shadow of her father

The population of Dominica consists almost entirely of the descendants of African slaves who were imported by British plantation owners in the 1800s, most Catholic and very many poor. Both women and men worked in agriculture, trade and skilled occupations and were active locally in village matters. But men dominated in the high positions in the churches and plantations, and in formal political decision-making at all levels.

Eugenia Charles was the granddaughter of a former slave, but unlike most people, her family was well-situated. And even if she did not inherit her political position directly from her father, J.P. Charles, he played an important role as guide and mentor. In an interview in 1994, Eugenia credited her father with being her major political influence, though she admitted that he was not her model for politics (Guy, 1995: 136–7). J.P.'s parents were humble farmers, and J.P. left home early to become a mason. He emphasised self-sufficiency, hard work and thrift and became a wealthy landowner and fruit exporter. He had a strong sense of social responsibility and established, among other things, a cooperative bank. In 1923, J.P. became member of the Town Board of Roseau, and in 1928, of the Dominica Legislative Council. He served for more than two decades, defending small farmers, criticising plantation owners and challenging the colonial system. At the age of 83 he was also elected to the Federal Council of the Leeward Islands as a senator.

The boss at home was Eugenia's mother, Josephine. She impressed the children with her strong will, and in addition to the house and family, she managed a grocery in Roseau and a bakery in Pointe Michel. 'In Dominica we really live women's lib', Eugenia Charles noted (Stratton, 1996). Neither of her parents had more than an elementary school education, and they placed great emphasis on education. They encouraged the development of their children's full potentialities and Eugenia's two brothers became doctors. Her sister, however, went to France to become a nun.

Eugenia was the youngest child, born in 1919, and had a privileged upbringing. At the dinner table at home, they always talked about things that mattered in Dominica. Her father took her to political meetings and on travels around the island, showing her the living conditions of the not-so-well-off Dominicans. Eugenia received her early education at the Convent school for girls in Dominica and finished her secondary schooling in Grenada. Her father suggested that she learn shorthand, which she practised at court proceedings and became interested in law. She undertook a degree at the University of Toronto and was the first Dominican woman called to the bar in the UK in 1947. She took a course on juvenile delinquency at the London School of Economics, and in 1949, was admitted to the bar in Barbados and Dominica. Her parents persuaded her to settle down as the first woman lawyer in Dominica. She practised law and business for

30 years, bringing many neglected issues to public notice and earning a reputation as a resolute and fearless advocate of human rights and the rule of law. As she remained unmarried and childless, she stayed with her parents, and her father died in 1983, at the age of 107 years.[4]

'Shut-Your-Mouth-Bill'

Dominica is one of the smallest states in the Caribbean, with only 70,000–80,000 inhabitants. During British colonial rule, conditions were primitive. People said that the only things the island had plenty of were bananas and drug dealers. During the 1700s, a local parliament was established for white people. Black people joined later, but the development was characterised by strong antagonism between the black majority, on one hand, and the colonial power and a small group of wealthy plantation owners, on the other. Natural disasters and the abolishment of slavery contributed to decline in colonial agriculture, but not to social change. Tensions mounted, and demands were raised for self-government. This was eventually granted, but only after tough political battles and, at times, violent clashes. In the 1940s, measures were implemented to improve living conditions, education and health. Universal suffrage was introduced in 1951. Workers and farmers got together in the Labour Party (DLP), won the elections in 1961 and formed a government. In 1967, Dominica got self-government, and in 1978, the island became an independent republic.

In Dominica, the president is elected by the Assembly and appoints a prime minister on the basis of support in the Assembly. The House of the Assembly (parliament) consists of a single, 30-member chamber: 21 representatives are elected by simple plurality and nine senators are usually appointed by the president, five on the advice of the prime minister and four on the advice of the leader of the opposition. The prime minister chooses the cabinet from among the members of the Assembly and all are collectively responsible to the Assembly. Although the president formally has executive power, the real power lies with the prime minister.

J.P. and Josephine Charles were keen to help people in need, and as a lawyer, Eugenia was engaged in the problems of children and youth, the elderly, and the disabled. From the late 1950s, she wrote letters to newspaper editors criticising the government, but had no political ambitions. A bill in 1968 from the increasingly authoritarian Labour prime minister suddenly got her going. There were signs of social unrest, and the bill aimed at gagging the opposition. It became known as the 'Shut-Your-Mouth-Bill'. Eugenia Charles just had to protest. 'I made up my mind I would do everything to prevent the government from continuing to rule, because I felt democracy would die', she said (Stratton, 1996). Thus, a comet-like political career began that made her prime minister 12 years later.

They called themselves 'Freedom Fighters', the people who came together in the office of Eugenia Charles to oppose the government bill. They were professionals and businessmen, in addition to some dissidents from the Labour Party. In 1968, the centre-right Dominica Freedom Party (DFP) was formed, and Eugenia Charles along with five others, one woman and four men, were appointed to a steering committee. In 1969, Charles was elected leader of the DFP. Like the majority of the population, she was black. Her father had a good reputation, and she was known for her determination and hard work. Moreover, it was essential that the leader was not identified with plantation owners. Through her work as a lawyer, Charles had contact with different social groups and supported both business and common people. But for the most part, the DFP had a class background that was radically different from that of the majority of Dominicans and was viewed with suspicion by the working class. Eugenia Charles was not elected to the House of Assembly in 1970, but entered as a nominated member after the elections. In 1975, however, she was elected as a member of parliament (MP) for the DFP (Barrow-Giles, 2006: 70–89; Gill, 2011).

'Danger lady'

Women had been politicians on the island before, but Eugenia Charles was not only an MP. She became leader of the opposition and was in an exposed position. Although it was claimed that her gender was no more peculiar than all the other strange things that happened on the island at the time, she was criticised both for her gender and her class. She was 49 years old and unmarried when she joined active politics and was called an 'Eminent Professional Virgin', 'Lady Dracula', 'Danger Lady' and 'That Bitch of a Woman'.[5] At the time, party politics had a pattern of abusive exchanges and Charles usually answered virulent attacks with a quick-witted reply. When she was accused of not understanding other people's suffering because she had never felt the pangs of childbirth, she replied: 'Mr Speaker, all these men should be put in a zoo because they all feel the pangs of childbirth' (Guy, 1995: 138). The public gallery was hysterical with laughter. When the male-biased decision was made that shirt jack suits should be the only legal dress in the Assembly, Charles demonstrated by appearing in the House with a bathing suit under her robes (Higbie, 1993: 109–10).

In the elections in 1975, the DFP lost two of the five seats in the Assembly despite an overall increase in the number of seats (from 13 to 21). The leadership of Eugenia Charles was challenged. People thought that the hostility towards her weakened the party. However, no one obtained greater support than she did, and Charles continued as party leader.

Eugenia Charles came to power in the most turbulent and difficult period in Dominica's modern political history. There were economic problems, with unemployment and a decline in the banana industry. In addition, scandalous measures by the DLP government attempting to stop trade unions and the press led to riots and confrontations. Strikes spread, and when shots were fired against demonstrators in May 1979, workers, farmers, business people, churches and the opposition declared that the government had to go. It was the first time that an elected government was overthrown by means other than an election. The prime minister resigned in June and a broad interim cabinet was formed. But Charles refused to join and demanded new elections. In August, the island was hit by the worst hurricane in over a hundred years. Most of the banana and coconut palms were destroyed. Three quarters of the population became homeless and essential public services were damaged.

People were tired of misrule and problems, the DLP was split by bitter antagonisms and many put their trust in the DFP. The party ran an election campaign in 1980 directed against economic mismanagement, corruption and oppression. Now the party won 17 of the 21 seats. At 61 years old, Eugenia Charles became Dominica's third prime minister, a position she retained until 1995, after she was re-elected in 1985 and by a narrow margin again in 1990. In 1985, the DFP obtained 15 seats, but in 1990, it only got 11 of the 21 seats. The cabinet was small. In addition to being prime minister, Charles was minister of finance, partly also minister of development, and for many years, foreign minister and minister of defence. Nobody in Dominica has been later able to measure up to this, and no women in the Caribbean.

Caribbean matriarch

The election secured the party leader and the DFP control. After 1980, Charles was Dominica's powerful and domineering matriarch. Her supporters called her 'Moma Charles' or 'Mother of the Nation', who took care of the country and protected the weak (Barriteau, 2006a: 15). She came to power without any long apprenticeship in national politics and lacked education in economics and the social sciences. The newly independent state was in deep crisis, and as if this was not enough, Dominica was hit by a new hurricane in 1980, albeit weaker than the previous one. In addition, the prime minister was exposed to two coup attempts during her first year and declared a state of emergency three times during 1981–83. Her predecessor, the DLP Prime Minister Patrick John, was later arrested for involvement in the coup attempts and sentenced to 12 years in prison. Eugenia Charles dissolved Dominica's security forces, which were involved in the unrest, and went ahead with reconstructing the country. She got assistance from the US, the World Bank and the International Monetary Fund (IMF) and focused on rebuilding agriculture and infrastructure, particularly roads and electricity, and developing industry, education and health.

Eugenia Charles is described as a rugged leader who tried to tame a physically rugged, politically rebellious and economically regressive country (Barriteau, 2006a: 10). She was ideologically conservative, portraying herself as an advocate of democracy against communism, and promoted a neo-liberal economy where the government should mainly facilitate a private sector that would create jobs and reduce poverty. She implemented economic reforms with structural adjustment, privatisation and a reduction in the role of the state, and was compared with the British Margaret Thatcher. But, in practice, Eugenia Charles was closer to the centre. To strengthen Dominica's position, she fought to preserve the international agreement that gave bananas from the Caribbean preferential access to European markets. And when revenues fell, unemployment rose and public services deteriorated, she supported welfare programmes and cooperative initiatives. She also banned casinos, nightclubs and duty-free shops, which could attract negative elements to the island.

Charles received credit for her righteous and steadfast management. She was never accused of corruption or ostentatious living. Her efforts to combat corruption and promote economic growth were also appreciated, but she was criticised for her piecemeal approach and failure to deliver a vision or blueprint for the development of the country. She governed like a headmistress, her enemies said. She described herself as a 'pragmatist' – 'looking after the things that needed looking after' (*Economist*, 2005). Such an attitude was probably logical in light of her character and qualifications, but to obtain very much-needed financial assistance from international donors, a flexible approach was also required.[6]

During the 1980s, political stability, the economy and social conditions improved. Dominica did not achieve a living standard that was as high as some of the neighbouring states, but disparities were smaller, life expectancy higher and there was relatively little crime. However, the basic problem of poverty remained unresolved. For a small and vulnerable economy like Dominica, it was not sufficient to facilitate the private sector. The country could not rely on traditional tourism and the banana industry was in decline. With falling export revenues and a rising debt burden, the situation in the 1990s also became more difficult. Charles was blamed for an autocratic leadership style, not listening to the grassroots and a lack of emphasis on social welfare and jobs. The Labour opposition grew stronger. In 1993, Eugenia Charles withdrew as party leader. She continued as prime minister, but in 1995, the DFP lost the elections. The party got 36 per cent of the votes, but only five seats in the Assembly, while the two opposition parties obtained 16 seats. The political career of Eugenia Charles was over. She was also more than 70 years old.

Reluctant feminist

Living in a society where women in politics are very few and their activity is perceived as improper by many people, it is not surprising that Eugenia Charles was ambivalent to gender and feminism and often expressed inconsistent views. Researchers called her a 'reluctant feminist'. She said herself: 'I don't think I'm a feminist, really. I just felt that women had the right to do what they wanted to do. Men couldn't think they had the world in their pocket' (Mondesire, 2006: 259–81). In politics, it was an advantage to be a woman, Charles thought, because it attracted more attention. At the same time, men abused female politicians, so they had to be very stubborn not to give up. With regards to political decisions, Charles insisted that gender was irrelevant. The problems were the same, and a job had to be done. At the same time, she explained her willingness to battle for the defenceless as 'the instinctive part of womanhood' (Guy, 1995: 137–40).

Insisting that she was not an advocate for women, Eugenia Charles nevertheless promoted equal rights in her statements and actions. Women's groups and associations blossomed, and in 1986, they formed an umbrella organisation, the National Council for Women, to promote women's issues. Charles herself became president of the International Federation of Women Lawyers. Charles gave women opportunities to work at senior levels of government and exercise public leadership. As the speaker of the Assembly did not have to be an elected member, one of the first things Charles did as prime minister was to appoint the first woman speaker. But she stressed: 'I did so not because she was a woman, but because she was the most knowledgeable person on the Parliamentary rolls' (Barriteau, 2006a: 18). She also appointed two women as parliamentary and permanent secretaries and a female High Court judge, but no women ministers. The Assembly had few members and the electoral system of plurality vote made it difficult for women to be elected. They could be appointed, as senators, but there was minimal representation of women generally at decision-making levels in the Dominican power hierarchy. Thus, there were a total of only four women in the Assembly while Charles was in power: three from the opposition in addition to herself. And male dominance continued after Charles withdrew. In 1995, all in all, there were only three women in the Assembly and none were from the DFP. In 2011, there were still extremely few women in governing bodies: four (13 per cent) in the Assembly and two (13 per cent) in the cabinet.

Margaret Thatcher and Golda Meir were models for Eugenia Charles. She had great confidence in herself as a politician. She was sure of her leadership skills, enjoyed power and was proud of her ability to make decisions, even if they were unpopular. As prime minister, she dominated the party, cabinet and Assembly. It was said that she had 'a female commanding presence' and exhibited feminine as well as masculine traits. She was known for her good heart and generous support of people who came to a bad end. At the same time, her leadership style was characterised as autocratic and incorrigible. To exert power as a woman in a male-dominated political world and combat the violence that had gained ground in society when Charles came to power, it can be argued that a tough political stance was necessary, but it was not always in the spirit of a democracy (Cuffie, 2006: 143–7; Mondesire, 2006: 265–9; Gill, 2011).

While Eugenia Charles was prime minister, Dominica became party to the CEDAW, and the women's desk in the government administration was upgraded to a Women's Bureau. In 1989, a National Policy on Women was adopted, but Charles believed that Dominica had come further than CEDAW and it took time before action was taken (Mondesire, 2006: 69–73). Nevertheless, the development of housing and education benefited women, and more women entered the labour marked. At the same time, unemployment increased far more for women than for men, and jobs the government considered as 'women's work' were characterised as the 'feminisation of poverty' by the women's movement.

With strengths and weaknesses, the political leadership of Eugenia Charles was unprecedented in the Caribbean. And with her background and achievements, she became an inspiration and role model, first of all, for women in the Caribbean, but also for women of colour in other parts of the world.

Three Haitian women in the turmoil: Ertha Pascal-Trouillot, Claudette Werleigh and Michèle Pierre-Louis

Poverty, Tonton Macoute and AIDS

After Charles became prime minister of Dominica, more women went to the top in the Caribbean, but no one got anywhere near as much influence as Charles. Haiti distinguished itself by being a French colony.[7] The Spanish came first and virtually wiped out the Indians on the island. To get labour, both French and Spanish colonisers imported several hundreds of thousands of slaves from Africa, and sugar, rum, coffee and cotton were produced. The slaves were brutally treated, rebelled in 1791 and defeated the colonial power in the only successful slave revolution in world history. After 13 years of struggle, Haiti became independent in 1804 and formed the first black republic. But the violence did not stop. Independence was followed by conflict between the light mulattos who dominated the economy and the black majority, quarrels with the neighbouring state of Santo Domingo, periods of extensive political and economic chaos, and a series of dictatorships. In 1915, the US invaded the country. Infrastructure, agriculture, health and education were developed, but 50,000 farmers were killed before the Americans left the country 20 years later.

There were elections and a coup, and in 1957, Jean François Duvalier, known as 'Papa Doc', established a family dictatorship that ruled with an iron hand until 1986, using terror police (*Tonton Macoute*), with support of the US. The population of about 6 million was terrorised. Thousands were murdered or forced into exile. The economy was characterised by patron–client relationships and corruption, and resources were exploited. Haiti was one of the few countries in the world that did not have economic growth during most of the 1950s and 1960s. Catholicism was Haiti's official religion, and most people also practised voodoo (a domestic cult of family spirits). CEDAW was ratified in 1981, and schools and health services were strengthened in urban areas. But most people lived in the countryside, and in the 1980s, two thirds of the population were without schooling. Life expectancy was a mere 50 years. Haiti was the poorest country in Latin America and the Caribbean. About 80 per cent of the population, which had increased to about 7 million, lived in miserable conditions, and, in addition, the island was greatly affected by AIDS. The situation became so desperate that massive crowds finally forced the dictator to leave the country.

A number of short-lived governments followed, and in 1987, a new constitution was adopted. Parliament consisted of a Senate of 27 members and a Chamber of Deputies of 83 members, both elected directly by second ballot majority vote.[8] A dual executive was established, with a directly elected president who could not serve two consecutive terms. The president appointed a prime minister, who did not have to be an MP, but was approved by parliament (Haggarty, 1989; Nicholls, 1998; Girard, 2010).

However, the military overthrew the civilian government. People reacted and demonstrated, so it was decided to hold elections in 1990. Along with a State Council, with representatives from different sectors, an interim cabinet headed by a Supreme Court judge was given the task of organising free and fair national elections. The Supreme Court judge was a woman.

Female supreme court judge

Female protest and activism go far back in Haitian history, from involvement in the slave revolution to guerrilla warfare, public demonstrations, political organisation and a 'revolutionary literature' in later centuries. Haitian women participated in the labour market to a greater extent than other women on the continent, and on the farms, spouses shared work and income. From 1930, women joined both social movements for justice and feminist organisations. As men, they were subjected to repression, disappearances, killings and torture by the authorities, and, in addition, they were opposed by fathers, husbands and other men. The feminists were intellectuals from the middle class first of all, but under the Duvalier dictatorship, the movement got larger breadth. Women organised themselves in exile or in secret in urban and rural settings. When the regime fell in 1986, thousands of women from all walks of life demanded justice for all, and women's organisations became more active. Few women got political positions, but, gradually, pressure from both inside and outside the government contributed to the enactment of laws and decrees against discrimination against women (Bell, 2010).

Ertha Pascal-Trouillot was a rarity. She was born in 1943 as the ninth of 10 children in a poor family. Her father, Thimoclès Pascal, was a blacksmith and her mother, Louise Dumornay, was a seamstress. But they lived in a well-to-do suburb of Port-au-Prince, and Ertha could go to school. Here, she met her future husband, Ernst Trouillot. He was her teacher, a journalist and lawyer, and 21 years older than her. He encouraged her to study law and she became Haiti's first female lawyer in 1971. Soon after, they married and had a daughter. Ernst Trouillot came from the elite and had a flourishing career under Duvalier. Ertha joined the family firm, travelled abroad with her husband and published texts on legal questions. She became the country's first female judge, and when Duvalier was thrown out, she was appointed as the first woman to the Supreme Court due to her skills. Despite her husband's links with the deposed dictator, Ertha Pascal-Trouillot also became a member of the commission to revise legislation after the fall of the despot. The year after, her husband died of a heart attack.

According to the Constitution, the leader of the Supreme Court should act as the provisional president, but both the leader and the deputy leader were rejected because they were too close to the Duvalier regime. The 46-year-old Ertha Pascal-Trouillot, however, was politically acceptable, and the fact that she was a woman underlined the change that was about to take place. She hesitated, but accepted the 'heavy task' in the name of Haitian women (Opfell, 1993: 158). She also promised to introduce democracy as soon as possible without bloodshed. The task was brief, but demanding. Ertha Pascal-Trouillot was inaugurated in March as Haiti's fifth president after Duvalier's fall. She appointed a cabinet of 13 members, including a woman minister of social affairs, but the ministers alternated several times. There was no prime minister (Johnson, 1993).

In December 1990, elections were held – the first really free, fair and democratic elections in Haiti. The leftist Catholic slum priest Jean-Bertrand Aristide was elected president, with 68 per cent of the votes. But before he could take office, Pascal-Trouillot was captured and forced to declare on the radio that a former security officer of Duvalier was the new head of the nation. Thousands of outraged Aristide supporters poured into the streets. The security officer fled, and Aristide was inaugurated as president on 7 February 1991. He arrested Pascal-Trouillot for complicity in the attempted coup, though she denied any wrongdoing. Under pressure from the outside, she was released and left the country.

Movement for change

After about seven months, Aristide was deposed in another coup and went into exile in the US. The military regime caused great consternation in the international community, which sought to re-establish democracy in Haiti. In 1994, UN forces led by the US were stationed in the country and Aristide was reinstated. He appointed a businessman, Smarck Michel, as prime minister.

Haiti was in a very difficult situation, not only politically, but also socially and economically. While poverty, illiteracy and human rights violations were widespread, the World Bank and IMF required austerity measures and privatisation to provide loans. Public sector workers and students hit the streets to protest against low salaries and neo-liberalism and clashed with UN troops.

In the parliamentary elections in June 1995, the Aristide coalition won a overwhelming victory, with 67 out of the 83 seats in the Chamber of Deputies. Women got three of the seats (4 per cent). Aristide reduced trade tariffs, which aggravated the crisis in the agricultural sector, and dissolved the armed forces, so Haiti only had a police force and a coastal guard. A year after his return from exile, demonstrations against foreign occupation and foreign demands made Aristide replace Prime Minister Michel with the more leftist Claudette Werleigh.

In exile, Claudette Werleigh was deputy prime minister and minister of finance in the Aristide government. She was well known both inside and outside government circles. She was born in 1946 in a wealthy family. Her parents, Marc Antoine and Clara Lespinasse, exported coffee, and, in addition, her mother had a shop. Her father was a former MP, but withdrew from politics before Claudette was born. Both parents emphasised that the children, five girls and two boys, should receive an education. Claudette was also inspired by her grandmother, who was a strong, intelligent and independent businesswoman who supported a crowd of children and got all of them to school.

Claudette went to elementary and secondary schools run by nuns, then studied diverse subjects, including medicine and pedagogy, in Spain, the US, Mexico and Haiti and undertook university degrees in law and economics. In 1970, she married George Werleigh, who was a professor of economics and a prominent figure in the social-democratic party PANPRA (The National Progressive Revolutionary Haitian Party), but later resigned. The couple had two daughters and with the help of a maid, Claudette Werleigh engaged in social and educational work. "I was part of a broad popular movement for change: democracy, human rights and social justice after Duvalier", she said when I interviewed her in Uppsala, Sweden, in 2006. It was important to reduce the gap between the rich and poor, women and power structures, Werleigh pointed out: "Women are the backbone of society and have great capacity for peace-making." For 11 years, Werleigh worked as secretary general of the Catholic development organisation Caritas and travelled all around Haiti. She was calm and quiet by nature, but created one of the country's most important educational organisations and was leader of a group of women who worked for political and economic equality.

In Pascal-Trouillot's cabinet, Claudette Werleigh was minister of social affairs. She was well-qualified, and as she did not belong to any party, she was accepted in the interim government. She wanted very much to make a contribution in the social field, but disagreement about policy made her withdraw after a short time. When Aristide became president, Werleigh joined the private cabinet of Prime Minister René Préval and was engaged in the Lavalas movement in support of the president. Because of her international contacts, she became foreign minister during 1993–95, partly in exile in the US, and promoted contacts with the Americans (Haiti Progres, 1995).

One hundred days

Claudette Werleigh was 49 years old when she became prime minister. In consultation with the president, she appointed a cabinet with 17 ministers, including four women, and went to work. Her ambitions were high, but it was a tough situation. Time was short and little help was available. She got 100 days from 7 November 1995 to strengthen the leadership of the country and elect a new president, as Aristide's term was ending. She declared that 'my main goal is political, social, cultural and economic justice' (Haiti Info, 1995), received financial support for energy, agriculture and road construction, improved relations with Cuba and Taiwan, and organised democratic elections. She also tried to reduce Haiti's economic dependence and halted the privatisation process. But when it became clear that there would be no privatisation, the IMF held back loans, sparking a political crisis (Toussaint, 2006).

René Préval was a Belgian-trained agronomist and did not belong to any party. He was elected president with 88 per cent of the vote. It was the first peaceful change of president since Haiti became independent. Préval was an ally of Aristide and would have liked Claudette Werleigh to continue as prime minister. But the majority in parliament, which needed to approve the prime minister, had changed, so she withdrew. Her successor initiated an economic reform programme that triggered massive loans from the IMF, but also an opposition in parliament and the population that paralysed the government for a long time.

Claudette Werleigh left the country and became director dealing with conflict issues at the Institute of Life and Peace of Uppsala. Later, Werleigh became secretary general of the Catholic peace organisation Pax Christi International.

New attempt

Claudette Werleigh was not the last woman to go to the top in Haiti. After René Préval, Aristide was elected president again in 2000, in elections that were boycotted by the opposition. Aristide, who began as a charismatic champion of democracy, became increasingly authoritarian, and conditions in the country did not improve. In 2004, protests and riots became so large-scale that an international force led by the US intervened, and Aristide was forced to resign. At the same time, the country was hit by a hurricane and lawlessness spread.

After many delays, new parliamentary and presidential elections were held in 2006, and René Préval was declared president, with 51 per cent of the vote. In the electoral decree, an article reduced by two thirds the registration cost for all candidates of parties presenting electoral lists on which women represented at least 30 per cent. But in the Chamber of Deputies, only two women were elected of the now 98 members, and in the Senate, four women of 30 members (13 per cent).

The situation was difficult, and when food prices soared in 2008, sparking a series of riots, the Senate forced the prime minister to resign. Préval suggested two other men as prime ministers, but they were not accepted. Despite the large male majority, parliament then approved a woman, the independent economist Michèle Pierre-Louis, in September.

Pierre-Louis had a good reputation. Since the 1980s, she had been asked to take up ministerial posts several times, but refused. The international donor community also believed that she was well-suited to improve the conditions in the country. She was born in 1947 and got an education, first, in Haiti, then New York, where she earned a master's degree in economics, and later in Vermont, where she got a PhD in humanities. She married the businessman Eduard Pierre-Louis and had a daughter, but later divorced. At the time of Duvalier, she was assistant director general of the Civil Aviation Authority. Afterwards, she worked to strengthen the social structure of society. She was engaged in education and literacy and emphasised equal access to education for women and men. She was director of a human rights centre, a financial development company and a credit bank. She became a business partner with René Préval and together they started a large bakery. In 1991, she became a member of President Aristide's cabinet. Since 1995, Pierre-Louis has been executive director of FOKAL, a private foundation organising educational programmes and supporting human rights and cultural activities, and in 2003 and 2004, FOKAL criticised Aristide's government because it was oppressive, intimidating and hostile to education. When she was appointed prime minister, at 61 years old, in addition to leading FOKAL, she was professor of pedagogy at a private university in Port-au-Prince.

Prime Minister Pierre-Louis was approved despite the fact that a smear campaign was launched questioning her sexual orientation. She underlined in her declaration of August 2008 that there must be a way out of the crisis:

> I will fight for values: solidarity, honesty, responsibility, transcendence of self, openness and respect for others combined in an idea of this country, an idea that this country has suffered and still suffers too much. We have to fight for education, health, work, justice and children and young people and against corruption, political intrigues and high living costs. (http://iham-chrd.org)

That the country was experiencing a humanitarian crisis contributed to her approval by parliament. In the course of a year, Haiti was hit by no less than four tropical hurricanes, with an extensive loss of lives and damaged bridges, crops and buildings.

Pierre-Louis did not focus specifically on women in her declaration, and in her cabinet, with 17 ministers, three were women. But they managed to amend the constitution to ensure that women fill at least 30 per cent of elected and appointed positions at the national level, though implementation of the amendment afterwards was delayed (Bouchard, 2009; Shaw, 2013; Vilardo, 2013).

After a year, senators from Préval's party complained that people's living standards were not improving. Others thought that it was unfair to place the blame in Pierre-Louis for 200 years of poverty and social inequality, but the prime minister and her cabinet were voted down and out in November 2009. In January 2010, the country was devastated by unusually violent earthquakes, taking over 200,000 lives.

Portia Simpson-Miller: up and down in Jamaica

Matriarchs in a male-dominated country

Women who rose to the top in other parts of the Caribbean did not stay in office very long, either. In 2006, Jamaica got a woman prime minister. It was only a few days after Michele Bachelet became president of Chile, but even if it was the first time a woman obtained Jamaica's most important political position, little attention was paid to the event in the world press. Jamaica was not as important as Chile and Portia Simpson-Miller did not come to power through a suspenseful direct election with wide media coverage. She made her way more quietly up through the party and parliament. But it was quite an achievement.[9]

Jamaica has a turbulent history, with a Caribbean record in slave revolts. When slavery was abolished, the black people on the island started to strive for independence. During the recession after World War I, trade unions, women's organisations and political parties were formed, and the British colonial authorities accepted a certain level of self-governance. The first elections with universal suffrage were held in 1944. Jamaica was the first English-speaking country in the Caribbean to give women the right to vote. In 1962, the island became independent, and Jamaica adopted a constitutional monarchy with a parliamentary democracy, following the British model. The 60 members of the House of Representatives were elected by simple plurality, while the governor appointed the 21 members of the Senate: 13 on the advice of the prime minister and eight on the advice of the leader of the opposition. The prime minister chose the cabinet members from parliament, but not more than four must be from the Senate.

In the new state, political life was marked by a two-party system based on rivalry between the Jamaica Labour Party (JLP) and the People's National Party (PNP). The JLP was considered a moderate right-wing party, while the PNP was social-democratic and left-wing – the party names were therefore quite misleading. Power alternated between the two parties. There were economic problems, unemployment, violence and crime. In 1989, the PNP got the majority. The two parties reached an agreement on economic austerity policies, and after that, the PNP was re-elected three times. In 1992, Prime Minister Michael Manley retired for health reasons, and Deputy Prime Minister Percival J. Patterson was promoted. Jamaica got the reputation of being a stable political democracy. Economic and social conditions improved slowly, although problems with drugs, violence and unrest continued, and many highly skilled people left the island.

It was claimed that the 'Jamaican matriarch' was at the centre of society (Harman, 2006). She played an important role at home, in the church and in the local community. There were also prominent women leaders and artists. But society as a whole was characterised by discrimination on the basis of both gender, class and skin colour. Men dominated and had privileges, while many women were single parents, had heavy, poorly paid work (if they had paid work at all), and were hit hard by economic and social problems.

Jamaica established a women's office in the state administration in 1976, became party to the CEDAW in 1984 and adopted a national women's policy in 1987. Women's organisations criticised the government because it did not implement the policy, but more women got education and they began to make themselves felt in the administration and services. Few acquired high positions, however, especially in politics. In 1993, the PNP only had two women (18 per cent) in the party leadership, while the JLP had five (31 per cent). There were seven women in the House of Representatives (12 per cent) and one in the cabinet (5 per cent). And the situation did not change significantly in the years that followed (Meditz and Hanratty, 1987; Stone, 2010).

Captain disembarks

In 2002, Patterson declared that he would resign before his term was over. The PNP obtained 52 of a total of 60 seats in the House of Representatives in 1993,

50 in 1997 and then only 34 in 2002. In 2006, the PNP elected his successor, and it was an emotionally charged battle. In a population of approximately 2.5 million, the party had about 60,000 members, and as many as possible were mobilised to ensure proper participation in the election. The plan was that the (male) minister of national security should take over the party leadership and the post as prime minister. But he suddenly faced fierce competition from two men and a woman. All the candidates were experienced party members and former ministers. The two men had a PhD, while the woman had only a bachelor's degree in administration, but she won nevertheless. Portia Simpson-Miller got 1,775 votes, 190 votes more than the runner-up. For the first time, a woman became president of a major party in Jamaica. Admittedly, the majority was not overwhelming, and it was the first time a head of the PNP was elected with less than 50 per cent of the vote, but she was elected.

Portia Simpson-Miller did not lack qualifications. She had been active in the party since the early 1970s. In the local government elections in 1974, she became the first PNP councillor from her division, and in the parliamentary elections in 1976, she won her constituency for the PNP for the first time. She became one of the longest-serving MPs in Jamaica. She became the party's first woman vice-president and held the office for 28 years. She was president of the party's women's movement, senior cabinet minister for 17 years with different responsibilities (labour, social welfare, sports, tourism, local government, and community development) and acted in the capacity of prime minister on several occasions. There were allegations of mismanagement and corruption regarding her ministerial portfolios and some claimed that she was not intellectually up to the task. But she was appreciated for her efforts at reforming local government, industrial relations and the overseas farm workers programme, expanding the national insurance fund, developing a plan for sustainable tourism, and constructing kindergartens. At the polls, she was frequently the most popular politician.

It was not common that women went to the top. Jamaica had the reputation of being a 'macho' country, which was reinforced by the party structure and mode of operation. Simpson-Miller was the PNP candidate for president and prime minister in 1992 and lost. Why did she win now? She had far more experience and was known for her efforts for women, the poor and the marginalised. She was not afraid of anything, her voters said: Sista P. 'has balls'. Some also wanted a new deal, something else than the corrupt gang of old guys who filled the corridors of power. Even sceptics felt that it was hard to do worse than the men who in the name of modernisation had served the middle and upper classes during four decades while the masses lived in poverty (Bellanfante, 2005; Williams, 2006; Patterson, 2007).

Sista P. takes over

In March 2006, Portia Simpson-Miller was appointed prime minister, at 60 years old. There was national jubilation, particularly among women, when the nation's beloved mother and sister – 'Momma', 'Auntie Portia' or 'Sista P.', as she was called – took over. In a country where there were supposed to be 'matriarchs', where 70 per cent of university students were women, and where women had long constituted more than half of the labour force and were about to get leading positions in economic life, but not in politics, many felt that it was time for a woman at the helm (Harman, 2006). After more than 60 years with the right to vote, there were still not more than seven women in the House of Representatives (five from the PNP and two from the JLP), four in the Senate and three in the cabinet.

Portia Simpson-Miller not only had her gender, but also her class, against her. She was born in 1945 in a rural working-class family. They were poor, but the eight children were well taken care of, according to Portia. Her mother was strong, physically and spiritually, and her father was determined and hardworking. They were politically active and PNP groups often had meetings in their home. Portia was one of her father's favourites, and at a young age, she started speaking out for her rights in the family and wider community. She went to high school and worked as a secretary, married businessman Errald Miller and had four children. Later, they divorced. As a politician, Sista P. was criticised for her populist viewpoints, Creole dialect and lack of education. 'How dare this uppity woman …', it was said. She did not have a PhD, but she took a bachelor's degree in public administration and acquired a number of certificates in management and leadership training (Patterson, 2007; Bean, 2011).

Percival J. Patterson had problems with declining living standards, a trade deficit, strangling public debt, widespread unemployment and violent crime, and was accused of scandals and corruption. Portia Simpson-Miller met sky-high expectations, and these were not reduced by the fact that she was a woman of the people. When she was sworn in, she asked the people of Jamaica to go into partnership with her to promote human rights, combat corruption and crime, strengthen education, create jobs, and give the poor a better life. The goals were vague, and the only thing that was said about women was that sexuality, fatherhood and motherhood had to be responsible, and women had to be protected (Inaugural Address, 30 March 2006). In the new cabinet, in addition to being prime minister, Simpson-Miller took responsibility for defence, women's affairs and sport, and she was later honoured for her contribution to promoting women's activities in Jamaican sports. She kept most of her predecessor's ministers, which was criticised. She did not have good enough collaborators, and she did not get rid of people who obviously worked against her. The women ministers Portia Simpson-Miller included were the same three as before (25 per cent).

Defeat and revenge

Forbes placed Portia Simpson-Miller as number 89 of the world's 100 most powerful women in 2006, and 81 in 2007. But she was only prime minister for 18 months. She strengthened the police and improved the justice system. Crime went down, and the economy grew. But then the PNP was accused of corruption, and when hurricane 'Dean' struck the island, the prime minister was reproached because she did not react quickly enough to the disaster.

At the 2007 elections, which were held at about the time of the hurricane, the PNP lost with the smallest imaginable margin: the party got 49.8 per cent of the vote against 50.1 per cent for the JLP. The JLP defeated the PNP after 18 years of unbroken governance. The distribution of seats was 32–28, and Simpson-Miller had to withdraw. Key men in the PNP were opposed to the woman prime minister and also attempted to depose her as party leader. But they did not succeed. 'Momma' was re-elected with a larger margin than before after an even tougher battle. She got 2,332 votes, 373 more than the rival male candidate. So, she continued, now as head of the PNP in opposition, in a political environment that was as male-dominated as before.

In the elections in 2012, Simpson-Miller got her revenge. She promised to reduce poverty, strengthen the economy, calm down political antagonisms and break the remaining colonial ties to Britain, and the PNP obtained 42 seats in the House of Representatives, while the JLP only got 21. It was a great victory, and the 'outspoken and charismatic' Portia Simpson-Miller became prime minister for the second time – the second individual to serve non-consecutive terms (the first was Michal Manley). When she was sworn in, roughly 10,000 people filled up the garden of the governor general, probably for the last time, as the new prime minister intended to make Jamaica a republic. *Time* magazine ranked her among the 100 most influential persons in the world (Associated Press, 2012).

But the victory was not complete. The number of women in parliament remained extremely low: still only eight (13 per cent) in House of the Representatives (five from the PNP and three from the JLP) and six (29 per cent) in the Senate (four from the PNP and two from the JLP). And Simpson-Miller only appointed one woman minister with a portfolio (youth and culture) and two without (20 per cent in total). The prime minister was also minister of defence, development, information and sports. It was evidently not easy to reduce the dominance of men in high-level positions.

Kamla Persad-Bissessar in Trinidad and Tobago

East Indians and Africans

While Portia Simpson-Miller struggled as opposition leader in Jamaica, Kamla Persad-Bissessar went to the top in Trinidad and Tobago.[10] The two small twin islands, with a bit more than 1 million inhabitants, were among the most prosperous in the Caribbean, known for their oil resources, carnivals and cocaine trade. The islands were colonised by the British, who cultivated sugarcane, first, with African slaves, then with contract workers from India. Following demands from trade unions, limited electoral representation was introduced in the 1920s and 1930s, and in 1945, universal suffrage was adopted. Gradually, the islands got internal self-government. In 1956, the 'Father of the Nation', Eric Williams, won the elections with the People's National Movement (PNM), a nationalistic, moderate centrist party, and they had a long run of electoral successes.

The country became independent in 1962 and a republic in 1976, with a president as head of state and a parliament with two chambers: the House of Representatives with 41 members and the Senate with 31. The members of the House were elected by universal adult suffrage using a simple plurality vote, while the members of the Senate were appointed by the president. The president was elected by an electoral college drawn from both chambers. The president appointed the prime minister and the cabinet from the MPs, and they were accountable to the House of Representatives. The prime minister had executive political power.

Women gradually acquired education and professional positions, but they had low wages and little power. About 80 per cent of the population was shared nearly equally between Afro-Trinidadians and Indo-Trinidadians, and the gender gap was particularly large in the Indo-Trinidadian community. The role of an Indo-Trinidadian woman was intrinsically linked to her family and her duty to her husband. Kamla Persad-Bissessar was born in 1952 in an Indo-Trinidadian family in a rural community and went to Hindu and Presbyterian schools. Contrary to the usual domestic mould, Kamla's parents encouraged her to pursue higher education. She obtained a bachelor's degree in law, an executive master's in business administration and a diploma in education. She pursued a career in education before becoming an attorney-at-law to promote social justice and equality for all. She married Dr Gregory Bissessar and had a son.

There were tensions between Indo-Trinidadians and Afro-Trinidadians. When economic conditions worsened in the 1980s, the PNM was ousted by a coalition of opposition parties. However, the coalition was troubled and Basdeao Panday quit to form the United National Congress (UNC), a centre-left party mainly supported by Indo-Trinidadians. The PNM mostly attracted Afro-Trinidadians. In 1991, the PNM won again at the elections, but lost in 1995 in a close race with the UNC (Drayton, 2011).

'Government of compassion'

Kamla Persad-Bissessar entered politics at the local level in 1987, and in 1995, she was elected as UNC member of the House of Representatives, having failed the first time she ran for election. As the UNC formed the government, Persad-Bissessar became a cabinet member and the first woman attorney general. She contributed to the establishment of a Family Court and, due to the plural nature of society, an Equal Opportunities Commission. Afterwards, she became minister of legal affairs and minister of education, and she acted as prime minister when he was absent, being the first woman to do so. In addition, she was deputy political leader of the UNC.

The UNC won a majority again in 2000, but the PNM challenged the results. New general elections in 2001 resulted in political deadlock, and only in the third general elections, in 2002, was the PNM declared the winner, again in a very close race with the UNC. The PNM also won the elections in 2007. During this period, the UNC leader, Basdeao Panday, had to stand trial several times and was sentenced to prison for economic mismanagement. Many felt that the UNC would only gain power if Persad-Bissessar became the political leader of the party.

When Basdeao Panday was in prison, Persad-Bissessar acted as leader of the opposition, and in December 2009, she challenged Panday as party leader. It was a courageous step to run against her guru and mentor, the founder of the party, an old political stalwart, and a charismatic leader in the region. She also did the unheard of in a patriarchal party, setting a male leader in competition with a woman. In was a fight between the lion and the lioness. But the country and the party were in trouble. Many wanted a change and youth in the party stated that if democracies were to function, women's voices must be heard (Drayton, 2011: 188). Kamla Persad-Bissessar was very well-qualified, calm, strong and independent. In January 2010, she won a landslide victory and scored another first by unseating Panday as party leader.

With a strong message of good governance, anti-authoritarianism, anti-corruption and unity across the ethnic and political divide, Persad-Bissessar immediately engaged with the other opposition parties and trade unionists to mount a joint campaign and present a single platform against the PNM at the forthcoming elections. In the snap elections in May 2010, the PNM lost. The People's Partnership led by Persad-Bissessar got 27 of the 41 seats in the House of Representatives, and she became the country's first woman prime minister, at 59 years old. When she was elected, she said on 26 May 2010:

> I will lead a government of compassion. As a mother and grandmother, I will not let you down.... We leave the labels behind and we move forward as one nation – all committed to the same goal: a safer, more prosperous and just Trinidad and Tobago where we all have opportunity and equality. No more labels. No more prefixes of Afro and Indo nor North and South nor East and West. (www.news.gov.tt)

With a plurality vote, it was difficult for women to get access to the House of Representatives and the cabinet, but women activists put on pressure and representation in the House increased from 11 per cent in 1995 to 27 per cent in 2010. In the Senate, the percentage of women was 13 per cent. Persad-Bissessar fought for gender equality and women's political participation, but in her cabinet, there were, first, only four, then five, women ministers, while her predecessor had 10. The People's Partnership only had four women in the House of Representatives and one in the Senate. But Persad-Bissessar created a new Ministry of Gender, Youth and Child Development and appointed envoys for women and children.

Male-dominated democracy

Intricate path to the top

Despite the fact that the Caribbean states went through lengthy democratisation processes with active women's organisations and formally worked in a democratic way after they became independent in the latter half of the 1900s, women did not easily gain access to high positions.[11] Before 1980, there were no women top leaders, and in the 30 years that followed, six women rose to the top in only four of the 13 countries.

In most of the Caribbean countries (nine of the 13), no women obtained top leadership positions at all. This was the case with communist Cuba[12] and eight liberal-democratic island nations.

While many countries in the world had both a president and a prime minister, most of the Caribbean countries did not. Eight only had a prime minister (with a governor appointed by the British Queen), two had a president and prime minister combined, and only three countries had both a president and a prime minister.

In all three countries with two elected top leaders, women got one of the positions. In Haiti, one woman was president and two were prime ministers. Both positions entailed political power, but the president was the most important. In Dominica and Trinidad and Tobago, the president had a more formal role, and the two women managed to become prime ministers with executive power. Jamaica was the only country where a woman acquired the only top position. She was elected prime minister with executive power, and it happened twice. In total, four of the women obtained the most important political position, while two shared power with a (male) president.

In a parliamentary system, the prime minister is usually elected by parliament among the MPs. But in all the Caribbean countries, except two, the parliaments/lower houses were elected by majority vote, which made it difficult for women to be nominated and elected. In addition, the parliaments/lower houses were often small, with few members. So, the proportion of women in parliaments/lower houses in the Caribbean generally remained very low. And this was not all. Several countries had rules entailing that part or all of the members of the cabinet had to be MPs. In this way, parliaments could be an effective barrier to women's rise to the top. In some cases, this was offset by women being appointed to the senates. The senates often had less importance than the lower houses and the share of women was sometimes higher.

In 2012, countries in the Caribbean had, on average, a low one sixth to one fifth women in the parliaments/lower houses, senates and cabinets.[13] At the same time, direct strategies to increase women's representation in parliaments, for example, by using quotas, met with considerable opposition. Quotas are more complicated with majority votes than proportional representation, but affirmative action can be carried out, among other things, by using reserved seats. And electoral systems can be changed.

Analysing the low representation of women, the political scientist Cynthia Barrow-Giles (2005) noted that it was a function of both supply and demand. The socialisation of women into care-giving and their burdens as single supporters with limited income reduced the pool of women available for national politics, while political parties did not address the challenges facing women, did not view the inclusion of women as necessary to winning elections and did not seek or promote them as candidates. If women's under-representation is to be effectively addressed, Barrow-Giles concluded, political parties must take affirmative action deliberately designed to increase women's presence in national parliaments (Barrow-Giles, 2005: 58).

Their own achievement

Although the majority of countries were relatively democratic, authoritarian tendencies made themselves felt, and the first women rose to the top in connection with unrest and demands for democratisation. Eugenia Charles came to power in an exceptionally turbulent situation in Dominica, and in Haiti, women did so during a tense period of change between authoritarian and elected rulers. In Jamaica and Trinidad and Tobago, however, the women ran for office in regular elections and won – or lost.

Caribbean societies were relatively small and transparent. Politics easily became very personalised, and parties were generally characterised by male leaders who ruled in a more or less personal and self-willed way. They were 'men's clubs'. Often, political life was dominated by rivalry between two strong men, each with their own party. Patron–client relationships were widespread. It has been argued that such relationships were advantageous in linking different socio-economic and ethnic strata together and contributing to political stability. But they could also effectively keep women out because the networks were closed and controlled by male leaders, who did not see benefits in including women. In the various parties, the participation of women varied, but there were generally very few in leadership positions.

In the Caribbean, none of the women rose to the top as substitutes for male political leaders, and neither as widows or daughters. But in Haiti, the two women prime ministers were launched by male presidents with whom they had worked closely, but they did not stay long in office in troubled situations. The woman president in Haiti was independent and came to power by mere coincidence, and she only acted in the interim. All the three Haitian women were more or less political outsiders, though Werleigh and Pierre-Louis were cabinet members before they became prime ministers. The other women national leaders fought their way up through political parties, participated actively for a considerable period of time, stood for election, got positions and finally rose to the top. In addition to being party leaders, they were MPs and Simpson-Miller was also a minister with different portfolios. The women belonged to different political tendencies. While Charles was clearly to the right, the others were to the left (three) or centre-left (one).

All the women top leaders were exceptionally well-qualified and acquired top positions on the basis of their expertise and efforts. Simpson-Miller and Pascal-Trouillot came from humble circumstances, but Pascal-Trouillot married into the elite and had the support of her husband to get an education. Simpson-Miller took supplementary training as an adult. The others came from well-to-do families, and all received higher education. Charles and Persad-Bissessar had advanced education in law, and Pierre-Louis had a PhD in the humanities. The others had lower university degrees, and some more than one. Charles and Persad-Bissessar became lawyers, and among the others, there was a judge, professor, secretary general and secretary. It is not surprising that professionals succeed in a context where women have traditionally not been business owners and are primarily care-givers, lacking independent sources of income.

The women did not have the same basis for their political careers, but all contributed to democratisation of their countries. Pascal-Trouillot became provisional president in her official capacity as Supreme Court judge in a transitional period. Werleigh and Pierre-Louis were independent, but they supported the elected male presidents, were drawn into their circles and became prime ministers. Charles was in opposition to an authoritarian government and co-founded the party that she became the head of. The others joined existing parties. Charles and Simpson-Miller had to fight to keep their positions as party leaders, but both managed to beat their opposition, though Simpson-Miller had to do several rounds.

The women were mature in age when they reached the top. Most were in their 50s or 60s, while Pascal-Trouillot and Werleigh were in their late 40s. Charles was single and childless, but all the others were married with one or two children, two were also divorced. All the children were adults when the mothers became top politicians.

One real leadership

Of the top political women leaders in the Caribbean, only one really got to exercise proper leadership. That was Eugenia Charles of Dominica, who was prime minister for 15 years. None of the others exceeded one-and-a-half years in power, and many were in power for just a few months. Three worked briefly during the tumultuous times in Haiti, while one lost the election that she was supposed to win as the newly appointed prime minister of Jamaica. Later, she was re-elected and Simpson-Miller and Persad-Bissessar were both in office at the end of 2010.

The women leaders rose to the top with very few women in the parliaments/lower houses as well as the cabinets, and the two were usually connected. In Dominica, very few women were elected to the Lower House, and besides Eugenia Charles, all belonged to the opposition. Women could be nominated to the Senate, but there were few with sufficient qualifications. So, Charles had practically no basis for recruiting women to the cabinet. In Jamaica, Simpson-Miller appointed, first, two, then three, women ministers, though there were more women in parliament. But the male majority must have given men priority. Persad-Bissessar appointed all four elected women MPs and the woman senator from her alliance as ministers. Contrary to these countries, Haiti could also recruit ministers outside of parliament. But this did not lead to an increase in the number of women. First, a woman minister was appointed when there was no parliament. Later, three women ministers were appointed and then four, while there were three in parliament.

The women top leaders were both appreciated and attacked, idolised and despised. For Pascal-Trouillot, it was an advantage to be a woman, as a positive sign of renewal. Charles and Simpson-Miller also got support. They were called 'Moma Charles', 'Auntie' and 'Sista P', and Simpson-Miller was even admired because she 'had balls'. But they were also criticised: Simpson-Miller as an 'Uppity Woman' and Charles as a 'Bitch of a Woman' and other negative characteristics. Their gender was used against both Charles and Simpson-Miller as party leaders.

Due to constraints, the top women generally got little opportunity to influence policies in general, or those related to women in particular, regardless of their qualifications and positions. Most could only deal with the most pressing matters. Four of the women were engaged in women's organisations and gender equality. But it was mainly Charles who managed to implement measures of significance for the benefit of women, though there were few women around her and she was perceived as a 'reluctant' feminist. Actually, both her economic and women-related policies were complex and controversial. She also governed one of the smallest states in the Caribbean. However, she stood out in the political landscape, both nationally and regionally, and was an inspiration and role model for many women.

The President of Liberia Ellen Johnson Sirleaf at a press conference in the United Nations in New York on 19 September 2006. She was elected as president in 2005 and took office in January 2006.
125461: UN Photo/Erin Siegal

Chapter Eight

'Big Chiefs' in sub-Saharan Africa

Ruth Perry ends Liberia's civil war

Mother of warlords

She did not look like a tough politician, more like a kind grandmother: an elderly woman with a colourful headscarf and twinkling eyes behind the glasses. But in 1996, after 17 years of conflict and seven years of war, Ruth Sando Perry was assigned the task of bringing peace to Liberia and organising the elections of a legislature and a president.[1] As Ruth Sando Perry told me when I met her in Oslo in 1999:

> "Women wanted peace in Liberia. We wanted fighting to stop. Women started forming themselves into groups to talk about peace in 1992 before elections. We held peaceful marches – Christian, Moslem, rural, women from all over. A widowed mother of seven heading a household with 15 children, I was not politically active after the civil war broke out in 1989. I was doing my business at home in Paynesville and tried to survive as best I could with my children and the family."

From the beginning of the war, women were active in calling for peace in public meetings, and they required to be heard at peace conferences. It took time before this was accepted, but in August 1996, a women's delegation was invited to attend the Abuja peace conference organised by the Economic Community of West African States (ECOWAS). Ruth Perry explained to me that she was willing to go because women in the country wanted peace. But she did not know that she was going to play a special role before a Nigerian ambassador suddenly arrived at her hotel with a car to take her to the conference. She had to dress in a hurry, and before she knew it, she found herself in front of the Council of State of the transitional government. And they asked her to take over as chairwoman of the Council of State. The warlords said to her: 'As a mother. Take us as your children, and we will cooperate.'

Ruth Perry admitted that she experienced some trepidation. But she accepted the task:

> "I thought that the good Lord had made his choice, and I would continue to pray for guidance. So I replied: 'Some mothers are overbearing and some are strict. I belong to the last. I love my children, but I discipline them. If the war shall end, you have to cooperate with me'." (interview, 1999)

Everybody promised to cooperate, and Ruth Perry said 'yes'. The peace and stability of the country were at stake. The ECOWAS leaders unanimously supported Perry as the interim Liberian head of state. Men had long had the opportunity to make peace, they said, but they had not succeeded. Now, it was time to try a woman. In August 1996, Ruth Perry, aged 57 years old, became the first woman head of state not only in Liberia, but also in contemporary Africa as a whole (African Women and Peace Support Group, 2004: 84–6).

Blood everywhere

The appointment of Ruth Perry was a great victory for the Liberian women peace activists, and they supported her. But some were sceptical. They thought the warlords had settled on Ruth Perry because she was known in Liberia, but since the events of 1989, had been a private and uninvolved citizen. They considered her perhaps as more flexible than others who might be chosen and no threat to themselves (Sirleaf, 2009: 210). The international press was alarmed: how could a weak woman cope with the dangerous warlords? It was a challenging task. Perry was head of both state and government, with a council including the leaders of a number of warring factions – all men. And she was supposed to bring peace and tranquillity: disarm the combatants; repatriate, resettle and reintegrate refugees and displaced people; get people's everyday lives going; and organise transparent elections.

There was unrest, confrontations and tension. The warlords refused to give a woman leader the authority, personnel and money she needed to do the job. There were clashes and shooting in the council offices with blood everywhere. But Perry was undaunted. She used the moral authority of her office and went fearlessly forward. She declared that she was 'hard as steel' and demanded that the warriors lay down their arms and accept elections. Women, who had been sceptical, acknowledged that Perry represented them well, and she dispelled the myth that women cannot be leaders (African Women and Peace Support Group, 2004: 31).

The former head of state chuckled when she talked about her relationship with the warlords:

> "Along the way, sometimes you tell them a little truth, and a little something else, always reassuring them with the ballot box. I used my womanly, my

motherly, touch and everything that you apply within your community, your church and your home." (interview, 1999)

Perry was a skilled organiser, mobilising and cooperating with different parties. Over the radio, she urged people to maintain discipline and peace, and she got women together to help. She got water, biscuits and portable radios from the business community and travelled around the country to inform people about their rights and persuade youngsters to hand in their weapons. Fortunately, Liberia is a very small country, for roads and communications were in bad shape after the war. In addition to the United Nations (UN), voluntary organisations engaged in relief work and reconstruction, and Perry went to the US, where she received clothing, medicine and school supplies.

Eleven peace attempts

Liberia has a long history of exploitation and conflict. The country grew out of a settler colony for freed African slaves from the US and gained its independence as a republic in 1847, though the US continued to exert considerable influence. A constitution was approved by referendum. It was largely modelled on that of the US, with an elected president and a legislature with two chambers. Only land-owning men had the right to vote. Thus, the former slaves established themselves as a ruling class governing the people living on the small coastal strip (around 100,000 square kilometres). There were 16 ethnic groups, with different traditions, religions and languages. But the Americo-Liberians regarded themselves as civilised masters, while the original inhabitants were treated as a barbaric underclass. For more than a century, the Americo-Liberian elite, comprising only 2.5 per cent of the population, ruled the country in a strict colonial way as a one-party and apartheid state.

The Americo-Liberian elite monopolised the state and used the resources for personal consumption and to protect its own position. The soil was fertile, and rubber, iron ore and diamonds gave large revenues that ended up in the pockets of foreign investors and the ruling class. The vast majority got neither political nor economic rights, were deprived of land, and were recruited as labour by force. Resistance and uprisings were brutally suppressed. While poverty and illiteracy prevailed among ordinary people, the well-to-do could attend West Africa's first college in the capital, Monrovia. Here, women had already gained access in the 1880s.

After World War II, President William Tubman governed Liberia more or less like his own plantation and the whole country was tied up in extensive patron–client relations. In fact, the relations were so intricate, both vertical and horizontal, and deep that researchers preferred to give them a special name: 'Big Man networks' (Utas, 2008, 2012). But Tubman's successor, President William Tolbert, had problems when he took over in 1971. Resources dwindled and networks started to collapse. An increase in the price of rice led to violent riots in Monrovia in

1979, and in 1980, there was a coup. Samuel Doe, a non-commissioned officer from the inland, took power. He suspended the constitution, and the president and most of the ministers were killed.[2]

The Americo-Liberian Charles Taylor supported Doe's coup and worked in the government, but was charged with embezzlement and fled to the US. Here, he was jailed, but managed to escape. The new government turned out to be no less despotic than the former, and the brutality got worse and worse. In 1989, Charles Taylor invaded the country from the Ivory Coast as the head of the National Patriotic Front of Liberia (NPFL) to get rid of Doe. Soon, a civil war was in full swing, with up to seven different warring factions competing for power and resources, looting, killing, molesting and raping the civilian population. With a population of about 2.5 million, more than half became refugees, while as many as 200,000 (8 per cent of the population) died in fighting or massacres.

In 1990, ECOWAS sent in 'peace-keeping forces'. ECOMOG, the Economic Community of West African States Cease-fire Monitoring Group, numbered 12,000 personnel from several states, led by Nigeria. However, unofficially, their mandate was to prevent Taylor from taking power, and the forces soon became part of the conflict, collaborating with Taylor's enemies. The war continued and Doe was arrested and executed by the warlord Prince Johnson, who captured Monrovia. An interim government was established. And after 11 international attempts at peace between 1990 and 1995, it finally seemed to succeed. Charles Taylor and Nigeria's military President Sani Abacha agreed to let the leadership of Liberia be decided democratically. Then, the head of the interim government had to resign and be replaced by a 'neutral' person. Many were suggested, but there was always a faction that vetoed the proposal. The only person that everyone could agree on was Ruth Sando Perry.

'You can't stay away'

Even though she was seen as 'weak' by some, Ruth Perry was not just anyone. She belonged to the *Vai* people, who were one of the few African tribes to have developed a script, and they were less involved in the war than many other ethnic groups. She had experience and competence, both from politics and economics, and as an elderly woman, she enjoyed special respect.

In Liberia, women played important roles in the economy, household, society and peace-building. After independence, women organised themselves and actively contributed to the establishment of schools and churches. Some women got higher education and became politically active. After voting rights became universal in the 1940s, a few also obtained important positions. Several women were ministers and members of the legislature. In 1969, a Liberian woman, Angie Brooks Randolph, became the first African president of the UN General Assembly, and Mary Antoinette Brown Sherman became the first woman president of an African university. Liberia acceded to the UN Convention on the Elimination of All Forms of Discrimination against Women (CEDAW) in 1984.

When armed conflict broke out, women were injured, beaten, abused and raped. But they also launched counter-attacks. Some took up arms and joined the various warring factions. Others – and they were by far the most numerous – took on peace-building tasks, mobilised and demonstrated against the war.

Ruth Perry was the daughter of Marjon and Alhaji Semil Fahnbulleh and was born in 1939 in a rural area in Grand Cape Mount in Western Liberia. The family was Moslem, and in addition to traditional training in the secret women's association Sande, Ruth went to a Roman Catholic school for girls run by missionary nuns and undertook teacher training at the University of Monrovia. She worked for a time as a teacher and married the lawyer Perry McDonald, who later became a judge and MP. They had four sons and three daughters. When the youngest reached school age in 1971, Ruth took a job in a bank in the capital. Here, she worked for 14 years, with increasing responsibility, until the bank had to close as a result of political tensions.

When her husband became involved in politics, Ruth Perry was engaged in the electoral campaign and tried to get women to vote for him. Doe's government revised the Constitution and it was approved by referendum in 1984. The system of government was basically maintained and elections were held in 1985. As Ruth Perry's husband had died, the Unity Party asked the widow to run as a senator from their home district. No one was opposed, and she was elected. In response to the extensive fraud during the elections, the opposition, including Ellen Johnson Sirleaf, decided to boycott the Senate, but Perry did not agree. 'You can't solve the problems by staying away', she told me. She was the only representative of the opposition in the Assembly. She participated in various committees and sponsored legislation to protect the rights of women and children. In particular, she went against Doe's efforts to legalise polygamy. When the war put an end to political activities, she launched a retail business, took care of refugee children and became involved in the women's peace efforts. But she had to flee several times and stayed for a while in the US (Brennan, 1997; Jensen, 2008: 67–8).

Failed success

As Liberian head of state, Ruth Perry managed to establish peace and organise elections. It was quite an achievement. She might just as well have been murdered. But she survived, and not only that, she disarmed 70 per cent of the troops, and elections were held according to schedule in 1997. They took place peacefully, and Perry was satisfied. According to the peace agreement, she could not run for office herself, but there were 12 candidates: faction leaders and former members of the Doe regime. The wealthiest and the leader of the strongest faction was Charles Taylor. His most well-known challenger was Ellen Johnson Sirleaf, a Harvard-educated economist and dissident under Doe. She wanted civilians to take back control of their country, a message that sounded good to educated Liberians and the West, but gave little assurance to the poor, uneducated masses. She was also associated with former President Tolbert and the urban elite and lived abroad during the war (Turshen and Twagiramariya, 1998: 133–4).

The preacher, warlord and showman Charles Taylor was elected president, with 75 per cent of the vote. After seven years of ECOMOG presence, the result was exactly what the ECOWAS countries had set out to prevent in 1990. Taylor's movement, the NPLF, embraced the greatest number of ethnic groups. He controlled commercial transactions rather than a specific territory. Further, he was the only candidate with the resources to conduct a real campaign. He had motorcycles and helicopters, and controlled several newspapers and the only radio that reached outside Monrovia. Many people were afraid. They believed that if Taylor was not elected, he would continue fighting. Taylor himself appealed to socio-religious notions and argued that he was destined by God to be president. He dressed all in white to appear like a Messiah and used the slogan: 'Better the devil you know than the angel you do not'. Young supporters sang: 'He killed my Pa. He killed my Ma. I'll vote for him' (Ellis, 1999: 104–9, 273–80).

Liberians who voted for Taylor thought that the one who had destroyed the country should also repair it again. But there was no peace and development with the warlord as president. The situation deteriorated, human rights were violated and Taylor got involved in war in Sierra Leone. In 2000, the UN adopted economic sanctions against him. Liberians United for Reconciliation and Democracy (LURD) rebelled in northern Liberia with support from Guinea, and a new civil war was a fact.

Authoritarian rule in poor countries

'Big Chiefs' take over

Africa is as big as Asia and rich in natural resources. The large majority of the population are black Africans, but the continent is sparsely populated, and at the turn of the millennium, most states were low-income countries.[3]

Contact with the Europeans goes way back in time. The transatlantic slave trade was eventually replaced by a varied exchange of goods. Christian missionary activity expanded in addition to Islamic influence, and from 1880 to 1918, Africa was colonised by seven European powers, notably, Britain and France, but also Belgium, Germany, Italy, Portugal and Spain. The colonial powers pursued somewhat different policies, but all exploited the resources of the countries. Authoritarian colonial states were established. The population was oppressed and resistance was struck down. At the same time, the original population was supposed to be 'civilised'. But apart from missionary schools, only a small minority got secondary or higher education. Portugal differed from the other colonial powers in that it did less to develop the countries and their colonial rule lasted longer and ended in bloody wars.[4]

Although the colonisation was relatively short-lived, it left deep traces. When the countries became independent national states – mostly in the 1950s and 1960s, but for the Portuguese colonies, only in the 1970s – government institutions were established according to the Western European model, and the colonial set-up, with legislation and central administrations, armies, and Western education, was continued.

Political parties and elected bodies created in the late-colonial period functioned poorly in societies organised on the basis of tribes. After independence, the forms of government changed and were adapted to local conditions. Thus, the systems differed from country to country. Most states introduced authoritarian presidential systems, and in many cases, the military took power. There was a need to consolidate the nation-state and keep ethnic, regional, cultural and religious antagonisms in check. A one-party system had some similarity with traditional African forms of decision-making, and the state was used as an engine for development. Various kinds of corruption and patron–client systems were very widespread. 'The Big Chief' (autocratic president) was at the centre and controlled extensive networks and state resources. Compared to other regions of the world, African governance was less bureaucratic, informal networks were more important, rulers were less encumbered by legal restrictions and the battle over the state and its resources was harder. Changes of regime were more often forced through by political protest movements than ruling elites. When presidents left office, it was often as a result of coups.

Pseudo-democracy

The end of the 1980s and the beginning of the 1990s saw the emergence of demands for democracy inspired by developments in other parts of the world. Student organisations, trade unions, human rights activists and women's organisations objected and demonstrated against corrupt and oppressive regimes. At the same time, the collapse of the Soviet Union brought an end to the support by superpowers of authoritarian African leaders just because they were on the 'right' side of the Cold War. Economic problems and a lack of resources also reduced the possibilities for rulers to suppress or adapt to protests. A wave of democratisation swept across the continent (see Figure 11).

The processes of change were often incomplete, turbulent and uneven during the transition of authoritarian regimes to democracy. In a quarter of the countries, there was internal armed conflict: coups or war. In others, democratic systems more or less collapsed. Eventually, most of the countries became multiparty states, and elections were held. But the same men who had previously taken power by coups, were often elected as presidents. They were more legitimate, but just as 'autocratic' as before. Corruption remained widespread, and the presidents would not retire. They used all sorts of methods to win elections and often continued sitting. The majority of the presidential elections after 1990 ended with re-election. Democratisation made regimes less oppressive. There was more personal freedom and more room for competing political groups, a critical media and activist organisations. But in presidential systems, the power and control remained with

Figure 11: Sub-Saharan Africa: regimes by type, 1946–2012

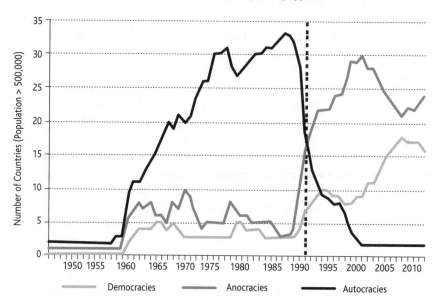

Note: Anocratic governance is a system placed somewhere between democracy and autocracy. The power is spread
between elite groups competing for power.
Source: Center for Systemic Peace, Polity IV Project (www.systemicpeace.org)
© Center for Systemic Peace 2014

the autocratic president. Usually, the president had extensive executive, legislative and budgetary powers. There was little separation of powers and members of the legislatures, which were elected with varying electoral systems, were weak and passive. The opposition was also weak and often part of the political elite, which was more preoccupied with gaining personal power than changing the system. In addition, the judiciary lacked the strength to prevent injustice and misuse by 'The Big Chief'. The result was a situation of strong presidents in weak, even more or less failed, states.

Observers believed that there were positive developments: new generations came forward, more people got access to mobile phones and the Internet, elections and formal rules became more important than before, and governments became more democratic and accountable. But unrest in connection with elections was increasingly a problem that hindered democratisation.

In 2000, 13 African states were characterised as 'authoritarian'. The rest (32 states) were 'democratic'. With the exception of two 'liberal democracies' (Botswana and Mauritius), all were 'emerging democracies', and practically all (except Ethiopia, Lesotho and Mauritius) had presidential political systems (Derbyshire and Derbyshire, 2000). In these systems, the president appointed the cabinet, possibly also a prime minister, and the prime minister could appoint the ministers or present proposals. Cabinet members could not be MPs. The president delegated tasks to the prime minister, but the distribution of roles between the two varied. Often, the president was designated 'head of government' even though there was a prime minister as well.

The world's poorest region

When they became independent, sub-Saharan African countries were economically and socially far behind Asia, Latin America and the Caribbean. During the first years, things went relatively well. Production and exports increased, and infrastructure, health and education were developed. But, with few exceptions, the economies remained just as dependent, one-sided and vulnerable as before, and the countries were poorly prepared when commodity prices dropped in the 1970s while the prices of oil and industrial products rose. The 1980s became Africa's 'lost decade'. The continent struggled, with debt burdens, budget deficits and inflation. Production, the supply of goods and real incomes fell. Structural adjustment measures were implemented, entailing a weakening of the state, liberalisation and the privatisation of the economy.

When economies started doing better, and income per capita began rising again in the 1990s, many countries were back to the level they had been at 20 years earlier. And development made commercial interests take precedence, while concerns for social justice and gender equality gave way.

The crisis hit sub-Saharan Africa harder than other regions of the world, and despite substantial international development assistance, it was the world's poorest region at the turn of the millennium. Population growth was unusually high. There were great disparities, and about half of the population, especially women and children, were poor. The mortality rate was high. Although urbanisation was rapid, most people lived in the countryside, where both women and men worked as farmers. There was progress in health and education, also for girls, and in the towns, some women got secondary education and became teachers, midwives, nurses and clerks. But most had odd jobs in the informal sector (UNDP's annual human development reports, 1995-2013).

Queens who disappeared

There are between 500 and 2,000 ethnic African groups, with partly different languages, histories and cultures. Traditional religions exist in countless variations, together with Christianity and Islam. The cities are affected the most by modern Western thinking, while traditional culture is more rooted in the countryside. The position of women varies greatly. While they traditionally were strongly oppressed in some ethnic groups, they had a high position in others. Among farmers in Central Africa, descent was matrilineal, while patrilineal descent was widespread among cattle people affected by Islam. Queens, queen mothers, empresses, female chiefs and co-rulers exercised power throughout the ages in groups of people scattered across the continent. Women leaders could alternate with men having control. There were dual-sex political systems, and systems that gave women a distinctive role. Ethnic groups along the coast of Guinea in West Africa were noted for the political authority women could possess.

The male dominance that existed in traditional African societies was reinforced by the introduction, first, of Islam, then Christianity and, finally, European colonial rule. Developments entailed some progress for the women who were worst off, but, in general, the status of women was weakened. This was particularly tangible in societies where they previously had a strong position. Women lost the right to customary land. Only men were given credit and training, and when they took up export-oriented sales agriculture, as colonial powers wanted, women's workload in subsistence agriculture became heavier.

The European colonial masters were just that – masters – and they often neglected or opposed women's leadership where it existed, while men were recognised or appreciated as leaders. Women protested and demonstrated against discriminatory decrees, sometimes alone, sometimes together with men, and they participated in the fight against colonialism. At the end of the colonial era, universal suffrage was introduced, but when the states became independent, African men took over the leadership positions that the European men had before, and women were excluded from national government.

The independent African states were among the states in the world with the lowest representation of women in parliaments and cabinets. But CEDAW was ratified by about half of the countries in the 1980s and the others became party to the Convention later. In particular, the third UN International Women's Conference, which took place in Africa (Nairobi) in 1985, had an impact on the continent. Women's organisations were strengthened and regional organisations like the Organization of African Unity (OAU) and the South African Development Community (SADC) focused on the status of women. In connection with the democratisation of the 1990s, women's activism flourished. Women presented claims and more got engaged in politics. They founded and headed political parties and stood for election as presidents and vice presidents in addition to MPs.[5]

Explosion in Rwanda and Burundi: Agatha Uwlingiyimana and Sylvie Kinigi

Arrangement for conflict

Apart from Elisabeth Domitien, women did not become heads of state and government in sub-Saharan Africa before democratisation began in 1990. The first two women came to power at about the same time, in the summer of 1993. It was during the ethnic-based conflicts in Rwanda and Burundi, and both women wished to contribute to national reconciliation. Their role as top politicians was, however, short-lived and stormy. One was killed and the other had to go into exile.[6]

Rwanda and Burundi are 'twin states' in Central Africa. Both were German colonies and, after World War I, Belgian-mandated territories. The countries are small, but the fertile mountains and hills are among the most densely populated on the continent and the depletion of natural resources creates serious problems. Traditionally, the Hutus cultivated the land while the Tutsis were cattle farmers. They belonged to the same ethnic group, spoke the same language, intermarried and had a common culture. In both countries, the Hutus have been and still are in the majority while the Tutsis have been in the minority. Nevertheless, there have been Tutsi kingdoms and the Hutus have had lower status. The Belgian government increased the tensions between the groups by establishing social segregation. Everybody was classified as either Hutu or Tutsi, and the Tutsis were systematically privileged in education and administrative positions.

Many in the two countries became Catholics, while others kept to traditional religions. Both women and men were farmers, but women were subordinated, and most power positions were reserved for men. In Rwanda, the queen mother was influential, but the status of women was weakened by the colonial power.

Universal suffrage was introduced in 1961 and the countries became independent in 1962. The antagonisms flared up immediately. In Rwanda, a Hutu nationalist movement was created and seized power, while a Tutsi military junta took over control in Burundi. Both the Hutu rule in Rwanda and the Tutsi rule in Burundi lasted for about 30 years in a situation of tension, violence, armed conflict, power struggles and oppression. The governance of Burundi was described as a form of tribal apartheid. At the same time, both countries were very poor, with widespread illiteracy and low life expectancy. In a few decades, the population doubled. In the 2000s, Burundi had 8 million and Rwanda 9 million inhabitants, and the pressure on scarce resources increased (Longman, 2006; Stanford, 2010).

Tutsi woman in Burundi

Sylvie Kinigi was born in 1953 in a family with six children in the countryside of Burundi. The oldest child was a girl. Then came a boy and Sylvie was number three. Her father was a merchant, and her mother cultivated the soil and kept the house. The oldest daughter had to help her mother, but Sylvie was allowed to attend a Belgian school for girls run by nuns. After independence, the authorities placed great emphasis on the education of girls, so Sylvie got both primary and secondary education and afterwards went to the capital, Bujumbura, to study economics. At 19 years old, she married one of the professors and they rapidly had four children. Nevertheless, Sylvie continued with her studies. Her husband supported her, and a maid took care of the house and children. During the 1980s, Sylvie Kinigi was engaged in the woman's organisation of the governing Tutsi party (the only party that was allowed) and managed to get laws changed and economic and social measures implemented for women. She headed the group in the capital and was a member of the national executive board of the women's branch.

After she graduated in economics, Sylvie Kinigi got a job in Burundi's central bank and, at the same time, taught at the university. A good number of women obtained important positions in working life, but not in politics, and in the bank, women had to fight for their rights. Yet, Kinigi claimed, when I interviewed her in Malabo in 1999, that she personally never felt discriminated against. She was Tutsi, was promoted and given responsibility for research and studies. In 1991, she became advisor to the prime minister and was responsible for reducing military expenditures and carrying out an economic reform programme. She negotiated with Western donors, the International monetary Fund (IMF) and the World Bank. In 1992, Burundi became party to the CEDAW.

There was armed conflict between Hutus and Tutsis, violence and mass murder, coups and military rule until the summer of 1993. Then, elections were organised as a transition to democracy. Opposition was permitted and, to great surprise, Melchior Ndadaye, a university-educated banker who was the leader of the opposition, was elected as the country's first Hutu president. The incumbent Tutsi president, who came to power in a coup in 1987, had expected to win with ease. The legislative elections took place with proportional representation, and the opposition got an overwhelming majority (almost three quarters) in a national assembly with 10 per cent women. A coup was tried before Ndadaye took office, but it failed.

To reduce tensions between the ethnic groups, the new president appointed a cabinet with two thirds Hutu and one third Tutsi members. It was the first ethnically mixed cabinet formed after a democratic election. Two ministers were women: the minister for women and human rights and Sylvie Kinigi, who was prime minister. Ndadaye knew her from the bank and was well aware of her competence. Besides, he wanted to show his respect for Tutsis and women. Kinigi was very surprised and thought that she could make best use of her skills in the administration (not in politics), but was persuaded. At 40 years old, she was a widow (her husband died in 1992) and her children were adults. She emphasised that her highest political priority was to help bring about ethnic reconciliation between the Tutsis and Hutus, which was essential for her economic development plans (Hill, 1996b: 119). Most of the cabinet members had studied and worked together, so they knew each other. They were not personal enemies, but some were angry because Sylvie Kinigi had been appointed prime minister. Not only was she a woman, but she belonged to a different party that, in addition, had lost the elections.[7]

Abrupt end

Sylvie Kinigi did not stay long in office. She was appointed in July, and in October, there was a coup attempt. Tutsi soldiers stormed the National Palace and killed the president and six senior politicians. At the same time, ethnic violence broke out around the country. Kinigi and part of the cabinet survived the massacre and sought refuge in the French embassy.

The violence and the international condemnation made the coup fail. And suddenly Sylvie Kinigi was not only prime minister, but also acting president. She managed to get 15 of the 22 ministers together to continue to govern and try to stop the turmoil and bloodshed. Two former military presidents supported her, but it was a very difficult situation, with a deeply divided country and a cabinet that was both temporary and very complex. A certain order was established in the capital, but the killings continued throughout the country. In January 1994, Sylvie Kinigi made the National Assembly amend the constitution so that the Assembly could elect a new president and thus get a head of state with proper authority. But the election of the former minister of agriculture, the Hutu Cyprien Ntaryamira, caused negative reactions among Tutsis.

When Ntaryamira was inaugurated in February, Sylvie Kinigi resigned as prime minister. She was the object of criticism, attacks and threats from all sides, and it was not long before she left the country.

On 6 April 1994, President Ntaryamira was shot and killed along with the president of Rwanda, Juvenal Habyarimana. It happened when the presidential plane came back from regional peace negotiations and was to land in the Rwandan capital Kigali. It is not clear who fired, but the incident led to widespread massacres, both in Burundi and Rwanda. In Burundi, the civil war lasted several years and the Tutsi army again took power. Following protracted peace negotiations, the Arusha Agreement was signed in 2002 with power-sharing between ethnic groups, and in 2005, elections were held.

Meanwhile Sylvie Kinigi was employed in the UN system, where she worked for development, peace and reconciliation, and she remained abroad. When I met her in 1999, she was resident representative of the UN Development Programme (UNDP) in Malabo, the capital of Equatorial Guinea, and had no thoughts of moving back to Burundi. "Here, I can use my knowledge in a constructive manner", she said. Then, she added:

> "When things got most serious in Burundi, I do not know where I got the strength from. Providence must have guided me. I wanted peace and normal conditions, but my collaborators wanted me to declare a coup d'état! You can't carry on like that. When I managed to get a successor elected in a reasonably acceptable manner, I resigned." (interview, 1999)

But now, several years later, how did she see her time as a top political leader? Sylvie held the view that it had not been in vain. Her term in government made people realise "that a woman can do even more than a man can do, with a soul of a mother and strong will, at the highest level of politics" (interview, 1999).

Hutu woman in Rwanda

Agathe Uwlingiyimana was also born in 1953 and grew up in Butare in southern Rwanda. Her family were farmers, but she got an education and acquired the right to teach in the humanities in her early 20s. Thereafter, she studied mathematics and took a bachelor's degree in chemistry in 1985. This was unusual for Hutu women, and many criticised her. But she taught chemistry at the university and various schools, including a secondary school for girls. She married a fellow student from the village. He became a laboratory assistant at the university, and they had five children. Agathe was interested in societal issues and fought actively against ethnic polarisation and for education for girls. When she taught at academic schools in Butare, she started a self-help organisation among the employees that was so successful that she was appointed director in the Ministry of Trade and Industry in 1989. The authorities wanted to have decision-makers from the dissatisfied population in the south of the country, and, in addition, she was a Hutu and woman. Rwanda became party to the CEDAW in 1981.

Under Hutu rule, Tutsis were massacred and expelled. In 1990, the country was invaded by the Rwandan Patriotic Front (RPF), which was created by Tutsi refugees in neighbouring Uganda. They demanded an end to the authoritarian rule of the Hutu president, General Habyarimana, and the right to return home. Habyarimana permitted opposition parties and established a coalition government, with separation of powers between the president and the opposition. Agathe Uwlingiyimana joined one of the opposition parties. The new opposition parties put pressure on the government to address women's issues, and in 1992, Habyarimana brought in women for the first time: Agathe Uwilingiyimana as minister of education and another woman as minister of family and women. As a minister, Uwilingiyama abolished the ethnic quota system in schools, a decision that made Hutu extremists hate her, despite the fact that she, herself, was Hutu.

In July 1993, Agathe Uwlingiyimana became prime minister, at 40 years old, after negotiations between the president and the opposition. Two women ministers were also appointed. Uwlingiyimana was probably chosen because Habyarimana wanted to split the opposition, while the opposition parties thought that they could control her. The appointment entailed that she was suspended from her own party, which was opposed to any government without the RPF. Thus, she lacked a power base. And the president humiliated her by publicly addressing her as 'You, woman!' at a political meeting in Kigali. This made Uwlingiyimana replicate: 'Don't talk to me like that. I'm not your wife!' (Reuters, 1994).

It was crucial for the Hutu-dominated government to get a peace agreement with the RPF. This was extremely challenging, but the prime minister stressed: 'I'm Rwandan and I'm a person. I have a role to play for my country, and it is irrelevant whether I am male or female, Hutu or Tutsi' (Attar, 2000). An agreement was signed in August. Formally, Agathe Uwlingiyimana then resigned as prime minister, but the transition period dragged on, and in the meantime, she acted in the position. When the president was killed in the plane crash, the bloodbath in Rwanda cost about one million lives, mostly Tutsis and moderate Hutus. Agathe Uwlingiyimana and her husband were shot and killed by presidential guards on 7 April 1994. At that time, Agathe Uwlingiyimana had not been prime minister for more than nine months. But she is remembered as a pioneer for women's rights, education and national reconciliation (Hill, 1996a; Hoogensen and Solheim, 2006: 48–50; Jensen, 2008: 68).

Female record

The RPF conquered the capital, Kigali, and a transitional government was established with representatives from different parties. The president was Hutu and the vice president Tutsi. Four of the 20 ministers were women, a number of patriarchal laws were repealed and new laws were enacted to strengthen the position of women. The genocide created a special situation. Women became the majority of the population and took over duties that men had previously had as community leaders, breadwinners and heads of the family. They were actively involved in peace-building and reconciliation, and with the help of international donors, they received training in administration and governance. Well-educated and well-to-do women also came back from exile to contribute to the reconstruction of the country. The transitional government recognised women's importance and introduced women's councils, a women's ministry and 30 per cent quotas for women in the legislature and the cabinet.

In 2000, the president resigned and the vice president, Paul Kagamé, became president. In 2003, a constitution was adopted with a presidential system, and in the years that followed, the security situation improved, the economy grew and social services were developed. But the regime was criticised because freedom of expression was limited and opposition groups were marginalised. The quotas for women, however, were more than filled up, and important decisions for women were adopted, for example, a law against gender-based violence. The Lower House consisted of 80 members: 53 representatives of the political parties, 24 women elected by special bodies and two representing youth and the disabled. The Senate had 26 members: 12 representatives of the provinces, eight appointed by the president and six appointed by others. In 2012, Rwanda had a world record, with 56 per cent women in the Lower House. In the Senate, there were 39 per cent women, and in the cabinet, 32 per cent.[8]

In Burundi, quotas were also introduced, leading to 31 per cent women in the Lower House in 2012. In the Senate, the share was 46 per cent, and in the cabinet, 35 per cent.

Mame Madior Boye: change of elites in Senegal

Change of regime

Africa's fifth woman top leader came to power under very different circumstances than her predecessors. Senegal was one of the most stable countries south of the Sahara, though there were violent clashes in the north on the border with Mauritania and in the south in Casamance. For 300 years, Senegal was a French colony. After the slave trade ended, the focus was on the production of peanuts. The French did little to provide Africans with schooling. At independence in 1960, 90 per cent of the population were illiterate. Only those who were worked in the colonial administration received education in Dakar, which was the capital of French West Africa as a whole. After independence, Senegal maintained a close relationship with France, among other things, with a military agreement. Africans went to France to study, and Senegalese became members of the French National Assembly.[9]

After independence, the economy grew, health services and education were developed, and Senegal became classified as a middle-income country. But during the last decades of the 20th century, financial conditions became more difficult. The economy deteriorated, large populations were poor and life expectancy was low. Many children did not go to school and illiteracy was widespread.

Senegal includes different ethnic groups, but almost all are Moslems. During four decades, the country was ruled by the Socialist Party (PS), with close ties to the Moslem Brotherhood. The country's first president was the poet politician Léopold Sédar Senghor, and Senegal was for a long time a one-party state. But democratisation began earlier here than in the rest of Africa. The Senegalese Democratic Party (PDS) became a legal opposition party in 1974, and a few years later, a multiparty system was established. The president was elected directly and the legislature was elected with a mixture of proportional representation and majority vote. The president was head of state and government and appointed a prime minister who proposed members of the cabinet. In 1980, Senghor retired and Abdou Diouf, also from the PS, took over.

In 2000, there was a change of regime for the first time. The veteran politician Abdoulaye Wade, with a PhD in law and economics, was elected president at the head of a front of more than 20 opposition parties. He had been in opposition for years, had been exiled and imprisoned several times, but had also been a member of the cabinet. He founded the PDS and led the party since its founding in 1974. He ran for president four times before he finally was elected in 2000. Wade promised 'change' and was elected with 59 per cent of the vote in the second round. But nobody expected the change to be a woman prime minister.

Astonished lawyer

Senegalese women's organisations participated in protests against the colonial administration and were active in labour and student strikes. Women got the right to vote in 1945 and worked on such issues as health, education and labour rights for women. But few acquired positions in the political institutions. In 1982, the PS reserved 25 per cent of all posts in the party for women, and in 1985, the CEDAW was ratified. But in the 1990s, the PS only had three women (10 per cent) and the PDS only two (7 per cent) in their party bureaus. In the legislature women reached 12 per cent, and in the cabinet, 7 per cent. Mame Madior Boye was not appointed prime minister at once, either. Wade first appointed a man, while Mame Madior Boye became minister of justice.

Mame Madior Boye was surprised by her appointment as a minister. As a specialist in law, she is a typical professional. She was born in 1940 to a family of lawyers in Saint Louis, and like her three brothers, she was educated as a lawyer in Dakar and Paris. She spent most of her career in the Senegalese administration of justice and worked to strengthen women's rights. She was a founder and the first woman president of the Federation of African Lawyers and vice president of the International Federation of Women Lawyers. For the previous 10 years, she worked in a West African bank. She had a strained relationship with the Diouf regime and did not accept high positions in the judicial system to preserve her integrity and independence.

When Wade took over as president in April 2000, he was in a delicate position because he lacked a majority in the legislature. Elections were scheduled only a year later, and the broad front he represented was loosely assembled. Tensions soon arose between the president and the prime minister, who came from a different party. Two months before the elections, in March 2001, the prime minister was fired and 61-year-old Mame Madior Boye was appointed instead.

With the appointment of a woman as prime minister, Wade killed two birds with one stone: he got rid of a bothersome prime minister at the same time as he appealed to women voters. A non-partisan prime minister also looked good, in that the cabinet did not only come from the PDS. It was a widespread view that the appointment of Mame Madior Boye was only temporary. The cabinet was practically unchanged and she kept her portfolio as minister of justice. She was a brilliant lawyer and a practising Moslem, but as a woman and, in addition, a feminist and being divorced with two children (a son aged 22 and a daughter aged 28), she was highly unusual as prime minister. Her own comment was only: 'This is a vote of confidence in women. I'll do my best for the country, whether it is for two months, a year or ten' (Champin, 2001a; see also Thiam, 2005: Jensen, 2008: 67).

Sacked without justification

The elections gave Wade a large majority, with 89 of the 120 seats in the National Assembly. Before the elections, more than 30 non-partisan women's organisations organised a broad campaign demanding at least 30 per cent women in the legislature and this was supported by 14 political parties recommending at least 30 per cent women on candidate lists. The representation of women increased, but not to more than 19 per cent. And to people's amazement, Mame Madior Boye continued as prime minister without being minister of justice at the same time. The cabinet was moderately changed to give the PDS a dominating role and strengthen the position of women and representatives of civil society.

Of 25 ministers (besides Boye), there were now five women (20 per cent) against two previously. It was a nice victory for Boye and the new ministers were important for women. The director of the UN Programme for HIV/AIDS in Geneva, Awa Maria Coll-Seck, became minister of health and initiated far-reaching reforms in the health sector. The former director of the Fund for Economic Development, Aïcha Agne Pouye, was responsible for small and medium enterprises, where women were particularly involved, and Thiéwo Cisse Doucoure was responsible for local communities. The three ministers were reappointed to the cabinet after Boye left (Champin, 2001b).

The government faced considerable economic and social challenges. In 2001, Senegal was classified as a Low Development Country (LDC). Efforts were made to strengthen education and health, improve salaries, reduce unemployment among the young, and support the agriculture sector. But the ministers were new and inexperienced, taking over from a long-lasting well-established regime. The coalition promised 'change', but before the elections, it did not elaborate a programme and views differed. Boye kept a low profile outwards, but it was evident that she did not always agree with the president's views. When he enthusiastically cheered the Senegalese football team, 'the Lions', she was more concerned with northern drought victims. Many thought Boye's legal competence, impartiality and rigour were qualities that would come in handy in an unstable political situation. She could ensure good governance, and when it came to defending the common good, she was not afraid of taking difficult decisions. She was no 'Iron Lady'. She showed compassion and supported the weak. But when she followed her principles in practice, she soon got the reputation of being 'as straight and cold as the penal code' (Thiam, 2002: 28; see also Dioh, 2001; Fadjiri, 2002a).

Before two years had passed, in November 2002, both Mame Madior Boye and the cabinet were fired without delay and without justification. It was assumed that the reason was the *Joola* disaster. Wade was abroad when the state-owned ferry *Joola* sank and more than 1,800 people died. It was one of the worst shipping disasters of all times and the prime minister had to confront the media. She claimed that the accident was due to the weather and thus excluded failures of ship or crew. Soon, however, there were allegations of high-level errors and omissions. The head of the navy was dismissed and two ministers had to resign. A French court issued an arrest warrant because of Boye's role in the *Joola* disaster, but it was later withdrawn.

'Poor communication'

Wade stated that the bad impression people had of him as president was not due to his own efforts, but Mrs Boye's 'poor communication' (Afro1 News, 2002a, 2002b). And he appointed the male vice president of the PDS, Idrissa Seck, as prime minister to 'sell' the victories of the party in government in a better way. Eight women ministers (26 per cent) were also appointed. But it was not long before Seck also had to go. In total, Wade appointed five prime ministers in the course of seven years.

Mame Madior Boye remained as prime minister longer than expected when she was appointed, but still not very long. She rarely delivered press releases and the president's strong position makes it difficult to know what she actually did. Boye was supposedly close to Wade, but it is an open question how much leeway and support he gave her. As prime minister, she was subordinate to the president, and he was a hands-on, dynamic leader, showing clear authoritarian tendencies when he came to power. His reaction to disagreement, for example, tended to be submit or leave (Dioh, 2001; Mbow, 2008). Mame Madior Boye was the first woman prime minister. She was an expert in law, but not in socio-economic development and she lacked administrative experience. In politics, she was an outsider. She had never participated in political activities and her civil society involvement was also limited. Her power base and supportive networks were probably minimal.

From the outside, it looks like Wade mostly used Boye as a symbolic transition figure. Her strength as a person – being honest, independent, principled and strong – made her act differently than most of the male politicians, and this was probably appreciated more in theory than in practice. Boye did not give in, however. Even if the situation was difficult, she kept her dignity and integrity, representing another kind of politician than the dominating men.

It required courage for an independent, professional woman like Mame Madior Boye to accept the challenging position as top political leader surrounded by nearly only strong male politicians. And she showed that a woman could be prime minister. Even if she made mistakes, she was not considered a failure. She did not make a big deal of herself, but people thought that the president, as the superior, had considerable responsibility for what happened. When she was sacked, the media noted that 'She left as she came'. The Senegalese would keep an image of her as a stern lady, an atypical woman, without proclaimed political affiliation, not letting herself be pushed around (Thiam, 2002). It was assumed that this was the real reason why Boye was sacked, not the *Joola* disaster as such.

Boye was also a feminist. This was rare and the effect is not clear. But the prime minister raised women's concerns in inter-ministerial meetings and the women ministers brought them into their work (Fadjiri, 2002b). After she left the government, Boye was appointed special representative of the African Union for the protection of civilian populations in countries with armed conflict and travelled around the world promoting the status of women in meetings and seminars (Guèye, 2007).

In 2010, gender balance on the candidate lists for local and national elections was made compulsory, and in the elections in 2012 a record number of 64 women became members of the legislature (43 per cent). A new president was elected, Macky Sall, who belonged to the PDS until 2008, but then founded his own party, Alliance for the Republic. He first had a male prime minister and five women ministers (20 per cent). Then, on 1 September 2013, he appointed a second woman prime minister: Aminata Touré from the Alliance for the Republic.

Aminata Touré was hailed by women activists as an economist and anti-graft campaigner, and a human rights and women's rights activist. She was born in Dakar in 1962. Her father was a physician and her mother a midwife. After secondary school Aminata studied in France, took degrees in economics and business administration and a PhD in international financial management. She got involved in politics and was active on the left in the French university milieus. She was employed in the public transportation sector in Dakar, but from 1995 her career took place in the United Nations Population Fund (UNFPA), where she promoted family planning and reproductive health. In 2003 she became director for the human rights department in New York. She had three children and two divorces, and in 2010 she left the UN to work with Macky Sall in his new party. In 2012 she became Senegalese minister of justice and then prime minister. She immediately appointed her cabinet, but to the disappointment of the women activists she only included five women ministers (16 per cent) (Carayol, 2013).

Political squeeze in São Tomé and Príncipe: Maria das Neves and Maria do Carmo Silveira

Africa's smallest nation

The small São Tomé and Príncipe islands were uninhabited when the Portuguese arrived in the 1400s. They started up plantations using slaves to primarily produce cocoa. Working and living conditions were terrible, and rebellions were forcefully suppressed. A liberation movement was formed in exile in the 1950s. It did not organise guerrilla warfare, but the islands became independent in 1975 after the Portuguese dictator Salazar fell. São Tomé and Príncipe became Africa's smallest nation. It was a low-income country populated by about 100,000 inhabitants, mostly Catholics with Portuguese-African backgrounds. About 80 per cent were illiterate. A few families of African descent controlled policies and resources with deeply rooted patron–client networks.[10]

The new state instantly had problems. It only had one product for export – cocoa – in order to finance the import of essential basic goods. When the islands became independent, a few hundred residents returned from exile, some with higher education, but thousands of Portuguese settlers and professionals left. Exports went down and although the islands received exceptionally large amounts of development aid, São Tomé and Príncipe became heavily indebted. With the help of external donors, considerable investments were made in health and education for girls as well as boys, but the islands did not have institutions for higher education until the 1990s. Until then, people had to travel abroad to attend university or college.

The new state established a socialist-oriented one-party rule with a strong president, Manuel Pinta da Costa, and the plantations were nationalised. But ideological and personal differences led to schisms and coup attempts, and moderate politicians went into exile. At the end of the 1980s, policies were liberalised, and in 1990, a multiparty constitution was approved by a referendum. It provided for an executive president and a single-chamber parliament with 55 representatives. The president was elected directly and appointed the prime minister and 14 ministers on the latter's advice. The prime minister must be ratified by the majority party in parliament.

Three parties fought for power, and there were repeated changes in leadership. Economic reforms and privatisation were carried out, but there were protests and unrest and the policies were unstable. Sometimes, the military intervened. The living conditions of the underprivileged did not improve. Half of the population was poor. In the new millennium, hopes were created for a new deal due to hydrocarbon resources in the sea, but the petroleum policies led to renewed antagonisms.

There were not many women politicians. Male chauvinism prevailed in society and the 'old boys' networks' in the political parties. However, women were economically independent, and some engaged in politics. For several years after independence, São Tomé and Príncipe had a woman president in parliament who was also the country's vice president (Aldo Graça [1980–1991]). During the 1990s, the three political parties had from 10 to 20 per cent women on their executive boards (CIA, 2008; IRIN, 2008; Eyzaguirre, 2010).

President against parliament

In 2001, a wealthy businessman and cocoa exporter, Fradique de Menezes, was elected president, with the support of the Centre Party. But, at this time, the parliament had a socialist majority. To change it, the president called new elections in 2002. But the socialists obtained 24 and Menezes only 23 of the 55 seats. There was no clear majority, and the result was an unstable cohabitation, with a number of short-lived cabinets headed by the opposition. First, a three-party coalition was formed under the socialist Gabriel Costa. But it soon broke down. The Socialist Party then designated Maria das Neves as prime minister.

Maria das Neves Ceita Baptista de Sousa, born in 1958, was a key figure in the Socialist Party and was close to the leader. Having received education as an economist in Cuba, with specialisation in public finances, she worked in the Ministry of Finance, the World Bank and the UN Children's Fund (UNICEF). She married, and when her two daughters had grown up, she became minister of economics during 1999–2001, minister of finance in 2001/02 and minister of industry, trade and tourism in 2002. She was a member of the Costa cabinet when she was appointed prime minister in October 2002. Das Neves was a competent technocrat, skilled at negotiations and also keen on women's issues. For many years, she fought to make physical violence against women a criminal offence. In the coalition government, she included more women ministers than before: four out of a total of 11 (36 per cent). São Tomé and Príncipe became party to the CEDAW and later established a women's office and a minister for women. In parliament, five women were elected (9 per cent) in total: two socialists and three centre liberals.

São Tomé and Príncipe were in a difficult situation, being heavily indebted and dependent on aid. The economy, oil policy and relations with the numerous donors and petroleum interests dominated the political agenda. Das Neves stated that a reduction of foreign debt was her 'priority of priorities' and warned people against believing that oil was a lifeline for the country's economy. To obtain sustainable development, investments had to be made in agriculture, fishing and tourism (São Tomé and Príncipe, 2011). But she was only prime minister and number two, the president was from a different party and the cabinet included several parties. There were disagreements and power struggles.

When an oil agreement was signed with Nigeria, there was a military coup. While the president was abroad, the army and mercenaries took action in July 2003 and Maria das Neves and other government officials were arrested. The coup leaders complained about corruption and said that the forthcoming oil revenues would not be distributed fairly. Following international pressure, a settlement was reached, with the result that Menezes was reinstated after a week. Maria das Neves was admitted to hospital and resigned as prime minister. The president asked her to continue, nevertheless, and she retained her position with a new 'national unity government'.

But the tug of war between the president and the prime minister and internally within the cabinet continued, and when it was claimed that Maria das Neves had misused aid, both she and the cabinet were dismissed in September 2004. Maria das Neves denied any wrongdoing and argued that it was all part of a political cabal, asserting that the president was the country's main lawbreaker. Das Neves had been elected as an alternate to parliament and now she moved up as an MP (Afrique-express, 2002; Afrique Centrale Info, 2004; Jensen, 2008: 58–9).

Second woman

It did not take long before another woman became prime minister. Strikes and conflict about the distribution of oil fields made the president also dismiss the male prime minister who succeeded Maria das Neves. The Socialist Party demanded new elections, but the president refused. So, the Socialists proposed Maria do Carmo Trovoada Pires de Carvalho Silveira as the new prime minister. Why a woman was brought forward again is unclear. But there was a lack of people with higher education on the islands. Maria do Carmo Silveira was born in 1960 and was educated as an economist at the University of Ukraine. She was not only a member of the party executive board, but became head of the central bank in 1999 and was considered a 'reconciliation person'. The cabinet consisted mainly of members from the Socialist Party, with Maria Silveira as minister of planning and finance as well as prime minister. Besides her, there were two women and seven men.

Maria do Carmo Silveira declared that macroeconomic stability was her priority (Sao Tome and Principe, 2011). She worked from June 2005 to April 2006 and made her mark by, among other things, resolving the wage dispute with the unions in the public sector, securing assistance from the IMF and obtaining an agreement with Angola on cooperation in the oil sector. But then she had to resign.

There were presidential and parliamentary elections in 2006, and Menezes was re-elected as president. This time, his party got more seats in parliament than the Socialists (23 to 20), although not a majority. There were still changes of government, but less frequently. Now, the prime minister could come from the president's own party, and all the cabinets were headed by men. There were no quotas, and the number of women in parliament was reduced to four (7 per cent). Maria das Neves was elected as an MP together with three centre liberals. Das Neves chaired the committee on human rights and gender issues and finally managed to get a law against violence against women.

In 2011, Menezes could not continue as president, and the former President Manuel Pinto da Costa was elected again by a narrow margin. Ten women (18 per cent) became MPs. Das Neves stood for election as president, but only obtained 14 per cent of the vote. Silveira was governor of the Central Bank. In the cabinet, there was only a single woman (9 per cent) (Afrique Centrale Info, 2005; Jensen, 2008: 59).

Luisa Diogo: assistant to the boss in Mozambique

Independence and war

The first woman top leader in Africa to function for some time came to power in Mozambique. As prime minister, Luisa Dias Diogo was subordinate to the president, but she served for six years before she was replaced by a man.[11]

Mozambique is an agricultural country 800 times larger than São Tomé and Príncipe. The population consists of about 60 different ethnic groups, mainly small farmers. Cultural variety is huge, with descent following both the maternal and the paternal line, polygamy, and female family providers. There are differences between the north, the centre and the south, and the religions span from traditional African beliefs to Islam and Christianity. From the 1500s, the Portuguese gained control of more and more land. Colonists established themselves, but there was little societal development. In the 1900s, large private companies came in, often owned by the British, built railways to neighbouring countries and supplied the nearby British colonies with cheap African labour, often by force. Little was done to build infrastructure or provide the population with education.

The brutal treatment of the population led Mozambicans in exile to form the Mozambique Liberation Front, FRELIMO, which started a guerrilla war against the Portuguese in 1964. FRELIMO was supported by China, the Soviet Union and Nordic countries and won control of large parts of the country. In 1975, Mozambique became independent.

Mozambicans took over an impoverished country, and, in addition, the economy broke down when the country became independent. Practically all the Portuguese left. Few Mozambicans had an education and almost nobody had higher education. Much of the existing infrastructure was destroyed and more was to be. FRELIMO established a socialist one-party state with the liberation leader and military commander Samora Machel as president and tried to develop the country with international assistance. Private enterprises were nationalised,

301

healthcare was developed and literacy campaigns were organised. But the new state was faced with sabotage from neighbouring states and armed opposition by the anti-communist Mozambique National Resistance, RENAMO, which received support from the white Southern Rhodesia and the then minority regime in South Africa. The civil war lasted for 16 years, and of a population of about 10 million, it is estimated that 1 million died, 1.7 million became refugees and several millions were internally displaced (CIA, 2005, 2009).

Women of the revolution

FRELIMO soon formed a women's organisation. The women were needed, and they were to be liberated by breaking with traditional roles, participating in production and defending the revolution. According to the constitution of the new state, women and men were equal, and the government followed up. Women got education and access to agricultural technology and participated in decision-making at the local level. In the elections in 1977, women obtained 28 per cent of the seats in the district assemblies and 12 per cent in the legislature. It was a record in Africa at the time. But although women fought side by side with men, many were later abandoned to cooking and child care, while positions of power in the party and the government were occupied by men. There was only one woman minister, and national policy took little account of women's needs.

The civil war destroyed schools and health centres. Women had to take up arms both in FRELIMO and RENAMO, and throughout the countryside, they were strongly affected, as single providers, victims of violence and abuse, combatants, and refugees (Disney, 2008).

Luisa Dias Diogo was born in 1958 in the rural areas in north-western Mozambique. Her father was a nurse, and her mother took care of the house and family. There were eight children, five boys and three girls. Luisa was number three. She got a basic education in Tete, but to attend secondary school, she had to go to the capital, Maputo. She received a little support from her parents, and together with her 11-year-old brother, she lived in a tiny shed in the capital, fetched water and coal every morning, and went to school during the day. After secondary school, she had to work to be able to study. She learned accounting, business management and economics. She joined FRELIMO and began working in the Ministry of Finance in 1980, while she was still studying. She wanted to assist in developing education and health in Mozambique. She earned a bachelor's and a master's degree in economics, rose quickly through the ranks of the ministry, and became national budget director in 1993. Afterwards, she got a job in the World Bank in Maputo. At 23 years old, she married one of Mozambique's leading lawyers, Albano Silva, and they had three children, but were later separated.

In 1986, President Machel was killed in a plane crash, and the former minister of foreign affairs, Major General Joaquim Chissano, took over. The country was in ruins. Vast areas were covered by landmines. There were flooding disasters and HIV/AIDS spread rapidly. To receive international assistance, a new constitution was adopted in 1990. It entailed free elections and a multiparty system. A strong president was elected directly, and a legislature, using proportional representation. The president appointed the prime minister and the cabinet. The prime minister chaired the cabinet meetings, coordinated the ministers and helped the president to rule the country. Women's rights were maintained, and possibilities for a market economy were opened up.

In 1992, a peace agreement was signed with RENAMO, and elections were held in 1994. Chissano was elected president by a narrow margin (53 per cent), and FRELIMO got 52 per cent of the seats in the National Assembly. Before the elections, FRELIMO fixed a women's quota for the party of 30 per cent and proposed a number of women as candidates. In the new assembly, the total representation of women amounted to 25 per cent, the vast majority from FRELIMO, but there was only one woman in the cabinet.

Freedom fighter and financial expert

Chissano asked 36-year-old Luisa Dias Diogo to be state secretary in the Ministry of Finance. She was thus central in the elaboration of the country's first development plan, which involved a large-scale repatriation operation and development of agriculture, healthcare and schools. At the same time, the CEDAW was ratified. Despite widespread poverty, in the 1990s, Mozambique was regarded as one of the more successful countries with regards to development in Africa south of the Sahara.

At the elections in 1999, FRELIMO and Chissano were re-elected, but it was by a narrow majority. Diogo became minister of finance as one of three women in the cabinet (13 per cent). In the party leadership, women constituted 28 per cent. Mozambique was heavily indebted and dependent on aid, and the focus was on poverty reduction, economic growth and reform. Diogo received recognition from international donors for her efforts to bring about economic change, accountability and good governance in a country with a failed state and ruined economy heavily marked by corruption (Freeman, 2002). In 2004, the magazine *The Banker* named Luisa Diogo the 'Finance Minister of the Year' for Africa. Revenue per capita doubled in 10 years, and Diogo was given the primary responsibility for this. The World Bank praised her efforts for poverty reduction.

In 2004, Prime Minister Pascoal Mocumbi resigned to accept an international position. Presidential and legislative elections were to be held in nine months, and the 46-year-old Diogo was asked to serve as prime minister in the meantime. Chissano emphasised that she was capable and also a woman. She appreciated the confidence and added: 'Mozambique's women are doing progress, but we still have a long journey ahead of us' (Agencia de Informacao de Mocambique, 2004). In her new position, she would try to achieve real economic change and poverty reduction. One of the first things she did was to launch a comprehensive programme to combat HIV/AIDS. She also requested that the government's next five-year plan should strengthen its focus on health and education and include reforms of the police and the judiciary.

Chissano did not stand for re-election, and the former minister of the interior, FRELIMO General Armando Guebuza, who had become a wealthy businessman, was elected president. FRELIMO and Guebuza got more than 60 per cent of the vote in both elections. The president asked Luisa Diogo to continue as prime minister (without being minister of finance at the same time), with one quarter women in the cabinet. In the National Assembly, the representation of women amounted to more than a third, the vast majority from FRELIMO.

Mozambique was gradually described as a 'patrimonial democracy', with tensions between patron–client networks and democratic decision-making processes (Braathen and Orre, 2001). Over the years, economic and political power was increasingly linked. FRELIMO acquired an increasing power monopoly at all levels, and the country was characterised by a one-party system. In the 2009 elections, FRELIMO and Guebuza were both re-elected, with 75 per cent of the vote. But the elections were considered so undemocratic that Mozambique was removed from Freedom House's international list of 'electoral democracies'.

Diogo continued as prime minister until January 2010. Two days after Guebuza was sworn in as the new president, he appointed the former minister of education (a man) as prime minister. Diogo was no longer a member of the cabinet.

Dinner without ingredients

Luisa Diogo was widely perceived as a strong and energetic person, but the president was head of both state and government. To maintain her position and get political results, Diogo depended on the support of Guebuza. At the same time, with her financial education and experience, she possessed a key competence for management of the state that he lacked. She also got a growing reputation as an able negotiator and managed to secure numerous grants from international financial institutions. Foreign development aid amounted to 60 per cent of government revenues. Further, she was not a male rival, and could appeal to women (Notable Biographies, 2010).

Diogo created a network of female ministers and legislators to promote women-friendly laws and measures, and the government followed a line of policy that was actively supportive of women. Special emphasis was placed on education and healthcare. Diogo also participated in networks across borders. She was recognised internationally and stood forth as a driving force for the improvement of women's reproductive and sexual health, although she was a Catholic.

In 2010, peace was secured in Mozambique, but democracy was inadequate. The economy grew, but so did the population and inequalities. Since independence, the population more than doubled. Although fewer were poor, the proportion remained very high, and Mozambique was one of the world's poorest countries. Health and education were better, but improvement was slow. Women's position in public life was considerably strengthened, but far less had happened in the economy, culture and the family.

Luisa Diogo got the reputation of being a progressive reformer, passionate advocate and smart businesswoman. She was called the 'Iron Lady' and was included on the *Forbes* list of the 100 most powerful women in the world. She was number 73 in 2004, 96 in 2005, 83 in 2006 and 89 in 2007. In 2007, she was also awarded the Global Women's Leadership Award as one of the most powerful women in Africa. Under her leadership, the government developed Mozambique from economic ruins to Asian Tiger-like growth. She, herself, said that the job of prime minister was 'like making dinner for a large family, often without ingredients' (Fleming, 2005).

In 2008 and 2009, she was not on the *Forbes* list, and it is unclear whether she resigned in 2010 at her own request. She had worked for Mozambique's economy for 30 years, and it was claimed that the country needed 'a renewal and a fresh approach to accelerating implementation' (Johnson, 2010). Most of the ministers were reappointed, but Diogo was to work in the legislature, not the government. She also became a high-level adviser nationally and internationally. The new cabinet had 28 per cent women, and in the National Assembly there were 39 per cent, with a woman president of the Assembly. Mozambique was number 12 on the world-ranking list of women in parliament in 2012.

Ellen Johnson Sirleaf to the top in Liberia

By a hair's breadth

In 2005, a woman finally went to the very top in African politics. It happened when Ellen Johnson Sirleaf was elected president of Liberia. She was 67 years old and a divorced grandmother. But she only just managed to survive long enough to be able to obtain such a position: more than once, she was about to be murdered by President Samuel Doe.[12]

The first time was under Doe's coup in 1980. President William Tolbert and his cabinet were brought down to the beach at Monrovia, where all were shot. Ellen Johnson Sirleaf was minister of finance, but she was spared. Maybe it was sheer coincidence. Sirleaf herself thinks that it was because she had criticised the government and the injustice in society (Sirleaf, 2009: 99). There were four ministers who survived the massacre.

The next time was five years later. Elections were going to be held, and Sirleaf came home from the US to participate. She was immediately arrested and accused of having said that the Liberian leaders were 'idiots'. It could easily have gone wrong. But the US government reacted, and women's groups in Liberia collected 10,000 signatures to get her released.

Sirleaf was elected senator in 1985, but was arrested again shortly after the elections. She describes in her autobiography (Sirleaf, 2009) that in jail there was a group of men in the neighbouring cell, and they were all taken out and shot. A soldier came to Sirleaf saying, 'I'm going to fuck you.' But just as he was about to unlock the gate, a soldier of higher rank turned up. 'Retreat,' he ordered. The soldier closed the gate, locked it and went out. The superior asked if Ellen Sirleaf was *Gola*.[13] When she confirmed it, he said: 'OK. I will stay here all night. Nobody will trouble you.' He stayed, and no one did.

Early the next morning, they came to take Ellen Sirleaf to President Doe. It could only mean one thing: immediate execution. Sirleaf's refusal to take her Senate seat in protest against the fraudulent elections was causing the president international embarrassment. The soldiers drove her to the back of the presidential villa. Here, the man in charge of the Executive Mansion Guard asked why she was making all this trouble. Sirleaf replied that she had no intention of making trouble, but she could not take up her Senate seat. The guard looked at her. Then, he ordered: 'Don't take her to the President. You know what will happen if you do. Put her in prison.' And they were told not to harm her (Sirleaf, 2009: 141–53). So, she lived.

Hundreds, maybe thousands, of Liberians were murdered at this time. But not Ellen Johnson Sirleaf. After nine months in prison, she was released.

African countryside and the US

Ellen Johnson Sirleaf's background evidently played a role when she survived. She was often perceived as an Americo-Liberian, but, in fact, she was half *Gola*, a quarter *Kru* and a quarter German. Both parents came from poor conditions in rural Africa. Her father was the son of a *Gola* chief and his wife, while her mother was the daughter of a *Kru* market woman and a German. But both were adopted by Americo-Liberians in Monrovia while they were young and acquired an education that few ordinary Liberians got. Ellen's father served as an apprentice to a jurist and became what was called a 'poor man's lawyer'. He did very well and became the first Liberian from the original population who was elected to the legislature. Ellen's mother got to travel and go abroad to school for a year. When she came home and the two were married, she opened a school nearby and also worked as an itinerant Presbyterian priest. The couple had four children, two boys and two girls.

Ellen was the second-youngest and was born in 1938. She undertook basic and high school education, became a Methodist and wanted to be a schoolteacher. But she married as soon as she graduated, at only 17 years old. Doc Sirleaf was seven years older. His father was Mandingo, his mother belonged to the elite in Liberia and he studied agriculture in the US. They soon had four sons and Ellen took care of them with the help of various women in the family, while she worked as a secretary to earn a living. Then, both she and her husband got scholarships to go to the US: Doc to study agriculture at the university and Ellen to learn business practice at a specialised college. It was not easy. The children were small, the youngest just one year old. But two were placed with Doc's mother and two with Ellen's and the young parents left in 1962. The economy was tight, and Ellen worked as a waitress in parallel with her studies. After a year, Doc passed his exam and went home, while Ellen stayed in the US for another year to complete hers (Sirleaf, 2009: 7–42).

An obstinate woman

When Ellen Sirleaf returned to Monrovia, she joined the Treasury Department. There was a shortage of professionals and the family had good connections and a respected name, even though her father was disabled by a stroke. Thus, an unsettled career began. Liberia's economy was in bad shape. Ellen Sirleaf spoke candidly about the situation and accused the government of corruption among other things. This was not well received and she was advised that she had better move on. She got a scholarship for Harvard and travelled to the US again in 1969. Now, she took her second-youngest son with her. The marriage was breaking up, and in a male-dominated society like that of Liberia, the custom was that the father kept the children after a divorce. Two were sent to missionary school, while two stayed with their father for a while before moving to Doc's brother, and one came back to Ellen. In the US, she studied economics and took a master's degree in public administration. When she came back to Monrovia after a year, she became state secretary in the Ministry of Finance in the government of President William Tolbert.

As state secretary, Sirleaf was critical of the policies being followed and was eventually pushed aside. She used her contacts and got a job at the World Bank in Washington DC in 1973. The work in the bank was instructive, but after a few years, she began to feel homesick. At the same time, she was sceptical of the government. The solution was that she assisted the Liberian government in the capacity of a World Bank expert, which did not prevent Tolbert from appointing her as minister of finance in 1979 – as the first woman in the country. She introduced measures to curb the mismanagement of government finances, but the work was soon interrupted. After Samuel Doe seized power in 1980, he asked Sirleaf to take responsibility for Liberia's development bank. But she had to leave before a year had passed when she pointed out that Doe's policies were financially irresponsible. Again, she went to Washington DC, but then she became the first African woman vice president of CITICORP's Regional Office in Nairobi, Kenya.

International pressure on the Doe regime made him hold elections in 1985. That was when Ellen Sirleaf went home to participate and only just avoided being raped and murdered. After her time in prison, she returned to the US and became a senior loan officer at the World Bank and vice president for the Equator Bank in Washington DC. In 1992, she was appointed director for Africa in the UNDP, based in New York (Jensen, 2008: 132–3; Notable Biographies, 2008; Sirleaf, 2009: 43–187).

Roots in the African soil

Ellen Johnson Sirleaf could have stayed in the US. She had a high position in the UN that was both exciting and well-paid. She had an apartment in the centre of the metropolis, and she had every possibility for a bright career in the UN system. But she wanted to go home.

Initially, Ellen Sirleaf supported the rebellion of Charles Taylor, but changed her stand and later backed the LURD uprising. The Truth Commission, established in order to clarify human rights violations during the war, criticised Sirleaf for being associated with former warring factions and recommended that she, along with 50 others, should be banned from public office for 30 years (see: www.usip. org). Sirleaf apologised publicly to Liberians, pointing out that she joined Taylor to get rid of Samuel Doe and went against him when she understood what kind of a man he actually was (Sirleaf, 2009: 171–85). And in 1997, she ran against Taylor in the presidential elections, but only got 9.5 per cent of the vote.

Nevertheless, Ellen Sirleaf would not give up. She established a small company in the Ivory Coast and awaited the course of events. Sometimes, she went to Liberia and held public speeches. She also assisted the OAU to investigate the genocide in Rwanda and contributed to a UN report on women, peace and war.

The situation in the region led the Special Court for Sierra Leone to accuse Taylor of crimes against humanity, and ECOWAS tried to bring about peace negotiations. Women's organisations, such as the Mano River Women's Peace Network, Women in Peace-building Network and the Liberian Women's Initiative, actively pressed for peace. And when negotiations were held in Ghana, they peacefully occupied arenas around the premises, blocked the exits and threatened to undress if negotiators did not come to an agreement. A deal was, in fact, reached, and the women co-signed the 2003 Accra Comprehensive Peace Agreement. Taylor was forced to resign and went into exile in Nigeria. Later, he was brought to the Special Court in The Hague and sentenced to 50 years in prison.

But although they demonstrated and participated as observers in the proceedings, women were marginalised in the subsequent process. Only three women (14 per cent) were included in the transitional cabinet, and only four (5 per cent) in the interim legislature. Women activists proposed an electoral gender quota, but this was rejected. However, Ellen Sirleaf was asked to head the Governance Reform Commission (Sirleaf, 2009: 187–243).

'Ellen is our man'

Nobody expected Ellen Sirleaf to be elected president in 2005. She ran on her own, not as the substitute for an established male politician. There were 22 candidates, including two women. And Sirleaf was not just a woman; she had links with the elite, too light skin and too much education. Admittedly, she had long experience, but she was also old and had gained political enemies. Sirleaf ran with a male vice president and mobilised the family, the Unity Party, networks of various kinds, US contacts and particularly Liberian women. In the first round, she ended second after the 'gold ball' George Weah – a young, rich, former football star – but achieved only 20 per cent of the vote. The second round was a thriller, but Ma Ellen (as she was called) won with 60 per cent of the vote. She became Africa's first elected woman president (Perry was appointed, not elected) and the world's first black woman elected head of state.

It was an advantage for Sirleaf that there was not any party or male candidate in power who wanted to be re-elected, and members of the transition government were barred from running. Ellen represented both continuity and change. And her weaknesses were turned into merits. She was better qualified than Weah, who was politically inexperienced and dropped out of high school. Who could be better able than Ellen to rebuild the country's shattered economy? She had a long career in economics and development and knew the national terrain, as well as international institutions and donors. She had also learnt her lesson in the male-dominated institutions and explained:

> If a woman is competing with men as a professional, she has to be better than they are and make sure she gets their respect as an equal. It's hard. Even when she gains their acceptance, it's in a male dominated way. They say, 'Oh, now she's one of the boys'. (Sirleaf, quoted in Pittman, 2005)

Ellen's supporters took to the streets and shouted: 'Ellen, She's Our Man' (Jensen, 2008: 159).

At the same time, Sirleaf benefited from being a woman. Men had governed and failed. Now, a woman had to put things straight. Ellen underlined that she was a professional, a technocrat and politician – who happened to be female. She was not going to establish a women's government, but she promoted women's rights and values and used the power that lay in the symbol of a mother. She wanted, in particular, to bring 'motherly sensitivity and emotion to the presidency' as a way of healing the country's wounds (Price and Tonpo, 2005). Typically, she was called both 'Iron Lady' and 'Mum' – tough and tender. Later 'Old Ma' and 'Grandmother' were added.

Ellen's long-lasting involvement in issues concerning women at the grassroots level meant that many were there for her. Women's organisations ran a campaign that made the share of women among registered voters rise from 24 to over 50 per cent. Among other things, they took over the market stalls for a day so that the women owners did not lose money when they went to register and vote. Women knew more than anyone what a war was. They ignored the threats of Weah supporters, saying 'No Weah, no peace', and voted for Ellen. The other female candidate in the presidential election only ended up as number 13 (Adams, 2008, 2010; Sirleaf, 2009: 245-73; Jalalzai, 2013a: 207-12).

'Queen of Africa'

Ellen Sirleaf's victory aroused great attention and joy. First and foremost, Liberian women were happy. The Election Commission, which had a majority of women, urged the political parties to include 30 per cent women on their candidate lists. But with an electoral system using simple plurality, the new House only got eight women members (13 per cent) and the Senate only five (17 per cent). All in all, of the 110 female candidates mobilised by the women's organisations, only 14 were elected (Sirleaf included). This was more than before, but certainly not enough. The fact that one became 'Queen of Africa' was good compensation. Among women in Africa and around the world, the election was seen as a major victory and a demonstration. For once, an African woman was directly elected and obtained the most important position in the country. And it was an unexpected woman, an elderly grandmother, who, in addition, had women's rights on her programme.

In her inaugural address, Sirleaf pledged 'to give Liberian women prominence in all affairs of our country' (Sirleaf, 2009: 271). Her predecessors had a few women ministers. Now, Sirleaf appointed many more. Ministers were not drawn from the legislature in Liberia, but appointed by the president and approved by the Senate. There was no prime minister, but women became ministers of finance, commerce and industry, foreign affairs, gender and development, justice and youth and sports. In 2006, there were five women out of 21 ministers (24 per cent), but the numbers varied over the course of the years. In addition, 27 women were appointed as deputy and assistant ministers, 40 per cent of the total. Such a broad range of women connected with the executive was exceptional for an African country, or any country in the world. In addition, Sirleaf appointed two women (of five) to the Supreme Court and five women (of 15) as county superintendents. Further, it was her intention to recruit 20 per cent women into the armed forces and the police, take special measures against gender-based violence, and implement national programmes to support school girls, market women and women farmers (Bauer, 2011).

Breakneck task

The challenges were overwhelming. The country was in ruins and the population was deeply divided. Water and electricity supplies, roads and bridges, schools and health services were destroyed. Three quarters of the population were poor and diseases flourished. Unemployment was 80 per cent, and illiteracy 70 per cent. Many educated people had left the country. At the same time, Liberia had nearly USD 5 billion in debt to the World Bank, IMF and other donors.

Particularly in rural areas, men were sceptical of the newly elected president. 'Liberia is not ready to have a woman leader yet', it was said, 'only a man can be strong enough to deal with all the ex-combatants' (BBC News, 2005a). Sirleaf did not get a majority in the legislature, either. In addition to the independent candidates, 21 parties ran for election and about half managed to be represented.

The Unity Party only got eight (13 per cent) of the 64 seats in the House, while Weah's party got 15. In the Senate, the Unity Party only got four (13 per cent) of the 30 seats. Decision-making implied extensive negotiations and bargaining. 'It is time that we, regardless of our political affiliation and beliefs, get together to heal and rebuild the country', Ellen Sirleaf declared (Olinga, 2006), and she appointed both supporters and representatives of the opposition from various sectors to the cabinet.

A new Liberia had to be created with peace and security, and improvements were made, but it was not easy. The president started by demilitarising the country and demobilising the armed forces, but most of the former combatants were unable to find suitable employment afterwards. Sirleaf demanded that former President Taylor be handed over to the Special Court for Sierra Leone and managed to get the sanctions against the country annulled. But it took time to get war criminals to justice, and Sirleaf was criticised because she did not follow up on the recommendations of the Truth Commission in a more active way. Generally, peace was maintained, even if it was fragile and occasionally broken, but violent crime remained rampant. The UN contributed peacekeeping forces and police while a new police corps and a new army were being built up. However, there were problems with control and responsibility, salaries and capacity, equipment and training. A total of 20 per cent women were recruited to the police and a special police unit and court were set up for the protection of women and children. But lack of resources hindered the work. By 2011, very few sentences had been passed and sexual assault was escalating.

Since independence, Liberia had only had authoritarian rule. After decades of conflict, despair and pain, Liberians were deeply demoralised, with a collapsed state that failed to deliver security and services. During Ellen Sirleaf's first term, Liberia showed the greatest improvement in governance of Africa's 53 states, but the country nevertheless remained in the bottom half of the continent's rankings (AllAfrica, 2010). A central administration was built up and corruption was reduced, but not eliminated. To stop corruption, Sirleaf ordered a financial audit of the transitional government, and all the 300 employees in the Ministry of Finance were laid off and only allowed to return after closer investigation. But the established Big Man networks could not be rapidly dissolved or changed. In fact, the president had to deal with them to be able to maintain power and get things done, and they included many kinds of people, from clean businessmen to former warlords. Sirleaf was not accused of being corrupt herself, but officials and people close to her were, among others, her own sons. Some were forced to resign, but not all.

International and private donors gave a helping hand. Liberia got debt relief, and the state budget was quadrupled. A reconstruction process was set in motion. Mines were reopened and the airport repaired. Internally displaced persons returned home. Roads, health clinics and schools were built. Primary education was made compulsory and free, and many children, especially girls, went to school. Monrovia got electricity and water for the first time in many years, and the construction of a new university started. Efforts were made to promote forest and agricultural industry, but Sirleaf was criticised because a large part of Liberia's land was handed over to foreign and private investors. The economy grew, but it mostly reflected the reconstruction of Monrovia, financed by international aid. In 2011, life expectancy in Liberia was still low, on average, Liberians only got four years of education and nearly two thirds of the population lived below the poverty line.[14]

Re-election

Ellen Sirleaf not only became a role model for African women; she became a symbol of women's empowerment. She was controversial and criticised, but she made herself respected by dealing with overwhelming challenges and doing what she thought was right for the country. In 2007, she was awarded the Medal of Freedom by the US president, the highest honour a civilian can receive. *Forbes* ranked her as number 51 of the world's most powerful women in 2006; as 100 in 2007; 66 in 2008; 67 in 2009; 86 in 2010; 62 in 2011; 82 in 2012; and 87 in 2013.

In 2010, Liberia received the prestigious UN Millennium Development Goal Award for outstanding leadership, commitment and progress toward achievement of the goals by promoting gender equality and women's empowerment across the country (goal number three). The magazines *Newsweek* and *Time* considered Sirleaf to be one of the 10 best leaders in the world, and *The Economist* thought that she was the best president Liberia had ever had. The same year, Ellen announced that she would stand for re-election to ensure the continuity of policies. She highlighted the progress made in several areas since she was elected, and emphasised the value of women leaders:

> When a woman is equally qualified, competent, committed and courageous, she excels. She performs better than men, because women bring an extra dimension to the task. They carry their sensitivity towards humankind. They display greater concerns about children and the welfare of people. (Sirleaf, quoted in Yedder, 2009)

Opponents protested, claiming that she had been mediocre as president and could have done more. Besides, she was too old, at 73 years in 2011.

But things went as Sirleaf wanted, even though it came as a surprise that she had won the Nobel Peace Prize for her 'non-violent struggle for women's security and their right to participate fully in peace-building efforts' (The Nobel Institute, 2011) four days before the presidential election. There were also critical comments from Western experts and Liberian opponents due to her previous support of armed opposition.

There were pre-election controversies and violence, but against 15 candidates, Sirleaf obtained 44 per cent of the vote in the first round, while 33 per cent voted for Winston Tubman, a relative of the former president. Tubman then boycotted the second round of the elections because he believed that there had been fraud. As a result, the turnout was low. But international observers approved the conduct of the elections, and Sirleaf was elected in the final round with 91 per cent of the votes cast. The Unity Party increased its representation in the legislature and got a plurality in both the House and the Senate, but only with 33 per cent of the seats, while Tubman's party got 15 and 10 per cent, respectively. When Sirleaf was inaugurated, Winston Tubman declared that his party was nevertheless ready to collaborate with the president to unite the country and bring it forward.

The re-elected president stated that reconciliation would be a priority for her (Bøås, 2011), and that continued efforts were required. After the elections, there were only seven women members (10 per cent) in the House and only four (13 per cent) in the Senate. With a mixture of old and new ministers, but with the same number of women and men, Sirleaf got going with her second term.

Rose Rogombé, Gabon's master of ceremonies

Between two male presidents

After Liberia, Gabon got a female head of state – but it was, typically enough, a substitute. Rose Francine Rogombé ensured a smooth transition when the old president of the country died. Gabon was a French colony, and the small, oil-rich state became a republic after independence in 1960. Omar Bongo was elected vice president in 1961, and when the president died in 1967, Bongo moved up. During more than 40 years, Bongo and his close circle decided most of what was to be decided in the country. In 1990, a multiparty system was introduced, but Bongo was still the boss. He served as president longer than anybody else in the world.[15]

The conservative party in power, the Gabon Democratic Party (PDG), had a women's branch and Gabon became party to the CEDAW, but there were few women in the legislature. Only after 2000 did the proportion of women in parliament exceeded 10 per cent, and in Bongo's cabinet, there were 17 per cent. In 2010, there was 15 per cent in the National Assembly and 18 per cent in the Senate.

In June 2009, Bongo died, and 66-year-old Rose Rogombé took over in her capacity as president of the Senate. There were several in the PDG leadership who raised their eyebrows when Bongo made Rose Rogombé president of the Senate. Bongo knew Rogombé well, but she had not been in the limelight much. She ran as the party's only candidate and received 90 of 99 votes. It was the first time a woman got such a position.

Rose Etomba, which was her first name, was born in 1942 and grew up on a plantation in Lambarene. She was the oldest of six siblings and went to a nun's school and undertook secondary education in Libreville. She married in 1963 and had two boys and two girls, partly while she was studying law in Nancy in France. She became Gabon's first female judge in 1967, at 25 years old, and served in a number of posts as judge. She joined the PDG, was a member of the Central Committee and the first female minister. For a long time, she was minister of women's affairs in the 1980s. In the 1990s, she went back to working as a judge and also passed an exam in theology. In 2008, she was elected to the local council in Lambarene, and the following year, to the Senate. The elections to the Senate were indirect, by local and departmental councillors. As president of the Senate, it was her duty not only to act in the president's absence, but also to organise new elections.

The job took four months. Rogombé reappointed the cabinet, with only some internal changes, and went to work. Soon, she was called the 'Iron Lady'. They were three women, surprisingly enough, who ensured the transition from one (male) president to another. Besides Rogombé, the head of the Constitutional Court was a woman, and Omar Bongo's daughter was responsible for the president's office. It was said about Rogombé that the man who was the longest in power was succeeded by a short-lived woman who expected to be succeeded by the late president's son. Of the 17 presidential candidates who stood for election, there were three women, though none with a chance of succeeding. Omar Bongo's son, Ali-Ben Bongo, was elected with 42 per cent of the vote. He appointed a male vice president and prime minister, but three of the four deputy prime ministers were women, in addition to two of the 30 ministers (15 per cent).

Overshadowed by 'Big Chiefs'

In war and peace

In spite of the importance of women leaders traditionally and women's activism in recent decades, there were fewer women top leaders in sub-Saharan Africa after World War II than in other regions. Indeed, 10 African women rose to the top, but there are 45 countries in the region. Including Elisabeth Domitien in the Central African Republic, only eight of the 45 states (18 per cent) had national women leaders until 2010, and there was usually only one, except Liberia and São Tomé and Príncipe, where there were two.

The countries where women rose to the top found themselves in different situations. In four, there was authoritarian rule or difficult transitions in connection with armed conflict. The Central African Republic had a brutal dictatorship, and the dictator appointed a female prime minister to strengthen his appeal abroad in the International Women's Year. Burundi, Rwanda and Liberia were struggling to get out of civil war, and the women were given high positions as part of the peace efforts. In Liberia, warlords could not agree on a man as temporary president and gave Ruth Perry the task of implementing the agreed ceasefire. When armed conflict broke out again after a few years, Ellen Sirleaf was elected president to complete the peace process. In Rwanda and Burundi, Sylvie Kinigi and Agatha Uwlingiyimana became prime ministers to contribute to the reconciliation between Hutus and Tutsis.

Sub-Saharan Africa has been hit by a series of armed conflicts over the past decades, and researchers note that in various parts of the world, women relatively often became decision-makers after armed conflicts (Tripp et al, 2006). Unrest and war shake up existing social and cultural norms, and legislation and political institutions are often reformed after a conflict. There may also be fewer established male leaders for women to compete with for positions. Many of the African countries with the highest proportion of women in parliaments in the early 2000s had recently undergone liberation struggles or civil war.[16] But the same countries did not always perform as well with regards to other political positions, such as women ministers, and only a few had women top leaders. If the angle is changed, it is clear that as many countries recently affected by war had low female representation in parliaments as those who had high. This means that unrest and armed conflict can give women more opportunities than before to assert themselves politically, but not necessarily so. Conflicts may turn out differently, and various factors come into play. With regards to top leaders, they are also on the whole so few that a great deal is required for everything to fall into place.

With the exception of the Central African Republic and the three war-torn countries, no women went to the top in authoritarian regimes. Neither did they in the two 'liberal democracies' (Botswana and Mauritius), only in 'emerging democracies'. Here, there were six women top leaders in five countries.[17] One was elected president, and one acted temporarily in the position. Four were appointed prime ministers. But by far the most 'emerging democracies' let no women rise to the top, whether they were large countries such as Nigeria, Ethiopia and Kenya, or relatively small countries such as Benin, Gambia and Namibia.

Thick layer of men

Women were national leaders in diverse countries in southern, western and eastern Africa. Except the three countries with parliamentary governments, all the African countries had presidential systems – democratic or authoritarian. Even in the democratic systems, only a single woman was elected president and one acted for a short time to organise elections.

Due to the way the presidential systems worked even after democratisation, it was extremely difficult for women to go to the top. With so much power concentrated in one position, the battle was very hard. Often, male presidents tried to be re-elected, while women were newcomers. In the countries that only had a president, women were virtually excluded from rising to the top. Quite a few tried. From 1990 to 2010, 45 different women ran for president in 48 different elections in 26 different countries. Several stood for election more than once. They represented different parties or were independent. Very few were close relatives of politically powerful men. Only one succeeded. The vast majority received very few votes, often less than 1 per cent (Christensen, 2014).

Most often, several male candidates participated in each election. The total number of candidates ranged from five to 33, and the incumbent president, or a man close to him, usually came out on top, if it was not a male opposition leader. It was all the more remarkable that Ellen Sirleaf was elected president. Ruth Perry was also head of state, but she was appointed and functioned only temporarily. Rose Rogombé was also only temporary. When Sirleaf was elected, she was not brought forward by a male relative or predecessor. There was no male predecessor. She was not under the patronage of any other man, either. She fought her way herself and succeeded, among other things, because she worked in a country where women traditionally had a strong position and woman actively mobilised to get a woman president.

Women had greater success as vice presidents. While 35 different women ran for vice president from 1990 to 2010 in 14 different elections in 10 different countries and lost, eight managed to be elected in six countries.[18] But even if the position was formally very high, it did not necessarily mean that the women acquired great influence. Often, the position mainly had a symbolic character. The vice president was subordinate to the 'Big Chief', and the women could also fall outside the established patron–client networks. But the president could give the vice president a certain latitude if he wanted to.

More women in politics

The women's movement put on pressure. International and regional agencies, as well as local women's organisations, demanded an increase in women's representation in political decision-making in Africa south of the Sahara. Even if women rarely succeeded in presidential and vice presidential elections, more and more got involved in politics and tried to gain influence. In total, the number of women in parliaments rose, although the electoral systems in some countries were unfavourable. Two fifths of the African countries gradually introduced quota systems of various kinds, and some became worldwide leaders with regards to the number of women ministers and parliamentarians. They proved that with political will, it was possible to give women a fast track to decision-making. In 2014, Africa surpassed both Arab states, Asia and the Pacific with regards to women's representation. On average, African women constituted 23 per cent of the MPs and 21 per cent of the cabinet members. Some countries were up to 30 per cent and more. Five were included among the 12 countries in the world with the highest representation in parliaments and cabinets, respectively.[19] This implied a recognition of women's political importance and gave them possibilities of exerting influence, but in many African countries, the parliaments and cabinets did not play very active roles politically. And women top leaders remained most unusual.

Women mainly had a chance of obtaining a position as top leader if the country had a prime minister in addition to the president. Of the democratic countries, about half had both a president and a prime minister, while half only had a president. All the women top leaders – with one exception – acquired their top positions in countries with both a president and prime minister. And the women were not elected. They were appointed or approved as prime ministers by the president and they were usually not MPs at the time, but had various professional and political posts. Rogombé, who became president temporarily, was indirectly elected to the Senate, and then the president gave her the position that made her interim president when he died. Liberia had no prime minister, and here was where a woman was elected president.

Even with a prime minister, the president could in fact be both head of state and government, and the prime minister functioned almost as his assistant or servant, with greater or lesser scope for action. This was the situation for the women prime ministers in Senegal and Mozambique. In São Tomé and Príncipe, the situation was different, because parliament had to approve the prime minister and, at the time, the president did not have a majority in parliament. The two women prime ministers were therefore appointed by the majority party.

Exceptional qualifications

In sub-Saharan Africa, none of the women top leaders came to power through family ties; all were recruited on the basis of their own qualifications. Certainly, there were several widows (Perry, Kinigi and Sirleaf), and, in a number of cases, the husbands supported their wives' political participation, but none of the women went to the top as substitutes in their capacity as widow or wife. Perry 'inherited' a position as senator, but that was all.

Sub-Saharan Africa lagged behind other continents in terms of living standards, particularly women's health, education and resources, but it does not take many people to fill key political positions. Although the women top leaders came to power in different situations, they had exceptional qualifications, which were in demand. With the exception of Domitien, all had long formal education, with university degrees, most often in economics, but also in law and science. The women's parents usually came from rural areas, many with modest backgrounds. Only in the case of Boye is it noted that her parents had higher education. Nevertheless, the families ensured that the daughters went to school and, with one exception, acquired higher education. Six of the women went to university in Western or Eastern industrialised countries, while three studied in Africa. With such high formal qualifications, the women were also in a strong position in countries with generally low levels of schooling. In addition, the women had valuable work experience: from agriculture, education, commerce, banking, the finance ministry and the judiciary. In some cases, other qualities played a role, such as ethnic background. It could also be an advantage to be a woman in order to symbolise peace and reconciliation and appeal to the female part of the population.

All the women except one (Boye) had political experience, some from central offices, though only one was party leader (Sirleaf). Party landscapes in Africa varied. Often, the parties functioned mainly as private clubs around a male leader, where it was not primarily joint policies, but a common desire for access to state resources, that held them together. The women top leaders had different motives for their party activities. Most joined parties in government to help create a better society, while some became members of opposition parties.

Party affiliation was not always essential. It was mostly on a personal basis that the women came to power. In Liberia, parties played a relatively minor role. In the Central African Republic, Mozambique and Gabon, ties to the ruling party and the strong male leader were decisive. In São Tomé and Príncipe, the women were associated with a socialist party, which formed the basis for their appointment as prime ministers, and were opposed to the president, who belonged to a different party. In Rwanda and Burundi, the women prime ministers were drawn from the opposition to head coalition cabinets with another majority party. The only woman outside the parties was in Senegal, where the president was looking for an independent expert. With quotas, parties could possibly become better channels for the recruitment of women politicians to top decision-making levels.

The majority of the women top leaders were married with children, and some were divorced or widowed. If necessary, relatives and hired assistants helped with child care, but the mothers did not rise to the top in politics before the children had grown up. About half of the women were in their 40s, one was 50 and four were in their 60s.

Women's woman

Of the three women top leaders who were required to contribute to peace (Perry, Kinigi and Uwilingiyama), only Perry succeeded – at first. Kinigi resigned because of threats and Uwilingiyama was murdered. Rogombé managed to organise an acceptable presidential election, but three of the women prime ministers were dismissed (Domitien, Boye and Das Neves), while Silveira and Diogo had to resign in connection with elections. Apart from Diogo, all of them functioned for a relatively short period. Diogo and Sirleaf were the only who were in office for some length of time: Diogo for six years under a strong president and Sirleaf for five until 2011, when she was re-elected. Most of the women top leaders thus had little or limited opportunity to develop or implement their own policies. The exception was Sirleaf.

Only one of the top women leaders was described as 'feminist' (Boye), but the women's lives and work give the impression that women-related social and political efforts were not as problematic as in many other places. In traditional villages, there could be a strong sisterhood, and girls and women participated in women's groups and associations that solved tasks together and defended the rights of women. Older women could have special status. In towns, women's organisations flourished in connection with democratisation. Apart from two, where information is missing, all of the women top leaders were associated with women's societies and organisations. Before they advanced in politics, they worked to mobilise women and strengthen their status. Often, the activity of women's organisations, both locally and internationally, was essential in the women's political career.

For five of the top leaders, the fact that they were women was clearly a positive factor when they acquired a top position. Perry and Sirleaf were supposed to step in where men had failed, and they were clearly perceived as maternal figures: 'Ma' or 'Mum'. Perry, herself, referred to her 'motherly grip' and Sirleaf used the fact that she was a woman and mother as a reason for her becoming the country's highest leader. The president of Rwanda wanted to show respect for women when he appointed Kinigi, while the president of Senegal thought that Boye would appeal to female voters. In Mozambique, the president needed a woman to lead active woman-friendly policies supported by the party. But the signals were not always unambiguous or positive. Sirleaf should be 'one of the boys', and in Burundi, Uwilingiyimana was met with clear misogyny.

If they did not become 'feminists', the women top leaders at least supported women as far as they could. Several managed to increase the number of women ministers. In countries affected by war, this was difficult, but in other countries, they obtained 20–30 per cent women in the cabinet. Further, the top leaders got woman-friendly laws and administrative arrangements approved, established women's networks, fought against violence and the sexual abuse of women, and strengthened education and health services. It was, above all, Diogo and Sirleaf who implemented policies of importance for women. Diogo did it even though she was subordinate to a male president, because the promotion of women's interests was part of the party programme. To help her in her work, Diogo, among other things, established women's networks. In Liberia, women's organisations had a strong position, and both Perry and Sirleaf undertook extensive mobilisation of women to build peace and implement policies. Women took action, first, to get Sirleaf out of jail and then to get her elected and re-elected. Sirleaf responded by appointing many women in important positions and supporting women-oriented activities.

Roza Otunbayeva in Kyrgyztan was first acting president and then elected in 2010. Here she is speaking at the symposium of the UN secretary general on international collaboration against terrorism in New York on 19 September 2011.
484894: Un Photo/Rick Bajornas

Chapter Nine

Eastern Bloc:
from communism to capitalism

The countries in Eastern Europe and the former Soviet Union[1] have in common that they all underwent extensive social changes in the 20th century and became 'socialist states'. The regimes were based on Marxist ideology and established 'people's democracies', with the Communist Party in a dominant role and state control of the economy. With the exception of Yugoslavia and later Albania, all the countries in Eastern Europe became members of the Warsaw Pact and part of the Eastern Bloc.

In 1990/91, the communist regimes collapsed, and the world region went through some of the biggest political and economic upheavals since World War II. The Eastern Bloc was dissolved. The Soviet Union, Yugoslavia and Czechoslovakia were split up and the number of states tripled.

Liberation becomes oppression

Promising socialism

In 1917, a quite extraordinary thing happened: a social upheaval had as an explicit goal to liberate women. After the Tsar was overthrown in Russia, a socialist republic was established based on the writings of Karl Marx, Friedrich Engels and Vladimir Lenin. Socialism was supposed to liberate the people from the yoke of capitalism. The working people should rule, and a revolutionary transformation of society would abolish the oppression of class society, including men's oppression of women. Women should be liberated and become financially independent.[2]

Russian rule was autocratic. The population consisted of different ethnic groups and the Russian Orthodox Church had a strong position. In the 1800s, the country was economically underdeveloped and poor. Most people ran farms in the traditional way. The population grew rapidly, and the soil was a sought-after resource. Around 1900, large-scale industrialisation was launched, and people flocked to the cities. But the Tsar was unable to introduce democratic reforms like other European countries did. The miserable conditions led workers to protest and go on strike, which culminated in the revolution of 1905. In the election of the first parliament, special groups of men got the right to vote.

In the cities, many women played an active role, were engaged in politics and academic life, created their own organisations, and fought for the right to vote. Engels and August Bebel encouraged the formation of an independent socialist women's movement, and central feminists such as Clara Zetkin in Germany and Emmeline Pankhurst in England were socialists. It was a demonstration of female textile workers that triggered off the February Revolution in 1917. Women obtained the right to vote, and Countess Sofia Panina was appointed 'deputy minister' in the provisional cabinet.[3] When the Bolsheviks took over in October, the feminist Alexandra Kollontai became the world's first female minister. It was established in the constitution of 1918 that all citizens were equal regardless of gender, and family laws went further than any other laws in Europe and the US in the direction of equality for women. Among others, divorce and abortion were permitted (Jancar, 1978; Voronina, 1994).

From right to duty

When system changes broke down established hierarchical structures and allowed for real reforms, women's political activity could increase, the political scientist Barbara Wolfe Jancar (1978: 113–14) noted. In Russia, women got involved and took on tasks that were assigned to men, such as warfare. Many women joined the Bolsheviks and served in the Red Army, where they sometimes held high positions. But women's expectations regarding a different relationship between women and men after the Communist Party took over power were not met. New hierarchical structures emerged where the old were torn down and the patriarchal order of priority was maintained, albeit in other forms. Women disappeared again from the political arena.

The new Bolshevik regime was met with armed resistance, and the war lasted several years. Antagonisms arose within the Communist Party. Kollontai came into opposition with Lenin and was sent to Norway as the world's first woman ambassador, which probably saved her life.[4]

The revolution and the war ruined the economy. Millions lost their homes, and distress was widespread. To develop the nation from an agricultural society to an industrial power, between 1922 and 1953, Josef Stalin implemented forced collectivisation and heavy industrialisation within the framework of firm party-controlled central planning. Until World War II, industry and the economy had record growth, but millions of peasants were killed or sent to camps in Siberia. The Communist Party was turned into a totalitarian, ruling force, taking over all the state functions, both the legislative and executive power, and controlling all aspects of society. Religion and political, social and cultural opposition were banned. Extensive purges were conducted, and fear and suspicion spread. The political structure with a parliament (the Supreme Soviet), presidency and cabinet were retained at the national level and in the republics. But the candidates were chosen by the party and elected without contest. The party and the bureaucracy developed into a powerful caste that established patron–client networks and controlled the distribution of goods.

Industrialisation required much labour. Stalin declared that the 'woman question' was resolved, and women's possibility for paid labour now became a duty, at the same time as motherhood was emphasised. Health services, mother–child care, institutions for children and schools were developed. Women received education and were encouraged to become engaged in 'masculine professions'. But the right to abortion and divorce were abolished and access to contraception was removed.

Double burden

When Stalin died in 1953, almost all Russian women participated in the labour force, and half of the highly educated Soviet experts were women. This was significantly more than in Western Europe and the US at the time. But women generally had lower status than men. Very few women obtained high positions. They first of all got unskilled jobs, often heavy and poorly paid in 'male professions' such as metallurgy and mining. Trained women usually worked in traditional 'female fields' such as education and health.

It was important to maintain the size of the population and family life was re-established according to the bourgeois pattern. Women were not freed from domestic duties. On the contrary, they were supposed to be workers, mothers and political activists. Women remarked that it was difficult to carry three melons under one arm, but women actually had five roles: wife, house worker, child educator, worker and activist. Although there was a focus on social services, it was not sufficient. There were many more institutions for children than in the West, but they in no way covered needs, and the quality was often poor. At the same time, women often had long working hours, both outside and at home. 'Liberation' became a double, even triple, workload (Rosenthal, 1975; Lapidus, 1976).

Under Nikita Khrushchev (1953–64), party control was somewhat reduced, and the standard of living rose after the first difficult post-war years. Women benefited from the improvements, but their status and role were not significantly changed. A woman's organisation was established (under the party's leadership), and abortion and divorce were allowed. The textile worker and chemical engineer Ekaterina Furtseva was the first female member of the Politburo during 1957–61 and minister of culture from 1961 to 1974 in a cabinet with 103 members. But that was all. And despite a reduced birth rate and productivity, Leonid Brezhnev (1964–82) continued with the traditional Soviet economy based on cheap labour and women's dual role as workers and mothers.

Sham 'liberation'

It was not easy to liberate women with the economic problems the Soviets had to struggle with. But the Communist Party's view of the 'woman question' was also an obstacle. The emancipation of women could only take place as part of larger social changes. These had to come first, and to implement them, women's efforts were needed. So as not to weaken the struggle, they had to adapt themselves to the joint labour movement. An independent women's organisation was as inadmissible as an independent trade union, and feminism was considered as divisive and 'bourgeois'. Units and mass organisations were created for women, but they were under tight control of the party.

Many women enthusiastically supported the revolution, but the leadership of the Communist Party was only interested in 'liberation' as long as women followed the party's policies and participated in the building of society. The male elite did not care about the issues women raised, such as women's identity and problems in the family. So, women got rights and education, paid employment and income, yet were still not equal. It was a sham liberation. Some women got good jobs, but the vast majority remained on the lowest levels of the economic ladder, and social differences were greater than in the West. In addition, women stood outside of government.

Outside the country's leadership

According to socialist thinking, women should participate in the leadership of the country on the same level as men. But the totalitarian state led to widespread political apathy. Patriarchal norms were strong, and men in power were not eager to give up control. Women were, in turn, often overworked, lacked motivation and shrank from the use of time and the power struggle required by a political career. Thereby, women were excluded from the political institutions. But as they did not participate in government, they lacked the possibilities to change the situation.

Up to about half of the members of the local workers' councils could be women, but then the percentage fell the further up the system you went. Like workers, farmers, minority ethnic groups and other groups, women were also given a certain representation in the Supreme Soviet – first, up to a quarter, then a third. It was more than in Western democracies at the time. But the representatives were elected by the party, and the Supreme Soviet was essentially a body rubber-stamping decisions made elsewhere.

The power was with the Communist Party's Central Committee and Politburo. Some women joined the party, but they did not get high positions. In the pre-revolutionary period, women formed over 7 per cent of the total Central Committee membership at a time when only 8 per cent of party members were women. This figure was never reached again during the Soviet period, although the number of women party members eventually rose to 30 per cent (in 1990). Only two women became full members of the Politburo and five were ministers. None was head of the legislature or the cabinet. The lack of an independent women's movement also entailed that women with political positions had difficulties representing the female part of the population (O'Neill, 1979: 59; Moses, 1986; Aivazova, 2002).

Satellites and collapse

Eastern European people's democracies

While Russia had to cede large areas of land after World War I, the Soviet Union emerged as one of the victors after World War II, despite enormous human losses and extensive destruction. Soviet troops were located from Manchuria to Berlin. Baltic and Polish territories and significant areas in Moldova and Western Ukraine were annexed. Eastern European states were reconstructed with Soviet help, and the same structure of society as that of the Soviet Union was forced upon them. This was not done by means of military coups, but with strong political pressure, and the communist regimes were established with varying popular support. During the Cold War, from 1949 to 1989, there were nine socialist states: Albania, Bulgaria, Czechoslovakia, East Germany, Hungary, Poland, Romania, the Soviet Union and Yugoslavia.

The Eastern European countries had different sizes and economies, and the population varied socially and culturally. Most of the states were established at the end of World War I, with representative political structures and universal suffrage. However, with the exception of Czechoslovakia, which was the most economically and socially advanced, democratic government was replaced by authoritarian regimes of a semi-fascist nature during the interwar period. Industrialisation started later than in Western countries, and the development of economic activity was generally slow.

Whatever the differences, the countries became 'people's democracies' under the leadership of authoritarian communist parties. National leaders, including women pioneers, were killed during the war, but opposition movements encouraged women to participate, and women got political rights after the war that they did not have before. Mass organisations for women were established, and millions went into paid labour. Gradually, industrialisation accelerated and the economy grew. Education and social services were developed and social indicators went up, but not as much as in Western countries. The regulation of marriage, divorce, motherhood and abortion varied with the perceptions that the leaderships had of the demographic situation.

As the years went by, progress stagnated. Right after World War II, some women became ministers. But, gradually, women's 'double burden' became heavier, women's organisations were dissolved and the number of women cabinet members decreased. All countries had female ministers, but rarely more than one at a time. Quotas for women were introduced in legislatures, and women were recruited to the Communist Party. But in the Central Committees, the proportion of women did not exceed 10 per cent. Many of the Politburos did not include any women at all, and in case they did, there were never more than a total of four in the course of 40 years.

Opposition to the regime was expressed by workers' revolts and campaigns organised by intellectuals. The protests in East Berlin in 1953, Poland and Hungary in 1956, Prague in 1968 and Poland in 1981 were particularly large in scale.

Decline and tensions

Towards the end of the 1980s, the Soviet Union was about to fall apart. Decline in the union's economic and political structures became increasingly noticeable, and Mikhail Gorbachev (1985–91) changed the policies. Military support to the satellite states was brought to an end. The economy was restructured (*perestroika*) and greater political openness was accepted (*glasnost*). But production sank. Built-up nationalist and ethnic-religious tensions broke out, and democratisation movements forced the communists out of power. In the course of some years, the Soviet Union was split up into 15 separate sovereign states: seven Eastern European and eight in Central Asia and the Caucasus. Czechoslovakia was divided in two, and East Germany merged with the Federal Republic of Germany.

The leaders of all the socialist countries committed themselves to promoting gender equality, and those who had not done so before became party to the United Nations (UN) Convention on the Elimination of all forms of Discrimination Against Women (CEDAW). All claimed that their countries had reached the UN's goals, but statistics showed that if women and men were formally equal, they were not in practice. The picture varied somewhat from country to country, but the main features were the same. Generally, women had considerable education, and their economic activity was greater than in the West. But they earned less and worked more than men. Women usually had a representation in parliaments of 20–30 per cent, which was higher than in the West, but there were very few in key power positions in government and party leaderships. Unlike the West, the Eastern Bloc had no female top leaders until 1990/91 (Rueschmeyer, 2011).

Croatia's Milka Planinc and Jadranka Kosor

Neither East nor West

Yugoslavia was special, with a unique form of 'self-management socialism'.[5] But women were not liberated here, either. After World War I, southern Slavs (Serbs, Croats and Slovenians) were united in a kingdom dominated by the Serbs. In 1941, the country was occupied by the Axis powers, and, eventually, great parts of the population were organised to fight under Josip Broz Tito. With limited support of the Red Army, the Axis powers were defeated, and Tito's Republican Popular Front, led by the Communist Party, won an overwhelming majority at a referendum on the form of government in 1945.

Tito was both prime minister and minister of foreign affairs in the new socialist republic. The country was ruled by the Communist Party and was initially centrally placed among the Eastern countries. But in 1948, Tito broke with Stalin because he wanted to follow his own road to socialism. Yugoslavia was supposed to be independent of both the East and the West and was a founding member of the movement of non-aligned states.

The population of Yugoslavia was very complex, with different cultures and ethnic groups. The country became a federal state, with six republics and two autonomous provinces. Each republic and province had its own constitution, assembly, executive council and president, and above these there were a federal assembly, executive council and president/presidency. To develop and modernise the economy, collectivisation of agriculture was carried out and industry and major businesses were taken over by the state.

New form of society

Then, Tito launched what he called 'socialist (or workers') self-management', a new and distinctive form of society. It entailed a profound revolution, which the leadership tried to implement step by step and unevenly over 30 years. It was not easy to make changes with a population mainly consisting of poor farmers with little education and a history marked by war and dictatorship, and there were large differences between the regions.

The new form of society was not a socialist planned economy, but neither a capitalist market economy. It was a third alternative, with different kinds of property. Enterprises were directed by the workers' councils, and communes were established with significant political autonomy governed by the citizens and working people. Economics and politics were woven together through a complicated system of delegations from workplaces, communes and socio-political organisations. The delegations attended assemblies, which were the highest bodies of the communes, republics, provinces and the federation. At the same time, Yugoslavia was a one-party state ruled at the highest level by a controlling Communist Party, which functioned as a tough cadre party.

Industrialisation and urbanisation, together with economic and political reforms, led to improved living conditions, health, education and cultural life. Self-management socialism attracted international attention and became an inspiration for leftists in both industrialised and developing countries. Industrial democracy was a fine way of strengthening the participation rights of employees. The employees were both women and men, but what was the status of women (Cordellier and Didiot, 1981–92; Morgan, 1984)?

Self-management for the 'working people'

From the most industrialised areas of Catholic Slovenia and Croatia, via the Moslem-influenced Bosnia and Herzegovina, to the economically backward Kosovo and Montenegro, women had their traditional place. Particularly in rural areas, they were often more subordinate than in other parts of Europe. The Communist Party included gender equality in its programme at an early stage, and feminists joined. Thousands of women were partisans, and many got important military and organisational positions. In the constitution of the new state, it was determined that women and men had equal rights economically, politically and in the family. Women got the right to vote, but the woman question was not given much attention. The reconstruction after the war, the strengthening of the economy, the break with the Soviet Union and the development of an independent political course took its toll. A political programme related to women that differed significantly from other Eastern European countries was not elaborated, and, in practice, the position of women was weaker.

Women benefited from the development of schools, and some received higher education. Increasing numbers got paid employment, but they were hampered by traditional attitudes and the lack of jobs. During the 1970s, women made up about one third of the total labour force. This was significantly less than in other Eastern European countries, and the proportion varied greatly from republic to republic. Without institutions for children, technical facilities and men who took part in the housework, women paid a price for 'liberation'. They did not get the best jobs or positions of authority, either.

The economic and political elite consisted mostly of men. Women made up about 30 per cent of the members of the workers' councils, but only 5 per cent of the leaders. The different delegations were supposed to mirror the population, but in the 1970s, women made up only between 10 and 20 per cent of the delegates to the assemblies in the communes, republics and the federation, and they were even fewer in the bodies that were elected by the assemblies.

It was a complicated, partly indirect, electoral system, with an emphasis on traditional male workplaces. There were no direct elections to the Federal Assembly. Delegates were chosen from self-management organisations and the assemblies in the republics and provinces. This meant that many women could neither vote nor be elected. Many housewives, for example, did not participate in any self-management organisation. Women were more under-represented than in other Eastern European countries, at the same time as the Yugoslav assemblies had more influence. In the Communist Party, about one fifth of the members were women, but there was no one in the Politburo. There were none in the federal presidency, either, but in the Executive Council, they constituted 8 per cent. In the republics, women sometimes obtained power positions in party organisations, but it was rare. One example was Croatia (Springer, 1986; Jancar, 1978).

Reward of loyalty to Milka Planinc

It was a woman from Croatia who unexpectedly made her way right to the top of the Yugoslav political elite. Milka Planinc became the country's first and only female prime minister. When the Communist Party took over control of Yugoslavia, it cracked down on nationalistic movements to prevent ethnic violence. And peace was largely maintained as long as Tito was alive – with the exception of the 'Croatian Spring' during 1968–70.

Croatia was one of the wealthiest and most modern republics. Although patriarchal traditions were maintained, particularly in rural areas, women in urban areas got higher education and obtained academic and professional positions.

The population had a certain liberty, and poets and linguists started cultivating Croatian culture. At the end of the 1960s, a movement was created demanding more rights for the republic, and students demonstrated in the streets.

Central in the movement was a woman, Savka Dubčević-Kučar. She belonged to a young and reformist generation, and with the support of Tito, she became the first woman leader of the Croatian Communist Party. She was very popular in the republic because she supported greater autonomy and liberty and was called 'Queen Savka'. Tito tried to get local party leaders to restrain the nationalists, but the unrest continued. Eventually, the police went in and arrested the student leaders, and Tito (who was himself Croatian) conducted a purge of Croatian organisations. Savka Dubčević-Kučar was forced to resign.

Dubčević-Kučar was replaced by another woman of about the same age. Milka, with the family name Malada, was born in 1924 in the Dalmatian city Drnis. The population was mixed, and Milka had Croatian–Serbian background. She went to school until her education was interrupted by World War II. She became a member of Tito's communist-led resistance movement in 1941, and when she was 19, she joined the partisans, who carried out guerrilla war in the mountains. 'Those were dangerous times, and I vividly recall very hard, very dramatic moments that left deep scars' (Opfell, 1993: 115; Jensen, 2008: 134). But she would not go into detail about what it was. She became an enthusiastic supporter of Tito. In 1944, she became a member of the Communist Party and district commissioner for the 11th Dalmatian shock brigade. When the war was over, she was 21 years old and a hardened partisan veteran, with a degree as a lieutenant and several decorations. She completed her education at the Higher Management School in Zagreb, married a civil engineer, Zonk Planinc, and had a son and a daughter.

Milka Planinc wanted to play an active role in the Communist Party to support Tito's road to socialism and specialised in training and propaganda. From 1949, she worked full time for the Zagreb party as secretary for culture and education and became Croatia's minister of education in 1965. She became member of the Central Committee of the Croatian Communist Party in 1959, of the Presidium in 1966 and of the Executive Committee in 1968. Then, in 1971, she became head of the party of the republic. An important reason was her unfailing loyalty to Tito. She contributed, among other things, to the suppression of the Croatian independence movement.

Before the storm

After Tito's death in 1980, his policies were supposed to be carried on at national level by a collective presidency, with a representative for each republic and province and a federal executive council elected by the Federal Assembly. As the representative of Croatia, 57-year-old Milka Planinc was elected as the head of the federal council in 1982, which means that she became the Yugoslav prime minister. It was the first time in the 64-year history of the country that a woman got such a high position, and it happened just a few weeks after Yugoslavia became party to the CEDAW, without there necessarily being any connection. Planinc had a high status as a partisan veteran, came from an important republic that was considered to be 'liberal' and had more political experience than most people. Planinc was the only woman top leader of a socialist state, while Margaret Thatcher was the only woman top leader in the West. Planinc formed an executive council with 29 ministers, half of whom were representatives of the republics and provinces, and the others also represented different nationalities. All were newcomers, except five, and there were only men, apart from Milka Planinc herself.

Yugoslavia had serious financial problems, and the federal government had limited authority. Much of the power was delegated to the republics. Milka Planinc was previously perceived as a conservative Titoist, but joined the 'liberals' in terms of economic development. She was not primarily guided by ideology, but by concrete realities, and promoted radical reforms to get the economy into shape. She was hindered by internal strife in the Council, but gets credit for implementing austerity measures that reduced debt and stabilised the Yugoslav economy. Although the measures hit Yugoslavs hard, it was said in 1985 that she was the country's most popular political leader. A traditionally male-dominated society respected a strong female leader, especially as she stood in sharp contrast to the increasingly inefficient rotating collective presidency that came after Tito.

But the differences between the republics increased and nationalism blossomed. Planinc collided with party leaders in the republics and the federal institutions lost in the power struggle. In 1986, she retired and was replaced by a male leader from Bosnia (Jensen, 2008; Djokic, 2010).

When Milka Planinc was asked how it felt for her, as a woman, to do a job that was usually attributed to men, she wondered why she should be perceived differently than men. She quoted Indira Gandhi, who said: 'Are not we women human beings too? Do we not belong to the same species?' And then Planinc added:

> And in fact, why should we be perceived differently? The people itself elected me. I did not force myself on them. I had been politically active for many years, from the liberation movement. On the way up to the position of Prime Minister, I was often the only woman on the various management levels. I feel totally at ease with this. (Planinc, quoted in Opfell 1993: 119)

One state becomes seven

Tensions between ethnic groups and republics increased. In 1990, armed conflict broke out, and in the stormy years that followed, Yugoslavia split up into a number of independent states: Bosnia and Herzegovina, Croatia, Macedonia and Slovenia, and the Federal Republic of Yugoslavia were established in 1992. But the Republic of Yugoslavia broke up again, and Montenegro and Serbia became separate states in 2006 and Kosovo in 2008. The conflicts arose between different groups of the population, but were also related to various forms of governance in the republics and the relationship between them. War broke out in Croatia and Slovenia, Bosnia and Herzegovina. When Albanians formed a liberation army in Kosovo and Serbs led a regular war in the province, the North Atlantic Treaty Organization (NATO) intervened, and a separate state of Kosovo was proclaimed.[6]

New Croatian woman: Jadranka Kosor

Developments varied from state to state, but all were headed by men, although they became party to the CEDAW soon after independence. In Croatia, antagonisms between Catholic Croats and Orthodox Serbs were of old date, and when the area was established as an independent state in 1990/91, civil war broke out, followed by 'ethnic cleansing'. Along with the conflict in neighbouring Bosnia, this led to large displacements of the population, with hundreds of thousands of people becoming refugees and internally displaced. The UN intervened, but it was only in 1996 that Croatia was recognised as a state by the Serb-dominated Yugoslavia.

During the war, Jadranka Kosor made programmes about refugees on Croatian radio and was honoured by the journalist organisation and the European Union (EU) for her work. She also published two collections of poetry and two books about the war. Kosor was born in 1953 in Pakrac in Western Croatia, undertook secondary education in the neighbouring town Lipik and graduated from the Faculty of Law in Zagreb. In 1972, she began working as a journalist for the press and radio. She divorced twice and was a single mother with a son.

In the first Croatian multiparty elections in 1990, the former partisan and general Dr Franjo Tudjman, who led the right-wing nationalistic party the Croatian Democratic Union (HDZ), was elected president. A mixture of a parliamentary and presidential system was adopted, and Tudjman was elected by the parliament. But with his charismatic authority, politics was determined by the president in practice.

In the new state, the electoral system was mixed and female representation in parliament was dramatically reduced. Previously, 16 to 25 per cent women were MPs. Now, they were down to 5 per cent, and under Tudjman, there were only 3 per cent women in the cabinet. But in 1992, Croatia confirmed its adherence to the CEDAW, and in 1995, the UN held its major International Women's Conference in Beijing. To appeal to women voters, Tudjman urged Jadranka Kosor to stand for parliament for the HDZ, and she was elected in 1995, became vice-president of the parliament, where there were now 8 per cent women, and became deputy leader of the party. Since other parties had women's sections, one was now created in the HDZ to strengthen the position of women in the party, and Kosor headed it from 1998 to 2002. She got the credit for doubling the number of female candidates in the elections of 2000. The women's section also worked as an effective lobby group in the party and contributed to Kosor's career.

Pleasing the European Union

Croatia had problems with a war-ravaged economy, and nearly 20 political parties competed for power. In 1999, Tudjman died and the HDZ developed major problems. After an internal battle, the relatively moderate Ivo Sanader was elected as the new leader, but the HDZ lost in the elections in 2000, and a centre-left coalition took over. It introduced a parliamentary system. The president was directly elected, but given limited authority. Executive power was attributed to the prime minister with the consent of parliament, which was elected by proportional representation. During the centre-left coalition, the economy improved, and a national gender equality policy was adopted. But in 2003, a coalition led by a moderated, but still centre-right, HDZ took over again, and Ivo Sanader became prime minister.

The number of women in parliament increased to 21 per cent in 2000, many from the Social Democratic Party (SDP), and the number of female ministers also increased, in part to mark a break with the Tudjman era. Moreover, as Croatia was seeking to approach the EU, the perception spread in political circles that more women should be involved in government. In the HDZ cabinet in 2003, the number of women rose to four (27 per cent). Jadranka Kosor became one of several deputy prime ministers and minister of family, war veterans and solidarity between generations. In addition, there were female ministers of justice, environment and European integration. A gender equality law was adopted, a commissioner was established and the national gender policy was continued.

In 2005, Kosor stood for election as president for the HDZ. She lost. The centre-left president in office was re-elected, but Kosor came second, with 34 per cent of the vote in the second round. In the parliamentary elections in 2007, the HDZ alliance won by a narrow margin, and the Sanader government continued. A second gender equality law was adopted, recommending, among other things, female quotas in politics, but without sanctions (Jurjević, 2009).

Time of crisis

Suddenly, in July 2009, Sanader resigned after six years in power. Croatia had just become a member of NATO. The country was experiencing the most severe economic problems since independence, and a border conflict with Slovenia hindered the negotiations with the EU about accession. Sanader proposed that the 56-year-old Jadranka Kosor should take over as prime minister.

Kosor promised to continue her predecessor's policies and lead the government with 'a strong female hand'. Economic recovery and membership in the EU were priorities. 'Croatia will become a full-fledged member of the European family... despite historical shortsightedness of our northern neighbours (Slovenia),' Kosor declared. And she appealed to women MPs to support her: 'Women should be given a chance where there is real power and money. This is a right opportunity for that' (Veselica, 2009). In parliament there were a total of 24 per cent women, and in the HDZ parliamentary group, 19 per cent. But Kosor retained most of the cabinet ministers and there were only two women among them. Later the number was reduced to only one in addition to Kosor herself. The parliament approved the new prime minister with 83 out of 153 votes. Kosor also became head of the party.

Troubled times followed. Kosor began by introducing an emergency budget to reduce spending and debt. This gave rise to negative reactions. Then, she launched a campaign against corruption and arrested a number of people, also connected to her own party. In the presidential elections in 2009/10, the SDP won (European Forum, 2010). And until the parliamentary elections in December 2011, the economic problems continued, with high unemployment. In addition, there was a series of corruption scandals linked to the government. Ivo Sanader was arrested, and the HDZ as a whole was put under scrutiny. Kosor replaced ministers, resolved the conflict with Slovenia and obtained an accession agreement with the EU. In addition, she supported measures for unemployed women, opposed gender violence and stereotypes, and gave rights to gays and lesbians. The country's strong Catholic Church reacted very negatively to the last measure.

In the parliamentary elections in 2011, the HDZ only got 24 per cent of the vote, and the Kosor cabinet had to resign. A centre-left coalition led by a male prime minister took over, and Kosor became leader of the opposition. In the leadership election in the HDZ afterwards, in 2012, Jadranka Kosor only got 18 per cent of the votes as leader of the party, competing against four men, and Tomislav Karamarko, former minister of the interior, became both party leader and leader of the opposition. All in all, in parliament, there were 36 women (24 per cent), and in the cabinet, four women (20 per cent) (Forrest, 2011).

'Shock therapy' in the East

Painful restructuring

The collapse of the Eastern Bloc led not only to the creation of new states, but also to the restructuring of political systems.[7] Free elections were introduced, with several parties, and new structures, actors, constellations and opportunities sprang up. Many of the political actors were also new and inexperienced, groups changed and policies became unstable. Although women participated actively in the upheavals, they were marginalised in the political processes that followed. The new political systems were just as male-dominated as the former. The representation of women in parliaments was greatly reduced when the established quotas were abolished. At the same time, the countries were exposed to greater influence from abroad than before, not only from the UN, but from the EU and international women's networks.

The economic system was reorganised from central planning and control to market liberalism. This meant the privatisation of state-owned enterprises, the creation of new businesses in accordance with capitalist principles and the restructuring of production and services. Although most were middle-income countries, the transition processes were difficult and uneven, often painful. The communist states were based on full employment, social security and welfare for the masses. Now, state-owned enterprises were reorganised to make a profit, and the goal of full employment and the use of price subsidies were abandoned. What counted was to own capital. Antagonisms, economic and social problems, unrest and turmoil, and partly armed conflict broke out. People talked about a 'shock therapy' with a lot of shock and not much therapy. The tendency was to throw away everything that had been before. Wages fell and inflation rose. In some cases, unemployment increased dramatically, at the same time as welfare services were weakened. Suddenly, some people got rich, while living standards deteriorated for large groups. Some became desperately poor.

Generally, women were hit harder than men. Very many women were dismissed and encountered more problems than men trying to get new jobs. Typically, women got jobs with lower wages and poorer working conditions. As social services, including day care for children, deteriorated, it became more difficult for women to take paid work, and the burden of combining home and occupation increased. It was easier than before for young women to go abroad and study, but some became victims of human trafficking, which was unknown before. Single parents got a tougher life, and elderly women especially suffered. No one would hire them, and they had little or no pension. They were the poorest of the poor.

Differences between states

The transition processes lasted longer in the Balkans and the countries further east than in the Baltics, Poland, Hungary, the Czech Republic and Slovakia. The reduction in living standards was more drastic in the Balkans and the eastern countries, economic growth started later and social inequalities were greater. The Central Asian states constituted a separate group, marked by nomadic people and cultures, and most continued with authoritarian regimes after the fall of communism.

The political institutions that were established differed and changed over time. Developments were rarely smooth, but after a period of transition, there was often a time of democratic consolidation. Some countries introduced presidential rule, while others preferred a dual system. Parliamentary systems were rare, but became more frequent over time. Parties and governments often changed. The regimes spanned from highly autocratic to more democratic. Many countries were initially characterised by a conservative wave as a reaction against communism. But when living conditions did not improve, quite the contrary, dissatisfaction spread. Voter preferences swung back and forth, and sometimes former communists came to power again in a reformed version.

At the turn of the millennium, the macroeconomy had begun to stabilise in the Baltics and Central Europe, and the average standard of living rose. But there were still considerable economic and social problems. Only Slovenia was considered a

Figure 12: Europe: regimes by type, 1946–2012

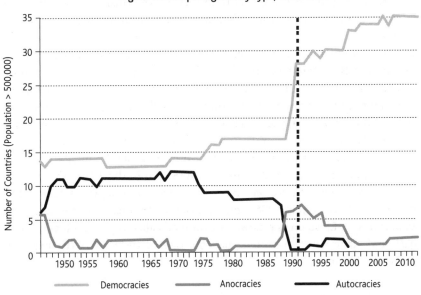

Note: Anocratic governance is a system placed somewhere between democracy and autocracy. The power is spread
between elite groups competing for power.
Source: Center for Systemic Peace, Polity IV Project (www.systemicpeace.org)
© Center for Systemic Peace 2014

high-income country. In 1998, negotiations began with the EU about the accession
of eight Central and Eastern European countries. This affected not only economic
and political, but also social and cultural, developments in these countries.

Lithuanian relay: Kazimiera Prunskienė and Dalia Grybauskaitė

Women's protest and nationalism

Despite the obstacles, some women went to the top in Eastern European countries
in connection with or after the fall of the communist regimes – something that
had not happened before, with the exception of Milka Planinc in Yugoslavia. In
1990, Kazimiera Prunskienė became prime minister of Lithuania. "Men can give
women a chance when there are difficult times", she commented later with a
cunning smile when I interviewed her in Vilnius in 2006.[8]

Historically, Lithuania was a deeply Catholic agricultural country. But at
independence in 1918, the country was one of the first in Europe to give women
political rights. The Catholic women's organisation contributed greatly to this.
From 1920 to 1926, women were elected to parliament on joint Catholic lists
and accounted for 3–5 per cent of the MPs. But then the regime became more
and more authoritarian, and there were financial problems. In 1929, a Lithuanian
Women's Council, with 20 organisations, was created to defend women's rights

to paid work during the recession. With limited job opportunities, a number of women went to university, and in 1930, they made up more than a quarter of the students.

In the 1940s, Lithuania was occupied by the Red Army, then Hitler's troops and again by the Red Army, and finally made a Soviet republic. The remainder of a Lithuanian resistance movement fought against the superior Soviet force until 1953. Hundreds of thousands of people were killed or deported. Priests and bishops were imprisoned and political parties were banned, while the Communist Party consolidated its power and carried through industrialisation and the collectivisation of agriculture. An opposition movement led by intellectuals and the Catholic Church was established in the 1960s, and in the 1970s, the protests attained a massive scale. With the *glasnost* policy, freed political prisoners began to demonstrate for liberty, and in 1988, a number of mainly conservative intellectuals got together in the 'Lithuanian renewal movement' called Sajŭdis. A few women took part, and Kazimiera Prunskienė became one of the leaders (Krupavičius and Matonyté, 2003).

Kazimiera Prunskienė, economic expert

Kazimiera Danutė, with the family name Stankevičiūtė, was born in the countryside in 1943. Her father was a forest ranger and owned some plots of land, but was killed when Kazimiera was two years old. Her mother got a job at a children's sanatorium and struggled hard to provide for the family. Kazimiera and an older brother, but not an older sister, got an education, and Kazimiera had to work as a secretary while she studied. She acquired a sense of responsibility and felt that it was important to help other women. In 1961, she married Povilas Prunskus and took his family name. They had a son and two daughters, whom Prunskienė took care of. She divorced and remarried in 1990, to Algimantas Taryvydas, but divorced again.

In 1965, Kazimiera Prunskienė undertook a degree in economics and worked for nearly 20 years as a lecturer and associate professor of industrial economics at the University of Vilnius, the capital of Lithuania. In between, she worked at universities in Hungary and West Germany, experienced other conditions than those in her home country, and became keen to change the Lithuanian economy. She took two PhDs in economics, first, in 1971 and then in 1986. Out of consideration for her career, she joined the Communist Party in 1980 and became deputy director of Lithuania's Research Institute on Rural Economy in 1986 and principal of an institute for economic education in Vilnius in 1988. She became involved in public debate, fought for economic independence for Lithuania and was noticed due to her vitality and eloquence.

Solitary 'Amber Lady'

The demonstrations for independence became increasingly widespread. In protest, more than 1 million women and men formed a 'human chain' from Tallinn in Estonia to Vilnius in Lithuania. The Communist Party of Lithuania adopted a more nationalistic approach, and in 1989, Prunskienė was appointed deputy prime minister. Then the Communist Party liberated itself from the Soviet mother party, gave up its political monopoly and accepted the free exercise of religion and a multiparty system. In the elections in February 1990, Sajūdis and its allies obtained a majority in the new pro-independence parliament, and Prunskienė was among those elected. Full independence from the Soviet Union was proclaimed. The Sajūdis leader Vytautas Landsbergis became president, and Prunskienė, prime minister. A woman as prime minister was noteworthy. The representation of women in parliament had increased to 36 per cent in the course of a few decades, but few had higher positions, and in the elections in 1990, representation dropped to just 10 per cent.

But the men did not mind handing over the job as head of government to Prunskienė. She was 47 years old, publicly known as an independent and critical voice and of generally recognised ability, and she had – unlike most others – participated in government before. Not least important was the fact that she had studied economics in the West and become knowledgeable about reform measures that could develop Lithuania in a more liberal direction. "I wanted to change the economic system and make Lithuania economically independent of the Soviet Union," she explained to me when I interviewed her in Vilnius in 2006. This was essential for a government that wished to become more oriented towards the West. But when Prunskienė proposed to include another woman in the cabinet, she got a flat refusal: "You are an exception. We will not have any more." And people constantly remarked that she was the "first of the nineteen male ministers".

Despite *glasnost*, Gorbachev absolutely wanted to keep Lithuania within the Soviet Union. When political pressure did not work, economic blockade followed, and the Soviet military intervened. Both Prunskienė and Landsbergis travelled around the world to get help. Independence was put on hold and negotiations were started with the Kremlin. As prime minister, Prunskienė became very popular and was called the 'Amber Lady', 'Lithuania's Thatcher' and the 'Iron lady from the East'. But this did not help much when she announced price increases on imports to strengthen the poor economy. There was a storm of protests, and while Prunskienė was in Moscow, the price increases were defeated in parliament. The prime minister and the cabinet immediately resigned, in January 1991, after only having been in office for 10 months. Prunskienė was criticised because she withdrew at a time of crisis in the country, but she replied that she could not continue without support from the president and parliament (Opfell, 1993: 161–8; Liswood, 2007 [1995]: 132–4; Jensen, 2008: 52–3).

A new (male) prime minister was appointed, and the crisis was resolved after the international community condemned the Soviet action, and 90 per cent of the Lithuanians voted for independence in a referendum.

Special women's party

When I spoke with Kazimiera Prunskienė later, she commented:

> "It was not easy to rise in the ranks as a woman. You had to have faith in yourself and prove that you were more competent than others. Opposition made me strong. But I would have liked to have more women with me so we could have dealt not only with the most pressing current issues, but focused on strategic priorities for women." (interview, 2006)

Because of disagreement with Sajūdis, Prunskienė became leader of the Party for Democracy, and in the elections in 1992, Sajūdis suffered a scathing defeat. The former Communist Party – having become social democratic and a supporter of market economics – took over power. But not a single woman was included in the cabinet, although there had been one in 1991/92. Only 10 women (7 per cent) were elected to parliament, although the electoral system had become more favourable, with a mixed arrangement of proportional representation rather than majority vote.

Prunskienė was upset: this was not acceptable! She founded a women's organisation and became involved in the emerging women's movement. "A country only ruled by men cannot be considered a true democracy", she declared, "and such a masculine regime cannot be desirable. Women are not able to develop on their own terms, and their resources are not utilized" (interview, 2006). Soon there were more than 60 active women's organisations. They mobilised women to participate in society, but were sceptical about political parties. In turn, the parties gradually stabilised and made contact with European sister parties, especially in Scandinavia, which had a significant proportion of women. In 1994, Lithuania became party to the CEDAW.

In 1995, Prunskienė founded a special Women's Party, of which she was the president. It contributed to setting women's issues on the agenda and strengthening women's position in politics. The party also put emphasis on issues related to children, family and education, opposed destruction of the economy, and supported free enterprise with social responsibility and a strong welfare state. In the parliamentary elections in 1996, the party only obtained 3.7 per cent of the vote, but Prunskienė was a prominent figure and was elected. A female minister was appointed shortly before the elections, two conservative parties established women's sections and the proportion of women in parliament increased to a total of 18 per cent. The conservatives won the elections, but even though governments changed until the year 2000, there was always one woman minister. For a while, there were two, and Irena Degutienė acted as head of government twice when the prime minister resigned, before a new one was appointed (Ishiyama, 2003: 291–3; Krupavičius and Matonyté, 2003).

Dalia Grybauskaitė across the finish line

Prunskienė was admired as a role model for women in Lithuanian politics, and she was a tireless advocate, being dynamic and persevering. In addition to being an MP from 1996 to 2008 and party leader for a long period,[9] she stood for election three times as presidential candidate. Lithuania had a dual political system, with a directly elected president and a prime minister who was approved by both the president and parliament. The prime minister was head of government, while the president had special responsibility for national security and foreign policy.

In the 2002 presidential elections, Prunskienė was the first and only woman candidate and got only 5 per cent of the vote. But in 2004, she obtained 47.4 per cent in the second round and lost by a hair's breadth to the former president, Valdus Adamkus, who received 52.6 per cent. Afterwards, she became one of two women ministers in the centre-left cabinet, with responsibility for agriculture. When I met her, I wondered why she was minister of agriculture. Prunskienė thought that it was an important job. "The farmers and the food sector are vital for the economy of a country like Lithuania", she underlined. "Women farmers work hard, but are not sufficiently appreciated."

After four years in the ministerial chair, Prunskienė stood for election as presidential candidate again in 2009. But then the situation had changed dramatically. After several years of exceptionally high economic growth, the global financial crisis hit hard in 2007, with deep recession and widespread unemployment. People lost confidence in the political leadership and wanted new faces. There were three women and four men as presidential candidates and now Prunskienė only got 4 per cent of the vote. But another woman, Dalia Grybauskaitė, won a great victory, with 69 per cent. She was not only Lithuania's first women president, but also the one elected with the largest margin (Hyndle-Hussein, 2009; Forrest, 2011).

'Steel Magnolia'

Grybauskaitė was 53 years old, a solid bureaucrat and politician, known to be independent and outspoken, and with a black belt in karate. Originally, she was from the working class. She was born in 1956 in Vilnius, and her father, Potikarpas Grybauskas, was an electrician and a driver, while her mother, Vitalija Korsakaitė, was a saleswomen. Under the Soviet regime, Vitalija supported the Lithuanian resistance movement by providing food. Dalia got an education, joined the Communist Party and studied political economy at the University of Leningrad while she worked in a factory. She graduated in 1983 and taught at the party college in Vilnius. But her role models were Margaret Thatcher and Mahatma Gandhi, so she resigned from the Communist Party in 1988 at the same time as she got her PhD at the Moscow Academy of Social Sciences. Later, she stayed outside the parties. She also remained unmarried. And when Lithuania became independent, she went to the US and undertook management courses at Georgetown University.

From 1991, Dalia Grybauskaitė worked in Lithuania's Foreign Service. She became a director stationed in the EU and US. In 1999, she came home and was state secretary, first, in the Ministry of Finance, then in the Ministry of Foreign Affairs. In 2001, she became minister of finance in the social-democratic government. When Lithuania became a member of NATO and the EU in 2004, Grybauskaitė was appointed as a member of the European Commission and EU budget chief. After a year, she was chosen as the 'commissioner of the year' for her efforts in making the EU administration more effective.

Grybauskaitė returned to Lithuania in 2009 to run as a presidential candidate. 'In difficult times I can use my experience and my knowledge for the benefit of the country,' she declared (BBC News, 2009). She wanted to create a Lithuania ruled by the people and stressed the need for measures to subdue the economic crisis, reduce unemployment and protect those with the lowest incomes. She stood for election as an independent, but was supported by the conservatives. Although, according to the constitution, the president had limited impact on economic policy, people had confidence in Grybauskaitė's competence and experience in the financial area and emphasised her contacts, both on the Right and the Left, with European elites and the EU.

The new president immediately put her stamp on politics. She was honest, plain speaking and hard-working and was called the Lithuanian 'Iron Lady' or 'Steel Magnolia'. When it came to foreign policy, Grybauskaitė tried to create dialogue so that the relationship with the Soviet Union became less confrontational, and the relationship with the East, EU and US became more balanced. She particularly wanted to contribute to European integration and strengthen Nordic–Baltic cooperation in various areas. Together with the prime minister, Grybauskaitė pursued rigorous economic austerity policies, with cuts in public spending and tax increases to master the financial crisis. In addition, she supported women's rights and managed to get a European Institute for Gender Equality in Vilnius.

The conservative male prime minister in office, who was elected in 2008, continued with a very male-dominated cabinet. There was only a woman minister of defence, but Grybauskaitė got in a woman minister of finance. Thus, the percentage of women in the cabinet rose to 14 per cent for a while. But when the Social Democrats won the parliamentary elections in 2012 and formed a coalition government, there was only one woman minister (7 per cent), who was responsible for the economy. In parliament the share of women was 24 per cent.

The presidential elections in 2014 took place amid rising concerns regarding neighbouring Russia's foreign policies. Grybauskaitė ran for re-election as the only woman among 7 candidates and won 58 per cent of the votes in the second round against a Social Democratic man. It was the first time a president was elected twice in a row. The 58 year old 'Iron Lady' inspired confidence, particularly by her courage and determination, clearly condemning Russia's aggressive actions in Ukraine.

Sabine Bergmann-Pohl, the last head of East Germany

Mixed history

In East Germany (the German Democratic Republic, GDR), Sabine Bergmann-Pohl emerged as acting head of state in 1990.[10] Germany had an active women's movement in the 19th century that worked to give women an education, more power in the family and political rights. Women got the right to vote in 1918, and between the world wars, a multiplicity of female unions and feminist and left-wing organisations flourished. Clara Zetkin founded the socialist women's movement, Rosa Luxemburg became leader of the Second International and the artist Käthe Kollwitz spoke through her pictures. In 1926, 32 women were elected to parliament. But the Nazis banned feminism, birth control and abortion. Now, it was *Kinder, Kirche, Küche* (children, church, kitchen) that counted. In the 1930s and 1940s, women were forced out of paid jobs and denied political office. Millions of Jews and others were sent to concentration camps, put to forced labour, abused and killed. The war also led to extensive destruction of German cities and inflicted great suffering on the population.

After the German defeat in 1945, the country was divided. East Germany was occupied by the Soviet Union and a communist state (the GDR) was established in 1949. Conditions were difficult: a destroyed country, war reparations that had to be paid to the Soviet Union and a lack of labour, even if foreign workers were imported. In addition, there was political oppression. Many people fled to the West, and the number of inhabitants went down. In 1961, the GDR regime built the Berlin wall to stem the flow. But women got education, employment and access to contraception, abortion and public child care. In 1989, the GDR was the European country with the most women in the labour market.

Although an independent women's movement was banned, women were active in the official trade unions and the communist-dominated women's federation. During the 1980s, women for peace and human rights groups were created under the protection of the Protestant Church. Some activists were deported or imprisoned, but others participated in the leadership of the movement that toppled the regime (Lemke, 1994).

Head of state for six months

Unrest and changes in 1989 led to protest demonstrations against the regime, bringing together up to half a million people, and the Berlin Wall fell. At the same time, women formed groups criticising the lack of gender equality in society. Despite resistance, a women's group managed to participate in the roundtable discussion on the further development of the country. But the women's views were scarcely able to be heard. Unification of Germany was the only theme that leading men would talk about, and objections from women were quickly brushed aside. The women wanted to have political and civil rights (freedom of speech, assembly and movement), but, at the same time, they were afraid of losing the social and economic rights they had under the communist regime (guaranteed jobs, affordable housing, free health care and education, paid parental leave, and child care).

Sabine Bergmann-Pohl was born in 1946 and graduated in medicine in 1972. She became a lung specialist, undertook a PhD in 1980 and got a job as a medical director. She married and had two children. As a Protestant, she got involved in social activities, and in 1981, she joined the Christian Democratic Union (CDU), which was part of the Communist Party's National Front. Here, she became a board member in the Berlin district in 1987. After the Wall fell, elections were held in March 1990 – the first and last free elections in the GDR. And Bergmann-Pohl became member of the People's Chamber (parliament).

The Alliance for Germany, where the CDU took part, demanded a rapid unification of Germany and got 48 per cent of the votes. A five-party cabinet was formed, with four women (15 per cent), and the male CDU leader became the new prime minister. Although the elections used proportional representation, the number of women in parliament went down (from 32 to 21 per cent). None of the parties were willing to follow the agreed rule of one-third women any longer. But Bergmann-Pohl was elected, and at the age of 44, she became president of the parliament. Thereby, she came to function as GDR's last head of state, from April 1990 until the reunification with West Germany took place in October of the same year (Deutscher Bundestag, 2005).

Women pay the price

The reunification was dramatic. When Western goods flooded the East German market, a wave of bankruptcies followed. Production and income declined, while unemployment rose. The Bonn government refused to provide sufficient support, and all the new East German states went bankrupt. Women, children and the elderly were hit the hardest, and women's activists pointed out that a joint attack on women's rights was taking place during the process. West German women and family law was conservative and favoured housewives. Women with paid jobs in the East lost salaries and pensions, health services, and child care.

In the transitional cabinet, two women activists were appointed ministers: a Social Democrat was responsible for labour and social policy and a woman from the CDU for women and family. The last got a special state secretary for gender equality. The minister for women was a party colleague of Bergmann-Pohl, but it is not known if the two women collaborated with regards to women's issues. Bergmann-Pohl was not a member of the cabinet, and the state secretary for equality complained that she was expected to restrain women activists, not promote women's interests.

The situation of women was not mentioned in the first unification agreement. Following pressure from women in both parts of Germany, women and the family were included in the second agreement, but it did not lead to much. Some women's studies were undertaken. Hostels were established for abused women, and the more liberal East German abortion law was extended for a couple of years. The minister for labour and social policy resigned in protest because the transition from a socialist welfare state to a social market economy hit women hard and disproportionately (Rosenberg, 1991).

After reunification, Bergmann-Pohl participated in the joint German Bundestag and the chancellor's cabinet. Later, she became parliamentary secretary for health. But it was another woman from the East: Angela Merkel, who went to the top in the Federal Republic of Germany (see Chapter Ten).

Polish compromise: Hanna Suchocka

Obstinate people

Poland was struck hard during World War II. More than 6 million ethnic Poles and Polish Jews perished. In addition, almost half of the country was taken over by the Soviet Union, while Poland acquired some German territories. Millions of people had to move. Eventually, a communist regime was established, and in 1948, the country became a one-party state and Soviet satellite. But the people's republic was characterised by an 'obstinate political culture'. Josef Stalin once said that the introduction of socialism in Poland was like saddling a cow. Many Poles reacted negatively to the Stalinist regime, persecution of the Catholic opposition and bad living conditions. There were political and economic crises in 1956, 1968, 1970, 1976 and 1980. The authorities responded with fierce repression mixed with some concessions.[11]

The crisis in 1980 was triggered by a woman crane operator who wanted to honour the workers who were killed 10 years before. Workers all over the country demanded 'solidarity' and the independent trade union Solidarity was formed. The organisation quickly got more than 10 million members, half of them women. But there were only 7 per cent women at the first national congress. Two women were included in the strike committee with 18 members, and only one in the leadership. Men took power as a matter of course. On the walls, they wrote: 'Women, don't disturb us – we are fighting for Poland.' The only demands the trade union presented on behalf of women workers were maternity leave and children's institutions so that they could be better mothers. The agreements with the authorities included nothing about empowering women, either politically or in the workplace.

The government first responded to the turbulence with persecution and a state of emergency, but deterioration of the economy gradually reduced the pressure. There was a new wave of strikes in 1988, and in light of the reform policy of the Soviet Union, the authorities and Solidarity entered into a compromise in 1989, entailing that elections were to be held in 1989, 1990 and 1991. In 1989, the elections were partly controlled, but for the first time in 40 years, voters in Eastern Europe could freely express their views. The result was a disaster for the communists. In the parliament (Sejm), Solidarity got all the seats that were not predetermined for the communists and their allies. But women only accounted for 13 per cent. The elections were based on majority vote, and the key players did not consider women's issues as important. In 1990, the founder of Solidarity, Lech Wałesa, was elected as president of Poland. A myriad of political parties were formed, between 100 and 200, and with elections with proportional representation in 1991, no fewer than 29 parties were represented in parliament. But the women's movement was weak, and the fragmentation of parties was unfavourable. The proportion of women in parliament was only 9 per cent (Siemeńska, 1994).

Clever idea

There was a dual political system. The president was directly elected, while the prime minister had to be approved by parliament. There were antagonisms between the parties and between the president and parliament. Governments were based on various coalitions and changed constantly. In 1992, Wałesa was so frustrated that he threatened to take over the role of prime minister himself if parliament failed to agree on a government. To the amazement of everybody, the majority suggested a cabinet headed by a woman. During the communist regime, few women got high posts, and apart from being vice president of the Council of Europe, Hanna Suchocka had not had any special positions.

It is reported that Lech Wałesa was confused when he heard about Hanna Suchocka. He had no idea who she was, even though she had been an MP for several years. He asked: "A woman?" There was silence. "A woman", he repeated, and his voice rose: "See, that was clever." In a country where men should be chivalrous and kiss women on the hand, Wałesa probably thought that Poland's male-dominated parties would be reluctant to start intriguing against a woman prime minister (Liswood, 2007: 41). Later Wałesa described Suchocka as the 'best premier we have had' (*Current Biography*, 1994: 52; Jensen, 2008: 51). But she did not remain in power very long.

Solid and acceptable

Hanna Suchocka's background was solid. She was born in 1946 in a Catholic family of chemists and was taught to work hard by her mother, who was a pharmacist. Her grandfather was a university teacher and her grandmother, Anna, became a member of the first Polish Parliament after independence in 1918, when women got the right to vote. Her father's sister was also an independent woman who had considerable influence on Hanna. Hanna had no brothers, and her parents wanted her to be a pharmacist. But she ended up in law school. She remained unmarried and became a researcher at the University of Poznan, but she was fired because she refused to join the Communist Party. She wanted the liberty to go to church. A few years later, she was hired again. She was preoccupied by human rights, studied in West Germany and undertook a PhD in constitutional law in 1975.

In 1969, Suchocka joined a small non-Marxist 'satellite party', the Democratic Party (SD), and was elected to parliament during 1980–85. At the same time, she was a member and legal adviser in Solidarity. She was one of only a few MPs who had the courage not to vote in favour of martial law in 1981 and the criminalisation of Solidarity in 1984. The party suspended her (or she resigned). With the support of Solidarity, she was elected to parliament again in 1989.

Solidarity supporters split up into several parties. Suchocka joined the centre-liberal Democratic Union (DU) and was re-elected to parliament in 1991. When she was nominated as prime minister, it was because she could be accepted by people who had antipathy towards the more prominent leaders of DU. Suchocka was known for her low profile and willingness to make compromises and promote reconciliation. In addition, she was accepted politically by both sides of the spectrum because she was considered left-wing while, as a Catholic, she opposed abortion. Thus, she could represent a broad coalition of seven parties, including a Christian and a liberal party (Opfell, 1993: 212–22).

Reconciliation – for a while

The thought of becoming prime minister made Hanna Suchocka hesitate at first. She was 46 years old, but felt unprepared and was of the opinion that she was not competent enough (Jensen, 2008: 51). But she was persuaded. It was said that, as a woman, she might have better chances of forming a cabinet than her predecessors because women often curb antagonisms.

At her inauguration in parliament, Poland's first women prime minister stated: 'My task is to calm down the controversies between the political parties. This is a government for social reconciliation.' Moreover, she promised to lead the country forward in the transformation from Communism to capitalism. MPs were 'shocked' and 'surprised' by the suggestion that a woman should head the government, but none could come up with a reason to oppose her candidacy. Some had high expectations and Suchocka was approved by 233 against 61 votes and 113 abstentions (*Current Biography*, 1994: 52).

The new prime minister quickly formed a cabinet. People Wałesa wanted were appointed as ministers of defence and foreign affairs, while she took charge of the economy. But she did not get any female ministers, even though she wanted to. None of the coalition parties were willing to accept another woman. On the other hand, to strengthen support for the new government, they gave her two male deputy prime ministers, one for economic affairs and one for politics.

Hanna Suchocka became prime minister in July 1992, put a photograph of Margaret Thatcher on the wall and stayed in office longer than any of her four predecessors. But if she was protected as a woman, it did not last long. In parliament and the cabinet, disagreement and strife arose. There was a wave of strikes. Hanna was a warm supporter of market reforms and followed a hard line against the strikers. Production and exports increased, and inflation fell. But when she would not give salary increases to teachers and health workers in 1993, parliament adopted a vote of no confidence by a majority of one vote. One of the MPs who would have voted in her favour, arrived only moments too late to cast the crucial vote. Wałesa dissolved parliament and held new elections, and Hanna resigned as soon as the new parliament was in place (Lewis, 1992; *Who's Who in Poland*, 1994).

No feminist

There was a widespread view – supported by national trends and the Catholic Church – that a Polish woman's place was in the home, where she was supposed to raise the next generation. When Suchocka became prime minister, the attitudes towards women politicians became more positive, but this did not last long. And Suchocka was no champion of gender equality. In 1991, women parliamentarians formed a bipartisan caucus to promote equality, and the cabinet appointed a special representative for family and women. She was very active, but her contract was brought to an end in 1992. When Suchocka became prime minister, women's organisations requested her to appoint a new special representative. But Suchocka replied that she saw no need for it or other measures to improve the position of women. She was opposed to sex education and the distribution of condoms, and supported a restrictive anti-abortion law that active feminist groups were against, despite the fact that more than 80 per cent of the population wanted a more liberal law. But there was no effective women's lobby, and Wałesa approved the restrictive law in 1992.

Suchocka was personally very popular, but people disliked her economic policy. With 15 per cent unemployment and increasing inequality between rich and poor, Suchocka was re-elected to parliament in 1993, but her party only received 10 per cent of the votes. In total, the representation of women was 13 per cent. Few women candidates were nominated, and those who were elected, came from the main parties and electoral alliances. In 1994, Suchocka was one of the founders of a liberal and social-democratic Liberty Union, which became the country's third-largest political force. And in 1995, she tried to be nominated as a candidate in the presidential election, but the party would not support her. However, she was minister of justice in a coalition government during 1997–2000. Afterwards, she became ambassador to the Vatican (Siemieńska, 2003).

Latvia's queen: Vaira Vīķe-Freiberga

Disney fairy tale

Ten years passed after the communist regimes began to collapse before a woman in one of the eastern states acquired a top political position 'for real', a position she held for a normal period of time – yes, even for two periods. Vaira Vīķe-Freiberga was president of Latvia for eight years, from 1999 to 2007.[12] However, unlike many of the other countries, the president had a relatively weak position in Latvia. The country adopted a parliamentary system, with parliament elected by proportional representation. The president was elected by parliament and had essentially a ceremonial role. The most important task was to nominate the prime minister.

Vaira Vīķe-Freiberga's life was like a fairy tale, people said. The little girl escaped from her war-torn home country and came back 50 years later to become president. And, actually, that was the way it was.

Vaira's childhood was dramatic. She was born in Riga in 1937 just before her father, Kārlis Vīķis, who was a sailor, perished at sea. Later, her mother Annemarija married a fire-fighter, Edgars Hermanovičs. In 1940, Latvia was invaded by the Russian army. The Nazis took over a year later, until the Soviet army returned in 1944. Vaira experienced two occupations, where the front line went back and forth across her grandfather's farm. Just before the Soviet troops came back, the Hermanovičs family fled in a hurry with the two little girls. They found room on a ship full of refugees. It was one of the last ships that were not sunk by Soviet aircrafts, and they arrived safely in Gdynia. Approximately 200,000 Latvians fled to Germany in 1944/45, and they were gathered together in hundreds of camps. The Vaira family ended near Lübeck, where Vaira went to a Latvian school. She got dysentery, but survived. Her little sister, however, died at 10 months old. At the same time, Vaira got a little brother.

In 1949, it was decided to dismantle the camps and people had to get out. Vaira's stepfather got a job as a mechanic in a French company building a dam in Morocco, and they moved there. Vaira attended a French school for five years before the family moved to Canada. The transition to Canada was tough, with changes in climate, environment and language, and Vaira Vīķis had to work as a cashier in a bank to help the family economy. She went to evening classes, took courses by correspondence on weekends and obtained a master's degree in psychology in 1960. Toronto was the 'capital' of Latvians in exile, and Vaira married a countryman, Imants Freiberg. They moved to Montreal, where Vaira undertook a PhD in 1965 alongside a variety of jobs, became university professor and taught psychology and linguistics. Imants was a professor of computer science. They, first, had a son, then a daughter.

Vaira Vīķe-Freiberga had an active professional life. She did research, taught and wrote articles and books in English and Latvian. She became the leader of several professional organisations and travelled at home and abroad, including to Latvia, to lecture. In addition to working as a psychologist, she was interested in the Latvian language and culture and published books on Latvian folklore. When she resigned from her position in 1998, she was requested to head the new Latvia institute in Riga, Latvia's capital, which was supposed to spread knowledge of Latvian culture abroad. A year after, she was elected as the country's president, at 61 years old.

Seven election rounds

Vaira Vīķe-Freiberga was not a candidate in the presidential election. But parliament was unable to obtain a majority for any of the proposed candidates. The party situation was messy, with a divided parliament where several smaller parties entered into shifting alliances. Both male and female politicians and cultural personalities ran as presidential candidates, but none got enough votes. The media suggested the name of Vīķe-Freiberga, and when she was asked, she replied that she could imagine being president. Well-known intellectuals wrote to parliament recommending her, and frustrated MPs from three parties launched her as a compromise candidate. She was independent, highly respected and after seven election rounds, she obtained a majority (53 out of 100 votes) ahead of six better-known candidates. There were 17 per cent women in the parliament.

Many Latvians had never heard of Vīķe-Freiberga and were shocked, not so much because she was a woman, but because she lacked political experience and had lived abroad for 55 years. However, it was precisely these qualities that got her elected. People appreciated that she stood outside of the political games and never had anything to do with the Communist Party. With the election of Vīķe-Freiberga, the post-Soviet period was definitely over. Moreover, for a country that more than anything wanted to approach the West, it was an advantage that she knew Western democracy, culture and language, spoke several languages, and had good training in presenting Latvian interests abroad. She also had broad management experience and was a wise person with extensive knowledge of people and society. She, herself, noted: 'There was a price to pay in becoming President. But in order to serve the land of my birth, I decided I was willing to pay that price' (Tarm, 1999). In artistic circles, she was called the Latvian 'Vaclav Havel'.

Vaira Vīķe-Freiberga did not doubt that she could handle the job: 'If I didn't feel fully confident that I had the skills and resources to do this job properly, I never would have considered taking it,' she said (Tarm, 1999). More than usual was also required of her. The economy was in trouble, there were tensions between Latvians and Russians, who constituted a large part of the population, and the country had to clarify its relationship with the West and the East. In her inauguration speech, the newly elected president said:

> We must have economic growth, we must have social justice and we must have legal and moral order. Latvia must become a partner in the negotiations for accession to the European Union, Latvia must become member of NATO …
> I call on every citizen and resident of Latvia to remember that our destinies are inextricably linked, that we will walk side by side through the course of our lives.…Let us live so that we respect one another, understand one another, enrich one another's lives. (Vīķe-Freiberga, quoted in Dixon, 2006: 92)

With ever-changing cabinets, the president became important not least as a mediator in order to stabilise the situation.

Role model

As president, Vaira Vīķe-Freiberga tried to avoid political conflict, but during her first period, she sent seven laws back to parliament for further consideration. In public, she was very visible and active. She had a striking appearance, which many found reminiscent of Margaret Thatcher – both had reddish hair – and Vīķe-Freiberga was immediately called 'Latvia's Iron Lady'. She also made plain-spoken statements and attracted special attention with her harsh criticism of the Soviet Union. Foreign policy was her main area. She became one of Latvia's most popular politicians and was re-elected after four years by a large majority (88 out of 96 votes) (Jensen, 2008: 215).

The president was only supposed to publicly promote policies that were approved by the prime minister, and the interaction between them usually took place behind closed doors. And while Vīķe-Freiberga was president, there were six different prime ministers from four different parties. But all were heads of coalition governments, and Vīķe-Freiberga stood out almost as a centre politician. She could express controversial views, but she mostly went out with messages based on broad agreement, at least in theory. She received universal recognition for the leading role she played in relation to the EU and NATO. She declared: 'I changed Latvia so it became a country with stable democratic values, a safe position within NATO and a continually growing economy' (iKNOW Politics, 2008).

Vīķe-Freiberga was aware that she was a role model for women, in Latvia as well as abroad. Women's issues received little attention in Latvia after independence in 1991, although CEDAW was accepted in 1992 and women's situation was generally difficult. Women were a majority of the labour force, but also a majority of the unemployed. The income of 80 per cent of the population was below the poverty line. The maternal allowance was miserably low and pre-school care was essentially non-existent. At the same time, women were not empowered politically to protect their rights in the labour market and to struggle for social programmes (Novikova, 1995). Vīķe-Freiberga supported women's rights. Women should have, among other things, the same access to higher positions as men. But she noted:

> Gender is just one of the attributes that defines me as a human being and I don't see it as playing a primordial role either in my decision-making or in the sense of my country's priorities. I tend to view my commitments as humanistic ones in the fullest sense of the word. For me, democracy is a service to human beings regardless of their gender, and in that sense my own gender is not an important issue. (Vīķe-Freiberga, quoted in Sorensen, 2002).

During the time Vīķe-Freiberga was president, from 1999 to 2007, the representation of women in parliament increased from 17 to 22 per cent and in the cabinet from 12 to 21 per cent. In 2014, there were 25 per cent women in parliament and 31 per cent in the cabinet.

In 2004, *Forbes* rated Vīķe-Freiberga as number 70 of the world's 100 most powerful women; in 2005 as number 48; and in 2006 as number 63. But after two terms, Vīķe-Freiberga could not be re-elected. After she retired, she travelled around the world giving lectures, accepted international positions regarding literature and research, and worked with future studies, tolerance and reconciliation. In particular, she joined a group of senior politicians in Brussels drawing up plans for the EU in the future. The Baltic countries proposed her as secretary general of the UN, but she was not elected. She also ran, as the only woman candidate, for the post of president of the European Council, but, again, male candidates were preferred. However, Vīķe-Freiberga received numerous medals, awards, orders of merit and honorary doctorates (President of Latvia, 2005; Liswood, 2007: 145-7).

Reneta Indzhova: Bulgarian episode

'Non-party' interim leader

The first woman top leader in South-Eastern Europe was hardly noticed. The Bulgarians demanded an end to the communist regime in 1990. A new constitution was adopted, with a parliamentary system and multiparty elections. More than 40 parties were formed, and the new parliament had no clear majority in 1991. In the first direct presidential election in 1992, Zhelyu Zhelev, leader of the liberal-conservative Democratic Union (UDF), was elected. Previously, he was professor of philosophy, and he ran with a famous female poet, Blaga Nikolova Dimitrova, as vice president.

Dissatisfaction spread as the economy deteriorated and the cabinet had to resign. A new one was formed, but received little support in parliament. The prime minister withdrew after there had been seven votes of no confidence against him. No one else obtained a majority, and the president dissolved the parliament. In anticipation of new elections in 1994, he appointed the 41-year-old Reneta Indzhova, also a member of the UDF, to head a 'non-party' interim cabinet.

Reneta Indzhova was born in 1953, received a PhD and became a professor of political economy. She married and had a child, but later divorced. She worked as a financial expert for the UDF and led the government office of privatisation. There were not many women politicians. With weak women's organisations and a changing party system, the share of women in parliament did not amount to more than 14 per cent in 1991, with proportional representation. And there was only one woman minister (of culture) in 1991/92. Indzhova acknowledged that she was an exception in modern Bulgarian history, but she got another woman to join the otherwise totally male-dominated expert cabinet. A female employee from the ministry of finance was appointed deputy prime minister. The cabinet worked for three months, and the only action that is noted is that Indzhova made progress when it came to combating the high crime rate in the country.

In the elections in December 1994, the proportion of women in parliament was reduced to 13 per cent, and only one woman minister (of health) was appointed. In 1995, Reneta Indzhova ran as an independent candidate for mayor in the capital Sofia and finished third. In 2001, she ran as the only woman for president on behalf of the Party of Rights and Freedoms, but only got 5 per cent of the votes (Kostadinova, 2003).

Rose Revolution with Nino Burjanadze

Protest against fraud

Suddenly, a slender, dark-haired woman came forward in front of the agitated masses of people. Western media broadcast the picture all over the world. The pale, but resolute, woman declared herself to be Georgia's interim president and urged people to be calm. It was Nino Burjanadze, aged 39 years and just retired as Speaker of the Parliament of Georgia.[13]

People took to the streets in Tbilisi, Georgia's capital, to protest when it became clear that extensive fraud was supposed to ensure President Eduard Shevardnadze a majority in the legislature in the 2003 elections. More than a 100,000 people gathered and carried out what has been called the 'Rose Revolution'. When Shevardnadze tried to install the new legislature the head of the opposition, Mikheil Saakashvili, led the protesters into the building with roses and demanded their political rights. During the days that followed, Shevardnadze resigned and the elections were annulled. The rebellion was one of the so-called 'velvet revolutions' because it took place without bloodshed.

Secession from the Soviet Union led Georgia into civil war and anarchy until Shevardnadze was elected president in 1992. Shevardnadze was previously the president of the Georgian Communist Party and became minister of foreign affairs of the Soviet Union under Gorbachev. Georgia had a presidential system, and as the country's powerful president, Shevardnadze gained a reputation as the nation's saviour because he defeated warlords and began to build a stable state. Political parties, the Georgian Church, the media and industry flourished. But as the years went by, conflicts remained unresolved. There were tensions between regions and clans, power crises, widespread poverty, and corruption. Discontent spread and burst into active protest when the elections were manipulated after Shevardnadze had been in power for 11 years.

Law and order

Nino Burjanadze tried to pour oil on troubled waters. Even though she appeared to be small and frail in the floodlights, she was respected. She was born in 1964 into a wealthy and influential family. Her father was a businessman and supported Shevardnadze financially. As a child, Nino wanted to be an ambassador and she became an expert on international law and got her PhD in 1990. She married a peer, Badri Bitsadze, who became Georgia's acting attorney general, had two children, and worked as a professor at the university from 1991. In addition, she worked as a consultant for the state administration. Her mother took care of the housework and grandchildren.

Nino Burjanadze was preoccupied with law and justice. In 1994, Georgia became party to the CEDAW, and in 1995, she stood for election to the legislature for Shevardnadze's party as one of very few women. The electoral system was mixed, but most were elected by proportional representation and Burjanadze got in. But there were only 6 per cent women legislators in all. Burjanadze served as the chair of a number of committees and was re-elected in 1999, in a national assembly with 7 per cent women members. In 2001, she became Speaker of the Parliament of Georgia. Burjanadze was known for her pro-Western values and wanted Georgia to try to get into the EU and NATO. She supported Shevardnadze's foreign policy (especially with regards to Russia), but became increasingly critical of inefficient domestic governance. In 2002, she formed her own opposition party – the Burjanadze-Democrats – which later joined Saakashvili's party.

One crisis after the other

When elections were held in 2003, Nino Burjanadze was formally no longer the Speaker because the national assembly was dissolved, but she was one of the leaders of the opposition, declared the elections invalid and called for new ones. When Shevardnadze withdrew, she served as the country's interim leader. In two months, she became one of Georgia's most popular politicians. She was compared with Margaret Thatcher and was called the 'Iron Lady'. But she did not run for president because she felt that she was not ready to take on such a responsibility. In January 2004, Mikheil Saakashvili was elected by an overwhelming majority. Nino Burjanadze continued as the speaker in the new legislature, now with 9 per cent women MPs (Jensen, 2008).

President Mikheil Saakashvili strengthened the state and public services and implemented economic reforms. But he extended the president's power, limited freedom of speech and introduced unjust election rules, which led to a crisis in 2007. There were mass demonstrations and protests. Saakashvili declared martial law and refused to resign, but promised to hold early presidential elections. According to the constitution, the president had to resign 45 days before the elections. For the second time, Nino Burjanadze acted as president. Then, Saakashvili was re-elected and took over again.

Legislative elections were planned to be held in May 2008, but to everyone's surprise Nino Burjanadze refused to stand for election. She was supposed to be on the top of the list of Saakashvili's party, but was frustrated over the president's policies. He used brutal methods to govern the country. Corruption was widespread, wages were low and unemployment was sky-high. And the war between Georgia and Russia about Abkhazia and South Ossetia made Burjanadze form a declared opposition party, Democratic Movement – United Georgia, where she was the chairperson, this time against Saakashvili. In the years that followed, she headed mass demonstrations to make her former ally step down as president. In 2011, there were clashes with the police and four demonstrators were killed.

The opposition came to power in the legislative elections in 2012, and in 2013, Georgia finalised a change of power and political system, introducing a parliamentary republic. The authority of the president was reduced in favour of the prime minister and the government. Saakashvili's time as president was over, and Burjanadze ran for president against 22 candidates at the elections in 2013. She ended third (after two men), with 10 per cent of the vote. In parliament, there were only nine women (7 per cent) and four women were appointed to the cabinet (21 per cent) (Kobaladze, 2008; Lanskoy and Areshidze, 2008).

Yulia Tymoshenko: Ukraine's Orange Princess

Strikes for democracy

A year after Georgia's Rose Revolution in November 2004, the Orange Revolution in Ukraine was suddenly on the front page of all the newspapers.[14] Nearly a million people dressed in orange crowded together in the centre of the capital, Kiev, to protest against the presidential election. The election campaign had been intense, and the atmosphere was energised when a second round was organised between the two main candidates: the pro-Western opposition leader, Viktor Yushchenko, who was prime minister during 1999–2001, and the pro-Russian Viktor Yanukovych, who took over as prime minister in 2002. When Yanukovych was declared the winner in 2004, with foreign observers reporting extensive fraud, the Yushchenko campaign immediately appealed for demonstrations and strikes for democracy. The protests were so widespread that the election was annulled and new elections were held in December. Viktor Yushchenko emerged victorious by a narrow majority: 52 per cent of the vote.

As in Tbilisi, a woman also stood centre-stage during the demonstrations in Kiev. Yulia Volodymyrivna Tymoshenko was just as fair-headed as Nino Burjanadze was dark, with a large braid around her head. She was not speaker of the national assembly, but party leader and a key figure in the opposition. When Yushchenko was prime minister, she was deputy prime minister and played an important role in the Yushchenko campaign. Western media baptised her the 'Joan of Arc'.

Competent but controversial businesswoman

Opinions differed with regards to Yulia Tymoshenko. Supporters called her the 'goddess of the revolution', a 'superstar' and a 'beauty queen', while opponents said that she was 'dominating', 'power-seeking' and 'nationalistic' (Schmidt, 2006). Before she became involved in politics, she was a successful, but controversial, businesswoman in the gas industry. She was born Yulia Grigyan in an ordinary

Orthodox family in Dnipropetrovsk in Eastern Ukraine in 1960. She was an only child, and her father left them when she was little, so her mother had to have several jobs to support herself and her daughter. Yulia learned early that a woman had to be strong to manage and was diligent at school and university. In 1979, she married Oleksandr Tymoshenko, the son of a Communist Party bureaucrat, and they had a daughter the following year.

Yulia rose in the ranks of the Komsomol, the official communist youth organisation, and undertook a university degree in economics in 1984. She began working in a machine factory, but then started a chain of video rental shops with her husband. In 1991, she became managing director of Ukraine Oil, a private company that was involved in the sale of fuel, and in 1995, president of another private company called United Energy Systems of Ukraine, which managed to get a near-monopoly on the import of gas from Russia. As a consequence, she was called the 'Gas Princess' and 'Energy Queen'. Her husband worked in the export of metal, and both got very rich. They were accused of illegal business operations, and Yulia Tymoshenko was in prison for a short period, while her husband stayed abroad for long periods of time.

From oligarch to reformer

Ukraine's independence entailed neither political reforms nor immediate restructuring of the economy. The country's leadership was heavily influenced by Russia, and for a long time a social equilibrium was established based on patron–client relationships that were not easy to change. Politics was dominated by 'political machines', organisations in which different forms of bribery made people do as the leaders wanted. In that way, the president could exert control over the media, industry, regional leaders and political opponents. Ukraine was marked by extensive corruption and little real law and order (Hale, 2010).

An oil company Yulia Tymoshenko owned received a fine of USD 300 million for violating currency laws, and Tymoshenko realised that she either had to continue doing big business and constantly get into confrontations with the state or go into politics and fight to liberate business from state intervention. In 1997, she was elected to the legislature with great support. There were 4 per cent women, and she became vice president for the 'Hromada' party of the incumbent Prime Minister Pavlo Lazarenko. He was a business partner and a very corrupt prime minister. But in 1999, she founded her own party, the All-Ukrainian Union Fatherland Party. She also undertook a PhD in economics.

Then, Tymoshenko moved from oligarch to reformer. 'I do not seek power', she declared, 'I only offer the policies that can give new life to my country' (Internet Press Service of Yulia Tymoshenko, 2009). Her priority was economic reform: 'Taxes must become inevitable, but affordable', she stated, 'I want to say to people, "Forget about paying bribes. Pay taxes"' (Zarahkovich, 2005).

She became deputy prime minister for energy during 1999–2001 in Prime Minister Yushchenko's cabinet. The revenues from the electricity industry increased by several thousand per cent so that the state got money to pay the administration and increase wages. But she came into conflict with powerful interests in the coal and natural gas industry and was dismissed by President Leonid Kuchma. After that, she became an active street protester against Kuchma – a 'passionara chic' (stylish passionate person) demanding 'Ukraine without Kuchma' – and attacked him for, among other things, his alleged involvement in the murder of the journalist Heorhyi Gongadze in 2000 (Dedet, 2005; Limoncelli, 2011).

On 24 January 2005, a record high number of representatives of the Supreme Council (legislature), 373 of 450, voted for 44-year-old Yulia Tymoshenko as prime minister according to the proposal of President Yushchenko. Of the 450, 5 per cent were women. The president, who was directly elected, proposed the prime minister, but both the prime minister and the cabinet had to be approved by the Supreme Council, though cabinet members may not sit in the Council. The Council was elected by a mixed system of proportional representation and majority vote. Many tens of parties and independents stood for election. The relationship between the president and prime minister was problematic, and in 2006, the president was stripped of key powers in favour of the prime minister, who was now elected by the Council and accountable to it.

The appointment of Tymoshenko was perceived as 'a continuation of the revolution', because she was considered to be radical and West-oriented. She formed a coalition cabinet and declared that as prime minister, she would work to get Ukraine into the EU without alienating Russia, cleanse the country of corruption, get rid of the grey economy and create an independent judiciary (Selmer, 2005). Tymoshenko was now called the 'Iron Lady' or 'Iron Angel', and in July 2005, Forbes rated her as the third most powerful woman in the world (after US Secretary of State Condoleeza Rice and Chinese Deputy Prime Minister Wu Yi).

Top leaders fight

Ukraine struggled with a huge foreign debt, unemployment and poverty, and the president disagreed with the prime minister over economic policy. Tymoshenko wanted to cancel and renegotiate or relaunch a large number of privatisation deals and was accused of being a state socialist and populist. Moreover, there were antagonisms within the cabinet, and there were accusations of corruption. After seven months, in September 2005, President Yushchenko dismissed both Tymoshenko and the cabinet. However, the Supreme Court annulled the corruption charges against Tymoshenko in November, and she travelled around the country to win the parliamentary elections in March 2006. She strengthened her position, and Tymoshenko's election alliance became the second-largest, but only got 129 seats against 186 for the party of Yanukovych and 81 for the party of Yushchenko.

Several months of government negotiations between the former Orange partners ended in deadlock, and the loser of the presidential election in 2004, Viktor Yanukovych, took over as prime minister. He manoeuvred skilfully and was suspected of 'buying' support from MPs to undermine the president. Spurred by Tymoshenko, Yushchenko renewed the alliance with her and they boycotted the Supreme Council to force new elections. There was agitation and demonstrations, but in the elections in September 2007, Tymoshenko strengthened her position further. Now, her alliance obtained 156 seats against 175 for the party of Yanukovych and 72 for the alliance of Yushchenko. In December, Yushchenko appointed Tymoshenko as prime minister for the second time, with the narrowest margin possible in the Council – 226 votes out of 450 – after several rounds of voting. Now, 8 per cent of the members were women. In 2006 and 2007 *Forbes* did not include Tymoshenko on the ranking list of the world's most powerful women, but in 2008 she was rated as number 17 and in 2009 as number 47.

Tymoshenko became head of a coalition government, but disagreement arose again between the prime minister and the president. When Russia invaded Georgia, Yushchenko condemned Russia's actions, while Tymoshenko took a more cautious stance. At the same time, Yushchenko was opposed to legislation aimed at reducing the power of the president. The Supreme Council was divided, not least in the approach towards the East and the West. A motion for a vote of no confidence and threats of new elections were put forward.

During January–February 2010, presidential elections were held. Against 18 candidates, Yulia Tymoshenko lost in the last round with a narrow margin. She got 45.4 per cent of the votes, while Viktor Yanukovych got 48.95 per cent. Yanukovych, who was overthrown by the Orange Revolution in 2004, now became president and Tymoshenko had to resign after a vote of no confidence in the council. Of the 450 members, 243 voted against her (Stratfor, 2010).

Imprisoned 'political atom bomb'

Tymoshenko's political career was not over in 2014, and what will be her legacy as a Ukrainian top politician is unclear. In autumn 2010, Tymoshenko was indicted for abuse of her position in connection with a gas deal with Russia. She was arrested and sentenced to seven years in prison. Tymoshenko denied any wrongdoing and said that President Yanukovych was involved in political persecution. In addition to Tymoshenko, charges were also brought against a number of high-ranking politicians and officials from the previous government. The government's actions provoked international condemnation. EU politicians spoke of 'selective prosecution of political opponents' and the EU demanded Tymoschenko's release as a condition for signing an EU-Ukraine trade and partnership agreement. After two and a half years in prison, partly in hospital, Tymoshenko was released in February 2014 during the 'Maidan revolution' in Kiev. She appeared in a wheelchair and gave a speech to the crowds where she declared that a new era had begun of free people in a free, European country. But she did not become member of the transitional government.

There is no doubt that Tymoshenko is exceptionally charismatic, articulate, energetic and competent, with special organisational and administrative capabilities. She climbed to the top in business as well as in politics in an extremely male-dominated society. In high administrative positions, there were less than 5 per cent women in the mid–1990s. Representation in parliament was constantly less than 10 per cent, and women ministers were a rarity. Tymoshenko was called a 'political atom bomb', one of the 'most cunning politicians in Ukraine' and 'the most efficient politician in Ukraine's recent history' – extremely rare descriptions when it comes to a woman politician. She was not criticised for being a woman, but was perceived as politically equal with the two central male politicians Yanukovych and Yushchenko. This alone was an accomplishment for a woman in a society like that of the Ukraine (IPU, 1997; Birch, 2003; Stratfor, 2010).

But, like the other two, Tymoshenko was also controversial. All three had their 'political machines', were criticised for their policies and blamed for engaging in personal rivalry at the expense of the interests of the nation. In the foreign press, Tymoshenko was accused of being a 'charming, but tyrannical Machiavelli in skirts' (Dedet, 2005). Tymoshenko, herself, lists a number of achievements during her time in power, among other things, the recovery of the 2008/09 Ukrainian financial crisis (see: www.tymoshenko.ua). But her former partner, Yushenko, declared in 2010 that his worst mistake was to give the power to Tymoshenko twice (UNIAN, 2010).

No woman-friendly policies

The fact that Tymoshenko became a renowned politician and nearly won the presidential election in 2010 says a lot about her appeal to voters, tactical abilities and financial resources, but does not mean that she proposed effective policies. Conditions were extremely complicated, and she was criticised, among other things, for failing to promote woman-friendly policies.

After independence, civil and political associations were formed, and women began to engage in politics. Some parties had a woman in the leadership, and a few even got a woman leader, of which three in particular (including Yulia Tymoshenko) gained some influence. None of the women's parties that were created obtained significant voter support. The number of parties increased to a total of more than 100, so the women leaders and parties represented only a minority. The women party leaders were not perceived as part of the women's movement. Women who explicitly supported women's issues did not get such positions, and the women party leaders did not focus specifically on questions related to women. Here, Yulia Tymoshenko was no exception (Sverdljuk and Oksamynta, 2006).

Tymoshenko took advantage of her role as a woman and changed her attire, behaviour and speech according to the political context. She was aware that women faced greater resistance than men in politics, and she presented herself as the nation's mother, a national heroine, victim/martyr, faithful Christian, stylish lady, sexy woman, partner and doll. And her appearance made an impression. But she denied being a 'feminist' and attacked the women's movement despite the fact that women's organisations supported her when she was imprisoned in

2001. Tymoshenko did not regard herself as a representative of women's interests, and her party voted against a women's quota in 2003 (which was rejected) and opposed a law on gender equality in 2005 (which was adopted). In 2006, while Tymoshenko was in the opposition, the government adopted an action plan for gender equality up to 2010. During the trial against Tymoshenko, the woman's organisation FEMEN demonstrated with the slogan: 'Tymoshenko and Yanukovych are one' – none of them had done enough for women's rights in Ukraine (Kis, 2007; UNDP BRC, 2010; Limoncelli, 2011).

It is significant for the situation that the representation of women in Ukraine's parliament remained below 10 per cent until 2014. There was only one woman minister during the period Tymoshenko was prime minister. In 2012, there were none, but in 2014 the number had increased to three (14 per cent).

'Communism' in Moldova: Zinaida Greceanîi

Red election winner

'A new colour revolution!', exclaimed reporters when angry young men began throwing stones at the police in Ukraine's neighbouring country, Moldova, during Easter in 2009.[15] The protesters in the capital, Chisinau, accused the communists of 'fraud' because they had won the elections. But there was no 'revolution', though nearly 30,000 people gathered in the streets. International observers noted that the elections were largely 'free and fair'. The police cracked down on protesters and the opposition was unable to get together to provide a common front.

Many were amazed at the developments in Moldova. For the first time since the collapse of communism, a non-reformed Communist Party came to power in an Eastern state. Earlier, Moldova was a province of Romania, then became a Soviet republic and declared independence in 1991. But there was disagreement over whether the country should become a part of Romania again, the relationship with Russia and the border area Transnistria. The majority of the population were Moldovan, with significant Russian and Ukrainian minority groups. Most people belonged to the Russian East Orthodox Church. Moreover, Moldova was Europe's poorest country, with serious economic problems.

After independence, Moldova introduced universal suffrage and popular elections. After a few years, a parliamentary system was introduced, with a president elected by parliament, which was elected by proportional representation. First, non-socialist liberal parties were in power. In 2001, the Communist Party won a majority, with 71 of the 101 seats in parliament. The Communist Party leader, Vladimir Voronin, became president and Vasile Tarlev became prime minister. Although the party was 'communist', it considered itself as part of the European Left and based its policies on 'the common good, justice and the law'. The party supported a multiparty system and economic modernisation and committed itself to work for EU integration at the same time as it maintained a good relationship with Russia.

The government had an absolute majority and was accused of authoritarian rule. But people's living standards improved. In 2005, the communists obtained 55 seats in parliament. Election of the president required a three-fifths majority, and with the support of other parties, Voronin was re-elected and Tarlev continued as prime minister.

Communist woman head of government

In 2002, Zinaida Greceanîi became minister of finance as the only woman in Tarlev's cabinet. She was born in Siberia in 1956, where her parents, Marioara Ursu and Petrea Bujor, were deported because they were Jehovah's Witnesses. Her brother died, but Zinaida and her parents returned to the family's village in the north of Moldova when Zinaida was 12 years old. Her mother's mother had her baptised in the Orthodox Church. She went to school, got a university degree in economics in 1974, joined the Communist Party, married Alexei Greceanîi and had two children. From 1974 to 1994, she held various positions in the county administration, and from 1994, in the Ministry of Finance, where she eventually became director of the budget department. In 2000, she became secretary of state for finance.

Moldova acceded to the CEDAW in 1994, and women's organisations became more active. The representation of women in parliament increased from 9 per cent in 1998 to 21 per cent in 2005. Most were elected from the Communist Party. The government presented a national gender equality plan in 2003 and a gender equality law was adopted in 2006. In 2005, Greceanîi became first deputy prime minister and when Tarlev resigned as prime minister in March 2008, Europe got a communist woman as head of government. She was the second, after Milka Planinc.

When 52-year-old Zinaida Greceanîi became prime minister, she declared that the government would focus on 'freedom of the media, an active dialogue with civil society and an independent judiciary' (Associated Press, 2008), and she increased the number of women ministers from two to five (25 per cent). The cabinet was approved (by 56 votes) and, among other things, followed up on the laws on gender equality.

New parliamentary elections were to be held in a year, and the opposition was sure that it would now be able to beat the communists, even though it lacked a common programme. But the communist cabinet, which mostly consisted of experts, was more competent than the previous one and it had effective media strategies. Zinaida Greceanîi scored high in the polls, and the party attracted youngsters and a multi-ethnic electorate. In the elections in April 2009, the communists won 60 seats in parliament. Greceanîi was re-elected and continued as prime minister, with 24 per cent women in parliament (Mungiu-Pippidi and Munteanu, 2009).

Power and boycott

When street protests did not help, the opposition decided to boycott the presidential election. Voronin could not run again, and as fate would have it, the Communist Party only lacked one vote to get a president elected. Now, no one would give a helping hand, and Greceanîi ran for president twice and lost. According to the constitution, new elections had to be held. In July 2009, the Communist Party got 48 seats in parliament. Greceanîi continued as interim prime minister. But no one could muster enough votes to get a president elected. In September, Voronin and Greceanîi withdrew, and Moldova got an interim president and prime minister until a referendum could be organised in 2010 to change the voting system and then call an election. However, the referendum was unsuccessful, and in the elections in November 2010, the communists only obtained 42 seats in parliament. However, Zinaida Greceanîi was elected. Neither the communists nor the opposition had enough votes to get a president elected, and the deadlocked constitutional situation continued with an interim president and government until March 2012, whereupon an independent male politician was elected president, with 62 votes out of 101 (with 61 needed). The communist opposition boycotted the vote (IPU PARLINE database, 2010).

What difference the fact that Zinaida Greceanîi was a woman made for the boycott of the presidential election by the rightists is not known. An alternative communist man also stood for election as president, but he received no votes at all. The right-wing candidates for president and prime minister were all men, and in the interim cabinet that was established, they were all men except for one. Zinaida Greceanîi continued in parliament, but the representation of women was only 19 per cent in 2014. In the cabinet there were 28 per cent women (5 out of 18), of which two were deputy prime ministers (IPU and UN Women, 2014).

Exceptional Roza Otunbayeva in Kyrgyzstan
From one dictator to another

In April 2010, Kyrgyzstan made the headlines in the world's media. Demonstrations against mismanagement, corruption and high prices spread across the country, and in the capital, Bishkek, many were wounded and killed in confrontations with the police. A woman with glasses and a scarf appeared on television and reported that a transitional government had taken control. It was the opposition leader Roza Otunbayeva, and she was immediately called the 'Thatcher of Central Asia', although there was little that they had in common except their gender. Some chaotic days followed until President Kurmanbek Bakiyev resigned and left the country.[16]

Central Asia was considered an economically and politically underdeveloped region, and four of the five states had authoritarian regimes after independence. But the small mountainous and water-power country Kyrgyzstan was different. The country was poor, with severe economic problems, but after independence in

1991, it went from being a totalitarian state to an emergent democracy, though was more emerging than democratic. A new constitution in 1993 made the country a democratic republic with a presidential system, and Kyrgyzstan became a member of the regional Collective Security Treaty Organisation (CSTO). A large number of non-governmental organisations (NGOs) and political parties were created, and elections were held. Askar Akayev became Kyrgyzstan's first president.

Patron–client relationships, clan politics, corruption and abuse of power were widespread, and no real party system was established. Akayev's rule became increasingly authoritarian and elections were manipulated. In 2005, the opposition launched a 'Tulip Revolution', inspired by the Orange Revolution in Ukraine, and forced Akayev to resign. Roza Otunbayeva was one of the leaders of the revolution.

Kurmanbek Bakiyev from the opposition was elected as the new president, and Roza Otunbayeva became minister of foreign affairs. But Bakiyev soon started to develop a family dictatorship characterised by nepotism, corruption, persecution of political opponents and human rights violations. The country was marked by regional divisions and economic deprivation. A large part of the population found themselves below the poverty line, and many were migrant workers in neighbouring countries.

Active women

In Moslem Kyrgyzstan, women traditionally lived secluded in the religious elite. But nomad women participated both in the production, cooking and child care. Within the traditional roles, women worked as virtual equals with men and elderly women and mothers were respected. But men had higher status. In the Soviet period, education and healthcare for all were introduced. Kyrgyz women got the right to vote in 1918, and they played a more prominent role after independence than women elsewhere in Central Asia. But economic problems led to a decline in social services, and women were hit particularly hard.

Women's organisations of various kinds were created, and several women's parties demanded woman-friendly policies. Patriarchal attitudes persisted, but following the UN Women's Conference in Beijing in 1995, a state commission for women and the family was established and a gender equality programme for 1996–2000 was adopted. In 1997, Kyrgyzstan became party to the CEDAW. Elections based on proportional representation were held and six women entered the legislature in 2000. Two of them represented the Women's Democratic Party and they made the legislature adopt laws on gender equality and domestic violence in 2003.

But in 2005, no women were elected. Under pressure from civil society, a representative of the president on gender issues was appointed in the legislature, and a 30 per cent quota for women in political positions was adopted. As a consequence, Kyrgyzstan went to the top in Central Asia, with 27 per cent women in parliament in 2007. Kyrgystan's Development Strategy for 2007–2010 had further provisions for gender parity in the civil service, and by the end of 2008, 42 per cent of civil servants were women. There were five women ministers (22 per cent), including the vice prime minister of social affairs and the minister of finance, and women held the following posts: chair of the Supreme Court, the Constitutional Court and the National Academy of Sciences (Momaya, 2009b; UNDP BRC, 2010).

Philosopher, politician and diplomat

Roza Isakovna Otunbayeva (named after Rosa Luxemburg) was born in the south, in Osh, in 1950. Her father was a Supreme Court judge, and she graduated in philosophy from Moscow University in 1972 and became professor and head of the philosophy department at the University of Kyrgyzstan. She married B.K. Sadybakasov and had two children, but divorced later. She was an agnostic, and in 1981, she joined the Communist Party and became secretary of the party in the capital. In the years that followed, she alternated between political and diplomatic positions.

At the end of 1980s, she was vice president of the Council of Ministers in the Soviet republic and then went to Moscow, where she became head of the National Commission for the United Nations Educational, Scientific and Cultural Organization (UNESCO), and the first woman in the cabinet of the Soviet Ministry of Foreign Affairs. After independence, she was sent as Kyrgyzstan's ambassador to the US, where she stayed for two years before becoming Minister of Foreign Affairs in Akayev's government. However, she reacted negatively when Akayev's rule developed in an authoritarian direction and went as ambassador to Great Britain. Afterwards, she was a UN observer in Georgia to assist in peace-building.

Otunbayeva came home in 2004 and became involved in politics. She wanted a more democratic system, with a stronger parliament. Along with other members of the opposition, she founded the Ata-Jurt (Fatherland) Party in 2004 in preparation for the 2005 elections, but she could not stand for election herself having lived too long abroad. In 2007, she was elected to the legislature for the Social Democrats and became the opposition leader of the party in 2009 (Collins, 2011; Markelova, 2011).

Advocate for democracy

The choice of Otunbayeva as caretaker president was a compromise. All the men in question were perceived as corrupt and dictatorial. She was the only one who was 'clean'. And people knew that she placed the struggle for democracy above her own ambitions. She wrote in the newspaper about establishing democracy after the revolution: 'Having paid such a high price, we cannot squander the historic opportunity we have to right past wrongs and to build a better state and a more just society ... The path to democracy is not easy, but it is the only way forward' (Otunbayeva, 2011). She was known to be unifying, and in the transitional cabinet, she had four male vice presidents, two ministers, including a woman, and a male head of national security.

The transitional government reintroduced political and civil rights. The legislature, which was the result of fraudulent elections, was dissolved and corrupt judges were deposed. All political parties and a wide array of civil society leaders were brought together to draft a new constitution. It was agreed to transform the country into a parliamentary republic, and on 27 June, a referendum was held, and 90 per cent voted in favour. Otunbayeva was confirmed as interim president until December 2011, without possibility of re-election. She started to ensure that political parties could compete around the country and have access to voters, that there was a free press to provide for national dialogue, and that civic associations had space to advocate their interests. Women were employed in the ministries and received training in business management. Most urgently, the rule of law had to be provided for. Otunbayeva reformed the ministries dealing with security, limited the power of the president and developed a programme against corruption. The problems of trafficking and violence were addressed and a special organisation was established for policewomen.

It takes time to change a culture of corruption, patron–client relationships and contempt for law and order. Bakiyev's supporters opposed the transitional government, and an extremely difficult situation arose, with violent clashes between Uzbeks and Kyrgyz in the south of the country. Houses were burned down, hundreds were killed, thousands were wounded and 400,000 became internally displaced and refugees. It is described as a massive anti-Uzbek pogrom, where the Kyrgyz military and security forces failed to defend Uzbek victims. The transitional government asked Russia for military assistance, but Russia refused. Otunbayeva declared martial law and managed to calm the situation, but the devastation was enormous and the relationship between ethnic groups was clearly aggravated.

In October 2010, parliamentary elections were held. This was perceived as a democratic step forward, but led to an extremely divided parliament, with many extremist Kyrgyz nationalists. The Social Democrat Almazbek Atambayev eventually became head of a coalition government with executive political power. Despite the fact that there were 23 per cent women in parliament, none were included in the cabinet to begin with, but in 2012, there were two women ministers (11 per cent) and in 2014 three (14 per cent).

The Social Democrats were considered to be the strongest supporters of liberal democracy, and in the presidential election in 2011, Atambayev was elected in the first round with a large majority. Otunbayeva resigned – being the first president of Central Asia who did not change or break with the constitution to stay in power. On 8 March, the US State Department gave her the 2011 International Women of Courage Award, and the last thing Otunbayeva did before she left office was to launch a campaign against bride kidnapping, which was an old custom in Kyrgyzstan (Kilner, 2011).

Iveta Radičová, sociologist in Slovakia

Promoting rights

Slovakia is a middle-income country in the heart of Europe with a majority of Catholics. When the country became an independent state after the 'velvet divorce' from the Czech Republic in January 1993, a parliamentary system was introduced, with a parliament elected by proportional representation. Changing the social structure led to major economic problems and a fragmented party landscape, with a dozen political parties. The first prime minister, Vladimír Mečiar, headed several nationalistic-populist coalition cabinets and was accused of being authoritarian. In 1998, a rainbow coalition led by Mikuláš Dzurinda took over with the aim of strengthening democracy, implementing economic reforms and improving the position of minority groups. But after the country became a member of NATO and the EU, a centre-left coalition led by Robert Fico won in 2006, with an emphasis on social welfare.[17]

Slovak women had considerable education, many had paid employment and some took part in politics. Support for CEDAW was confirmed at independence in 1993, and inspired by the UN Women's Conference in Beijing in 1995 and the EU, institutions were established, plans were elaborated and policies were adopted to promote gender equality. But all was only advisory. In 2004, a law against discrimination was passed, but it did not allow quotas, so even if women's organisations put on pressure, women remained under-represented in society's power positions. In parliament, the proportion did not exceed 20 per cent, and in the cabinet, 15 per cent (Bitušíková, 2005; Zvončeková, 2008).

Then, suddenly, something happened. After the elections in 2010, a woman, Iveta Radičová, became prime minister in a centre-right coalition government, despite the fact that the proportion of women in parliament fell to 15 per cent.

Iveta Radičová was born in Bratislava in 1956, studied sociology at the Comenius University, obtained a PhD in philosophy in 1981 and completed her postdoctoral studies at Oxford. She specialised in social issues, family policy and children's rights, and coordinated family research at the Slovak Research Academy for a decade. She married a famous actor, Stano Radič, and had a daughter, but her husband died in 2005. In 1991, she founded an independent centre for analysis of social policies, which she headed at the same time as she taught social studies at the Comenius University. She became a member of the public movement against violence and was known as a defender of women's rights, human rights and the rights of minority groups such as the Romany people and ethnic Hungarians.

From university to politics

In 2005, Iveta Radičová was Slovakia's first woman professor of sociology. That same year, she became minister of labour, family and social affairs in the cabinet of Mikuláš Dzurinda. Then, she was elected to parliament in 2006 for Dzurinda's liberal-conservative, Democratic and Christian Union (SKDU-DS). The party had to go into opposition, and Radičová was deputy leader of the party. In 2009, she ran for president and did surprisingly well, even if she lost. She got 44 per cent of the vote in the final round. It was the first time a woman got so far in a presidential election.

In 2010, Dzurinda withdrew as election leader of the party because of questions about party financing. Radičová defeated the former finance minister and became the new election leader. In June, she stood for election, emphasising tax discipline and the strengthening of the economy. The SKDU-DS was the second-largest party in parliament, with 15 per cent of the vote. When Robert Fico, the leader of the largest party, was unable to form a government, Radičová was asked, and she was approved as prime minister by 79 of the 150 votes. The government was a four-party centre-right coalition, including, among others, the conservative Christian Democratic Movement, which limited the government's action with regards to questions relating to women and gender. Radičová declared: 'We are ready to take responsibility over the country at a time when it is coping with the impact of a deep economic crisis and the irresponsible decisions of our political predecessors' (McLaughlin, 2010). There were 23 per cent women in parliament, but the cabinet only included two women (14 per cent).

Radičová's government improved relations with neighbouring Hungary, which Fico had weakened. A series of tightening measures to stabilise the economy were adopted. Entrepreneurship was encouraged and labour was made more flexible. But Slovakia was not only a member of the EU. In 2009, the country was also part of the Eurozone. The financial crisis struck, and on 11–12 October 2011, the government lost the vote to enable them to support the Eurozone rescue fund by 21 votes. The cabinet had to resign, but served as a caretaker government until new elections in March 2012. Then, Robert Fico's party got an absolute majority and the rescue fund was approved. But the representation of women in parliament was reduced to 19 per cent. In the cabinet there were still two women ministers to begin with, but in 2014 the number was reduced to one (7 per cent).

Patriarchy continues

Transformation controlled by men

Socialism promised to liberate women, but when the ideals were implemented, politics, economics and social conditions were changed, but not patriarchal traditions. Women got education and paid employment, but were underpaid and double-working and remained subordinate to men. Men controlled society, and women's participation was hampered by authoritarian structures, traditional roles and lack of resources. In the countries in the Eastern Bloc, no women rose to the top of the political leadership while communist parties were in power. Yugoslavia tried its own form of socialism, but workers' self-management did not make women heads of state or government either. An exception was Milka

Planinc, who became prime minister, but, typically enough, only in a collective leadership after Tito's death.[18]

The fall of communism led to extensive and sometimes painful transformations. Not only was democracy to be introduced, but also, at the same time, market liberalism. The political system, the economy and social arrangements were changed at a pace and at a scale that led to major problems, especially for vulnerable groups, and women more than men. At the same time as unemployment and poverty increased among women, they lacked political representation and reproductive rights, and woman-friendly measures were eroded or discontinued. The representation women had in legislatures during the communist era was now considered as 'illegitimate' and helped to discredit them as politicians. With the abolition of quotas, representation was dramatically reduced.

As before, the political leaders were men, and gender equality was no major objective. The societal transformations were worked out on men's terms. Nationalism, democratisation and market liberalism dominated the agenda. These questions concerned women to the greatest extent, but they were kept outside the decision-making forums. For the changes to take women and their needs into account, they had to be formulated and carried forward by an independent women's movement. But no such movement existed under communist regimes.

Democratisation gave women increased importance as voters, and new opportunities for participation opened up. With fluid political conditions and a myriad of major and minor parties, women could, in theory, assert themselves. Several Eastern countries established large national assemblies elected by proportional representation, which should have given women relatively good chances of being elected, and there was no lack of interest. However, in practice, it was extremely difficult to break through. The new parties were mostly founded and led by men. Often, they were prominent personalities who had resources and based themselves on patron–client networks consisting exclusively of men. Politics was not for women, according to prevailing opinion, and they were often met with scepticism. They lacked experience, did not have the right skills and were not tough enough. A large number of parties also led to tougher competition. Small parties rarely ventured to nominate a woman. It was mostly larger political parties that sometimes could afford to invest in such a special person.

From allergy to adaptation

The political scientists Richard Matland and Kathleen Montgomery (2003: 19–42) point out that women in Eastern Europe after the fall of communism were allergic to Western-influenced feminism. The communist regimes annexed feminism's goals and rhetoric, and 'equality' was associated with the sham liberation that had been forced upon them in the discredited past. Along with the socialist ideals of the past, gender equality was also rejected, both in principle and in practice. The baby was thrown out with the bath water. But women thus lacked acceptable terms to promote their legitimate demands and they could be accused of being 'man haters', 'anti-family', 'lesbian', 'communist' and 'unpatriotic' when they tried to do it.

Surveys after the fall of communism showed that women, as well as men, were much more traditional in their views of gender roles in Eastern than in Western industrialised countries. It was emphasised in the East that a woman's place was primarily in the home, where she fulfilled her role as housewife and mother, produced future citizens, and strengthened the nation. Many believed the societal transformation was an appropriate occasion for women to return home after communism had forced them into the labour market and weakened the family. Further, economic problems after the fall of communism and the loss of social services in connection with neoliberal reforms forced women to invest in the domestic sphere to a greater extent than before.

Although women participated in the regime changes, they only managed to a small extent to organise themselves to promote their own interests or even define specific 'women's problems'. Gradually, a large number of women's organisations emerged, but these were usually neither 'feminist' nor politically oriented. They were based on the traditional female role. The parties were not subject to active pressure either from the outside or from within to support female candidates, or 'women's issues'. The few women's political parties that were established seldom became particularly effective.

The new states reaffirmed their adherence to the CEDAW, and the large UN Women's Conference in Beijing in 1995 made an impression. Women's networks were established across borders, both regionally and internationally. Centres for women's and gender studies were established at several universities, and national and international conferences were held on women's rights, improvement of the position of women, domestic violence and trafficking.

The rapprochement with the EU led to a 'Europeanisation' of countries in Eastern and Central Europe. This had a significant impact on women's access to political power, according to the political sociologist Maxime Forrest (2011:80–1). 'Europeanisation' led to gender equality being placed on the political agenda, with the adoption of new laws and the establishment of new institutions. Moreover, the feminisation of politics was perceived as a sign of increased commitment to European values. After negotiations with the EU began in 1998, there was a significant increase of women in senior positions in the candidate countries.

Transitional figures

Apart from Milka Planinc, who came to power at the end of communist rule in Yugoslavia, women went to the top in the course of various democratisation processes. Four women became leaders during the difficult and fluid situation in the 1990s. Whether it was determined in advance or not, they remained in office for a very short time as typically transitional figures. For Bergmann-Pohl in the GDR and Indzhova in Bulgaria, this was clear when they were appointed, while Prunskienė in Lithuania and Suchocka in Poland had to resign because of political disagreement – Prunskienė after 10 months and Suchocka after 15.

In the 2000s, there were also some transitional figures, but only two, and they were typically now further to the east: Burjanadze in Georgia and Otunbayeva in Kyrgyzstan. Burjanadze acted for four months in all and Otunbayeva for one-and-three-quarter years before she retired. Theoretically, the other six top leaders could have remained in office longer, but it did not always happen. Vîķe-Freiberga in Latvia was special and sat for eight years. Then, Tymoshenko functioned for nearly three years altogether, Kosor for about 2.5 and Greceanîi for 1.5. Radičová resigned after one-and-a-quarter years, while Grybauskaitė was re-elected for a second term in 2014 after her first term of five years.

After the fall of communism, one quarter of the Eastern countries remained authoritarian and no women went to the top. The democratic countries were relatively evenly distributed between parliamentary, presidential and dual systems, and, with one exception (Georgia), all had both presidents and prime ministers. Five women became top leaders in parliamentary, four in presidential and three in dual systems. Most of the women (seven) were prime ministers, while five were presidents. Compared with the other top leader in the same country, five women acquired the most powerful position, four women got the weakest and three shared power with their colleague.

The type of position, in addition to the time in office, reinforces the impression that the top women were not particularly powerful. The two who were in office the longest both had positions with relatively little power. Planinc was the head of a much-weakened collective central government, while Vîķe-Freiberga had a presidential position that was essentially ceremonial. This was also the case with Bergmann-Pohl. The only woman who obtained the role as a strong president was Burjanadze, and she only acted for a very short time. Otunbayeva also had a certain authority as president, but it was only as an interim leader during an unclear transitional situation. Tymoshenko was prime minister under a strong president. In the dual systems, Prunskienė and Suchocka as prime ministers and Grybauskaitė as president had to share power with male colleagues. Only Indzhova, Kosor, Greceanîi and Radičová were prime ministers in parliamentary systems, where they had considerable executive power, and Indzhova was only temporary.

Overqualified women

The women who went to the top in the Eastern countries after the fall of communism had exceptional backgrounds. None of the women inherited a top position from their family. Their fathers had very different occupations: Supreme Court justice, self-employed businessman, electrician, sailor and forest ranger, as far as we know. There is reason to believe that most of their mothers also had paid employment, but only three of the jobs are noted: saleswoman, pharmacist and nurse. There is no information about significant political activity in the family, except for the fact that Suchocka's grandmother was an MP.

What made the 13 female heads of state and government special were their personal qualifications. All of them except Milka Planinc had university degrees, and eight had PhDs. Planinc was educated at college. Four of the women were economists, four specialised in philosophy and the social sciences, three were lawyers, one was a physician, and one was a management expert. With the exception of Vîķe-Freiberga, who was educated in Canada, all the others received their education under communist rule, some with additional studies abroad.

All the women had a profession. Some even started to work before they finished their education. So they had 10, 20 or even 30 years of experience in various occupations, and many had senior positions. Five of the top women leaders were university professors, four were directors, one was a principal and one was a researcher. In addition, one was a journalist and one was a full-time party leader (in a Yugoslavian republic).

The women had lived for quite some time before they rose to the top. Eight were more than 50 years old, with Vîķe-Freiberga as the oldest. She was 62 when she became president. The others were in their 40s, with the exception of Burjanadze, who was only in her 30s. Most had a husband and children. Ten of the women got married, often with men with intellectual professions, but three were later divorced. One was married and divorced twice. Ten of the women had children (one, or more often two, while one had three), of which one was a single mother. Most probably, the women were completely or partially double-working during periods before they became heads of state or government.

Professionals

The Communist Party regime prevented most of the future top women leaders from pursuing a party-political career. The only one was Planinc. She became a partisan at an early age and worked in the Communist Party all her life, but at the level of a republic, before she became prime minister at the national level. Tymoshenko joined the communist youth movement, and Greceanîi, Grybauskaitė and Prunskienė were also members of the Communist Party, but only Greceanîi after independence. In the communist era, Bergmann-Pohl and Suchocka were members of what were called 'satellite' parties of the Communist Party (the Christian Democratic Party in the GDR and the Democratic Party in Poland).

After independence, the women joined different and sometimes varying parties. Three participated in the creation of their own. But if they were party members, they were not really party workers. Only three were national leaders before or at the same time as they rose to the top (Tymoshenko, Kosor, Radičová). The women's political activity took place first of all in the parliaments and governments. Nine of the top women were MPs, while three became presidents or vice presidents. Eight were ministers, some in several fields, and three were deputy prime ministers. Here, party affiliation was important, but professional background also weighed heavily.

Some of the women went to the top primarily due to their academic and professional careers. Vîķe-Freiberga was elected as an independent intellectual and cultural worker. Grybauskaitė also stood for election as an independent even though she had held political office before, and Indzhova headed a 'non-party' government. Kosor and Radičová were recruited to the parliaments and governments on the basis of their academic performance and only then joined parties.

The women participated in parties with varying, sometimes indefinable and changing, colours, marked by the situation and key actors. As the point of departure, the parties spanned a wide range: four belonged to the Left and centre-left, three to the centre and three to the Right and centre-right. But, in practice, the political emphasis often turned out to be in the centre, because it was necessary to establish government alliances.

Coincidences

Three of the women rose to the top just before or in connection with a change of regime (Planinc, Bergmann-Pohl and Prunskienė). The others did so afterwards. Nevertheless, the women obtained positions in a situation where very few women did. After the fall of communism and the abolition of quotas, the Eastern countries were clearly placed lower than the West with regards to women's representation in parliaments and cabinets – actually, lower than the world average. And although representation increased somewhat over time, the Eastern countries clearly lagged behind the West up to 2014.

Often, mere coincidences gave women a chance. Tito's death, the fall of the Wall and the Orange Revolution contributed to the sudden promotion of Planinc, Bergmann-Pohl and Tymoshenko to top positions. And Burjanadze, Indzhova and Otunbayeva functioned temporarily in positions that unexpectedly became vacant. Suchocka and Vīķe-Freiberga were brought in as compromise candidates because the men could not agree among themselves. Prunskienė became prime minister because she had knowledge that was invaluable for a new cabinet that was suddenly created, and Greceanîi and Kosor stepped in when their predecessors abruptly withdrew. Grybauskaitė and Radičová were those who were elected in the most 'normal' way.

Although coincidences played a role, women had to be available and be considered as qualified and acceptable. They had to be active and seize chances that arose. But the fact that women were more modest and less greedy for power than their male colleagues could also be an advantage. They could play important roles as neutral and stabilising figures in transitional phases. But they did not come to power in deadly earnest. They were allowed to sit for a while because they were not seen as a threat.

Who might have rejected or lost a top position is not known. Burjanadze said that she would not run for president, but later did so anyway, in 2013. After 1990, there were 65 women who ran in 46 presidential elections in 22 Eastern countries and lost. Six women (Greceanîi, Indzhova, Kosor, Prunskienė, Radičová and

Suchocka) who had top positions tried to acquire others, but failed. Tymoshenko was prime minister twice, but lost the battle for the presidency.

Various profiles

Women were able to assert themselves in politics, even though it was only to a certain extent, and those at the top did not always manage to achieve much in practice. This was true in general and particularly with regard to women's issues. Some of the top leaders were in office for only a short time (Bergmann-Pohl, Burjanadze, Indzhova), while others had more than enough to deal with, with urgent economic and national problems (Prunskienė and Radičová). Others shared the widespread view that women politicians should not promote women's interests (Planinc, Tymoshenko and Suchocka).

Often, there was no basis that could support the top leaders as women, either inside or outside the formal political institutions. It took time to establish an active women's movement and women's organisations had little contact with political parties. During reunification, women's groups in the GDR actively attempted to influence policies, but with little result. After she resigned as prime minister, Prunskienė made efforts to build up a women's base. Later, parties in Croatia established women's sections that contributed to the strengthening of the representation of women, and Kosor led the section in her party. But other top leaders were not active in this way.

Planinc, Prunskienė, Suchocka and Tymoshenko were the only women in their cabinets. Prunskienė and Suchocka tried to get another woman in addition to themselves, but this was turned down. Indzhova, however, managed to have one, and Otunbayeva also had a woman colleague. Radičová had two, while Kosor reduced the number in her cabinet from three to two, then one. Although she was not a member of the cabinet, Grybauskaitė increased the number from one to two. The exception was Greceanîi, who had 25 per cent women cabinet members.

At the same time, the representation of women in the parliaments was also low, on average, one sixth, when the women top leaders rose to power. In Georgia, Poland and Ukraine, there were less than 10 per cent on the whole, while Kyrgyzstan, Croatia, Moldova and Slovakia had about a quarter.

Although they would not consider themselves as 'feminists', some of the top leaders nevertheless promoted the interests of women. As presidents, Vîķe-Freiberga and Grybauskaitė supported women's rights, while Kosor and Otunbayeva as heads of government helped to give women paid employment and positions and fought against violence of different kinds. Greceanîi followed up broad woman-friendly policies while she was in power.

As top leaders, some of the women conformed to the prevailing male culture, while others pursued policies than benefited both men and women. The atmosphere changed over the years, and all of them came to power in the 2000s, when attitudes towards female politicians and woman-friendly policies were more positive.

No women at the top: Russia

In 12 Eastern countries, including the former GDR and the former Yugoslavia, women went to the top in politics. But in most of the former Eastern Bloc countries, 18 in all, they did not. These included Russia, four Central Asian republics, Albania, Armenia, Azerbaijan, Belarus, Bosnia, the Czech Republic, Estonia, Hungary, Macedonia, Montenegro, Romania, Serbia and Slovenia. Of these, eight had authoritarian regimes and the others were mostly emerging democracies.

In Russia, the years following the collapse of the Eastern Bloc were characterised by political and economic turmoil.[19] The country still had the world's largest territory, with vast resources, particularly oil and gas, and a population of about 140 million. There were many different ethnic and religious groups, but most were Russian and Orthodox Christians.

The dissolution of the Soviet Union created tensions due to different views on the country's development and the formation of powerful 'oligarchs' in connection with rapid privatisation. There were constitutional crises, economic collapse, armed conflict and war.

Russia was established as a federal republic, with a presidential system. The president is directly elected and appoints the prime minister and government with consent of the lower house (the Duma). The lower house is elected using a mixed electoral system, while the upper house (Federation Council) is indirectly elected. It was not easy to change the culture and institutions after 75 years of Soviet rule, and the regime acquired an authoritarian character. As the economy gradually improved under President Putin, the national policies were also more marked by superpower tendencies and an emphasis on military strength.

Regimes change, oppression of women persists

The status of women was no less problematic after the dissolution of the Soviet Union than before. They were described as breadwinners at home and outcasts in politics. The lack of social support forced women into the labour market, where they were poorly paid, less than men. Although women had more education than men on average, they remained a minority in higher positions. Most were double-working. The family was weakened and violence increased. During the 1990s, several state bodies were established for women, children and the family, but they were weak and inefficient. A number of independent women's organisations were founded, but they encountered considerable resistance from a socially conservative population that lacked a culture with an active civil society. The Russian Women's Party obtained 8 per cent of the vote at the legislative elections in 1993. But then the party fell below the limit for the minimum percentage of votes required for representation in 1999, with only 2 per cent.

Generally, the representation of women in the legislature and the cabinet was very low, 'scarcely visible' according to Russian feminists. There were no women among leaders of the major political parties. An exception was the Union of Right Forces, a liberal opposition party. In 2014, the representation of women in the lower house was only 14 per cent, and in the upper house, not more than 8 per cent. Usually, a symbolic woman was appointed to the cabinet as minister of social affairs. In 2012, there were three women ministers in all (16 per cent), but in 2014 it was reduced to two (7 per cent).

Official photo of the Prime Minister of New Zealand, Helen Clark, in 2005. She was prime minister from 1999–2008. Afterwards she became administrator of the United Nations Development Programme.
Image: http://en.wikipedia.org

Chapter Ten

Western industrial countries (II): womanpower and defeat

The Western countries had the majority of women top leaders during the 1990s and later. Eight new countries got women as national leaders, and five had more than one. Of the seven countries that had women top leaders earlier (Germany included), four got one more. In all, 17 women rose to the top in this part of the world during the period 1990–2010.[1] However, it was no straightforward or consistent development, despite the relatively peaceful conditions, high living standards, well-established democracies and increasing participation of women in politics in general.[2]

Irish surprise: Mary Robinson and Mary McAleese

Against all odds

It attracted attention both nationally and internationally when the conservative Catholic Ireland chose a woman, and, in addition, a radical advocate for women, as president in 1990.[3] People outside of the country knew little about women's political activity on the island: that women participated in the uprisings against British royal power, were active in political and intellectual circles in the 19th and 20th centuries, and took action in the 1960s and beyond against poor economic conditions, rape, abuse of women and restrictions on contraception and abortion. Women were also involved in the political–religious conflict in the north of the island. Some fought and were imprisoned, while others marched for peace or made their mark in political parties.

Mary Robinson was warned in advance: if she ran for president, she had no chance of being elected. A woman had never run before. The position was usually viewed as a reward for loyal service to one of the major parties and Mary Robinson insisted on running as an independent (O'Callaghan, 1996: 262). The governing party, Fianna Fáil, had never lost a presidential election, and now the party presented the experienced and popular

Minister of Defence Brian Lenihan. In Ireland's parliamentary system, the president had little power. The main task was to protect the constitution. But the position enjoyed considerable prestige. And to the surprise of many, a woman newcomer was elected.

Mary Robinson, born Bourke, grew up in a well-off Catholic family characterised by high performance, independent thinking and social responsibility. Both parents, Aubrey and Tessa Bourke, were physicians, and Aubrey took up practice at home. Tessa was involved in her medicine, but few patients trusted a woman and she reared the family. They had five children. Mary was born in 1944 as the middle child and only girl. Seeing poor patients early in her life gave her a desire to promote greater equality. She was talented and ambitious and was sent to boarding school in Dublin and Paris. She wanted to follow in her grandfather's footsteps and become a lawyer. Along with her brothers, she was sent to Ireland's top university, Trinity College, to study law as one of only a few women, with special permission from the Archbishop because the institution was Protestant.

Mary graduated with the highest grade at the same time as she was active in student associations. After graduation, she went to Harvard University in the US. The period was marked by the Vietnam War and the civil rights movement and the stay became a watershed for a young Irish woman because of the debates about socialism, equality and rights, poverty, race, and gender. Mary Bourke took a master's degree in law while she was politically engaged and saw how legislation could be used to promote social change (O'Callaghan, 1996: 257–8; Horgan, 1997: 13–28; Siggins, 1997: 18–44).

Young, liberal, lawyer and woman

In 1969, Mary Bourke got a part-time job as a professor of constitutional and criminal law at Trinity College. It was a prestigious temporary position as a junior lecturer and the appointment of Bourke was unusual because of both her gender and her age. She also addressed an unusual theme: reproductive rights. At the same time, she ran as the first woman candidate for one of the three seats that the university had in the Senate. In the Senate, 11 were appointed by the prime minister, six elected by the universities and 43 by a panel representing most sectors of Irish society.

It happened by chance that Mary Bourke ran. Senators were mostly older men, and when Bourke argued in a discussion that there should be representatives of different generations, her friends turned towards her and said that she therefore had to run. She ran as an independent and introduced herself as 'young, liberal, lawyer and woman' (Horgan, 1997: 24; Siggins, 1997: 54). It was a sensation when she got the third seat. She became the youngest senator and one of only four women in the assembly (7 per cent). She got to sit in the Senate for 20 years.

The year after, Mary Bourke married Nick Robinson, a Protestant fellow student who became a lawyer, artist and writer. He also became a quiet, but important, supporter of his wife's political activities. They had three children, a girl and two boys. A nursemaid, who took care of Mary when she was a child, helped the family so that Mary could continue with her work and politics, although it was certainly rather laborious to combine the different roles.

Radical 'enfant terrible'

It was a special time. Fianna Fáil had been in power for decades. The economy went well, and the flow of emigrants decreased. In 1973, a coalition of Fine Gael and Labour took over, and, later, the political blocs alternated.[4] Regarding security, Ireland was neutral, but it joined the European Union (EU), which resulted in economic benefits, but also social requirements. At the same time, TV and reforms in the Vatican brought new ideas into the conservative Irish society and helped energise and focus the women's movement. In Northern Ireland, tensions led to protests and increased violence.

Mary Robinson worked tirelessly to liberalise Irish society, which comprised 4 million people. As for feminism, she did not belong to the most extreme and was criticised by women's activists for this. But she was conscious of the discrimination that took place, and became leader of the Women's Political Association. The Senate had little political influence, but could be used as a rostrum. She focused on human rights and pursued a kind of guerrilla activity in which she championed women's causes: legalisation of family planning, divorce and homosexuality; abolition of illegitimacy; equal pay; and social and pension rights. Although the proposals obtained little support, they attracted attention. And she became an increasingly familiar figure in the Supreme Court, where she promoted family and women's issues to change legal practice.

Twenty frustrating years passed as a radical *enfant terrible*. In the mid-1970s, Mary Robinson joined the small Labour Party and became a member of the City Council of Dublin. She also ran as a candidate for the House of Representatives in 1977 and 1981, but lost, although it is uncertain as to whether it was due to lack of support for the party, that she was a woman or that she was too unconventional and liberal. Women won full voting rights in 1922, when Ireland became independent, and elections were based on proportional representation. But in 1977 and 1981, women obtained only six (4 per cent) and 10 (6 per cent) of the seats in total. However, Ireland became party to the United Nations (UN) Convention on the Elimination of all forms of Discrimination Against Women (CEDAW) in 1985.[5]

Unusual campaign

Mary Robinson fell out with Labour, and in 1989, she decided to leave the Senate to concentrate on her law practice. To her surprise, Labour asked her to run in the presidential election in 1990. Elections had not been held in 1976 and 1983. The other parties accepted the Fianna Fáil candidate uncontested. Labour had not presented any candidate before, but now the party wanted to assert itself, provoke debate about important issues and create competition so that the position was not only used to reward faithful toilers in the two main parties. Robinson was young and energetic, known throughout the country and associated with forces that wanted reform. On her side, Robinson thought the position would be an opportunity to give a voice to the voiceless: women, young people, the poor, the disabled and the unemployed (Opfell, 1993: 185). Parties and politics were strongly male-dominated, and in the Fianna Fáil cabinet, there was only one woman.

Mary Robinson ran as an independent even though she had the support of Labour. She conducted the most unusual election campaign in Irish political history. It lasted more than six months (compared with the usual three weeks) and brought her all over the country, even to the most remote corners. Robinson promised to change the presidential role: the president should be more active and work for an open, manifold, generous and tolerant Ireland. She also criticised the 'patriarchal, male dominated Catholic Church, which sought to keep women down' (O'Callaghan, 1996: 262), and opponents called her the 'red horror'. Women supported Mary Robinson as the only woman candidate, and when a minister criticised her for mismanaging the family, several women went to her defence. And although she had resisted at first, Robinson agreed to be the subject of a number of magazine stories featuring her in domestic settings, such as the kitchen (Jensen, 2008: 155). Further, it was to Robinson's advantage that the candidate for Fine Gael was weak, and the Fianna Fáil candidate was caught in an obvious lie. In the elections, Mary Robinson obtained 39 per cent of the first choices, while Brian Lenihan got 44 per cent. When the second votes for the third candidate were divided between the first two according to the electoral system, Robinson ended as the winner (Horgan, 1997: 124–63; Siggins, 1997: 118–44).[6]

Popular president

When 46-year-old Mary Robinson became president, it was a shock to the establishment in Ireland. In her inauguration speech, she said that she wanted to be president for all the people, to represent:

> A fifth province, which is not anywhere here nor there, north or south, east or west. It is a place within each of us – that place that is open to the other, that swinging door which allows us to venture out and others to venture in. I would like to be a symbol of reconciling and healing. (Robinson, quoted in O'Callaghan, 1997: 263; see also Siggins, 1997: 148–49)

Robinson wished to represent all the 70 million people of Irish descent in the whole world, give people self-confidence as Irish and, at the same time, work for international protection and the promotion of human rights.

She changed the presidency from belonging to the political parties to belonging to the people. She insisted that she was placed above politics, at the same time as she was unstoppably political. But she focused on universal values and rights. She also made the presidency more accessible, collaborative and inclusive than before. She went where presidents had never been before and invited the most marginalised to the president's residence. She was the president of the weak: homeless, disabled, women activists and Irish abroad. She worked for reconciliation between ethnic groups in the north and improved relations with England. She travelled tirelessly. In the course of a year, she gave 700 speeches. While she was president, she visited Northern Ireland 18 times (more than all her predecessors combined); England, 15 times; and the US, 13 times. She was the first Irish president who visited the British monarch. She also went to the Third World, to countries affected by humanitarian disasters, such as Rwanda and Somalia. Afterwards, she wrote the book, *A voice for Somalia* (Robinson, 1992).

Mary Robinson took greater liberty than her predecessors when it came to expressing herself publicly, speaking to and on behalf of the citizens. This led to friction between the president and especially the Fianna Fáil government, but Mary Robinson was persistent, visible and influential. At the end of her term, she had greater support from the public than any other elected leader in Europe and, in addition, extraordinary moral authority.

A radical female president was elected out of a desire for change, and she became a force in this direction. She was an inspiration for other women and affected the parties even though she had no special resources. In the general elections in 1992, Labour doubled their number of seats, while Fianna Fáil had the worst result in decades. Labour participated in different coalition governments,[7] and although the representation of women in the leadership of the parties did not exceed one quarter and there were only 23 women (14 per cent) in the House of Representatives and one to two women ministers, comprehensive legislation was introduced to strengthen women's welfare. Homosexuality was decriminalised. Contraceptives were made available and divorce was allowed. Abortion was not permitted, but it was possible to get information and travel overseas to have the intervention carried out.

In the elections in 1997, the two major parties did well, while the support for Labour diminished and Fianna Fáil formed a coalition government. The representation of women in the House of Representatives was reduced to 20 (12 per cent), but three women joined the cabinet (21 per cent). Mary Robinson resigned as president shortly before her term expired and was appointed as the UN Commissioner for Human Rights. In the following years, she had an extensive international career.[8]

Mary number two

The election of a new president in 1997 turned out to be a 'women's competition'. There was growing resentment against traditional male politicians, and Mary Robinson had shown what a talented woman could do. There were more candidates than ever, five in all, including four women: Fine Gael presented Mary Banotti, a member of parliament (MP), and Fianna Fáil presented Mary McAleese, the pro-vice chancellor of the University of Belfast. In addition, there were three independent candidates: a woman singer and two human rights activists (a man and a woman). In both political parties, the internal fight for nomination was fierce. In Fine Gael, there were two women contestants, while 46-year-old Mary McAleese surprisingly won the battle in Fianna Fáil against two established male politicians.

Fianna Fáil wanted desperately to win back the presidency. However, it was difficult to find a suitable candidate, one who could win. Mary Robinson had changed the presidency into a much more active and visible role. Fianna Fáil was criticised because the party gave the position to old-timers who were not particularly enthusiastic. The two male candidates seemed to fit this pattern. Both were elderly, represented much the same views and had pursued long political careers. They had also made mistakes and gained enemies.

Mary McAleese was different: a newcomer, but educated, likeable and trustworthy. She was the first woman pro-vice chancellor of the University of Belfast. She had done a brilliant job and her supporters did extensive networking in the party before the nomination. Some people said it was worrying that McAleese was from Northern Ireland, but she had lived during long periods in the south, and with her background, was particularly suited to narrow the gap between the different parts of the island. She ran with a special emphasis on peace and reconciliation. Launching the election campaign, she said: 'My dream is for a presidency which will capture and hold in its embrace this large, colourful family, which is the Irish people' (BBC News, 1997). In the first round, McAleese obtained 42 votes, while the two men respectively got 49 and 21. In the second round, McAleese received 62 votes, while the male opponent attained 48.

With the support of the country's largest party, Mary McAleese won the presidential election, with 45 per cent of the first choices and well over half of the second. She came forth with a high profile and with her experience as a TV journalist, did well in the debates. The only male candidate came last, with less than 5 per cent of the vote (McCarthy, 1999: 152–217; McGarry, 2008: 143–85).

Outsider in the North and South

Mary McAleese benefited from her predecessor's popularity, even if they belonged to different political camps. Like Mary Robinson, Mary McAleese was a lawyer, a professor at Trinity College and supported liberal causes. But she had another background socially and geographically. Mary McAleese was born in 1951 in a Catholic working-class family in a predominantly Protestant area of Belfast. The family came from the countryside to find work in the city and moved around a bit. Finally, her father, Paddy Leneghan, managed to buy a pub, and as the oldest of nine children, Mary helped her mother, Claire, take care of younger siblings. Her father was interested in history and had a lot of books. Mary went to convent school and enjoyed the work, but as a girl and a Catholic, she felt excluded and marginalised in the surrounding world. She wanted to study law, but when she said so, the family priest explained to her that she could not because she was a girl. This made her otherwise quiet-mannered mother pull the chair from under the priest and scream: 'You – out!' And then she told Mary: 'And you – ignore!' (McAleese, 1999: 46).

Mary did so well in school that she became the first in her family to study law at university. But the violence in Belfast increased. Several acquaintances were killed. Mary's deaf brother was accosted and the house was peppered with bullets. In 1972, the family had to leave the pub and their home. Mary completed law school in 1973 and became a lawyer both in Northern Ireland and the Irish Republic. But the hateful atmosphere in Belfast made her move to Dublin in 1975. Here, she got a permanent full-time job at Trinity College and was drawn into discussions about equality, human rights and gender awareness. At the same time, she married her childhood sweetheart Martin, who was a dentist and accountant, and they had three children, a girl and twin boys. Mary McAleese worked as a lawyer, professor and journalist on radio and TV. She worked to have the law prohibiting homosexuality repealed and to strengthen prisoners' rights. She participated in the Fianna Fáil party and the Catholic Church. In 1987, she ran as a candidate for Fianna Fáil in the general elections, but lost and fell out with the party.

There was an outcry when Mary McAleese and her family returned to Belfast the same year, and McAleese became head of the legal department at Queens University. A woman, a Catholic and former Fianna Fáil representative gave the establishment shivers. The situation was not helped by the outspoken criticism by Mary McAleese of the conditions in Northern Ireland while she was in the South, and the fact that at Queens, she ousted an established male senior university teacher who was a Protestant and a member of the Ulster Unionist Party. It had been difficult to get applicants for the position, so there were just two: a man who had taught law at Queens for 19 years, and a woman who had taught criminology at Trinity for nine years. But the pro-vice chancellor insisted that McAleese was best qualified for the position. On the job, McAleese invited colleagues home, kept a low, friendly profile and emphasised diplomacy, fairness and competence. In 1994, she got her reward. 'Mother Mary' was the youngest of three university pro-vice chancellors, the first woman and the second Catholic. She also became the director of the TV Channel 4 and the Northern Irish power company (McAleese, 1997; McCarthy, 1999: 7–151; McGarry, 2008: 45–142).

'Love in chaos'

It is difficult to place Mary McAleese politically. She is both radical and conservative and sometimes changes her point of view. As president, she supported values that her predecessor, Mary Robinson, also sought to promote: equality and justice, social inclusion, reconciliation, and anti-sectarianism. For many years, she fought for peace in Northern Ireland, and in 1997, she published the book *Love in chaos – spiritual growth and search for peace in Northern Ireland* (McAleese, 1997).

Mary McAleese was Ireland's first president from Northern Ireland. The slogan she chose as president, 'Building bridges', aimed particularly at the relationship between Catholics and Protestants. As president, she travelled frequently to Northern Ireland. She highlighted important days for both faiths and also took communion in the Anglican Church. McAleese thought that the peace process had a clear relation to the modern-day embrace of women's rights, stating:

> It is absolutely no accident that the peace and reconciliation, and indeed the economic progress, that eluded us generation after generation for hundreds of years, has at last come to pass in an Ireland where the talents of women are now flooding every aspect of life as never before. (Merkelson and Swift, 2010)

McAleese was deeply involved in the debate in the Catholic Church on the role of women. She had a much closer relationship to the Church and was less radical than Mary Robinson. She was against both abortion and divorce, but she deviated from the Church in her view on homosexuality and women priests.

It was a male supporter who made Mary McAleese run for president. And as president, she became so popular that no one would run against her after her first seven-year term. In 2004, she was 're-elected' as an independent for another period without further ceremony. She continued to build bridges and travelled on state visits to the US, Russia and China. She met the Pope and invited Queen Elizabeth to Ireland as the first British Monarch since 1911. But she could also express strong views, as when she criticised the Central Bank of Ireland for its role during the financial crisis (McGarry, 2008: 186–310).

In 2004, *Forbes* rated Mary McAleese as number 33 of the 100 most powerful women in the world. In 2005, she went up to number 21, but then she fell down to the bottom half of the list: number 55 in 2006, 58 in 2007, 74 in 2008, 69 in 2009 and 64 in 2010. There were no more than 14 per cent women in the House of Representatives. In the Senate, women amounted to 22 per cent, and there were three women (21 per cent) in the cabinet. This was far less than in most Western countries. When her period expired in 2011, McAleese could not be re-elected. A man from the Labour Party took over, and the representation of women increased to 16 per cent in the House and 32 per cent in the Senate. But in 2014, there were only two women ministers in the cabinet (14 per cent).

Edith Cresson: caught in a French trap

Country of Joan of Arc

It is said that Mary Robinson and Mary McAleese could exercise power as women because they initially had very little power. The story of Edith Cresson shows how difficult it can be for a woman to really penetrate the corridors of power.[9]

France has been a European superpower for several centuries, and in the 1990s, had about 60 million inhabitants in Europe in addition to colonies, possessions and external territories on other continents. Formally, the country had a parliamentary system with dual executive power, but, in practice, the government largely worked as a presidential system. The president was directly elected and appointed the prime minister after nomination by a majority in parliament. During almost the whole of the Fifth Republic (from 1958), the National Assembly was elected by majority vote in single-member constituencies, which favoured men.

In 1991, Edith Cresson became prime minister, chosen and appointed by the president, but before a year had passed, she was dismissed without ceremony by the same president. She was abused by her party friends, lynched by the press and ruined by television – as the chief editor of the newspaper *Nouvel Observateur*, Elisabeth Schemla, describes in her book *Edith Cresson, la femme piégée* (the trapped woman) (Schemla, 1993).

The country was predominantly Catholic, with centralised power and large class differences, but it was also the country of Joan of Arc, the French Revolution and the Declaration of Women's Rights by Olympe de Gouges. Here, the feminist pioneer Simone de Beauvoir lived and wrote and the students rebelled and demanded democracy in 1968. And then the first woman top leader was treated as a pariah in 1992? Had the French learned nothing?

The president's mascot

When Edith Cresson became prime minister, she was 57 years old and had a long political career. She was born in 1934 in a bourgeois Catholic milieu in Paris. Her father, Gabriel Campion, was a tax inspector and member of the Socialist Party. Her mother, Jacqueline, was strict, conservative and mundane, and hired an English nanny for her daughter. When World War II broke out, Campion was posted in the French Embassy in Belgrade. He returned to Paris, but settled his family in the Alps, where Edith was enrolled in a convent boarding school, Sacre Coeur. After the war, she went to a religious school in Paris. Edith's younger brothers were sent to school in England. Edith was attached to her father and rebelled against her mother and the bourgeois milieu she came from. She wanted to be free and independent. At the age of 17, she was admitted to one of France's most prestigious schools – the Haute École Commerciale (HEC) – where she earned a business degree. She got a job in a research office while she oriented herself in politics. In 1959, she married a businessman, Jacques Cresson, had two daughters and moved to Nantes. She hired a maid and undertook a doctorate in demography, studying the lives of Breton farm women.

They moved back to Paris in 1965. Edith Cresson worked as a consultant in private industry and did well. She had a very active life, with both paid work and children. In addition, she did volunteer work for the Socialist Party in the presidential election in 1965. She did not think of becoming a politician herself, but in 1967, she became acquainted with the almost 20-year-older Socialist Party leader François Mitterrand. He became her hero and she his protégée, 'my little soldier', as he called her. He was particularly impressed with her intelligence, energy and pragmatism. She joined the Socialist Party in 1971, and in 1975, Mitterrand's 'mascot' was given the responsibility for students and youth in the party secretariat and became a member of the executive committee. She ran twice for election to the Chamber of Deputies and lost, but became mayor of Thuré, south-west of Paris, in 1977 and member of the European Parliament in 1979 (Opfell, 1993: 200–6; Schemla, 1993: 31–49; Liswood, 2007: 120–3).

When the Socialist Party came to power in 1981, Edith Cresson became a member of the National Assembly. She was mayor of Châtellerault, a conservative stronghold not far from Thuré, and was the first woman to become minister of agriculture, of external trade, of industry and of European affairs under the three Socialist Party prime ministers: Pierre Mauroy (1981–84), Laurent Fabius (1984–86) and Michel Rocard (1988–91). The tasks were challenging, and even more so when a woman was in charge. Cresson had to be not only skilful, but also thick-skinned and tough. The landscape was strongly male-dominated and marked by patriarchal norms. Few women managed to enter the leaderships of the political parties or acquire high political positions. There were only 6 per cent women in the National Assembly, elected by majority vote, and 3 per cent in the indirectly elected Senate. In the Socialist Party cabinet, there were a handful of women ministers, 10–20 per cent, while the conservative cabinet only had 4 per cent. As a minister, Cresson was exposed to resistance and harassment due to her gender. She was, among other things, excluded from the prime minister's regular breakfast meetings with ministers, and in 1990, she retired as minister for European affairs because the government would not pursue the active industrial policy that she believed was necessary for France to assert itself in international competition.[10]

New thrust

Mitterrand was the first – and only – socialist who became president in the Fifth Republic. The Left had a majority in the National Assembly for five years, but in the elections in 1986, the Right won, and Mitterrand had to govern with the conservative Jacques Chirac as prime minister for two years. In 1988, Mitterrand was re-elected as president. His coalition strengthened its position in the National Assembly, but did not have a majority alone. Michel Rocard was prime minister, but he and Mitterrand partly disagreed, and Rocard had difficulties getting proposals through in the National Assembly.

There was a recession and unemployment. The voters did not trust politicians, and the Socialist Party struggled to transform its policy from nationalisation to market economy. The party was also affected by political scandals, and the internal dissension and rivalry grew as Mitterrand became older. He wanted a 'new thrust' that could generate enthusiasm and support.

Despite protests, France lagged behind other European countries, including the Catholic and Latin, with regard to women in politics. After the French Revolution, men got the right to vote (in 1848), but not women, in spite of the

Declaration of Women's Rights and women's participation in the revolution, the Paris Commune and World War I. A women's rights movement emerged in the late 1800s and women gained access to education and economic activities. But political rights were denied. Women demonstrated, and in 1936, the Socialist Prime Minister Léon Blum appointed three women as deputy ministers. Then, universal suffrage was proclaimed by the Provisional Government of Alger in 1944 and included in the new constitution in 1946.

But government was still centralised and the male elite was strong. Conservative tendencies made themselves felt and political life was characterised by hard antagonisms between Right and Left, the well-off and underprivileged. In 1949, Simone de Beauvoir wrote *The second sex* (2010 [1949]) and an activist feminism asserted itself, especially on the Left. Following the student and labour rebellion in 1968, women's groups addressed issues such as abortion, divorce, abuse and rape. Women's occupational activity was greater than in other European countries, but in politics, they were kept down. And here, the Socialist Party was no exception, even though the party introduced quotas in non-legislative elections in the 1970s[11] and France became party to the CEDAW under the Socialists.

When it was so hard to get access, women had to be appointed directly to political office by male leaders. This was called 'co-optation from above'. Mitterrand brought forth a number of women in that way. He was one of the few men in the political milieu who had faith in women's ability to govern. When Rocard resigned in 1991, Mitterrand launched Edith Cresson as prime minister.

There had been three male Socialist prime ministers since 1981, and according to Mitterrand, there were no more men who met the requirements. And he wanted a prime minister who would promote his own policies, with competence in trade and business, a person he knew well, and was friends with – an intelligent and brave person who could rise above the petty, vicious quarrels within the party and give it a new and dynamic thrust (Opfell, 1993: 208; Schemla, 1993: 73–93).

Alone and different

Mitterrand had reason to believe that it was a smart move to appoint Edith Cresson. He proved himself as a radical and modern leader, and women voters in particular responded with enthusiasm. The polls showed that 73 per cent of the population was positive. But Cresson was aware of the male chauvinism of the 'Barons' of the Socialist Party. She asked Mitterrand to appoint one of them as prime minister instead of her (Schemla, 1993: 81–5). But the president refused. As Cresson foresaw, the 'Barons' immediately responded negatively when an 'outsider' came and took 'their' leadership position. And the arrogant male opinion formers in the media condemned her even before she opened her mouth. They overlooked her intelligence, knowledge and experience. As Cresson noted: 'If a man was elected to such a position it is because he is competent … A woman who has been elected for ten years at the National Assembly, at the "Conseil General", that is to say at the regional level, who is the mayor of a city, it is as if she were coming out of nowhere' (Liswood, 2007: 47). According to the media, Cresson was just a media bluff from an aging president and a poor puppet of her party colleague Pierre Bérégovoy, who was the strong man in the government. And the intelligent men must not hand over control to a pitiful woman without ideas, it was claimed (Opfell, 1993: 209; Schemla, 1993: 93–131).

They did not. The new prime minister got many 'Barons' in her cabinet. In principle, she was supposed to select her ministers herself, but there was a cut-throat battle for ministerial office. Mitterrand rejected her proposals and put his weight in the bowl to get the most experienced, although the aim was a 'new thrust' (Schemla, 1993: 86–91; Jensen, 2008: 179). The cabinet included five female ministers, one more than before, but, in practice, Edith Cresson was essentially alone and 'different', without supporters either in the government or in the party apparatus.

Cresson wanted to revitalise French industry, strengthen workers' qualifications, decentralise state power and, at the same time, confirm the role of the state. But Elisabeth Schemla describes how the members of the cabinet continually failed to follow up on the prime minister's initiatives and projects, and gradually became clearer and clearer in their opposition to her. The Minister of Finance Bérégovoy carried out what Schemla calls 'a permanent coup', without Mitterrand intervening. Externally, Cresson was criticised for increasing charges despite the fact that she had gone against it, and failing to find a solution to unemployment (Schemla, 1993: 133–64).

Mitterrand's sexy slave

Edith Cresson did not hide her femininity and had a positive approach to women and their demands. She did not try to stick with the policies of the male-dominated party, like Margaret Thatcher did, though Cresson was compared with Thatcher. During her time as prime minister, Cresson proposed a law against sexual harassment, granted funds to cover the contraceptive pill, improved the working conditions of nurses and reduced the taxes for child care and housekeeping. But she was no 'feminist' and did not realise that gender was a significant factor in politics and what was happening around her, something that weakened her. It was, above all, her combative and rough leadership style that sparked criticism – a style her previous experience had brought out and that could have won acclaim if she had been a man. Cresson remarked: 'What they [her colleagues] want is a male. Well I'll make like a male. They want me to shout. I'll shout' (Jensen, 2008: 208). She was called 'la Dame de fer' (Iron Lady) and Mitterrand constantly urged her to 'keep going' (Schemla, 1993: 116). But instead of her courage and dynamism being a strength, it became a weakness.

For Cresson, what was essential was that something was done, not what others said. Facts were more important than appearance, honesty more important than rhetoric. She remained passive regarding her image in the media, had little sense of the nuances of political discourse and made hasty and inappropriate statements, which the media cynically exploited. She was particularly held up to ridicule for her comments that the Japanese 'lived like ants' and that there were more homosexuals in Britain than in France. She was parodied on TV as Mitterrand's sexy, slave-like servant and was ridiculed because of her 'frivolous' jewellery and high-pitched voice (Schemla, 1993: 114, 120–31, 165–202).

Reviewing Schemla's book, the political scientist Danielle Dufresne draws the following conclusion (1995: 71):

> Edith Cresson was caught in a trap because of her gender in a political environment dominated by men's power, where a woman is received like a dog in a bowling game: different, strange and impossible to integrate. Therefore, chased away.

Dramatic aftermath

When regional elections in March 1992 gave the Socialist Party a bad result, Edith Cresson's days in power were numbered, after only 10-and-a-half months – shorter than any other prime minister in the Fifth Republic. She was described as France's most unpopular prime minister. Pierre Bérégovoy succeeded her, but he was prime minister for only a year.

The parliamentary elections in 1993 were the Socialist Party's worst since the 1960s. Their number of seats in parliament was reduced from 260 to 53, and Mitterrand had to govern with the right-wing Edouard Balladur as prime minister until he retired himself in 1995, and the conservative Jacques Chirac became president. Bérégovoy committed suicide, and Edith Cresson got a stormy career in the EU Commission. She was appointed to the Commission in 1995, in charge of education, research and development, and human resources. After four years, she and several other commissioners resigned due to corruption allegations. Later, the allegations were withdrawn, but the EU stated that Cresson had neglected her official duties, though she was not punished.

Equality, parity and affirmative action became hot topics in French politics throughout the 1990s. In 1999, the constitution was amended, and in 2000, the election law, so that a 50 per cent quota was possible. But the follow-up and practice in different elections were highly variable. In 2007, the first woman from a major party ran for election as president. Ségolène Royal was a former MP and minister and ran for the Socialist Party, but lost with 47 per cent of the vote against 53 per cent for the male candidate (the conservative Nicolas Sarkozy) in the second round. In 2012, the Socialist Party won the presidential election, this time with a male candidate of its own (François Hollande). When the parliamentary elections resulted in only 26 per cent women in the National Assembly and 23 per cent in the Senate – one of the lowest levels in Western countries – Hollande promised to respect gender parity in the cabinet and appointed 50/50 female and male ministers, in addition to a male prime minister.

Kim Campbell: an impossible task in Canada

First top woman in North America

On the other side of the Atlantic and the other side of the political spectrum, things went even worse for the next top woman leader, Kim Campbell, in Canada. She was the first and, so far, only woman head of government in North America and sat for less than half a year.[12]

Like Edith Cresson, Kim Campbell was supposed to restore a party in power with an unpopular male leader. Canada is the world's second-largest country, is bilingual and multicultural, and has a population of over 30 million. The country is a federation of 10 states and three territories, with a parliamentary system following the British model. The House of Commons is elected by majority vote, while the Senate is appointed by the governor general on advice of the prime minister. The Conservatives came to power in 1984, and after nine years, Prime Minister Brian Mulroney was very unpopular, by many, almost hated. There were political scandals, economic depression, taxes and the North American Free Trade Agreement (NAFTA). Moreover, the welfare system needed reform, and there was tension between the French-speaking Quebec and the English-speaking majority.

A women's movement developed in Canada during the 1970s and 1980s, but regional and cultural differences (European, Indian and Inuit, English- and French-speaking) made it difficult to agree on common demands, and the system of strong states and a relatively weak federal government dominated by two parties (the Liberal and the Progressive Conservative Party) also contributed to division. Women who engaged in political parties preferably worked at the local level. Upwards in the hierarchies, they were filtered out. Several women headed parties with no chances of winning or ran for election as leaders in other parties and lost. Canada was quick to become party to the CEDAW, but in the late 1980s, there were only 11 per cent women in the House of Commons, 13 per cent in the Senate and 17 per cent in the cabinet.

Kim Campbell was born in British Columbia in 1947. Her mother served in the navy and her father in the army during World War II. They married in 1943 and had their first daughter in 1945. While George Campbell studied and became a lawyer, his wife, Phyllis, had various jobs and went to art school when she could. They separated when Kim was 12. Kim and her older sister were sent to boarding school, while their mother left what had become an intolerable marriage for her, leaving the children with their father. It took 10 years before Kim saw her mother again.

Kim's mother was a feminist and her daughters took for granted that they were going to study. Kim Campbell was interested in social issues and engaged in student politics, serving as president of the student council at high school and vice president of the student government in college. She took a bachelor's degree in political science. She got a scholarship and studied towards a doctorate in Soviet government at the London School of Economics, but met her future husband, Nathan Divinsky, a divorced mathematics professor, before completing her degree. After marrying in 1972, she taught and studied in British Columbia and received a bachelor of law degree in 1983.

In 1980, as a first-year student of law, Kim Campbell successfully sought a seat and became chairman and vice-chairman of the Vancouver School Board. After she graduated and divorced from Divinsky, she ran for the state legislature, representing the British Columbia Social Credit Party. She lost, but instead became adviser to the state premier. In 1986, she ran as a candidate for the leadership of the state party and lost, but became a member of the state legislature. Then, in 1988, she ran and became a member of the federal House of Commons from the Progressive Conservative Party. At the same time, she joined the cabinet. Her second husband, the attorney Howard Eddy, moved with her to Ottawa, but it was difficult to reconcile marriage and a political career and they divorced three years later. They had no children (Campbell, 1996: 3–93: Liswood, 2007: 110–11; Jensen, 2008).

Party leader's last resort

Mulroney needed to increase the female presence in government and strengthen representation from the West Coast. He also needed to foster a successor, so he appointed Campbell as minister of state for Indian and northern affairs in 1989. In 1990, she was appointed as the first woman minister of justice and attorney general. She made no secret of the fact that she was a feminist and promoted 'inclusive justice', focusing on women and aboriginal people (Campbell, 1996: 165). She convened the first-ever national symposium on women, law and the administration of justice and obtained several legislative successes, passing a tough law on sexual assault and strengthening Canada's gun-control laws. She also distinguished herself by fighting for a liberal abortion law. In 1993, she became the first woman minister of national defence, and soon after, Mulroney resigned with an all-time low approval rating.

Kim Campbell was encouraged by fellow party members to run as the new party leader (and thus prime minister). New, different policies and leadership style were required. Campbell had made her mark as an able minister. The voice of the districts should be strengthened, and women's groups demanded a woman on top. Her supporters conducted a broad election campaign and presented her as an outsider in relation to the unpopular Mulroney. She said herself:

> I'd like to change the way people think about politics in this country by changing the way we do politics in this country. In my view, we must reduce the distance between our people and the government. We must create a partnership between citizens and the government because, without that partnership, we cannot do the things necessary to build our future. (Campbell, 1996: 269)

At the party congress, Campbell defeated four male candidates. In the first round, she obtained 48 per cent of the vote against 39 per cent for the strongest opponent. In the second round, she won in a very close vote. She became the first woman to lead the Progressive Conservative Party.

Dent in the glass ceiling

On 25 June 1993, Kim Campbell took over as Canada's first woman and first West Coast prime minister. She was also unusually young, at 46 years old. She reduced the size of the cabinet and appointed 24 ministers, of which four were women (16 per cent). That a relatively unknown politician suddenly became top leader created a sensation, the first from the baby boom after World War II and, in addition, a divorced woman from the West Coast. The fact that the leader was a woman was appreciated by many hoping for a change. Although Campbell underlined that she represented an 'inclusion policy', it was not easy to promote a policy that differed from the one she and the party had supported earlier. Campbell was soon criticised for having the same views as her hated predecessor. 'New Tory, old story', people said. Although women politicians were not an unusual sight, people were unfamiliar with a woman top executive, and Kim lacked experience as head of government. She expressed herself in a clumsy way and made public relations blunders, which were mercilessly exploited by the media. And four months after she took office, there were elections.

It was an impossible task to reverse the current, counter the policies of nine years and improve living conditions in such a short period of time. The Conservatives suffered the bitterest defeat any party had ever experienced since Canada was founded in 1867. The Liberals simply swept the Conservatives off the field. Almost all the cabinet members, including Kim Campbell herself, lost their seats in the House of Commons, and the party was left with only two seats. This was primarily a result of Mulroney's failed policies and lack of popularity, but Kim Campbell resigned as party leader and left politics. Later she was appointed as Canadian consul general to Los Angeles, before she returned to lecturing in political science and served in various international positions (Campbell, 1996: 305–407; Liswood, 2007: 111–12).

In spite of her short term, Kim Campbell was of the view that her tenure as prime minister had broken ground, changing the sense of what is possible for women and girls and making possible an increase in the number of women cabinet ministers and the appointment of the first woman member of the Supreme Court (Campbell, 1996: 416). In 2014, Canada had 25 per cent women in the House of Commons, 40 per cent in the Senate and 32 per cent in the cabinet.

Ambitious Turkish economist: Tansu Çiller

Turkey becomes modern

Very few would have thought that one of the most prominent women top leaders in the 1990s would come from Turkey – a Mediterranean country at the crossroads between Europe and Asia, with 99 per cent Moslems, economic problems, political turmoil, military rule and a questionable human rights record.[13]

Turkey boasts of its 'feminist' reforms after the Republic was founded in 1923. In the middle of the 19th century, the Ottoman Empire started a reform policy that was influenced by Europe and addressed women's issues as part of 'modernisation'. Girls' schools, teacher's colleges for women and midwife training were established. Women organised, helped each other, discussed 'women's issues', questioned the patriarchal system and demanded women's rights. When the Ottoman Empire was broken up after World War I, women publicly addressed the masses and participated actively in the war of independence.

Mustafa Kemal Atatürk was the victorious leader of the war. He became 'Father of the Nation', the first president of the independent Turkish state. He headed an authoritarian regime, but pursued a policy of gradual 'modernisation', a transition towards a modern, liberal state, with European values, secularism and democracy. In 1926, sharia law was repealed and Western systems of law were adopted as a whole. The new laws forbade polygamy, instituted civil marriage, gave women inheritance rights and the right to divorce, and guaranteed equality of women before the law. In addition to a group of influential women in the capital, Istanbul, Turkish men carried out what was perhaps the most far-reaching women's revolution ever realised in a Moslem Mediterranean society.

Religious schools were closed, but education was seen as the engine of progress and was promoted for both women and men. Before the second wave of feminism in the West in the 1970s, the proportion of women in the high-status professions of law and medicine was higher in Turkey than in many Western countries.

In the first days of the Republic, a notable feminist activist, Nezihe Muhuittin, founded a women's party, but it was not legalised. Women gained full universal suffrage in 1934. This was earlier than many countries and 18 women (5 per cent) were elected to the National Assembly in 1935. But women entered a political arena set in a patriarchal society. The country was underdeveloped, traditional roles and values persisted, and women depended strongly on the patriarchal family structure. The 'woman question' was subordinate to the larger topic of modernisation, and political life was dominated by parties only sometimes interested in women or women-friendly policies. So, further on, women did not come through in politics. Their representation in parliament went down, and they remained – as in the West in general – a small minority.[14]

'Mission inborn'

Tansu Çiller was born in Istanbul in 1946 in a middle-class family. Her father was, first, a journalist, then a provincial governor with an unfulfilled desire to be a politician. The couple invested a lot in their only child. Tansu said: 'I was born with political ambition and vision, starting with a dream. At the age of 14, I wanted to be Minister of Finance. I always took time to read books on economics. It is a mission inborn' (Tan-Wong, 1998). She was sent to the American College for Girls, a private high school in Istanbul, where she felt out of place with her wealthier friends. At Robert College (also an American institution, later Boğaziçi/Bosphorus University), she earned a bachelor's degree in economics and married, at 17 years old, a fellow student. Özer took her surname and became an important supporter. They travelled to the US, where Tansu Çiller got a master's degree and a PhD in economics. Afterwards, she came back to Turkey and taught in the economics department of the Boğaziçi University, where she became a professor in 1983, at an exceptionally young age. At the same time, she helped the business community with economic analyses. This attracted political attention because she criticised government policies. Özer went into business, and the couple had two sons.[15]

Unstable politics

Turkey's military had a special status in law, tasked with protecting the state and the state's constitution. One-party rule lasted until 1950. Then, multiparty politics were permitted. But the system was unstable, and civilian and military rule alternated. There were military coups in 1960 and 1971, followed by democratic restorations. The competition in politics increased and the number of women MPs remained at a low level. The third military coup was in 1980 and banned political activity. But an independent women's movement mobilised for democratic restoration and a new constitution was adopted in 1983, returning to the multiparty system.

The system was parliamentary, with a single chamber elected by proportional representation, and the parliament elected both a president and a prime minister. Almost all parties included women in their elected organs, and in 1985, Turkey became party to the CEDAW, with some objections. The women's movement followed up to ensure the realisation of necessary measures. Following European practice, the Social Democrat Populist Party (SHP) adopted a 25 per cent quota in favour of women in the party and on candidate lists (Abadan-Unat and Tokgöz, 1994: 712–15; Gündüz, 2004: 117–21; Bennett, 2010: 111–29).

Turkey was a middle-income country of around 60 million people, and the economy was restrained by high unemployment and inflation. In 1990, Tansu Çiller was enlisted in the True Path Party (DYP) to become economic adviser to the former Prime Minister Süleyman Demirel. He founded the pro-Western centre-right DYP and asked Çiller to join because of her expertise. Heading a rural-based party, Demirel also wanted to benefit from Çiller to increase support within the business community and the urban elite, as well as women. Soon,

Demirel ensured Çiller's election to the executive board of the DYP and the position as deputy chair. Besides being interested in economics, Çiller told friends that she was entering politics to prevent the spread of Islamic fundamentalism, defending Turkish laicism (Reinart, 1999: 2).

The DYP defended both traditional culture and secularism. The party promoted economic growth, but not unrestrained liberalism. In the 1991 general elections, Demirel placed Çiller at the top of the DYP candidacy list in Istanbul and she was elected as one of a total of eight women MPs (2 per cent). The DYP became the largest party, with 27 per cent of the seats. The aging Demirel became prime minister for the fifth time and formed a coalition government with the SHP, which obtained 21 per cent of the seats. Tansu Çiller was appointed economics minister (Arat, 1998: 5–7; Jensen, 2008: 41–2, 131).

Çiller strikes

Coincidence provided Tansu Çiller with unexpected opportunities. The president died in 1993, and Demirel was elected president, a position that was largely ceremonial. All of a sudden, the important executive position of prime minister and leader of the DYP was vacant. Çiller was no obvious candidate. She was a newcomer and politically inexperienced. In spite of her formal qualifications, she performed poorly as economics minister. But Çiller was ambitious and declared her candidacy for the leadership of the party.

Demirel headed the party for 29 years, in and out of power, and the leadership needed renewal. Economic liberalisation caused social cleavages among the DYP's core supporters, but the coalition government failed to address the social and economic problems. The party found itself in an identity crisis. Demirel did not support Çiller as the new leader, having seen her performance, but he did not actively oppose her either and was reluctant to endorse other candidates. The three male contenders could not muster the resources, skill and support to compete effectively. Party members declared that a woman could not be prime minister since a woman could not even lead a funeral prayer. And her rival's supporters underlined his 'man-like' qualities (Arat, 1998: 8; Cizre, 2002: 201–2; Jensen, 2008: 139).

But Tansu Çiller was a professional urban woman, young and smart, with higher Western education. She spoke fluent English and had an international perspective. She was seen as part of a new beginning after the 1983 democratic restoration and appealed to modern-minded voters and women. She could draw on images of motherhood and sisterhood, and in 1992, she was elected woman of the year in Turkey. The media supported her, as well as the business community, while, externally, she gave the impression that Turkey was a progressive Moslem country. During her campaign, Margaret Thatcher came on a personal visit to support her. In June 1993, the 47-year-old Çiller fell 11 votes shy of a majority in the first ballot for party leader. Her opponents withdrew, and she won the contest. She became the first woman head of the DYP and Turkey's first woman prime minister. She was also the first woman top leader of a Moslem country who came to power on her own merit, not through the family (Arat, 1998: 6; Cizre, 2002: 201–2; Bennett, 2010: 110, 129).

Mixed record

Tansu Çiller continued Demirel's coalition government, but replaced most of the ministers from her own party. She was the only woman in the cabinet until 1995, when a woman state minister for women and family affairs was appointed. However, Çiller did not continue Demirel's policies. Before the elections in 1991, Demirel emphasised social welfare, civilianisation, democratisation and human rights. But as prime minister, Çiller promoted a conservative populism and economic liberalism. Her approach to the military oscillated, but she spent money on modernising the army and took a hard line on defeating a Kurdish insurgency. The armed struggle entailed both violence and illegal methods, and by the autumn of 1995, the Kurdish question was not resolved. Çiller managed to sign a customs union with the EU, but there were economic problems. An austerity package was initiated, but policies were not coherent, the economy shrunk and inflation rose.[16]

The government coalition broke up and Çiller resigned in September 1995. Afterwards, she formed a minority government, but it failed in less than a month. Then, she established a new coalition government with her former partner, which fell in March 1996 after general elections in December 1995.

Iron woman and mother

To deal with contradictory expectations, Tansu Çiller juggled 'masculine' and 'feminine' styles. She was called Turkey's 'Iron woman' and boasted of her 'decisiveness', 'toughness' and 'steely determination'. At the same time, she wanted to be the nation's mother and sister (Cizre, 2002: 206). Commenting on her experience as prime minister afterwards, she said: 'Women possess inherent love and that love easily overflows to the country when women become government leaders' (Tan-Wong, 1998). Çiller cultivated her feminine image, which could vary from elegant costume dresses with colourful scarfs to traditional attire with her head covered, depending on the occasion and the impression she wanted to give. And before elections, she brought the female constituency to the foreground.

Tansu Çiller became a new role model for a woman politician with clout who did not deny her femininity. But her image was ambiguous and contradictory. She had success, but also created confusion, distrust and disgust. Çiller was typical of Turkish women politicians in the sense that she had her father as a role model, a supportive husband and a senior male politician as mentor. And she pursued established male policies. As a top leader, she emphasised to begin with that she did not want to be any different from a man and was uninterested in women's issues. Although she was considered as a symbol of modern Turkey, she did not care to change women's traditionally subordinate position in the family. With a conservative constituency in the DYP, she assured them that she would not rock the boat in the family and promised help to improve women's conditions as housewives (Arat, 1998: 3, 9–10).

By her self-confidence and independence, Tansu Çiller stood out from other woman politicians. She would not remain circumscribed by the men surrounding her. She demonstrated that women, not only men, could rule authoritatively, took control of the party organisation and used co-optation, divide-and-rule and expulsion strategies. In practice, she took the DYP from the male patriarchs, who did not really know how to deal with a strong woman. It is said that she used 'Machiavellian' methods (Jensen, 2008: 217) and showed that women politicians could be as motivated by 'power, egoistical interests, aggression, clientelism and political intrigues' as men (Cizre, 2002: 207; see also Arat, 1998: 3, 9–10, 12–14).

Chameleon under all-round pressure

Elections were held in 1995. Tansu Çiller pledged to promote equality and defend secularism and called the Islamist Party 'murderous merchants of religion' (Reinart, 1999). But the elections did not go well. The DYP only got 25 per cent of the seats. Of 13 elected women (3 per cent), seven were from the DYP. A coalition of the two secular Right parties, the DYP and The Motherland Party (ANAP), formed a minority government, where the ANAP had the prime minister. Çiller became deputy prime minister and minister of foreign affairs. But the government did not last many months.

Then, the DYP entered into a coalition with the pro-Islamist Welfare Party. Now, Çiller became deputy prime minister and minister of foreign affairs in the government of Turkey's first Islamist prime minister. This was the beginning of the DYP's and Çiller's decline. She lost credibility as a person and a political leader because she joined forces with those she criticised the most. When women's groups blamed her, she explained: 'I am in this struggle, against all kinds of interest groups for my young people and my women. I am your defender and guarantee. I am also the guarantee of the secular republic' (Arat, 1998: 18).

When the Welfare Party joined the DYP in government, corruption charges against Çiller were dropped. But she became involved in the Susurluk scandal, where it was revealed that the government and armed forces collaborated with organised crime. After a year, the government resigned due to pressure from the military. The Welfare Party was declared illegal by Turkey's Constitutional Court. According to an agreement between the DYP and the ANAP, Çiller was supposed to take over as prime minister, but President Demirel asked the leader of the ANAP to do it instead. He formed a minority coalition government without the DYP, which lasted until the 1999 elections.

Tansu Çiller's manoeuvres, political excuses, failed policies and scandals made her increasingly unpopular. She was condemned for, among other things, acting like male politicians and failing to achieve a higher standard than them (Bennett,

2010: 113, 132, 135). Many leading DYP members left the party. Feminists, who supported her to begin with, caricatured her as a male imposter who pretended he was a woman, and 35 women's organisations took her to court because she lacked principles, leading to the emergence of the belief that women would be inconsistent and unsuccessful in politics (Arat, 1998: 18). She was also criticised for undermining democracy and the representative institutions because she gave the impression that there were no legal or moral constraints on the power of a political leader (Cizre, 2002: 213). No corruption charges led to conviction, but Tansu Çiller and her husband became multimillionaires.

In the elections in 1999, the DYP only got 15 per cent of the seats, and Tansu Çiller became minority leader of the opposition. At the next elections, in 2002, 18 parties participated, but only two got over the threshold of 10 per cent. The DYP only got 9.5 per cent of the vote and remained without representation. Tansu Çiller resigned as leader and soon withdrew from politics.[17]

Later, after Turkey became a candidate for the EU, the Civil Code was revised so that all legal inequalities were removed. In 2014, women amounted to 14 per cent in parliament for the first time, and there were 4 per cent in the cabinet. Turkey belonged to the Western countries with the lowest representation of women.

Women's top two in New Zealand: Jenny Shipley and Helen Clark

From welfare to market liberalism

On the other side of the globe, in New Zealand, a forward movement of women of a completely different kind took place.[18] Together with the Nordic countries, New Zealand was highlighted as one of the most well-run welfare states in the world after World War II. The islands were about the size of the British Isles, but they were geographically isolated and had a population of only 4 million, mostly Europeans, with varying Christian affiliation, and Māori. In the 1930s, New Zealand was relatively little affected by the international crisis and developed the economy and the social system, with a 40-hour working week and national insurance. In 1951, the country entered into a security agreement with Australia and the US, which was extended to also include Malaysia, Singapore and the UK in 1971. In 1987, New Zealand declared that it was a nuclear-free zone.

But in the 1970s, there were economic problems, compounded by the energy crisis, and the state budget had a deficit. This led to more widespread economic and social reforms than in any other Western country. Now, New Zealand became a Western model of neo-liberalism. The welfare state was scaled down in order to get a minimal state. One of the largest privatisation waves that the world has ever seen was begun. Just about everything was sold that could be: coal mines, power stations, forestry, postal service, railways, airlines and telecommunication networks. An attempt was made to privatise healthcare, but this failed. Almost all the hospitals went bankrupt. However, user fees were introduced in education and social and welfare services.

New Zealand had a stable parliamentary system, with a governor general who represented the British queen, and a House of Representatives elected by majority vote. Two parties, the centre-right National party (NP) and the social-democratic Labour Party alternated being in power. The NP failed to solve the economic problems in the 1970s and 1980s and Labour took over the government in 1984. It was this party that began the 'modernisation' by liquidating much state control and introducing a liberal market economy, entailing significant social costs for the party's voters. The NP claimed that the Labour policies were too drastic, without human consideration, and demanded 'A Decent Society'. Labour was divided, and in 1990, the NP did better than ever before in the general elections and obtained nearly half of the vote and more than two thirds of the seats (Castles et al, 1996).

Elaborate neo-liberalism

In power, however, the NP government continued the Labour policies to a great extent and carried on with privatisation. Virtually all government subsidies were abolished and drastic cuts were made in public services, including family support. Furthermore, individual employment contracts were made the norm, so trade unions were put out of action and efforts to establish a minimum wage stopped. Although this had negative consequences for women and children, the policies were pushed not least by two of the cabinet's three women members: the country's first woman minister of finance, Ruth Richardson, and Jenny Shipley, minister of women's and social affairs, then health. Unemployment rose at first, but fell when the economy picked up. However, inequalities increased. Dissatisfied voters established alternative parties and demanded a new election system giving them the opportunity of being represented.

In 1996, the electoral system was changed from majority vote to mixed-member proportional representation. A number of smaller parties were established in addition to the two large ones and the NP had to form a coalition government to stay in power. The internal criticism grew stronger – the reforms did not go fast enough and Prime Minister Jim Bolger was not tough enough – and the government's popularity sank. When there were also allegations of misuse of public funds, Jenny Shipley masterminded a discreet party coup in 1997, while Bolger was abroad. Of the 44 MPs, 30 agreed to back her. The NP had relatively weak representation of women – with only eight women MPs (18 per cent) – but a woman had been elected as leader of the opposition (Helen Clark). So, in December, 45-year-old Jenny Shipley became the first woman leader of the NP and the first woman prime minister.

Free market farmer

While New Zealand was still a British colony, women got the right to vote in 1893 after two decades of struggle, becoming the first in the world. But they could not be elected to the House of Representatives until 1919. Elections by majority vote contributed to the fact that 40 years passed from the right to vote until a woman was elected (instead of her deceased husband). Before the 1960s, representation did not exceed 5–6 per cent. Then, a dynamic women's movement arose. In particular, the women's branches in the Labour Party took action. A Labour Women's Council was established in 1975, elected by women at the party conference. It supported women candidates and women's activity in the party and held Labour Women Conferences at three-yearly intervals. This enabled a feminisation of the party. And since 1984, there were four women party presidents and one woman party leader (the party has both a president and a leader). By the late 1990s, women formed a majority of the party membership.

The representation of women in parliament rose steadily from the beginning of the 1980s, mainly women from Labour. In 1984, New Zealand became party to CEDAW, and in 1986, a Women's Ministry was established. When the electoral system was changed in 1996, it led to a record number of women in parliament: 35 in all (29 per cent). Several small parties put forward women candidates and the traditionally strong position of women among the Māori contributed to the increase. Of the major parties, Labour was ahead, with 35 per cent women, while the NP had 28 per cent, and in the years that followed, Labour became increasingly woman-friendly, while the NP lagged behind (Curtin and Sawer, 1996: 150–4; Curtin, 2008, 2011: 58–60, 2012).

Jenny Shipley came from a middle-class family where both parents were staunch supporters of the NP. Her father, Len Robson, was a Presbyterian minister and known for his eloquence. He instilled confidence and the values of leadership in the tomboy Shipley. Her mother, Adele, took care of her four daughters, of whom Jenny was the oldest, born in 1952. Although her father died when she was 18 years old, Jenny got teacher training and passed the exam in 1972, the same year as she married a fifth-generation farmer, Burton Shipley. After four years, she quit teaching to take care of her children, a daughter and a son. She farmed with her husband, participated in the farmers' association and worked as a volunteer in programmes for children in the community. In 1983, she began teaching at a secondary school nearby and, at the same time, became a county councillor. Jenny Shipley was known for her tenacity, capacity for work and persuasion skills. Against all odds, she persuaded a majority of the elderly conservative farmers in the County Council to declare the county in favour of a nuclear-free zone.

Jenny Shipley joined the NP in 1975 and held various positions at the NP's lower echelons. She belonged to the right-wing, with strong support for a free market economy and a social policy based on personal, not state, responsibility. In 1987, she was elected to parliament as one of the youngest members, at 35 years old, and it was not long before she leapfrogged to a position of power. Her husband sold the farm to devote himself to child care. He also went back to school and got a good position as a business development manager in one of New Zealand's major banks (*Current Biography,* 2000a: 78–9; Liswood, 2007: 138–40).

'Perfumed bulldozer'

Jenny Shipley became minister of social welfare in the NP's shadow cabinet, and when the party won the elections in 1990 and Jim Bolger was elected prime minister, she took over the position in earnest. She was also minister of women's affairs at the same time. She proposed a bill against domestic violence, but was criticised when she cut social security benefits. 'The welfare state is not an unconditional right', she declared. People demonstrated and she was burned in effigy. But Shipley only responded: 'I'd rather do what's right than what's popular' (*Current Biography*, 2000a: 77, 79).

Increasing unemployment and crime, along with reductions in welfare, gave the NP a setback in the elections in 1993, and the party only just got a majority (with one seat). Prime Minister Bolger appointed Jenny Shipley as minister of health and of women's affairs. During much of the time, women's affairs was also supported by an associate minister outside cabinet. Shipley was popular when she distributed free birth control pills to reduce abortions and authorised sex education in schools, but negative reactions were strong when she attempted to introduce market competition in the public health service. After the elections in 1996, when the NP had to form a two-party centre-right coalition government, Shipley asked for a less controversial ministry and got (like most other ministers) the responsibility for several. She became minister of transport, of state services and state-owned enterprises, of accident rehabilitation and compensation insurance, and of broadcasting.

A woman prime minister was a novel and unexpected event in New Zealand's politics. Women, old and young, suddenly got a new role model. And Jenny Shipley promised to make a difference as a woman leader by promoting consensus politics and women's role in that process. 'Women and men together make the best decisions,' she declared, 'the skills and knowledge (a mother) brings are very important in understanding the hopes and aspirations of your people. A mother who understands how to draw the best out of her child, I'm sure can contribute the future of this country' (Jensen, 2008: 12, 157).

Shipley inherited a cabinet with only one woman minister (responsible for senior citizens and consumer affairs) who resigned in 1998. To begin with, the prime minister took responsibility for women's affairs herself, but in 1998, another woman was appointed to take over. There were no other women ministers. Shuffling the portfolios, Shipley placed those who shared her market-oriented approach to head critical departments such as health, welfare, education and commerce. Her initial proposals as prime minister included simplification of the tax system, a new highway toll, obligatory community service for welfare recipients and narrower eligibility requirements for disability benefits. Shipley also became the first New Zealand prime minister to attend the gay and lesbian Hero Parade.

Although Shipley supported a consensus policy, she pursued her own course and was named the 'perfumed bulldozer' because of her ability to push until she got what she wanted (Jensen, 2008: 207). Soon, she fell out with her coalition partner, who wanted less privatisation and more emphasis on health and education. In 1998, the coalition disintegrated, and Shipley ruled on with a minority government, surviving two parliamentary votes of confidence.[19]

Time for change

Before the 1999 elections, Labour accused the NP of conducting an extreme policy that had led to growing inequalities and social disintegration. Shipley replied that the budget was in balance, new jobs were created (although unemployment had increased) and the crime rate was down. She promised to increase interest rates and reduce taxes (*Current Biography*, 2000a: 81). Labour, on the other hand, wanted to increase taxes to improve health services.

In the elections, two women were vying for the premiership for the first time in an industrialised country. Prime Minister Jenny Shipley emphasised her experience: 'I'm a politician, but I'm also a Mum' (Trimble and Treiberg, 2010: 125), in contrast to Helen Clark's childlessness and allegedly cold and formidable leadership style. Clark portrayed herself as a 'caring, modern social democrat', and after a decade of conservative rule, it was time for a change (BBC News, 1999).

This time, Labour did well and took over the government. The party got 49 seats, while the NP only got 39 (out of 120). At 49 years old, Helen Clark was the first woman who won the parliamentary elections in New Zealand. She became prime minister and succeeded another woman prime minister. There were 37 women (31 per cent) in parliament, with Labour having 20. And before a year had passed, a record was set, with women in five key public positions: prime minister, leader of the opposition, attorney general, chief justice and governor general. Not many countries, if any, could match this. But the record did not stand long. In the elections in 2002, the NP obtained the worst results in 70 years, and Jenny Shipley resigned as party leader and left politics.

It was no novice who took over as prime minister in 1999. Like her predecessor, Helen Clark was the eldest daughter of four in a long-established well-to-do farming family. Helen's mother, a former teacher, was active in community groups and a 'strong, no-nonsense, enormously practical, hugely efficient woman' (Jensen, 2008: 91). Her father was a dairy farmer, who was active in the affairs of the centre-right NP. Helen was born in 1950. She attended a high school for girls, and when she came home from boarding school on holidays, she would argue with her father about political issues, rebelling against his conservative views. She began to study in 1968, read history, English and German, and took a master's degree in political science. She worked as a university lecturer, but did not complete her PhD. Her interest in politics took over, and she became involved in opposition to the Vietnam War, apartheid in South Africa and nuclear tests in the South Pacific. She realised that the conservative government would never share her views and became a member of the Labour Party in 1971.

Experienced party boss

In the Labour Party, Helen Clark got positions at all levels. She became president of the youth council, chair of the university branch, executive member of the regional council, secretary of the women's council and, from 1978, a member of the party executive. She ran for election to parliament in 1975 and lost. In 1981, she married the medical sociologist Peter Davis, her partner for five years at the time. He became a university professor and a great support in her career. Later, in 1981, she was elected to parliament as one of four women. She was one of the youngest, at 31 years old, and in 1999, she was the woman who had been in office the longest and was given the unofficial title 'Mother of the House'. To begin with, Helen Clark was not particularly concerned with women's issues and she never headed the Women's Ministry. But she became interested when she attended international women's conferences, received inquiries from women voters about their problems and was met with suspicion and hostility from male colleagues when she became an MP (Curtin, 2008: 496).

Helen Clark and a good portion of the women Labour members were critical of the country's embrace of the free market, and women ministers ensured that support for families with children and legislation on fair wages were not abolished in a neo-liberal economic reform period. Clark joined the cabinet in 1987 and was, first, minister of housing and conservation, then labour and health. Although she did not speak very loudly of women's equality, she specifically addressed the housing needs of women, removed restrictions on midwifery practice and promoted employment equity legislation. She became the first woman deputy prime minister in 1989, and when Labour lost the elections in 1990, she was deputy leader of the opposition. After the NP won the elections in 1993 with an extremely small margin, less 0.5 per cent, intense fighting arose within Labour. Women activists challenged the party leader, and the consequence was that 43-year-old Helen Clark became the first woman party leader (of the parliamentary group) of a major political party – a position she held for 15 years.[20]

Cleaning up the mess

In the election campaign in 1999, Helen Clark expressed the same goals as she had when she started in parliament. She said:

> My objectives for, and the demands of, the Government are relatively simple. They centre on the right to work and be adequately housed, the need for better living standards, for access to health care at a price everyone can afford, for free and public quality education, for recognition of the rights

of minorities and for tolerance and social peace within the society. (Clark, quoted in *Current Biography*, 2000b: 9)

Clark was the first prime minister of New Zealand who stayed in office during three subsequent periods as the head of a stable government. She was called the 'Iron Lady' because of her firm and effective leadership, but she was leader of a centre-left coalition or alliance throughout – first, with the Alliance Party, then with the Progressive Party (both breakaway groups from Labour), and finally with several small parties – and this required a great capacity for collaboration. Clark's cabinet included a myriad of different members: women and minority group representatives, especially Māori, elected by the parliamentary group. With seven women ministers out of 20 (35 per cent), the country was placed at the top of the world, but participation varied over the years and was, at times, down to 23 per cent.

The prime minister was known to be an ardent advocate for the arts, convinced pacifist, strong environmental supporter and outdoor enthusiast. In the cabinet, Clark took responsibility for the Ministry of Arts, Culture and Heritage and got a comprehensive strategy for the conservation of biological diversity adopted, promoted a national anti-nuclear policy and refused to participate in the US-led war in Iraq.

The government was committed to reducing inequalities in society and improving people's living conditions. Close cooperation was established with trade unions to carry out a new programme and 'clean up the mess', as it was said colloquially. The policy was to change the economy, halt further privatisation and strengthen the unions and workers' rights. With strong participation by women ministers, a reform programme was implemented within the health, education and housing sectors. A minimum wage, paid parental leave, better pensions and vacation pay were introduced. Vocational training and primary healthcare were developed. It was not always possible to buy back enterprises that were sold, but the state took over a destroyed railway and an airline on the verge of bankruptcy. The 'cleaning up' was more about improving the welfare system than changing the ownership structure in industry and transport. New Zealand became an example of how difficult it is to restore a welfare state.

There was special emphasis on strengthening the position of the Māori population, and a number of women-friendly measures were carried out, often referred to as measures of 'national interest' to boost economic growth. They centred particularly on women's participation in the labour market: paid parental leave, child care and recreation for children. But a unit for gender equality was also established in New Zealand's Human Rights Commission, prostitution was legalised, a partnership law for both homosexuals and heterosexuals was adopted, and reasonable property distribution upon dissolution of cohabitation was introduced.[21]

Strong or too strong?

The Clark government was not universally popular; it was criticised for taxation of the rich, a liberal immigration policy and worker-friendly laws. But the NP had difficulties and the number of small parties increased, so Labour continued in power in 2002. The economy also had a long unbroken period of growth and unemployment was low. In 2005, the NP did better at the elections, but Clark still continued as prime minister. Eventually, economic growth slowed down, and before the 2008 elections, there were signs of a recession. Furthermore, the media reproached the government for not listening to voters any more. The NP stood for election promising tax cuts, and now it was Labour that suffered defeat. The party got 43 seats against the NP's 58 (of 122), and John Key formed a conservative minority government. Helen Clark resigned both as party leader and prime minister.

It was very unusual for governments to have more than three terms in office. But in addition to political problems, media representations of the prime minister contributed to Labour's defeat in 2008. As a top woman politician, Helen Clark was in an exposed position. Before becoming prime minister, she was extremely unpopular, but, in time, she became one of the most popular leaders in New Zealand. To succeed, Helen Clark felt that she had to be 'tough': 'If women are seen to be emotional, they are almost written off as unfit to do the job' (Jensen, 2008: 208), she noted. As well as a growing economy, Clark's leadership style accounted for her increased popularity. She was admired for her 'decisiveness, down-to-earth style and personal manner' (Jensen, 2008: 216).

Opponents raised questions with regards to Clark's sexuality because of her husky voice, status as single (before she married) and childlessness. Analysing the media coverage of the elections from 1996 to 2008, the political scientists Linda Trimble and Natasja Treiberg (2010) found that the majority of stereotypes applied to Clark and her opponents were masculine. And Clark was as, or even more, likely than her male opponents to be described with masculine stereotypes. The only leader portrayed as more masculine than Clark was another woman – Jenny Shipley. Being described as 'strong' and 'assertive' might have benefited Clark early in her career. But the masculine stereotypes were used more and more, positioning her as oddly unfeminine, even dangerous, and ultimately depicting her as too masculine, ruthless and dictatorial, a 'political dominatrix'. According to Trimble and Treiberg (2010: 126–30), such representations likely contributed to Labour's defeat in 2008 by undermining the legitimacy of Clark and her government.

'Queen Helen' to the United Nations

Welfare in New Zealand improved from the mid-1990s, but income levels were lower than in many countries in the OECD (Organisation for Economic Cooperation and Development) even though the country had relatively high employment. Women accounted for a growing share of the labour force, approaching half, but despite the fact that they generally had better health and increasingly were better educated than men, they received lower wages. And New Zealand was not at the forefront of an area such as paid parental leave. When it came to women in politics, New Zealand ranked in the top half of the Western group, with 34 per cent women in parliament and 30 per cent in the cabinet in 2014. But in other higher positions, the representation of women was lower. Only a quarter of the judges and a tenth of the directors of major companies were women.

When she resigned, Helen Clark had been the longest leader of Labour and was one of the prime ministers in New Zealand who had been longest in office. In 2004, Clark was ranked by *Forbes* as number 43 among the 100 most powerful women in the world. She rose to number 24 in 2005 and 20 in 2006, but then fell to number 38 in 2007 and 56 in 2008.

In April 2009, she was appointed the first woman head of the United Nations Development Programme (UNDP), the third highest position in the UN, and was now ranked by *Forbes* as number 61 of the world's most powerful women. In 2011, she was number 50; in 2012, number 34; and in 2013, she became number 21 after the UN secretary general had reappointed her for a second term.

Switzerland lets women in: Ruth Dreifuss, Micheline Calmy-Rey and Doris Leuthard

Collective leadership

People were startled when Switzerland got a woman president in 1999. The country was considered one of the most reliable male bastions in Europe. Women starting fighting for the right to vote in 1886. Trade unions and Social Democrats supported the claim, but women did not get the right to vote nationally before 1971.[22]

Upon closer inspection, it turned out that the presidency was not quite as grand as one might think. Switzerland has a distinctive political system. The country consists of four linguistic regions, with the great majority of inhabitants being Christian, equally divided between Catholics and Protestants. The country has a long history of armed neutrality and is constructed as a federation. The cantons have considerable autonomy, although more responsibility has gradually been placed at the federal level during the 20th century. The constitution provides for a two-chamber Federal Assembly. The 200-member National Council is elected directly by proportional representation, while the 46-member Council of States consists of representatives of the cantons. Most parliamentary decisions may be submitted to a general vote of all citizens.

The Federal Council is a seven-member executive council operating as a combination of cabinet and collective presidency. The seven members are elected one by one by the Federal Assembly, but do not have to be members of the Assembly. Councillors are elected for four-year terms and are each responsible for a large department. Every year the Assembly elects one of the councillors as president and one as vice president for a year. By convention, the positions rotate so that each councillor becomes vice president and then president every seven years while in office.

All major political parties are usually represented in the Federal Council, which acts as a collective. The president is the first among equals, chairs the council meetings and represents the state externally. From 1959 to 2003, the council consisted of the same four-party coalition, with a fixed distribution of seats. Then, it was a bit changed.

After women got the right to vote, it took time before they acquired positions. In 1983, there were 11 per cent women in the National Council and 7 per cent in the Council of States. The failed election of the first official woman candidate for the Federal Council, a Social Democrat, was controversial and the Social Democrats considered withdrawing from the Council. The next year, in 1984, the first woman was elected. Elisabeth Kopp, a lawyer from the Free Democratic Party (FDP), became councillor to replace a party colleague who resigned for health reasons. She got 124 votes (of 244), held the Department of Justice and Police and was vice president before she resigned in 1989. The second woman was elected in 1993. Ruth Dreifuss was member of the Socialist Party (SP). She was the first Jewish woman to be elected to the Council and she was re-elected twice. In the Council, she was responsible for the Department of Home Affairs. In 1998, she was vice president, and in 1999, she became president of the confederation, becoming the first woman to do so (Stämpfli, 1994: 690–704).

Jewish feminist

Although the president is mainly a formal and ceremonial position and Ruth Dreifuss was already a councillor and vice president, it seemed at first as if she would not be president when, according to convention, it was her turn. Women were only a minority in the National Council (23 per cent). Dreifuss was the only woman in the Federal Council and she was both a distinguished and controversial person. In addition to being a woman, she was a Jew, and it would be the first time that a Jew was president. Switzerland was the last country in Western Europe that recognised the rights of Jews.

Ruth Dreifuss belonged to one of the oldest Jewish families in the country. Her father was a merchant, and because they lived near the border with Nazi Germany, he helped refugees. Ruth was born in 1940, but in 1942, the family had to move and settled, first, in Bern, then in Geneva. Here, Ruth and her older brother went to school. After business education, Ruth worked as a secretary, a journalist and a social worker active in the field of the social integration of people with psychiatric disorders. She joined the SP in 1964. In 1970, she undertook a master's degree in economics and worked for two years at the university. From 1972 to 1981, she was a civil servant in the Department of Foreign Affairs, working for the Swiss Development Agency. Then, she was elected secretary of the Swiss

Trade Union, where she dealt with questions related to social insurance, labour law and women's issues.

Ruth Dreifuss was unmarried and a strong and outspoken feminist. She fought for equality, education, motherhood, abortion rights, health, elderly insurance and the environment. She received warm support from women voters in 1989 and became a member of the Bern legislative council. She did not become a member of the National Council in 1991, but was elected to the Federal Council in 1993. For the first time, there were two women candidates from the same party (the SP). Dreifuss was elected in the third round, with 144 votes (of 246). In the Federal Council, she was responsible for home affairs, including health, social security, research, gender equality, culture and the environment. During the 10 years she was minister, she introduced comprehensive reforms of the health service, social security and pension systems. In particular, she managed to implement paid maternal leave.

As Dreifuss was vice president in 1998, she should become president in 1999. But women and the SP were not sure whether Dreifuss would really get the position and initiated actions, although this was unusual in presidential elections, and 58-year-old Ruth Dreifuss was elected. In addition, another woman became a councillor: Ruth Metzler from the Christian Democrats (CVP). For the first time, there were two women.

The election of Ruth Dreifuss attracted great attention. Although the president did not have great power, the position had symbolic significance. Furthermore, at the same time, Switzerland celebrated both 150 years as an independent state and the 50th anniversary of the UN Declaration of Human Rights. When she was elected, Dreifuss declared: 'I won't be satisfied if I'm the last woman President for decades. I'm just opening the door for other women' (Cohen, 2001). But it was not straightforward. When Ruth Metzler ended her vice presidential year in 2002, she did not become president because she was not re-elected to the Council (Baker-Siroty, 1999; Jensen, 2008: 55–6).

Women take over

Ruth Dreifuss served as president for a year, as the custom was. Then, she continued as minister of home affairs until the end of 2002. When she retired from the Federal Council, she was replaced by her five-year-younger party colleague Micheline Calmy-Rey. She was born in 1945 and took a university degree in political science. While studying, she married André Calmy and had two children. She ran a small enterprise in the book distribution business, joined the SP and got political positions in the Geneva canton in 1981. She was a member and president of the great council of the canton, president of the canton SP and head of the finance department, and president of the state council (Jensen, 2008: 56).

The women in the National Council amounted to 26 per cent in 2003. Calmy-Rey was elected to the Federal Council and became head of the Department of Foreign Affairs during 2003–2011. In 2006, she became vice president, and in

2007, president, at 62 years old. Now, it was taken for granted that she should be elected president when it was her turn, even though she was a woman. Soon, the Federal Council included three women. In addition to Calmy-Rey, a woman from the Christian Democrats and one from the Conservative Democrats were elected.

In 2010, the representation of women in the National Council was 34 per cent. When an additional woman from the SP was elected councillor, for the first time, women were in a majority in the Federal Council, with four of the seven members (57 per cent). A majority was highly unusual, even in a Western context, and, in addition, a woman became president. Doris Leuthard was born in 1963, studied law, married an academic and worked as a lawyer. In 1999, she was elected to the National Council, and after a few years, she became leader of the Christian Democratic Party. When a party colleague withdrew from the Federal Council in 2006, Leuthard was elected instead and took responsibility for the Department of Economic Affairs. In 2009, she became vice president, and in 2010, president.

Switzerland was no longer the most reliable bastion of male domination in Western Europe, but gender-balanced political decision-making was not ensured, either. In 2012, the representation of women was 29 per cent in the National Council and 20 per cent in the Council of States. Micheline Calmy-Rey took over as president for the second time, and Eveline Widmer-Schlumpf, a lawyer from the Conservative Democrats, became vice president and then president in 2012. But women were no longer the majority in the Federal Council in 2012 and a man was elected vice president. In 2013, both the president and the vice president were men. In 2014, the male president was supplemented by a female vice president (Simonetta Somaruga).

Finland's three national leaders: Tarja Halonen, Anneli Jäätteenmäki and Mari Kiviniemi

Pioneer country

Finland has been known for its strong presidents and active women's movement. In contrast to the other Nordic countries, where executive political power is given to the prime minister, Finland introduced a parliamentary system with a dual executive.[23] President Urho Kekkonen dominated Finnish politics for a generation (1956–81), steered Finland's foreign policy towards neutrality and signed the Agreement of Friendship, Cooperation and Mutual Assistance with the Soviet Union. After he resigned, the system became more parliamentary.

In the 1880s, Finnish women began to fight for political rights, and even before the country became independent in 1906, they received the right to vote and be elected to parliament. From 1907 to World War II, there were between 7 and 13 per cent women in parliament. Worldwide, this was exceptional. It was not until the 1980s that other Nordic countries got on a par with Finland, and from then on, the Nordic region as a whole was at the forefront globally. The first Finnish woman minister was appointed in 1926, but it was not until the 1970s that there was always at least one woman in the cabinet. In the 1990s, there were seven women ministers (40 per cent), and the percentage of women in parliament was over a third (37 per cent) in 1999.

It was perceived as a major victory for women when Tarja Halonen was elected president of Finland in 2000, although it happened at the same time as the constitution was amended so that the presidency lost some of its power. Now, the president was to be responsible for national security and foreign policy in cooperation with the cabinet, while the prime minister was responsible for domestic and EU policy.

Some said that the presidency was weakened because a woman rose to the top. But this is not correct. The constitutional amendment had been prepared for a long time and was adopted before the presidential election (Holli, 2008). It was also claimed by a former female presidential candidate, Elisabeth Rehn, that 'there was so little power left after the change that even a woman could be president' (interview by Halgeir Opedal, 2000: 31). But the position was far from merely ceremonial. The president was head of state, was commander-in-chief of the military, issued decrees and made appointments. In particular, the president appointed the prime minister on the advice of parliament and the cabinet on the advice of the prime minister. The cabinet was accountable to parliament.

In all, three men and four women competed for the presidency in 2000. The number of women was extraordinary, but it was not the first time that a woman ran for president. Helvi Sipilä had already run as a presidential candidate for the Liberal People's Party in 1982.[24] In 1994, when the first direct presidential election was held, Elisabeth Rehn ran for the Swedish People's Party against the Social Democrat Martti Ahtisaari but was pipped at the post, with 46 per cent against 54 per cent.

Unmarried single mother outside the state Church

It was not at all obvious that Tarja Halonen would become president. Elisabeth Rehn ran again. The woman president of the National Assembly and a woman European parliamentarian also ran – not to speak of the former male Prime Minister Esko Aho, who was the obvious favourite in the polls.

Tarja Halonen was born in Helsinki in 1943. Her mother worked in a shoe factory and her father, who was a welder, was fighting at the front. After World War II, they separated, and Tarja grew up in humble circumstances. Her mother worked as a set-dresser and her stepfather was an electrician and very active in the labour movement. Tarja went to high school and undertook a master's degree in law at the university in 1968. She got a job as social affairs secretary and general secretary of the National Union of Finnish Students, which made her more interested in politics. In 1970, she became a lawyer in the Central Organization of Finnish Trade Unions (FFC), and in 1971, she joined the Social Democratic Party. She withdrew from the Lutheran state Church in protest against the Church's attitude towards women priests. Halonen worked in the FFC until 1979, with the exception of 1974/75 when she was parliamentary secretary of the Social Democratic prime minister. She was a member of the city council in Helsinki for five periods, from 1977 to 1996.

In 1979, Tarja Halonen ran for parliament as the single mother of an infant child, though it was difficult, and she was elected. She became a member of the Social Affairs Committee and came forward as a generalist, raising issues related to women and children along with other issues. In particular, she tried to get the provisions on homosexuals in the Penal Code repealed. The Finnish governments were typically coalition governments, and from 1987, Halonen was a member of several, as minister of social affairs, health and equality, minister of Nordic cooperation, the first woman minister of justice, and the first woman minister of foreign affairs. In fact, she was minister for longer than any other woman (for nine years) and promoted 'soft values' such as human rights and the interests of discriminated groups in a factual way, sometimes even with a heavy hand.

When 57-year-old Halonen said that she would run for president in 2000, there were many who wondered why, because she was so unconventional. She was known for her political Left orientation and break with the state Church, in addition to the fact that she lived in cohabitation as a single parent with a daughter. But she was one of Finland's most experienced politicians, and the party supported her with a clear majority. Martti Ahtisaari said he would not run for re-election, and Halonen received 60 per cent of the vote in the primary elections in the Social Democratic Party against two male candidates: a former party leader and the European ombudsman.[25] She scored low in the polls to begin with, but got most votes in the first round, with 40 per cent. Esko Aho from the Centre Party got 34 per cent. In the second round, she won by a small margin: 51.6 per cent against 48.4 per cent for Aho.

According to media comments, Halonen won because she appeared as broad-minded, tolerant, internationally aware and a champion of solidarity, human rights, equality and minority groups. She received bipartisan support from women and young voters. The crude, underhanded political criticism of her as an unmarried single mother was met with criticism of Aho as a 'mobile phone dad', with his wife in their home county taking care of the children.[26]

'Moomin Mamma'

When Halonen took office as president on 1 March 2000, she said:

> As well as I can, I will promote the Finnish people's welfare. I really want
> to be the President of the people as a whole. I will do my best so the Finns
> in six years are able to feel that they live in a country with greater equality.
> (Norwegian Embassy Helsingfors, 2000b)

As president, Tarja Halonen quickly became popular. In 2003, she obtained nearly 90 per cent support in the polls. She broke with the heavy row of stalwart male presidents and came forward as a humorous, warm, down-to-earth and uncomplicated mother of the nation, a 'Moomin Mamma' in political life.[27] She had to develop a new role as president with less power than before, but she held on to the authority she had, and seemed to manage well, according to public opinion. Although she did not belong to the state Church, as president, she was member of the leadership of the Church, but only occasionally intervened in domestic politics. With regards to foreign policy, the collaboration with the cabinet went smoothly. Both the prime minister and the minister of foreign affairs were Social Democrats during the first years and agreed to oppose EU plans for common defence.

In addition to welfare and social security for the Finnish people, Halonen emphasised international solidarity. Themes regarding human rights, the environment, women's rights and the rule of law recurred constantly. She was perceived as an interpreter of the people's feelings and was in this way similar to both Vigdís Finnbogadóttir in Iceland and Mary Robinson in Ireland. Soon after her appointment, she agreed to marry her partner of more than 15 years, Pentti Arajärvi, to prevent complications during official visits abroad. Arajärvi resigned his position as committee counsel of the parliamentary Social Affairs Committee, obtained a PhD and became a part-time professor of social work at the University of Joensuu. He had a son from a previous relationship and actively supported Tarja's political career. The marriage was one of the few adaptations Halonen was willing to make for the sake of the presidency. Otherwise, she stood her ground and was respected for it.

Traditionally, there was broad consensus on Finnish foreign policy, but Halonen was a peace activist. She was opposed to Finnish North Atlantic Treaty Organization (NATO) membership and described herself as a 'relative pacifist', meaning that she did not support unilateral disarmament. As president, she joined the leadership of defence and accepted this role. She also supported Finland's participation in the NATO-led International Security Assistance Force (ISAF) operation in Afghanistan, emphasising that the aim was to reconstruct the country and ensure democracy and human rights, including the rights of women and girls. But after the cabinet changed in 2003, and the prime minister came from the Centre Party, disagreement arose with regards to landmines. Halonen said that they were inhumane. Yet, Finland refused to sign the Ottawa Treaty banning the use of landmines.[28]

More than half

Tarja Halonen was re-elected as president with the same margin in 2006 as in 2000. Six men and one woman ran for president in addition to Halonen herself. She got most votes in the first round, 46 per cent, but it was not enough to be elected. The second round was exciting and Halonen emerged victorious, with 52 per cent of the vote against 48 per cent for the male candidate from the conservative National Coalition Party (NCP).

In the general elections in 2007, the NCP was successful and became as large as the Centre Party. The coalition government nevertheless continued under the leadership of Matti Vanhanen from the Centre Party, with members from the NCP, the Swedish People's Party and the Green Party. In parliament, there were 42 per cent women, and the cabinet caused a stir when 12 (60 per cent) of the 20 ministers were women, and three of them were pregnant. It was a world record – and all the more surprising since themes related to women and gender equality were virtually absent from the electoral campaign. It was also noted that the minister for equality was a man, and heavy ministerial posts such as foreign affairs, finance and defence went to men from the NCP, which increased tensions between the cabinet and the president.

In 2008, Halonen also made the unusual decision to reappoint the woman permanent undersecretary in the Interior Ministry, in spite of the fact that the cabinet wanted a man as new permanent undersecretary. During the previous 50 years, it had only happened once that the president did not accept a nomination by the cabinet. In this case, the cabinet said that the man had more suitable experience. But there were no objections to the woman's performance, so Halonen kept her in the post. Since the woman was a Social Democrat, Halonen was accused of cronyism. But it might also have been a case of preventing discrimination due to gender.

As president, Tarja Halonen received a great number of decorations from foreign countries. Her second term ended in 2012 and she could not be re-elected. In 2004 and 2005, *Forbes* ranked her as number 31 among the 100 most powerful women in the world, but then she fell further down the list: to number 44 in 2006, 50 in 2007, 71 in 2008, 68 in 2009 and 62 in 2010. After she retired, she served in various international capacities.

'Voters' queen'

In sharp contrast to Tarja Halonen's presidential idyll was the storm around Prime Minister Anneli Jäätteenmäki. She became Finland's first woman prime minister in 2003 – a 'voters' queen' who had to resign after two months in office.

Anneli Jäätteenmäki was born in 1955 on a small farm in the forests of Ostrobothnia. The family's son was to take over the farm, so the daughters went to school. Anneli became a member of the Centre Party and active in student politics. She came from one of the most conservative districts in Finland, but was herself liberal and courageous enough to go against public opinion in her own district. For unknown reasons, she was called 'The crow'. Maybe it was due to her haircut or her insistent voice.

Having taken a master's degree in law in 1980, Jäätteenmäki became a lawyer for the party's parliamentary group. She also took the aspirant course at the Ministry of Foreign Affairs. In 1987, she was asked by the local party in her home district to run for a seat in parliament and was both elected and later re-elected. In parliament, she specialised in international issues and voted for a controversial law on partnership. She married a journalist, Jorma Melleri, in 1994, but had no children. The same year, the post of minister of justice became vacant and Jäätteenmäki was elected with a majority of one vote in the Centre Party parliamentary group. But after a year, the party went into opposition.

In 2000, Jäätteenmäki was surprisingly elected as temporary leader of the party for a year. Having lost the presidential election against Halonen, the party leader, Esko Aho, decided to go to the US for a year to work as a university professor at Harvard. Jäätteenmäki had not previously had front-line party tasks, but showed herself as a skilled debater. She led the party's success in the local elections the same year. The popular support for Jäätteenmäki made Aho resign after he returned, and Jäätteenmäki was elected party leader in 2002 by a large majority, the first women leader of the party (Government of Finland, 2005).

In the same year, Jäätteenmäki published a book called *Sillanrekentaja* (The bridge-builder) about women of the past and her own generation, and wrote: 'We women in the 2000s will be the fighters who do not give up. We are ready to fight, tolerant, humorous – and utterly irrepressible' (Hämäläinen: 2003: 4).

'Up like a sun, down like a pancake'

Before the parliamentary elections in 2003, Jäätteenmäki stated that the country needed 'a safe change' and 'a brighter alternative'. She did not support large tax cuts, but wanted to develop the welfare state. It was a thriller, and the Centre Party won with just two seats more than the Social Democrats. The difference was not more than 6,000 votes. The Centre Party got 24.7 per cent against 24.5 per cent for the Social Democrats. Anneli Jäätteenmäki was 48 years old, but a new face in Finnish politics, and her personal popularity was one of the party's strongest cards. She criticised the government for high unemployment and attacked the prime minister for being too pro-US in his Iraq policy.

Jäätteenmäki became, first, speaker of parliament for a few weeks, then stepped down to take over a coalition government with the Social Democrats and the Swedish People's Party as prime minister. She stated that she wanted 50/50 women and men in the cabinet (Associated Press, 2003; Hämäläinen, 2003).

Two women in the country's two main political positions was unique in Europe, and the Finns sunned themselves in their gender-equality record. Half of the cabinet members were women, but the prime minister had to push some younger women through in spite of opposition from older, male party veterans and this created ill-feeling in the Centre Party.

However, a brilliant political career ended before it really began. The media tried to find out from where Jäätteenmäki got her information when she attacked the prime minister for his Iraq policy. Questions were raised as to whether the information she had received from a party colleague, who was advisor to the president, was confidential and obtained in an 'illegal' way. In parliament, Jäätteenmäki got entangled in half-truths, denials and outright lies. There was also an outcry in the Centre Party, and after 68 days at the helm, the new prime minister resigned, citing the lack of political trust and without admitting any wrongdoing. She also stepped down as party leader.

Afterwards, many said that if Jäätteenmäki had expressed herself a bit differently and failed to lie in parliament she would not have been obliged to resign. It was a small issue that grew into a political bombshell. When Jäätteenmäki was later tried in court, she was acquitted. She was supported by many women in her career, but when she used 'wrong' words, male politicians in both her own party and among the Social Democrats saw their chance to 'get' her. As she said herself: 'My greatest sin was that I won the elections. Certain circles can never forgive me' (Bruun, 2004: 20). Later, Anneli Jäätteenmäki ran for the European Parliament and was elected (Jensen, 2008, 55).

Centre Party women get even

When Jäätteenmäki resigned, her male party colleague Matti Vanhanen became prime minister. Seven years passed and then the Centre Party women got revenge. Vanhanen had to step down, and Finland got a new woman prime minister. But there was a fly in the ointment: Mari Kiviniemi got the job not only because of her own competence, but because of scandals related to Vanhanen.

Mari Kiviniemi was born in the countryside in 1968. Her father was a chicken farmer, and Mari got to go to school. She studied economics and took a master's degree in the social sciences at the university. She married a businessman, Juha Louhivuori, had two children and became the leader of an organisation for the physical education of children and youth. By 1991, while she was secretary general of the Centre Party's student union, she had already run for parliament and lost. But in 1995, she was elected and later re-elected. In 2003, she became deputy leader of the Centre Party and served as special adviser to Prime Minister Vanhanen. Then, she stepped in as minister of foreign trade and development (2005/06) and of public administration and local government (2007–10).

After seven years in power, Matti Vanhanen suddenly withdrew as party leader and prime minister. The reason was a political scandal in connection with the financing of the party's election campaign. Suddenly, a new leader had to be elected. The 41-year-old Mari Kiviniemi ran against two male party veterans and won in the second round, with 1,357 against 1,035 votes. Kiviniemi was relatively young, but she was a capable, knowledgeable and serious politician, and it was only a matter of 10 months until parliamentary elections would be held in April 2011. Under Prime Minister Vanhanen's leadership, the Centre Party had lost confidence, and many hoped a new leader without any scandals would increase support for the party in the elections.

Kiviniemi took over Vanhanen's four-party coalition and declared that she would follow her predecessor's political course, get Finland out of the financial crisis and reduce the high unemployment. She also continued with Vanhanen's cabinet, with a majority of women (12 of 20) (Prime Minister's Office Finland, 2011).

But the parliamentary elections did not go well for the Centre Party. The Party of the True Finns had a roaring victory and the Centre Party went from the largest to only the fourth-largest party, with 35 seats against the 51 before. Mari

Kiviniemi had to resign as prime minister in June 2011. The NCP appointed a male prime minister in a new coalition government. There were 43 per cent women in parliament and the cabinet got 50/50 women and men (*Good News*, 2010; Government of Finland, 2011).

Angela Merkel: the world's quiet leader

West German reunification

No one would have believed that a quiet scientific researcher from the former communist East Germany (GDR), who was a woman, a Protestant, childless and divorced, should become leader of Germany's powerful Christian Democratic Party (CDU) and, in addition, chancellor of the Federal Republic of Germany. The CDU was known for its conservative Catholic roots and was dominated by men. But at the party congress in 2000, something happened that everyone would have thought was impossible just six months earlier: Angela Merkel was elected president of the CDU, with 96 per cent of the vote. And in 2005, she became chancellor.[29]

When the Federal Republic was established as a separate state in 1949, it was stated in the constitution that men and women were equal. But traditional gender roles were strong. Feminism was weak and the women's movement was divided between those who sought change through institutional politics and radical feminists striving for autonomy. In the 1970s, feminism gained in strength, and during the 1980s, women engaged in political parties, primarily on the Left. In the Social Democratic Party (SPD), women pressed for change, and a new party, the Greens, were trailblazers for equality. When the CDU lost women's votes in the elections, the interest in women's issues increased in this party as well.

In 1983, the Green Party adopted women's quotas. Gradually, other parties followed suit. Several hundred equal rights offices were established locally, and in 1986, a Ministry for Women was created. In the mid-1990s, about half of the central committee members in the Green Party and the SPD were women, while they amounted to a third in the CDU and a quarter in CDU's sister party the CSU, the Christian Social Union of Bavaria (IPU, 1997). The electoral system was a mixture of proportional representation and majority elections, and the representation of women in the Federal Assembly increased from 8.5 per cent in 1980 to 26 per cent in 1994. The SPD had a third in its parliamentary group, while the CDU only had a sixth and the CSU even fewer. In the CDU coalition government, there were two women ministers (11 per cent).

In the 1990s, West Germany had about 80 million inhabitants and was one of the world's largest industrialised countries. When East and West Germany were reunified, it was not by forming a new, third state: East Germany became part of the existing Federal Republic. The West German constitution was also applied to the former GDR, and with some modifications, the West German economic and political system was introduced throughout the common nation. Five new *Länder* (states) were created. Parliament was expanded, and the political parties in the East were incorporated into the West German ones. As before, parliament consisted of two chambers: a directly elected Federal Assembly and an indirectly elected Federal Council. The Federal Assembly elected the chancellor (prime minister) and the cabinet from the majority party or coalition, but ministers did not have to be members of the Assembly. The chancellor was given a strong position, while the federal president was essentially ceremonial, elected by members of the Federal Assembly and an equal number of representatives from the *Länder* legislatures (Morgan, 1984; Kolinsky, 1993; Lemke, 1994; Henig and Henig, 2001).

Convenient scandal

The reason why Angela Merkel became the CDU president in 2000 was dramatic. The new unified German government had to deal with deep economic, social, political and cultural differences between the East and West. The long-serving and highly respected Chancellor Helmut Kohl from the CDU oversaw the unification. But the economy faltered and problems arose. In 1998, the CDU coalition lost the elections for the first time since 1982. The party had internal troubles and a financial scandal was about to destroy the CDU as a whole. Disclosures of corrupt and illegal practices brought down both CDU President Helmut Kohl and his successor, President Wolfgang Schäuble. In such a crisis, the party bosses were at a loss about what to do. Angela Merkel, who was deputy leader, first tried to find out what really happened, and when she became convinced that Kohl had done wrong, she went public, said what her view was and demanded a fresh start for the party without him. She was accused of betraying Kohl's trust, but for Merkel, Kohl had betrayed her trust. And the party was more important than the individual (Mills, 2008: 57). She turned according to the wind in the right second, and thereby she flew to the top – as a transitional solution, according to many people.

   In such an extraordinary situation, traditional attitudes did not block a woman as usual, but assisted her politically. The party bosses thought that Merkel could be suited to do the cleaning up and rebuild the CDU's moral reputation, and then they could take over again afterwards. Merkel stood near the central party circles, but as a woman, she was not part of them. She was not struck by the financial scandal and was considered to have a clean record. This was strengthened by the regional party meetings she organised when the crisis broke out. Here, Merkel was reminiscent of a *Trümmerfrau*, a woman who cleaned up house ruins after World War II bombings. The CDU needed a new deal. Merkel was at the right place at the right time when a path opened up to the top.[30]

Advantageous weaknesses

Angela Merkel was no novice in politics. She had held important positions since 1991. Helmut Kohl made her his protégée, or 'chicken', as she was called. In a broad, unifying popular party like the CDU, it was important to have different groups represented in the party leadership, and a type of informal quotas were used to achieve this. Features many perceived as Angela Merkel's weaknesses thus became her strength. After reunification, the CDU needed to be more attractive to East Germans. There was pressure to attract more young people and women, especially Protestants. Merkel thus fulfilled several important requirements. In addition, Kohl wanted industrious, adaptable and obedient staff. The modest young Merkel seemed to be an excellent fit.

Kohl appointed Angela Merkel as minister for women and youth. She was Germany's youngest cabinet minister since World War II. Merkel had not been involved in women's issues in the past, but was determined and quick to learn. She worked to preserve the extensive network of child care that existed in the GDR, and a law on gender equality was passed. She focused on family-friendly practices in the workplace, gave scholarships to women and kept a moderate course on the issue of abortion. Even if she was not particularly interested in the issues, she wished to do a good job to promote her career. Neither her predecessor nor her successor succeeded in this (Wiliarty, 2008a: 86–7).

A few months after she became a minister, 'das Mädchen' (the girl), as Kohl called her, was elected deputy leader of the party, with 86 per cent of the vote. Then, in 1994, she was appointed minister for the environment, nature conservation and nuclear safety. In addition to her professional competence, she demonstrated that she was an astute and practical politician.

When the CDU lost the elections in 1998, Angela Merkel became the party's secretary general. She was appointed by the new party leader, Wolfgang Schäuble, after pressure from women activists in the party. With 18 per cent women, the CDU was the party in the Federal Assembly that was most male-dominated, and the party's own decision in 1996 to have one third women in party positions was not met. In addition, the CDU did particularly poorly among women voters. The only available woman that could serve as secretary general was Angela Merkel, and she helped the party do well locally, with victory in six out of seven *Länder* elections.[31]

Diligent pastor's daughter

There was considerable confusion when Angela Merkel abruptly rose up through the ranks and became party president. She had not distinguished herself with political initiatives or stances. With clear discrimination against women, the media described her 'bland hairstyle', her 'drab appearance', her subservience to Kohl and her 'greyness' as a candidate (Wiliarty, 2008a: 82).

Angela Merkel's background did not give many indications of where she stood politically, either. She was born in 1954 in Hamburg in West Germany, where her mother, Herlind, came from. When Angela was three months old, the family moved to East Germany, where her father, Horst Kasner, who was born in Berlin, took over a country church near Brandenburg. Kasner was both a Lutheran pastor and an idealistic socialist and thought that he was particularly needed in the East.

He soon moved to Templin and became head of a seminar for further education for pastors. The Church was not banned, but the priests and their families were discriminated against in many ways. Herlind was also a socialist and a teacher of English and Latin, but the wife of a priest could not get teaching posts in the GDR.

Angela was the eldest of three siblings, and her parents had high hopes for her. Her father's expectations fuelled her later political ambitions. She also felt that she had to excel as the daughter of a pastor (Thompson and Lennartz, 2006: 101). She was diligent and did exceptionally well, learnt Russian and participated in Freie Deutsche Jugend, the communist youth movement, like young people usually did at the time. Membership was important to being allowed to study at the university. Actually, Angela wanted to be a teacher, but she could not, so she chose physics (Mills, 2008: 33–4). The family often visited relatives in the West and Angela came to reject the East German system as inhumane. But she did not show it outwardly and therefore did not face major obstacles in her studies and career. Natural science was also a prestigious and non-ideological subject. After a PhD in science at the academy in East Berlin, she became a researcher. She married a fellow student, Ulrich Merkel, in 1977, but after a few years, they divorced. Angela lived for a long time with her second husband, Joachim Sauer, a professor of chemistry, who was her mentor, before they married in 1998. The couple had no children together, but Sauer had two sons from a previous marriage.[32]

From grey mouse to lioness

When she was young, Angela Merkel appeared as fairly apolitical, even though she participated in the Freie Deutsche Jugend. The dramatic events in connection with the fall of the Berlin Wall got her involved. She joined a group called Democratic Awakening (DA) and she soon became the group's spokesperson in the media. She was not a candidate in the East German elections in March 1990, but the DA and CDU formed a partnership, and she was a media contact for the CDU-led transitional government. After reunification, she went from physics to politics. 'For me, three things were immediately clear after reunification', she stated, 'I wanted to get into the *Bundestag* [parliament], I favoured rapid German unity and supported a free-market economy' (*Berliner Morgenpost*, 1998, cited in Niethammer, 2000). She joined the CDU and got a job in the press office of the federal government. Then, she ran for election in a CDU-dominated district in northern Germany in December 1990, defeated two West German candidates and became a member of the Federal Assembly.

It has been claimed that Angela Merkel's journey to the top in German politics was unlikely, accidental and unexpected. There were evidently a number of coincidences and strikes of luck. Among the fortuitous circumstances, attention has been called to: the family's move to the GDR and Angela Merkel's education there; the fall of the Wall and her role as deputy spokesperson of the pre-unification government; her choice of the CDU and contact with Chancellor Kohl; the pressure for women, 'Ossis' (people from the East) and Protestants in the government; her appointment as minister; and her election as deputy leader of the CDU and as secretary general before the CDU financial crisis led her to the top in the CDU.

Although many sheer coincidences played a role, Merkel had to grasp the opportunities that arose and exploit them to her advantage. She had to do the jobs in a satisfactory way and then be able to advance further. The CDU had long been an unwieldy alliance of clashing political traditions and views. Merkel's working methods and management style helped her. She was extremely industrious and efficient, acquainted herself well with the issues, and listened to others before she took a stand. Her approach was more pragmatic than ideological. She voiced broadly liberal views, had a sense of power and could vary her leadership according to the circumstances. As a leader, she was first and foremost the party administrator. She was concerned with problem-solving and action. To build consensus, she balanced views and tensions between various party groups at the same time as she did not associate with any particular group and thereby reject others. In this way, she got relatively few enemies and could preserve and represent the whole. She was also ready to accept new ideas and promote change. Her strategy was one of small steps. Furthermore, she represented a new manner with her calm, thoughtful, honest, direct and clear way of speaking.

As was the case with many women leaders, a male top politician helped Angela Merkel advance. But Helmut Kohl, like many of Merkel's male political colleagues, mentors and opponents, tended to underestimate her talent and drive. Not only her gender, but also her reserved manner, contributed to this. However, this tendency did not hurt her. On the contrary, Merkel managed to take advantage of it and use it in her rise to the top.

Leading the CDU without her prominent mentor was no bed of roses for Angela Merkel. She enjoyed considerable popularity among ordinary people, but many in the party were against her, especially male party bosses who, for years, had elbowed their way forward under Kohl and suddenly found themselves overtaken by a young female upstart from the East. The intrigues against her were described as 'Machiavellian'. But Merkel learned to turn critics' attacks against them and could be pretty tough – 'Merkiavellian' or 'Lady Merciless' – and she used her position to sweep challengers aside. Nevertheless, before the chancellor elections in 2002, she was outmanoeuvred, with the CDU presenting the male leader of the CSU as a candidate instead of Merkel against the SPD's Gerhard Schröder. Despite a huge lead initially in the polls, the CSU leader lost and Merkel took over as leader of the conservative CDU/CSU opposition in the Federal Assembly. The year after, she was re-elected as party leader with a massive majority and her preferred candidate, Horst Köhler, became federal president.[33]

The 'grey GDR mouse' became a 'lioness', the most powerful woman in German politics. People called her 'Maggie Merkel' and 'Iron Frau', after Margaret Thatcher, although the two women scarcely had more in common than the fact that they were conservatives. Merkel guided the CDU in a more social-liberal direction, and it was said that she was 'a little bit of Margaret Thatcher and a little bit of Tony Blair' (Klinkert, 2005).

In the crossfire

When Chancellor Gerhard Schröder suddenly announced early elections in 2005, a year before schedule, Angela Merkel was the CDU's candidate for chancellor. It was the first time that a woman ran in a chancellor election. With record-high unemployment, virtually no growth in the economy, huge budget deficits and significant uncertainty about the country's future, one would think that the election campaign was straightforward for the opposition. But it was not. From a lead for the CDU of 20 percentage points in the polls, the difference shrank to almost zero.

Merkel was criticised for an unclear policy because she promised market-friendly reforms and, at the same time, a 'social market economy' with less unemployment. She was not a very catchy speaker, committed factual errors and scared people with unpopular tax proposals (Mills, 2008: 62–74; Wiliarty, 2010a: 137–54).

For a long time, Merkel tried to avoid women's issues, thinking that being associated with femininity or feminism could have detrimental effects on public opinion. But in the media, the female novice was lined up against the male champion, with questions raised as to whether she could cope with him and be his equal. Towards the end of the campaign, Merkel began talking about child care and women in positions of power: 'Never in my political career has my gender played as big a role as in the last few months', she said, 'In return, I have been much more open about my woman-ness than I used to. And I'm not just talking about my makeup' (Hawley, 2005; see also Schwarzer, 2006).

Top of Europe

When the result was clear, the CDU had received only one percentage point more votes than the SPD (35 per cent versus 34 per cent). Except for one election, the result was the poorest for the CDU since 1949. An intense tug of war went on for several weeks. Both the CDU and the SPD wanted the job as chancellor, and men on both sides used the tricks they knew to prevent a woman from going to the top. But what Merkel lacked in public charisma, she now made up with in efficient negotiation skills, and to the surprise of many, she managed to become chancellor. Schröder finally gave in on the condition that the SPD got half of the new cabinet: the deputy chancellor and seven ministers. A government platform was elaborated with tax increases, higher retirement ages, reductions of government spending and an investment plan to fight unemployment. In parliament, Merkel obtained 397 of 614 votes. Fifty representatives of the government coalition voted against or abstained.

At 51 years old, Angela Merkel became not only the first woman chancellor of Germany, but also the youngest since World War II. And she was the top leader in a great European power. It was bitter victory, though, observers noted, as she had to lead a coalition that she had rejected, and implement a policy that she had gone against. But a bitter victory was much better than a defeat.

The new chancellor quickly put the doomsday predictions to shame. As soon as she was appointed, she travelled to London, Paris and Washington and managed to gather an EU summit together to find a solution to the budget crisis. One hundred days after she had taken office, she had 80 per cent support in the polls, the highest any chancellor had received. 'From duckling to the eagle', observers commented. And it was at the international level that she made her mark the strongest. She became known for her ability to resolve crises and create consensus and shaped herself into a European leader with a centre of gravity in Berlin, strengthened Germany's relations with the US and made relations with Russia more sober. She was the second woman, after Margaret Thatcher, who led the group of eight leading industrialised countries (the G8) meetings and made progress with regards to climate change, poverty and support to Africa (*Economist*, 2006; Mills, 2008: 72–94).

Woman and hostess

Angela Merkel's rise to power was at least partially *because* of her gender, not in spite of it. Merkel benefited from gender stereotypes and hopes related to women's political role, and the women's movement and the impact it had on issues, expectations and political institutions (Ferree, 2006). Merkel, herself, never made a political issue of her gender or placed women's issues at the centre of her public policies. But her appearance was the subject of an enormous amount of discussion. She made significant changes over time: from 'Ossi–Frau' (Eastern woman) to more stylish hair and clothing. And it was noted that she became both more feminine and more Western – that is, both more and less competent at the same time (Wiliarty, 2010a: 146–7).

However, Merkel was never provocative in her appearance, always discreetly feminine, quiet and polite. She was generally perceived as a rational technocrat, stemming from her scientific training and East German background. At the same time, she was referred to as the nurturing 'Mutti' (mother) by her colleagues and gradually also by voters (though she is childless). The political scientist Sarah Elise Wiliarty (2010a) notes that in the press, Merkel was more and more portrayed not only as mother, but also 'Landesmutter' (mother of the country), as well as mother and hostess. The last may be a new positive stereotype allowing women politicians to be gracious, generous and powerful at the same time (Wiliarty, 2010a: 152–3).

Female activists in Germany have supported Angela Merkel as chancellor. Although she never called herself a 'feminist', her appointments, allies and policies slant towards feminism. As CDU president and chancellor, Merkel's closest advisors were women, more women were employed in higher positions and she appointed women in the cabinet. In 2005, there were 32 per cent women in the Federal Assembly and the cabinet included five women (one third). Following pressure from the women's movement, Germany tabled equality on the agenda at the G8 meeting in 2007 and became an active defender of women's rights internationally.

Merkel has quietly advocated gender equality and supported policies favourable to women. She has attempted to modernise the welfare state in terms of family policies and promote women as workers. There has been a strong focus on increasing the number of kindergartens so that parents have a real choice between working at home or having an occupational career with children. Parental leave was also introduced with a quota for fathers.

The measures were criticised because they challenged traditional policy in the West. But compared to other European countries, Germany clearly lagged behind with regard to equality, employment among mothers and child care, though a general law against discrimination was adopted in 2006. Merkel thought that the pay gap between women and men was a real problem, but state power should not, according to her, be used to promote equal pay. Women had to ask for a raise themselves, and the law against discrimination provided a basis for such claims.[34]

Victorious loser

Leading a grand coalition of the CDU and SPD was anything but easy. But as chancellor, Merkel gradually enjoyed great respect from politicians of all parties. She followed up the environmental policy of the Greens, the social responsibility of the SPD and strengthened the German economy. The growth figures were solid. Unemployment went down, and greenhouse gases were reduced. But there was conflict within the government, and there were warnings that the reforms in the economy were too small and the social costs too large. Merkel was accused of being too cautious, focusing on welfare instead of reform to win the favour of the voters. But she revolutionised the CDU and conservative policies. She changed the party's views on family and child-rearing, stimulated the integration of Moslems in German society, and attached less significance to Catholic views on homosexuality, divorce and abortion. As a party, the CDU became solidly placed in the centre, and the SPD had problems with its position.

In the elections in 2009, Angel Merkel was the candidate for chancellor from the CDU and her message was that she, safe and competent as a mother of the country, would guide the Germans out of the worst economic crisis since World War II by reducing taxes, creating jobs and deregulating the labour market. This required a centre-right coalition.

There was widespread uncertainty and dissatisfaction among the voters. The election campaign was unusually dull and voter participation was low. Merkel's CDU got less support than previously, at 34 per cent, but the SPD experienced a disastrous election, obtaining only 23 per cent. The two major parties only got a total of 57 per cent of the vote, against 69 per cent in 2005. The opposition parties were the election winners: the liberal Free Democratic Party (FDP) on the Right went up to 15 per cent, while the Greens and the Left (a breakaway party from the SPD founded in 2005) got 11 and 12 per cent, respectively.

Although the CDU obtained fewer votes, the party won 13 more seats in the Federal Assembly. Merkel could get rid of the grand coalition, which was heavily criticised within the CDU, and instead go into a government alliance with the FDP. This represented a clear shift of policy towards the Right, with an emphasis on tax cuts and business reforms.

Unlike in 2005, more women voted for the CDU than the SPD in 2009. But women's representation in the Federal Assembly was about the same, at 33 per cent. Angela Merkel – now being called 'Supermerkel' – became chancellor, with a man from the FDP as vice chancellor and five women ministers (one third) in the cabinet. She was described as 'Europe's quiet leader', and while she was in power, Germany became more powerful and more dominant.[35]

Crisis and success

When the financial crises arose in Greece and other European countries, Merkel's role became crucial, and she was perceived as a strict accountant and mother. 'Madame Europe' was replaced by 'Madame No', 'Madame Germania' and 'The Empress of Berlin'. Germany was Europe's largest economy and had got rid of its debts. Merkel did not want the country to become a cash cow for others, while she prevented the Eurozone from collapsing. She held strictly to the rules, reviewing costs and benefits, demanded discipline for solidarity, and did not give in.

As the crises deepened, Germany's chancellor became increasingly controversial. When Germany gave financial assistance to other EU countries, Merkel also wanted Germany to have a say. 'Germany takes over the EU', observers noted, and Merkel was harshly criticised because she was leading Europe further down into the abyss. By demanding savings and cuts in public expenditures, European countries were stricken by unemployment, reduced living standards and social problems. People demonstrated and gave the chancellor a Hitler moustache on drawings of her.

But at home, Angela Merkel was popular. The German economy moved relatively easily through the stormy weather, with economic growth and high employment. In fact, German industry was growing at the expense of the economies in other European countries. Although many Germans had low salaries and the gap between the rich and poor was increasing, the CDU/CSU had one of its most decisive victories in the elections in 2013, obtaining 42 per cent of the vote. The CDU's ally, the FDP, on the contrary, lost all its seats. The SPD got 26 per cent. With 311 seats in the Federal Assembly, Angela Merkel only lacked five seats for a majority. But a coalition government was required and collaboration was established again with the SPD. The representation of women in the Federal Assembly increased to 37 per cent, but the cabinet included one third of women ministers as before (five of 15).

Angela Merkel became a role model for women worldwide, and *Forbes* placed her on top of the list of the world's most powerful women in 2006, 2007, 2008 and 2009, as number 4 in 2010, and again on top in 2011, 2012 and 2013. She was also considered to be one of the most powerful people in the world, regardless of gender.

Jóhanna Sigurðardóttir rescues the Saga island

The elite must go

Twenty-nine years after Vigdís Finnbogadóttir attracted international attention by being elected president of Iceland, the country was again in focus. A woman, Jóhanna Sigurðardóttir, became prime minister. Although women had gradually obtained one third of the seats in parliament and the cabinet, the prime minister was an important step. The position was more powerful than the president. And Sigurðardóttir was not only a woman; she was openly lesbian and living in a civil partnership with another woman. She not only became Iceland's first woman prime minister, but also the world's first openly gay head of government. In Iceland, the lesbian relationship was no issue. Laws against gay sex were repealed in 1940 and, becoming one of the first nations in the world to do so, civil partnerships for same-sex couples were legalised in 1996. But the international media gasped.

However, it was not the woman top leader first of all that brought Iceland to the media headlines. It was Iceland's spectacular economic collapse in connection with the international financial crisis in 2008. The country's three commercial banks, having grown to 10 times the country's gross domestic product (GDP), failed in quick succession. External debt, unemployment and inflation shot up. Both households and businesses were struck. In the capital, Reykjavik, people went to the streets to protest, week after week, against the government's handling of the situation. At its highest, the 'Saucepan Revolution', as it was called, because the demonstrators were beating pots and pans, included 32,000 people, more than 10 per cent of Iceland's total population. After 14 weeks, the (male) Prime Minister Geir Haarde from the centre-right Independence Party resigned with the whole coalition government.

That was when a woman came in. In such an exceptional situation, all the political parties were consulted before the president asked the head of the centre-left Social Democratic Alliance to be prime minister. She refused due to health reasons, but suggested her woman colleague, Jóhanna Sigurðardóttir, instead. At 66 years old, she had been a member of the Althing (parliament) the longest and was the only minister who had increased her popularity during the crisis. When Prime Minister Haarde's limousine was pelted with eggs, Jóhanna Sigurðardóttir had 73 per cent support in the polls. In February 2009, Jóhanna (as Icelanders called her) was sworn in as head of a minority coalition government and set about organising new elections.[36]

From stewardess to prime minister

Jóhanna Sigurðardóttir had a surprising life, from airline stewardess to trade union official, parliamentarian, cabinet minister and then prime minister. She was born in 1942. Her grandmother was one of the earliest Icelandic female labour leaders in the 1920s and 1930s and her father, Sigurður Egill Ingimundarson, was an MP in the 1960s. Jóhanna undertook a degree at the Commercial College of Iceland in 1960 and courses at academic level in 1962. She worked as an airline stewardess for nine years and then as an office worker for seven, and was strongly involved in trade union activities. She headed the Icelandic Cabin Crew Association in 1966 and 1969 and was responsible for the first strike carried out by Icelandic airline stewardesses. Then, she sat on the board of the Commercial Workers' Union from 1976 to 1983. She married the banker Thorvaldur Jóhannesson in 1970 and had two sons, but the couple divorced. In 2002, Sigurðardóttir entered into a homosexual partnership with a female writer, Jónína Leósdóttir, who had a son from a previous marriage.

In 1978, Jóhanna Sigurðardóttir was elected as a Social Democratic representative to parliament from Reykjavik and was subsequently re-elected eight times. The women's movement was strong, especially in the capital. Jóhanna was a member of the presidency of parliament for several periods, vice president of the Social Democratic Party for eight years and minister of social affairs from 1987 to 1994. She ran for election as the leader of the Social Democratic Party, but lost. She then gave a speech, clenching her fist and declared: 'My time will come!' (*Current Biography*, 2010: 79). She resigned as a minister and formed her own party, Þjóðvaki (the nation's awakening), in 1995, which got four seats in parliament. In 2000, the party joined forces with the Social Democrats in the Social Democratic Alliance, and Jóhanna Sigurðardóttir became minister of social affairs in 2007 in the coalition government with the Independence Party. While she was a minister, a gender balance of 40/60 was adopted for public boards and committees. When she ran for election as leader of the Social Democratic Alliance for the second time in 2009, she was elected practically unanimously. Her time had come (*Current Biography*, 2010; Prime Minister's Office Iceland, 2013).

The Left sweeps in

As a politician, Jóhanna Sigurðardóttir was known as a tireless fighter for gender equality, champion of the underprivileged and advocate of progressive social welfare policies. She said: 'I'm in politics because I believe that progress can be made and that the struggles of the underprivileged and of the minorities are moving our communities forward' (Morán, 2013). She became known as 'Saint Jóhanna'.

Taking over as prime minister, Jóhanna declared that the nation had to learn from the mistakes that had brought the country into a deep economic downturn. A paradigm shift was needed. The government would therefore be a liberal welfare government, seeking to combine social responsibility with the advantages of the market to benefit public rather than individual interests. For the first time, the government comprised an equal number of women and men, and the constitution would be changed to increase the involvement of the general public in the governance of the country and ensure greater social justice. The financial system would be restructured to develop healthy financial activities directed primarily at serving the needs of customers, and special efforts would be made to assist individuals facing economic difficulties, create jobs and promote welfare (Prime Minister's Office Iceland, 2009a).

Although the media and politics in Iceland were still clearly male-dominated and women politicians were usually criticised more harshly than men, the appointment of Jóhanna was generally greeted with enthusiasm. In the media, she was presented as a capable, efficient leader. She was widely hailed as one of the few uncorrupted politicians Iceland had left and Icelanders liked her quiet, steady personality in contrast to the 'New Viking' menfolk. Some conservatives were critical, but decent in their criticisms. The former prime minister said: 'Jóhanna is a good woman – but she likes public spending, she is a tax raiser' (Byers, 2009; see also Mundy, 2013). In the elections in April 2009, the Left got an overwhelming victory. Iceland took the largest leap to the left in the country's history and got a predominantly Social Democratic government for the first time. The Independence Party, which had been in power for 18 years, received the lowest support ever. The party lost nine of its 25 seats.

The Left won a majority in parliament, with 20 seats for the Social Democratic Alliance and 14 for the Left–Green Movement (out of a total of 63). Jóhanna continued as prime minister with a strengthened coalition government of Social Democrats and Left–Greens. The elections were based on proportional representation and the number of women in parliament increased from 21 to 27 (43 per cent). Among the 10 cabinet ministers, four were now women, but the number fell to three or two later.

The government managed to calm the waters as it actively started to gain control of the finances, seek solutions to the debt and rebuild the economy. Fifty important actions were set in motion in the first 100 days after the elections. Chief executive bank officers were forced out and central banks were nationalised. The country applied for EU accession and started to review monetary policy and the fisheries management system. Loans amounting to thousands of millions were obtained from the International Monetary Fund (IMF) and various countries. In addition, a marriage equality law was passed and Jóhanna married her partner. In the middle of it all, the government had to deal with an erupting volcano that stalled travel around the world (Prime Minister's Office Iceland, 2009a, 2009b, 2009c; Munday 2013).

Feminists strike

Even if Jóhanna did not become prime minister primarily because she was a woman, in the wake of the economic collapse and the women in government, there arose a debate about gender and female leadership. It was pointed out that men had created a mess that women had to clean up. Studies of the collapse were initiated, and researchers pointed out that a male norm, with emphasis on exaggerated gambling, hegemonic masculinity and nationalist manliness ideals, were behind the development that led to the crisis. The banking sector was controlled by a small group of financial princes who supported each other and had the support of politicians, and important decisions were taken in informal networks. One conclusion was that there had to be more openness and diversity in the top layers of economic activity. Feminists in parliament jumped at the chance and gender quotas for women on company boards were adopted.[37]

Labour force participation among Icelandic women was widespread, and several women were now promoted or brought in to lead banks. Women also led the financial companies that were established to do business in a different way, with emphasis on balance, transparency and accountability, justice, social responsibility, and sustainability. Further, budget-making was gendered, the rights of children were strengthened and it was decided to combat the sex industry by prohibiting the purchase of sex, shutting strip clubs and acting against trafficking in women (Momaya, 2009a; Bindel, 2010; Carlin, 2012; Møller, 2013).

Jóhanna's role in promoting gender equality and gay rights was historic and admired across the globe. In 2009, *Forbes* placed Jóhanna Sigurðardóttir as number 75 among the world's 100 most powerful women and as number 80 in 2010.

Inspired by the women's activism three women ran as candidates for president in the elections in 2012. In total there were six candidates, all independent, including the incumbent president, Ólafur Grímsson, a man who was running for his fifth term. The woman who got the most votes, Thóra Arnórsdóttir, was a journalist emphasising the need for change; however, Ólafur had shown his capacity to steer the country in a time of crisis and obtained 53 per cent of the vote, while Thóra only got 33 per cent.

Backlash

In 2013, Iceland was one of the crisis-ridden West European countries making the most progress. In late 2011, the country exited recession. Considerable debt was paid back, and the economy was growing rapidly. Taxes were more progressive, unemployment was less than 5 per cent and the welfare state was maintained. A great number of bankers, financiers, businessmen and bureaucrats were brought to court. And in April 2013, Jóhanna signed a historic free trade agreement with China.

Internationally, the country was praised for its efforts, but in Iceland, opinions differed. In 2009, the government faced a practically impossible task, and many people thought that no politicians could have done a better job than Jóhanna and her team. The fact that things could have been a lot worse was 'a policy triumph', and it was a 'miracle' that the government managed to stay in office until the elections. But others were dissatisfied because the government had failed to live up to expectations. It promised to shield households, but many still had economic problems. Healthcare and social benefits were cut, while taxes rose. The government promised a new constitution, but a long and broadly democratic process had not yet led to a decision. The government agreed to repay foreign debts, but was defeated, first, by the people in two referendums and, finally, by the court of the European Free Trade Association (EFTA). Disagreement about the EU and internal divisions in the government did not make things better (Carlin, 2012; Sæther, 2012; Møller, 2013; Ring, 2013).

In 2012, Jóhanna Sigurðardóttir declared that she would not run for parliament again. At the age of 70, after 35 years in politics, it was time to end her 'long and eventful' political career, she stated (Ring, 2013). A male colleague replaced her as leader of the Social Democratic Alliance.

General elections were held in April 2013 and the main choice seemed to be between the centre-right parties that led the country into economic disaster and the Left–Green coalition that had not managed to lead it out again. Twice as many political parties participated in the elections as before, but the leaders of the largest parties were all men. The two centre-right opposition parties, the Independence Party and the Progressive Party, won the election. They obtained 51 per cent of the vote, promising, above all, a great reduction in household debt. A male prime minister from the liberal-agrarian centrist Progressive Party took over with three women and six men in the cabinet. But in parliament, there were 40 per cent women, and the women's movement inside and outside the political parties continued to be strong and well organised (Styrkársdóttir, 2013: 142). Using referendums a new constitution was adopted, the distribution of fishing rights was made more transparent and special rules were introduced for the appointment of top bureaucrats and judges.

Australian Prime Minister Julia Gillard under attack

Women's struggle

In the late 18th century, British convicts and other 'undesirables', mainly men, were sent to 'settle' in Australia, where they developed a tough masculine immigrant society. Explorers, gold diggers and farmers also came, while the indigenous Aborigines were weakened by discrimination and expropriation. In 1901, the six British colonies formed a common federal state, with a mainly European population.

In 1902, Australia was the first country in the world to give majority women the right both to vote and be elected at the national level. But Australia then had the longest gap of any country (41 years) before the first woman was elected to parliament and even longer before one entered the cabinet. The House of Representatives did not have women members continuously before 1980. Aboriginal people did not get uniform voting rights in federal elections until 1962. Those surviving European settlement now form some 3 per cent of the population.

Australia became an immigrant nation with largely British immigrants up to the mid-20th century, but then sources of immigration became more diverse, particularly after the final dismantling of the 'White Australia policy' in the 1970s. The population grew to more than 20 million. The federal state comprised six states and a political system inspired by the British. A governor general represented the queen, and the federal parliament had two chambers: a House of Representatives elected by majority vote and a Senate representing the states and territories, where elections were based on proportional representation. Both had roughly equal power. Voting became compulsory, and a winning candidate for the House of Representative had to have at least 50 per cent of the vote after distribution of preferences, making it difficult for newcomers and people differing from the norm to be elected. The prime minister and the cabinet were recruited from parliament and were accountable to it.

Female activists struggled for voting rights and women's organisations worked to improve the situation of women, but activism was limited until the second feminist wave at the beginning of the 1970s. Increasing levels of education made women from the majority more frustrated with their traditional role as mothers and they began to demand economic and reproductive rights and services such as child care. They formed associations and groups, including a non-partisan lobby, the Women's Electoral Lobby, to get political parties and politicians to respond to the new demands. Indigenous women had their own demands, such as the right to land, healthcare and housing, and the women's movement also took up these demands.[38]

Labor accepts the challenge

At the federal level, the centre-left Labor Party and a conservative coalition of the Liberal and the National Parties alternated in power. The Women's Electoral Lobby was founded in 1972, and made women's demands an important part of the campaign, coinciding with a more general desire for change after 23 years of conservative rule. Labor formed the government and began to create women's policy machinery in government.

But the party suffered a dramatic defeat in 1975 after coming under sustained attack by the Murdoch press. The lack of appeal to women voters by a party dominated by male trade unions was defined as a major reason, and Labor started to address the 'gender gap'. The party adopted affirmative action and developed comprehensive women-friendly policies. Later (from 1994), the party adopted enforceable candidate quotas for winning seats. While women became increasingly important in the leadership of progressive minor parties and then the Labor Party, the coalition parties did not accept quotas and put fewer women into parliament.

The Labor Party came to power again in 1983 and tried to combine deregulation of the economy with moves towards greater gender equity. The number of women ministers increased. Australia became party to the CEDAW. Women's policy machinery was strengthened, including at the intergovernmental level. A law against discrimination on the basis of gender was adopted, as well as affirmative action for women in education and economic life. More women received higher education, and they participated extensively in the labour force, but were discriminated against in terms of positions and wages. Funding for child care was increased, but commercial provision was encouraged at the same time. Funding was also increased for a range of women's services, including those dealing with gender-based violence. But women's representation in the House of Representatives remained low: in 1996, it was only 16 per cent, while it amounted to 30 per cent in the Senate.

Unexpected change

The coalition parties came to power again in 1996 and remained until 2007. The representation of women in the House of Representatives gradually increased to a quarter, but the gap between the representation of women in government and in opposition parties grew during this period, thanks to Labor quotas.

In 2007, Labor took over again with 27 per cent women in the House of Representatives and 36 per cent in the Senate. Kevin Rudd became prime minister and set a record with four women ministers in the inner and three in the outer cabinet, amounting totally to 24 per cent, and one of them was deputy prime minister. Australia managed to avoid economic recession after the global financial crisis and Rudd was named the most popular prime minister in 30 years. Nevertheless, before the election in 2010, he was replaced by a woman.

Julia Gillard was known to be determined, astute and persistent. She was born in Wales in 1961. Her father, John Gillard, came from an impoverished background and did not get much education. His wife, Moira, did not either. In 1966, the family migrated to Australia with their two daughters. Julia was the youngest and only four years old. They settled in a suburb near Adelaide, where John got a job as a psychiatric nurse and Moira in a nursing home. Both worked hard and emphasised achievement and career. They were also great readers and interested in Labor politics. But when Julia was 16, she told her mother that she did not want to have children. She could not see how marriage, a family and a demanding job could be combined (Kent, 2010: 17). Julia went to university, was an outstanding student and graduated with a combined arts–law degree. But student politics was her great interest and she became, first, vice president, then president, of the student union, as the second woman to do so, and participated in the Labor club.

After university, Gillard worked in a law firm and did well. But politics was what she wanted to do. She tried twice to be selected for parliament, but failed. She then became chief of staff of the Labor leader in Victoria, the second most populous state. She learned a lot and drafted the constitution of EMILY's list, a US-inspired feminist fund-raising organisation that helped Labor women candidates who had made commitments on abortion and gender equity.

In July 1998, Gillard was elected to the House of Representatives, and in 2001, she became a member of Labor's shadow cabinet, with responsibility for population and immigration, indigenous people and health. She allied herself with her party colleague Kevin Rudd, who entered parliament at the same time, so when he became party leader in 2006, she became deputy. The following year, when Labor came to power, Kevin Rudd became prime minister and Julia Gillard became deputy prime minister and minister of education, of employment and social inclusion. She served as acting prime minister during the prime minister's frequent overseas trips.

The government started with a break from the past: it apologised for the suffering inflicted on the indigenous people and signed the Kyoto protocol for climate change. But then there were problems in follow-up, priorities and management. Labor went down in the polls and when Rudd shelved the centrepiece of his environmental strategy, people thought that he was a coward. In addition, he came into conflict with the resources sector. As the 2010 elections approached, the faction leaders in Labor thought that it would be better to go to the elections with Julia Gillard as prime minister than Kevin Rudd. Gillard had made herself popular with her efforts to reform education and obtain decent wages for workers and was a more effective decision-maker (BBC News, 2010, 2013a, 2013b; Bryant, 2010; Kent, 2010).

Tough time

It was an extremely hard decision to make, but in order to save the party and party policies, Julia Gillard agreed to take over as prime minister. 'I love this country, and I was not going to sit idly by and watch an incoming opposition cut education, cut health and smash rights at work,' she said (BBC News, 2010; Kent, 2010: 361–5). Kevin Rudd resigned, and Gillard was unanimously elected as party leader and became prime minister in June 2010. She was not only the first woman prime minister, but the first unmarried – she was cohabiting with Tim Mathieson – and the first since the 1920s that was born in another country. She kept Rudd's cabinet generally unchanged and prepared for elections.

The election campaign was tough on many levels and Julia Gillard struggled. Statements she made created negative reactions. She avoided gender issues because they were considered an electoral liability. But she was subjected to sexist misrepresentation focused on her marital status and her decision not to have children. She was attacked for being 'deliberately barren' and without the ability to understand society because she had no children (Sawer, 2013a: 11). At the elections in August, Labor only obtained 72 of the 150 seats in the House of Representatives, the same as the conservative coalition. It was the first hung parliament in decades at the federal level.

After negotiations, Julia Gillard nevertheless continued as prime minister with a minority government supported by one Green and three independents. Kevin Rudd became foreign minister. There were 25 per cent women in the House of Representatives and 36 per cent in the Senate. Gillard appointed three women in the inner and two in the outer cabinet, five in all (17 per cent), fewer than her predecessor. She also had a male deputy. She started to increase the public hospitals, health services and support to parents to cover the costs of their children's schooling.

After she became prime minister, the sexist attacks on Julia Gillard intensified. According to the professor of politics Marian Sawer, Gillard was the victim of appalling levels of sexism not seen before in Australian public life. She was called 'bitch' and 'liar'. There was hate speech and vilification on Facebook and cartoons were distributed with the PM naked wearing a dildo. Feminists reacted promptly and mobilised highly successfully against the sexism, but it continued. In October 2012, Gillard gave a 15-minute intervention in parliament where she described the leader of the opposition as a misogynist. Both the content and the passion made the speech a sensation and it won admiration around the world (Sawer, 2013a: 12–14; 2013b).

Ousted by a colleague

In addition to the hostile opposition and media, the internal battle for leadership in the Labor Party continued. Kevin Rudd fought a relentless battle to regain the prime ministership. In February 2012, Rudd challenged Julia Gillard, but lost the ballot 71 votes to 31. In March 2013, he declined to stand in another leadership challenge, but in June, exactly three years after Julia Gillard was installed as Australia's first women prime minister, she was ousted by Kevin Rudd as leader of the Labor Party, with 57 votes to 45. The change came ahead of the general elections in September 2013 (Walsh, 2013).

As Labor leader, Julia Gillard was, of course, politically controversial and she had problems communicating effectively. There was a very hostile reception in the print media to her raising issues of gender equality in the latter part of her prime ministership and this combined with a loss of male votes for Labor. The sexist attacks and rival jealousy did not make anything easier, and they overshadowed her impressive legislative record. In fact, according to her biographer Jacqueline Kent (2013), as prime minister, Gillard achieved a higher rate of passing legislation than any Australian prime minister, even though she headed a minority government. During her time in office, the economy grew and unemployment was reduced. She led landmark policies on climate change, school reform and the funding of care for the disabled. In addition, she supported the extension of equal pay to community service workers and the funding of their pay increases. In 2010, *Forbes* placed Gillard as number 58 among the world's 100 most powerful women; in 2011, as number 23; in 2012, as number 27; and in 2013, as number 28.

Julia Gillard declared that she would leave politics if she lost the leadership contest with Kevin Rudd. And with Rudd as leader, Labor lost the 2013 elections, obtaining only 55 seats. The centre-right Liberal–National coalition got 90 seats and a male prime minister from the Liberal Party took over. In the House of Representatives, there were 26 per cent women, and in the Senate, 41 per cent, but he only appointed one woman minister (in a cabinet of 19). Julia Gillard noted that the 'gender revolution' had failed. Australia was not ready for a woman leader. But she hoped more women would enter politics, though her own experience was 'mixed'. She was confident that it would be easier for the next woman and the next (BBC News, 2013a; Pearlman, 2013). After politics, the first woman prime minister became a visiting professor at the University of Adelaide (Attard, 2013; BBC News 2013a, 2013b; Pearlman, 2013; Totaro, 2013).

Breakers, walls and rising tide

By 2010, almost half of the Western industrial nations (15 of 31) had the experience of one or more female leaders. But although the phenomenon became more common, it was not at all self-evident that women should go to the top. More than half of the Western countries have never had a woman head of state or government in modern times. This included Nordic countries such as Denmark and Sweden, where women generally made themselves strongly felt in politics, great powers such as the US and Japan, Southern European countries such as Italy and Spain, and small states such as Luxembourg and Monaco. Denmark got a woman prime minister in 2011.

And the 17 women who rose to the top during the last two decades did not always obtain power and glory. Some were treated roughly and only remained in office for a short period of time. Others were defeated or lost elections. But some became national leaders of considerable importance.[39]

More or less power

Since 1990, seven women in Western countries were elected presidents, which mostly entailed a relatively weak position. The three in Switzerland (Dreifuss, Calmy-Rey and Leuthard) were part of a collective leadership, while the presidents in Israel (Itzik) and Ireland (Robinson and McAleese) had mainly ceremonial roles in parliamentary systems. In addition, Itzik only got a short-term temporary position and the presidents of Switzerland did not function for more than a year. Although the Irish president had limited political power, Robinson strengthened the position and used it to influence public opinion, which was followed up by McAleese to some extent. The seventh president was in Finland, with a dual system, so she had more power, though she shared it with the prime minister.

The Irish presidents remained in office for nearly one and two terms, respectively (seven and 14 years), while the Finnish president served for two terms (12 years).

Ten women obtained top positions with considerable power because they were prime ministers in countries with parliamentary systems. But the situations were, in many cases, exceptionally challenging. Four women were given the task of saving government parties losing support under male leadership (Campbell, Cresson, Gillard, Kiviniemi). Three of them failed after a relatively short time, while the fourth (Gillard) kept going for three years. In addition, one woman was supposed to save the entire country because the male elite had driven it into a financial crisis. Iceland's prime minister (Sigurðardóttir) headed a turnaround for a bit more than four years. The sixth prime minister (Jäätteenmäki) resigned after a very short time.

Four women obtained top leadership positions under relatively normal circumstances. But two only functioned for two to three years. Both Shipley and Çiller were very controversial and resigned as heads of government because their parties lost the elections. But they continued as party leaders. When the Conservative Party in New Zealand then experienced the worst elections for 70 years, Shipley left politics. Çiller continued as a minister for a year after she resigned as prime minister, but then went into opposition. Two years later, her party lost again in the elections, it fell completely out of parliament and Çiller withdrew.

Clark and Merkel remained in office unusually long. Clark lost in elections, but she had then been in office for three consecutive terms, nine years in all. Merkel was re-elected, first, in 2009 and then again in 2013. She had then been chancellor for eight years.

Although the women could benefit from their gender in their recruitment, they had to be able to handle an alien, sometimes hostile, male-dominated world in order to succeed. Politics is a tough competition for men also. But because they were women, they were particularly visible, and they were faced with exceptionally high demands in a rough media-influenced political climate. This was also the case with relatively inexperienced national leaders. Hasty statements and blunders were blown up, and the women could be subjected to harassment and merciless criticism not only of their policies and statements, but also of their gender, appearance and private life. Campbell and Cresson were assigned almost impossible tasks and were subjected to harsh treatment by the media and politicians before they resigned. When Jäätteenmäki made a mistake, the criticism was so strong that she withdrew after a short while, though old-timers said that she did not have to. Gillard was also subjected to sexist attacks, which intensified during her time in office and contributed to her demise.

Resistance to gender quotas

Since the 1990s, the Western industrialised countries have had the highest standard of living in the world, and practically all became party to the CEDAW, established national gender equality machinery, often with a special minister for women, and carried out women-friendly reforms.[40] In comparison to other regions, Western women generally had the best health, lived the longest and had most education. Many had paid employment, but women's share of the labour force, and particularly their access to higher positions, varied from country to country. Almost all the states had liberal democracies, most with a parliamentary system and elections with proportional representation.

Despite an active women's movement in many countries, the participation of women in politics remained limited. More women joined political parties, and some got into the leaderships, but men continued to dominate in the governing bodies. There was great resistance in political circles, even in the Nordic countries, against statutory quotas for women. Recruitment was left to the political parties, and some adopted internal quotas, while others did not and eventually contented themselves with non-binding goals and recommendations. The representation of women in parliaments and the cabinets increased over the years, but unevenly and often slowly.

In Western Europe as a whole, the representation of women in political decision-making was a bit above the world average, but there were marked differences from country to country. With formally the same democratic system, the party structure, political processes and culture could vary greatly. While some countries, especially the Nordic ones, had thriving women's activities in political life and women in different positions, others had very few. The average percentage of women in parliament /lower house was 28 per cent in 2014, ranging from a low of 8 per cent (Japan) to a high of 45 per cent (Sweden). In cabinets there were on average 29 per cent women, ranging from a low of 0 per cent (San Marino) to a high of 57 per cent (Sweden).[41]

Well-equipped for action

None of the women leaders in the West went to the top through their families. Several had centrally placed male politicians as mentors, but the women were usually not launched as their substitutes.

In addition to luck, the women generally rose to the top on the basis of their competence. And it is striking what skills and persistence many of them had. Some came from humble beginnings, but most grew up in middle-class families, where their fathers were intellectuals, employees or self-employed. The majority of their mothers also had an occupation. The future top women were often the eldest or the only child and got lengthy education. Apart from Shipley, who was a teacher, all undertook academic courses and almost all also academic degrees, usually in law, political science or economics. Çiller and Merkel undertook PhDs.

Most of their parents were engaged in society and inspired their daughters. Some supported conservative parties, while others were socialists. Sigurðardóttir's father was an MP, while the father of Dreifuss helped refugees and Robinson's father treated poor patients. The McAleese family reacted against discrimination and violence in Northern Ireland. As a child, Çiller was pushed by politically ambitious parents, while her mother gave Campbell an introduction to feminism.

Many top woman leaders became politically active while they were studying. Campbell, Gillard and Robinson got involved in student politics, while Clark, Jäätteenmäki and Kiviniemi joined political parties. Dreifuss, Halonen and Sigurðardóttir engaged in trade union activity. In the GDR, the disintegration of the country suddenly gave Merkel a political awakening.

After finishing their education, all the top women were economically active, with solid occupations. Six were university teachers (including three professors and one researcher), three were teachers and four worked as lawyers. Two were self-employed, two were general secretaries and one was an office worker and trade union representative. McAleese had the highest position as pro-vice chancellor of a university.

Almost all of the women married. Only two were single (Dreifuss and Gillard, but Gillard was cohabiting), and one was cohabiting and married after she got the top position (Halonen). Ten of the women had children (two or three), while seven were childless. So, a good number of the women combined occupations, children and politics. At this time, the rationalisation of housework and the development of kindergartens had accelerated in many Western countries, and the top women could afford to get paid help, but some worked hard to reconcile the different roles. Four women were divorced, of which one twice (Campbell), and one entered into a lesbian partnership (Sigurðardóttir). The fact that women who were divorced, single mothers or even living in lesbian partnership could act as top politicians, were signs of traditional norms changing, and they occurred in Northern Europe and Canada.

The women's husbands had good occupations as intellectuals and self-employed. How much the men were engaged in the children and home is unclear, but it is reported that several actively supported the wife's political work (Clark, Halonen and Robinson). One went so far that he moved to the capital for her sake (Campbell), while another moved and then retrained for another profession (Shipley).

Party women

Although their professional careers were important, the women rose to top positions primarily through their political parties. They became party members when they were 20–30 years of age. The only exception was Çiller, who was over 40. But in Turkey, political activity was prohibited for a long time.

The women mostly engaged in party-political activity in the 1970s and 1980s, at a time when women's organisations demanded reforms and more women in politics. Only Ruth Dreifuss became a party member as early as 1965. Çiller and Merkel only joined in 1990 in connection with the democratisation processes in Turkey and the GDR, respectively. The women's movement gave women a basis for political activity and supported women politicians, but it also demanded that the parties should support woman-friendly policies.

The women joined various parties: nine participated in social-democratic parties, six in conservative and two in agrarian. The parties perhaps had the least importance for Mary Robinson and Mary McAleese. Both were members, but they acquired high status and visibility primarily on a personal, independent basis. The others had long party careers. It is not always clear exactly when they became members, but calculating from registration or the first time they ran for election, they were generally involved in party activities for more than 20 years before they acquired top positions. Apart from Çiller and possibly Leuthard, none had less than 10 years' service. Nine had from 20 to 34 years. Perhaps this much was required before women could be accepted at top level. And it meant that women had broad political experience. They were not very young, either, when they became top leaders. The youngest was 42 years and the oldest 67. Most were 40–50 years old.

Persistence and support

After they joined a party, it was not long before the women got positions of various kinds. The parties were under pressure by women's activists and voters to give women a chance and renew their policies and image. Most of the top women served in a series of posts before they rose to power. Half of them held positions at the municipal or regional level. All except three (Robinson, McAleese and Dreifuss) were MPs, and one became president of parliament (Itzik). Robinson was elected to the Senate. The majority of the women (14) served as ministers, from two to nine years, and six were party leaders.

The future women top leaders advanced step by step. Usually, they received support from male colleagues who thought that they were competent and served the party's interests. But Gillard had to fight continuously against a male rival to be able to stay in power as prime minister. On the other hand, some were helped by prominent male mentors (Cresson by François Mitterrand, Campbell by Brian Mulroney, Çiller by Süleyman Demirel and Merkel by Helmut Kohl). Nevertheless, the women had to be active themselves and exploit the chances that arose. Robinson, McAleese and Halonen ran for election as presidential candidates, and Dreifuss, Calmy-Rey and Leuthard as candidates for the Federal Council. Cresson, Campbell and Gillard agreed to be prime ministers even though their parties were doing poorly at the time. Çiller plunged ahead when the position as party leader was suddenly vacant, and Jäätteenmäki got her chance when the party leader went abroad. Kiviniemi and Merkel rose to the top in the wake of financial scandals, Itzik after a sex scandal and Sigurðardóttir during a financial crisis. Shipley rebelled against a male party leader who was not up to the task and took over herself, while Clark took over at the request of women activists.

At crucial points, several of the top women received support from other women. In Finland and Iceland, a bipartisan women's movement took action to get more women into politics. Women in the party also put on pressure so that Clark and Merkel would get important posts, while women voters voted for Dreifuss. Robinson carried out an extensive electoral campaign and got the support of women. And her success gave McAleese a basis on which to go forward. Women immediately responded positively when Cresson, Campbell and Çiller got top positions, and supported Gillard when she was subjected to sexist attacks. For Cresson and Gillard, resistance from the male elite was not reduced and Campbell was actually a victim of hostility caused by her male predecessor, not herself. Feminists eventually turned their back on Çiller because of her policies, and Shipley's course was also highly controversial.

In front for women

The women top leaders who were in office for some time had to rule with coalition or minority governments. This meant that they could not necessarily carry out what they wanted and often had to compromise. The policies were generally drawn towards the centre.

The situation of the national leaders also varied. There was no clear connection between women serving as top leaders and many women in the parliaments and cabinets. For some, this was the case, while others advanced and worked as leaders surrounded only or almost only by men. In a few cases, women were pushed forward by the male elites precisely because women top politicians were lacking. But unlike the top leaders who were part of a broad women's forward movement, these could be quite lonely in the political landscape.

For the majority of the top women leaders, their gender was an advantage when they rose to power. They represented something new and better and had particular appeal to women voters. Regarding the approach to gender equality, only one was clearly anti-feminist. She was also the only one from a predominantly Moslem country. Tansu Çiller declared explicitly that she would govern like a man – which did not prevent her from playing various female roles when she could benefit from it.

The other women leaders came from countries dominated by Christians: Catholics, Protestants or both. Here, there was a great number who proposed or supported measures benefiting women, although few called themselves 'feminists'. It seemed to be widely accepted that women leaders could or should promote women's interests in different ways as long as it was within reason and moderation. Gillard and Merkel actively avoided women's issues in the beginning of their election campaigns, but changed their attitudes later. Family and reproductive rights were more difficult in Catholic than in Protestant countries.

Campbell and Dreifuss were declared 'feminists', and in government, Dreifuss fought especially for paid maternity leave and Campbell for inclusive justice. Robinson championed women's issues, though she did not always agree with the women's activists. Cresson supported women's demands, but lacked insight into the character of discrimination. Only Robinson, Clark and Sigurðardóttir participated in women's organisations, but Halonen, Shipley and Merkel were ministers for women before they became prime ministers. Shipley did not bring any women into the cabinet, and her policies were controversial from a women's perspective. Merkel stressed that she was no 'feminist', but, in practice, carried out a number of equality measures. So did Clark and partly Sigurðardóttir. Clark, Jäätteenmäki, Kiviniemi, Merkel and Sigurðardóttir were those who had the highest number of women ministers. In addition, McAleese and Halonen fought for women priests, and Halonen, Jäätteenmäki, McAleese and Sigurðardóttir for gay rights. Sigurðardóttir entered into a lesbian partnership herself.

The President of Chile Michelle Bachelet shakes hands with the UN Secretary General Ban Ki-moon on 24 September 2007. After Bachelet retired as president (after her first term) she became the first under-secretary general for gender equality and the empowerment of women in the UN as well as director for the new entity UN Women, which was established in July 2010.

153480: UN Photo/Evan Schneider

Chapter Eleven

Where women came to power:
summary of the regional chapters[1]

Western countries

The Western industrialised countries – Western Europe, North America and some other countries with common societal features[2] – had the highest number of women top leaders during the half-century from 1960 to 2010, or, to be more precise, from 1969 to 2010. A total of 23 women became presidents or prime ministers in 15 states, or 48 per cent of the Western countries. In 2010, the representation of women in parliaments and governments in Western countries as a whole was 26 per cent and 29 per cent, respectively, but there were marked variations from one country another.

Wealth, democracy and feminism

Modern states were created relatively early in Europe and North America and developments in Australia and New Zealand came to resemble much of those in Western Europe and North America. In West European countries, ethnic diversity was not particularly large, although there were different peoples, languages and cultures. The Christian faith was widespread and patriarchal structures stood strong. Gradually, almost all the states established liberal democracies. The Industrial Revolution and capitalism led to major social changes. Both men and women became part of a new proletariat, but men got better jobs and higher salaries than women, in addition to higher education and positions of power. The first wave of feminism contributed to women obtaining the right to vote in most countries during the first decades of the 1900s.

Despite wars and changes in economic activity, the Western countries became the richest in the world, with unprecedented prosperity. The countries had different forms of mixed economies, with market forces and state intervention. Both women and men got paid employment, better health and more education, and technological advances made work easier. However, women were still

439

discriminated against in relation to men. Women's organisations protested, and from the end of the 1960s, the second wave of feminism emerged, with a broad front against male power and oppression of women. More women were engaged in societal issues and politics, and women-friendly measures were adopted.

Most of the Western countries developed into post-industrial societies.[3] They not only had high socio-economic levels, with extensive education and paid employment for women; but modernisation and the second feminist wave also promoted more rational ethical values, radical changes in gender roles and more positive attitudes towards women's political involvement. The liberal democracies were well-established, with rights for women, and the representation of women in political bodies increased, but not very fast.

Professional and party careers

Most of the women heads of state and government (20) from this part of the world belonged to 12 post-industrial countries, but a number of post-industrial countries had none. It was far from obvious that women should rise to the top, even if material conditions were good, the political system was democratic and attitudes developed in a positive direction. Much had to fall into place. Of the five Nordic countries, which had more women in parliaments and governments than most other countries in the world, there were three (Finland, Iceland and Norway) that did, and two (Denmark, Sweden) that did not, have a woman top leader until 2010. In 2011, Denmark got a women prime minister.

The countries that were not post-industrial were considered as 'industrial'. There, the modernisation of society was less advanced. In three of these countries, women rose to the top in situations where the democratic system was under pressure. Maria Pintasilgo in Portugal and Tansu Çiller in Turkey served as prime ministers in volatile situations between military and civilian rule, and Agatha Barbara had to step in as president in Malta to handle a constitutional crisis.

In the countries that were or became post-industrial, political conditions were usually stable when the women came to power. An exception was Israel, which in 1969, when Golda Meir became prime minister, was a newly formed state in conflict with neighbouring countries. Another dramatic situation was when Jóhanna Sigurðardóttir became prime minister in 2009 because Iceland was about to go bankrupt. But such events were rare. When women became national leaders, the countries could often have economic, political and social problems, but the political system was not in danger.

Most of the women went to the top because an opening was created by the fact that the position of president or prime minister became vacant. If chance factors played a role, it was not by chance that a well-qualified woman was ready to take over. The competition could be tough, but the women managed because they were knowledgeable, experienced and competent. In addition, there could be a desire for a new deal and a better policy. There were never family ties between the predecessor and the successor.

All the women heads of state and government had the advantage of an active women's movement in their political careers, which focused on women and demanded increased political representation at high levels. But the road to the top went through the political parties, and the women generally had to acquire long experience: 20 years, some up to 30 years or more, before they had served sufficient time to go to the top. Most were members of parliament (MPs), and a good number were ministers before they became heads of state or government. Apart from Switzerland, which had a collective leadership, and Finland, which had a dual executive, all the women rose to the top in parliamentary systems. Five became ceremonial presidents, while 12 were prime ministers, most of them with executive power. In all cases except five, the country had two elected national leaders

Two women were appointed as interim leaders, and three had brief careers at the top because of political problems. The rest remained in office until the end of their terms, and some were even re-elected. This means that almost half of the top women (11) served for a long time and could play significant roles. Five sat for 10 years or more (Presidents Vigdís Finnbogadóttir, Mary McAleese and Tarja Halonen, and Prime Ministers Margaret Thatcher and Gro Harlem Brundtland) and six for five to 10 years. At the end of 2010, six of the women were still in office.

Eastern countries (former Eastern Bloc)

There were fewer women presidents and prime ministers in the Eastern industrial countries (the former Eastern bloc) than in the Western.[4] No women went to the top in this part of the world before 1982. A total of 13 women became heads of state and government in 12 states, or 41 per cent of the Eastern countries. There were also fewer women in parliaments and cabinets. In 2010, the Eastern countries had only 18 per cent women in parliaments and 10 per cent in cabinets.

New openings and setbacks

As long as the Communist Parties were in power in the Eastern industrial countries, no women went to the top of the political leadership. Socialism promised liberation, but reality was different. The political system, economy and social conditions were changed, but patriarchal traditions remained. The countries were industrialised and living standards improved. Women got education and paid employment, but they were still subordinate, underpaid and, in addition, double-working. The Communist Party ruled in an authoritarian way, with men in all important positions. Women could be allocated a quota in the legislature, but the power was vested in the party, not the legislature. The introduction of self-management for working people in Yugoslavia did not bring women into government either.

Dissolution of the Soviet Union and Eastern Bloc led to the establishment of new states, and the fall of communism entailed extensive and partly painful restructuring. In a short time, not only democracy, but also market liberalism, was to be introduced. Generally, living standards were lower in Eastern than in Western industrialised countries, and, in addition, restructuring led to serious economic problems in the former Eastern Bloc countries. This particularly affected vulnerable groups and women more than men.

The restructuring of society took place on men's terms. Men dominated as before, and gender equality was no major objective. Under the communist regime, there was no independent women's movement, and when the regime fell, women only managed to a small extent to organise themselves to promote their interests or even define specific 'women's problems'. Along with the socialist ideals of the past, gender equality was also denied. While unemployment and poverty among women increased, they lacked political representation, and existing woman-friendly measures were eroded or discontinued.

Women were not encouraged to engage in politics under either communist rule or the emerging democracies that followed. In the new states, women and men were much more traditional in their views of gender roles than in Western countries. Women's place was in the home, not in politics. Democratisation gave new openings, but political life was often fluid, with a myriad of small and large parties, so competition was fierce. It was extremely difficult for women to break through. They were not appreciated very much as politicians and the new parties were mostly founded and led by men, often marked personalities with resources based on male patron–client networks.

Transitional experts

It was most often in connection with political changes, upheavals and turmoil that women went to the top. They participated in the struggle to establish new states and introduce democracy, and they played important roles in the transition between the regimes. Planinc became prime minister of Yugoslavia after Tito's death, Prunskienė when Lithuania seceded from the Soviet Union, and Tymoshenko in connection with the Orange Revolution in Ukraine. Bergmann-Pohl became president under the dissolution of East Germany (GDR), Burjanadze under the Rose Revolution in Georgia and Otunbayeva under the April uprising in Kyrgyzstan. During political crises, Indzhova was drawn in as prime minister in Bulgaria and Suchocka in Poland. Vaira Vīķe-Freiberga became president in Latvia when parliament could not agree on anybody else. Greceanîi in Moldova and Kosor in Croatia took over as prime ministers when their predecessors unexpectedly resigned. Grybauskaitė in Lithuania and Radičová in Slovakia were the ones who came to power in the most 'normal' way under calm conditions.

After the fall of communism, seven of the Eastern states continued with authoritarian rule. The rest became emerging democracies. With the exception of Planinc, who came to power at the end of the communist regime in Yugoslavia, all the women rose to the top during democratisation processes or more or less established democracies. Party experience was limited for almost everyone, but they distinguished themselves with exceptional education and high positions. All but one had university education, eight had PhDs. Very many were professors or directors.

The political systems were organised in different ways, and some eventually modified the system. Most often, the women obtained positions in parliamentary or dual systems. Some became presidents and a few more prime ministers. But it was a striking feature that no one became top leader alone, except for one. Nino Burjanadze was president of Georgia twice, but each time, it was for a very short period in a mainly formal transitory role. It was a typical feature that the women top leaders did not get much power. The positions had limited authority and/or were of short duration. One was a ceremonial president for eight years (Latvia), one a prime minister in a collective leadership for four years (Yugoslavia) and one a prime minister under a strong president for three years (Ukraine). Except for four who were still in office in 2010, the other women served for only a few months or little more than a year. They were given temporary positions or got involved in conflicts and crises that made them retire after a short period of time. Of the top leaders in 2010 three worked for 1½ to 2½ years, while Grybauskaitė was re-elected for a second term after five years.

Latin America and the Caribbean

With regards to developing countries, there were more women heads of state and government in Latin America and the Caribbean than in Asia and sub-Saharan Africa. On the continent, a total of 16 women became presidents or prime ministers in 13 states, or 36 per cent of the countries. Latin America had the highest number, with 10 women top leaders in nine states, or 45 per cent of the countries, while the Caribbean had six leaders in four states, or 31 per cent of the countries. Latin America also generally had more women in parliaments and cabinets than there were in the Caribbean. In 2010, there were 20 per cent women in the parliaments/lower houses in Latin America and 23 per cent in the cabinets, while in the Caribbean, there were 16 per cent and 14 per cent, respectively.

Early independent Latin American states

The vast majority of Latin American countries were Spanish colonies, while Brazil was Portuguese.[5] The native population consisted of various Indian groups, but the Spaniards and Portuguese became dominant in the new states with a Catholic Church and a gender order of *machismo*, an excessive, aggressive masculinity. The states became independent in the 1800s; the societies were modernised, urbanised and stratified, with large social and economic inequalities. Practically everywhere, power was centralised in a small upper class, which ruled by means of patron–client relationships and violence. Women's movements grew up across the continent, and women got the right to vote from 1929 onwards, but the male political elite was protective of its power.

Over the years, stability and instability, and democracy, dictatorship and mixed regimes, alternated. Authoritarian regimes were prevalent when a widespread wave of democratisation began in 1978. All the states adopted more or less democratic regimes, with presidential executives. In 11 countries, only men became heads of state and government, but in nine countries, women got a chance. With the exception of Isabel Perón, who inherited the position from her husband, no women came into power before democratisation. But there would probably not have been any women political leaders without the women's movement, which helped change traditional views of the role of women and strengthen women's rights.

In addition to traditional agriculture, meat, wheat, coffee, sugar, bananas, rubber, oil and metals were produced for export. The economy expanded, and the countries became middle-income countries. Both women and men got better health and more education. But then the oil prices on the world market rose, and the economic activities in the industrial countries declined. At the same time as democratisation swept over Latin America in the 1980s–1990s, the continent was struck by deep financial crisis. Neo-liberal reforms were implemented, with privatisation and the deterioration of social services. Poverty increased, and economic and social inequalities became larger in most regions.

Women fought for democracy and a woman, Lidia Güeiler Tejada in Bolivia, rose to the top while the military was still heavily involved in politics. In addition, women became national leaders in situations with more or less democratic rule. Violeta Chamorro implemented a peace agreement in Nicaragua, while Janet Jagan succeeded the first freely elected president of Guyana. The others ran for election as presidential candidates in democratisation processes that had gone on for a while. Beatriz Merino was the only one who was prime minister. She was appointed to assist the president in a crisis of confidence.

Successors of strong men

On the occasions that women in Latin America rose to the top in politics they always had to become presidents. Most countries only had one executive top leader, who was head of both state and government. Admittedly, it was an advantage that the presidents were elected by direct vote, where women voters could be mobilised, but the competition was fierce, and women had difficulties being accepted by political parties. They fell outside the male networks and lacked money to finance election campaigns.

In a *macho* culture like that in Latin America, strong men were decisive for the advancement of women. Four women came forward as substitutes for important male politicians in the capacity of widows (Perón, Chamorro, Jagan and Moscoso). One succeeded her husband as president while he was still alive (Fernández), and two were launched by the male presidents that they were to succeed (Chinchilla and Rousseff). The women had different qualifications, but only three went to the top basically on their own merits (Güeiler, Merino and Bachelet). Three were still in office in 2010. Fernández was re-elected in 2011, but Chinchilla could not serve a second consecutive term. Of the others, three were defeated and one resigned for health reasons after a short time. The rest completed their election periods, but then could not be re-elected. Michelle Bachelet was the only one who became a strong president on her own merits. She completed her first term, but then could not be re-elected. She got a high post in the United Nations (UN), and after another term had passed, she went back to Chile and was re-elected.

Heavy Caribbean male democracy

The Caribbean includes a number of large and small islands, with varying populations, ethnic groups, language, culture and religion, and they were colonised by different Western powers. Haiti and the Dominican Republic became independent long before the others and had a turbulent development, with conflict, interventions from the outside, elections and coups. The Duvalier dictatorship in Haiti lasted from 1956 to 1986. Cuba became communist, while the former British colonies underwent long-lasting democratisation processes, with active women's organisations, before they became independent in the 1960s–1980s and established parliamentary democracies. By then, most of the islands were incorporated in independent states, but 12 areas were still colonies.

People lived on agriculture, trade, tourism and a significant export of oil and bauxite. Little by little, the states became high- or middle-income countries, with the exception of Haiti, which remained a low-income country. The societies were characterised by economic dependence, population growth, illiteracy, unemployment, corruption, violence and rising inequality. The colonial powers strengthened men's domination and gave them high positions, while most women belonged to 'the invisible majority' at the bottom of the social ladder. After independence, women got education on the same level as men and generally did better than them, but economic problems increased women's family responsibilities at the same time as more women than men were unemployed.

Women got little access to politics. Many of the states are small, with less than a quarter of a million inhabitants. Politics easily became a personal affair, and the parties usually centred around male leaders who ruled more or less arbitrarily. Patron–client relationships were widespread, and women were generally excluded from the networks. The number of women's organisations and groups increased, but it was difficult to give the movement strength.

Democratic obstacles

In parliaments and cabinets, the representation of women generally remained at a low level.[6] The election of women to parliaments (the lower houses) was hindered by the electoral arrangement, with majority vote. In some cases, this was offset by the fact that women were appointed to the senates. The senates had less importance and the share of women could be higher. In 2010, there were generally only 16 per cent women in the parliaments (the lower houses) in the region, while there were 28 per cent in the senates. Women's access to political leadership was further hampered by the requirement that the prime minister and, in many countries, also the ministers had to be MPs. At the same time, direct strategies to increase the representation of women, for example, the use of quotas, met with considerable opposition.[7]

Six women were heads of state and government, but only in four of the 13 states. In most Caribbean countries, women did not rise to the top. This was the case in Cuba and the states with only one national leader. The exception was Portia Simpson-Miller, who became prime minister in Jamaica. But she did not remain long in office the first time, though in 2012, she came back. The three states with two national leaders, both a president and a prime minister, all got women top leaders. None rose to the top on the basis of family connections. They had professional and political qualifications. In Haiti, women got top positions during a tense period when authoritarian and elected governments alternated, and none functioned very long. Eugenia Charles came to power in Dominica in an unusually turbulent situation, with demands for democratisation, and was the only one of the top women leaders in the Caribbean that really got to exercise leadership. She served as prime minister with considerable power for 15 years. Prime Minister Persad-Bissessar of Trinidad and Tobago was still in office by the end of 2010.

Asia

There were a total of 11 women heads of state and government in seven Asian countries, or 32 per cent. They were very unevenly distributed, with significantly more in South than in East Asia.[8] In South Asia, there were seven women top leaders in four countries, or 44 per cent, while in East Asia, there were only four countries, or 21 per cent. In both regions, there were few women in political bodies in general. In 2010, there were 17 per cent women in parliaments and 8 per cent in cabinets in South Asia, and in East Asia, 18 per cent in parliaments and 9 per cent in cabinets.

Asia's historical experiences, religions, cultures and economic and political systems are the world's most diverse. More than half the world's population lives in Asia, with giant nations like India and China and small countries like the Maldives and Brunei, and the continent is the most densely populated on the globe. Many countries were British or French colonies and gained their independence only after World War II. Developments were marked by turbulence: revolutions, ethnic rivalries, armed conflict and superpower intervention. Some countries industrialised very rapidly, while the majority stayed as poor agricultural societies. Islam became the most influential religion in addition to Buddhism and Confucianism. Christianity was a minority religion. In some societies, women traditionally had a high position, while they were oppressed in others. Most states had different forms of authoritarian rule, but from the late 1980s, democratisation processes resulted in the majority becoming liberal or emerging democracies in the 2000s. Not all democracies had women national leaders, but only democracies had such leaders.

South Asian dynasties

South Asia distinguished itself by having relatively many women top leaders, despite the fact that they were populous agricultural countries dominated by feudal structures and poverty, and women's position was generally weak. Sri Lanka gradually became a middle-income country, while the others continued as low-income states.

The four countries with women leaders had been British colonies, and after independence, violent conflicts occurred between states and groups. Murders of political leaders were one manifestation of the violence. India and Sri Lanka introduced liberal democracy, with parliamentary systems, but Sri Lanka was marked by growing unrest and militarisation. After periods of military rule, Pakistan and Bangladesh underwent a certain democratisation: Bangladesh with a parliamentary system, while Pakistan had a somewhat varied, almost dual, regime. Whatever the form of government, democracy in the region largely became an empty ritual. At the turn of the century, independent experts wrote about a government crisis. Elections were held, but a few privileged elites and dynasties retained access to power and resources. Politics was characterised by patron–client relationships, manipulation, corruption, mafia activity and violence.

After independence, most people in India were Hindus; in Pakistan and Bangladesh, Moslems; and in Sri Lanka, Buddhists. Practically everywhere, patriarchal social structures entailed that women were subordinate to men. There were large gender inequalities, for example, in health and education, in addition to inequalities between castes and classes. The struggle for universal suffrage took a long time, and then women had to fight to benefit from the political rights.

Authoritarian, militarised regimes gave no room for women. From the end of the 1970s and the beginning of the 1980s, the breadth of women's organisations grew, but they kept away from the 'dirty game' of politics. Bangladesh and Pakistan established women's quotas at the national level,[9] but apart from quotas, it could be difficult for women to be nominated and elected. With the exception of Sri Lanka, the states used majority vote, which was unfavourable to women. Without entering the parliaments, the road to the top was almost impossible.

Family representatives

In the power elites in each country, there were first and foremost a few family dynasties that ruled the country. The women top leaders belonged to these families, and with one exception, the women rose to the top in politics because they were related to prominent political leaders. Following the resignation or death, often by political murder, of the leaders, the women took over. It was customary to go to the closest family, and women were accepted when they were family members. Two were widows, and four were daughters. Kumaratunga was appointed by her mother, Sirimavo Bandaranaike, while she was still alive. The daughters had considerable education, but the widows did not. The women leaders in Bangladesh and Pakistan fought for democracy against dictatorial regimes, while in India and Sri Lanka, they led democracies during sometimes difficult conditions. Pratibha Patil did not belong to the dominant family, but was close. Her role as president was mainly ceremonial and she only served a single term.

The women top leaders were mostly executive prime ministers. Only Bhutto struggled with a strong president. When Kumaratunga became president, the position was assigned considerable powers. The women remained in power for many years: Bandaranaike for 18; Gandhi, 15; Kumaratunga, 11; and Zia, 10. But belonging to ruling families did not necessarily imply that they could govern without opposition. All the women prime ministers were deposed or defeated in elections and then re-elected. Hasina was re-elected for the second time in 2014 after having served 10 years in office. In India and Pakistan, Indira Gandhi and Benazir Bhutto ended up being assassinated.

East Asian democracy movements

The East Asian countries are just as spread out as the South Asian are concentrated. However, in East Asia, women also rose to the top on the basis of family relations with prominent leaders. Cory Aquino was a widow, while Gloria Arroyo and Megawati were daughters. But women came to power in this way in only two of the 14 countries in the region.

The Philippines and Indonesia are large archipelagos of diverse ethnic groups, cultures and religions. Both were subjected to prolonged colonisation. People in the Philippines became essentially Catholic, and in Indonesia, Moslem. Indonesia was a low-income country for a long time, but in the 2000s, both were classified as middle-income countries. Education was relatively widespread, among women also, who were economically active to a great extent. In both countries, there were groups who traditionally had widespread social equality between women and men, but national politics were dominated by men.

As in South Asia, one could talk about a government crisis in the Philippines and Indonesia. After independence, democratic presidential systems were introduced according to a Western model, but control of the state was centralised in two realms with widely dispersed populations and large economic, social and ethnic/cultural differences. Politics were marked by elite rule and patron–client relationships. The army played a central role, and the countries soon got military dictatorships.

Democratic front figures

Like several of the South Asian women top leaders, the women in East Asia also rose to power in democratisation processes. The widow Cory Aquino had little education and political experience, and the same was true for Megawati to a certain extent, while Gloria Arroyo was well-qualified. Megawati led a popular uprising for democracy, while Arroyo, as the elected vice president, campaigned against a corrupt president. Aquino received the special support of women. All the three women presidents stayed in office until the end of their terms. Arroyo and Megawati ran for re-election, but only Arroyo succeeded and served two terms.

Han Myung Sook in South Korea was neither a widow nor daughter, but she also came to power in a democratisation process. She became prime minister in order to strengthen the position of the president and appeal to female voters. But she resigned after a few months.

Sub-Saharan Africa

Apart from the Arab states and the small Pacific islands, where there were no women top leaders, sub-Saharan Africa had the lowest number of women heads of state and government. There were 10 women top leaders in eight countries, or 18 per cent, and they were scattered all over the region. In 2010, there were, on average, 17 per cent women in parliaments and 20 per cent in cabinets. But some countries had up to 30 per cent and more in parliaments.[10]

Poorest region

Sub-Saharan Africa is rich in natural resources, but the region was colonised by European powers exploiting resources, and colonisation left deep marks. The countries became independent after World War II, and during the first years, things went relatively well. But then commodity prices fell in the 1970s, while the prices of oil and industrial products went up. This led to a prolonged economic crisis, with debt burdens, budget deficits and inflation, with sub-Saharan Africa hit harder than other world regions. Backed by Western donors, the International Monetary Fund (IMF) and the World Bank, major economic reforms were pushed through, with privatisation and market liberalisation, and poverty increased. Although substantial development assistance was provided, and income per capita began to rise again in the 1990s, the region was the world's poorest around the turn of the millennium. About half of the population, especially women and children, were poor, and the mortality rate was high.

There are between 500 and 2,000 African ethnic groups, with different histories, languages and cultures. Traditional religions coexist with Christianity and Islam. The traditional position of women was very variable. In some places, they had a high position. But the world religions, together with colonial rule, strengthened men's dominance. Urbanisation was rapid, but most people lived in rural areas, where women and men worked in agriculture. There was considerable progress in health and education, for women also, but most women only had odd jobs in the informal sector.

Democratisation began in the 1990s. Usually, presidential systems were established, but even if multiparty elections were held, men who had formerly come to power by coups were often re-elected as presidents. They became more legitimate, but continued to rule in a more or less authoritarian way, using patron–client relationships and corruption, and did everything they could to stay in power. To a great extent, it was a sham democracy.

In connection with democratisation, more and more women got involved in politics. The election arrangements varied, but the number of women in parliaments increased, and two fifths of the African countries gradually introduced quota systems of various kinds. This gave women possibilities for influence, but, in most countries, parliaments and cabinets did not play very active roles.

Assisting male power

Elisabeth Domitien was appointed prime minister of the Central African Republic while the country had a brutal dictatorship. Armed conflicts marked several countries, and in Burundi, Rwanda and Liberia, women obtained leadership positions as part of peace efforts. Two were supposed to contribute to reconciliation between ethnic groups, while one became a temporary head of state because the warlords could not agree upon anybody else to implement a ceasefire. The other women national leaders came to power in democratic regimes.

In the year 2000, 14 African countries had authoritarian rule. In addition to two liberal democracies, 29 were described as emerging democracies. In five of the emerging democracies, six women became heads of state and government.[11] About half of the African presidents had a prime minister, and four women acquired such a position. Even if they had unusually high education and political experience, they were subordinate to their presidents and assisted them with their background and knowledge. But they were never related to them. One woman was elected as president, and one moved up temporarily. But in the vast majority of democracies, women got no chance.

Due to the way the governments worked, it was extremely difficult for women to go all the way to the top. So much power was concentrated in the president, and they ran for re-election so often, that is was extremely hard for newcomers, not to mention women, to break through. When a woman became temporary head of state, it was to organise new elections. Otherwise, there was only one woman who managed to be elected president in a fairly ordinary way: Ellen Sirleaf in Liberia. She fought her way up and succeeded partly because she came from a country where women traditionally had a strong position, and women actively mobilised to get her as president. She thus became a strong president – and a notable exception in relation to the other women top leaders. She was re-elected in 2012. The African prime ministers worked for a relatively short time, with the exception of Luisa Diogo of Mozambique, who sat for six years.

Where women did not go to the top

It is not possible to provide an analysis here of all the states where women did not go to the top. However, a few examples will be briefly presented to help shed light on some of the reasons why women do not become national leaders, although the descriptions are rough. The examples include two regions – the Arab states in addition to the Pacific islands – and two of the world's most powerful states: China and the US.

Arab states

In the most ancient civilisations, including the Egyptian and Sumerian, women had a high status in many areas. Neither the thrones of gods nor secular positions as rulers were reserved for men. But the introduction of private property, slavery and, later, feudalism weakened the position of women. Greek, Roman, Christian, Arab and Turkish invaders throughout history also contributed to women losing their relatively favourable position and being subjected to discrimination based on both gender and class. From the 1500s, poor women had to cultivate the land, while well-situated women were locked up in their homes and had to wear a veil. When the Ottoman Empire collapsed after World War I, the Middle East and North Africa came under British and French control, and both men and women were exploited as cheap labour. Only after World War II were independent states created.[12]

The region was influenced by patriarchal traditions, tribalism, Islam and authoritarian regimes. There were ample natural resources, but the wealth was unevenly distributed. Gulf countries had a high income, while Yemen struggled with little. Many were middle-income countries. Nevertheless, there were great class differences, and people suffered under widespread unemployment and partly severe poverty. The regimes ranged from absolutist monarchies to revolutionary republics, but political power was extremely centralised in all cases. The head of state was the head of government, the army, the judiciary and the public services, and the regimes were more or less oppressive. Freedom of expression was limited, political parties were banned or gagged, and dissidents were jailed. There were also restrictions on non-governmental organisations. The situation was not helped by military conflict, civil war, superpower pressure and intervention. Many countries had long periods of military rule or martial law (see Figure 13).

Some countries introduced multiparty systems, but formal democracy from above made it easier for parties based on religion to participate in politics, and confrontations arose between the state and Islamic opposition. In the 2000s, most of the countries held elections. But they were marked by irregularities and manipulation. The legislatures had little political significance and represented

Figure 13: Middle East: regimes by type, 1946–2012

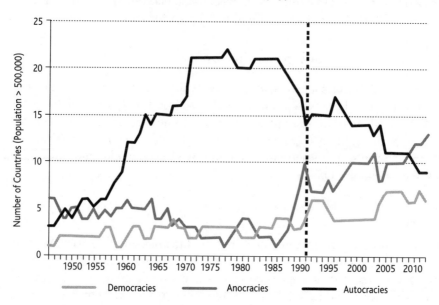

Note: Anocratic governance is a system placed somewhere between democracy and autocracy. The power is spread between elite groups competing for power.
Source: Center for Systemic Peace, Polity IV Project (see: www.systemicpeace.org)
© Center for Systemic Peace 2014

the ruling elites, not the people. The Arab states were in a deep development crisis, with repressive political systems at the centre. The 'Arab Spring' exploded in 2011 with demonstrations, riots and revolutions in a number of countries. Women played their part as leaders and participants and suffered arrests, sexual harassment and even death. The impact remains uncertain. Some progress was made on women's rights at the level of policy, but the changes did not influence entrenched patriarchal structures and the rise of Islamic fundamentalism.

Women were bound by patriarchal family structures, legal discrimination, social subordination and ingrained male dominance. The superior position of men was underlined by a traditional religious culture embodied, among other things, in family law. Women's personal freedom was limited and they were subject to direct and indirect violence. Modernisation meant that women, as well as men, got better health and education. But women ran high risks in connection with pregnancy and childbirth. Some women went to university, learned to master the art of modern communication and distinguished themselves in art, literature and research. However, half of the women were illiterate. Most worked hard, among other areas, in agriculture, and encountered significant obstacles when they tried to get gainful employment and decent wages. The economic activity of Arab women was the lowest in the world.

Some countries introduced the right to vote at independence, others later. Most often, women got the right to vote in the 1950s–1960s, but in several Gulf countries, it did not happen until after 2000. In 2014, women still lack the right to vote at national level in Saudi Arabia.

Women organised to obtain rights and participated to some extent in the forefront of reform movements and demonstrations for democracy and better living conditions. Especially after 1975, they presented special women's demands. Sometimes, they were listened to, and family laws were changed in a progressive direction, for example. But more often, the authorities struck down women's activists. Almost all the states became party to the UN Convention on the Elimination of All Forms of Discrimination against Women (CEDAW), but many held reservations, particularly with regards to the principle of equality between women and men. A few women were appointed as ministers, usually from the elite or the ruling party. But there was no general tendency to strengthen the position of women. Both the political parties and women themselves were divided. While some fought for social and political rights that could not fit into a religious social structure, others promoted a cultural identity based on a woman-oriented interpretation of Islam. Although several countries introduced quotas, there were not more than 10 per cent women in the legislatures and 7 per cent in the cabinets in the Arab states as a whole in 2010. A new activism by women made itself felt both during the uprisings and in the political processes that followed, among young and old, many of whom had never taken part in politics before. In 2014, the representation of women had increased to 16 per cent in the legislatures and 8 per cent in the cabinets, but it was still very low, and in addition neither had significant power.

Pacific islands

In the 12 independent Pacific island states (Australia and New Zealand excluded) democracy was introduced at independency.[13] Yet women were not accepted in government, and there have been no women top leaders in the region.

There are between 20,000 and 30,000 islands scattered throughout the Pacific. Until recently, a lot of the area belonged to the most remote and inaccessible places on the planet. Communication was a major problem, not only in relation to the outside world, but also between the different islands and, to some extent, within each island. The population was small and scattered. Only one state reached more than 1 million inhabitants. Most had about 100,000, some only 10,000–15,000. The majority of the people lived in Melanesia, with volcanic islands and steep mountains, while Micronesia and Polynesia consisted of low coral reefs. Communication was not made easier by the fact that there was a myriad of different ethnic groups, cultures and languages, and the states had varying histories and status. They were colonised by different Western powers and, disregarding Australia and New Zealand, there were 12 independent states in Oceania in 2010 and 13 semi-independent territories and colonies under various Western powers. The independent states have only had short time with their own governments, often only from the 1970s–1980s.

The islanders primarily worked in agriculture and fisheries, and they received considerable development assistance. Some states had a middle-income level, while others struggled with widespread poverty. The culture was diverse, with paternal and maternal inheritance, monogamy and polygamy, but women played an important economic role everywhere, cultivating the soil and collecting seafood. But land was in short supply in many places. The islanders had to fight for land against foreign interests, and women often lacked formal rights. In Melanesian societies, women traditionally had low status, which was reinforced by the bride price that gave their husbands family rights over the women's sexual services, children and labour. In Polynesian societies, however, women had high status and equality with men in different areas and could become leaders. When schools and healthcare were developed, women in Polynesia benefited from this as much or more than men, while women in Micronesia and Melanesia had poor health, education and income. Here, illiteracy among women could be substantial.

In addition to traditional religions, Christianity gained a strong position, and the churches helped to keep women 'in place'. The colonial powers promoted a monetary economy and urbanisation. Women had less access than men to paid labour, and women's rights were undermined. Men were allowed to dominate in the new economic and political structures. Even where women were traditionally able to hold leadership positions, they got no access to modern forms of status in politics and the economy. Usually, each village had its women's group, which was involved in sewing, cooking and crafts, and raising funds for the local community, but there was no focus on the women's own position. A number of women's projects supported by international aid organisations helped to improve women's situation. At the same time, awareness of the culture, traditions and their own powerlessness was neglected because the initiative and resources came from outside.

Women engaged in the struggle against the colonial powers and fought for land and a Pacific free of nuclear weapons. A feminist consciousness arose in connection with the International Women's Year in 1975 and was followed up with regional cooperation initiatives. But many of the islands were still under colonial rule. The population was small and it was difficult to create a movement of women across geographic, political, ethnic, cultural and linguistic divides and promote common claims. Most of the states acceded to the CEDAW, but little was done to change traditional attitudes. In some cases, customs protected by law were opposed to equality for women. Men's privileged status was maintained, and women had little influence beyond their traditional roles as mothers and food producers.

With two exceptions, the countries established liberal democracies, with parliamentary or presidential systems.[14] Usually, they were based on majority vote in single-member constituencies, which favoured men, and in several states, it was necessary to have a traditional title to run for election, something very few women had. The political parties were weak and little influenced by ideology. They mostly aimed at promoting the interests of a (male) leader or a district. No country introduced quotas for women. In 2010, there were, on average, only 4 per cent women in parliaments and 10 per cent in cabinets. But women's organisations were mobilising, using modern communication technology to give them a voice and influence in coming national elections (Femlinkpacific, 2012).

United States of America

Apart from India, none of the world's largest countries after World War II have had a top women leader. A look at two very different great powers, the US and China, aims to clarify some of the factors that play a role in accounting for this disparity.

The US was established as a federal state and liberal democracy. The country was large and the population diverse, and liberty was emphasised more than social cohesion. Liberty was primarily for the elite, not women, slaves, servants and the poor. The US became the birthplace for both the first and the second feminist wave. The first was interwoven with the struggle against slavery. In 1848, women met in Seneca Falls and demanded rights. In the state of Wyoming, where female settlers were both important and few in number, women got the right to vote in 1869. At the national level, they did not obtain the vote until 1920.[15]

After World War II, the US developed into an extraordinarily rich post-industrial society, but there were large differences between classes and groups. Women got education, but according to traditional gender stereotypes, they were often housewives or worked in low-paid occupations. The second feminist wave arose when Betty Freidan destroyed the false romanticised descriptions in her book *The feminine mystique* (Freidan, 1963) (see Chapter Two). The new women's movement became broad and manifold, and women gradually obtained the same level as men in education, income and health. But they rarely got the highest positions and had few channels to translate political demands into action.

The US has a presidential system, with a powerful directly elected president and a Congress with two chambers: the House of Representatives, elected by majority vote in single-member constituencies; and the Senate, elected by the states. The voting arrangement makes it difficult for women to be elected, and the party system does not make it easier (see Figure 14). Basically, there is a two-party system, with very large, loosely organised parties. At the federal level, they mainly function as umbrella organisations and election machinery. At the state level, there are in all 102 local parties of Democrats and Republicans in each state. The local parties are very independent, but weak, and resistance against women has been strong. For a long time, almost no women were elected to Congress, and neither President Truman, President Kennedy nor President Johnson had women in their cabinets.

At the same time as the feminist movement grew, the political parties, trade unions and non-governmental organisations (NGOs) were weakened under Republican rule, starting with the election of President Ronald Reagan in 1980. The central administration was reduced and social services were cut. The personality and finances of the candidates were increasingly important to being elected to Congress, which specifically hampered women, and Congress became the arena for wealthy lobby groups dominated by men. Attempts to include gender

Figure 14: Percentage of women in the US Congress 1917–2012

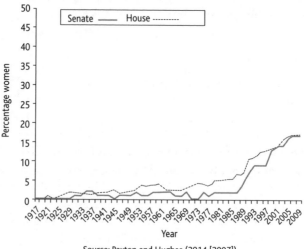

Source: Paxton and Hughes (2014 [2007]).

equality in the constitution in the early 1980s failed. When President George H.W. Bush left office in 1992 and the Democrats took over with President Bill Clinton, there were only 11 per cent women in the House, and of these, only a few came from minority ethnic groups. In the cabinet, women constituted 6 per cent and there were very few women in senior positions in the central administration. Under Clinton, the representation of women increased, and it continued partly under his successor George W. Bush. But in 2010, there were not more than 17 per cent women in the House. In the US, the members of Congress should not be cabinet ministers and President Obama appointed 27 per cent women, with varying backgrounds, in the cabinet.

The position as state governor is an important stepping stone to become president or minister. But until 2010, only 31 women had been governors. Women were candidates for the positions as national vice president and president. Geraldine Ferraro ran as the Democratic vice presidential candidate with Walter Mondale in 1984, but the Democrats lost to Ronald Reagan. No women have managed to be nominated as a presidential candidate by one of the two major parties. Hillary Clinton, who was the one who came the closest, was white, highly educated and politically experienced, and, in addition, the wife of a former president, but failed nonetheless. She was criticised, among other things, for preferring a profession to her family.

The power that is concentrated in the office of the US president makes it especially difficult for women to get there. The US is a mighty nation state, with 300 million inhabitants in 2010 and worldwide political and military engagement. According to prevailing gender stereotypes, women are primarily caring and compassionate, while presidents must be able to stand up as tough and fierce supreme military commanders. Hillary Clinton was described as 'the only real man' among the Democrats in the Senate, but it was not enough to be elected.

China

According to traditional Confucianism, the world consists of heaven and earth, and man is in between.[16] The woman is subject to the three Obediences – to her father, her husband and sons – and shall strive to achieve the four Virtues: humility; silence; purity and adornment to please her husband; and to work hard. In ancient China, women had no property or inheritance rights. They had no rights in the family, and the participation of women in political life was forbidden. Most women lived in ignorance and isolation. A few women manifested themselves, but it varied during the different dynasties.

Women participated in the bourgeois revolution in 1911 and also in the fight against the Japanese and Chiang Kai-shek. After the communist revolution, women got economic and political rights, a new marriage law was adopted, and old barbaric traditions were banned.

In 1964, Mao Tse-tung said: 'Times have changed, and today men and women are equal. Whatever male comrades can accomplish, women comrades can too' (Lu, 1972). Women should particularly take care of the family and build a socialist economy. According to needs, more or less emphasis was placed on one task or the other. During the 'Great Leap Forward' in 1958, with a shortage of labour, women were forced into production. Child care, communal meals and a policy of only one child to liberate women were established. They joined in political activities at the local level; eventually, a few also participated in wider contexts.

The Cultural Revolution brought confusion because women were supposed to participate on equal terms with men, but women's organisations were disbanded, kindergartens were no longer a priority, and women should enter men's domains, while men should not enter women's. The two most distinguished women were, typically enough, Mao's wife, Jiang Qing, who was deputy head of the central cultural revolution group in 1966, and Soong Qingling, the widow of the 'Father of the Nation', who, among other things, acted as a substitute for China's president from 1968 to 1972 together with Dong Bivu. In 1978, the party decided to work for 'Socialist Modernisation'. Greater emphasis was placed on the family, and a moderated women's movement re-emerged.

China is a vast country with many different ethnic groups. There are more than 1 billion people, most of whom live in rural areas. Formally, the Communist Party heads a cooperation of several parties, but, in reality, China is a one-party state controlled by the Communist Party. The state is governed by a People's Congress elected indirectly by local congresses. The election of delegates takes place at the city and village level, but is dominated by the Communist Party. The People's Congress elects the political leadership: president, prime minister and cabinet. The key political leaders are often also party leaders. The highest governing body of the Communist Party is the Party Congress. Then come the Central Committee, Politburo and, finally, the Politburo Standing Committee, which formulates party policies and ideology. In addition to the party and state bureaucracy, the army plays an important role.

In 2010, the Communist Party had about 80 million members, or 6 per cent of the population. A total of 22 per cent of party members were women, according to official statistics. In the People's Congress, women got a fixed share of about 20 per cent, while they amounted to 12 per cent of cabinet members in 2010. But it is the party that matters, and in the party's Central Committee, the representation of women never surpassed 10 per cent and was usually much lower. In 2010, there were not more than 6 per cent women in the Committee, and in the Politburo, only a single one (4 per cent). The Standing Committee consisted entirely of men.

Since the 1980s, China has restructured the government several times, decentralising and reducing the administration. A few elite women gained greater possibilities for obtaining administrative positions, but the cuts struck women first of all, and competition became harder so that it was more difficult for women to participate in decision-making and politics.

Chinese women did not fight for the right to vote. The revolution gave them rights. A women's federation was created in 1949 to promote equality, give advice on policy and provide women with training, but it was under the authority of the Communist Party. Women's committees were established at the local level, but women's consciousness as women was poorly developed. In 1980, China ratified the CEDAW, and state bodies were created for women and children. Women got better health and education, but less education than men, and they remained subordinate and supplemental in all parts of society. Only in the 1990s were different women's organisations established.

Patriarchal traditions are very strong in China, and the male-dominated Communist Party has made the country's leadership a reserve for men. Mao's statement that women are half the sky has remained a dream. Since the People's Republic was founded in 1949, only two women have been governors of the country's 31 provinces and four largest municipalities – far less than in the US. Only five women have served as full members of the Politburo and three of them were the wives or widows of senior male executives. A very special case was Wu Yi, who retired in 2008 as China's deputy prime minister with responsibility for international trade and financial services. In stark contrast to the absence of women in the government is their success in recent years in private business. Men have led China's large state-owned companies, but in 2010, many of the world's richest self-employed were Chinese women.

Women standing together claiming their rights and defending their status in the new constitution in Tunisia on 2 November 2011.

Image: www.demotix.com

Chapter Twelve

When women made it to the top: overview, variation, trends

Remarkable and limited

When Sirimavo Bandaranaike became the world's first woman prime minister of what was then Ceylon in 1960 it caused worldwide concern. How could a woman cope with such a demanding task?

Half a century later, the woman president of Liberia, Ellen Johnson Sirleaf, received the Peace Prize from an impressed Nobel Committee for her contribution to 'ensuring peace, promoting economic and social development and strengthening the position of women' (Norwegian Nobel Institute, 2011).

After Sirimavo Bandaranaike, 72 women have been presidents and prime ministers in 53 countries up to the end of 2010.[1] They were top leaders in great and small nations, rich and poor, in north and south, east and west. They exercised power during crises and economic growth, transitional regimes and democracy, war and peace (see Figure 15).

When Australia got a woman prime minister in June 2010, the British newspaper The Independent announced that 'Women are taking over the world' (Battersby, 2010). Australia is an important country, but the truth was that the total number of women heads of state and government rose to 16 when Julia Gillard was elected. Later in 2010 it rose to 18 – or about 6 per cent of the world's presidents and prime ministers. This was more than ever before, but there was certainly still a way to go before women had control of the planet.

Since World War II, 28 per cent of the world's 192 states have had a woman national leader for a longer or shorter period of time. Among the world's 11 most populous states, with more than 100 million inhabitants, Bangladesh, Brazil, India, Indonesia and Pakistan have had the experience of a women head of state or government. But of the 2.8 billion people who have had a woman as president or prime minister, often brief episodes of female leadership did not change men's dominant position. And states with a total of 4 billion people have never had a woman as a top leader.

Figure 15: Countries with women heads of state and government, 1945–2010

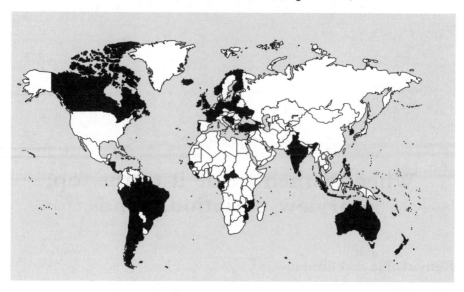

Source: Compiled by the author.

In the United Nations (UN) Security Council, only two of the five permanent member states have had women top leaders: Great Britain and, for a short period, France. The power forum of the eight leading industrialised countries (the G8) had, until 2010, only comprised three states with women national leaders – Britain, Canada and Germany – and not many more were represented at the larger meetings of the G20, the group of the most influential economies, representing both developed and developing countries. Here Argentina, Australia and Germany were headed by women. At the summit of developing countries, four countries had female leadership at some point in time: Argentina, Chile, Indonesia and the Philippines.

In such a thoroughly male-dominated political world, how did the 73 women succeed? Which circumstances contributed to their rise to the top, and what happened when they took over power positions?

Favourable conditions

Rich countries at the forefront

After the UN agreed that women and men should have equal rights in 1945, the number of nation states increased dramatically and economic and technological developments gave women and men across the globe greater income, more education and better health. Above all, it was in industrialised countries that people got a high standard of living. However, looking at the number of women heads of state and government, it seems at first glance that women went to the top as often in developing as in industrialised countries. A total of 37 women rose to power in developing and 36 in industrialised countries.[2]

But the absolute numbers are misleading. Taking the total number of countries into account, the picture changes completely. There are many more developing than developed countries. In 2010, there were actually twice as many developing countries. Whereas about 40 per cent of industrial countries have or have had one or more women heads of state and government, this has only been the case for about 20 per cent of developing countries. Thus, the conditions in industrial countries were more favourable for female leadership than in developing countries. People's health, education and income were important, though they were not necessarily the only factors of importance.

It may be objected that developing countries had the first women national leaders, and they rose to the top in countries with very low standards of living. But although standards were generally low, the elite in poor countries could live in abundance and form a basis for political leadership.

Necessary democracy

It has been to the advantage of women in politics that the number of democracies increased. Democracy is based on the principle that people are equal, and it is the people, not a limited elite, that should govern. As the government must be accountable to the people, it is often responsive to trends among the voters, and women constitute half of the electorate. This leads to the demand that women should participate in governing bodies that are supposed to be representative of the population as a whole. Democracy and increasing respect for human rights also expand the space for civil society, popular activity and opposition, not only political parties, but also community-oriented organisations, such as women's organisations of various kinds. At the same time, paradoxically enough, anti-democratic, religious fundamentalist and chauvinist ethnic movements can grow in strength in the space democracy provides.

It is a clear tendency that women did not generally get political power in totalitarian systems. Only two women became prime ministers in authoritarian countries (the Central African Republic and Yugoslavia), and the situations were special. Nine women rose to power in turbulent transition situations, where democratic systems were not in place or did not work, or where there were uprisings or civil war.[3]

But the great majority of women national leaders came to power in countries characterised as 'democracies', according to Derbyshire and Derbyshire (2000). There were 62 women leaders in 48 democracies, both liberal and emerging, but most in liberal democracies. There were 37 women leaders in 26 liberal democracies and 25 women leaders in 22 emerging democracies.[4] The differences between the two forms of democracy were, first of all, that the emerging democracies were less stable and civil rights were not as deeply rooted as in the more established liberal democracies.

As the number of democracies in the world changed significantly over the years, it is not possible to evaluate the distribution in relation to the total number of countries. But by the turn of the century, there were approximately the same number of liberal and emerging democracies. Most women leaders (23) rose to the top in liberal democracies in Western industrial countries. Then, some (10) got top positions in emerging democracies in Eastern industrial countries. Moreover, they were scattered over different regions.

Times of crisis

Simultaneously with the democratisation processes, there were economic crises of global proportions, among others: the debt crisis in the 1980s, which particularly affected Latin America and Africa; the Asian crisis in the 1990s; and the global financial crisis from 2007 onwards. It was particularly in developing and Eastern industrial countries that political transformations took place during the past few decades, and it was also here that the economic crises hit the hardest, and that changes were most extensive. In many places, women participated in democracy movements and fought for rights and better living conditions.

Earlier studies (see Chapter Two) noted that before 1990, many women leaders came to power in turbulent times of social or political distress.[5] It is not easy to define this type of situation in a clear manner, but also after 1990, women rose to the top under exceptionally difficult circumstances: with armed conflict, transition from authoritarian to democratic rule and economic crisis, with unemployment and social unrest. In fact, only about one third of the women were national leaders under stable, calm conditions. They worked mostly in liberal democracies in Western countries. The majority, about two thirds, came to power in unusually demanding situations. Along with political problems and the complications related to their gender, serious financial difficulties were an important challenge. As one might expect, the women primarily lived in developing and Eastern industrialised countries. In many cases, their go-ahead spirit was remarkable, but under such unfavourable circumstances, there were clear limits to what they could achieve and they could face painful dilemmas.

The crises were largely caused by economic forces that the leaders had little influence over. They were faced with strong public demands for better living conditions, while the countries were heavily indebted, with trade and budget deficits. Rich Western countries introduced neo-liberalism more or less gradually depending upon local conditions, but many of the developing countries were strongly aid-dependent and did not have the same possibilities for choice. Eastern countries were also often in difficult situations. To get support from the international financial institutions and wealthy Western countries, they had to change the economic policy in a neo-liberal direction. This entailed difficult adjustments. Popular control over the development of society was reduced and public authorities had their wings clipped. There was less emphasis on fairness and justice, and social and economic inequalities increased. While women's position in many countries was weakened and poverty was 'feminised', women-friendly policies were often harder to implement in spite of pro-equality rhetoric.

Women's movement

If a certain democracy was necessary for women's political participation, it does not follow that it was sufficient. After World War II, Western industrial countries had mostly liberal democracies, with political rights for women. But the systems were based on long-lasting male dominance, and women were not mobilised and welcomed into the political institutions.

Inspired by a new wave of feminism in the 1970s, more women started to participate in formal politics. Parties and governments were put under pressure to let women in, and especially from 1975, the UN and the international women's movement mutually supported each other. The women's movements presented demands and formulated policies, while the UN promoted change, collected data, organised debates and set standards. In many countries, political institutions became more open for women, women's influence increased and woman-friendly decisions were made. In addition to the UN and other intergovernmental and private organisations, the globalisation of modern mass media played an important role in spreading information about women's actions and women national leaders.

Generally, but unevenly, the number of women heads of state and governments increased at the same time as the number of women in parliaments and governments. Not unexpectedly, more women joined parliaments than cabinets, and more became cabinet ministers than top leaders (see Figure 16). Women participated in elections and the call for more power applied to all political governing bodies. The great majority of the women who became presidents and prime ministers had the advantage of being able to appeal to women voters, and when they rose to the top, at least half also benefited, directly or indirectly, from women activists specifically requiring more women in leading positions. Some also received support from women in parliaments and governments.

Christian, but not only

Patriarchal traditions based on religion are often a strong force against changes in women's role and participation in politics. It is hard to know exactly what role religion plays because it is intertwined with social and cultural factors. Looking at the women heads of state and government, it is striking that they came from countries where dominant ethnic groups had different religions: Hinduism, Buddhism, Judaism and Islam, as well as Christianity (Catholicism, Protestantism and Orthodox Christianity). In 2010, about half of the world's states had a majority of Christians in the population, while there was a Moslem majority in about a quarter. Only a few countries were marked by other religions.

To a great extent, the women national leaders came from countries where the majority of the population was Christian: 52 (71 per cent) leaders from 37 countries, most Western or Eastern industrialised countries. In many cases, the population was Catholic, but also Protestants, Orthodox or belonged to different movements. Although there were many countries marked by Christianity in total, this was an over-representation. As a religion, Christianity has clear patriarchal traits, but the influence of faith is reduced by the secularisation in many industrial countries, with relatively little religious involvement in the population and a secular state formally or in practice.

Of the women heads of state and government, 21 (29 per cent) lived in 16 countries marked by other religions. It is worth noting that two important Buddhist/Hindu countries had women top leaders – India and Sri Lanka – and they had two each. In addition, six countries with a Moslem majority had women top leaders – Bangladesh, Indonesia, Kyrgyzstan, Pakistan, Senegal and Turkey – though some of them encountered considerable resistance on a religious basis. Nevertheless, it was not impossible for women to become national political leaders.

Well-equipped women

Mothers with stamina

Normally, men took part in politics and a few became national leaders. How could it be that women entered such an unfamiliar, tough and distinctly 'male territory' and even obtained one of the most important positions? What background and qualifications did they have?

Data are lacking for some of the women top leaders, but in all regions, they came from varied economic and social conditions. The occupations of the fathers ranged from wealthy landowners and merchants to clergymen, lawyers, carpenters, boatmen and smallholders. Many were professional politicians and businessmen, while others were farmers, intellectuals, employees and workers. Most families belonged to the middle class, but all classes were represented. The very well-off were from different regions, while those who lived in poor circumstances were mostly workers in industrialised countries or small farmers in Africa. Several came from ethnic groups that were not in the majority in the country, but none from distinctive 'out-groups'.

In addition to the roles as wife, homemaker and mother, many of the top women's mothers also had an occupation and participated in activities outside of the home. There is information about the families of two thirds of the national women leaders, and of these, two thirds of the mothers had paid employment, while the rest were housewives.[6] The economically active mothers worked as farmers, teachers, seamstresses, social workers, nurses, pharmacists, medical doctors and shopkeepers. Several of the housewives had previously been economically active but stopped when they got married and had children. The number of children could be quite large.

Many of the mothers were energetic and strong-willed, exercised leadership in the family, were involved in the community, and active in organisations. Eugenia

Charles believed her mother was the boss at home, although her father was an important person. Hanna Suchocka learned to work hard from her mother, and Golda Meir's mother opened a shop in spite of her husband's protests. Some families could afford maids and nannies, as in the families of Indira Gandhi and Mary Robinson. Others toiled and moiled with little money, such as the mothers of Agatha Barbara and Mary McAleese, with nine children, and the daughters had to give a helping hand. A few of the top women lost their fathers early, and their mothers had to support the children alone, as was the case for Kazimiera Prunskienė and Ertha Pascal-Trouillot. Some, such as the mothers of Megawati and Kim Campbell, did not get along with their husbands and left both them and their children. It is only noted in the case of the mothers of Campbell, Finnbogadóttir and Gandhi that they were explicitly feminists.

Politics at the dinner table

In half of the families, we have information that the father, and sometimes the mother or grandparents, were politically active and had or had had political positions. Some fathers were prominent national politicians in parliaments and governments, while others worked at the local level. If they did not have formal positions, they could play an important role in informal consultations in the local community. Arroyo, Bhutto, Gandhi, Hasina and Megawati succeeded their fathers in the position of top leader. Brundtland's father was a cabinet minister; the father of Charles was a member of the local parliament; Thatcher's father was a mayor; and Halonen's was active in the labour movement. Suchocka's grandmother was a member of parliament (MP), and Sigurðardóttir's grandmother was a trade union leader. Kumaratunga was the only top woman leader to have a mother in office as national leader. But several of the mothers came from politically distinguished families, were engaged in political work, supported the activities of the spouse and sometimes influenced them. Bachelet's mother was an active socialist and Finnbogadóttir's was a trade union leader. Hasina's mother participated actively in shaping Mujib's liberation movement and Gandhi's mother made the family support Mahatma Gandhi.

When the parents were politically engaged, political issues were often discussed at home. In the cases where the father worked as head of state or government, the house could almost be like a public gathering place, with an intense political atmosphere. The daughters also got to participate in meetings or engage in other political activities. As a child, Thatcher helped her father in electoral campaigns, Bandaranaike accompanied her father when he travelled around to talk with people, and Charles could listen to debates in parliament. While they were travelling or imprisoned, the fathers of Indira Gandhi and Benazir Bhutto wrote long letters to their daughters, and Sheikh Hasina was a messenger between her parents when her father was in jail. This was an important stimulus, especially where the families were in favour of the involvement of girls in society. Several of the top women note that boys and girls were treated equally in the family, and that as young girls, they were encouraged to occupy themselves with societal issues.

But girls were not always encouraged to enter politics. Sometimes, they were discouraged because the activity was considered inappropriate for girls or boys had precedence. Aquino's parents took for granted that girls should not go into public service, and the father of Chamorro warned against the enmity that political debates could entail. Of the five daughters who were to take over the nation's leadership after their fathers, Benazir Bhutto was the only one who was deliberately formed as his successor. For the others, there was no intention of preparing them for such a career. And as children, some of the top women reacted negatively to politics because of the tension and insecurity it entailed and the frequent absences of one or both parents. When her father was murdered, Kumaratunga was only 14 years old.

From Tito to Thatcher

In the years after World War II, there was a shortage of living role models for future women politicians. Most of the women top leaders were the first in their country. There may have been women in other important positions, but there were very few cases. Many countries had active women's organisations who demanded that women should participate in politics, supported women who did or even provided opportunities themselves for women leadership, but the range was usually limited. As a child, some of the future women top leaders had Joan of Arc as a role model, but she was undeniably somewhat remote. Several therefore picked out male role models. Bandaranaike looked up to the Yugoslav leader Tito and the Egyptian leader Nasser, who both supported the non-aligned movement. Brundtland admired two Social Democratic leaders: Sweden's Olof Palme and West Germany's Willy Brandt. Robinson was inspired by India's Mahatma Gandhi, Martin Luther King in the US and the Czech Vaclac Havel, while Cresson had De Gaulle and Mitterrand in her own country, as well as Winston Churchill in Great Britain. Thatcher also worshipped Churchill and Grybauskaitė Mahatma Gandhi.

As the years passed, women could be inspired across the borders by other national women leaders. Women who became top leaders themselves mention Bandaranaike, Gandhi, Meir and Thatcher. As women, they attracted considerable attention as exceptions to the male-dominated leadership of nations. From 1975, the UN and the large international women's conferences, with prominent politicians from around the world demanding gender equality, contributed to changing the image of women and women's status in considerable parts of public opinion. Women should not only be mothers, but actively participate in the economy and politics and help to determine the development of society. This stimulated women to try new roles. At the same time, economic development and urbanisation gave rise to a more varied working life.

Social commitment

While some of the top women were swirled into politics as children through the family, many got engaged in societal issues as they grew up. Only a handful of women got top positions without having participated at all in political and social activities. Some women were engaged in the struggle for freedom and independence (as Barbara, Domitien, Meir and Planinc), others for democracy (as Bachelet, Güeiler, Han and Zia) or peace and reconciliation (as Kinigi, Kosor, McAleese and Perry). Brundtland and Tymoshenko participated in party-political youth movements, while Diogo, Fernández, Jagan, Jäätteenmäki and Otunbayeva became members of political parties at an early stage. Campbell, Cresson, Kumaratunga and Shipley got positions at local or regional level. Some of the women became interested in social issues during their studies and student activities (as Çiller, Gillard, Hasina, Prunskienė and Sirleaf) or experiences in professional work (as Arroyo, Chamorro, Dreifuss and Sigurðardóttir). Others were preoccupied with social problems, children and education (as Bergmann-Pohl, Itzik and Werleigh).

Long before any top leadership position was in question, about a third of the women were concerned with women's issues, mostly in Western countries, but also in Africa and Asia. Most were left-wing. They fought for women's rights and improved conditions through education, social services, higher wages and freedom from violence. They included, for example, Bandaranaike, Brundtland, Das Neves, Dreifuss, Han, Merino, Patil, Robinson, Sigurðardóttir and Uwilingiyimana. Some women founded, joined or led independent women's organisations (such as Barbara, Güeiler, Jagan, Meir and Perry) or the women's affairs wing of a political party (such as Domitien, Gandhi, Kinigi, Kosor, Kumaratunga and Simpson-Miller). A few got positions such as the head of a women's commission (Pintasilgo) or gender equality group (Werleigh).

Extraordinary qualifications

Regardless of their parents' occupations and economy, the daughters got to go to school. This was not obvious at the time when many of the top women leaders were young, especially in poor developing countries. But the women generally became an exceptionally well-qualified group. The great majority (66, or 90 per cent) not only went to primary and secondary school, but also got higher education at college and university.[7]

There were seven (10 per cent) of the women top leaders who did not have education beyond primary and secondary school. If we compare them with their male predecessors in the same position, there were about as many with limited education. The men were mostly workers, farmers and businessmen. The women with little education worked as housewives and had jobs such as bookkeeper, dancer, farmer, stewardess and unskilled teacher. In addition they participated in organisations for liberation, democracy and social justice, which entailed social activity. The women mostly went to the top before 1990. Three were widows in Asia and Latin America, and the others came from poor conditions in Africa, Latin America and the West.

Most of the women top leaders had far more education than the average in the population, not to mention the average women. Many of the women leaders climbed up the social ladder through education. They very often studied law, economics and political science in addition to other subjects. They came forward with qualifications that were very unusual, particularly in developing countries, and, at the same time, useful for politics and government. If we compare them with their predecessors, more women than men had higher education, but the difference was not very great. Of the male top leaders, approximately 80 per cent had such education, while this was the case for 90 per cent of the women.

The political scientist Farida Jalalzai (2013b: 83) noted in her study of women top leaders that, regardless of region, extensive education preceded the political careers of both women and men. Women increasingly fitted the traditional mould of the political elites and their entrance to executive posts did not signal a shift from the qualifications deemed necessary for the job. The largely male-defined pattern prevailed.

Eventually, the school system was developed in different parts of the world, but progress was slow and uneven. It is significant that almost all of the women top leaders from industrial countries received education in their home countries, while the majority from developing countries went abroad to study, often in Western countries. Thereby, they got an education that was not available where they grew up. But the families had to have resources to be able to send their daughters abroad.

The top women often had a long professional career before they became political leaders. Apart from a few housewives, all were economically active and most had different jobs over time. With their education, they usually could carry out a wide spectrum of occupations. Many were also professional politicians for varying lengths of time before they went to the top. The great majority had professional, technical jobs first, such as a teacher in basic or secondary school, nurse, lawyer, medical doctor, academic or expert, followed by administrative and leadership posts, such as cabinet minister, MP, civil servant and party and trade union official.[8] A few were engaged in office work, sales, agriculture or other production. A bit more than 40 per cent achieved high positions, such as director, professor, researcher, attorney general, judge, editor or ambassador. It was unusual that men had such jobs, and even more unusual that women got them. There was no basis for criticism of their experience and qualifications.

Looking at the women's male predecessors as top leaders, there were not more than 20 per cent who had similarly high positions as the women before they went into politics, even if a leader of high military rank is included. Women evidently had to have higher status than men to rise to power.

Married – and divorced

It is notable that the vast majority (64, or 89 per cent) of the women were or had been married or cohabiting when they became top leaders. Only eight (10 per cent) were unmarried and single. (Information is lacking for one.)

Marriage and children could be a complicated issue for politically active women. In many places, a middle-aged woman could be met with scepticism if she was not married. Doubts could be raised about her femininity and morals. Tactically, it was an advantage to stand forth as a 'real woman', 'wife' and 'mother'. This was particularly true in developing countries, and most single top leaders also found themselves in the industrial world.[9] Bhutto, Merkel and Halonen went so far as to formally marry due to their political career.

Some of the women married more than once, were divorced or widowed. In some milieus, divorce, especially for women, was condemned, but 19 (26 per cent) of the top women were divorced, and some more than once. They belonged to all regions, but in Asia, there was only one. Most of the divorced were Christians, mainly Catholics, but there were also a couple of Moslems. Despite the divorces, the women rose to national power in their countries.

The great majority of women top leaders lived in long-lasting marriages, where the husband usually had his own career and the wife had hers. The women frequently met their partners while they studied, and several of the women with a working–class or agricultural background hence married upward on the social ladder. Most of the spouses, where the occupation is known, were intellectuals in liberal professions: researchers, university teachers, professors, lawyers, economists, medical doctors, dentists or newspaper people. In addition, some were businessmen. Generally, they had jobs that were well-remunerated with considerable autonomy in their work.

Apart from the husbands of the widows, who, by definition, were extremely politically active, there were few men who had a political career of their own, and those who had were all in developing countries. In industrial countries, such a career would easily create problems for the wife's political activities. But in developing countries, it was more accepted that politics was a family affair, and the husbands of Bhutto, Gandhi and Megawati became MPs. Benazir also took her spouse into the cabinet. In Latin America, Cristina Fernández and Nestor de Kirchner and Janet and Cheddi Jagan were political couples (but both women ultimately became widows, Janet before and Cristina after being elected president). In some cases, discord arose in the marriage, for example, as Gandhi experienced, and some husbands caused political problems because they were accused of corruption, as happened with the spouses of Arroyo, Bhutto and Çiller.

Politician and mother

Three out of four of the women top leaders had children, usually one to three, but some had four, five and even seven (Perry). The women could be assisted by mothers, sisters and other female relatives, hire help in the house and benefit from day care institutions and boarding schools. In developing countries it was not uncommon for the extended family to contribute with housework and childcare. A few women, especially in Western countries, got active help from their husbands, who took on tasks that were unusual for men in order to support their wives. In addition to being political advisers and responsible for public relations, writing texts and taking photographs, they functioned as accompanying escorts and took care of the house and children. Examples were Denis Thatcher, Arne

Olav Brundtland, Nick Robinson, Pentti Arajärvi (husband of Tarja Halonen), Burton Shipley and Mike Arroyo.

Nevertheless, taking care of home and family required time and effort for the woman, and it could be claimed that the wives and mothers neglected their husbands and children because of their political activities. The Conservative Party did not allow Thatcher to run for parliament as long as her children were young, and Finnbogadóttir was told that she could be criticised because she was a single mother (with an adopted daughter) when she ran for president. But both Halonen and Kosor ran as single mothers and were elected to parliament, and, at times, Bachelet and Güeiler were also single parents. Although they were not single, several mothers, for example, Hasina, Meir and Sirleaf, felt that their involvement in politics caused their children to suffer. Bhutto gave birth to a son shortly before she became prime minister and a daughter a year later. She continued her political work unabated with the support of her mother as deputy prime minister, but, at times, she had a guilty conscience, and it became a joke among opponents that all Benazir managed to produce as head of government was a baby.

Usually, the women top leaders had passed child-bearing age when they came so far as to acquire their highest positions. The vast majority were in their 40-50s – on a par with male top leaders (see also Jalalzai, 2013b: 80–81). They no longer had responsibility for minors and had also gained considerable experience in professional and social life. In Western countries, older people were often met with scepticism, while age and authority were more related in the developing world. The oldest women national leaders were also from developing countries. Janet Jagan was 77 years old when she became president of Guyana and Sirimavo Bandaranaike was 78 when she was appointed prime minister for the third time in Sri Lanka. Only two women were under 40 when they rose to power. In addition to Benazir Bhutto, who was 35 years old when she became prime minister, a temporary top leader in an Eastern Bloc country (Nino Burjanadze) became president at 39 years old.

Struggling upwards

Three paths

There is usually a long way to go to acquire a national top position. As noted earlier (see Chapter Two; also D'Amico, 1995), three paths could be distinguished for national women leaders:

1. 'Substitutes', who take over a family member's position of power;[10]
2. 'Insiders' or climbers in the political parties, who obtain a position of power through the party; and
3. 'Outsiders', who obtain a position of power on the basis of occupational activities, participation in non-governmental organisations (NGOs) or at grassroots level outside the political parties.

Looking at the 73 women top leaders by the end of 2010, 14 (19 per cent) were substitutes, 48 (66 per cent) were insiders and 11 (15 per cent) were outsiders.

The paths to power varied from region to region. Asia and Latin America were the only regions with substitutes. On the other hand, there were no outsiders there. The existence of substitutes reflects the importance of elite family dynasties in society. Turbulent and violent upheavals also played a role. In Asia, there were only two women who obtained political top positions without being substitutes, and they had positions with limited power. In Latin America, there was about the same number of substitutes and insiders. Women could 'inherit' top positions, but also engage in the parties and go to the top in this way. In the other regions – the Eastern and Western industrial countries, the Caribbean, and sub-Saharan Africa – the women mainly rose to the top through political parties. The exception was 11 outsiders, who were distributed among the four regions.

Penetrating labyrinths

The three paths may seem simple, but they do not tell us anything about the obstacles women face while rising to the top. It has almost become a standard expression that women butt against a 'glass ceiling' that blocks the way to leadership positions (US, 1991). It is possible that there were absolute barriers in places against women leaders due to their gender, particularly in the past and even now in some countries. But the barriers have been more or less broken in a lot of places. And the study of the women top politicians shows that the image of a glass ceiling is far too simple. It gives the impression that there is only a single barrier that stops women, not that they encounter obstacles all the way, and it says nothing about what it takes to reach the glass ceiling. A ceiling is a plain construction, and the metaphor gives the idea that one can break it with a blow, once and for all, and then it is done. Although pioneers can reduce obstacles, it does not mean that it is easy for women to follow in their footsteps. In fact, there are complex interactions between different factors that make it possible for a woman go to the top or not. Various barriers must be overcome, perhaps one barrier several times, in different ways, and when one is overcome, there are new ones.

In their book about women leaders in the US, the psychologists Alice Eagly and Linda Carli (2007) provide a more appropriate metaphor. They believe that women have to go through a *labyrinth* to reach their goal. The labyrinth provides a better picture of the varied challenges women can face when they try to move up in society and politics, and labyrinths can be formed in different ways. With regards to the women top leaders, this image seems to be far more accurate than a glass ceiling. The women constantly encounter barriers that they must overcome in order to progress. They have to take detours, go back and find their way along intricate and often hidden paths. Many factors come into play. To be successful, societal conditions must be right, and the political system must be accessible. Moreover, women must have appropriate expertise and a supportive environment.

Unless there are special circumstances, most men also have to go through a labyrinth to advance to the top in politics. But labyrinths for men are often simpler than those that women have to go through, with fewer dead ends, nooks, crannies and barriers, less insecurity and resistance and more support. Women most often start with a handicap due to their gender. They not only find themselves in uncharted territory, but in an area that is deemed inappropriate for women, where their skills and training are often unsuitable or undervalued. Nevertheless, some have succeeded.

For people and fatherland

What motivation did the women have to pursue an extremely demanding political career and take on a difficult top position that was usually reserved for men? In speeches and interviews in connection with their inaugurations, they usually indicated vague and general reasons. Substitutes represented the family and wished to carry on the political inheritance from their relative. Only a few, like Sirimavo Bandaranaike and Benazir Bhutto, emphasised that they were women. The outsiders wanted to serve the country and promote peace and democracy. In addition, several said that they would support women, for example, Vigdís Finnbogadóttir, Ruth Perry, Maria Pintasilgo and Mary Robinson. The insiders underlined that they would follow the policies of the party and contribute to the solution of societal problems. Some presented a variety of tasks, but there were not many who specifically mentioned women and gender equality, and in the cases where they did, it was usually in general terms: women should participate in government or their needs should be addressed. Some thought that it was important to improve conditions for children and the family. Only a few came forward as pronounced feminists: Michelle Bachelet, Mame Badior Boye, Kim Campbell, Ruth Dreifuss, Maria des Neves, Maria de Lourdes Pintasilgo and Ellen Sirleaf.

Although coincidences could play a role in women's access to top positions, it was no coincidence that there were women available who were both well-qualified and willing to assume office. There were long and determined efforts behind the women's availability. When they became political top leaders for the first time, 11 of the women were vice presidents or deputy prime ministers, five were presidents of parliament, 18 were ministers, 18 were party leaders or deputy leaders, six were MPs, and two were leaders at the state level in a federal country.[11] One was retired, but had recently been secretary general in the government party (Meir). The outsiders had high positions in different areas of society, with the exception of Perry, who ran a shop at home because of the civil war.

Smart with a woman

But how did it happen that some women rose to the top in the political hierarchies instead of men, who usually did this? There were plenty of men and very few women among potential leaders.

Sometimes, a woman rose to the top when the male leader in office suddenly disappeared: fell ill, died or withdrew for one reason or the other. Suddenly, there was an unexpected opening and a political power vacuum, because no (male) successor stood ready to take over. In some cases, the women had a position that made it natural to move up. This happened to eight women (11 per cent). Or they were asked to fill the role until a new leader could be elected: six women (8 per cent). In most cases (39, or 53 per cent), the women were requested by the party or top leader to run for office or act as a leader in a crisis situation or in the case of a change. Some women, but fewer (20, or 27 per cent), ran for election more or less on their own initiative and won. It happened that the male top leader was challenged by a woman in the party, and a woman then took over the position (Clark and Shipley).

Why were the women asked or why did they receive support to take on such an important power position? The substitutes brought a positive force that stemmed from the earlier leaders. Moreover, for almost all the top women, it was emphasised that they were personally competent, with knowledge, capacity for work and experience, and had held high positions. As the importance of democracy increased and women's movements became stronger, this was reflected in the fact that many of the male leaders saw the women's gender as a positive aspect because they could appeal to women voters. In some cases, there were no suitable and willing men, or there was no agreement on any man. In situations characterised by antagonisms and conflicts, women were often appreciated as a neutral, stabilising and unifying force. It was an advantage that they stood outside the ordinary political fighting between men. They could therefore be accepted by the different (male) parties and play a special role as mediator, peace negotiator or innovator. Often, the women were seen as less greedy for power than their male colleagues. They were not discredited, either, as some male leaders were (they were 'clean') and could provide a new deal.

But if women's 'purity' and distance from conflicts was an advantage before they acquired a top position, it was rarely any advantage afterwards, when they moved from symbolic value to political leadership. Then, on the contrary, it could be a disadvantage. To succeed as leaders, it was not sufficient to be clean, modest and neutral. They had to take a stand, get involved in political power struggles, handle various challenges and deal with conflicting expectations. And it was not easy. Often, the women did not get access to the 'real' power, or were only allowed to sit as long as the male elite did not perceive them as a political threat.

Substitute struggle

The substitutes started with an advantage: the legacy of an influential relative. At the same time, they were often criticised because they came to power due to connections, not skills. Very few men could benefit from the same kind of family connections climbing to the top (Jalalzai, 2013b: 92, 109–10). Looking closer at the substitutes, it is clear that there was only one who actually inherited the top position directly. Before President Juan Perón died, having appointed his wife Isabel as vice president, he gave her all the powers so that she automatically became president. Otherwise, the family relationship was an important, perhaps necessary, but not sufficient, condition for the women's political career. They followed in the footsteps of their husband or father (in one case, mother). The relatives could serve as mentors before they died, as S.W.R.D. Bandaranaike, Jawaharlal Nehru and Zulfikar Ali Bhutto did, and after their death, they could function as a kind of spiritual guide. The association gave the women status and strength, but it did not entail that they acquired certain political positions or went straight to the top. They had to be appointed or elected to the important offices. Some succeeded their father or husband rather quickly, but they had to run for election and be accepted. Others had to struggle, sometimes for many years, for example, Benazir Bhutto in Pakistan and Khaleda Zia and Sheikh Hasina in Bangladesh, before they got positions as national leaders, and they had to continue struggling to keep their position afterwards.

Some 'heirs' were told that they were ignorant and had little political experience. Six had only primary or secondary education, but eight had attended college or university. Moreover, belonging to an active political family often entailed insight and support, and several had a significant political career before they became top leaders. Most became party leaders and had to learn the game quickly to be able to assert themselves in the political competition. Some had to fight both within and outside the party and the government because central male politicians wanted to carry out the real leadership. Their approach was that 'A woman should only be for decoration' or 'Women know nothing about politics'. There could also be political disagreement. The women got help from friends and allies, but this could also lead to accusations of nepotism. In many countries, there was a tradition of autocratic party leadership, and the women could follow up. Violeta Chamorro refused to give the vice president an office in the government building, Hasina and Zia replaced opponents in the party leadership, and in India, it went so far that the Congress Party split up.

Unexpected assignments

Those who did not get to the top by means of the political parties – 'the outsiders' – were more experts than activists. They were either unexpectedly drawn into politics because of specific circumstances or chosen on a personal basis. In general, they did not obtain positions of central political importance. In industrialised countries, four independent women became presidents in parliamentary systems and had essentially ceremonial duties (Ireland [two], Iceland and Latvia). Two women were requested to head temporary 'non-party' cabinets during a transitional period pending elections (Portugal and Bulgaria). In Africa, a versatile woman outside the warring factions was brought in to bring peace to Liberia, while an 'expert' woman was appointed as prime minister to strengthen Senegal's president before the elections. Three Caribbean women were given short-term top positions during the tumultuous democratisation processes in Haiti because they were independent and competent. All the outsiders were valued for their status and skills, but it was primarily on a professional or personal basis.

Political experience was often limited. Four were elected specifically because they were women: Vigdís Finnbogadóttir, Mary McAleese, Ruth Perry and Mary Robinson.[12]

Laborious inside journeys

In most countries,[13] political parties were the gateway to political office. Parties have been criticised for being closed male clubs that keep women out, but the top women participated extensively in party activities. They got or gained admission in some way or other and went to the top. But it was neither fast nor easy. Most were members for a very long time, climbed up the ranks of the established hierarchy and became experienced insiders. But though the vast majority of the women top leaders acquired extensive political experience, the political credentials of male top leaders were generally greater (Jalalzai, 2013b: 85).

None of the political parties was a women's party. Some top women – Lidia Güeiler Tejada, Chandrika Kumaratunga and Yulia Tymoshenko – formed their own parties, but these did not differ significantly from the others. The representation of women in the party leaderships varied, but, as far as is known, the predominance of men was solid across the board.

In political parties, 28 women insiders (38 per cent of the top women leaders) acquired office at the national level. They were members of the central committee, deputy leaders or leaders. Sixteen women (22 per cent) were party leaders. Most (10) were in Western countries and the others in Eastern countries (three) and the Caribbean (three). No insiders were party leaders in sub-Saharan Africa, Asia or Latin America. But, in addition to the insiders, substitutes also became party leaders. They often went straight into the leadership position without having to climb up through the hierarchy first. Eight of them were in Asia and one in Latin America. In all, 28 (52 per cent) of the women presidents and prime ministers were party leaders.

It has been noted earlier (in Chapter Two), that left-wing parties were more open to women politicians than right-wing ones because they placed greater emphasis on equality and justice and were more positive to changes in social structures.[14] The political colour of various parties was not always clear, but 38 (52 per cent) of the women national leaders were left-oriented and 18 (25 per cent) were oriented to the right. The remaining 17 (23 per cent) were independent, belonged to the centre or other parties. Looking at the women who obtained considerable power in their countries, the political distribution was about the same. Women heads of state and government with different political colours were found all over the globe, but in sub-Saharan Africa, Latin America and the Caribbean, almost all were left-wing. The right-wing and centrists lived, first and foremost, in Western and Eastern industrial countries and in Asia.

Sex with a mentor?

However male-oriented the internal dynamics of political parties were, a sufficient number of influential men had to see it as in their interest that women became leaders and support them so that they managed to rise to the top. (The same was true for male recruits.)

It is often stressed that new and inexperienced party members need the help of a mentor, an experienced and preferably powerful party colleague, to make a career in politics. It was very common among men to provide such support. Often, it was not democratic decision-making, but patron–client relationships, that decided who would get positions. This was complicated for women. They were so few, especially at higher levels, that when it came to men's networks, women were not easily accepted and given access. The norms of interaction were different, depending on the participation – only men, only women or both – and women had fewer goods and services to offer. A special 'service' could be to enter into a sexual relationship, but this could lead to unpredictable complications, and in many cultures, it entailed considerable risk for a woman, who could be severely condemned.

It was typical that rumours arose in some places of a sexual relationship as soon as a woman had a distinct male mentor or obtained a high political position, whether this was true or not. Edith Cresson went public against the rumours before she was appointed prime minister to get ahead of the gossip. We know little about the informal relationships top women had with male colleagues, but most of the women were married and were unlikely to enter into extramarital sexual relations without further ado, although one cannot rule out that it may have happened. It is known that Golda Meir had romances with several of the leading men of the Zionist movement. She was not divorced, but had separated from her husband. The men opened doors for her and promoted her career, but this did not prevent her from being obliged to show that she was competent, again and again.

In presidential systems, women had to be proposed by the president to become prime ministers, whereas in parliamentary systems, they had to be chosen by the party. The party also endorsed presidential candidates. But it was usually a long time before they came so far. In the reports on the top women leaders, a number of important male mentors are mentioned who promoted the women and gave them positions. President Tito ensured that Milka Planinc became leader of the party in Croatia, Prime Minister Heath took Margaret Thatcher into the cabinet, while President Lula built up Dilma Rousseff as his successor. President Mitterrand's role as a mentor for Edith Cresson and Chancellor Kohl's for Angela Merkel are used as examples of established male leaders recruiting women who are eager to learn as presumably loyal protégées.

But politics is an unpredictable world. After Mitterrand and Kohl had made sure that the two women obtained important positions, Mitterrand changed his mind and fired the protégée and Merkel, in turn, criticised Kohl publicly and was elected as party leader in his place. Party leader Demirel appointed Tansu Çiller as minister, but did not support her when she wanted to become party leader (something that she was anyway). President Toledo went further and dismissed Beatriz Merino shortly after he had appointed her as prime minister. In New

Zealand, the opposite happened: Jenny Shipley managed to remove party leader and Prime Minister Bolger after he had appointed her to several ministerial posts.

Many women top leaders said that they got support from 'the people', people they met around the country, voters and sympathisers. Often, they could also travel internationally and meet fellow sisters, get encouragement and inspire others. The parties had international organisations, and politicians met regionally and in the UN. Top leaders could also go on visits to other countries. Sirimavo Bandaranaike and Indira Gandhi, for example, became good friends. Politicians in the Nordic and Baltic countries were in regular contact, and regional cooperation in Latin America and the Caribbean was well-developed. Thatcher met Gandhi and Bhutto, visited Brundtland in Norway, and helped Çiller in her election in Turkey. But there was not only appreciation. Golda Meir, for example, condemned both Sirimavo Bandaranaike and Indira Gandhi. As the years went by, international and regional relations were developed, the women's movement expanded, and special meetings and networks were organised for women top leaders within and outside of the UN.

Openings and obstacles

Parliaments and cabinets are central bodies in a democratic system. In addition to being important decision-making forums, they provide arenas for training and influence and form recruitment bases for national leaders.

However, with the partial exception of the Nordic countries, the cabinets in the 1980s and 1990s had few or no women ministers and the representation of women in parliaments was generally below 10 per cent. It was only after the new millennium that the proportions, on average, began to rise. But by 2010, there were still not more than 19 per cent women in parliaments globally and 17 per cent in cabinets (see Figure 16).

Figure 16: Percentage of women in parliaments, cabinets and top leader positions worldwide

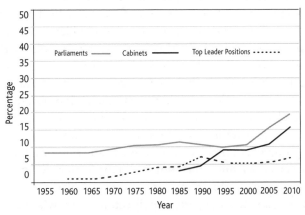

Source: Compiled by the author.

Countries with women top leaders generally had relatively high percentages of women in parliaments and cabinets. In these countries, women's rights were relatively strong and living conditions were good. But there were no clear patterns of countries getting a woman national leader as the result of a certain representation of women in parliaments and cabinets, or that a women top leader automatically led to an increase in the number of women ministers or MPs. For a woman to become a top leader, many factors had to fit together, and even if they could have a positive effect, there was no automatic 'trickle up' or 'trickle down' between the national leaders and parliaments or cabinets.

Recruitment to the various bodies took place in different ways. There were usually direct elections to parliaments, but the recruitment of women was hampered by little goodwill in the parties, few women candidates and unfavourable electoral systems.

The electoral system is a key factor. In different countries, it is of essential importance for women's access to the parliaments. Majority vote in single-member constituencies and proportional representation on the basis of party lists have been the most widespread systems, majority vote being most prevalent by the turn of the millennium. But proportional representation is generally more favourable for women (see Chapter Two).[15]

Among the women national leaders, considerably more rose to the top in countries using proportional representation (42 women, or 58 per cent) than those using majority vote (15, or 12 per cent). In other cases (16, or 22 per cent) there was a difficult situation of transition or elections were not held. Majority vote could thus inhibit women's access not only to the parliaments, but also to further advancement, particularly in parliamentary systems where top leaders had to pass through the parliaments.

Cabinet ministers had to be well-qualified politically and professionally and fit into a complicated ministerial puzzle. In parliamentary systems, they also usually had to be MPs. In presidential systems, ministers were most often brought in from the outside, among people who had distinguished themselves in their professions and society. Nevertheless, women were in short supply.

Of the women national leaders, six out of 10 were MPs before they advanced to the top. Some were also presidents or vice-presidents of their parliaments. Half had experience as a minister. Most of these had also been MPs. As central as parliaments and cabinets have been in most countries throughout the last half of the 20th century, it is notable that there were not more of the women heads of state and government participating in these bodies. It is probable that parliaments with unfavourable electoral systems have, in many cases, worked more as an obstacle than an opportunity for future women national leaders.

Only one group of countries exhibited broad and significant women's progress over a long period of time: the Nordic countries. The countries were small, wealthy and relatively egalitarian, with strong popular movements in general and women's organisations in particular. Electoral systems also gave openings for women. From the 1970s and 1980s, the proportion of women in parliaments and cabinets increased in all five countries, and the Nordic countries acquired a worldwide position at the forefront. Six women also became national leaders by the end of 2010, and in 2011, number seven arrived (in Denmark). From the late 1990s, New Zealand followed a similar trend, although not quite as consistently, and some other countries eventually followed slowly.

To create a faster track to power, gender quotas were introduced. Women could get important political positions without long-term efforts by a broad women's movement. In 2010, around 100 countries had quotas in some shape or form, though they were not always sufficiently ambitious to make a difference. Above all, it was in countries in Latin-America and sub-Saharan Africa that the fast track worked, with marked rises in the representation of women in parliaments. But the countries had presidential systems, so this did not automatically translate into increasing numbers of national women leaders. Particularly in Argentina, Costa Rica and Mozambique, the use of quotas increased support for women leaders, contributing to the rise to power of Fernández, Chinchilla and Diogo.

More or less power

Male partners

Some of the women top leaders were presidents, while others were prime ministers. These positions are allocated more or less power in different countries. What kind of political power did the women top leaders acquire?

From 1960, a total of 32 women became presidents and 41 became prime ministers. Three were both.[16] As noted earlier (see Chapter Two; see also Jalalzai, 2013b: 48-49), it was easier for women to acquire positions as national leaders when the positions had a lower degree of autonomy and they shared power with others. Our material confirms this picture.[17]

Many countries in the world, in fact, most of them in 2010, had only one politically elected top leader, whether a president or a prime minister. In countries with a presidential system, the president was therefore the combined head of state and government. In countries with a parliamentary system, the prime minister was head of government and had an appointed, not elected, head of state (monarch or governor-general) with a mainly ceremonial role. The other countries had both a president and a prime minister who were head of state and head of government, respectively, with a somewhat variable distribution of power.

Of the women top leaders, two thirds (50, or 68 per cent) rose to the top in countries with both a president and prime minister. This is a clear over-representation. There were two top positions to compete for, so the chances of success were often greater, and it was perhaps reassuring for the establishment that something as unusual as a woman top leader necessarily had to collaborate closely with a male colleague. Women obtained roles both as presidents and prime ministers, and it was particularly in industrialised countries, Asia and partly sub-Saharan Africa that they were part of a 'top leader pair'.

Only 23 women (32 per cent) acquired top positions alone, and of these, not more than 15 became strong executive presidents. They lived in Asia and Latin America. The others (eight) were executive prime ministers, mostly in Western countries. Thus, it was extremely rare that women got the political leadership position with the most executive power and greatest autonomy.

Most with least

The titles 'president' and 'prime minister' cover varying realities. In countries with a presidential system, the president is usually the country's most powerful person, and the prime minister – if the role exists at all – functions mostly as an advisor. In a parliamentary system, the roles are reversed. Then, the president – if the role exists – preferably performs ceremonial duties, while the prime minister has political executive power. In dual systems, executive power is more or less evenly divided between the president and prime minister.

At the beginning of the 2000s, presidential systems were more common than parliamentary systems around the world, but women more often rose to the top in countries with parliamentary systems. However, the difference was not great: 24 women (33 per cent) became national leaders in presidential systems and 28 (38 per cent) in parliamentary systems. Only a few (10, or 14 per cent) were leaders in dual systems.[18] These systems were not very common, either. Eleven women (15 per cent) came to power in authoritarian or transitional regimes. There were most women leaders in presidential systems in Latin America and sub-Saharan Africa, and in parliamentary systems in Western and Eastern industrialised countries and Asia.

But women did not necessarily become presidents in presidential systems and prime ministers in parliamentary systems. In presidential systems, 17 women were presidents and seven prime ministers, while seven were presidents and 21 prime ministers in parliamentary systems. Apart from the three presidents of Switzerland, where there was a collective leadership, 35 women (48 per cent) had executive positions with considerable power, while 17 (23 per cent) had mainly ceremonial or positions with limited power. Ten (14 per cent) shared power more or less evenly with a president or prime minister in dual systems. In authoritarian or transitional regimes, five women had relatively strong positions, while six were clearly limited.

All in all, a bit more than half of the women top leaders (40, or 55 per cent) obtained positions that were given considerable power. The other 33 (45 per cent) did not. Their influence was limited by the character of the post or by a male politician in a senior position. In addition, many experienced that they had to exercise leadership in a situation where they not only faced serious problems in the country, but where the party did not have a majority in parliament and had to work with a coalition government in which different political parties, factions or group representatives participated. In some cases, women headed minority governments. Often, extensive negotiations were necessary to implement policy measures. A compromise had to be reached or the top leaders simply had to give up on getting the support of the cabinet regarding specific views or measures.

Another limitation was related to the term of office. Regardless of the position, it was clear from the beginning that 16 (22 per cent) of the women would only work temporarily as top leaders pending elections or the appointment of a permanent leader. The fact that they would only work for a short time certainly contributed to their rise to the top. Some acquired the position on a permanent basis afterwards, but most had to resign. Of the women who got a position with considerable power, there were seven who only got it temporarily. So, all in all, less than half (33, or 45 per cent) of the women obtained a position with considerable power that did not begin with a clear time limit. For the majority of the women top leaders, their power was thus formally more or less limited.

Of the 33 women heads of state and government with the most power, the greatest number were from Western countries (10), Latin America (eight) and Asia (eight). From the other regions, there were very few: Eastern industrialised countries (three), the Caribbean (three) and sub-Saharan Africa (one). Of these women, four were the heads of some of the world's most populous states – Bangladesh, Brazil, India and Indonesia (all developing countries) – nine were the heads of large- and medium-sized states, and 15 of small states.[19] Power was also limited for many in this perspective.

Short terms with exceptions

Politics is no bed of roses, and the top leaders could fall out of favour, be fired or lose elections. Half of the women heads of state and government were directly elected when they came to power for the first time. The others were elected or approved by their parliaments or appointed by leading male politicians. The women top leaders stayed in office for varying periods of time. Quite a few (29 women, or 40 per cent) only served for a year or less. They lived in all regions, but most in Western countries. A good portion (23, or 32 per cent) functioned from one to five years, and they were also to be found in all regions. Finally, there were some (21, or 29 per cent) who remained in power for more than five years until the end of 2010. Of these, 10 had a career of 10 to 17 years. There were five in Western countries (Brundtland, Finnbogadóttir, Halonen, McAleese and Thatcher), four in Asia (Bandaranaike, Gandhi, Kumaratunga and Zia) and one in the Caribbean (Charles).

If we compare the women top leaders with their male predecessors in the same position,[20] the men remained in power longer than the women. The women worked, on average, for three years and nine months before the end of 2010, while the men worked for just over four-and-a-half years before the women took over. This is somewhat more than the women, but the difference is not very large. Some women also continued in office after 2010. Looking at the individual leaders, however, different patterns emerge. About twice as many women as men worked for a very short time, one year or less. Often, women apparently inspired less confidence than men in taking power. But when it came to leaders who remained in office for a very long time, there were actually more women than men. Only four men sat for 10 years or more. Two were prime ministers in the Caribbean and two presidents in Western countries.

Regarding the 33 most powerful women top leaders, six were in office for a year or less, 13 from one to five years and 14 for more than five years until the end of 2010. The 14 who worked the longest were: Aquino, Arroyo, Bandaranaike, Gandhi, Hasina, Kumaratunga and Zia in Asia; Brundtland, Clark, Meir, Merkel and Thatcher in Western countries; Chamorro in Latin America; and Charles in the Caribbean. The six who had a very short career were all still functioning by the end of 2010, with the exception of Campbell.

With and against their will

By the end of 2010, a total of 18 women heads of state and government were still in office.[21] For the others, the role as women top leader was finally or provisionally concluded by 22 retiring when the election term or the temporary appointment ended, 19 being deposed or losing elections, and 11 withdrawing for various reasons. Three were murdered: Bhutto, Gandhi and Uwilingiyimana.

Those who were appointed temporarily lived in different regions. Some continued in office after the interim period was over, but 10 had to leave – actually two were deposed by a coup (Güeiler and Pascal-Trouillot). Those who resigned at the end of the election term had positions where a limited time was fixed that could not be extended, even if they wanted to. They were mostly strong presidents in Asia and Latin America (six) and presidents with limited power in Eastern and Western industrialised countries, including Switzerland (six). In some cases they could make a come-back at a later stage and before 2014 two had done so (Bachelet in Chile and Calmy-Rey in Switzerland).

Of those who resigned, just over half (six) referred to health reasons or preference for other activities. The others (five) experienced political problems. They were all prime ministers and mostly in industrialised countries. Only Kinigi was from a developing country, and she withdrew because of the difficult political situation in Burundi. Prunskienė did something similar in Lithuania. Thatcher was criticised in the UK, Greceanîi came up in a political crisis in Moldova, and Jäätteenmäki committed a political blunder in Finland.

Regarding dismissals, there were always political disagreements behind them. Perón was deposed by the military, and strong presidents deposed subordinate prime ministers: Boye, Das Neves, Diogo and Domitien in Africa, and Merino in Latin America. In addition, Cresson and Pierre-Louis got into trouble in dual systems in France and Haiti.

The women top leaders who lost elections were all prime ministers who had served for a period of time and sought a new vote of confidence. They worked in various regions, except Latin America. Some had been elected before, such as Charles, Clark, Shipley, Tymoshenko and Zia, while others were appointed during the election period and ran for the first time, such as Campbell, Çiller, Megawati, Silveira, Simpson-Miller and Suchocka. Several could come back later, but did not do so before the end of 2010. Simpson-Miller was re-elected in 2012.

For a total of 27 national leaders (37 per cent), their careers ended against their will for political reasons. It was obviously not easy to have a role as a top leader. It was not easy for men, either. But there is reason to believe that women were more vulnerable because leadership was more unusual for them, and the demands were often stricter for women than for men. Women also came to power in many cases in times of crises. However, data do not exist for comparisons between men and women leaders.

Women's leadership

Justice and interests

The importance of the women top leaders can be assessed in different ways. From the point of view of justice, the fact that women become part of the political leadership is significant in itself. Women have the right to participate in the governance of the country on an equal basis with men, and the election of women national leaders is a step in this direction. Because women leaders have been and still are so few, it is also important that the women top leaders constitute role models for women by showing that women, not only men, are willing and able to get to the top and exercise political power.

But the next claim, that the interests of women should be safeguarded as well as those of men in the political arena, is not necessarily met by a few women being included in the political leadership. It is even an open question as to what extent women who become top leaders are on the whole able or willing to promote the interests of women. Although they should appeal to women voters, they are ordinarily supposed to represent the nation as a whole, being elected with a general mandate worked out to a large extent by male politicians, particularly where issues concerning women usually do not have priority. Women have generally gone to the top as more or less solitary swallows, feeling that they had to follow men's leadership to be able to retain power. And on their laborious way through the male-dominated political institutions, they have usually been obliged to compromise and adapt in order to succeed. In addition, the question arises as to which women's interests top leaders with an upper-class background or super qualifications are able or willing to promote.

The whole story of the efforts of the women top leaders as leaders cannot be told here. They endeavoured to solve tasks they were assigned: conduct ceremonial duties, fulfil constitutional and legal requirements, and act as the role required on a par with men. In new and ambiguous situations, when policies and decisions were not determined in advance, in emergencies or when there was disagreement, they had greater possibilities of making a difference. They also engaged in a wide range of issues and problems. Here, the focus is directed specifically towards their work in their capacity as women.

Woman or politician

Politics is about the struggle for power and influence. The women top leaders got into a turbulence of conflicts and dilemmas, as male colleagues also did. In addition, the women were often newcomers in politics and found themselves in an area that was traditionally reserved for men. How should a 'women politician' behave? Expectations were characterised by uncertainty, confusion and contradictions. The roles of a man and a politician/leader, as they were usually defined, corresponded well. Politicians, and especially leaders, should preferably be ambitious, energetic, conflict-oriented and tough. Based on the gender division of labour, however, it was expected that women should be cooperative, caring, compromise-oriented and peaceful. In politics, women should be both 'women' and 'political leaders', roles that were not easy to combine. If the women were persistent and strong, they could be criticised for being 'unfeminine' and 'arrogant'. If they were cooperative and 'weak', they affirmed their femininity, but proved at the same time that they were unable to govern.

To be a top leader, it was required that women politicians should be at least as competent as male, be leaders of society as a whole, men as well as women, and pursue the same policies that men usually pursued. At the same time, it was often said that women had to make a *difference* to justify their leadership position – behave differently and 'better' than men, whatever this might entail.

In political parties, women generally had to advance or defend their positions on men's terms. They obtained central positions through prolonged work in parties, parliaments and governments, where they were more or less co-opted into the system: acted in such a way that they were accepted by men, and fought for issues that were prioritised by them. Often, they had to more or less deny their femininity to be 'one of the guys'. At the same time, they distanced themselves from the women voters they were presumably supposed to represent.

Whatever they did, the women top leaders could be subject to criticism, abuse and harassment. Male politicians were also attacked because of their views and behaviour, but women were exposed to condemnation not only of their policies, but also of their person and gender. Bandaranaike was described as a 'weeping widow' and Thatcher as the 'lady nobody loved'. Brundtland was called the 'nagging woman from Bygdøy' and Bhutto a 'punk little girl'. Gandhi was a 'dumb doll', Chamorro a 'useless old bag of bones', Charles a 'savage old woman' and Tymoshenko a 'tyrannical Machiavelli in skirts' – just to give a few examples.

And the top women were not only subjected to derogatory remarks. Several experienced that they were intensely opposed by those who should be their closest associates because they were women. These included, among others, Aquino, Bhutto, Chamorro, Cresson, Gandhi, Perry and Simpson-Miller.

Also, where relationships were positive, the women got derogatory nicknames: Mitterrand called Cresson 'my little soldier', and Merkel was Kohl's 'chicken'. Praise was often ambiguous. The stereotype 'iron woman' became a standard phrase used in many countries over the years. It is both positive and negative and clearly illustrates the tension between the role of 'woman' (soft) and 'iron' (hard). Often, women were described as men. Several were praised for being 'a proper man' or 'the only man in the government' (where they were actually the only woman). Others were turned into 'superwomen': 'mother of the nation', 'Virgin Mary', 'Joan of Arc' or 'Queen'.

Many of the women national leaders also attempted to exploit their role as women and appeal to women while they performed their role as politicians. A good deal not only had problems because of, but also benefited from, their gender. They were elected because a woman was needed, and they gained influence by behaving differently from men. Some of the women supplemented the men, were exciting and innovative, for example, Bachelet, Brundtland, Diogo, Hasina and Vīķe-Freiberga. Others exploited the fact that they were women to manipulate men. Thatcher, for example, was an expert in using and changing women's roles so that men got confused, and she got her way. Some top women emphasised values of women roles, especially women's importance in peace and reconciliation, cooperation, and caring. Kinigi was an example of this. In many cultures, the role as mother could be used to strengthen the top women's position. This was particularly done in Asia, where Bandaranaike was the 'Mother of the People', Megawati 'Mother Earth' and Aquino 'Mother of Democracy', but also in Africa, where Perry was the 'Mother' of the warring factions and Sirleaf became everyone's 'Ma Ellen'.

Surrounded by men

It is assumed that women can influence policies and the political culture if they constitute a 'critical minority' of, for example, 30–40 per cent (see: quotaproject. org). Especially when women enter politics not as individuals, but in the capacity of *women*, as members of a discriminated group and representatives of their gender, they have possibilities of changing norms and values, policies, and the system, and the possibilities increase with increasing numbers. The women get more self-confident and can bring their diverse experiences as women into processes and decisions to a greater extent. They can also support one another.

But the concrete impact of a particular number depends upon the circumstances: how they are recruited, how the institution is organised, which women they are, if they are interested in change (and, if so, what kind) and the extent to which they can collaborate to make something happen. Arroyo said that women ministers formed a unified block that got proposals through, while Cresson felt 'alone', with five women ministers. However, very few women national leaders experienced something approaching 30–40 per cent women in the decision-making bodies they had to deal with.

The leaderships of political parties were generally extremely male-dominated. When it came to the parliaments, 20 of the women top leaders experienced that the representation of women was below 10 per cent while they were in office, 23 that it was 10–19 per cent, 13 that it was 20–29 per cent and only 11 that it was 30 per cent or more.[22] None enjoyed gender balance or a majority of women. How many women MPs supported the national women leaders is not known. Often the MPs belonged to different parties, and the relationship the leaders had to the parliaments also varied according to their positions as presidents or prime ministers. In any case, the women MPs most often represented an extremely limited number and gave top leaders little to play on or with. This was particularly true in developing countries and, to some extent, Eastern industrialised countries.

Regarding the cabinets, 27 of the women top leaders worked with fewer than 10 per cent women ministers. In some cases, there were only men, with the exception of the head of government, while in others, there were one, two, three or a maximum of four women, depending upon the size of cabinet. Twenty-one women top leaders had 10–19 per cent women ministers, 11 had 20–29 per cent and 14 had 30 per cent or more. It was particularly in Western countries that there were women ministers. But the composition of the cabinets could change: ministers turned out to be unsuitable; some resigned; and there was internal strife and conflicts. Often, ministers were replaced, women as well as men.

Looking at the overall picture, only nine (12 per cent) of the women top leaders worked with 30 per cent or more women in both the parliaments and the cabinets. With one exception, all were from Western countries: Brundtland, Clark, Halonen, Jäätteenmäki, Kiviniemi, Leuthard, Merkel and Sigurðardóttir. In addition, there was Chinchilla from Latin America. And all, except Brundtland, were in office from 1999 or later. Five top leaders in different regions had many women in the cabinets, but not in parliaments: Arroyo, Bachelet, Calmy-Rey, Das Neves and Sirleaf. In two cases, there were many women in the parliaments, but not in the cabinets. That was while Diogo and Fernández were heads of government.

Despite the increase in women's representation, particularly in some of the Western countries, most women top leaders were rather solitary swallows in national politics. In relation to this, 30–35 per cent women can be perceived as significant progress. But women are still a minority.

Somebody holding the pen

It is surprising that, generally, there should be so few women in the cabinets. The top women leaders, themselves, participated in the suggestion, nomination and approval of ministers. But the role of the ceremonial presidents was essentially formal, and the prime ministers in dual systems or subordinated to a strong president had to find ministers in consultation with the president. Executive presidents and prime ministers had most power, but, in many cases, they had to get approval from the parliaments. In addition, the party, or parties if it was a coalition government, played an important role. It was required that the appointment of cabinet members should include key party members, reward supporters, ensure representation of different interests and provide people with skill and experience.

Cresson and Gandhi were forced to take male party bosses into the cabinet. Jäätteenmäki was also put under pressure, but resisted. When Chamorro and Aquino refused to include certain men, they were attacked by the rejected men afterwards, sometimes with violence. Merino had to resign when she would not accept the ministers proposed by the president. Male colleagues also opposed the appointment of women. Güeiler, Prunskienė and Suchocka wished to bring in a woman minister, but strong men around them refused.

If the top leaders had to stick to MPs, and there were few or no women there from their own party, this set clear limits for the composition of the cabinets, which Bandaranaike and Charles experienced, for example. Pintasilgo found that women in parliament refused to become ministers. They did not feel competent or were ambivalent in relation to the political work. Some women heads of government (15) took over one or more ministerial posts themselves, primarily finance or defence. This was especially in South Asia and Western countries, a few also in the Caribbean and sub-Saharan Africa. In South Asia, it happened that the prime minister appointed her mother and husband (Bhutto) and a sister (Zia) as ministers, and Zia's son went so far as to set up a parallel cabinet in his mother's office. In Latin America, the president's son-in-law became de facto prime minister (Chamorro).

Not all the national women leaders were actually interested in appointing women ministers, for example, Chamorro, Megawati, Thatcher and Tymoshenko. Some did not think that there was any point in having women, while others did not find women who they thought were sufficiently qualified. A few reduced the number of women in the cabinets when they took over. But looking at the overall picture, there was a tendency that cabinets had more women ministers the stronger the impact that the top women leaders had on the appointment.

And there were possibilities, especially as time passed. Brundtland created worldwide sensation with her 'women's cabinet' in 1986. It was formed on the basis of a party decision, demanding 40 per cent women in decision-making bodies. It took time, but then others followed, among others: Clark in New Zealand in 1999, with 35 per cent women in the cabinet; Jäätteenmäki in Finland in 2003, with 50 per cent; Bachelet in Chile in 2006, with 50 per cent; and Sigurdardóttir in Iceland in 2009, with 46 per cent. In 2007, the male Prime Minister Matti Vanhanen of Finland created a stir by appointing 60 per cent women in the cabinet, and in 2010, to general astonishment, women were 57 per cent in the Federal Council of Switzerland.

Making a difference

The women did not become top leaders primarily because they were women, but because they should lead the nation. Many were valued in their capacity as women, but it was unclear what this really meant: if it mostly had to do with tactical considerations to attract voters or it implied that women could pursue special women-oriented policies.

Although the national women leaders made a career in male-dominated political institutions, the majority – especially as the women's movement grew – were conscious of the fact that they were women, and that women's status differed from that of men. With the exception of a handful, they all persistently denied that they were 'feminist', whatever they meant by the word. Men generally reacted in a negative way to women's emancipation and advocates for women's rights, and in the public debate, the term 'feminist' was often used as an insult. Many of the top leaders therefore denied being 'feminist' for tactical reasons so that they would not be rejected. But there were also leaders who were sceptical of the women's movement and denounced 'women's interests'.

As noted earlier (see Chapter Two; also Krogstad, 1999b), women top leaders can be placed in three categories:

1. *Conforming* to the norms and values of male-dominated politics, acting in the same way as their male colleagues, fighting on their terms and becoming the first among equals. They were usually not engaged in 'women's issues', whatever they might be.
2. *Compromising* between men's and women's interests, trying to look after both, being as matter of fact as possible, both 'tough and caring'.
3. *Challenging* male domination and explicitly promoting women-friendly or feminist policies: recruiting women, introducing gender quotas, passing laws or adopting measures supporting women.

It is not quite straightforward to apply the categories in practice. What does it mean to promote women's interests? What interests and how? Some women's issues are also highly controversial, particularly those relating to sexuality and procreation: divorce, contraception and abortion, homosexuality, prostitution, and sterilisation. Here, support to the implementation of the UN Convention on the Elimination of All Forms of Discrimination against Women (CEDAW) and the Beijing Platform will be considered as a 'woman-friendly policy'.

Some national women leaders both strengthened and weakened women's position. Arroyo promoted women's economic rights, for example, but opposed family planning. Kosor declared that she would lead the government with a 'strong female hand', but reduced the number of women ministers. Shipley went against domestic violence, but cut down on social security benefits.

Detailed information is lacking with regards to some of the women top leaders, and many worked for such a short period time or in such a difficult transitional situation that there was no room for anything but the most pressing. Of the 48 women that we have been able to place according to a rough evaluation, about one fifth were 'conforming'. Among others, Chamorro, Çiller, Megawati, Meir, Suchocka and Thatcher pursued a policy that partially weakened women's position.

Nearly half played a 'compromising' role, among others, Das Neves, Diogo, Fernández, Gandhi, Greceanîi, Hasina, McAleese and Merkel. Finally, one third can be described as 'challenging', among others, Bachelet, Bhutto, Brundtland, Clark, Güeiler, Perry, Pintasilgo and Robinson. Some of the top women leaders did more, some less, but the vast majority did something to support women in particular. So, it made a difference that a woman rose to the top instead of a man.

The three kinds of politicians were to be found in different regions, and women from various political parties were both 'conforming' and 'compromising'. However, no right-wing leaders were 'challenging', only left-wing and centre leaders.

Women's office and crisis shelter

A good deal of the women top leaders were involved in women-related activities before they went into politics in earnest, and the acceptance of CEDAW meant that governments got a larger and more comprehensive responsibility for strengthening women's status and rights. Several of the top women worked as ministers for women or supported women in their capacity as ministers for other sectors before they rose to power. Examples include Barbara, Campbell, Greceanîi, Han and Merkel. Three were ministers for women at the same time as they were national leaders (Dreifuss, Simpson-Miller and Shipley), but others got top positions under such difficult conditions that it was impossible to deal with other issues than the most urgent on a national basis.

There is information about speeches that have been given, proposals that have been made and decisions that have been taken with the aim of empowering women by more than half of the women top leaders (38). In ceremonial roles, Finnbogadóttir, Robinson and Vīķe-Freiberga, for example, tried to influence public opinion in a woman-friendly direction. Executive presidents and prime ministers supported various measures. Several participated in the approval of CEDAW, such as Bhutto, Brundtland, Charles and Das Neves, and Hasina managed to get reservations regarding the Convention removed. Aquino got gender equality into the constitution, while Clark succeeded in passing a partnership law and paid maternity leave. In addition, Bandaranaike, for example, created a women's office and ministry, and Gandhi established a women's commission and headed India's activity in the International Women's Year. Brundtland appointed a 'women's cabinet' and both she and Merkel promoted the building of kindergartens, among other things. Hasina introduced a women's quota in local politics, Güeiler created a women's hospital, and Bachelet established shelters and provided access to contraception. Diogo made efforts to improve the health and education of women, and Kumaratunga and Sirleaf fought against violence against women.

Male politicians could also have promoted woman-friendly policies and supported measures to improve the situation of women. Some did, but most did not. It was a common experience that, in practice, women were necessary to address women's concerns (IPU, 2008).

Democratic challenges

Many expect women leaders to be especially democratic and cooperative. None of the national women leaders came to power through a coup or established an authoritarian regime. On the contrary, many actively contributed to combating dictatorship and establishing or strengthening democracy.

It can be said that, by itself, the fact that women came forward and were accepted in important positions in male-dominated politics helped strengthen democracy. But it went further than this. Often, the top women took responsibility as leaders in demanding transition situations and comprehensive democratisation processes, and most pursued an active policy to improve democratic institutions. Among others, Güeiler, Pascal-Trouillot and Rogombé organised elections. Aquino, Bhutto and Domitien released political prisoners and Chamorro and Sirleaf opened up the government of the country to the opposition. Arroyo, Bhutto, Hasina, Simpson-Miller and Sirleaf improved the rule of law, and Barbara and Otunbayeva introduced a more democratic electoral system. But several who tried to change the law, especially the constitution, in a more democratic direction failed because they did not have sufficient support. This was the case for Aquino, Arroyo, Bhutto, Bachelet, Chamorro and Kumaratunga.

Many of the women top leaders travelled around the country to win votes, but also to bring politics to the people, especially where mass media could not. This was the case with Bandaranaike, Finnbogadóttir, Gandhi, Hasina, Robinson and Zia. But it was generally a democratic problem that very many of the women top leaders (as the men) came from the elite and were surrounded by people who also belonged to the elite. Some on the Left sought to strengthen the position of weak groups, among others, Bandaranaike, Barbara, Clark, Diogo, Fernández, Hasina and Jagan, but it was no easy task.

Although the countries were formally more or less democratic when the women came to power, it happened especially in the emerging democracies that institutions functioned badly. Democratic governance was a tough challenge. Such governance was not introduced by magic in countries with established authoritarian structures, different ethnic groups and major economic, social and cultural differences. The women top leaders experienced coup attempts. Armed conflict arose in various parts of the country, and the military intervened in politics. The parliaments and governments were paralysed by internal strife, and the administrative and judicial systems were inefficient. Corruption and abuse of power were widespread.

Some of the national women leaders were criticised for their authoritarian leadership style, generally or in periods. This included, among others, Çiller, Gandhi and Perón. Some of the women went so far as to declare martial law during their term of office, such as Bandaranaike, Charles, Gandhi and Otunbayeva, but all repealed it after a while. There is also a question as to how democratic Arroyo's 'people power' number two actually was, and when she later ran in regular presidential elections and was elected, she was accused of fraud.

Clean or dirty

All in all, 14 (19 per cent) of the women national leaders were accused of corruption. This included especially leaders in Asia and Latin America, among others, Bandaranaike, Bhutto, Gandhi, Hasina, Moscoso, Simpson-Miller, Tymoshenko and Zia, in addition to Arroyo. Some of their relatives (particularly husbands) were also accused. The allegations may have been well-founded. Typically enough, they were expressed in countries that were known for widespread corruption and abuse of power in politics. This could be so extensive and ingrained that political leaders could hardly avoid it if they should manage to govern at all. At the same time, the charges came from people and bodies that could also be corrupt, and they were often used politically. It belongs to the nature of corruption that the actors try to conceal what they are doing, and in countries where the press and the judicial system are not vigilant and independent, it is difficult to discover the truth and even more difficult to stop the abuse of power.

Some women top leaders received special support because they were 'clean' – as opposed to the 'dirty' political environment. Several also took action against corruption, launching anti-corruption campaigns, establishing anti-corruption commissions and so on (Kosor, Otunbyeva, Charles, Megawati, Persad-Bissessar, Diogo and Sirleaf). But the results are not known.

In a report in 2008/09, United Nations Development Fund for Women (UNIFEM) presented global research related to gender and corruption. The conclusion was that the key factor to avoid corruption was the political structure, not gender. According to the research, both women in government and liberal democracy were significant and inversely related to corruption. But if these were put together, the effects of women's participation became insignificant, whereas liberal institutions remained powerful predictors of low corruption. Freedom of the press and the rule of law had the strongest influence on corruption. Democratic and transparent politics were both correlated with low corruption and created an enabling environment for more women in politics. Effective checks and balances on power were needed, whatever the gender of the politicians (Goetz et al, 2008: 27).

Military frameworks

Many believe that women are more suited than men to make peace. Generally boys are physically stronger than girls and are culturally moulded into tough and brave, dominating men. Women are seen as having a more caring role, and their approach to the use of force is more negative than that of men. Peace has been a basic claim in the international women's movement since early in the 20th century. Women have participated in peace conferences, collaborated with the League of Nations and the UN, fought against military armament and nuclear weapons and demanded room for women in cease-fire and peace negotiations.

But women politicians went to the top in a world that was anything but peaceful and pacifist. During the Cold War, an unprecedented arms race took place between the North Atlantic Treaty Organization (NATO) and the Warsaw Pact. Afterwards, armament continued with NATO in the lead in addition to other collective and bilateral military alliances, primarily with the US, entailing worldwide militarisation.

In addition to international wars, conflicts arose internally in a number of countries or between neighbours, often with external interference, entailing great suffering for the civilian population. With the exception of a handful of countries, all had more or less developed military forces.

The women top leaders often rose to power in countries that were part of military alliances. Others were neutral (Malta, Moldova, Panama, Switzerland); nevertheless, all had stronger or weaker standing armies, with the exception of Costa Rica and Iceland (Iceland was a member of NATO). Haiti and Panama had very limited forces. In any case, the women top leaders entered frameworks that were very difficult to change, at least in the short term. The military could be a very strong political force and a mighty military industry exerted pressure for profit. The peace movement, on the other hand, was often weak and had difficulties making itself felt. A striking exception was Liberia, where women generally had a strong position. During the armed conflict they organised for peace, demanded influence for women and collaborated with Ruth Perry and Ellen Sirleaf (see Chapter Eight).

Stands on war and peace are often difficult to analyse. All wish to stand forth as promoters of peace, so the use of violence and military power can often be concealed or described with opaque terms such as 'protection', 'military engagement', 'peacekeeping operation' or 'intervention to secure democracy and human rights, including the rights of women'.[23] Of the national women leaders, only a few explicitly endeavoured to promote non-violence, for example Aquino, Clark, Halonen and Megawati. Clark supported an anti-nuclear policy and refused to participate in the US-led war in Iraq. Halonen opposed joint EU defence, but accepted the NATO intervention in Afghanistan. At the same time, ten of the women presidents constitutionally became supreme commanders of the military, and eight prime ministers and one president were also ministers of defence. Their aim could be to control and influence the military, not necessarily to strengthen it. It was particularly so in South Asia, where armed forces were active and powerful, and women top leaders were ministers of defence.

When the women came to power, the situation in many countries was difficult. In 45 cases (62 per cent) there was turbulence and violence related to militarisation, armed conflict, military regimes, the assassination of political leaders or economic crises. Some of the women top leaders, like Aquino, Arroyo, Charles and Kinigi, were exposed to bomb attacks and armed coup attempts that failed, but four others were ousted by the military: Güeiler, Pascal-Trouillot, Perón and Zia. Aquino began her political career fighting against the military dictatorship, but continued by bringing in parts of the army and even American fighter planes to quell armed uprisings, and when the US bases in the Philippines were closed, it was against her wish. Bandaranaike and Çiller also used armed force against insurgents and Bandaranaike was helped by Indian and Pakistani troops. Gandhi and Perón swooped down upon political opponents, and Bhutto and Han strengthened the military. Arroyo supported the US war against terror. Regarding conflicts between states, Gandhi assisted Bangladesh/East Pakistan in the liberation war against Pakistan/West Pakistan. With US aid, Meir fought off Egyptian and Syrian attackers and supported settlement on the West Bank, and Thatcher defended British sovereignty when Argentina invaded the Falkland Islands. So, it was not the case that women top leaders were peaceful in any situation.

Peace and reconciliation

In spite of the often unfavourable circumstances, many women top politicians contributed to peace and reconciliation. Many were active promoting international collaboration, for example Bandaranaike, Brundtland, Gandhi, Grybauskaitė, Merkel and Vike-Freiberga. Bandaranaike mediated between India and China and Merkel solved difficult political conflicts. Hasina, Kinigi, McAleese and Robinson reduced tensions between ethnic groups, Güeiler, Burdsjanadze and Pascal-Trouillot assisted with peaceful regime changes and Barbara prevented civil war. Kosor and Radi ova improved relations with neighbouring states, Hasina and Uwilingiyimana signed peace agreements, and Chamorro, Perry and Sirleaf implemented demobilisation and reduction of the military. Finnbogadóttir organised a summit meeting between the USSR and the US. Some women came into situations where peace efforts failed and they resorted to force of arms instead, for example, Arroyo and Kumaratunga. But if Kumaratunga can be criticised for use of the military, her male successor was far worse. Charles dissolved the army in Dominica, but she asked the US to intervene militarily on the neighbouring island of Grenada.

What men would have done in the same positions we do not know, nor what the reactions would have been towards a man instead of a woman. The women top leaders were surrounded by men and depended on their acceptance of the policy they carried out. Most probably they encountered considerable resistance. It is a prevailing perception worldwide that men and masculinity are closely related to violence and war. There are also examples of women top leaders being defeated by male colleagues in connection with security issues. This happened when Finnbogadóttir went against the US bases in Iceland and Halonen opposed the use of landmines.

Although the countries did not disarm and pursue pacifist policies, the women top leaders achieved something in the direction of peace and reconciliation. And where they failed, they could still have contributed more to peace than male leaders would have done. Even if the women did not go against all use of armed force, they could, for example, have tried peaceful possibilities for a solution first to a greater extent than men or waited longer before they used power. We do not know, but conditions were obviously important for a women's 'peace potential' to be utilised, including the role of peace movements, the number of women in politics and their power and room for action as women.[24]

Important pioneering

Whatever the women top leaders did, many were criticised by the women's movement because they 'betrayed women'. The leaders could possibly have done more to promote women's issues, but they encountered significant resistance. There were few feminist supports and the women's movements often lacked strength. Nevertheless, all the women top leaders contributed to a strengthening of women as political actors by accepting a top position. They demonstrated that women were willing and able to lead a nation under varying and often very difficult circumstances and became models for others. Many showed personal courage and determination by going in new directions and undertaking extremely demanding tasks. They broke with prevailing patterns and showed that women were (mostly) able to handle the tasks. Some came forward as a new kind of (woman) politician. Thus, they could inspire both women and men.

A woman politician in South Africa once said: "I disagree with everything Margaret Thatcher stands for, but if she could do what she wanted, I can too." In addition, the majority of the women top leaders contributed to strengthening the position of women. They spoke in favour of women's causes and supported measures benefiting women. Although one could wish for more, many did important pioneering work in practice. On the whole, it made a difference that top leaders were women, and they became an important part of the slow but generally increasing participation of women in national governments and the strengthening of woman-friendly policies worldwide during the last decades.

Woman-friendly democracy

Still far to gender parity

A small, but growing, number of women have become heads of state and government in the world. They had qualifications out of the ordinary and had to go through extremely demanding careers to reach their goals. All in all, very few women made it, and although some exercised considerable power for a long time many only worked for short periods in less important positions. Female leadership is not as strong as the number of leaders would suggest. Moreover, in most cases, women climbed to the top on men's terms. They got top positions primarily to implement a national policy or party agenda set by men, where there was little room for women's demands. The fact that women obtain top leadership positions does not mean that policies necessarily become more egalitarian or woman-friendly. The possibilities of pursuing woman-friendly policies have been severely limited, and the top leaders had to resist significant counter-forces to help strengthen the position of women.

The role of chance is striking when one reads the biographies of the women top leaders. This is particularly the case with the substitutes. But if these women had the benefit of chance, it is no coincidence that the number of women leaders increased in the years after World War II. The development was the result of the sustained efforts of individual women and men, a growing women's movement and the efforts of the UN and governments to implement the basic right for everyone to participate in the governance of the country and equality between women and men. Few causes promoted by the UN have generated more intense and widespread support. One can say that the women's movement has come through to a certain extent. Without women activists, there would not have been so many women top leaders. But the women's movement did not achieve these results alone. The democratisation of politics has been essential, along with a socio-economic development that has contributed to women getting better health and more education and participating in the labour market to a greater extent. Often, crises and upheavals also facilitated women's rise to the top.

There is still far to go to obtain gender parity in the leadership of nations. If the hitherto slow pace continues, it will take over 200 years to get 50/50 men and women in the world's governing bodies.

Walk the talk

Numbers are important. More women must become top leaders, cabinet ministers and MPs to promote democracy and social justice. But impact is about more than numbers. Women must be able to assert themselves, and they must be able to do it in their capacity as women and feminists.

Deep-rooted patriarchal norms and social structures that systematically lead to men being accorded and women deprived of power are persistent. And in some milieus, they are being reinforced on the basis of fundamentalist religious beliefs. But if women and men shall be equal citizens, it is essential that traditional power relations between the genders are changed. To achieve this, a broad and vibrant women's movement must exist that clarifies women's situation and views, questions the established gender system, promotes demands for change, and is heard. Moreover, men must be engaged in a positive way in order to achieve a more gender-just society. Groups of voters must exert political pressure, but governments must also take seriously that they have accepted the CEDAW and the Beijing Platform. It is not sufficient to sit in the UN General Assembly and urge all states to eliminate laws and practices that prevent or restrict women's participation in politics and take action to ensure women's equal participation in government (see Resolution 66/130 [2012] on women and political participation). Governments must go home and walk the talk, actively putting the recommendations into practice. So far, nobody has done enough. And the UN system must pay attention and follow up.

In particular, UN Women (2011) and IPU (2014a, b) request governments to introduce effective gender quotas and make electoral laws more woman-friendly. Women activists note that the UN has not organised any world women conferences since 1995 and call for such a conference or similar action.

In recent years, through its programme on Gender and Development, the UN Research Institute for Social Development (UNRISD) has been studying women's political effectiveness in working for justice in various countries (UNRISD, 2005; Goetz, 2009). The conclusions are in line with those that arise from the study of the women top leaders. To strengthen gender equality, a woman-friendly democratisation process must be pursued. In the research and efforts to develop 'democracy' and 'good governance', the role of women and gender equality must have a central place, instead of being marginalised, as is often the case now.

Institutional change

Woman-friendly democratisation is a complex process that requires institutional changes:

- To ensure that women can promote their interests on equal terms with men, focus must be put on the *political culture* and *political parties*: recruitment to the parties, internal processes, elections and decision-making, training and policy development, financing of political activities, and forms of political competition. Here, the mass media play an important role. It is essential to have an open, democratic and inclusive political life where women are welcome, as women, and activities are not spoiled by abuse of power, corruption and patron–client relationships, distortions of reality, and the utilisation of stereotypes and degrading approaches towards women.
- Parliaments and governments must become more *representative*. In many countries, the electoral system must be changed to facilitate the access of women to elected bodies. A whole election science is beginning to flourish in order to find the best technical solutions. Introduction of proportional representation instead of majority vote is a measure that may have a significant impact without costing much. In addition, to recruit women to governments, positive 'critical measures', such as special stimulus programmes and support groups for women, must often be implemented. Particularly important are quotas for the composition of governing bodies. In elections at local, regional and national levels, the quotas must be designed so that they are effective, and failure to follow up must entail sanctions.
- Should a woman-friendly democratisation succeed, 'good governance' must mean *democratic governance*, with emphasis on participation, human rights and social justice. Feudal power structures, class and caste distinctions, and ethnic differences must not prevent both women and men from participating in public decisions; the voices of weak groups from being heard so that they can make claims; private and public institutions from being responsive, open and accountable; and resources and services from being organised so that a just access is ensured. For women to participate on a par with men, the status and valuation of caring work must be increased and men must assume their share.
- Furthermore, there must be *an efficient state*. Only the state can safeguard the interests of the community, protect human rights and promote social equality. But it must be a democratic state characterised by social justice and equality that has the capacity, expertise and resources to meet women's needs, implement measures and be accountable for woman-friendly policies. Fragile, weak and conflict-ridden states may give room for a women top leader once in a while, but they generally pose a threat to dedicated work for welfare and equality. There must also be an incorrupt and independent judiciary and audit system that is characterised by and ensures justice and equality.

- It is unlikely that gender equality can become a reality in societies where primarily market-liberal thinking and pressures determine policies, and *social and economic inequalities increase*. In the short term, market forces can promote economic growth, but in the longer term, if they are not brought under societal control, they can contribute to increased insecurity and poverty, poor social cohesion, and extremist activities. To put women's rights into practice in all countries of the world, *global economic justice* is an important prerequisite. Particularly in poor countries, the strengthening of women's health, education, job situation and economy remain essential.

Unconventional and courageous activists and women top leaders have stepped into the breach and shown what can be done. More people need to follow up if female leadership is not to be an exception for a few special, but a democratic right for many. Women leaders are important, but it is also important that they are supported so that they can pursue woman-friendly policies. As the women top leaders who met at the UN on 19 September 2011 underlined: 'Women's political participation and decision-making across the world is fundamental to democracy and essential to the achievement of sustainable development and peace in all contexts – during peace through conflict and post-conflict and during political transitions' (unwomen.org).

Notes

Introduction

[1] Here 'presidents' and 'prime ministers' are heads of state and/or government in sovereign nations. The prime minister can also be a principal minister. The 'cabinet' is the body of persons appointed by the head of state or government to help manage government. The names of the elected representative national assemblies with power to legislate vary. Here the term 'parliament' will be used for the assemblies in general, in line with the Inter-Parliamentary Union. More specifically, 'parliament' will designate the assemblies in parliamentary systems, where the assemblies hold the power, while the term 'legislature' will designate those in presidential systems, where executive and legislative functions are separated. In dual or semi-presidential systems terms will be chosen according to the role of the national assembly.

Denmark, Netherlands and the UK had ruling queens after World War II. Luxembourg also had a grand duchess. Governors-general representing the British queen, head of the Commonwealth of Nations, are not included as national top leaders here.

[2] UN (1945: 1; 1948: art 21; 2001: 181).

[3] Sykes (1993: 119–24).

[4] Watson et al (2005) studied 52 top leaders, Jensen (2008) described 64, while Jalalzai and Krook (2010) first analysed 71 and then Jalalzai later increased the number to 79 (2013b).

[5] In the group of 73 women top leaders, Dilma Rousseff is included, because she was elected in 2010, although she only took up office on 1 January 2011. Cynthia A. Pratt in The Bahamas, Rosalia Arteaga in Ecuador, Carmen Pereira in Guinea Bissau, Irena Degutienė in Lithuania, Radmila Šekerinska in Macedonia, Cécilie Manorohanta in Madagascar, Nyam Osoryn Tuyaa in Mongolia, Anne Enger Lahnstein in Norway and Ivy Matsepe-Casaburri in South Africa are not included due to their short time in office. The captain regents in San Marino are excluded because two persons serve jointly as heads of both state and government. In the 53 states the German Democratic Republic (East Germany) and unified Germany are considered as one state, and Croatia and the former Yugoslavia also as one.

Chapter One: Breakthrough on several continents

[1] In 1953/54, the widow of Mongolia's revolutionary leader and national hero Damdin Sügnaatar, first Vice President S. Yanjmaa (1893–1962), acted on a temporary basis as the ceremonial president until the position was filled again. She is not included here because she was not the head of an independent state acknowledged by the United Nations (UN). Mongolia declared itself to be an independent people's republic in 1924, but the real sovereignty of the state was contested internationally and it only became a member of the UN in 1961.

[2] The section on Sirimavo Bandaranaike is particularly based on Seneviratne (1975), Morgan (1984), Gooneratne (1986), IPU (1987), Manor (1989), UN (1991, 1995, 2000), Opfell, (1993),

Current Biography (1996), De Silva (1999), Kiribamune (1999a), Abeysekera (2000), Kirinde (2000), Rettie (2000), Malhotra (2003), Werakoon (2004), Basu (2005, 2009), Liswood (2007), Attanyake (2008), Rupesinghe (2008), Christensen (2014) and Parliament of Sri Lanka (2014).

3. Gooneratne (1986: 160), Manor (1989:324-6), Kiribamune (1999b: 78), Abeysekera (2000) and Malhotra (2003: 236-7).

4. The section on Indira Gandhi is particularly based on Jacobsen, D. (1974), Jain (1975), Mankekar (1975), National Committee on the Status of Women (1975), Masani (1976), Gandhi (1980), Omtvedt (1980), Morgan (1984), Malhotra (1989, 2003), Manor (1993), Opfell (1993), Swarup et al (1994), Carras (1995), Jayakar (1995), Adams and Whitehead (1997), Marshall (1997), Hasan (1999), Frank (2002), Basu (2005), Steinberg (2008), Gupte (2009), Everett (2013) and Christensen (2014).

5. Masani (1976: 1-31), Gandhi (1980: 11-29), Malhotra (1989: 26-42), Jayakar (1995: 3-63), Frank (2002: 13-33, 46-7), Steinberg (2008: 18-19), Gupte (2009: 129-82) and Everett (2013: 147-8).

6. Masani (1976: 31-96), Gandhi (1980: 49-56, 69), Malhotra (1989: 46-71), Jayakar (1995: 135-61), Frank (2002: 200-25, 231-44), Steinberg (2008: 19-23), Gupte (2009: 182-248) and Everett (2013: 149-51).

7. Masani (1976: 97-121), Gandhi (1980: 85-90, 115), Jayakar (1995: 156-60), Adams and Whitehead (1997: 153-6), Datta-Ray (1999) and Frank (2002: 249-57).

8. Masani (1976: 122-42), Malhotra (1989: 79-89), Jayakar (1995: 170-80), Adams and Whitehead (1997: 172-8), Frank (2002: 289-93), Steinberg (2008: 21-6), Gupte (2009: 248-70) and Everett (2013: 151-3).

9. Masani (1976: 143-256), Gandhi (1980: 111-49), Malhotra (1989: 134-41; 2003: 67-75), Jayakar (1995: 183-217), Adams and Whitehead (1997: 181-205), Frank (2002: 289-347), Steinberg (2008: 26-36), Gupte (2009: 271-422) and Everett (2013: 155-9).

10. Masani (1976: 257-320, Gandhi (1980: 153-73), Malhotra (1989: 130-81, 192-200; 2003: 80-91), Jayakar (1995: 221-321), Adams and Whitehead (1997: 206-37), Frank (2002: 348-414), Steinberg (2008: 34-41), Gupte (2009: 422-42) and Everett (2013: 159-64).

11. Malhotra (1989: 201-308; 2003: 92-128), Jayakar (1995: 325-492), Adams and Whitehead (1997: 238-79), Frank (2002: 415-501), Steinberg (2008: 41-5), Gupte (2009: 45-105) and Everett (2013: 164-7).

12. According to the UN, during the period 1970-90, the number of births per woman was reduced from 5.7 to 4.3, life expectancy for women increased by 10.6 years, the gross primary school enrolment of girls nearly doubled, and the literacy rate for adult women rose from 20 to 34 per cent. Women's employment increased in absolute numbers, but the rate was reduced from 38 to 29 per cent (UN, 1991: 24, 28, 69, 106; UNICEF, 1993a: 74).

13. The section on Golda Meir is particularly based on Syrkin (1969), Meir, G. (1976), Meir, M. (1983), IPU (1987), Martin (1988), Opfell (1993), Sharfman (1994), Butt (1998), Hitzeroth (1998), UN (2000), Burkett (2008), Steinberg (2008), IPU and UN DAW (2005, 2010), Thompson (2013) and Christensen (2014)

14. Golda used Meyerson as her last name from 1917 to 1956, when she changed it to Meir because Ben-Gurion asked her to take a Hebrew name as minister of foreign affairs (Steinberg, 2008: 128). For the sake of simplicity, Meir will be used in the text as a whole.

15. Meir (1976: 1–55), Hitzeroth (1998: 11–42), Burkett (2008: 13–43), Steinberg (2008: 115–18) and Thompson (2013: 177–80).

16. Meir (1976: 56–186), Martin (1988), Hitzeroth (1998: 52–75), Burkett (2008: 45–146), Steinberg (2008: 118–25) and Thompson (2013: 180–6).

17. Meir (1976: 164–210), Hitzeroth (1998: 70–8), Burkett (2008: 125–61), Steinberg (2008: 124–7) and Thompson (2013: 185–7).

18. Meir (1976: 210–91), Hitzeroth (1998: 78–84), Burkett (2008: 163–217), Steinberg (2008: 127–32) and Thompson (2013: 187–8).

19. Meir (1976: 291–388), Hitzeroth (1998: 84–97), Burkett (2008: 217–385), Steinberg (2008: 132–44) and Thompson (2013: 188–92).

[20.] The section on Isabel Perón is particularly based on *Current Biography* (1975), Morgan (1984), IPU (1987), Opfell (1993), Selmer (2007a, 2007b), Nymark (2008), Weir (2013) and Christensen (2014.

[21.] The section on Elisabeth Domitien is based particularly on Booth (1979), World Bank (1980), Lique (1993), Chebabi and Linz (1998), UN (2000), Skard (2001, 2003), Fandos-Ruis (2005) and IPU and UN DAW (2005, 2008) in addition to an interview with Elisabeth Domitien and Marie Serra in Bangui, 8 December 1999.

[22.] Information from Marie Serra. Other sources claim that the three male leaders were also Ngbaka (Mbaka).

[23.] A contemporary sultanistic regime is defined by H.E. Chebabi and Juan J. Linz (1998: 7) as a non-democratic regime 'based on personal rulership, but loyalty to the ruler is motivated not by his embodying and articulating an ideology, nor by a unique personal mission, nor by any charismatic qualities, but by a mixture of fear and rewards to his collaborators'.

Chapter Two: Women in politics

[1.] Mathiasson (1974), Reiter (1975), Rohrlich-Leavitt (1975), Hafkin and Bay (1976), Iglitzin and Ross (1976, 1986). More references relating to different regions are found in the relevant regional chapters.

[2.] Waylen (1996), Coquery-Vidrovitch (1997), Ashcroft et al (1998) and Skard (2003).

[3.] Boulding (1976), Pietilä and Vickers (1996), Walters (2005), Pietilä (2007: 1-8), Paxton and Hughes (2007: 29-62; 2014: 31-61).

[4.] Lovenduski (2005a: 20-1), Pilcher and Whelehan (2005: 93-6) and Wharton (2005: 1–9).

[5.] UN (1975, 1995/96, 2003), Galey (1995), Pietilä and Vickers (1996), Antrobus (2004: 28-66). Fraser and Tinker (2004: 3-61) and Jain (2005).

[6.] UN (1995/1996, 2001, 2003, 2006), Winslow (1995), Jain (2005) and Squires (2007).

[7.] Nelson and Chowdhury (1994: 6-8), Derbyshire and Derbyshire (2000: 4-8), Coquery-Vidrovitch (1997) and Skard (2003).

[8.] World Bank (1978a-2012a), UNDP (1996a-2013a) and UNRISD (2005).

[9.] The analysis of Kenworthy and Malami includes the parliaments in 146 countries, while Reynolds studied both parliaments and cabinets in 180 countries.

[10.] Measured with the Gender-related Development Index (GDI) of the UN Development Programme (UNDP), or where this was lacking, the Human Development Index (HDI). HDI measures education, life expectancy and income, and the GDI adjusts the index with regard to gender differences (UNDP, 1998: 128–33).

[11.] ILO (1968) and UN (1991, 1995).

[12.] Dahl (1989), Linz and Stepan (1996) and Linz (2000).

[13.] Based on the scale constructed by Freedom House (1997). Here, the focus is especially on free and just elections according to law and practice, the degree of competition during elections, the possibilities for minority groups, and the real capacity to govern of the elected representatives.

[14.] Lister (2003).

[15.] Global surveys/overviews of women's political representation include UN (1991, 1995, 2000, 2010), UNDP (1995a-2010a), IPU (1997, 1999, 2000, 2008, 2010), Karam (1998), Matland (1998), Inglehart and Norris (2003), Ballington and Karam (2005) and Bauer and Tremblay (2011).

[16.] Antrobus (2004: 80–186), Fraser and Tinker (2004: 65–148), Ferree (2006: 93–4), McBride and Mazur (2002: 27-31) and Tremblay and Bauer (2011: 171-86).

[17.] Elson (2002), Antrobus (2004), Boltanski and Chiapello (2005), Lovenduski (2005b), UNRISD 2005, Hawkesworth (2006), Holst (2008), Fraser (2009), Goetz (2009), Walby (2009, 2011), Krook and Childs (2010), McBride and Mazur (2010: 27-34), Lethbridge (2012) and Wichterich (2014).

[18.] IPU (1997), Krook and Childs (2010), Lovenduski (2010) and Ballington (2012).

[19.] See Lovenduski (2005a), Krook (2009), Dahlerup and Friedenwall (2010) and Franceschet et al (2012)

[20.] Kenworthy and Malami (1999), Reynolds (1999), Norris (2004), Matland (2005) and IPU (2013).

[21.] This applies to all 'deviants', also people from minority ethnic groups, lower social strata and so on, but representatives from different groups can experience the problems differently, and this will also be the case with women from different backgrounds.

[22.] Jalalzai's and this book cover the same period, but the case selection is a bit different. Jalalzai's selection includes women chief executives who were only in office for a few days or weeks, whom I have excluded.

Chapter Three: Western industrial countries (I)

[1.] The chapter as a whole is based on Deckard (1975), Haavio-Mannila et al (1985), UN (1991, 1995, 2000), Kaplan (1992), UNDP (1995a-2013a), Davis (1997), Derbyshire and Derbyshire (2000), Henig and Henig (2001), Dahlrerup (2006), Jensen (2008), IPU and UN DAW (2005, 2008, 2010), IPU and UN Women (2012, 2014), Christensen (2014) and Schemmel (2014).

[2.] Due to common societal features, the following countries are considered here as Western industrial countries: Western Europe (Andorra, Austria, Belgium, Denmark, Finland, France, Germany, Greece, Iceland, Ireland, Italy, Lichtenstein, Luxembourg, Monaco, Netherlands, Norway, Portugal, San Marino, Spain, Sweden, Switzerland, UK), together with Canada, the US, Australia, New Zealand, Japan, Cyprus, Malta, Israel and Turkey (31 countries in total).

[3.] The Netherlands had Wilhelmina (1890-1948), Juliane (1948-80) and Beatrix (1980–2013). Margrethe II of Denmark has ruled from 1972–present. In addition, Luxembourg had ruling grand duchesses from 1912 to 1964. Norway and Sweden only recently changed their laws of succession so that the oldest child inherits the throne regardless of gender.

[4.] Ratification implies that the country accepts to be bound by the convention, usually by the national assembly endorsing it and adopting laws that implement it. By signing the convention, the government accepts to start the ratification process and abstain from acts that go against it. The US has stated that it is a problem for ratification that the country is a federal state.

[5.] The section on Thatcher is based particularly on Morgan (1984), Young (1989), Ogden (1990), Opfell (1993), Lovenduski (1994), Harris (1995), Paton et al (1995d), Thatcher (1995a, 1995b), Krogstad (1999a), Liswood (2007), Steinberg (2008), Campbell (2009), Dale (2010), Genovese (2013) and Moore (2013).

[6.] Steinberg (2008: 238), Campbell (2009: 500–2) and Genovese (2013a: 270).

[7.] Thatcher (1995a: 3–34), Steinberg (2008: 211–12), Campbell (2009: 1–8), Genovese (2013a: 273–6) and Moore (2013: 3–39).

[8.] Thatcher (1995a: 35–60), Steinberg (2008: 212), Campbell (2009: 8–19), Genovese (2013a: 275–7) and Moore (2013: 4–114).

[9.] Thatcher (1995a: 61–84), Campbell (2009: 19–27, 495), Genovese (2013a: 276–7) and Moore (2013: 115–40).

[10.] Thatcher (1995a: 94–101), Steinberg (2008: 213), Campbell (2009: 27–31), Genovese (2013a: 277) and Moore (2013: 115–40).

[11.] Thatcher (1995a: 165–93), Steinberg (2008: 214, 242), Campbell (2009: 54–65) and Moore (2013: 143–228).

[12.] Thatcher (1995a: 240–81), Steinberg (2008: 215), Denham and O'Hara (2008), Campbell (2009: 66–76), Genovese (2013a: 280) and Moore (2013: 229–95).

[13.] Thatcher (1995a: 435–61), Steinberg (2008: 216–18), Campbell (2009: 103–13), Genovese (2013a: 281) and Moore (2013: 296–416).

[14.] Thatcher (1995b: 17–304), Steinberg (2008: 216–25), Campbell (2009: 184–228), Genovese (2013a: 286–7) and Moore (2013: 419–758).

[15.] Thatcher (1995b: 305–588), Steinberg (2008: 225–9) and Campbell (2009: 228–336).

[16.] Thatcher (1995b: 589–862), Steinberg (2008: 229–36) and Campbell (2009: 352–475).

17. Steinberg (2008: 239–300), Campbell (2009: 491–3, 499–502) and Genovese (2013a: 290–304).

18. Young (1989: 303–12), Harris (1995: 62–3), Pilcher (1995: 493–7) and Genovese (2013a: 297–301).

19. Webster (1990: 1–2), Thatcher (1995a: 150–2), Mackay (2004), Genovese (2013a: 297–301) and Moore (2013: 184, 353).

20. The section on Barbara is based particularly on Lane (1995), Dunn (2001), Adami (2002), Notable Biographies (2006) and President of the Republic of Malta (2013).

21. From Maria Isabel Barreno et al (1975: 96), also presented in Pintasilgo (1984: 572–3) and Brill (1995: 129).

22. The section on Pintasilgo is based particularly on Morgan (1984), Pintasilgo (1984), Brill (1995), Opfell (1993), O'Shaughnessy (2004) and an interview in Paris on 28 October 1978.

23. I participated with Pintasilgo at the UNESCO General Conference in Paris in the autumn of 1978 and heard her speech. The text is from my notes.

24. Based on O'Shaughnessy (2004) and an interview with Pintasilgo in 1978.

25. The section on Finnbogadóttir is particularly based on Dahlerup (1985), Opfell (1993), Paton et al (1995b), Styrkarsdóttir (1999, 2013), Haugstad (2006), Liswood (2007), Jensen (2008) and a conversation with Vigdís Finnbogadóttir on 25 January 2012.

26. The correction is based on the conversation with Vigdís Finnbogadottír on 25 January 2012.

27. The section on Brundtland is based particularly on Morgan (1984), Dahlerup (1988), Hansson and Teigene (1992), Opfell (1993), Van der Ros (1994), Bystydzienski (1995), Skjeie (1995), Brundtland, A.O. (1996, 2003), Brundtland, G. H. (1997, 1998, 2002) and Liswood (2007) in addition to correspondence with Gro Harlem Brundtland in November 2011.

28. Opfell (1993: 101–4), Brundtland (1997: 51–124; 2002: 21–67) and Henderson (2013: 55–8). I went to the same secondary school in Oslo as Gro and Arne Olav and got to know them both.

29. Brundtland (1997: 125–49, 182–214; 2002: 67–77, 92–110) and Henderson (2013: 58–9).

Chapter Four: South Asia

1. South Asia includes nine countries: Afghanistan, Bangladesh, Bhutan, India, Iran, The Maldives, Nepal, Pakistan and Sri Lanka. Chapter Five includes the rest of Asia. The title of the chapter: 'Roaring She-Tigers' was used by Ehrum Kawja in The Herald (Karachi) in July 1999. The description of South Asia is based particularly on Jain (1975), Mankekar (1975), Morgan (1984), Jahan (1987, 2000), Richter (1990-91), UN (1991, 1995, 2000, 2010), Nelson and Chowdhury (1994), UNDP (1995a-2010a), Hodson (1997), Haq (1999, 2000), Derbyshire and Derbyshire (2000), Thompson (2002/03, 2004), Kabir (2003), Basu (2005, 2009), IPU and UN DAW (2005, 2008, 2010), Fleschenberg (2008, 2011), Iwanaga (2008), Jatrana (2008), Jensen (2008), Ayaz and Fleschenberg (2009), Bennett (2010), IPU and UN Women (2012, 2014), Christensen (2014) and Schemmel (2014).

2. The section on Bhutto is based particularly on Bhutto (1988, 2008), Mernissi (1993), Opfell (1993), Dreifus (1994), D'Amico and Beckman (1995), Chitkara (1996), Hodson (1997), Academy of Achievement (2000), Akhund (2000), Shaikh (2000), Weaver (2002), Thompson (2002/03), Malhotra (2003), Cohen (2004), Graff (2004), Padrino (2004), PILDAT (2004), Liswood (2007), Stan (2007), Bhatia (2008), Filiquarium Publishing (2008), Gall (2008), Bennett (2010) and Anderson (2013).

3. With the support of her older brother, Fatima got an education and became a dentist. She participated in the Moslem League and founded the first All-Indian Federation of Moslem Women (later, the All-Pakistani Women's Organisation). She took care of her brother when he became a widower, and participated in extensive humanitarian work. Due to her courageous leadership in a critical period, she was called 'Mother of the Nation' (Padrino, 2004: 68).

4. Bhutto (1988: 3–17), Malhotra (2003: 245–76), Bennett (2010: 62–6) and Anderson (2013: 82–4).

5. Bhutto (1988: 21–79), Shaikh (2000: 22–76), Malhotra (2003: 277–80) and Anderson (2013: 84–7).

6. Bhutto (1988: 80–214), Shaikh (2000: 77–91), Malhotra (2003: 280–83) and Anderson (2013: 88–90).

7. Bhutto (1988: 217–42, 266–302), Akhund (2000: 1–38), Shaikh (2000: 92–121), Malhotra (2003: 283–6) and Anderson (2013: 90–5).
8. Bhutto (1988: 303-16), Dreifus (1994), Padrina (2004: 85-6), Gall (2008) and Anderson (2013: 93–4, 102).
9. Shaikh (2000: 122–8), Krook (2009: 68–9), Bennett (2010: 69) and Anderson (2013: 95–9).
10. Shaikh (2000: 128–86), Bhutto (2008: 167–8, 203), Krook (2009: 69–73), Bennett (2010: 71–2, 80) and Anderson (2013: 97–101).
11. Shaikh (2000: 187–227), Bhutto (2008: 203–5), Filiquarium Publishing (2008), Bennett (2010: 71, 74), Malhotra (2003: 288–98) and Anderson (2013: 96, 102–4).
12. Malhotra (2003: 294–8) and Anderson (2013: 105–8).
13. Akhund (2000: 315–26), Shaikh (2000: 247–51), Graff (2004), PILDAT (2004) and Krook (2009: 76–80).
14. The section on Bangladesh is based particularly on Jahan (1987, 2000, 2007), IPU (1991), Hakim (1992), Opfell (1993), Chowhury (1994), Hodson (1997), Father of the Nation Bangabandu Sheikh Mujibur Rahman Memorial Trust (1999), Haq (1999, 2000), Awami League President's Press Wing (2001), Bangladesh Awami League Election Steering Committee (2001), Thompson (2002/03), Hasina (2003), Kabir (2003), Malhotra (2003), Ahmed (2005, 2008), Bangladesh Awami League (2007, 2008), Kumar (2007), Alamgir (2009), Bennett (2010), Eicher et al (2010), Reuters (2010), Majumdar (2012), Bangladesh Government (2013), Islam (2013) and UNB (2013) together with an interview with Sheikh Hasina in Dhaka on 26 April 2003 and an account by Begum Shamsun Nahar, convenor in the women's organisation Naripokkho, in Oslo on 7 May 2008.
15. Datta-Ray (1999) and also Bennett (2010: 137-63) and Bangladesh Government (2013).
16. Hakim (1992: 1-15), Opfell (1993: 189-99), Current Biography (2003), Liswood (2007) and Bennett (2010: 81-108).
17. The ranking started in 2004 and was done annually by different editors. Selection was on the the basis of influence, not fame or popularity. Forbes looked for women who led countries, large companies or influential NGOs and considered their visibility (presentations in the press) and the size of the country or organisation (see: www.forbes.com).
18. The section on Sonia Gandhi and Prathiba Patil is based particularly on Embassy of India (2007), Guha (2007), Kidwai (2010), Gayathri and PS (2013) and PS (2013).
19. The section on Kumaratunga is based particularly on Current Biography (1996), Gluckman (1996 Hodson (1997), BBC News (2005b), BBC (2007b), Attanayake (2008) and PresidentCBK (2008).
20. The JVP tried to defeat Sirimavo Bandaranaike in 1971 and was considered to be responsible for the murder of Kumaratunga's husband several years later, but Kumaratunga claimed that the group had now changed.
21. The partition of India and Pakistan in 1947, the conflict between India and Pakistan about Kashmir in 1949, 1965 and 1999 and the partition of East and West Pakistan in 1971.
22. Anura Bandaranaike was an MP from 1977 until he died in 2008. He was minister of education in the UNP cabinet in 1993/94, was speaker in the lower house in 2000/01, joined the SLFP in 2001 and was minister for tourism during 2004–07. For a short period, he was also minister of foreign affairs.
23. Quotas were also introduced in Nepal, but the introduction of quotas failed in India at the national level despite great efforts, although quotas were accepted at the local level.

Chapter Five: East Asia
1. Here, countries are included that are considered as both East and South-east Asian. Japan is considered a Western industrial country. Taiwan is not included because it is not member of the United Nations (UN) and, in addition, the country is often excluded from international statistics. The chapter thus covers 14 countries: Brunei, Cambodia, China, Indonesia, North

Korea, South Korea, Laos, Malaysia, Mongolia, Myanmar (Burma), the Philippines, Singapore, Thailand and Vietnam. The description of East Asia is particularly based on Morgan (1984), Atkinson and Errington (1990), Richter (1990/91), Nelson and Chowdhury (1994), UN (1991, 1995, 2000, 2010), UNDP (1995a-2010a), Derbyshire and Derbyshire (2000), Asian Development Bank (2002), Thompson (2002/03, 2004), IPU and UN DAW (2005, 2008, 2010), Fleschenberg (2008, 2011), Iwanaga (2008), Jensen (2008), Ayaz and Fleschenberg (2009), Bennett (2010), IPU and UN Women (2012, 2014, Christensen (2014) and Schemmel (2014).

2. See, among others, H.E. Jacobsen (1974), Tanner (1974), Bacdayan (1977), Errington (1990) and Blackburn (2004).

3. The section on Aquino is based particularly on Crisostomo (1987), IPU (1987, 2010), Komisar (1988), Richter (1990/91), Opfell (1993), Aquino (1994), Boudreau (1995), Reid and Guerrero (1995), Roces (1998a, 1998b), Thompson (1998, 2002/03, 2004), Veneracion-Rallonza (2001, 2008, 2009), Aquino, C. C. (2002), Whaley (2002), Rogers (2004), Liswood (2007), Fleschenberg (2008), Jensen (2008) and Col (2013).

4. Thompson (1998: 226–29; 2004: 18–34).

5. Crisostomo (1987: 1–135), Komisar (1988: 3-76), Opfell (1993: 127-34), Reid and Guerrero (1995: 1–33) and Col (2013: 14–25).

6. Veneracion-Rallonza (2001: 82) and Thompson (2004: 22–7).

7. Crisostomo (1987: 136-238), Komisar (1988: 77-123), Opfell (1993: 134-6) and Col (2013: 26–8).

8. Crisostomo (1987: 239-78), Komisar (1988: 124-252), Opfell (1993: 136-40, Reid and Guerrero (1995: 33–243) and Col (2013: 33–40).

9. The section on Arroyo is particularly based on Roces (1998a, 1998b), Veneracion-Rallonza (2001, 2008, 2009), Crisostomo (2002), Current Biography International Yearbook (2002), Rogers (2004), Thompson (2004, 2010), Fleschenberg (2008), Hutchcroft (2008), Jensen (2008), Mamot (2008) and Tarcyznski (2009), in addition to an interview with Gloria Macapagal-Arroyo in Manila on 7 May 2003.

10. See, among others, Bernas (2007) and Mamot (2008).

11. Observation by the Norwegian Embassy in Manila on 22 August 2013.

12. The section on Megawati is based particularly on Morgan (1984), IPU (1987, 1988), *Current Biography* (1997), McIntyre (2000, 2005), BPS et al (2001), Doorn-Harder (2002), Thompson (2002/03, 2004), Famous Moslems (2003), Fic (2003), Holden (2003), Suryakusuma (2003), Asia Finest Discussion Forum (2004), Parawansa (2005), Sitasari (2006), Anderson (2007), Jensen (2008) and Bennett (2010).

13. The revolts that were not headed by women took place in South Korea in 1987, China in 1989 and Nepal in 1990. In Myanmar (Burma), Aun Sung Suu Kyi led a democracy revolution and was elected prime minister in 1990, but was prevented from taking office. In Malaysia in 1999, Wan Azizah Wan Ismail headed the newly created Reformasi movement after her husband, who was vice prime minister, was dismissed and arrested, but did not manage to make the prime minister retire.

14. With exception of Afghanistan and Brunei, all other countries in South Asia and South-east Asia marked by Islam have had a prominent woman politician as top leader or leader of the opposition.

15. The section on Han Myung-sook is particularly based on Morgan (1984), Sohn (1994) and BBC (2002).

Chapter Six: Latin America

1. The chapter as a whole is particularly based on UN (1991, 1995, 2000, 2010), UNDP (1995a-2013a), Htun (1997, 1998a, 1998b, 2000, 2005), Derbyshire and Derbyshire (2000), Hagopian and Mainwaring (2005), IPU and UN DAW (2005, 2008, 2010), Llanos and Sample (2008), Bull (2010), IPU and UN Women (2012, 2014), Christensen (2014) and Schemmel (2014). The

chapter includes Central America with eight and South America with 12 independent states, 20 states in all. French Guyana is not included.

[2.] The section on Chamorro is particularly based on Morgan (1984), Close (1988, 1999), Bye (1990), Opfell (1993), Saint-Germain (1994, 2013), Williams (1995), Chamorro (1996), IPU (1997), Booth (1998), Tan-Wong (1998), Craske (1999), Skidmore and Smith (2005), Hoogensen and Solheim (2006), Liswood (2007), Disney (2008) and Jensen (2008).

[3.] Booth (1998), Close (1988), Skidmore and Smith (2005) and Saint-Germain (2013: 110–16).

[4.] Opfell (1993: 169-75), Williams (1995), Chamorro (1996: 9-201), Liswood (2007: 112-5) and Saint-Germain (2013: 118-21).

[5.] Morgan (1984: 485–9), Close (1988), Saint-Germain (1994) and Skidmore and Smith (2005).

[6.] Pedro left Nicaragua in 1984 to join the contras. Carlos became editor of the newspaper of the Sandinistas, *Barricada*, while Claudia became ambassador. At one time, the Chamorro family operated three daily newspapers in Nicaragua, spanning from complete support of the FSLN to uncompromising criticism.

[7.] Opfell (1993: 178-80), Chamorro (1996: 297-331), Close (1999: 37-173), Hoogensen and Solheim (2006: 109–14) and Saint-Germain (2013: 118–43).

[8.] This has become the standard name for the global democratisation revolution that started in Portugal in 1974/75, spread to Spain and Greece, and then to Latin America. But according to the literature, how many democratisation waves there actually were in Latin America is somewhat disputed. It has, among other things, been asserted that there have only been two since World War II: 1956–62 and 1978–92 (Hagopian and Mainwaring, 2005). The section on the third wave of democratisation is based particularly on Htun (1998a, 1998b, 2000), Craske (1999), Valdés and Palacios (1999), Buvinic and Roza (2004), Skidmore and Smith (2005), Araújo and García (2006), Bouvier (2009) and Mainwaring and Scully (2010b).

[9.] Hagopian and Mainwaring (2005), Skidmore and Smith (2005) and Mainwaring and Scully (2010b).

[10.] Valdés and Palacios (1999), Buvinic and Roza (2004), Araújo and Garcia (2006), Llanos and Sample (2008) and Bouvier (2009).

[11.] The section on Güeiler Tejada is particularly based on Bonner (1980), Salinas (1994), Mayorga (2005), Jensen (2008) and Davison (2011).

[12.] The section on Jagan is based particularly on Jagan (1962, 1975), Merrill (1992), Valdés and Palacios (1999), Das (2000), Jensen (2008), Miller et al (2009) and Hinds (2011).

[13.] The section on Moscoso is based particularly on Bye (1990), Gonzalez (1999), Navarro (1999), Valdés and Palacios (1999), Skidmore and Smith (2005: 367-71), Hoogensen and Solheim (2006: 116–18) and Jensen (2008).

[14.] The section on Merino is based particularly on Morgan (1984), Vargas and Villanueva (1994), Barrig (1998), Blondet (2000), BBC (2003), Fournier (2003), Reuters (2003), Tanaka (2005), Araújo and García (2006) and Jensen (2008).

[15.] The section on Bachelet is particularly based on Morgan (1984), Htun (1998b, 2000), Valenzuela (1998), Valdés and Palacios (1999), Contreras (2005), Dahlerup (2006), Hoogensen and Solheim (2006), Reel (2006), Jensen (2008), Tobar (2008), Worth (2008), Angell (2010), Franceschet and Gwyn (2010) and Barnes and Jones (2011).

[16.] The section on Fernández is particularly based on Feijoó (1994, 1998), Carrio (2005), Levitsky (2005), Araújo and García (2006), Levitsky and Murillo (2008), Nymark (2008), Weissenborn (2009), Human Rights Watch (2010), Piscopo (2010), Barnes and Jones (2011), Cicco (2011), Forero (2011) and Hyland (2011).

[17.] Faujas (2007), Padgett (2007), Selmer (2007a), Sturcke (2007), Weissenborn (2009) and Piscopo (2010: 197–219).

[18.] The section on Chinchilla is particularly based on González-Suárez (1994), Cicco (2010), International Museum of Women (2010), News Wires (2010) and Goudreau (2011).

[19.] The section on Rousseff is based particularly on Tabak (1994a, 1994b), Araújo (2003), Sacchet (2009) and Osava (2011).

[20.]The following section is based on, among others, Jaquette (2001), Fukuyama (2008), Mainwaring and Scully (2010a), Zetterberg (2009), Bouvier (2009), Costa (2010) and Roza (2010).

[21.] In Ecuador, Rosalia Arteaga acted as head of state during two days in February 1997.

Chapter Seven: The Caribbean

[1.] Here, the Caribbean includes the 13 independent island states: Antigua, Bahamas, Barbados, Dominica, Dominican Republic, Grenada, Haiti, Jamaica, Cuba, St. Kitts and Nevis, St. Lucia, St. Vincent, and Trinidad and Tobago. The chapter as a whole is based on Morgan (1984), Meditz and Hanratty (1987), UN (1991, 1995, 2000, 2006, 2010), UNDP (1995a–2013a), Htun (1997), Derbyshire and Derbyshire (2000), IPU and UN DAW (2005, 2008, 2010), Duncan and Woods (2007), Barrow-Giles (2011), IPU and UN Women (2012, 2014), Shaw (2013), Christensen (2014) and Schemmel (2014).

[2.] In addition to the 13 independent states, there are still 12 colonies, dependencies and external territories in the Caribbean under the control of different Western powers, which are not included in the present account. Several of these have had female heads of government.

[3.] The section on Charles is based particularly on Walter (1983), IPU (1987, 1997), Higbie (1993), Opfell (1993), Guy (1995), Paton et al (1995a), Stratton (1996), Valdés and Palacios (1999), CARICOM (2003, 2011), Economist (2005), Barriteau (2006a, 2006b), Cobley (2006), Mondesire (2006), Liswood (2007: 115–8), Jensen (2008), Christian (2010, 2013) and Gill (2011).

[4.] Barrow-Giles (2006: 75–7), Cuffie (2006: 137–9), Mondesire (2006: 260–3), Christian (2010, 2013) and Gill (2011).

[5.] Higbie (1993: 5, 219), Barrow-Giles (2006: 90), Miller (2006: 239-56) and Mondesire (2006: 265).

[6.] Walter (1983), *Economist* (2005), Barriteau (2006b: 183–213), Lashley (2006: 214–35) and Christian (2010, 2013).

[7.] The section on Haiti is based particularly on Haggarty (1989), Johnson (1993), Haiti Info (1995), Haiti Progres (1995), Nicholls (1998), Toussaint (2006), Pierre-Louis (2008), Bouchard (2009), Bell (2010), Girard (2010), Shaw (2013) and Vilarda (2013), in addition to an interview I had with Claudette Werleigh in Uppsala on 10 February 2006.

[8.] A simple majority election is held, and if no one gets more than 50 per cent of the total vote, the candidate with the least votes is eliminated and a second election is held. The candidate who then receives a plurality is elected (Derbyshire and Derbyshire, 2000: 92).

[9.] The section on Simpson-Miller (written both with and without a hyphen) is based particularly on Meditz and Hanratty (1987), Bellanfonte (2005), Harman (2006), Simpson-Miller (2006), People's National Party (2006), Williams (2006), Patterson (2007), Government of Jamaica (2008), Stone (2010) and Bean (2011).

[10.] The section on Persad-Bissessar is based particularly on Caribbean Media Corporation (2010), Persad-Bissessar (2010) and Drayton (2011).

[11.] The following section is based on, among others, Barrow-Giles (2005) and Valdés and Palacios (1999).

[12.] The communist regimes are discussed more closely in Chapter Nine on the Eastern Bloc.

[13.] Cuba was an exception, being approximately gender-balanced (see Chapter Nine).

Chapter Eight: Sub-Saharan Africa

[1.] The section on Perry is based particularly on Konneh (1993), Klotchkoff (1996), Brennan (1997), AFELL (1998), Africa Recovery (1998), Turshen and Twagiramariya (1998), Ellis (1999), Skard (2003), Bøås (2003, 2004), African Women and Peace Support Group (2004), UNIFEM (2006), Jensen (2008: 67–8), Sirleaf (2009) and an interview with Ruth Sando Perry in Oslo on 22 June 1999.

[2.] The Americo-Liberians created what researchers call a '*neopatrimonial* state': the state operates somewhere between the legal, bureaucratic structure, based on impersonal laws, rules and standards, and the informal reality of personalised, unaccountable power and pervasive patron–client ties. There is a formal distinction between office and person, between politics and economy, but only on paper. In practice, the spheres are closely interwoven by patron–clients exchanges and between exchanges equals. Bratton and Van de Walle (1997: 61–96), Reno (1998: 79–111), Ellis (1999), Bøås (2003, 2004), Diamond (2008) and Utas (2008, 2012).

3. Here Africa comprises the 45 states south of Sahara (not including Djibouti, Somalia and Sudan, which are grouped with the Arab states). The chapter is based on Sweetman (1984), UN (1991, 1995, 2000, 2010), Bayart (1993), Stenseth et al (1995), UNDP (1995a-2013a), Bratton and Van de Walle (1997), Coquery-Vidrovitch (1997), IPU (1997), Bayart et al (1999), Chabal and Daloz (1999), Derbyshire and Derbyshire (2000), Tripp (2001), Van de Walle (2001), Skard (2003), Bøås (2004), Simensen (2004), IPU and UN DAW (2005, 2008, 2010), Bauer and Britton (2006), Lindberg (2006), Tripp et al (2006, 2009), Posner and Young (2007), Barkan (2008), Diamond (2008), Fallon (2008), Joseph (2008), Prempeh (2008), Musembi (2009), Radelet (2010), Akech (2011), Bauer (2011), IPU and UN Women (2012, 2014), Utas (2012), Christensen (2014) and Schemmel (2014).

4. In Angola, Guinea Bissau and Mozambique. There were also liberation wars in Kenya and South Africa.

5. Sweetman (1984), Coquery-Vidrovitch (1997), Tripp (2001), Tripp et al (2009) and Bauer (2011).

6. The section on Burundi and Rwanda is particularly based on Reuters (1994), Hill (1996a, 1996b), Attar (2000), Remmert (2003), Marsaud (2004), Vesperini (2004), Hoogensen and Solheim (2006), Longman (2006, 2010), Tripp et al (2006), Devlin and Elgie (2008), Jensen (2008), Stanford (2010) and Bauer (2011), in addition to an interview with Sylvie Kinigi in Malabo on 9 December 1999.

7. Reuters (1994), Hill (1996b), Hoogensen and Solheim (2006: 50-2) and Jensen (2008: 68).

8. Remmert (2003), Vesperini (2004), Tripp et al (2006), Devlin and Elgier (2008) and Bauer (2011).

9. The section on Boye is based particularly on Morgan (1984), Amundsen (2001), Champin (2001a, 2001b), Dioh (2001), Afro1 News (2002a, 2002b), Fadjiri (2002a, 2002b), Simpson (2002), Tanama (2002), Thiam (2002), Guèye (2007), Jensen (2008) and Mbow (2008).

10. The section on São Tomé and Príncipe is particularly based on UNICEF (1995b, 2006), Afrique-express (2002), Afrique Centrale Info (2004, 2005), UNDP (2005c), Leraand (2006), CIA (2008), IRIN (2008), Jensen (2008) and Eyzaguirre (2010).

11. The section on Diogo is particularly based on Braathen and Orre (2001), Freeman (2002), Agencia de Informacao de Mocambique (2004), CIA (2005, 2009), Fleming (2005), Disney (2008), World Bank (2008b), Johnson (2010), Manning (2010) and Notable Biographies (2010).

12. The section on Ellen Sirleaf is based particularly on BBC News (2005a) Cooper (2005), Pittman (2005), Price and Tonpo (2005), Ejime (2006), Hammer (2006), Olinga (2006), Polgreen (2006), Tonpo (2006), UNIFEM (2006), Liswood (2007), Meunier (2007), Sirleaf (2007, 2009), Notable Biographies (2008), Utas (2008), J. Bauer (2009), Yedder (2009), United States Institute of Peace (2009), Adams (2010), Bauer (2011), Executive Mansion (2011) and Jalalzai (2013a).

13. An ethnic group in Liberia.

14. Utas (2008), Sirleaf (2009: 275-308), Bauer (2011), UNDP (2011a) and Jalalzai (2013a: 213-16).

15. The section on Rogombé is based particularly on Tripp et al (2006), Adams (2008) and Dougueli (2009).

16. Angola, Burundi, Eritrea, Mozambique, Namibia, South Africa and Uganda.

17. Liberia became an 'emerging democracy' in 2000.

18. Burundi (two), Gambia, Malawi, South Africa (two), Uganda and Zimbabwe.

19. Rwanda, South Africa, Seychelles, Senegal (parliament), Cape Verde (cabinet) (IPU and UN Women 2014).

Chapter Nine: Eastern Bloc

[1.] The chapter includes the Eastern Bloc countries Albania, Bulgaria, Hungary, Poland, Romania, the former Czechoslovakia, the Soviet Union and Yugoslavia and the states these have been split up into up to 2010 (Armenia, Azerbaijan, Belarus, Bosnia and Herzegovina, Croatia, the Czech Republic, Estonia, Georgia, Kazakhstan, Kyrgyzstan, Latvia, Lithuania, Macedonia, Moldova, Montenegro, Russia, Slovakia, Slovenia, Tajikistan, Turkmenistan, Ukraine, and Uzbekistan). In 2010, this included 28 countries in all. In addition are the former East Germany (GDR) and the former Yugoslavia. The chapter is based on World Bank (1978a-2012a), IPU (1987), UN (1991, 1995, 2000, 2010), Seim (1994, 1999), UNDP (1995a-2013a), Derbyshire and Derbyshire (2000), LaFont (2001), Matland and Montgomery (2003), IPU and UN DAW (2005, 2008, 2010), Jensen (2008), UNDP BRC (2010), Bunce and Wolchik (2011), Wolchik and Curry (2011), IPU and UN Women (2012, 2014), Christensen (2014) and Schemmel (2014).

[2.] The section on the Soviet Union is based particularly Duverger (1955), Rosenthal (1975), Lapidus (1976), Jancar (1978), O'Neill (1979), Morgan (1984), Moses (1986), Voronina (1994), LaFont (2001) and Rueschemeyer and Wolchik (2009).

[3.] She was arrested by the Bolsheviks as an 'Enemy of the People' and put on trial. She was sentenced, but had done extensive humanitarian work, so she was released and went into exile.

[4.] Kollontai not only talked about economy and class, but also sexuality, marriage and family. As a member of the Central Committee of the Communist Party and minister for social affairs, she promoted radical family and marriage laws, collective housing, and institutions for children. But the economic crisis prevented money being spent on public services, and she resigned in March 1918. Her ideas also aroused resistance in a traditional rural population. After she became ambassador in 1923, she remained abroad, stationed in different countries, until 1945. Thereby, she survived Stalin's terror.

[5.] The section on Yugoslavia and Croatia, Milka Planinc and Jadranka Kosor is based particularly on Springer (1986), Jancar (1978), Cordellier and Didiot (1981-92), Morgan (1984), Opfell (1993), Jensen (2008), Jurjevi (2009), Djokic (2010), European Forum (2010), Bunde and Wolchik (2011), Forest (2011) and Veselica (2014).

[6.] Until 2014, Kosovo had not become a member of the UN.

[7.] The section on shock therapy is based particularly on Bakke (2002), Matland and Montgomery (2003), Rueschemeyer and Wolchik (2009) and Forest (2011).

[8.] The section on Lithuania is based particularly on Opfell (1993), Ishiyama (2003), Krupavi ius and Matonyté (2003), Liswood (2007: 132-4), Jensen (2008), Hyndle-Hussein (2009), Forest (2011) and an interview with Kazimiera Prunskienė on 27 March 2006 in Vilnius.

[9.] The name of the Women's Party was later changed to New Democracy. This party joined the Farmer's Party, and Prunskienė was, from 2001, leader of the Farmer's and Democracy Union. This later became the Farmer's Popular Union. Prunskienė stood as a presidential candidate for this union in 2008, while somebody else was head of the party. Politically, Prunskienė was centre-left.

[10.] The section on GDR is based particularly on Rosenberg (1991), Lemke (1994) and Deutscher Bundestag (2005).

[11.] The section on Poland is based particularly on Lewis (1992), Opfell (1993), *Current Biography* (1994), Siemieńska (1994, 2003), *Who's Who in Poland* (1994), Liswood (2007, 140-2) and Jensen (2008).

[12.] The section on Latvia is based particularly on Novikova (1995), Tarm (1999), Sorensen (2002), President of Latvia (2005), Dixon (2006), Liswood (2007) and iKNOW Politics (2008).

[13.] The section on Georgia is based particularly on Jensen (2008), Kobaladze (2008), Lanskoy and Areshidze (2008) and Parliament of Georgia (2009).

[14.] The section on Ukraine is particularly based on IPU (1997), Birch (2003), Dedet (2005), Zarakhovich (2005), Schmidt (2006), Sverdljuk and Oksamytna (2006), Kis (2007), Jensen (2008), Internet Press Service of Yulia Tymoshenko (2009), Hale (2010), Stratfor (2010),

UNDP BRC (2010), UNIAN (2010), Bunce and Wolchik (2011), Limoncelli (2011) and BBC News (2013c).

[15.]The section on Moldova is based particularly on Mungiu-Pippidi and Munteanu (2009), IPU PARLINE database (2010) and Parliament of the Republic of Moldova (2010).

[16.]The section on Kyrgyzstan is particularly based on Momaya (2009b), UNCP BRC (2010), Collins (2011), Kilner (2011), Markelova (2011), Otunbayeva (2011) and Tuttle (2011).

[17.]The section on Slovakia is based particularly on Bakke (2002), Bitušíková (2005), Zvončeková (2008) and Archive of Women's Political Communication (2013).

[18.]Communist states in Asia and the Caribbean did not give women a proper place in the top political leadership either. With the exception of wives, widows and sisters-in-law (Sühbaataryn Yanjmaa in Mongolia, Song Qingling and Mao Zedong's wife, Jiang Qing, in China, and Vilma Espin Guillois de Castro in Cuba), few women got central political positions. A single woman could become member of the Politburo in the Communist Party or become vice prime minister, and a few could become members of the cabinet, but that was all. The female revolutionary leader Nguyen Thi Binh was vice president in Vietnam during 1987–2002, but in 2010, there were only 4 per cent women in the cabinet. China is described in more detail in Chapter Eleven.

[19.]The section on Russia is based particularly on Linz and Stepan (1996), Shvedova (1998), Aivazova (2002), Matland (2003) and Moser (2003).

Chapter Ten: Western industrial countries II

[1.]These women will be described in the following text with one exception: Dalia Itzik (Israel) who was head of state during a few months in 2007, is already described in Chapter One.

[2.]'Western industrial countries' encompasses Western Europe, North America and in addition some countries with similar societal features: Cyprus, Malta, Turkey, Israel, Australia, New Zealand and Japan, 31 countries in all. The chapter is based on Haavio-Mannila et al (1985), IPU (1987, 1997), UN (1991, 1995, 2000, 2010), UNDP (1995a–2013a), Bergqvist et al (1999), Derbyshire and Derbyshire (2000), Henig and Henig (2001), IPU and UN DAW (2005, 2008, 2010), Krook et al (2006), IPU and UN Women (2012, 2014), Christensen (2014) and Schemmel (2014).

[3.]The section on Ireland is particularly based on Morgan (1984), Opfell (1993), Paton et al (1995c), O'Callaghan (1996), Horgan (1997), McAleese (1997), Siggins (1997), McCarthy (1999), Liswood (2007), Jensen (2008), McGarry (2008) and Merkelson and Swift (2010).

[4.]Fianna Fáil and Fine Gael emerged as a result of the split in Irish politics during the civil war of 1922/23, after the Irish Free State was established. Fianna Fáil was traditionally the largest party, earlier to the Left, but then to the Right of centre, and they often governed together with the right-wing Progressive Democrats. Fine Gael was earlier to the Right, but then to the Left, and governed together with Labour.

[5.]O'Callaghan (1996: 259–62), Horgan (1997: 29–123, 136) and Siggins (1997: 45–117).

[6.]The voters ranked the candidates as number one, number two and so on. The votes for the third candidate were distributed according to who their voters had placed as number two.

[7.]With Fianna Fáil (for the first time) in 1993/94, and then with Fine Gael and the Democratic Left during 1994–97.

[8.]O'Callaghan (1996: 262–4), Horgan (1997: 164–99) and Siggens (1997: 145–229).

[9.]The section on Cresson is based particularly on Morgan (1984), Opfell (1993), Schemla (1993), Jenson and Sineau (1994), Dufresne (1995), Liswood (2007), Jensen (2008), and Sineau (2008).

[10.]Opfell (1993: 207-8), Schemla (1993: 49-72), Liswood (2007: 46-7) and Jensen (2008: 129, 136).

[11.]A quota for 10 per cent women was introduced in the Socialist Party in 1974 for local and regional elections and for the European Parliament, and was raised to 15 per cent in 1977 and 30 per cent in 1990.

[12.]The section on Campbell is based especially on Morgan (1984), Bashevkin (1994), Campbell (1996) and Liswood (2007).

13. The section on Çiller is based particularly on Abadan-Unat and Tokgöz (1994), Arat (1997, 1998), Reinart (1999), Cizre (2002), Gündüz (2004), Liswood (2007 [1995]), Jensen (2008) and Bennett (2010).

14. Abadan-Unat and Tokgöz (1994: 707-9), Arat (1997, 1998: 3-5), Gündüz (2004) and Bennett (2010: 110–14).

15. Cizre (2002: 199-200), Liswood (2007: 119), Jensen (2008: 105, 131) and Bennett (2010: 128–9).

16. Arat (1998: 3, 11), Reinart (1999), Cizre (2002: 202–3, 210–13), Jensen (2008: 42, 176–7) and Bennett (2010: 129–30).

17. Arat (1998: 14–18), Reinart (1999), Cizre (2002: 203–5, 213), Jensen (2008: 123, 160, 216–18) and Bennett (2010: 130–6).

18. The section on New Zealand is particularly based on Morgan (1984), Castles et al (1996), Curtin and Sawer (1996), Brokett (1997), Current Biography (2000a, 2000b), Edwards (2001), Blaiklock et al (2002), Liswood (2007), Curtin (2008, 2011), Jensen (2008), Ministry of Women's Affairs (2009) and Trimble and Treiberg (2010).

19. Current Biography (2000a: 77-81), New Zealand National Party (2001), Liswood (2007: 138–40, 189–95), Jensen (2008: 43, 137, 157, 207) and Curtin and Teghtsoonian (2010: 556–60).

20. Current Biography (2000b: 9-11), Edwards (2001: 11-260) and Jensen (2008: 87, 137).

21. Current Biography (2000b: 12-13), Edwards (2001: 261-352), Jensen (2008: 43–4) and New Zealand Labour (2009).

22. The section on Switzerland is based particularly on IPU (1987), Stämpfli (1994), Baker-Siroty (1999), Cohen (2001), Jensen (2008: 55–6) and written contributions from Ruth Dreifuss (dated 28 July 2013) and Micheline Calmy-Rey (dated 5 August 2013).

23. The section on Finland is based especially on Morgan (1984), Haavio-Mannila et al (1985), Bergqvist et al (1999), Holli (2008), Korppi-Tommola (2008) and President of the Republic of Finland (2010), in addition to written information from Anneli Jäätteenmäki (dated 22 November 2011) and Mari Kiviniemi (dated 8 December 2011).

24. Helvi Sipilä became the first woman assistant secretary general in the UN system in 1972.

25. Elected by the European Parliament to mediate between EU citizens and authorities.

26. Norwegian Embassy Helsingfors (2000a), Government of Finland (2005), Jensen (2008: 54, 156) and Lähteenmäki (2008: 180–3).

27. A popular motherly figure in a cartoon drawn by the Finnish artist and writer Tove Jansson.

28. Jensen (2008: 113, 214), Korppi-Tommola (2008: 274–9) and Von der Lippe and Väyrynen (2011).

29. The section on Merkel is particularly based on Morgan (1984), Kolinsky (1993), Lemke (1994), IPU (1997), Henig and Henig (2001), Klinkert (2005), Clemens (2006), Economist (2006), Ferree (2006), Thompson and Lennartz (2006), Mills (2008), Wiliarty (2008a, 2008b, 2010a, 2010b), Buckley and Galligan (2011) and Steckenrider (2013); see also Chapter Nine about the GDR.

30. Thompson and Lennartz (2006), Mills (2008: 56–8), Wiliarty (2008a: 89–91) and Steckenrider (2013: 238–9).

31. Thompson and Lennartz (2006: 104–5), Mills (2008: 40–61), Wiliarty (2008a: 86–9) and Steckenrider (2013: 236–8).

32. Thompson and Lennart (2006: 101), Jensen (2008: 105, 120, 123), Mills (2008: 21–39) and Steckenrider (2013: 228–31).

33. Clemens (2006), Thompson and Lennart (2006), Mills (2008: 99–103), Wiliarty (2008a, 2010a) and Steckenrider (2013: 231–45).

34. Ferree (2006), Mills (2008: 95–106), Wiliarty (2008a, 2008b, 2010a) and Steckenrider (2013: 244–5, 248–53).

35. Jensen (2008: 177, 198, 215), Mills (2008: 75-94), Wiliarty (2008b, 2010a: 137-57) and Steckenrider (2013: 245–8).

[36.] Burns (2009), Byers (2009), Prime Minister's Office Iceland (2009a, 2009b, 2009c, 2013), Current *Biography* (2010), Munday (2013) and Styrkársdóttir (2013).

[37.] The research was carried out by Dr þorgerður Einarsdóttir and Dr Gyða Margrét Pétursdóttir and presented in an article by Erla Sigurðardóttir (2010). See also Westlund (2010) and Mundy (2013).

[38.] The section on Gillard is based particularly on Morgan (1984), Curtin and Sawer (1996), Australia. gov.au (2010), Kent (2010, 2013), Sawer (1994, 2013a, 2013b) and Curtin (2011).

[39.] The following summary comprises the women described earlier, and, in addition, Dalia Itzik, who served as president of Israel for six months in 2007 (see Chapter One).

[40.] The small states of Andorra, Liechtenstein, Malta and San Marino became party to the CEDAW after 1990. The US signed the Convention in 1980, but did not ratify it.

[41.] At the beginning of the 1990s, all were high-income countries with the exception of Greece, Malta and Turkey, which were middle-income countries. In 2010, only Turkey was a middle-income country. Among Western countries, only Andorra was considered an emerging democracy by Derbyshire and Derbyshire (2000). The rest were liberal democracies.

Chapter Eleven: Regional summary

[1.] References are mainly found in the regional chapters.

[2.] The Western industrial countries included here are Andorra, Australia, Austria, Belgium, Canada, Cyprus, Denmark, Finland, France, Germany, Greece, Iceland, Ireland, Israel, Italy, Japan, Lichtenstein, Luxembourg, Malta, Monaco, Netherlands, New Zealand, Norway, Portugal, San Marino, Spain, Sweden, Switzerland, Turkey, UK, US, making a total of 31 countries.

[3.] Inglehart and Norris defined post-industrial societies as the 21 countries with the highest gross domestic product (GDP) and Human Development Index (HDI) in 1998, according to the United Nations Development Programme (UNDP). All the countries were Western industrialised countries: West European countries, the US, Canada, Japan, Australia and New Zealand. On the whole, they have topped the list for HDI over the past 30 years (UNDP, 2003a: 241–4), and also topped the list of gender-related development (GDI) (UNDP, 2003a: 326-9; 2007a; 2008a: 310-3). These countries accounted for two thirds of the Western industrialised countries as defined here. Israel was not included in the survey of Inglehart and Norris, but is considered here as post-industrial since, in 1998, the country was number 23 on the list of HDI and number 22 on the list of GDI (Inglehart and Norris, 2003: 127–46, 169).

[4.] Here, the Eastern industrial states include the Eastern Bloc countries of Albania, Bulgaria, Czechoslovakia, Hungary, Poland, Romania, the Soviet Union and the former Yugoslavia, and the states that these have been divided into up to 2010, a total of 28 countries.

[5.] The Latin American countries include Central America, with eight, and South America, with 12 independent states, in all 20 states.

[6.] Cuba introduced communism and established an unusually large parliament, with over 600 members, with significant female representation. But parliament played a relatively small role in the communist country. For more about communism in connection with the Eastern industrial countries, see Chapter Nine.

[7.] Using quotas is more complicated with majority vote than proportional representation, but they can be introduced, among other ways, in the form of reserved seats.

[8.] South Asia comprises nine countries, while East Asia comprises 14. Central Asia is included among the Eastern industrialised countries.

[9.] India only had quotas at the local level despite great efforts to also introduce them nationally.

[10.] Africa comprises the 45 states south of Sahara.

[11.] Liberia became an 'emerging democracy' in 2000.

[12.] Here the area covers 19 Arab states: Algeria, Bahrain, Djibouti, Egypt, Iraq, Jordan, Kuwait, Lebanon, Libya, Morocco, Oman, Qatar, Saudi Arabia, Somalia, Sudan, Syria, Tunisia, United Arab Emirates and Yemen. The Palestinian territories are not included. Turkey and Israel are regarded here as Western countries. The section on the Arab states is especially based on Bonnevie (1964), Morgan (1984), Saadawi (1984), Afifi and Msefer (1994), Hatem (1994), UNDP (2002b, 2003b, 2004b, 2005b, 2006b, 2009b), Sabbagh (2005), IPU and UN DAW (2005, 2008, 2010), Lazreg (2009), Pinto (2011), IPU and UN Women (2012, 2014), Paxton and Hughes (2014: 315-20) and Schemmel (2014).

[13.] The following independent Pacific states are included: Fiji, Kiribati, Marshall Islands, Micronesia, Nauru, Palau, Papua New Guinea, Samoa, Solomon Islands, Tonga, Tuvalu and Vanuatu. Australia and New Zealand are here considered as Western countries. The section is especially based on Morgan (1984), UNDP (1999b, 2010b), Asian Development Bank (2008), IPU and UN DAW (2010), FemlinkPacific (2012), IPU and UN Women (2012, 2014) and Christensen (2014).

[14.] Tonga had a hereditary paternalistic monarchy and Fiji was an emerging democracy.

[15.] The section on the US is specifically based on Dahlsgård (1975), Deckard (1975), Morgan (1984), Nelson and Carver (1994), Paxton and Hughes (2007: 257-308; 2014: 249-73), Jalalzai and Tremblay (2011) and Fox and Oxley (2013a, 2013b).

[16.] The section on China is especially based on Lu (1972), Dahlsgård (1975), Morgan (1984), Daiyun and Jin (1994) and Du (2009). The widow of the 'Father of Modern China', Sun Yat-sen, Vice President Song Qingling (1893–1981), acted on a temporary basis as co-president in the People's Republic of China during 1968–72. She is not included here because she did not fill the position alone, but together with a male vice president.

Chapter Twelve: When women made it to the top

[1.] The German Democratic Republic (GDR) and the Federal Republic of Germany are considered as one country, and Croatia and the original Yugoslavia as one. Dilma Rousseff in Brazil is included because she was elected in 2010, although she first took office on 1 January 2011.

[2.] The United Nations (UN) has for operated with a fundamental distinction between developing and industrial countries for many years, but the difference has become less pronounced over the past decades. Here, the countries are classified as it is done by the UN Statistical Office and the UN Development Programme (UNDP).

[3.] Argentine in 1974; Bolivia in 1979; the GDR, Haiti and Lithuania in 1990; Rwanda and Burundi in 1993; Liberia in 1996; and Kyrgyzstan in 2010.

[4.] Some countries are listed under both difficult transitions and then democracy, as there were women leaders in both types of situations, so the total exceeds 53.

[5.] Tripp (2008), Genovese (2013b: 336-7) and Jalalzai (2013b: 14-21).

[6.] The information is most inadequate concerning mothers in Eastern industrial countries, but there is reason to believe that all of these were economically active.

[7.] Tertiary medium education (bachelor's degree) and tertiary high (master's degree and PhD). Women are included who studied at higher educational institutions without taking the final exam.

[8.] International Standard Classification of Occupations Codes (ILO, 1968). The occupational backgrounds correspond to that of members of parliament (MPs), according to previous research (Kenworthy and Malami, 1999).

[9.] Three in Western countries, three in Eastern, one in Latin America and one in the Caribbean.

[10.] In addition to the women who succeeded deceased husbands or fathers, Kumaratunga is also included, who succeeded her mother, and Cristina Fernández, who succeeded her husband while he was still alive.

[11.] Here, the highest position is included. Among ministers are also included ambassador to UNESCO (the United Nations Organisation for Education, Science and Culture), member of the European Commission, and adviser to and chief of staff of the prime minister/president. Of those who had more than one position, first minister, then party leader, are placed ahead of MP.

[12.] Outsiders include: Vigdís Finnbogadóttir, Mary McAleese, Mary Pintasilgo and Mary Robinson in Western industrialised countries; Reneta Indzhova and Vaira Vīķe-Freiberg in Eastern industrialised countries; Mame Madior Boye and Ruth Sando Perry in Africa; and Michèle

Pierre-Louis, Ertha Pascal-Trouillot and Claudette Werleigh in the Caribbean. McAleese was formally a party candidate, but her entire career was academic. Perry had been a senator, but it counted more that she was a woman, came from a non-belligerent district, stood outside the warring parties and was active in women's peace initiatives.

[13.] Exceptions are countries with military rule or countries without political parties (12 countries in 1999; see IPU, 1997).

[14.] Reynolds (1999) and Tremblay and Bauer (2011: 184).

[15.] Chapter Two and, among others, Ballington and Karam (2005), Norris (2004) and Rule and Zimmermann (1994).

[16.] This applies to Sylvie Kinigi of Burundi in 1993/94, Chandrika Kumaratunga of Sri Lanka in 1994 and Janet Jagan of Guyana in 1997. Here, they are classified by the office they had for the longest period of time: Kinigi as prime minister and the other two as presidents.

[17.] Jalalzai's (2013b) study and this cover the same period of time, but the case selection is not quite the same.

[18.] Kumaratunga became president in a formally dual system, but it functioned almost as a presidential system in practice.

[19.] The 33 women were: Gro Harlem Brundtland, Kim Campbell, Tansu Çiller, Helen Clark, Julia Gillard, Golda Meir, Angela Merkel, Jenny Shipley, Jóhanna Sigurðardóttir and Margaret Thatcher in Western countries; Michelle Bachelet, Violeta Chamorro, Laura Chinchilla, Cristina Fernández, Janet Jagan, Mireya Moscoso, Isabel Perón and Dilma Rousseff in Latin America; Cory Aquino, Gloria Arroyo, Sirimavo Bandaranaike, Indira Gandhi, Sheikh Hasina, Chandrika Kumaratunga, Megawati and Khaleda Zia in Asia; Zinaida Greceanîi, Jadranka Kosor and Iveta Radičova in Eastern countries; Eugenia Charles, Kamla Persad-Bissessar and Portia Simpson-Miller in the Caribbean; and Ellen Sirleaf in Africa.

[20.] Assuming that power had not been acquired by means of a coup. In this case, the most recently elected male predecessors were selected.

[21.] Dilma Rousseff is included, although she first took office on 1 January 2011.

[22.] In six cases, there was no functioning parliament.

[23.] Von der Lippe and Väyrynen (2011) and Von der Lippe (2012).

[24.] Marshall and Marshall (1999), Breines et al (2000) and Goldstein (2001).

Bibliography
(in original languages)

Abadan-Unat, Nermin and Tokgöz, Oya (1994) 'Turkish women as agents of social change in a pluralist democracy', in B.J. Nelson and N. Chowdhury (eds) *Women and politics worldwide*, London/New Haven, CT: Yale University Press, pp 705–57.

Abeysekera, Manel (2000) 'Facets of leadership of an empowered woman', *The Sunday Times*, Colombo, 29 October.

Academy of Achievement (2000) 'Benazir Bhutto, interview, biography, profile', www.achievement.org

Adami, Sandro Schembri (2002) 'Agatha Barbara', www.maltatoday.com.mt

Adams, Jad and Whitehead, Philip (1997) *The dynasty, the Nehru–Gandhi story*, New York: TV Books.

Adams, Melinda (2008) 'Critical perspectives: Liberia's election of Ellen Johnson-Sirleaf and women's executive leadership in Africa', *Politics & Gender*, 4: 475–84.

Adams, Melinda (2010) 'Ma Ellen: Liberia's Iron Lady?', in R. Murray (ed) *Cracking the highest glass ceiling*, Santa Barbara, CA: Praeger, pp 159–76.

AFELL (Association of Female Lawyers of Liberia, & the Editors) (1998) 'Hundreds of victims silently grieving', in M. Turshen and C. Twagiramariya (eds) *What women do in wartime*, London/New York, NY: Zed Books, pp 129–37.

Afifi, Aicha and Msefer, Rajae (1994) 'Morocco', in B.J. Nelson and N. Chowdhury (eds) *Women and politics worldwide*, London/New Haven, CT: Yale University Press, pp 461–77.

Africa Recovery (1998) 'From Liberia to the African stage', *Africa Recovery*, August.

African Women and Peace Support Group (2004) *Liberian women peacemakers*, Asmara and Trenton, NJ: Africa World Press.

Afrique Centrale Info (2004) 'Maria das Neves n'est plus Premier ministre', 15 September.

Afrique Centrale Info (2005) 'Bons Baisers De Moscou', 8 June.

Afrique-express (2002) 'Maria das Neves de Souza', 17 October.

Afrol News (2002a) 'Senegalese govt sacked over ferry accident', 5 November, www.afrol.com

Afrol News (2002b) 'Senegalese President defends his "successes"', 19 November, www.afrol.com

Agencia de Informacao de Mocambique (2004) 'Luisa Diogo sworn into office for nine months', 15 March.

Ahmad, Reaz (2013) 'Hunger halved well before MDG time', *The Daily Star,* 14 June, 2 pages.

Ahmed, Kamal Uddin (2005) 'Women and politics in Bangladesh', www.asiaticsociety.org.bd

Ahmed, Kamal Uddin (2008) 'Women and politics', in K. Iwanaga (ed) *Women's political participation and representation in Asia,* Copenhagen: NIAS Press, pp 276–96.

Aivazova, S.G. (2002) 'Women and politics in Russia', *Research and Analytical Supplement,* 19(May): 3.

Akech, Migai (2011) 'Constraining government power in Africa', *Journal of Democracy,* 22(1): 96–106.

Akhund, Iqbal (2000) *Trial & error, the advent and eclipse of Benazir Bhutto,* Oxford: Oxford University Press.

Alamgir, Jalal (2009) 'Bangladesh's fresh start', *Journal of Democracy,* 20(3): 41–55.

Alexander, Harriet (2013) 'South Korean President Park Geun-hye', Telegraph, 4 April, www.telegraph.co.uk

AllAfrica (2010) 'Africa: governance improves in Liberia, Angola, Togo, declines in Eritrea, Madagascar', 4 October.

Amnesty International (2012) 'Reproductive rights gains for women in the Philippines', 17 December, www.amnesty.org

Amundsen, Inge (2001) 'The Limits of Clientelism: Multi-Party Politics in Sub-Saharan Africa', *Forum for Development Studies,* 28(1): 43-57.

Anderson, Benedict R.O'G. (2007) 'The idea of power in Javanese culture', in C. Holt (ed) *Culture and politics in Indonesia,* Jakarta, Kuala Lumpur: Equinox, pp 1–69.

Anderson, Nancy Fox (2013) 'Benazir Bhutto and dynastic politics: her father's daughter, her people's sister', in M.A. Genovese and J.S. Steckenrider (eds) *Women as Political leaders,* London/New York, NY: Routledge, pp 80–109.

Angell, Alan (2010) 'Democratic governance in Chile', in S. Mainwaring and T.R. Scully (eds) *Democratic governance in Latin-America,* Stanford, CA: Stanford University Press.

Antrobus, Peggy (2004) *The global women's movement,* London: Zed Books.

AP (2005) 'Former Premier who supported US invasion of Grenada dies', 7 Sept, www.usatoday.com

Aquino, Belinda A. (1994) 'Philippine feminism in historical perspective', B.J. Nelson and N. Chowdhury (eds) *Women and politics worldwide,* London/New York, NY: Yale University Press, pp 590–607.

Aquino, Belinda, A. and Corazon C. (2002) *Inspiration and images, selected speeches and paintings,* Makati City: Benigno S. Aquino Jr. Foundation.

Arat, Yeşim (1997) 'The project of modernity and women in Turkey', in S. Bozdoğan and R. Kasaba (eds) *Rethinking modernity and national identity in Turkey,* Seattle and London: University of Washington Press, pp 95–112.

Arat, Yeşim (1998) 'A woman prime minister in Turkey: did it matter?', *Women & Politics*, 19(4): 1–22.

Araújo, Clara (2003) 'Quotas for women in the Brazilian legislative system', www.idea.int

Araújo, Clara and García, Ana Isabel (2006) 'Latin America', in D. Dahlerup (ed) *Women, quotas and politics*, London/New York, NY: Routledge, pp 83–111.

Archive of Women's Political Communication (2013) 'Iveta Radicova', Iowa State University, www.womenspeecharchive.org

Ås, Berit (2008) 'Master suppression techniques'; kilden.forskningsradet.no

Ashcroft, Bill, Griffiths, Gareth and Tiffin, Helen (1998) *Keywords in post-colonial studies*, London: Routledge.

Asia Finest Discussion Forum (2004) 'Full version: what is the history of presidency in Indonesia?', www.asiafinest.com

Asian Development Bank (2002) *Sociolegal status of women in Indonesia, Malaysia, Philippines and Thailand*, Manila: ADB

Asian Development Bank (2008) *A pacific strategy for the new millennium*, Manila: ADB.org.

Associated Press (2003) 'Finland selects a woman to be prime minister', *International Herald Tribune,* 16 April.

Associated Press (2008) 'Moldova's Parliament approves new government', *International Herald Tribune,* 31 March.

Associated Press (2012) 'Portia Simpson Miller sworn in 2nd time', *The Washington Post*, 5 January.

Jane Monnig and Errington, Shelly (eds) (1990) *Power and difference: gender in island South East Asia*, Stanford, CA: Stanford University Press.

Attanayake, Anula (2008) 'Elitism in women's political participation in Sri Lanka within a South Asian context', in K. Iwanaga (ed) *Women's political participation and representation in Asia*, Copenhagen: NIAS Press, pp 253–75.

Attar, Amadou (2000) 'Agathe Uwilingiyimana', 15 August, www.afrik.com

Attard, Monica (2013) 'Julia Gillard: admired abroad vilified at home', 27 June; edition.cnn.com

Australia.gov.au (2010) 'Australian suffragettes', 5 March.

Awami League President's Press Wing (2001) 'Daughter of democracy, Sheikh Hasina', Dhaka.

Ayaz, Aazar and Fleschenberg, Andrea (2009) *The gender face of Asian politics,* Oxford: Oxford University Press.

Bacdayan, Albert S. (1977) 'Mechanistic cooperation and sexual equality among the Western Bontoc', in A. Schlegel (ed) *Sexual stratification: a cross-cultural view*, New York, NY: Columbia University Press, pp 270–91.

Bacon, Kathleen (2012) 'Five years of presidency, what should be remembered of Cristina Fernández de Kirchner?', *COHA Daily News*, 17 September, Council on Hemispheric Affairs, www.coha.org

Baker-Siroty, Lucas (1999) 'Ruth Dreifuss (1940–)', Women Leaders and Transformation in Developing Countries; http://people.brandeis.edu/~dwilliam/profiles/dreifuss.htm

Bakke, Elisabeth (ed) (2002) *Sentral-Europa and Baltikum etter 1989*, Oslo: Det norske samlaget.

Ballington, Julie and Karam, Azza (eds) (2005) *Women in parliament: beyond numbers: a revised edition*, Stockholm: International IDEA.

Ballington, Julie (2012) 'Empowering women for stronger political parties', UNDP and NDI, www.undp.org

Bangladesh Awami League (2007) 'I am a mother: Sheikh Hasina', www.albd.org

Bangladesh Awami League (2008) 'Biography of Sheikh Hasina', www.albd.org

Bangladesh Awami League Election Steering Committee (2001) 'Empowerment of women', Dhaka.

Bangladesh Government (2013) 'Sheikh Hasina'; bangladesh.gov.bd

Barkan, Joel D. (2008) 'Legislatures on the rise?', *Journal of Democracy*, 19(2): 124–37.

Barnes, Tiffany D. and Jones, Mark P. (2011) 'Latin America', in G. Bauer and M. Tremblay (eds) *Women in executive power*, London/New York, NY: Routledge, pp 105–21.

Barreno, Maria Isabel; Horta, Maria Teresa and Costa, Maria Velho da (1975) *The three Marias: new Portuguese letters*, Garden City, NY: Doubleday.

Barrig, Maruja (1998) 'Female leadership, violence, and citizenship in Peru', in J.S. Jaquette and S.L. Wolchik (eds) *Women and democracy, Latin America and Central and Eastern Europe*, London and Baltimore, MD: Johns Hopkins University Press, pp 104–24.

Barrionueva, Alexei (2007) 'Female politicians leading new wave in Latin-America', *The New York Times*, 10 November.

Barriteau, Eudine (2006a) 'Enjoying power, challenging gender', in E. Barriteau and A. Cobley (eds) *Enjoying power: Eugenia Charles and political leadership in the Commonwealth Caribbean*, Jamaica: University of the West Indies Press, pp 3–27.

Barriteau, Eudine (2006b) 'The economic philosophy of Eugenia Charles and Dominica's development, 1980–1995', in E. Barriteau and A. Cobley (eds) *Enjoying power: Eugenia Charles and political leadership in the Commonwealth Caribbean*, Jamaica: University of the West Indies Press, pp 183–213.

Barrow-Giles, Cynthia (2005) 'Political party financing and women's political participation in the Caribbean', in S. Griner and D. Zovatto (eds) *Funding of political parties and election campaigns in the Americas*, Stockholm: IDEA and OAS, pp 55–70.

Barrow-Giles, Cynthia (2006) 'Straight roads or bumpy rides? Eugenia Charles' path to the power', in E. Barriteau and A. Cobley (eds) *Enjoying power: Eugenia Charles and political leadership in the Commonwealth Caribbean*, Jamaica: University of the West Indies Press, pp 70–107.

Barrow-Giles, Cynthia (ed) (2011) *Women in Caribbean politics*, Kingston, Miami, FL: Ian Randle Publishers.

Bashevkin, Sylvia (1994) 'Building a political voice: women's participation and policy influence in Canada', in B.J. Nelson and N. Chowdhury (eds) *Women and politics worldwide*, London/New Haven, CT: Yale University Press, pp 142–60.

Basu, Amrita (2005) *Women, political parties and social movements in South Asia*, Occasional Paper 5, Geneva: UNRISD.

Basu, Amrita (2009) 'Women, political parties and social movements in South Asia', in A.M. Goetz (ed) *Governing women*, London/New York, NY: Routledge, pp 87–111.

Battersby, Matilda (2010) 'The 16 women taking over the world', *The Independent*, 24 June, www.independent.co.uk.

Bauer, Gretchen (2011) 'Sub-Saharan Africa', in G. Bauer and M. Tremblay (eds) *Women in executive power*, London/New York, NY: Routledge, pp 85–104.

Bauer, Gretchen and Britton, Hannah E. (eds) (2006) *Women in African parliaments*, London and Boulder, CO: Lynne Rienner.

Bauer, Jacqui (2009) 'Women and the 2005 election in Liberia', *Journal of Modern African Studies*, 47(2): 193–211.

Bayart, Jean-François (1993) *The state in Africa: the politics of the belly*, London: Longman.

Bayart, Jean-François; Ellis, Stephen and Hibou, Béatrice (1999) *The criminalization of the state in Africa*, Oxford/Bloomington and Indianapolis, IN: James Currey/Indiana University Press in association with the International African Institute.

BBC (2002) 'Korea's (only) woman on top', 11 July; 'S Korean Parliament bars female PM', 31 July; S Korea's Kim laments vetoed PM', 1 August, news.bbc.co.uk

BBC (2003) 'Popular Peruvian PM stands down', 15 December, newsvote.bbc.co.uk

BBC (2007a) 'Female president for India', 21 July; newsvote.bbc.co.uk

BBC (2007b) 'Women in power: Chandrika Kumaratunga'; bbc.co.uk/worldservice

BBC News (1969) 'Israel elects first female leader', 7 March, news.bbc.co.uk

BBC News (1997) 'Mary McAleese – profile', 29 Oct, news.bbc.co.uk

BBC News (1999) 'Profile of Helen Clark', 27 November; news.bbc.co.uk

BBC News (2005a) 'Profile: Liberia's "Iron Lady"', 10 November; newsvote.bbc.co.uk

BBC News (2005b) 'Profile: Chandrika Kumaratunga', 26 August, news.bbc.co.uk

BBC News (2009) 'Lithuania gets first woman leader', 18 May, news.bbc.co.uk

BBC News (2010) 'Profile: Julia Gillard', 7 September, bbc.co.uk

BBC News (2013a) 'Kevin Rudd ousts Australian Prime Minister Julia Gillard', 26 June, bbc.co.uk

BBC News (2013b) 'Profile: Julia Gillard', 27 June.

BBC News (2013c) 'Profile: Yulia Tymoshenko', 10 October; bbc.co.uk

Bean, Dalea (2011) 'Born to serve: the political life of Most Hon. Portia Simpson Miller', in C. Barrow-Giles (ed) *Women in Caribbean politics*, Kingston, Miami, FL: Ian Randle Publishers, pp 158–68.

de Beauvoir, Simone (1949) *Le deuxième sex*, Paris: Editions Gallimard and (2010) *The second sex*, New York, NY: Vintage.

Beckman, Peter R. and D'Amico, Francine (eds) (1994) *Women, gender and world politics; perspectives, policies and prospects*, London and Westport, CT: Bergin & Garvey.

Beckwitz, Karen (2005) 'A common language of gender', *Politics & Gender*, 1(1): 128–37.

Bell, Beverly (2010) 'A history of Haitian women's involvement', 10 March, www. huffingtonpost.com

Bellanfante, Dwight (2005) 'Portia Simpson Miller', *The Jamaica Observer*, 11 September.

Bennett, Clinton (2010) *Muslim women of power*, London: Continuum.

Bergqvist, Christina; Bochorst, Anette; Christensen, Ann-Dorte; Ramstedt-Silén, Viveca; Raaum, Nina C. and Styrkársdóttir, Auður (eds) (1999) *Equal democracies: gender and politics in the Nordic Countries*, Oslo: Scandinavian University Press.

Bernas, Joaquin G.S.J. (2007) *A living constitution, the troubled Arroyo presidency*, Manila: Ateneo de Manila University Press.

Bhatia, Shyam (2008) *Goodbye, Shahzadi, a political biography of Benazir Bhutto*, New Delhi: Roli Books.

Bhutto, Benazir (1988) *Daughter of the East [1989 Daughter of Destiny]: An autobiography*, London: Hamish Hamilton.

Bhutto, Benazir (2008) *Reconciliation: Islam, democracy and the West*, New York, NY: Harper Perennial.

Bindel, Julie (2010) 'Iceland bans strip clubs', *The Guardian*, 25 March.

Birch, Sarah (2003) 'Women and political representation in contemporary Ukraine', in R.E. Matland and K.A. Montgomery (eds) *Women's access to political power in post-communist Europe*, Oxford and New York, NY: Oxford University Press, pp 130–52.

Bitušíková, Alexandra (2005) '(In)Visible women in political life in Slovakia', *Czech Sociological Review*, 41(6): 1005–21.

Blackburn, Susan (2004) *Women and the state in modern Indonesia*, Cambridge: Cambridge University Press.

Blaiklock, Alison J.; Kiro, Cynthia A.; Belgrave, Michael; Low, Will; Davenport, Eileen and Hassall, Ian B. (2002) *When the invisible hand rocks the cradle: New Zealand children in a time of change,* Innocenti working paper no 93, Economic and Social Policy Series, Florence: UNICEF.

Blondet, Cecilia M. (2000) *Lessons from the participation of women in politics*, Lima: Institute of Peruvian Studies.

Bøås, Morten (2003) 'Borgerkrigen i Liberia', *Internasjonal Politikk*, 4: 425–48.

Bøås, Morten (2004) 'Vest-Afrika – regionale og nasjonale konflikter', *Internasjonal Politikk*, 4: 579–601.

Bøås, Morten (2011) 'Ellen Johnson Sirleaf', 9 December, www.dagsavisen.no

Boltanski, Luc and Chiapello, Eve (2005) *The new spirit of capitalism*, London/New York, NY: Verso.

Bonner, Ray (1980) 'President Lydia Gueiler Tejada', *Ms*, pp 83–6.

Bonnevie, Margarete (1964) *Fra likestilling til undertrykkelse*, Oslo: Dreyer.

Booth, Alice Lynn (1979) 'Women in politics and government: first woman prime minister of the Central African Republic', in L.D. O'Neill (ed) *The women's book of world records and achievements*, Garden City, NY: Anchor Books, pp 47–8.

Booth, Johns A. (1998) 'The Somoza regime in Nicaragua', in H.E. Chehabi and J.J. Linz (eds) *Sultanistic regimes*, London and Baltimore, MD: Johns Hopkins University Press, pp 132–52.

Bouchard, Jen (2009) 'Michèle Pierre-Louis', *International Affairs*, 3 November.

Boudreau, Vincent G. (1995) 'Corazon Aquino: gender, class, and the people power president', in F. D'Amico and P.R. Beckman (eds) *Women in world politics*, London and Westport, CT: Bergin & Garvey, pp 71–83.

Boulding, Elise (1976) *The underside of history, a view of women through time*, Boulder, CO: Westview Press.

Bouvier, Virginia M. (2009) 'Crossing the lines, women's social mobilization in Latin America', in A.M. Goetz (ed) *Governing women*, London/New York, NY: Routledge, pp 25–44.

BPS (Statistics Indonesia), BAPPENAS (National Planning Development Agency) and UNDP (United Nations Development Programme) (2001) 'Towards a new consensus, democracy and human development in Indonesia', *Indonesia Human Development Report 2001*, BPS, BAPPENAS and UNDP Indonesia.

Braathen, Einar and Orre, Aslak (2001) 'Can a patrimonial democracy survive? The case of Mozambique', *Forum for Development Studies*, 28(2): 199–239.

Bratton, Michael and Van de Walle, Nicolas (1997) *Democratic experiments in Africa*, Cambridge: Cambridge University Press.

Breines, Ingeborg; Connell, Robert and Eide, Ingrid (eds) (2000) *Male roles, masculinities and violence, a culture of peace perspective*, Paris: UNESCO.

Brennan, Carol (1997) 'Ruth Perry', in L.M. Mabunda (ed) *Contemporary black biography*, Detroit, MI: Gale Group, p 15.

Brill, Alida (ed) (1995) *A rising public voice: women in politics worldwide*, New York, NY: Feminist Press.

Brinkerhoff, Derick W. and Goldsmith, Arthur A. (2002) *Clientelism, patrimonialism and democratic governance: an overview and framework for assessment and programming*, Cambridge, MA: Abt Associates Inc (for the US Agency for International Development).

Brockett, Matthew (1997) 'New Zealand: NZ pioneers women in politics again, or does it?', Reuters, 12 October.

Brundtland, Arne Olav (1996) *Gift med Gro*, Oslo: Schibsted.

Brundtland, Arne Olav (2003) *Fortsatt gift med Gro*, Oslo: Gyldendal.

Brundtland, Gro Harlem (1995) 'Norway's agent of care – and change', www.imow.org

Brundtland, Gro Harlem (1997) *Mitt liv*, Oslo: Gyldendal.

Brundtland, Gro Harlem (1998) *Dramatiske år*, Oslo: Gyldendal.

Brundtland, Gro Harlem (2002) *Madame prime minister: a life in power and politics*, New York, NY: Farrar, Straus and Giroux.

Bruun, Staffan (2004) 'Hon kunde ha klarat sig', *Hufvudstadsbladet*, 29 February.

Bryant, Nick (2010) 'Kevin Rudd's rapid fall from grace', *BBC News*, 24 June.

Buckley, Fiona and Galligan, Yvonne (2011) 'Western Europe', in G. Bauer and M. Tremblay (eds) *Women in executive power*, London/New York, NY: Routledge, pp 141–5.

Bull, Benedicte (2010) *Latinamerikanske utfordringer*, Oslo: Høyskoleforlaget.

Bunce, Valerie J. and Wolchik, Sharon L. (2011) *Defeating authoritarian leaders in postcommunist countries*, New York, NY: Cambridge University Press.

Burkett, Elinor (2008) *Golda*, New York, NY: Harper Perennial.

Burns, John F. (2009) 'Iceland names new prime minister', *The New York Times*, 2 February, www.nytimes.com

Butt, Gerald (1998) 'Golda Meir', *BBC News,* 21 April, news.bbc.co.uk

Buvinic, Mayra and Roza, Vivian (2004) *Women, politics and democratic prospects in Latin America*, Washington, DC: Inter-American Development Bank.

Bye, Vegard (1990) *Forbuden fred*, Oslo: Cappelen.

Byers, David (2009) 'Jóhanna Sigurdardottir', *The Times*, 29 January, www.timesonline.co.uk

Bystydzienski, Jill M. (1995) *Women in electoral politics, lessons from Norway*, London and Westport, CT: Praeger.

Campbell, John (2009) *The Iron Lady, Margaret Thatcher, from grocer's daughter to prime minister*, London: Penguin.

Campbell, Kim (1996) *Time and chance, the political memoirs of Canada's first woman prime minister*, Toronto: Doubleday Canada.

Care (2013) 'Arab spring or Arab autumn?', 36 pages, www.care.org

CARICOM (Caribbean Community) (2003) 'Dame Mary Eugenia Charles – Citation for the Order of the Caribbean Community', CARICOM-UWI Project, www.caricom.org

CARICOM (Caribbean Community) (2011) 'Dame Mary Eugenia Charles', www.caricom.org

Carlin, John (2012) 'A Nordic revolution: the heroines of Reykjavik', *The Independent*, 21 April, www.independent.co.uk

Carras, Maria C. (1995) 'Indira Gandhi: gender and foreign policy', in F. d'Amico and P.R. Beckman (eds) *Women in world politics*, London and Westport, CT: Bergin & Garvey, pp 45–58.

Carribean Media Corporation (2010) 'Women power: Kamla creates history in TT', 25 May, www.cananews.net

Carrio, Elisa Maria (2005) 'Argentina: a new look at the challenges of women's participation in the legislature', in J. Ballington and A. Karam (eds) *Women in parliament: beyond numbers*, Stockholm: IDEA, pp 164–72.

Castles, Francis; Gerritsen, Rolf and Vowles, Jack (eds) (1996) *The great experiment, labour parties and public policy transformation in Australia and New Zealand*, St Leonards, Australia: Allen & Unwin.

Chabal, Patrick and Daloz, Jean-Pascal (1999) *Africa works – disorder as political instrument*, Oxford and Bloomington and Indianapolis, IN: The International African Institute.

Chamorro, Violeta Barrios de (1996) *Dreams of the heart*, New York, NY: Simon & Schuster.

Champin, Christophe (2001a) 'Une femme à la primature', 5 March, www.radiofrance internationale.fr

Champin, Christophe (2001b) 'Un gouvernement couleur "Sopi"', 13 May, www. radiofranceinternationale.fr

Chehabi, H.E. and Linz, Juan J. (eds) (1998) *Sultanistic regimes*, London and Baltimore, MD: Johns Hopkins University Press.

Childs, Sarah and Krook, Mona Lena (2009) 'Analysing women's substantive representation: from critical mass to critical actors', *Government and Opposition*, 44(2): 125–45.

Chitkara, M.G. (1996) *Benazir – a profile*, New Delhi: APH Publishing Corp.

Chowdhury, Najma (1994) 'Gender issues and politics in a patriarchy', in B.J. Nelson and N. Chowdhury (eds) *Women and politics worldwide*, London/New Haven, CT: Yale University Press, pp 92–113.

Christensen, Martin K.I. (2014) *Worldwide guide to women in leadership*, www. guide2womenleaders.com

Christian, Gabriel (2010) *Mamo! The life and times of Dame Eugenia Charles*, Pont Cassé: Pont Casse Press.

Christian, Gabriel (2013) 'Biography of Dame Mary Eugenia Charles, DBE', Dominica Academy of Arts and Sciences; da-academy.org/eugenia_charles.pdf

CIA (Central Intelligence Agency) (2005) 'The world factbook: Mozambique', www.cia.gov

CIA (2008) 'The world factbook: São Tomé and Príncipe', www.cia.gov

CIA (2009) 'The world factbook: Mozambique', www.cia.gov

Cicco, Gabriela de (2010) 'Costa Rica: a new president for Latin America', 25 February, awid.org

Cicco, Gabriela de (2011) 'Reflection ten years after the Argentinean economic crisis of December 2011', 16 December, awid.org

Cizre, Ümit (2002) 'Tancu Çiller: lusting for power and undermining democracy', in M. Heper and S. Sayari (eds) *Political leaders and democracy in Turkey*, Lanham, MD, Oxford, Boulder, CO, and New York, NY: Lexington Books, pp 199–216.

Clemens, Clay (2006) 'From the outside in – Angela Merkel as opposition leader, 2000–2005', *German Politics and Society*, 24(3): 41-81.

Close, David (1988) *Nicaragua: politics, economics, and society*, London: Pinter.

Close, David (1999) *Nicaragua, the Chamorro years*, London and Boulder, CO: Lynne Rienner.

CNN Staff (2013) 'Park Guen-hye becomes South Korea's first female president', 26 February, edition.cnn.com

Cobley, Alan (2006) '"We are kith and kin": Eugenia Charles, Caribbean integration and the Grenada invasion', in E. Barriteau and A. Cobley (eds) *Enjoying power: Eugenia Charles and political leadership in the Commonwealth Caribbean*, Jamaica: University of the West Indies Press, pp 108–30.

Cohen, Michael (2001) 'Ruth Dreifuss (1940–)', Women Leaders and Transformation in Developing Countries; http://people.brandeis.edu/~dwilliam/profiles/dreifuss.htm

Cohen, Stephen Philip (2004) *The idea of Pakistan*, Washington, DC: Brookings Institution Press.

Col, Jeanne-Marie (2013) 'Managing softly in turbulent times: Corazon C. Aquino, President of the Philippines', in M.A. Genovese and J.S. Steckenrider (eds) *Women as political leaders*, London/New York, NY: Routledge, pp 14–42.

Collins, Kathleen (2011) 'Kyrgyzstan's latest revolution', *Journal of Democracy*, 22(3): 150–64.

Connell, Robert (1987) *Gender & power*, Stanford, CA: Stanford University Press.

Contreras, Joseph (2005) 'Latina lift off', *Newsweek*, 22 August, pp 44–7.

Cooper, Helene (2005) 'An act of kindness 20 years ago, resonating today', *New York Times*, 18 December.

Coquery-Vidrovitch, Catherine (1997) *African women, a modern history*, Oxford and Boulder, CO: Westview.

Cordellier, Serge and Didiot, Béatrice (eds) (1981–92) 'L'état des Balkans: Ex-Yougoslavie', *L'état du monde*, Paris: Découverte.

Costa, Ana Alice Alcântara (2010) 'Quotas: a pathway of political empowerment?', *IDS Bulletin*, 41(2): 18–27.

Craske, Nikki (1999) *Women & politics in Latin America*, New Brunswick, NJ: Rutgers University Press.

Crisostomo, Isobelo T. (1987) *Cory, profile of a president*, Boston, MA: Branden.

Crisostomo, Isobelo T. (2002) *The power and the glory: Gloria Macapagal Arroyo and her presidency*, Quezon City, Metro Manila: J. Kriz Publishing Enterprises.

Cuffie, Joan (2006) 'Eugenia Charles and the psychology of leadership', in E. Barriteau and A. Cobley (eds) *Enjoying power: Eugenia Charles and political leadership in the Commonwealth Caribbean*, Jamaica: University of the West Indies Press, pp 133–48.

Currell, Melville (1974) *Political woman*, London and New Jersey, NJ: Croom Helm and Rowman & Littlefield.

Current Biography International Yearbook (1975) 'Isabel Perón', January, New York, NY: H.W. Wilson, pp 31-3.

Current Biography International Yearbook (1979) 'Golda Meir', February, New York, NY: H.W. Wilson, p 47.

Current Biography International Yearbook (1994) 'Hanna Suchocka', January, New York, NY: H.W. Wilson, pp 50-3.

Current Biography International Yearbook (1996) 'Chandrika Bandaranaike Kumaratunga', January, New York, NY: H. W. Wilson, pp 24-8.

Current Biography International Yearbook (1997) ' Megawati Sukarnoputri', September, New York, NY: H. W. Wilson, pp 43-4.

Current Biography International Yearbook (2000a) 'Jenny Shipley', March, New York, NY: H. W. Wilson, pp 77-81.

Current Biography International Yearbook (2000b) 'Helen Clark', Nov, New York, NY: H. W. Wilson, pp 9–13.

Current Biography International Yearbook (2010) 'Jóhanna Sigurdardottir', July, New York, NY: H. W. Wilson, pp 77–83.

Current Biography International Yearbook (2002) 'Gloria Macapagal Arroyo', New York, NY: H. W. Wilson, pp 28-31.

Current Biography International Yearbook (2003) 'Khaleda Zia', New York, NY: H. W. Wilson, pp 597-9.

Curtin, Jennifer (2008) 'Women, political leadership and substantive representation: the case of New Zealand', *Parliamentary Affairs*, 61(3): 490–504.

Curtin, Jennifer (2011) 'Oceania', in G. Bauer and M. Tremblay (eds) *Women in executive power*, London/New York, NY: Routledge, pp 45–64.

Curtin, Jennifer (2012) 'New Zealand', in M. Tremblay (ed) *Women and legislative representation: electoral systems, political parties, and sex quotas*, New York, NY: Palgrave Macmillan, pp 197–209.

Curtin, Jennifer and Sawer, Marian (1996) 'Gender equity in the shrinking state: women and the great experiment', in F. Castles, R. Gerritsen and J. Vowles (eds) *The great experiment*, St Leonards: Allen & Unwin, pp 149–69.

Curtin, Jennifer and Teghtsoonian, Katherine (2010) 'Analyzing institutional persistence: the case of the Ministry of Women's Affairs in Aotearoa/New Zealand', *Politics & Gender*, 6: 545–72.

Dahl, Robert A. (1989) *Democracy and its critics*, New Haven, CT, and London: Yale University Press.

Dahlerup, Drude (1985) 'Den første kvinedelige præsident', in D. Dahlerup (ed) *Blomster & Spark, Samtaler med kvindelige politikere i Norden*, Stockholm: Nordic Council of Ministers, pp 336–43.

Dahlerup, Drude (1988) 'From a small to a large minority: women in Scandinavian politics', *Scandinavian Political Studies*, 11(4): 275–98.

Dahlerup, Drude (2003) 'Quotas are changing the history of women', www.quotaproject.org

Dahlerup, Drude (ed) (2006) *Women, quotas and politics*, London/New York, NY: Routledge.

Dahlerup, Drude (2009) *About quotas,* International IDEA and Stockholm University, www.quotaproject.org

Dahlerup, Drude and Friedenvall, Lenita (2010) 'Quotas as a "fast track" to equal representation for women', in M.L. Krook and S. Childs (eds) *Women, gender, and politics*, New York, NY: Oxford University Press, pp 175–84.

Dahlerup, Drude and Leyenaar, Monique (ed) (2013) *Breaking male dominance in old democracies*, Oxford, UK: Oxford University Press.

Dahlsgård, Inga (ed) (1975) *Kvindebevægelsens hvem-hvad-hvor*, Copenhagen: Politikens forlag.

Daiyun, Y. and Jin, L. (1994) 'China', in B.J. Nelson and N. Chowdhury (eds) *Women and politics worldwide*, London/New Haven, CT: Yale University Press, pp 161–73.

Dale, Iain (2010) *Margaret Thatcher in her own words*, London: Biteback.

D'Amico, Francine (1995) 'Women national leaders' in F. D'Amico and P. R. Beckman (eds) *Women in world politics,* London and Westport, CT: Bergin & Garvey: 15-30.

D'Amico, Francine and Beckman, Peter R. (eds) (1995) *Women in world politics*, London and Westport, CT: Bergin & Garvey.

Das, Maitreyi (2000) 'Women's autonomy and politics of gender in Guyana', *Economic and Political Weekly*, 35(23): 1944–8.

Datta-Ray, Sunanda K. (1999) 'For some in Asia, it is hard to stand by their woman', *International Herald Tribune*, 3 August.

Davis, Rebecca Howard (1997) *Women and power in parliamentary democracies, cabinet appointments in Western Europe, 1968–1992*, London and Lincoln, NE: University of Nebraska Press.

Davison, Phil (2011) 'Lidia Gueiler Tejada', 12 May, www.independent.co.uk

Deckard, Barbara (1975) *The women's movement*, London/New York, NY: Harper & Row.

Dedet, Joséphine (2005) 'Joulia Timochenko', *J.A./L'Intelligent*, 2300, 6–12 February.

Denham, Andrew and O'Hara, Kieron (2008) *Democratising Conservative leadership selection, from grey suits to grassroots*, Manchester: Manchester University Press.

Derbyshire, J.Dennis and Derbyshire, Ian (2000) *World political systems*, New York: Sharpe.

De Silva, Chandra (1999) 'A historical overview of women in Sri Lankan politics', in S. Kiribamune (ed) *Women and politics in Sri Lanka, a comparative perspective*, Kandy, Sri Lanka: International Centre for Ethnic Studies, pp 19–69.

Deutscher Bundestag (2005) 'Dr. Sabine Bergmann-Pohl', www.bundestag.de

Devlin, Claire and Elgie, Robert (2008) 'The effect of the increased women's representation in parliament: the case of Rwanda', *Parliamentary Affairs*, 61(2): 237–54.

Diamond, Larry (2008) 'The rule of law versus the big man', *Journal of Democracy*, 19(2): 138–49.

Dioh, Tidiane (2001) 'Les vraies raisons d'un divorce', *Jeune Afrique/L'Intelligent*, 13–19 March.

Dixon, Nadine Vitols (2006) *Vaira Vīķe-Freiberga, President of Latvia*, Riga: Publishing House Pētergailis.

Djokic, Dejan (2010) 'Milka Planinc obituary', *The Guardian*, 10 October.

Doorn-Harder, Nelly Van (2002) 'The Indonesian Islamic debate on a woman president', *Sojourn*, 17(2): 164–90.

Dougueli, Georges (2009) 'Les dames de la transition', *Jeune Afrique,* 26 July–1 August.

Drayton, Josh with Barrow-Giles, Cynthia (2011) 'The Indo-Trinidadian woman in politics: Kamla 'Kamla' Persad-Bissessar', in C. Barrow-Giles (ed) *Women in Caribbean politics*, Kingston, Miami, FL: Ian Randle Publishers, pp 183–94.

Dreifus, Claudia (1994) 'Real-life dynasty: Benazir Bhutto', *The New York Times*, 15 May.

Du, Jie (2009) 'Public administration reform and women in decision making in China', in A.M. Goetz (ed) *Governing women*, London/New York, NY: Routledge, pp 257–73.

Duerst-Lahti, G. and Kelly, R.M. (eds) (1995) *Gender, power, leadership, and governance*, Ann Arbor, MI: University of Michigan Press.

Dufresne, Danielle (1995) 'Edith Cresson: La femme piégée', *Resources for Feminist Research*, 23(4): 70–1.

Duncan, Natasha T. and Woods, Dwayne (2007) 'What about us? The Anglo-Caribbean democratic experience', *Commonwealth & Comparative Politics*, 45(2): 202–18.

Dunn, Miriam (2001) 'Agatha, the true socialist', www.maltatoday.com.mt

Duverger, Maurice (1955) *The political role of women*, Paris: UNESCO.

Dzodan, Flavia (2011) 'A disobedient woman: Cristina Fernández re-elected President of Argentina', 25 October; globalcomment.com

Eagly, Alice H. and Carli, Linda L. (2007) *Through the labyrinth – the truth about how women become leaders*, Boston, MA: Harvard Business School Press.

Eagly, Alice H., Beall, Anne E. and Sternberg, Robert J. (eds) (2004) *The psychology of gender*, London/New York, NY: Guilford Press.

Economist (2005) 'Eugenia Charles', 17 September, p 94.

Economist (2006) 'Angela Merkel charms the world', 11 February, p 10.

Edwards, Brian (2001) *Helen, portrait of a prime minister*, Auckland: Exisle.

Eicher, Peter; Alam, Zahurul and Eckstein, Jeremy (2010) *Elections in Bangladesh 2006-2009: transforming failure into success*, Bangladesh: UNDP.

Ejime, Paul (2006) 'Liberia: all eyes on Ellen Johnson-Sirleaf', *PANA*, 15 January.

Ellis, Stephen (1999) *The mask of anarchy*, New York, NY: New York University Press.

Elson, Diane (2002) 'Gender justice, human rights and neo-liberal economic policies', in M. Molyneux and S. Razavi (eds) *Gender justice, development, and rights*, Oxford and New York: Oxford University Press, pp 78–114.

Embassy of India (2007) 'Prathiba Pratil is India's first woman president', *India Review*, August, p 2, indiaembassy.org

Errington, Shelly (1990) 'Recasting sex, gender, and power, theoretical and regional overview', in J.M. Atkinson and S. Errington (eds) *Power and difference, gender in island Southeast Asia*, Stanford, CA: Stanford University Press, pp 1–58.

European Forum (2010) 'Croatia', www.europeanforum.net

Evans, Judith (1995) *Feminist theory today*, London, New Delhi and Thousand Oaks, CA: Sage.

Everett, Jana (2013) 'Indira Gandhi and the exercise of power', in M.A. Genovese and J.S. Steckenrider (eds) *Women as political leaders*, London/New York, NY: Routledge, pp 144–75.

Executive Mansion (2011) 'Biographical Brief of Ellen Johnson Sirleaf', www.emansion.gov.lr

Eyzagirre, Pablo B. (2010) 'São Tomé E Príncipe', www.everyculture.com (accessed November 2010).

Fadjri, Wal (2002a) 'Mme le Premier ministre, "l'homme" de la providence!', 15 February; allAfrica.com

Fadjri, Wal (2002b) 'Politiques de population', 9 March; allAfrica.com

Fallon, Kathleen M. (2008) *Democracy and the rise of women's movements in sub-Saharan Africa*, Baltimore, MD: Johns Hopkins University Press.

Famous Muslims (2003) 'Ahmed Sukarno, Megawati Sukarnoputri', www.famousmuslims.com

Fandos-Ruis, Juan (2005) 'Elisabeth Domitien, première Premier Ministre Africain', 15 May, 2 pages, www.ideesplus.com

Father of the Nation Bangabandhu Sheikh Mujibur Rahman Memorial Trust (1999) 'Poet of politics, Father of the Nation Bangdabandu Sheikh Mujibur Rahman', Dhaka.

Faujas, Alain (2007) 'Le choix de Cristina', *Jeune Afrique*, 4-10 Nov.

Feijoó, María del Carmen (1994) 'From family ties to political action: women's experiences in Argentina', in B.J. Nelson and N. Chowdhury (eds) *Women and politics worldwide*, London/New Haven, CT: Yale University Press, pp 59–72.

Feijoó, María del Carmen (1998) 'Democratic participation and women in Argentina', in J.S. Jaquette and S.L. Wolchik (eds) *Women and democracy, Latin America and Central and Eastern Europe*, London and Baltimore, MD: Johns Hopkins University Press, pp 29–46.

FemLINKPACIFIC (2012) 'Here are the women', 69 pages, www.femlinkpacific.org.fj

Ferree, Myra Marx (2006) 'Angela Merkel – what does it mean to run as a woman?', *German Politics and Society*, 78, 24(1): 93–107.

Ferree, Myra Marx and Tripp, Aili Mari (eds) (2006) *Global feminism*, London/New York, NY: New York University Press.

Fic, Victor M. (2003) *From Majapahit and Sukuh to Megawati Sukarnoputri*, New Delhi: abhinav Publications.

Filiquarium Publishing (2008) 'Benzir Bhutto, female Muslim leader', www.biographiq.com

Fleming, Lucy (2005) 'Blazing a trail for Africa's women', BBC News, 11 November.

Fleschenberg, Andrea (2008) 'Asia's women politicians at the top: roaring tigresses or tame kittens?', in K. Iwanaga (ed) *Women's political participation and representation in Asia*, Copenhagen: NIAS Press, pp 23–54.

Fleschenberg, Andrea (2011) 'South and Southeast Asia', in G. Bauer and M. Tremblay (eds) *Women in executive power*, London/New York, NY: Routledge, pp 23–44.

Forbes (2004-2013) *The world's 100 most powerful women*, www.forbes.com

Forero, Juan (2011) 'Argentine President Cristina Fernandez de Kirchner is reelected', *The Washington Post*, 24 October.

Forest, Maxime (2011) 'Central and Eastern Europe', in G. Bauer and M. Tremblay (eds) *Women in executive power*, London/New York, NY: Routledge, pp 65–84.

Fournier, Vincent (2003) 'Toledo sauvé par une femme?', *Jeune Afrique/L'Intelligent*, 13–19 July.

Fox, Richard L. and Oxley, Zoe M. (2013b) 'Why no Madame President? Gender and presidential politics in the United States', in M. Genovese and J.S. Steckenrider (eds) *Women as political leaders*, London/New York, NY: Routledge, pp 306–35.

Franceschet, Susan and Gwynn, Thomas (2010) 'Renegotiating political leadership: Michelle Bachelet's rise to the Chilean presidency', in R. Murray (ed) *Cracking the highest glass ceiling*, Santa Barbara, CA: Praeger, pp 175–95.

Franceschet, Susan; Krook, Mona Lena and Piscopo, Jennifer M. (eds) (2012) *The impact of gender quotas,* New York, NY: Oxford University Press.

Frank, Katherine (2002) *Indira*, Boston, MA, and New York, NY: Houghton Mifflin.

Fraser, Antonia (2004) *The warrior queens*, New York, NY: Anchor Books.

Fraser, Arvonne S. and Tinker, Irene (eds) (2004) *Developing power, how women transformed international development*, New York, NY: Feminist Press.

Fraser, Nancy (2009) 'Feminism, capitalism and the cunning of history', *New Left Review*, 56 (March–April): 97–117.

Fraser, Nicholas and Navarro, Marysa (1996) *Evita: the real life of Eva Perón,* New York, NY: Norton.

Freedom House (1997) *Freedom in the world 1996-1997,* New York, NY, and Washington DC: Freedom House.

Freeman, Sharon T. (2002) 'Luisa Diogo' in *Conversations with powerful African women leaders, inspiration, motivation, and strategy*, Washington, DC: All American Small Business Exporters Ass. (AASBEA), pp 179-93.

Friedan, Betty (1963) *The feminine mystique*, New York, NY: Norton.

Fukuyama, Francis (2008) 'The Latin American experience', *Journal of Democracy*, 19(4): 8.

Galey, Margaret E. (1995) 'Women find a place', in A. Winslow (ed) *Women, politics, and the United Nations*, London and Westport, CT: Greenwood Press, pp 11–27.

Gall, Carlotta (2008) 'Bhutto spouse, divisive figure, asserts himself', *New York Times*, 1 January.

Gandhi, Indira (1980) *My truth*, New Delhi: Vision Books.

Gayathri and PS (2013) 'Prathiba Patil', 5 pages, nilacharal.com

Genovese, Michael A. (ed) (1993) *Women as national leaders*, Newbury Park, CA, and London: Sage.

Genovese, Michael A. (2013a) 'Margaret Thatcher and the politics of conviction leadership', in M.A. Genovese and J.S. Steckenrider (eds) *Women as political leaders*, London/New York, NY: Routledge, pp 270–305.

Genovese, Michael A. (2013b) 'Women as political leaders: what do we know?' in Michael A. Genovese and Steckenrider, Janie S. (eds) *Women as political leaders*, London/New York, NY: Routledge: 336–44.

Genovese, Michael A. and Steckenrider, Janie S. (eds) (2013) *Women as political leaders*, London/New York, NY: Routledge.

Gill, Markson (2011) 'Eugenia Charles: a biographic overview of her public life', in C. Barrow-Giles (ed) *Women in Caribbean politics*, Kingston, Miami, FL: Ian Randle Publishers, pp 147–57.

Gills, Barry K., Rocamora, Joel and Wilson, Richard (eds) (1993) *Low intensity democracy*, London: Pluto Press.

Girard, Philippe (2010) *Haiti*, New York, NY: Palgrave Macmillan

Gluckman, Ron (1996) 'Life under siege', *Asiaweek*, August, www.gluckman.com

Goetz, Anne Marie (2009) (ed) *Governing women*, London/New York, NY: Routledge.

Goetz, Anne Marie (2008) *Progress of the world's women 2008/2009: Who answers to women? Gender & accountability*, New York, NY: UNIFEM.

Goldstein, Joshua S. (2001) *War and gender*, Cambridge: Cambridge University Press.

Gonzales, David (1999) 'In Panama's new dawn, woman takes over', *New York Times*, 9 February.

González-Suárez, Mirta (1994) 'With patience and without blood: the political struggles of Costa Rican women', in B.J. Nelson and N. Chowdhury (eds) *Women and politics worldwide*, London/New Haven, CT: Yale University Press, pp 174–88.

Good News (2010) 'Mari Kiviniemi – Finland's new prime minister', 15 June, www.goodnewsfinland.com

Gooneratne, Yasmine (1986) *Relative merits, a personal memoir of the Bandaranaike family*, New York, NY: St. Martin's Press.

Goudreau, Jenna (2011) 'Costa Rica's first woman president fights invasions, drug cartels', 6 October, www.offnews.info

Government of Finland (2005) 'Personal details: Tarja Karina Halonen; Anneli Tuulikki Jäätteenmäki', www.government.fi

Government of Finland (2011) 'Personal details: Mari Kiviniemi', www.government.fi

Government of Jamaica (2008) 'The Most Hon. Portia Simpson Miller', www.opm.gov.jm

Graff, Irene (2004) 'Quota systems in Pakistan under the Musharraf regime', *NIAS News, Asia Insights*, 1, March.

Guèye, Cécile Sow (2007) 'Mame Madior Boye', *Jeune Afrique*, 12–15 August.

Guha, Seema (2007) 'Kvinnene som endrer India', *Ny Tid*, 6 July.

Gündüz, Zuhal Yeşilyurt (2004) 'The women's movement in Turkey', *Perceptions*, Autumn: 115–34, Center for Strategic Research, www.sam.gov.tr

Gupte, Pranay (2009) *Mother India, a political biography of Indira Gandhi*, New Delhi: Penguin.

Guy, Levis (1995) 'Dame Eugenia Charles, Dominica', in A. Brill (ed) *A rising public voice: women in politics worldwide*, New York, NY: Feminist Press, pp 136–40.

Haavio-Mannila, Elina; Dahlerup, Drude; Eduards, Maud; Gudmundsdóttir, Esther; Halsaa, Beatrice; Hernes, Helga Maria; Hänninnen-Salmelin, Eva; Sigmundsdóttir, Bergthora; Sinkkonen, Sirkka and Skard, Torild (1985) *Unfinished democracy: women in Nordic politics*, Oxford and New York, NY: Pergamon Press.

Hafkin, Nancy. J and Edna G. Bay (eds) (1976) *Women in Africa, studies in social and economic change*, Stanford, CA: Stanford University Press.

Haggarty, Richard A. (ed) (1989) *Haiti: a country study*, Washington: US Library of Congress, www.countrystudies.us/haiti/

Hagopian, Frances and Mainwaring, Scott P. (eds) (2005) *The third wave of democratization in Latin America, advances and setbacks*, New York, NY: Cambridge University Press.

Haiti Info (1995) 'Werleigh sworn in for "100 days"', *Haitian Information Bureau*, 4(2), 12 November.

Haiti Progres (1995) 'From Smarck Michel to Claudette Werleigh', *This Week in Haiti*, 13(32), 1–7 November.

Hakim, S. Abdul (1992) *Begum Khaleda Zia, a political biography*, New Delhi: Vikas Publishing House.

Hale, Henry E. (2010) 'Ukraine: the uses of divided power', *Journal of Democracy*, 21(3): 84–98.

Hämäläinen, Unto (2003) 'Kommer Anneli Jäätteenmäki til å skape historie?', 11 April, www.finland.no

Hammer, Joshua (2006) 'Healing powers', *Newsweek*, 3 April.

Hansson, Steinar and Teigene, Ingolf Håkon (1992) *Makt and mannefall, historien om Gro Harlem Brundtland*, Oslo: Cappelen.

Haq, Khadija (1999) *Human development in South Asia 1999: the crisis of governance*, Mahbub ul Haq Human Development Centre, Oxford, Oxford University Press.

Haq, Khadija (2000) *Human development in South Asia 2000: the gender question*, Mahbub ul Haq Development Centre, Oxford: Oxford University Press.

Harding, Sarah (ed) (1987) *Feminism and methodology*, Milton Keynes: Open University Press.

Harman, Danna (2006) '"It's woman time now" in Jamaica', *USA Today*, 19 March.

Harris, Kenneth (1995) 'Prime Minister Margaret Thatcher: the influence of her gender on her foreign policy', in F. d'Amico and P.R. Beckman (eds) *Women in world politics*, London and Westport, CT: Bergin & Garvey, pp 59–69.

Hasan, Zoya (1999) 'Power and powerlessness: women in Indian and South Asia politics', in S. Kiribamune (ed) *Women and politics in Sri Lanka: a comparative perspective*, Kandy, Sri Lanka: International Centre for Ethnic Studies, pp 181–202.

Hasina, Sheikh (2003) *Democracy in distress*, Dhaka: Agamee Prakashani.

Hatem, Mervat F. (1994) 'Egypt', in B.J. Nelson and N. Chowdhury (eds) *Women and politics worldwide*, London/New Haven, CT: Yale University Press, pp 226–42.

Haugstad, Tormod (2006) 'Førstekvinnen', *Dagbladet*, 29 April.

Hausmann, Ricardo; Tyson, Laura D.; Bekhouche, Yasmina and Zahidi, Saadia (2012) *The global gender gap report 2012,* Geneva: World Economic Forum, www.weforum.org

Hawkesworth, Mary E. (2006) *Globalization & feminist activism*, Lanham, MD: Rowman & Littlefield.

Hawley, Charles (2005) 'Angela Merkel realizes she's a woman', *Spiegel online*, 9 July, www.spiegel.de/international

Henderson, Sarah (2013) 'Gro Harlem Brundtland of Norway', in M.A. Genovese and J. Steckenrider (eds) *Women as political leaders*, London/New York, NY: Routledge, pp 43–79.

Henig, Ruth and Henig, Simon (2001) *Women and political power, Europe since 1945*, London/New York, NY: Routledge.

Hernes, Helga Maria (1987) *Welfare state and woman power, essays in state feminism*, Oslo: Norwegian University Press.

Higbie, Janet (1993) *Eugenia: the Caribbean's Iron Lady*, New York, NY: Macmillan Caribbe.

Hill, Kevin A. (1996a) 'Agathe Uwilingiyimana', in R.M. Salokar and M.L. Volcansek (eds) *Women in law*, Westport, CT: Greenwood Press, pp 323–8

Hill, Kevin A. 1996b) 'Sylvie Kanigi', in R.M. Salokar and M.L. Volcansek (eds) *Women in law*, Westport, CT: Greenwood Press, pp 118–22.

Hinds, David (2011) 'Janet Jagan and the politics of ethnicity in Guyana', in C. Barrow-Giles (ed) *Women in Caribbean politics*, Kingston, Miami, FL: Ian Randle Publishers, pp 195–208.

Hitzeroth, Deborah (1998) *Golda Meir*, San Diego, CA: Lucent Books.

Hodson, Piper A. (1997) 'Routes to power: an examination of political change, rulership and women's access to executive office', in M.A. Borelli and J.M. Martin (eds) *The other elites*, London and Boulder, CO: Lynne Rienner, pp 33–45.

Holden, Philip (2003) 'Imaged individuals: national autobiography and postcolonial self-fashioning', Asia Research Institute Working Paper Series 13, National University of Singapore.

Holli, Anne Maria (2008) 'Electoral reform opens to presidency for Finnish women', *Politics & Gender*, 4: 496–509.

Holst, Cathrine (2008) *Feminism, epistemology & morality*, Saabrücken: VDM Publishing.

Hoogensen, Gunhild and Solheim, Bruce O. (2006) *Women in power, world leaders since 1960*, London and Westport, CT: Praeger.

Horgan, Johns (1997) *Mary Robinson*, Niwor, CO: Roberts Rinehart.

Htun, Mala N. (1997) *Moving into power: expanding women's opportunities for leadership in Latin America and the Caribbean,* Washington DC: Inter-American Development Bank, 33 pages.

Htun, Mala N. (1998a) *Women rights and opportunities in Latin America: problems and prospects,* Harvard University: Center for International Affairs, 22 pages, www.idialog.org

Htun, Mala N. (1998b) *Women's political participation, representation and leadership in Latin America,* Harvard University: Weatherhead Center for International Affairs, 22 pages, www.idialog.org

Htun, Mala N. (2000) 'Women's leadership in Latin-America: trends and challenges', *Politics matter – a dialogue of women political leaders,* Washington DC: Inter-American Development Bank, Inter-American Dialogue, International Center for Research on Women, Women's Leadership Conference of the Americas, 89 pages, www.thedialogue.org

Htun, Mala N. (2005) 'Women, political parties and electoral systems in Latin America', in J. Ballington and A. Karam (eds) *Women in parliament: beyond numbers,* Stockholm: IDEA, pp 112–21.

Human Rights Watch (2010) 'Illusions of care. Lack of accountability for reproductive rights in Argentina', www.hrw.org

Hutchcroft, Paul D. (2008) 'The Arroyo imbroglio in the Philippines', *Journal of Democracy,* 17(1): 141–55.

Hyland, Jackie (2011) 'Second time's a charm: re-electing Cristina Fernandez de Kirchner in Argentina', *Gender across borders,* 31 October.

Hyndle-Hussein, Joanna (2009) *Dalia Grybauskaitė's victory in presidential elections in Lithuania,* Warsaw: OSW Centre for Eastern Studies.

Iglitzin, Lynne B. and Ross, Ruth (eds) (1976) *Women in the world: a comparative study,* Santa Barbara, CA/Oxford: Clio Books

Iglitzin, Lynne B. and Ross, Ruth (eds) (1986) *Women in the world, 1975-1985: the women's decade,* revised 2nd edn, Santa Barbara, CA/Oxford, ABC-CLIO.

iKNOW Politics (2008) 'Interview with H.E. Vaira Vike-Freiberga', 11 April, www.iknowpolitics.org

ILO (International Labour Organisation) (1968) *The international standard classification codes of occupations,* Geneva: ILO.

Inglehart, Ronald and Norris, Pippa (2003) *Rising tide, gender equality and cultural change around the world,* Cambridge: Cambridge University Press.

International Museum on Women (2010) 'Costa Rica – a model country for women?', http://imow.org

Internet Press Service of Yulia Tymoshenko (2009) 'Biography', www.tymoshenko.com.ua

IPU (Inter-Parliamentary Union) (1987) *Distribution of seats between men and women in national assemblies,* Geneva: International Centre for Parliamentary Documentation.

IPU (1988) *Participation of women in political life and in the decision-making process,* Geneva: International Centre for Parliamentary Documentation.

IPU (1991) 'Bangladesh' in Election Archives, Parline database, www.ipu.org

IPU (1995) *Women in parliaments 1945-1995: a world statistical survey,* Geneva: IPU.

IPU (1997) *Democracy still in the making: a world comparative study,* Geneva: IPU.

IPU (2000) *Politics: women's insights*, Geneva: IPU.

IPU (2005a) 'Women in national parliaments', www.ipu.org

IPU (2005b) *Women in politics 1945-2005,* Geneva: IPU.

IPU (2008) *Equality in politics: a survey of women and men in parliaments,* Geneva: IPU.

IPU (2009) *Is parliament open to women?* Geneva: IPU

IPU (2013) 'Increased women's political participation still dependent on quotas 2012 elections show', www.ipu.org

IPU (2014a) *Women in parliament in 2013: the year in review,* Geneva: IPU, 8 pages

IPU (2014b) 'Progress for women in politics, but glass ceiling remains firm', 11 March, www.ipu.org

IPU and UNDAW (Division for the Advancement of Women) (2005) *Women in politics 2005,* Lausanne: Presses Centrales.

IPU and UNDAW (2008) *Women in politics 2008,* Lausanne: Presses Centrales.

IPU and UNDAW (2010) *Women in politics 2010,* Lausanne: Presses Centrales.

IPU and UN Women (2012) *Women in politics 2012,* France: Courand.

IPU and UN Women (2014) *Women in politics 2014,* France: Courand.

IPU PARLINE (Parliamentary database) (2010) 'Republic of Moldova, Moldova, Parliament', www.ipu.org

IRIN (Integrated Regional Information Networks) (2008) 'Democratic Republic of São Tomé and Príncipe', UN Office for the Coordination of Humanitarian Affairs, OCHA, www.irinnews.org

Ishiyama, Johns T. (2003) 'Women's parties in post-communist politics', *East European Politics and Societies,* 17: 266–304.

Islam, Badrul (2013) 'Bangladesh elections 2013', *South Asian Outlook,* 14(2): 4.

Iwanaga, Kazuki (2008) *Women's political participation and representation in Asia,* Copenhagen: NIAS Press.

Jäättenmäki, Anneli (2002) *Sillanrakentaja,* Helsinki: WSOY.

Jackson, Guida M. (1998) *Women who ruled: a biographical encyclopedia,* New York, NY: Barnes & Noble.

Jacobson, Doranne (1974) 'The women of North and Central India: goddesses and wives', in C.J. Matthiasson (ed) *Many sisters: women in cross-cultural perspective,* London/New York, NY: Collier Macmillan and Free Press, pp 99–175.

Jacobson, Helga E. (1974) 'Women in Philippine society: more equal than many', in C.J. Matthiasson (ed) *Many sisters: women in cross-cultural perspective,* London/New York, NY: Collier Macmillan and Free Press, pp 349–77.

Jagan, Janet (1962) 'Guyana's women', *West Indian News,* www.jagan.org

Jagan, Janet (1975) 'Women in the struggle', www.jagan.org

Jagan, Janet (1999) 'Inaugural lecture', Toronto York University, 27 March, www.jagan.org

Jahan, Rounaq (1987) 'Women in South Asia's politics', *Third World Quarterly,* 9(3): 848–70.

Jahan, Rounaq (ed) (2000) *Bangladesh, promise and performance,* London/New York, NY: Zed Books.

Jahan, Rounaq (2007) 'Bangladesh at a crossroads', www.india-seminar.com

Jain, Devaki (ed) (1975) *Indian women*, New Delhi: Ministry of Information and Broadcasting.

Jain, Devaki (2005) *Women, development and the UN, a sixty-year quest for equality and justice*, Bloomington and Indianapolis, IN: Indiana University Press.

Jalalzai, Farida (2004) 'Women political leaders: past and present', *Women & Politics*, 26(3/4): 85–108.

Jalalzai, Farida (2008) 'Women rule: shattering the executive glass ceiling', *Politics & Gender*, 4: 205–31.

Jalalzai, Farida (2013a) 'Ma Ellen – the Iron Lady of Liberia', in M.A. Genovese and J.S. Steckenrider (eds) *Women as political leaders*, London/New York, NY: Routledge, pp 203–22.

Jalalzai, Farida (2013b) *Scattered, cracked or firmly intact? Women and the executive glass ceiling worldwide*, Oxford and New York, NY: Oxford University Press.

Jalalzai, Farida and Krook, Mona Lena (2010) 'Beyond Hillary and Benazir: women's political leadership worldwide', *International Political Science Review*, 31(1): 5–21.

Jalalzai, Farida and Tremblay, Manon (2011) 'North America', in G. Bauer and M. Tremblay (eds) *Women in executive power*, London/New York, NY: Routledge, pp 122–40.

Jancar, Barbara Wolfe (1978) *Women under communism*, Baltimore, MD, and London: Johns Hopkins University Press.

Jaquette, Jane S. (ed) (1974) *Women in politics,* New York, NY, London, Sydney, Toronto: Wiley & Sons.

Jaquette, Jane S. (2001) 'Regional differences and contrasting views', *Journal of Democracy*, 12(3): 111–25.

Jatrana, Santosh (2008) 'Gender issues in South Asia' in *South Asia 2008*, Europa Regional Surveys of the World series, London and New York: Routledge, pp 44–50.

Jayakar, Pupul (1995) *Indira Gandhi,* New Delhi: Penguin.

Jensen, Jane S. (2008) *Women political leaders: breaking the highest glass ceiling*, New York, NY: Palgrave Macmillan.

Jenson, Jane and Sineau, Mariette (1994) 'The same or different? An unending dilemma for French women', in B.J. Nelson and N. Chowdhury (eds) *Women and politics worldwide*, London/New Haven, CT: Yale University Press, pp 243–60.

Johnson, Anne Janette (1993) 'Ertha Pascal-Trouillot', *Gale Contemporary Black Biography*, www.answers.com

Johnson, Phyllis (2010) 'Mozambique: continuity with change', 21 January, www. allafrica.com

Joseph, Richard (2008) 'Challenges of a "frontier" region', *Journal of Democracy*, 19(2): 94–108.

Jurjević, Alina (2009) *Silent majority*, Zagreb: UNDP.

Kabir, Farah (2003) 'Political participation of women in South Asia', www. dawnnet.org

Kanter, Rosabeth Moss (1977) *Men and women of the corporation*, New York, NY: Basic Books.

Kaplan, Gisela (1992) *Contemporary Western European feminism*, New York, NY: New York University Press.

Karam, Azza (ed) (1998) *Women in parliaments: beyond numbers*, Stockholm: International IDEA.

Karl, Marilee (1995) *Women and empowerment,* London: Zed Books.

Kelber, Mim (ed) (1994) *Women and government,* London and Westport, CT: Praeger.

Kent, Jacqueline (2010) *The making of Julia Gillard,* Victoria, Australia: Penguin.

Kent, Jacqueline (2013) *Take your best shot – the prime ministership of Julia Gillard*, Victoria, Australia: Penguin.

Kenworthy, Lane and Malami, Melissa (1999) 'Gender inequality in political representation: a worldwide comparative analysis', *Social Forces*, 78(1): 235–69.

Kidwai, Rasheed (2010) *Sonia, a biography*, New Delhi: Penguin India.

Kilner, James (2011) 'Kyrgystan starts anti-bride-kidnapping campaign', *The Telegraph*, 29 November.

Kiribamune, Sirima (ed) (1999a) *Women and politics in Sri Lanka, a comparative perspective*, Kandy, Sri Lanka: International Centre for Ethnic Studies.

Kiribamune, Sirima (1999b) 'Climbing the greasy pole, opportunities and challenges in women's access to electoral politics in Sri Lanka', in S. Kiribamune (ed) *Women and politics in Sri Lanka*, Kandy, Sri Lanka: International Centre for Ethnic Studies, pp 71–100.

Kirinde, Chandani (2000) 'People's Mathiniya buried amidst people's tears', *Sunday Times*, 15 October.

Kirkpatrick, Jeane J. (1974) *Political woman*, New York, NY: Basic Books.

Kis, Oksana (2007) '"Beauty will save the world!": feminine strategies in Ukrainian politics and the case of Yulia Tymoshenko', *Spaces of Identity*, 7(2): 34.

Klinkert, Ulrich (2005) 'Profile: Angela Merkel', BBC News, 22 November, 2 pages, newsvote.bbc.co.uk

Klotchkoff, Jean-Claude (1996) 'Liberia: la mère de tous les combattants', *Jeune Afrique*, 14 October.

Kobaladze, Mikheil (2008) 'Georgia: an Iron Lady exits, for now', *Transitions Online*, 16 May, www.tol.cz

Kolinsky, Eva (1993) 'Party change and women's representation in Unified Germany', in J. Lovenduski and P. Norris (eds) *Gender and party politics*, London: Sage, pp 113–46.

Komisar, Lucy (1988) *Corazon Aquino, the story of a revolution*, New York: George Braziller.

Konneh, Augustine (1993) 'Women in politics in Africa: the case of Liberia', *Georgia Association of Historians: Proceedings and Papers*, 14, pp 107–15.

Korppi-Tommola, Aura (2008) 'Republikens President Tarja Halonen', in Irma Sulkunen, Maria Lähteenmäki and Aura Korppi-Tommola (eds) *Kvinnorna i Riksdagen,* Helsinki: Edita, pp 274-9.

Kostadinova, Tatiana (2003) 'Women's legislative representation in post-communist Bulgaria', in R.E. Matland and K.A. Montgomery (eds) *Women's access to political power in post-communist Europe*, Oxford and New York, NY: Oxford University Press, pp 304–20.

Krogstad, Anne (1999a) '"Lille speil på veggen der": Margaret Thatchers politiske image', in A. Krogstad (ed) *Image i politikken*, Oslo: Pax, pp 73–95.

Krogstad, Anne (1999b) *Image i politikken*, Oslo: Pax.

Krook, Mona Lena (2009) *Quotas for women in politics*, Oxford: Oxford University Press.

Krook, Mona Lena and Childs, Sarah (eds) (2010) *Women, gender and politics, a reader*, Oxford and New York, NY: Oxford University Press.

Krook, Mona Lena; Lovenduski, Joni and Squires, Judith (2006) 'Western Europe, North America, Australia and New Zealand: gender quotas in the context of citizenship models', in D. Dahlerup (ed) *Women, quotas and politics*, London/New York, NY: Routledge, pp 194–221.

Krupavičius, Algis and Matonyté, Irmina (2003) 'Women in Lithuanian politics: from nomenklatura selection to representation', in R.E. Matland and K.A. Montgomery (eds) *Women's access to political power in post-communist Europe*, Oxford and New York, NY: Oxford University Press, pp 81–104.

Kumar, Anand (2007) 'Caretaker government targets dynastic politics, South Asia Analysis Group', 10 pages, www.southasiaanalysis.org

Kyle, Younker (2010) 'Asignación Universal por Hijo, one year later', *The Argentina Independent*, 12 October.

LaFont, Suzanne (2001) 'One step forward, two steps back: women in the post-communist states', *Communist and Post-Communist Studies*, 34: 203–20.

Lähteenmäki, Maria (2008) 'Jurist Halonens ledamotskarriär', in I. Sulkunen, M. Lähteenmäki and A. Korppi-Tommola (eds) *Kvinnorna i Riksdagen*, Helsinki, Edita, pp 180–3.

Lane, John C. (1995) 'The election of women under proportional representation: the case of Malta', *Democratization*, 19 pages, maltadata.com

Lanskoy, Miriam and Areshidze, Giorgi (2008) 'Georgia's year of turmoil', *Journal of Democracy*, 19(4): 154–68.

Lapidus, Gail W. (1976) 'Changing women's roles in the USSR', in L.B. Iglitzin and R. Ross (eds) *Women in the world*, Oxford and Santa Barbara, CA: Clio Books, pp 303–17.

Lashley, Jonathan (2006) 'Enterprise development and poverty alleviation in Dominica: the role and motivations of Eugenia Charles', in E. Barriteau and A. Cobley (eds) *Enjoying power: Eugenia Charles and political leadership in the Commonwealth Caribbean*, Jamaica: University of the West Indies Press, pp 214–35.

Lazreg, Marnia (2009) 'Consequences of political liberalization and sociocultural mobilization for women in Algeria, Egypt and Jordan', in A.M. Goetz (ed) *Governing women*, New York, NY: Routledge, pp 45–62.

Lemke, Christiane (1994) 'Women and politics: the new Federal Republic of Germany', in B.J. Nelson and N. Chowdhury (eds) *Women and politics worldwide*, London/New Haven, CT: Yale University Press, pp 261–84.

Leraand, Dag (2006) 'São Tomé and Príncipe', in *Store Norske Leksikon*, Oslo: Kunnskapsforlaget, pp 825–7.

Lethbridge, Jane (2012) 'How women are being affected by the global economic crisis & austerity measures', Public Services International Research (PSIRU); congress.world-psi.org

Levitsky, Steven (2005) 'Argentina: democratic survival amidst economic failure', in F. Hagopian and S.P. Mainwaring (eds) *The third wave of democratization in Latin America*, New York, NY: Cambridge University Press, pp 63–89.

Levitsky, Steven and Murillo, Maria Victoria (2008) 'Argentina: from Kirchner to Kirchner', *Journal of Democracy*, 19(2): 16–30.

Levitsky, Steven and Roberts, Kenneth M. (2011) *The resurgence of the Latin American Left*, Baltimore, MD: Johns Hopkins University Press.

Lewis, Jone Johnson (1992) 'Hanna Suchocka government', October; womenshistory.about.com

Lijphart, Arend (ed) (1992) *Parliamentary versus presidential government*, Oxford: Oxford University Press.

Lijphart, Arend (1999) *Patterns of democracy. Government forms and performance in thirty-six countries*, London/New Haven, CT: Yale University Press.

Limoncelli, Mary Anne (2011) 'International women's issues: Yulia Tymoshenko and FEMEN: women, appearance and politics in Ukraine', *Persephone Magazine*, 13 October.

Lindberg, Staffan I. (2006) *Democracy and elections in Africa*, Baltimore, MD: Johns Hopkins University Press.

Linz, Juan J. (2000) *Totalitarian and authoritarian regimes*, London and Boulder, CO: Lynne Rienner.

Linz, Juan J. and Stepan, Alfred (1996) *Problems of democratic transition and consolidation, Southern Europe, South America, and post-communist Europe*, London and Baltimore, MA: Johns Hopkins University Press.

Lique, René-Jacques (1993) *Bokassa Ier, la grande mystification*, Paris: Chaka.

Lister, Ruth (2003) *Citizenship, feminist perspectives*, New York, NY: Palgrave Macmillan.

Liswood, Laura A. (2007) Women world leaders: great politicians tell their stories, Washington, DC: Council Press.

Llanos, Beatriz and Sample, Kristen (2008) *30 years of democracy: riding the wave? Women's political participation in Latin America*, Stockholm: IDEA.

Longman, Timothy (2006) 'Rwanda: achieving equality or serving an authoritarian state?', in G. Bauer and H.E. Britton (eds) *Women in African parliaments*, London and Boulder, CO: Lynne Rienner, pp 133–50.

Longman, Timothy (2010) 'Culture of Rwanda', www.everyculture.com (accessed November 2010).

Lovenduski, Joni (1994) 'Great Britain: the rules of the political game: feminism and politics in Great Britain', in B.J. Nelson and N. Chowdhury (eds) *Women and politics worldwide*, London/New Haven, CT: Yale University Press, pp 298–310.

Lovenduski, Joni (2005a) *Feminizing politics*, Cambridge: Polity Press.

Lovenduski, Joni (ed) (2005b) *State feminism and political representation*, Cambridge: Cambridge University Press.

Lovenduski, Joni (2010) 'The dynamics of gender and party', in M.L. Krook and S. Childs (eds) *Women, gender, and politics*, Oxford and New York, NY: Oxford University Press, pp 81–6.

Lovenduski, Joni and Norris, Pippa (eds) (1993) *Gender and party politics*, London, New Delhi and Thousand Oaks, CA: Sage.

Lu, Yu-lan (1972) 'Liberation of women', Peking Review, March 10: 10-12, www.marxists.org

Macapagal-Arroyo, Gloria (2004) 'Second inaugural address', Official Gazette, 30 June, www.gov.ph

Mackay, Fiona (2004) 'Gender and political representation in the UK: the state of the "discipline"', *The British Journal of Politics and International Relations*, 6(1): 99–120.

Mainwaring, Scott and Scully, Timothy R. (2010a) 'Democratic governance in Latin America: eleven lessons from recent experience', in S. Mainwaring and T. Scully (eds) *Democratic governance in Latin America*, Stanford, CA: Stanford University Press, pp 365–97.

Mainwaring, Scott and Scully, Timothy R (2010b) *Democratic governance in Latin America*, Stanford, CA: Stanford University Press.

Majumdar, Rozana (2012) 'Are Bangladeshi women politicians tokens on the political area?' The Asia Foundation, 27 June, 2 pages.

Malhotra, Inder (1989) *Indira Gandhi*, Boston, MA: Northeastern University Press.

Malhotra, Inder (2003) *Dynasties of India and beyond*, New Delhi: HarperCollins.

Mamot, Patricio R. (2008) *The rise and decline of President Gloria Macapagal-Arroyo*, Montgomery, AL: E-Book Time.

Mankekar, Kamala (1975) *Women in India*, New Delhi: Central Institute of Research & Training in Public Cooperation.

Manning, Carrie (2010) 'Mozambique's slide into one-party rule', *Journal of Democracy*, 21(2): 151–65.

Manor, James (1989) *The expedient utopian: (Solomon) Bandaranaike and Ceylon*, Cambridge: Cambridge University Press

Manor, James (1993) 'Innovative leadership in modern India: M. K. Gandhi, Nehru, and I. Gandhi', in G. Sheffer (ed) *Innovative leaders in international politics*, New York, NY: State of New York Press, pp 187–215.

Markelova, Katarina (2011) 'Putting Kyrgyzstan on the map', *The UNESCO Courier*, April–June, pp 13–4.

Marsaud, Olivia (2004) 'Politique se conjugue au féminin', *Jeune Afrique/L'Intelligent*, 25–31 January.

Marshall, Katryn (1997) *Indira Gandhi*, New York, NY: Exley.

Marshall, Monty G. and Marshall, Donna R. (1999) 'Gender empowerment and the willingness of states to use force', Center for Systemic Peace, Occasional Paper series #2.

Martin, Ralph G. (1988) *Golda – Golda Meir: the romantic years*, New York, NY: Charles Scribner's Sons.

Masani, Zareer (1976 [1975]) *Indira Gandhi, a biography*, New York, NY: Thomas E. Crowell Co.

Matland, Richard E. (1998) 'Women's representation in national legislatures: developed and developing countries', *Legislative Studies Quarterly*, 23(1): 109–25.

Matland, Richard E. (2003) 'Women's representation in post-communist Europe', in R.E. Matland and K.A. Montgomery (eds) *Women's access to political power in post-communist Europe*, Oxford and New York, NY: Oxford University Press, pp 32–42.

Matland, Richard E. (2005) 'Enhancing women's political participation: legislative recruitment and electoral systems', in J. Ballington and A. Karam (eds) *Women in parliament: beyond numbers*, Stockholm: International IDEA.

Matland, Richard E. and Montgomery, Kathleen A. (eds) (2003) *Women's access to political power in post-communist Europe*, Oxford and New York, NY: Oxford University Press.

Matthiasson, Carolyn J. (ed) (1974) *Many sisters: women in cross-cultural perspective*, New York, NY: The Free Press.

Mayorga, René Antonio (2005) 'Bolivia's democracy at the crossroads', in F. Hagopian and S.P. Mainwaring (eds) *The third wave of democratization in Latin America*, New York, NY: Cambridge University Press, pp 149–78.

Mazur, Amy G. (2002) *Theorizing feminist policy*, Oxford: Oxford University Press.

Mbow, Penda (2008) 'Senegal: the return of personalism', *Journal of Democracy*, 19(1): 156–69.

McAleese, Mary (1997) Love in chaos, New York, NY: Continuum.

McBride, Dorothy E. and Mazur, Amy G. (2010) *The politics of state feminism*, Philadelphia, PA: Temple University Press.

McCann, Carole R. and Kim, Seung-Kyung (2003) *Feminist theory readers, local and global perspectives*, London/New York, NY: Routledge.

McCarthy, Justine (1999) *Mary McAleese, the outsider*, Dublin: Blackwater.

McGarry, Patsy (2008) *First citizen, Mary McAleese and the Irish presidency*, Dublin: O'Brien Press.

McIntyre, Angus (2000) 'Megawati Sukarnoputri: from president's daughter to vice president', *Bulletin of Concerned Asian Scholars*, 32(1/2): 19.

McIntyre, Angus (2005) *The Indonesian presidency: the shift from personal toward constitutional rule*, Lanham, MD: Rowman & Littlefield.

McLaughlin, Daniel (2010) 'Sociologist Iveta Radicova becomes Slovakia's first female prime minister', *Irish Times*, 8 July.

Meditz, Sandra W. and Hanratty, Dennis M. (eds) (1987) *Caribbean Islands: a country study*, Washington DC: US Library of Congress, www.countrystudies. us/caribbean-islands

Meir, Golda (1976) *My life*, London: Futura.

Meir, Menahem (1983) *My mother Golda Meir*, New York, NY: Arbor House.

Merkelson, Suzanne and Swift, Andrew (2010) 'Women in control', *Foreign Policy*, 1 October, www.foreignpolicy.com

Mernissi, Fatima (1993) *The forgotten queens of Islam*, Minneapolis, MN: University of Minnesota Press.

Merrill, Tim (ed) (1992) *Guyana: a country study*, Washington, DC: US Library of Congress, www.countrystudies.us/guyana

Meunier, Marianne (2007) 'Nous ne décevrons pas', *Jeune Afrique*, 3–9 June.

Miller, Carmen Hutchinson (2006) 'Stereotyping women's political leadership: images of Eugenia Charles in the Caribbean print media', in E. Barriteau and A. Cobley (eds) *Enjoying power: Eugenia Charles and political leadership in the Commonwealth Caribbean*, Jamaica: University of West Indies Press, pp 239–56.

Miller, Federic P.; Vandome, Agnes F. and McBrewster, John (eds) (2009) *History of Guyana,* Lexington, KY: Alphascript Publishing.

Mills, Clifford W. (2008) *Angela Merkel*, New York, NY: Chelsea House.

Ministry of Women's Affairs (2009) 'Women in New Zealand', www.mwa.govt.nz

Møller, Iselin Stalheim (2013) 'Farvel til feminismen på Island', *Dagsavisen*, 26 April, pp 16–17.

Momaya, Masum (2009a) 'Can "feminine" leadership mend the economic crisis in Iceland?', 1 July, www.awid.org

Momaya, Masum (2009b) 'Kyrgyzstan – what is the status of women', www.awid.org

Mondesire, Alicia (2006) 'The reluctant feminist: Eugenia Charles on women and gender', in E. Barriteau and A. Cobley (eds) *Enjoying power: Eugenia Charles and political leadership in the Commonwealth Caribbean*, Jamaica: University of West Indies Press, pp 259–81.

Moore, Charles (2013) *Margaret Thatcher, the authorized biography, from Grantham to the Falklands*, New York, NY: Knopf.

Morán, María Pazos (2013) 'Interview with Jóhanna Sigurðardóttir', *El Pais*, 13 May, www.equalandnontransferable.org

Morgan, Robin (ed) (1984) *Sisterhood is global*, New York, NY: Anchor Books.

Moser, Robert G. (2003) 'Electoral systems and women's representation: the strange case of Russia', in R.E. Matland and K.A. Montgomery (eds) *Women's access to political power in post-communist Europe*, Oxford and New York, NY: Oxford University Press, pp 153–72.

Moses, Joel C. (1986) 'The Soviet Union in the women's decade', in L.B. Iglitzin and R. Ross (eds) *Women in the world 1975–1985*, Oxford and Santa Barbara, CA: ABC-CLIO, pp 385–413.

Munday, Dean E. (2013) 'Framing Saint Jóhanna', *Journal of Interdisciplinary Feminist Thought*, 7(1): 5–22; digitalcommons.salve.edu/jift/vol7/iss1/5

Mungiu-Pippidi, Alina and Munteanu, Igor (2009) 'Moldova's "Twitter revolution"', *Journal of Democracy*, 20(3): 136–42.

Murray, Rainbow (ed) (2010) *Cracking the highest glass ceiling: a global comparison of women's campaigns for executive office*, Santa Barbara, CA: Praeger.

Musembi, Celestine Nyambu (2009) 'Ruling out gender equality? The post-Cold War rule of law agenda in sub-Saharan Africa', in A.M. Goetz (ed) *Governing women*, London/New York, NY: Routledge, pp 274–90.

National Committee on the Status of Women (1975) *Status of women in India*, New Delhi: Indian Council of Social Science Research.

Navarro, Mireya (1999) 'Woman in the news: Mireya Elisa Moscoso; earnest icon for Panama', *New York Times*, 4 May.

Nelson, Barbara J. and Carver, Kathryn A. (1994) 'United States', in B.J. Nelson and N. Chowdhury (eds) *Women and politics worldwide*, London/New Haven, CT: Yale University Press, pp 737–57.

Nelson, Barbara J. and Chowdhury, Najma (eds) (1994) *Women and politics worldwide*, London/New Haven, CT: Yale University Press.

News Wires (2010) 'Laura Chinchilla', *International News,* 9 May, www.france24.com

New Zealand Labour (2009) 'Helen Clark and Helen Clark's valedictory speech', www.labourparty.org.nz

New Zealand National Party (2001) 'Rt Hon Jenny Shipley', www.national.org.nz

Nicholls, David (1998) 'The Duvalier regime in Haiti', in H.E. Chehabi and J.J. Linz (eds) *Sultanistic regimes*, London and Baltimore, MD: Johns Hopkins University Press, pp 153–81.

Niethammer, Ludwig (2000) 'Germany: a political profile of new CDU chairperson Angela Merkel', www.wsws.org

Norris, Pippa (2004) *Electoral engineering*, Cambridge: Cambridge University Press.

Norwegian Embassy Helsingfors (2000a) 'Tarja Halonen ny finsk president', 7 February.

Norwegian Embassy Helsingfors (2000b) 'President Tarja Halonens innsettelse', 2 March.

Norwegian Nobel Institute (2011) 'Nobel Peace Prize for 2011', Announcement, 7 October, nobelpeaceprice.org

Notable Biographies (2006) 'Agatha Barbara', www.notablebiographies.com

Notable Biographies (2008) 'Ellen Johnson Sirleaf', www.notablebiographies.com

Notable Biographies (2010) 'Luisa Diogo', www.notablebiographies.com

Novikova, Irina (1995) 'Women in Latvia today', *Canadian Woman Studies*, 16(1): 27–31.

Nymark, Johannes (2008) *Frå Evita til Cristina, Om anarkismen, peronismen and kampen mot nyliberalismen*, Bergen: Fagbokforlaget.

O'Callaghan, Jerome (1996) 'Mary Robinson', in R.M. Salokar and M.L. Volcansek (eds) *Women in law*, Westport, CT: Greenwood, pp 257–65.

Ogden, Chris (1990) *Maggie*, New York, NY: Simon and Shuster.

Olinga, Luc (2006) 'Une ère nouvelle', *Jeune Afrique/L'Intelligent*, 22–28 January.

Omtvedt, Gail (1980) *We will smash this prison! Indian women in struggle*, London: Zed Books.

O'Neill, Lois Decker (ed) (1979) *The women's book of world records and achievements*, Garden City: Anchor Books.

Opedal, Halgeir (2000) 'Kvinner på randen av gjennombrudd', *Dagbladet,* 15 January, pp 28-32.

Opfell, Olga S. (1993) *Women prime ministers and presidents*, Jefferson, NC: McFarland & Co.

Osava, Mario (2011) 'Brazil – new president's first steps create optimism in women's movement', *IPS*, 12 January.

O'Shaughnessy, Hugh (2004) 'Maria de Lourdes Pintasilgo, obituary', *The Independent*, 14 July.

Otunbayeva, Roza (2011) 'After the revolution, establishing democracy', *Washington Post,* 8 March, 2 pages, www.washingtonpost.com

Padgett, Tim (2007) 'Interview: Cristina Fernández de Kirchner of Argentina', *Time*, 29 September.

Padrino, Mercedes (2004) *Benazir Bhutto*, Philadephia, PA: Chelsea House.

Palmieri, Sonia (2011) *Gender-sensitive parliaments, a global review of good practice*, Geneva: IPU.

Parawansa, Khofifah Indar (2005) 'Case study: Indonesia', in J. Ballington and A. Karam (eds) *Women in parliament: beyond numbers*, Stockholm: IDEA, pp 82–90.

Parliament of Georgia (2009) 'The biography of the Chairperson of the Parliament of Georgia Nino Burjanadze', www.parliament.ge

Parliament of Sri Lanka (2014) 'Lady members 1931-2010', *Handbook of Parliament,* parliament.lk

Parliament of the Republic of Moldova (2010) 'Greceanîi Zinaida Depute', www.parlament.md

Paton, Kathleen; Madeson, Francis and O'Connell, Christopher (1995a) 'Dame Eugenia Charles', in A. Brill (ed) *A rising public voice: women in politics worldwide*, New York, NY: Feminist Press, pp 136–40.

Paton, Kathleen; Madeson, Francis and O'Connell, Christopher (1995b) 'Vigdís Finnbogadóttir', in A. Brill (ed) *A rising public voice: women in politics worldwide*, New York, NY: Feminist Press, pp 141–3.

Paton, Kathleen; Madeson, Francis and O'Connell, Christopher (1995c) 'Mary Robinson', in A. Brill (ed) *A rising public voice: women in politics worldwide* New York, NY: Feminist Press, pp 155–7.

Paton, Kathleen; Madeson, Francis and O'Connell, Christopher (1995d) 'Margaret Thatcher', in A. Brill (ed) *A rising public voice: women in politics worldwide*, New York, NY: Feminist Press, pp 158–60.

Patterson, Orlanda (2007) 'The troubles of Sista P.', *New York Times*, 9 January.

Paxton, Pamela and Hughes Melanie M. (2007) *Women, politics and power: a global perspective*, Los Angeles, CA/London/New Delhi/Singapore: Pine Forge Press/Sage.

Paxton, Pamela and Hughes, Melanie M. (2014) *Women, politics and power: a global perspective*, revised 2nd edn, Los Angeles, CA/London/New Delhi/Singapore: Sage.

Pearlman, Jonathan (2013) 'Julia Gillard hopes to inspire more women to enter politics', *Telegraph*, 25 September.

People's National Party (2006) 'Candidate Portia Simpson-Miller', 4 pages, www.pnpjamaica.com

Persad-Bissessar, Kamla (2010) 'Inauguration Speech', www.news.gov.tt

Peterson, V. Spike and Runyan, Anne Sisson (1999) *Global gender issues*, Oxford and Boulder, CO: Westview Press.

Petterson, Maria (2007) 'Førstedamen tar makten', *Morgenbladet*, 26 October–1 November, pp 16–17.

Philips, Anne (1991) *Engendering democracy*, University Park, PA: Pennsylvania State University Press.

Pierre-Louis, Michèle Duvivier (2008) 'Déclaration de politique générale', 30 pages, iham-chrd.org

Pietilä, Hilkka (2007) *The unfinished story of women and the United Nations*, New York, NY, and Geneva: UN.

Pietilä, Hilkka and Vickers, Jeanne (1996) *Making women matter, the role of the United Nations*, London: Zed Books.

Pilcher, Jane (1995) 'The gender significance of women in power, British women talking about Margaret Thatcher', *The European Journal of Women's Studies*, 2: 493–508.

Pilcher, Jane and Whelehan, Imelda (2005) *50 Key concepts in gender studies*, London: Sage.

PILDAT (Pakistan Institute of Legislative Development and Transparency) (2004) *Women's representation in Pakistan's parliament*, Lahore: PILDAT.

Pintasilgo, Maria de Lourdes (1984) 'Portugal: daring to be different', in R. Morgan (ed) *Sisterhood is global*, Garden City, NY: Anchor Books, pp 571–75 (reprinted in A. Brill [ed] [1995] *A rising public voice*, New York, NY: Feminist Press, pp 127–32).

Pinto, Vânia Carvalho (2011) 'Arab states', in G. Bauer and M. Tremblay (eds) *Women in executive power*, London/New York, NY: Routledge, pp 10–22.

Piscopo, Jennifer M. (2010) 'Primera Dama, prima donna? Media constructions Cristina Fernández de Kirchner in Argentine', in R. Murray (ed) *Cracking the highest glass ceiling*, Santa Barbara, CA: Praeger, pp 197–219.

Pittman, Todd (2005) 'Waitress to president: a Liberian odyssey', *New York Times*, 16 November.

Polgreen, Lydia (2006) 'Liberia's Harvard-trained "queen" is sworn in as leader', *New York Times*, 17 January.

Posner, Daniel N. and Young, Daniel J. (2007) 'The institutionalization of political power in Africa', *Journal of Democracy*, 18(3): 126–40.

Prempeh, H. Kwasi (2008) 'Presidents untamed', *Journal of Democracy*, 19(2): 109–23.

PresidentCBK (2008) 'Chandrika B. Kumaratunga', 4 pages, www.presidentcbk.org

President of Latvia (2005) 'CV Vaira Vike-Freiberga', www.president.lv

President of the Republic of Finland (2010) 'Halonen, Tarja Kaarina', 1 page, www.vnk.fi

President of the Republic of Malta (2013) 'Ms Agatha Barbara 1982–1987', www.president.gov.mt

Pribble, Jennifer and Huber, Evelyne (2011) 'Social policy and redistribution', in S. Levitsky and K. Roberts (eds) *The resurgence of the Latin American Left*, Baltimore, MD: The Johns Hopkins University Press, pp 117–38.

Price, Stuart and Tonpo, Jarlawah (2005) 'A lesson for Africa's big men', *New African*, December.

Prime Minister's Office Finland (2011) 'Prime Minister Mari Kiviniemi', www.vnk.fi

Prime Minister's Office Iceland (2009a) 'Platform of the government', 6 February; 3 pages, eng.forsaetisraduneyti.is

Prime Minister's Office Iceland (2009b) 'Government coalition co-operation statement', 10 May, 1 page, eng.forsaetisraduneyti.is

Prime Minister's Office Iceland (2009c) 'Prime Minister's opening address', 20 May, 5 pages, eng.forsaetisraduneyti.is

Prime Minister's Office Iceland (2013) 'Jóhanna Sigurðardóttir, Prime Minister, 2009-2013', 1 page, eng.forsaetisraduneyti.is

PS (2013) 'Sonia Gandhi', 3 pages, nilacharal.com

Quotaproject (2013) 'Global database of quotas for women', www.quotaproject.org

Radelet, Steven (2010) 'Success stories from "emerging Africa"', *Journal of Democracy*, 21(4): 87–101.

Randall, Vicky (1987) *Women and politics*, Chicago, IL: University of Chicago Press.#

Rauhala, Emily (2012) 'South Korea elects first female president', *Time,* 19 December, world.time.com

Raven, Susan and Weir, Alison (1981) *Women in history*, London: Weidenfeld and Nicolson.

Reel, Monte (2006) 'Bachelet sworn in as Chile's President', *Washington Post*, 12 March.

Reel, Monte (2007) 'The era of "la presidente"', *Washington Post*, 5–11 November.

Reid, Robert H. and Guerrero, Eileen (1995) *Corazon Aquino and the brushfire revolution*, London and Baton Rouge, LA: Louisiana State University Press.

Reinart, Ustun (1999) 'Ambition for all seasons: Tansu Ciller', *MERIA, Middle East Review of International Affairs, Journal*, 3(1): 4.

Reiter, Rayna R. (ed) (1975) *Toward an anthropology of women*, New York, NY, and London: Monthly Review Press.

Remmert, Consuelo (2003) 'Rwanda promotes women decision-makers', *UN Chronicle*, 4/2003.

Reno, William (1998) *Warlord politics and African states*, London and Boulder, CO: Lynne Rienner.

Rettie, John (2000) 'Sirima Bandaranaike', *The Guardian*, 11 October; guardian. co.uk

Reuters (1994) 'Sylvie Kinigi, Prime Minister of Burundi', Nairobi, 23 December.

Reuters (2003) 'First woman named Peru prime minister', 29 June; edition.cnn. com

Reuters (2010) 'UN Award for Bangladesh', *The Daily Star,* 21 September.

Reynolds, Andrew (1999) 'Women in the legislatures and executives of the world', *World Politics*, 51(4): 547–72.

Richter, Linda K. (1990/91) 'Exploring theories of female leadership in South and Southeast Asia', *Pacific Affairs*, 63(4): 524–40.

Ring, Trudy (2013) 'The legacy of the world's first out lesbian prime minister', 3 May, www.advocate.com

Roberts, Kenneth (2011) 'Chile: the Left after neoliberalism', in S. Levitsky and K. Roberts (eds) *The resurgence of the Latin American Left*, Baltimore, MD: The Johns Hopkins University Press, pp 325–47.

Robinson, Mary (1992) *A voice for Somalia*, Dublin: O'Brien Press.

Roces, Mina (1998a) 'The gendering of post-war Philippine politics', in K. Sen and M. Stevens (eds) *Gender and power in affluent Asia*, London: Routledge, p 312.

Roces, Mina (1998b) *Women, power and kinship politics, female power in post-war Philippines*, London and Westport, CT: Praeger.

Rogers, Steven (2004) 'Philippine politics and the rule of law', *Journal of Democracy*, 15(4): 111–25.

Rohrlich-Leavitt, Ruby (ed) (1975) *Women cross-culturally: change and challenge,* The Hague, Paris: Mouton

Rosaldo, Michelle Zimbalist and Lamphere, Louise (eds) (1974) *Woman, culture & society*, Stanford, CA: Stanford University Press.

Rosenberg, Dorothy J. (1991) 'Shock therapy: GDR women in transition from a socialist welfare state to a social market economy', *Signs: Journal of Women in Culture and Society*, 17(1): 129–51.

Rosenthal, Bernice Glatzer (1975) 'The role and status of women in the Soviet Union: 1917 to the present', in R. Rohrlich-Leavitt (ed) *Women cross-culturally: change and challenge,* The Hague, Paris: Mouton, pp 429–55.

Roza, Vivian (2010) *Politics and parties: without equality, far from parity,* Stockholm: IDEA.

Rueschemeyer, Marilyn and Wolchik, Sharon L. (2009) *Women in power in post-communist parliaments,* Bloomington, IN: Indiana University Press.

Rueschemeyer, Marilyn (2011) 'Women's participation in postcommunist politics', in S.L. Wolchik and J.L. Curry (eds) *Central & East European politics*, Lanham, MD: Rowman & Littlefield, pp 109–24.

Rule, Wilma and Zimmerman, Joseph F. (eds) (1994) *Electoral systems in comparative perspective*, London and Westport, CT: Greenwood Press.

Rupesinghe, Kumar (2008) Personal communication with Sirimavo Bandaranaike, 15 January.

Saadawi, Nawal El (1984) 'Egypt: when a woman rebels..', in Morgan, Robin (ed) *Sisterhood is global,* Garden City, NY: Anchor Books: pp 199-206.

Sabbagh, Amal (2005) 'The Arab states: enhancing women's political participation', in J. Ballington and A. Karam (eds) *Women in parliament: beyond numbers,* Stockholm: IDEA, pp 52–71.

Sacchet, Teresa (2009) 'Political parties and gender in Latin-America', in A.M. Goetz (ed) *Governing women,* New York, NY: Routledge, UNRISD, pp 148–72.

Sæther, Jens Marius (2012) 'Et mirakel at vi sitter ennå', *Dagsavisen,* 26 January.

Saint-Germain, Michelle A. (1994) 'The representation of women and minorities in the national legislatures of Costa Rica and Nicaragua', in W. Rule and J.F. Zimmerman (eds) *Electoral systems in comparative perspective,* London and Westport, CT: Greenwood Press, pp 211–21.

Saint-Germain, Michelle A. (2013) 'Women in power in Nicaragua, myth and reality', in M.A. Genovese and J.S. Steckenrider (eds) *Women as political leaders,* London/New York, NY: Routledge, pp 110–43.

Salinas, Gloria Ardaya (1994) 'Women and politics: gender relations in Bolivian political organizations and labor unions', in B.J. Nelson and N. Chowdhury (eds) *Women and politics worldwide,* London/New Haven, CT: Yale University Press, pp 114–26.

Sawer, Marian (1994) 'Locked out or locked in? Women and politics in Australia', in B.J. Nelson and N. Chowdhury (eds) *Women and politics worldwide,* London/New Haven, CT: Yale University Press, pp 73–91.

Sawer, Marian (2013a) 'Misogyny and misrepresentation: women in Australian parliaments', *Political Science,* 65: 105–17.

Sawer, Marian (2013b) 'Gillard right to play gender card', *The New Zealand Herald,* 25 June, www.nzherald.co.nz

Schemla, Elisabeth (1993) *Edith Cresson, la femme piégée,* France: Flammarion.

Schemmel, B. (2014) 'Rulers (heads of state and government)', www.rulers.org

Schlegel, Alice (ed) (1977) *Sexual stratification: a cross-cultural view,* New York, NY: Columbia University Press.

Schmidt, Dana (2006) 'Revolusjonens gudinne tilbake', *Dagsavisen,* 2 April.

Schwarzer, Alice (2006) 'A man sees red' and 'We are Chancelloress!', *Gender Forum, Special Issue: Women in Power,* 6 pages, www.genderforum.org

Scott, Joan W. (1988) 'Deconstructing equality-versus-difference or the uses of poststructuralist theory for feminism', *Feminist Studies,* 14(1): 33–50.

Seim, Jardar (1994) Øst-Europas historie, Oslo: Aschehoug.

Seim, Jardar (1999) Øst-Europa etter murens fall, Oslo: Aschehoug.

Selmer, Erik R. (2005) 'Oransjeprinsessen', *Dagsavisen,* 30 January.

Selmer, Erik R. (2007a) 'Argentinas nye Evita', *Dagsavisen,* 28 October.

Selmer, Erik R. (2007b) 'Ønsker Isabel Perón utlevert', *Dagsavisen,* 29 October.

Seneviratne, Maureen (1975) *Sirimavo Bandaranaike,* Colombo: Hansa Publishers.

Shaikh, Muhammed Ali (2000) *Benazir Bhutto: a political biography,* Karachi: Orient Books.

Sharfman, Dapha (1994) 'Women and politics in Israel', in B.J. Nelson and N. Chowdhury (eds) *Women and politics worldwide*, London/New Haven, CT:Yale University Press, pp 380–95.

Shaw, Robert (2013) 'Women politicians start to dismantle "men's club" across the Caribbean', *Alterpress*, 31 January.

Shifter, Michael (2011) 'A surge to the center, Latin America', *Journal of Democracy*, 22(1): 107–21.

Shvedova, Nadezhda (1998) 'The challenge of transition – women in parliament in Russia', in A. Karam (ed) *Women in parliament: beyond numbers*, Stockholm: IDEA, pp 57–63.

Siaroff, Alan (2003) 'Comparative presidencies: the inadequacy of the presidential, semi-presidential and parliamentary distinction', *European Journal of Political Research*, 42: 287–312.

Siemieńska, Renata (1994) 'Polish women as the object and subject of politics during and after the communist period', in B.J. Nelson and N. Chowdhury (eds) *Women and politics worldwide*, London/New Haven, CT:Yale University Press, pp 608–24.

Siemieńska, Renata (2003) 'Women in the Polish Sejm: political culture and party politics versus electoral rules', in R.E. Matland and K.A. Montgomery (eds) *Women's access to political power in post-communist Europe*, Oxford/New York, NY: Oxford University Press, pp 217–44.

Siggins, Lorna (1997) *Mary Robinson*, Edinburgh/London: Mainstream.

Sigurðardóttir, Erla (2010) 'Nationalcentriske mandighedsideal førte til bankers sammenbrud', *NIKK*, 2: 24–7.

Simensen, Jarle (2004) *Afrikas historie*, Oslo: Cappelen.

Simpson, Chris (2002) 'Senegal PM sacked over ferry disaster', *BBC News*, 4 November.

Simpson-Miller, Portia (2006) 'Inaugural address', www.jis.gov.jm

Sineau, Mariette (2008) 'France', in M. Tremblay (ed) *Women and legislative representation*, Hampshire and New York, NY: Palgrave Macmillan, pp 83–94.

Sirleaf, Ellen Johnson (2007) 'Liberia: emerging hope from Africa', *The Namibean*, 7 June.

Sirleaf, Ellen Johnson (2009) *This child will be great*, New York, NY: HarperCollins.

Sitasari, Amita (2006) *Women and Indonesian politics: modernization and its effect on public opinion*, West Virginia, WV: West Virginia University, Department of Political Science.

Skard, Torild (ed) (1979) *'Kvinnekupp' i kommunene*, Oslo: Gyldendal.

Skard, Torild (1980) *Utvalgt til Stortinget*, Oslo: Gyldendal.

Skard, Torild (2001) 'Rendons à Elizabeth …', *Jeune Afrique/L'intelligent*, 5–11 June.

Skard, Torild (2003) *Continent of mothers, continent of hope*, London/New York, NY: Zed Books.

Skard, Torild (2008a) 'Getting our history right: how were the equal rights of women and men included in the Charter of the United Nations?', *Forum for Development Studies*, 35(1): 37–60.

Skard, Torild (2008b) 'Promoting the status of women in the UN system: experiences from an inside journey', *Forum for Development Studies*, 35(2): 279–311.

Skard, Torild (2009) 'Gender in the malestream – acceptance of women and gender equality in different United Nations organisations', *Forum for Development Studies*, 36(1): 155–97.

Skidmore, Thomas E. and Smith, Peter H. (2005) *Modern Latin America*, 6th edn, New York, NY/Oxford: Oxford University Press.

Skjeie, Hege (1995) 'From movement to government: women's political integration in Norway', in A. Brill (ed) *A rising public voice: women in politics worldwide*, New York, NY: Feminist Press, pp 213–16.

Snyder, Margaret (1995) *Transforming development: women, poverty and politics*, London: Intermediate Technology Publications.

Sohn, Bong-Scuk (1994) 'Women's political engagement and participation in the Republic of Korea', in B.J. Nelson and N. Chowdhury (eds) *Women and politics worldwide*, London/New Haven, CT: Yale University Press, pp 436–47.

Sorensen, Jan Sand (2002) 'Interview with President Vaira Vike-Freiberga of Latvia', *International Journal of Humanities and Peace*, 18(1) January.

Soudan, François (2013) 'Centrafrique', *Jeune Afrique*, 24-30 March.

Soudan, François (2014) 'Centrafrique', *Jeune Afrique*, 26 January-1 February and 9-15 February

Springer, Beverly (1986) 'Yugoslav women', in L.B. Iglitzin and R. Ross (eds) *Women in the world, 1975-85: the women's decade*, revised 2nd edn, pp 415-38, Santa Barbara, CA/Oxford: ABC-CLIO.

Squires, Judith (2007) *The new politics of gender equality*, Hampshire: Palgrave Macmillan.

Stämpfli, Regula (1994) 'Direct democracy and women's suffrage: antagonism in Switzerland', in B.J. Nelson and N. Chowdhury (eds) *Women in politics worldwide*, London/New Haven, CT: Yale University Press, pp 690–704.

Stan, Adele M. (2007) 'Benazir Bhutto: an imperfect feminist', *The American Prospect*, www.prospect.org

Stanford, Eleanor (2010) 'Burundi', www.everyculture.com

Steckenrider, Janie S. (2013) 'Angela Merkel: from serendipity to global success', in M.A. Genovese and J.S. Steckenrider (eds) *Women as political leaders*, London/New York, NY: Routledge, pp 226–55.

Steinberg, Blema S. (2008) *Women in power, the personalities and leadership styles of Indira Gandhi, Golda Meir and Margaret Thatcher*, Montreal/Kingston: McGill-Queen's University Press.

Stenseth, Nils Chr.; Paulsen, Kjetil and Karlsen, Rolf (eds) (1995) *Afrika – natur, samfunn og bistand*, Oslo: Ad Notam Gyldendal.

Stone, Thalia S. (2010) 'Jamaican women'; debate.uvm.edu/dreadlibrary/stone.html

Stratfor (2010) 'Ukraine's presidential election', 9 March; stratfor.com

Stratton, Stephen (1996) 'Contemporary Black Biography: Mary Eugenia Charles 1919–', www.encyclopedia.com

Sturcke, James (2007) 'The art of the possible', *The Guardian*, 29 October.

Styrkársdóttir, Auður (1999) 'Kvindelister i Island – reaktion mod en stillestående politik', in C. Bergqvist (ed) *Likestilte demokratier? Kjønn and politikk i Norden*, Oslo: Universitetsforlaget, pp 83–90.

Styrkársdóttir, Auður (2013) 'Iceland: breaking male dominance by extraordinary means', in D. Dahlerup and M. Leyenaar (eds) *Breaking male dominance in old democracies*, Oxford: Oxford University Press, pp 124–45.

Suryakusuma, Julia (2003) 'Indonesia: Megawati hasn't helped her countrywomen', *International Herald Tribune*, 18 January.

Sverdljuk, Jana and Oksamytna, Svitlana (eds) (2006) *Women and politics in Ukraine*, Kiev: Atika.

Swarup, Hem Lata; Sinha, Niroj; Ghosh, Chitra and Rajput, Pam (1994) 'Women's political engagement engagement in India: some critical issues', in B.J. Nelson and N. Chowhury (eds) *Women and politics worldwide*, London/New Haven, CT: Yale University Press, pp 361–79.

Sweetman, David (1984) *Women leaders in African history*, Oxford: Heinemann.

Sykes, Patricia Lee (1993) 'Women as national leaders: patterns and prospects', in M. Genovese (ed) *Women as national leaders*, Newbury, CA: Sage: pp 219-29.

Syrkin, Marie (1969) *Golda Meir*, New York, NY: Putnam's Sons.

Tabak, Fanny (1994a) 'Women and politics in Brazil: legislative elections', in W. Rule and J.F. Zimmerman (eds) *Electoral systems in comparative perspective*, London and Westport, CT: Greenwood Press, pp 203–9.

Tabak, Fanny (1994b) 'Women in the struggle for democracy and equal rights in Brazil', in B.J. Nelson and N. Chowdhury (eds) *Women and politics worldwide*, London/New Haven, CT: Yale University Press, pp 127–41.

Tanaka, Martin (2005) 'Peru 1980–2000: chronicle of a death foretold? Determinism, political decisions, and open outcomes', in F. Hagopian and S.P. Mainwaring (eds) *The third wave of democratization in Latin America*, New York, NY: Cambridge University Press, pp 261–88.

Tanama, Josias T. (2002) 'Bilan du gouvernement: Silence sur l'investissement', 16 January; allAfrica.com

Tanner, Nancy (1974) 'Matrifocality in Indonesia and Africa and among black Africans', in M.Z. Rosaldo and L. Lamphere (eds) *Women, culture and society*, Stanford, CA: Stanford University Press, pp 129–56.

Tan-Wong, Nellie (1998) 'Conversation with eight women prime ministers', www.wimnet.org.my

Tarczynski, Stephen de (2009) 'Philippines: Women's rights laws in place', *IPS*, 28 October, ipsnews.net

Tarm, Michael (1999) 'Ms. President', City Paper, www.balticsworldwide.com/news/features/mspresident.htm

Thatcher, Margaret (1995a) *The path to power*, New York, NY: HarperCollins.

Thatcher, Margaret (1995b) *The Downing Street years 1979–1990*, New York, NY: Harper Perennial

The Nobel Institute (2011) 'Nobel Peace Prize 2011'; nobelpeaceprize.org

Thiam, Abou Abel (2002) 'Quand Wade sort son joker', *Jeune Afrique/L'Intelligent*, 11–17 November.

Thiam, Bachir (2005) 'L'exeption sénégalaise', www.maroc-hebdo.press.ma

Thompson, Mark R. (1998) 'The Marcos Regime in the Philippines', in H.E. Chehabi and J.J. Linz (eds) *Sultanistic regimes*, London and Baltimore, MD: Johns Hopkins University Press, pp 206–29.

Thompson, Mark R. (2002/03) 'Female leadership of democratic transitions in Asia', *Pacific Affairs*, 75(4): 535–55 (republished in M.R. Thompson [ed] [2004] *Democratic revolutions, Asia and Eastern Europe*, London/New York, NY: Routledge, pp 35–50).

Thompson, Mark R. (2004) 'The puzzles of Philippine "people power"', in M.R. Thompson (ed) *Democratic revolutions: Asia and Eastern Europe*, London: Routledge, pp 18–34.

Thompson, Mark R. (2010) 'Reformism vs. populism in the Philippines', *Journal of Democracy*, 21(4): 154–68.

Thompson, Mark R. and Lennartz, Ludmilla (2006) 'The making of Chancellor Merkel', *German Politics*, 15(1): 99–110.

Thompson, Seth (2013) 'Golda Meir, a very public life', in M.A. Genovese and J.S. Steckenrider (eds) *Women as political leaders*, London/New York, NY: Routledge, pp 176–202.

Tobar, Marcela Ríos (2008) 'Critical perspectives: seizing a window of opportunity: the election of President Bachelet in Chile', *Politics & Gender*, 4: 509–19.

Tonpo, Jarlawah A. (2006) 'A new beginning', *New African*, February.

Totaro, Paola (2013) 'Julia Gillard's demise shows Australia is not ready for a woman leader', *The Guardian*, 26 June.

Toussaint, Isabelle (2006) 'Women leadership report, Claudette Werleigh', unpublished report, Canada.

Towns, Ann (2003) 'Understanding the effects of larger ratios of women in national legislatures; proportions and gender differentiation in Sweden and Norway', *Women and Politics*, 25(1/2): 1–23.

Transparency International (2004) 'Political parties are most corrupt institution worldwide', Press release, 9 December, 5 pages, www.transparency.org

Tremblay, Manon and Bauer, Gretchen (2011) 'Conclusion' in G. Bauer and M. Tremblay (eds) *Women in executive power,* London/New York, NY: Routledge: 171-90.

Trimble, Linda and Treiberg, Natasja (2010) '"Either way, there's going to be a man in charge": media representations of New Zealand Prime Minister Helen Clark', in R. Murray (ed) *Cracking the highest glass ceiling*, Santa Barbara, CA: Praeger, pp 115–36.

Tripp, Aili Mari (2001) 'The new political activism in Africa', *Journal of Democracy*, 12(3): 141–55.

Tripp, Aili Mari (2008) 'Critical perspectives on gender and politics: what does the rising tide of women in executive office mean?', *Politics & Gender*, 4: 473–519.

Tripp, Aili Mari; Konaté, Dior and Lowe-Morna, Colleen (2006) 'Sub-Saharan Africa : on the fast track to women's political representation', in D. Dahlerup (ed) *Women, quotas and politics*, London/New York, NY: Routledge, pp 112–37.

Tripp, Aili Mari; Casimiro, Isabel; Kwesiga, Joy and Mungwa, Alice (2009) *African women's movements,* New York, NY: Cambridge University Press.

Turshen, Meredeth and Twagiramariya, Clotilde (eds) (1998) *What women do in wartime, gender and conflict in Africa*, London/New York, NY: Zed Books.

Tuttle, Tiffany (2011) 'Culture of Kyrgyztan', www.everyculture.com

UN (United Nations) (1945) *Charter of the United Nations*, New York, NY: UN.

UN (1948) *Universal declaration of human rights*, New York, NY: UN.

UN (1975) *Current trends and changes in the status and roles of women and men and major obstacles to be overcome in the achievement of equal rights, opportunities and responsibilities*, Mexico City: World Conference of the International Women's Year, E/CONF.66/3.

UN (1991, 1995, 2000, 2010) *The world's women, trends and statistics*, New York, NY: UN.

UN (1995/96) *The United Nations and the advancement of women 1945–1996,* New York: Department of Public Information.

UN (2001) *Beijing declaration and platform for action with the Beijing +5 political declaration and outcome document*, New York, NY: UN.

UN (2003) *Women go global, the United Nations and the international women's movement 1945–2000*, New York, NY: UN.

UN (2005) 'Review of the implementation of the Beijing platform for action and the outcome documents of the special session of the General Assembly entitled "Women 2000: gender equality, development and peace for the twenty-first century", report of the Secretary-General', E/CN.6/2005/2.

UN (2006) *Millennium development goals 2006 report: a look at gender equality and empowerment of women in Latin America and the Caribbean*, Santiago, Chile: UN.

UN (2010) *United Nations list of heads of state, heads of government and foreign ministers*, www.un.int

UN (2011) *The millennium development goals report*, New York, NY: UN.

UN (2012) 'Women and political participation', *Resolution adopted by the General Assembly,* New York, NY: UN, A/RES/66/130

UN (2014) 'Follow-up to the Fourth World Conference on Women', *Resolution adopted by the General Assembly on 18 December 2013,* New York, NY: UN, A/RES/68/140

UNB (2013) 'PM for equal participation of women in political decisionmaking', *Dhaka Tribune*, 2 pages, www.dhakatribune.com/politics/

UNDP (United Nations Development Programme) (1995a-2013a) *Human development reports*, Oxford and New York, NY: Oxford University Press/UNDP, www.undp.org

UNDP (1999b) *Pacific human development report*, New York: UNDP.

UNDP (2002b, 2003b, 2004b, 2005b, 2006b, 2009b) *Arab human development report*, New York, NY: UNDP.

UNDP (2005c) 'Bilan Commun de Pays, São Tomé e Príncipe', www.undp.org

UNDP (2010b) *Asia-Pacific human development report*, New York, NY: UNDP and Macmillan.

UNDP BRC (Regional Bureau for Europa and CIS) (2010) *Enhancing women's political participation, a policy note for Europa and the CIS*, Bratislava: UNDP BRC, www.undp.org

UNESCO (United Nations Educational, Scientific and Cultural Organization) (2003) *Gender and education for all, the leap to equality*, Paris: UNESCO.

UNESCO (2005) *Education for all: the quality imperative*, Paris: UNESCO.

UNESCO (2008) *Education for all 2009: overcoming inequality: why governance matters*, Paris: UNESCO.

UNESCO Courier (2011) 'Women conquering new expanses of freedom', April–June.

UNFPA (United Nations Population Fund) (2005) *The promise of equality: gender equality, reproductive health and the MDGs,* www.unfpa.org

UNIAN (2010) 'Yushchenko tells about his 'worst mistake'', www.kyivpost. com, 31 May.

UNICEF (United Nations Children's Fund) (1993a–2013a), *State of the world's children,* Oxford: Oxford University Press.

UNICEF (1995b) 'Recommendations for funding for short-duration country programmes in eastern & southern Africa region, II. São Tomé and Príncipe', E/ICEF/1995/P/L.27.

UNICEF (2006) 'Draft country programme document, São Tomé and Príncipe', E/ICEF/2006/P/L.10.

UNIFEM (United Nations Development Fund for Women) (2006) *Beyond numbers: supporting women's political participation and promoting gender equality in post-conflict governance in Africa*, New York, NY: UNIFEM.

United States Institute of Peace (2009) 'Truth commission: Liberia', www.usip.org

UNRISD (United Nations Research Institute for Social Development) (2005) *Gender equality, striving for justice in an unequal world*, Geneva: UNRISD.

UN Women (2011) *Progress of the world's women, in pursuit of justice, 2011–2012*, New York, NY: UN Women.

US Department of Labor (1991) *A report on the glass ceiling initiative*, Washington, DC: Department of Labor.

Utas, Mats (2008) 'Liberia beyond the blueprints', Lecture Series on African Security no 4, Swedish Defence Research Agency (FOI) and the Nordic Africa Institute.

Utas, Mats (2012) 'Introduction: bigmanity and network governance in African conflicts', in Mats Utas (ed) *African conflicts and informal politics: big men and informal networks*, London/New York, NY: Zed Books, pp 1–31.

Valdés, Teresa and Palacios, Indira (1999) *Participation and leadership in Latin America and the Caribbean: gender indicators*, Santiago: Economic Commission for Latin America and the Caribbean.

Valenzuela, Maria Elena (1998) 'Women and the democratization process in Chile', in J.S. Jaquette and S.L. Wolchik (eds) *Women and democracy, Latin America and Central and Eastern Europe*, London and Baltimore, MD: Johns Hopkins University Press, pp 47–74.

Van der Ros, Janneke (1994) 'The state and women: a troubled relationship in Norway', in B.J. Nelson and N. Chowdhury (eds) *Women and politics worldwide*, London/New Haven, CT: Yale University Press, pp 527–43.

Van de Walle, Nicolas (2001) 'The impact of multi-party politics in sub-Saharan Africa', *Forum for Development Studies*, 28(1): 5–42.

Vargas, Virginia and Villanueva, Victoria (1994) 'Between confusion and the law: women and politics in Peru', in B.J. Nelson and N. Chowdhury (eds) *Women and politics worldwide*, London/New Haven, CT: Yale University Press, pp 575–8.

Veneracion-Rallonza, Ma. Lourdes (2001) 'Engendering the state and imaging women political leaders: Corazon Cojuangco Aquino and Gloria Macapagal-Arroyo as cases to point', in Women and Gender Institute (ed) *Quilted sightings*, Quezon City, Manila: Miriam College, pp 67–83.

Veneracion-Rallonza, Ma. Lourdes (2008) 'Women and the democracy project: a feminist take on women's political participation in the Philippines', in K. Iwanaga (ed) *Women's political participation and representation in Asia, obstacles and challenges*, Copenhagen: NIAS Press, pp 210–52.

Veneracion-Rallonza, Ma. Lourdes (2009) 'A spectacle of masculine and feminine images of political leadership: feminist reflection on the current crises of leadership in the Philippines', in A. Ayaz and A. Fleschenberg (eds) *The gender face of Asian politics*, Oxford and New York, NY: Oxford University Press, pp 99–118.

Veselica, Lajla (2009) 'Croatia's first woman PM set to take office', 7 July, www.expatica.com

Vesperini, Helen (2004) 'Rwanda's parliament now leads world in gender parity', *Choices*, March.

Vilardo, Valeria (2013) 'Haitian women still waiting for a seat at the table', *IPS*, 07.

Von der Lippe, Berit (2012) 'Rhetoric of war, rhetoric of gender', in C. Kock and L. Villadsen (eds) *Rhetorical citizenship and public deliberation*, University Park, PA: Pennsylvania State University Press, pp 153–68.

Von der Lippe, Berit and Väyrynen, Tarja (2011) 'Co-opting feminist voices for the war on terror: Laura Bush meets Nordic feminism', *European Journal of Women's Studies*, 18(1): 19–33.

Voronina, Olga A. (1994) 'Soviet women and politics: on the brink of change', in B.J. Nelson and N. Chowdhury (eds) *Women and politics worldwide*, London/New Haven, CT: Yale University Press, pp 721–36.

Walby, Sylvia (1990) *Theorizing patriarchy*, Oxford: Basil Blackwell.

Walby, Sylvia (2009) *Globalization & inequalities*, London: Sage.

Walby, Sylvia (2011) *The future of feminism*, Cambridge: Polity Press.

Walsh, Kerry-Anne (2013) *The stalking of Julia Gillard*, Sidney: Allen & Unwin.

Walter, Greg (1983) 'President Reagan finds a fast friend in Eugenia Charles, Dominica's plucky PM', *People*, 20(20), 14 November, www.people.com

Walters, Margaret (2005) *Feminism*, New York, NY: Oxford University Press.

Watson, Robert P.; Jencik, Alicia and Selzer, Judith A. (2005) 'Women world leaders: comparative analysis and gender experiences', *Journal of International Women's Studies*, 7(2): 53–76.

Waylen, Georgina (1996) *Gender in third world politics*, Boulder, CO: Lynne Rienner.

Weaver, Mary Anne (2002) *Pakistan*, New York, NY: Farrar, Straus and Giroux.

Webster, Wendy (1990) *Not a man to match her: the marketing of a prime minister,* London: Women's Press.

Weerakoon, Bradman (2004) *Rendering unto Caesar, a fascinating story of one man's tenure under nine prime ministers and presidents of Sri Lanka,* New Delhi, Colombo: New Dawn Press Group/Vijitha Yapa.

Weiner, Tim (1986) 'Marcos pledges peaceful change if he loses election', *Inquirer*, 31 January.

Weir, Sara J. (2013) 'Perónisma, Isabel Perón and the politics of Argentina', in M.A. Genovese and J.S. Steckenrider (eds) *Women as political leaders*, London/ New York, NY: Routledge, pp 256–69.

Weissenborn, Odile (2009) 'Cristina vs Hillary: International Women's Day in Argentina', *Huff Post World*, 9 March.

Westlund, Jennie (2010) 'Ingen lag utan kris', *NIKK*, 2: 22–4.

Whaley, Floyd (2002) 'Corazon Aquino – lessons in power', *Reader's Digest,* June.

Wharton, Amy S. (2005) *The sociology of gender, an introduction to theory and research,* Oxford: Blackwell.

Who's Who in Poland (1994) 'Hanna Suchocka', *Directory of members of parliament, state and local government and the presidential chancellery 1994–95,* Warsaw, page II-497.

Wichterich, Christa (2014) '20 years reflection: the women's human rights paradigm in the current neoliberal context – EU', 4 January; wideplusnetwork. wordpress.com

Wiliarty, Sarah Elise (2008a) 'Angela Merkel's path to power: the role of internal party dynamics and leadership', *German Politics*, 17(1): 81–96.

Wiliarty, Sarah Elise (2008b) 'Chancellor Angela Merkel – a sign of hope or the exception that proves the rule?', *Politics & Gender*, 4(3): 485–96.

Wiliarty, Sarah Elise (2010a) 'How the Iron Curtain helped break through the glass ceiling: Angela Merkel's campaigns in 2005 and 2009', in R. Murray (ed) *Cracking the highest glass ceiling*, Santa Barbara, CA: Praeger, pp 137–57.

Wiliarty, Sarah Elise (2010b) *The CDU and the politics of gender in Germany*, New York, NY: Cambridge University Press, pp 163-84.

Williams, Carol (2006) 'Jamaica's "Mama" has hands full', *Los Angeles Times*, 30 March.

Williams, Harvey (1995) 'Violeta Barrios de Chamorro', in F. D'Amico and P.R. Beckman (eds) *Women in world politics*, London and Westport, CT: Bergin & Garvey, pp 31–43.

Winslow, Anne (ed) *Women, politics and the United Nations*, Westport, CT, London: Greenwood Press

Wolchik, Sharon L. and Curry, Jane L. (eds) (2011) *Central & East European politics, from communism to democracy*, 2nd edn, Lanham, MD: Rowman & Littlefield.

World Bank (1978a-2012a) *World developments reports*, Washington DC: World Bank, www.worldbank.org

World Bank (2008b) 'Mozambique millennium development goals'; ddp-ext. worldbank.org

World Commission on Environment and Development (1987) *Our common future*, Oxford: Oxford University Press, www.un-documents.net/our-common-future.pdf

Worth, Richard (2008) *Michelle Bachelet*, New York, NY: Chelsea House.

Yedder, Omar Ben (2009) 'I am proud of what we have achieved', *New African*, October, pp 38–43.

Young, Hugo (1989) *The Iron Lady: a biography of Margaret Thatcher*, New York: The Noonday Press, Farrar, Straus and Giroux.

Yue Daiyun and Li Jin (1994) 'China', in B. J. Nelson and N. Chowdhury (eds) *Women and politics worldwide*, London, New Haven, CT: Yale University Press, pp 161-73.

Zarakhovich, Yuri (2005) 'Ukraine's Iron Lady', *Time*, 7 February.

Zetterberg, Pär (2009) 'Do gender quotas foster women's political engagement? Lessons from Latin America', *Political Research Quarterly*, 62(4): 715–30.

Zvončeková, Janka (2008) 'Slovak women in politics till the end of the Dzurinda's government and the possible reasons for low women's political participation', *Actual issues in World Economics and Politics*, 3(1): 175–85.

Websites

CIA (Central Intelligence Agency), 'The world factbook', www.cia.gov

De Zárate, R.O., 'Women world leaders', www.terra.es/personal2/monolith/00women.htm

IDEA (International Institute for Democracy and Electoral Assistance), 'Women in politics', www.idea.int

IDEA and Stockholm University, 'Global database of quotas for women', www.quotaproject.org

IPU (Inter-Parliamentary Union) 'Women in national parliaments', www.ipu.org

Store Norske Leksikon, www.snl.no

The International Knowledge Network of Women in Politics (iKNOW Politics), www.iknowpolitics.org

United Nations, www.un.org and www.un.org/womenwatch

Wikipedia, 'The free encyclopedia'; wikipedia.org

Additional sources
African Elections Database
Africana – the encyclopedia of the African and African American experience
Encyclopaedia Britannica
Encyclopedia of world biography
Keesing's worldwide contemporary archives/record of world events
McGeveran: the world almanac and book of facts
The Europa world year book
The Europa regional surveys of the world
The international who's who of women

Chronological overview: women presidents and prime ministers (1960–2010)[a]: positions and terms of office (when first came to power)

Sri Lanka	Sirimavo Bandaranaike (1916–2000)	PM	21 July 1960–27 March 1965
			29 May 1970–23 July 1977
			14 Nov 1994–10 Aug 2000
India	Indira Gandhi (1917–84)	PM	19 Jan 1966–24 March 1977
			14 Jan 1980–31 Oct 1984
Israel	Golda Meir (1898–1978)	Acting PM	17 March–15 Dec 1969
		PM	15 Dec 1969–3 June 1974
Argentina	Isabel Martinez de Perón (1931–)	Acting Pres	During periods from Sept 1973
		President	1 July 1974–24 March 1976
Central African Republic	Elisabeth Domitien (1925–2005)	PM Acting Pres	2 Jan 1975–4 April 1976[b] During some periods
UK	Margaret Thatcher (1925–2013)	PM	4 May 1979–28 Nov 1990
Portugal	Maria de Lourdes Pintasilgo (1930–2004)	Acting PM	1 Aug 1979–3 Jan 1980
Bolivia	Lidia Güeiler Tejada (1921–2011)	Acting Pres	17 Nov 1979–18 July 1980
Dominica	Eugenia Charles (1919–2005)	PM	21 July 1980–14 June 1995
Iceland	Vigdís Finnbogadóttir (1930–)	President	1 Aug 1980–1 Aug 1996
Norway	Gro Harlem Brundtland (1939–)	PM	4 Feb–14 Oct 1981
			9 May 1986–16 Oct 1989
			3 Nov 1990–25 Oct 1996
Malta	Agatha Barbara (1923–2002)	President[c]	15 Feb 1982–15 Feb 1987
Yugoslavia	Milka Planinc (1924–2010)	PM	16 May 1982–15 May 1986
The Philippines	Corazon Aquino (1933–2009)	President	25 Feb 1986–30 June 1992

Pakistan	Benazir Bhutto (1953–2007)	PM	2 Dec 1988–6 Aug 1990
			19 Oct 1993–5 Nov 1996
Haiti	Ertha Pascal-Trouillot (1943–)	Acting Pres	13 March 1990–7 Feb, 1991
Lithuania	Kazimiera Prunskienė (1943–)	Acting PM[d]	11 March–17 March 1990
		PM	17 March 1990–10 Jan 1991
DDR	Sabine Bergmann-Pohl (1946–)	Acting Pres	5 April–2 Oct 1990
Nicaragua	Violeta Barrios de Chamorro (1929–)	President	25 April 1990–10 Jan 1997[e]
Ireland	Mary Robinson (1944–)	President	3 Dec 1990–12 Sept 1997
Bangladesh	Khaleda Zia (1945–)	PM	20 March 1991–30 March 1996
			10 Oct 2001–29 Oct 2006
France	Edith Cresson (1934–)	PM	15 May 1991–2 April 1992
Poland	Hanna Suchocka (1946–)	PM	8 July 1992–26 Oct 1993
Canada	Kim Campbell (1947–)	PM	25 June–4 Nov 1993
Turkey	Tansu Çiller (1946–)	PM	25 June 1993–7 March 1996
Burundi	Sylvie Kinigi (1953–)	PM	10 July 1993–7 Feb 1994
		Acting Pres	27 Oct 1993–5 Feb 1994
Rwanda	Agathe Uwilingiyimana (1953–94)	PM	18 July–5 Aug 1993
		Acting PM	5 Aug–7 April 1994
Sri Lanka	Chandrika Kumaratunga (1945–)	PM	19 Aug–14 Nov 1994
		President	12 Nov 1994–19 Nov 2005
Bulgaria	Reneta Indzhova (1953–)	Acting PM	17 Oct 1994–25 Jan 1995
Haiti	Claudette Werleigh (1946–)	PM	7 Nov 1995–6 March 1996
Bangladesh	Sheikh Hasina (1947–)	PM	23 June 1996–15 July 2001
			6 Jan 2009–
Liberia	Ruth Sando Perry (1939–)	Acting Pres	3 Sept 1996–2 Aug 1997
Guyana	Janet Jagan (1920–2009)	Acting PM	17 March–22 Dec 1997
		President	19 Dec 1997–11 Aug 1999
Ireland	Mary McAleese (1951–)	President	11 Nov 1997–11 Nov 2011
New Zealand	Jenny Shipley (1952–)	PM	8 Dec 1997–10 Dec 1999
Switzerland	Ruth Dreifuss (1940–)	President	1 Jan–31 Dec 1999[f]
Latvia	Vaira Vike-Freiberga (1937–)	President	8 July 1999–8 July 2007
Panama	Mireya Moscoso (1946–)	President	1 Sept 1999–1 Sept 2004
New Zealand	Helen Clark (1950–)	PM	10 Dec 1999–19 Nov 2008
Finland	Tarja Halonen (1943–)	President	1 March 2000–1 March 2012
The Philippines	Gloria Macapagal Arroyo (1947–)	President	20 Jan 2001–30 June 2010
Senegal	Mame Madior Boye (1940–)	PM	3 March 2001–4 Nov 2002
Indonesia	Megawati Sukarnoputri (1947–)	President	23 July 2001–20 Oct 2004
São Tomé and Príncipe	Maria das Neves (1958–)	PM	7 Oct 2002–16 July 2003 23 July 2003–18 Sept 2004
Finland	Anneli Jäätteenmäki (1955–)	PM	17 April–24 June 2003

Peru	Beatriz Merino (1947–)	PM	28 June–15 Dec 2003
Georgia	Nino Burjanadze (1964–)	Acting Pres	23 Nov 2003–25 Jan 2004
			25 Nov 2007–20 Jan 2008
Mozambique	Luisa Diogo (1958–)	PM	17 Feb 2004–16 Jan 2010
Ukraine	Yulia Tymoshenko (1960–)	Acting PM	24 Jan–4 Feb 2005
		PM	4 Feb–8 Sept 2005
		PM	18 Dec 2007–11 March 2010
São Tomé and Príncipe	Maria do Carmo Silveira (1960–)	PM	8 June 2005–21 April 2006
Germany	Angela Merkel (1954–)	PM	22 Nov 2005–
Liberia	Ellen Johnson Sirleaf (1938–)	President	16 Jan 2006–
Chile	Michelle Bachelet (1951–)	President	11 March 2006–11 March 2010
			11 March 2014–
Jamaica	Portia Simpson Miller (1945–)	PM	30 March 2006–11 Sept 2007
		PM	5 Jan 2012–
South Korea	Han Myung-sook (1944–)	PM	19 April 2006–7 March 2007
Switzerland	Micheline Calmy-Rey (1945–)	President	1 Jan–31 Dec 2007
			1 Jan–31 Dec 2011
Israel	Dalia Itzik (1952–)	Acting Pres	25 Jan–15 July 2007
India	Pratibha Patil (1934–)	President	25 July 2007–25 July 2012
Argentina	Cristina Fernández de Kirchner (1953–)	President	10 Dec 2007–
Moldova	Zinaida Greceanîi (1956–)	PM	31 March 2008–10 June 2009
		Acting Pres	10 June 2009-14 Sept 2009
Haiti	Michèle Pierre-Louis (1947–)	PM	5 Sept 2008–11 Nov 2009
Iceland	Jóhanna Sigurðardóttir (1942–)	PM	1 Feb 2009– 23 May 2013
Gabon	Rose Francine Rogombé (1942–)	Acting Pres	10 June–16 Oct 2009
Croatia	Jadranka Kosor (1953–)	PM	6 July 2009–23 Dec 2011
Lithuania	Dalia Grybauskaitė (1956–)	President	12 July 2009–
Switzerland	Doris Leuthard (1963–)	President	1 Jan–31 Dec 2010
Kyrgyzstan	Roza Otunbayeva (1950–)	Acting Pres	7 April–19 May 2010
		President	19 May 2010–1 Dec 2011
Costa Rica	Laura Chinchilla (1959–)	President	8 May 2010– 8 May 2014
Trinidad and Tobago	Kamla Persad-Bissessar (1952–)	PM	26 May 2010–
Finland	Mari Kiviniemi (1968–)	PM	22 June 2010–22 June 2011
Australia	Julia Gillard (1961–)	PM	24 June 2010– 27 June 2013
Slovakia	Iveta Radičová (1956–)	PM	8 July 2010–4 April 2012
Brasil	Dilma Rousseff (1947–)	President	1 Jan 2011–

Elected or appointed in 2011 or later

(not described in the book)

Peru	Rosario Del Pilar Fernández Figueroa (1955–)	PM	19 March–28 July 2011
Mali	Cissé Mariam Kaïdama Sidibé (1948–)	PM	3 April 2011–22 March 2012
Thailand	Yingluck Shiniwatra (1967–)	PM	8 August 2011– 7 May 2014
Denmark	Helle Thorning-Schmidt (1966–)	PM	3 Oct 2011–
Switzerland	Eveline Widmer-Schlumpf (1956–)	President	1 Jan–31Dec 2012
Guinea Bissau	Adiato Djaló Nandigna	Acting PM	10 Feb–12 April 2012
Mauritius	Monique Ohsan-Bellepeau (1942–)	Acting Pres	31 March–21 July 2012
Serbia	Slavika Đukić Dejanović (1951–)	Acting Pres	5 April–31 May 2012ᵍ
Malawi	Joyce Banda (1950–)	President	7 April 2012–
South Korea	Park Geun-Hye (1952–)	President	25 Feb 2013–
Slovenia	Alenka Bratušek (1970–)	PM	20 March 2013–
Senegal	Aminata Touré (1962–)	PM	3 Sept 2013–
Norway	Erna Solberg (1961–)	PM	16 Oct 2013–
Latvia	Laimdota Straujuma (1951–)	PM	22 Jan 2014–
Central African Republic	Catherine Samba-Panza (1954–)	President	23 Jan 2014–
Malta	Marie Louise Coleiro Preca (1958–)	President	4 April 2014–

Notes: ᵃ The overview includes acting, elected or appointed presidents and prime ministers in independent states that were members of the United Nations (UN) by the end of 2010. Colonies, dependencies and external territories such as Bermuda, the Faeroe Islands, the Netherlands Antilles, the Palestine Territories, Puerto Rica and Aaland are not included. Further, governors-general, queens, grand duchesses and traditional chiefs are not included. Only women acting for a least two months are listed. Aung San Suu Kyi in Myanmar, who won the election in 1990, is not included because she never acted. The dates indicate the time in office.

ᵇ According to www.rulers.org, Domitien, herself, said in 1999 that she was in office from 6 June 1974 to August 1976.

ᶜ There is information indicating that Barbara acted as prime minister for shorter periods during 1971–81, but no specific dates are available.

ᵈ Lithuania declared itself independent on 11 March 1990 and became a member of the UN on 6 September 1991.

ᵉ During the period 20 July 1979–19 April 1980, Chamorro participated in a government junta for national reconstruction with seven members.

ᶠ Switzerland did not become a member of the UN before 2002, but was for a long time, partly from 1945, member of most of the UN specialised agencies.

ᵍ Serbia became an independent state in 2006.

Sources: www.guide2womenleaders.com, www.rulers.org and others up to May 2014.

Index